CIMA

STUDY TEXT

GW00494218

Stage 2 Paper 6

Operational
Cost Accounting

First edition June 1994
Fifth edition July 1998

ISBN 0 7517 3105 6 (Previous edition 0 7517 3081 5)

British Library Cataloguing-in-Publication Data
A catalogue record for this book
is available from the British Library

Published by

BPP Publishing Limited
Aldine House, Aldine Place
London W12 8AW

http://www.bpp.co.uk

Printed and bound by Progressive Printing (U.K.) Limited, Leigh-on-Sea, Essex.

We are grateful to the Chartered Institute of Management Accountants for permission to reproduce past examination questions. The suggested solutions to the illustrative questions have been prepared by BPP Publishing Limited.

BPP Publishing

Contents

PREFACE

Professional exams aren't easy. And trying to fit in *study* as well as a *social life* around your *job* is difficult. But could you make better use of your *time*?

By using BPP study material you can be sure that the time you spend studying is time well spent.

The BPP Study Text

Our Study Texts provide you with the *knowledge and understanding, skills and application techniques* that you need if you are to be successful in your exams.

- The Study Texts are *comprehensive*. We do not omit sections of the syllabus as the examiner is liable to examine any angle of any part of the syllabus. But they are also *on-target* - we do not include any material which is not examinable.

- There are many useful exercises, quizzes and case examples to *help you learn*.

- We help you to *focus on the exam*, with recently-examined topics highlighted, new *exam focus points* (see below) and a bank of questions and suggested solutions.

- Our Study Texts are *up-to-date* as at 1 June 1998, the cut-off date for the November 1998 exam.

- Comprehensive updating notes in the January 1999 editions of our Practice & Revision Kits will bring you bang up-to-date if you are sitting the exam in May 1999, for which the cut-off date is 1 December 1998.

Operational Cost Accounting Study Text – July 1998

This edition of the *Operational Cost Accounting* Study Text has been significantly improved.

- A new feature! *Exam focus points* show you what the examiner is interested in, how topics have been covered in the past, and how to tackle future exam questions. You will find these exam focus points throughout this Study Text.

The BPP Effective Study Package

The Study Text ties in with the other components of the BPP Effective Study Package.

- Use *BPP Study Texts* to *acquire knowledge, skills and applied techniques*.

- *Revise and recap* using *BPP Practice & Revision Kits*, with updating notes to bring you up-to-date for May 1999 exams, tutorial questions, helpful checklists of key points and numerous exam questions with realistic solutions.

- *Focus* on what is likely to come up *in the exam with BPP Passcards*, clear and concise revision notes.

Help us to help you

Your feedback will help us improve our study package. Please complete and return the Review Form at the end of this Study Text; you will be entered automatically in a Free Prize Draw.

A final word

All in all, BPP Study Texts provide the most effective study material for your exams. It's about time. So choose BPP.

BPP Publishing
July 1998

For information about the products and services offered by BPP Publishing and other businesses in the BPP Holdings plc group, visit our website. The address is:

http://www.bpp.co.uk

HOW TO USE THIS STUDY TEXT

This Study Text has been designed to help students and lecturers to get to grips as effectively as possible with the content and scope of Paper 6 *Operational Cost Accounting*.

Syllabus coverage in the text is indicated on pages (viii) and (ix) by chapter references set against each syllabus topic. Syllabus topics are also identified within each chapter of the text. It is thus easy to trace your path through the syllabus. The CIMA 1998-99 Syllabus Guidance Notes give further insight into how the examiner sees this paper.

As a further guide - and a convenient means of monitoring your progress - we have included a *study checklist* on page (xviii) on which to chart your completion of chapters and their related illustrative questions.

Chapter format and contents

Each chapter of the Study Text is divided into **sections**.

- An *introduction* places the subject of the chapter in its context in the syllabus and the examination.
- The text gives clear, concise *topic-by-topic coverage*.
- *Examples* and *exercises* reinforce learning, confirm understanding and stimulate thought.
- *A chapter roundup* at the end of the chapter pulls together the key points.
- *Exam focus points* show you how the subject is examined.
- *A test your knowledge* quiz helps you to check that you have absorbed the material in the chapter.

Some features of the Study Text are worth looking at in more detail.

Exam focus points

Exam focus points show *what the examiner is interested in, how a topic* covered in the text *has been or might be examined*, and *how you could tackle exam questions* in the future.

Exercises

Exercises are provided throughout the text to enable you to *check your progress* as you work through the text. A suggested solution is usually given, but often in an abbreviated form to help you avoid the temptation of merely reading the exercise rather than actively engaging your brain.

Chapter roundup and test your knowledge quiz

At the end of each chapter you will find two boxes. The first is the *chapter roundup* which *summarises key points*. The second box is a *quiz* that serves a number of purposes.

- *Use it after the chapter roundup*. It is an essential part of the chapter roundup and can be glanced over quickly to remind yourself of key issues covered by the chapter.
- *Use it as a quiz*. Try doing it in the morning to revise what you read the night before.
- *Use it to revise*. Shortly before your examination sit down with pen and paper and try to answer all the questions fully.

Knowledge brought forward

The examiner's guidance notes explain that Paper 6 'is intended to build upon the knowledge gained from the study of cost accounting as part of the CQM paper at Stage 1'. We have therefore summarised the key facts of the more straightforward of those topics which you should have covered in *Cost Accounting and Quantitative Methods* and which are developed further in *Operational Cost Accounting*. This gives you the chance to decide whether you can rely on your existing knowledge and advance more quickly through the Study Text or whether you need to revise a particular topic. Those topics from Paper 2 which students often experience difficulties with are covered in depth again in this Study Text.

Illustrative questions

Each chapter also has at least one illustrative question, in the bank at the end of the Study Text. Initially you might attempt such questions with reference to the chapter you have just covered. Later in your studies, it would be helpful to attempt some without support from the text. Only when you have attempted each question as fully as possible should you refer to the suggested solution to check and correct your performance.

Following the suggested solutions, there are several class questions, without solutions. These are intended to be used by lecturers. The solutions are given in a separate lecturers' pack, available only to bona fide lecturers.

A number of the illustrative questions and class questions are in the style of full exam questions. These questions are provided with mark and time allocations.

Glossary and index

Finally, we have included a glossary to define key terms and a comprehensive index to help you locate key topics.

> **A note on pronouns**
>
> On occasions in this Study Text, 'he' is used for 'he or she', 'him' for 'him or her' and so forth. Whilst we try to avoid this practice it is sometimes necessary for reasons of style. No prejudice or stereotyping according to sex is intended or assumed.

SYLLABUS

The syllabus contains a weighting for each syllabus area, and a ranking of the level of ability required in each topic. The Institute has published the following explanatory notes on these points.

'Study weightings

A percentage weighting is shown against each topic in the syllabus; this is intended as a guide to the amount of study time each topic requires.

All topics in a syllabus must be studied, as a question may examine more than one topic, or carry a higher proportion of marks than the percentage study time suggested.

The weightings do not specify the number of marks which will be allocated to topics in the examination.

Abilities required in the examination

Each examination paper contains a number of topics. Each topic has been given a number to indicate the level of ability required of the candidate.

The numbers range from 1 to 4 and represent the following ability levels:

Appreciation (1)
To understand a knowledge area at an early stage of learning, or outside the core of management accounting, at a level which enables the accountant to communicate and work with other members of the management team.

Knowledge (2)
To have detailed knowledge of such matters as laws, standards, facts and techniques so as to advise at a level appropriate to a management accounting specialist.

Skill (3)
To apply theoretical knowledge, concepts and techniques to the solutions of problems where it is clear what technique has to be used and the information needed is clearly indicated.

Application (4)
To apply knowledge and skills where candidates have to determine from a number of techniques which is the most appropriate and select the information required from a fairly wide range of data, some of which might not be relevant; to exercise professional judgement and to communicate and work with members of the management team and other recipients of financial reports.'

Syllabus overview

This syllabus covers the underpinning knowledge necessary for a student to apply a range of cost accounting techniques within the context of organisation-wide databases and information systems.

Students should seek the opportunity to learn cost accounting techniques in a computer environment.

Aims

To test the candidate's ability to

- apply cost accounting principles and techniques to all kinds of organisations

- analyse and critically evaluate information for cost ascertainment, planning, control and decision making

- interpret cost accounting statements.

Content and ability required

		Ability required	Covered in Chapter
6(a)	**Cost accounting** *(study weighting 35%)*		
	Use of relevant, opportunity and notional costs; classification and coding of costs; cost behaviour	3	1, 2, 4, 12
	Cost accounting appropriate to service and production-based organisations; specification, design and operation of databases for the collection of and storage of cost accounting data; use of relevant applications software to extract data and prepare management information	3	1, 3
	Integrated and non-integrated systems, including their reconciliation	3	6
	Job, batch, contract and service costing, including work in progress	3	7, 8, 11
	Process costing: the principle of equivalent units; treatment of normal and abnormal losses and gains; joint products and by-products; problems of common costs	3	9, 10
6(b)	**Information for decisions** *(study weighting 25%)*		
	Marginal costing compared with absorption costing	3	5
	The concept of contribution; relevant costs	3	5, 12-15
	Product sales pricing and mix	2	13,14
	Breakeven analysis, breakeven and profit/volume graphs	3	14
	Limiting factors, single scarce resource problems including situations with demand constraints	2	15
	Decisions about alternatives, such as make or buy	3	13
6(c)	**Budgets and budgetary control** *(study weighting 20%)*		
	The budget manual; preparation and monitoring procedures; reporting against actual financial data	3	16, 17
	Flexible budgets	3	17
	Preparation of functional budgets for operating and non-operating functions, cash budgets; the master budget	3	16
	Principal budget factors	3	16
6(d)	**Standard costing** *(study weighting 20%)*		
	Types of standard and sources of standard cost information	3	18
	Evolution of standards: continuous improvement; keeping standards meaningful and relevant	3	18
	Variance analysis covering material (price/usage), labour (rate/efficiency), variable overhead (expenditure/efficiency), fixed overhead (expenditure/volume) and sales (price/volume) variances	3	19, 20
	Standard cost book-keeping	3	20

CIMA SYLLABUS GUIDANCE NOTES 1998-99

The following Guidance Notes will be published by the CIMA in the August 1998 CIMA Student *as an aid to students and lecturers.*

'The following guidelines have been drafted by the Chief Examiner for each of the subjects. They are intended to inform candidates and lecturers about the scope of the syllabus, the emphasis that should be placed on various topics and the approach which the examination papers will adopt.

Most of these guidance notes are applicable immediately, insofar as they provide a general guidance on each subject. Guidance specific to changes effective from the May 1999 examination will be applicable from that examination and are detailed at the end of these notes.

Introduction

Chartered management accountants are part of the management team of an organisation, whose role includes the preparation of management accounting information. The information which may be produced depends on the existence of a reliable cost accounting system which is suitable for the organisation concerned.

This paper is intended to build upon the knowledge gained from the study of cost accounting as part of the CQM paper at Stage 1.

The examination paper

The syllabus is divided into sections which represent the cost accounting functions of cost recording, providing information for management decision making, and control of revenues and expenditures. While it is easy to set a question which can be clearly identified within only one of these sections, it should not be assumed that this will always be done. Candidates will be expected to have a thorough understanding of the entire syllabus and to be able to relate the items within each part of the syllabus into a coherent whole.

Wherever possible, cost accounting systems should be considered in the context of a computerised environment, and questions may be set which require candidates to explain how a computer may be used to perform a particular cost accounting function.

The examination paper will be divided into three sections.

Section A will contain one compulsory question composed of ten multiple-choice sub-questions.

Section B will contain compulsory questions.

Section C will offer candidates a choice of questions.

Questions in Section B and Section C may be in either a numerical or essay format or in a combination of these styles.

Cost accounting

This section deals with the routine collection and classification of costs and their recording by a cost accounting system appropriate to the organisation concerned, which may be manufacturing, commercial or service-based.

In the examination, candidates may be required to:

- apply the knowledge of basic cost collection and classification from their Stage 1 studies to more complex situations involving detailed preparation and interpretation of cost accounting statements

- demonstrate a knowledge of modern approaches to absorption costing, as well as more traditional methods.

Information for decisions

This section builds upon the candidate's understanding from Stage 1 studies of cost behaviour, and the methods used to identify fixed and variable costs. This syllabus tests ability to apply this knowledge in decision making situations.

For the purposes of calculations in providing information for decisions, it should be assumed that the organisation's objective is cost minimisation and profit maximisation, unless information is provided to the contrary.

In the examination, candidates may be required to:

- make calculations and form a conclusion based upon the results of those calculations

- make decisions, or recommendations, as to the action to be taken in particular circumstances

- make comments concerning the non-quantitative (ie qualitative) aspects of the decision being made

- demonstrate an appreciation of the effects of pricing policies on decision making, applying basic economic knowledge to discursive elements of a question.

The following items are *not* examinable.

- The use of differential calculus to determine optimum selling prices
- Linear programming

Budgets and budgetary control

This section builds upon the knowledge gained at Stage 1 and requires candidates to demonstrate a thorough understanding of the budgeting process. Many of the topics are also examinable in the CQM paper at Stage 1, and candidates should not be surprised to learn that questions set at Stage 2 will be more complex and may emphasise the interpretative aspects of budget preparation.

In the examination, candidates may be required to:

- demonstrate an understanding of the role of forecasting, particularly in the determination of the principal budget factor.

The following items are *not* examinable.

- Calculations using quantitative forecasting techniques
- The behavioural aspects of budgeting

Standard costing

All of the topics within this section have an ability level of 3. Candidates will be expected to have understood the basic principles of standard costing from their earlier studies, and to be able to apply this knowledge to more complex and varied situations. The entire range of operating variances is within the syllabus at this level (except the fixed overhead volume sub-variances).

Introduction

In the examination, candidates may be required to:

- prepare profit reconciliation statements using either standard marginal costing or standard absorption costing principles
- prepare ledger accounts for a standard cost book-keeping system which uses either the integrated or interlocking method. In some questions the use of journal entries may be preferred to ledger accounts.

The following items are *not* examinable.

- The materials mix and yield variances
- The distinction between planning and operating variances

CREDIT ACCUMULATION

With effect from the November 1997 exams, CIMA has introduced a *more flexible and user-friendly* process to qualifying (Credit Accumulation). The structure of the qualification remains as four stages of four papers but, within these stages, you will have *more choice* over the *order* in which you attempt papers and the *number* of papers you take in one sitting.

Stages 1, 2 and 3

- You can choose to sit *between one and six papers* from Stages 1 and 2, or Stages 2 and 3, at any one examination sitting.
- You must *complete Stage 1 before you attempt Stage 3*.
- You must *complete Stages 1 to 3 before you attempt Stage 4*.
- *Core papers* must be taken in sequence.

  o Paper 2 *Cost Accounting and Quantitative Methods* must be taken before Paper 6 *Operational Cost Accounting*, which must be taken before Paper 10 *Management Accounting Applications*.

  o Paper 1 *Financial Accounting Fundamentals* must be taken before Paper 5 *Financial Accounting*, which must be taken before Paper 9 *Financial Reporting*.

- *Each paper* will be examined independently and will have a *pass mark of 50%*.

Stage 4

- At your *first sitting* of Stage 4, you must take all four papers. You will *pass* Stage 4 if you earn a *total of 200%* across all four papers.
- If you *fail to achieve 200%*, you will receive a *permanent credit* for any subject for which you achieved the *50% pass mark provided* you earned a *minimum of 30% in all other papers*.
- If you *do not pass* at your first attempt, you must *sit all papers for which you did not receive a credit at the same sitting*. You will pass Stage 4 if you earn a minimum of 50% for each paper taken.
- If you do not pass on your second attempt, the *credit accumulation process continues* until you have received a permanent credit for all four papers.

How many papers should you attempt each sitting?

This is really like asking how long a piece of string is. It will depend on whether or not you are enrolled on a course, the amount of study time you have available, your aptitude for the subject and so on.

If you are enrolled on a *course*, we suggest you *follow the advice of your course provider*. If you are *studying on your own* you should probably *attempt two papers every six months*. At each sitting we recommend that you combine a core paper with a non-core paper.

If you require any further information, contact our Customer Services Department. You will find details of how to do this at the back of the Study Text.

THE EXAMINATION PAPER

Assessment methods and format of the paper

		Number of marks
Section A:	one compulsory question composed of ten multiple choice sub-questions	20
Section B:	two compulsory questions	55
Section C:	one question from two	25
		100

Time allowed : 3 hours

Analysis of past papers

The analysis below shows the topics which have been examined in the seven sittings to date of *Operational Cost Accounting*, and those included in the CIMA Specimen paper.

May 1998

Section A (compulsory question, 20 marks)
1   Ten multiple choice questions covering various topics

Section B (2 compulsory questions, one worth 30 marks, one worth 25 marks)
2   Profit reconciliation and variances
3   Decision making: discontinuance, contribution breakeven chart

Section C (1 out of 2 questions, 25 marks)
4   Cash budget preparation
5   Overhead absorption, job costing and ABC

November 1997

Section A (compulsory question, 20 marks)
1   Ten multiple choice questions covering various topics

Section B (2 compulsory questions, one worth 30 marks, one worth 25 marks)
2   Process costing
3   Budgeting

Section C (1 out of 2 questions, 25 marks)
4   Variance analysis
5   Decision making

May 1997

Section A (compulsory question, 20 marks)
1   Ten multiple choice questions covering various topics

Section B (2 compulsory questions, one worth 30 marks, one worth 25 marks)
2   Contract costing; overhead absorption; process costing
3   Decision involving one limiting factor and limited sales demand; cost accounting terms

Section C (1 out of 2 questions, 25 marks)
4   Presentation of variances, difference between budgetary control and standard costing; uses of a database
5   Calculation of actual data from variances; explanation of variances

November 1996

Section A (compulsory question, 20 marks)
1 Ten multiple choice questions covering various topics

Section B (2 compulsory questions, one worth 30 marks, one worth 25 marks)
2 Absorption costing; uses of cost information
3 Variances under absorption and marginal costing; activity based costing

Section C (1 out of 2 questions, 25 marks)
4 Fixed and variable costs; breakeven and target profit analysis
5 Fixed and flexible budgets; uses of spreadsheets in budgeting

May 1996

Section A (compulsory question, 20 marks)
1 Ten multiple choice questions covering various topics

Section B (2 compulsory questions, one worth 30 marks, one worth 25 marks)
2 Contract costing (including balance sheet disclosures); differences between job, batch and contract costing
3 Variance analysis; standard cost bookkeeping journal entries; types of standards

Section C (1 out of 2 questions, 25 marks)
4 Marginal costing and absorption costing profit statements; marginal costing and absorption costing profit reconciliations; period-to-period absorption costing profit reconciliations; breakeven calculations; marginal costing and its advantages for decision making
5 Cash budgeting

November 1995

Section A (compulsory question, 20 marks)
1 Ten multiple choice questions covering various topics

Section B (2 compulsory questions, one worth 30 marks, one worth 25 marks)
2 Cost classification for decision making; limiting factor analysis; limiting factor analysis and make or buy decision
3 The application of job costing to a service industry (including cost classification and breakeven calculations)

Section C (1 out of 2 questions, 25 marks)
4 Use of high-low method and index numbers (taking account of inflation) to forecast costs; preparation of breakeven chart
5 Variance analysis and preparation of ledger accounts using standard cost bookkeeping

May 1995

Section A (compulsory question, 20 marks)
1 Ten multiple choice questions covering various topics

Section B (2 compulsory questions, one worth 30 marks, one worth 25 marks)
2 Process costing, joint products and by-products
3 Decision making: minimum pricing and opportunity costing

Section C (1 out of 2 questions, 25 marks)
4 Variance analysis, standard costing versus budgetary control
5 Cash flow forecasting: preparation, the usefulness of spreadsheets, control

Specimen paper

Section A (compulsory question, 20 marks)

1   Ten multiple choice questions covering various topics

Section B (2 compulsory questions, one worth 30 marks, one worth 25 marks)

2   Process costing and cost bookkeeping
3   Limiting factor decision making; the use of the graphical approach to linear programming in decision making

Section C (1 out of 2 questions, 25 marks)

4   Variance analysis and operating statements; budgetary control versus standard costing; absorption rates in service industries
5   Budget preparation; principal budget factors

THE MEANING OF EXAMINERS' INSTRUCTIONS

The examinations department of the CIMA has asked the Institute's examiners to be precise when drafting questions. In particular, examiners have been asked to use precise instruction words. It will probably help you to know what instruction words may be used, and what they mean. With the Institute's permission, their list of recommended requirement words, and their meaning, is shown below.

Recommended requirement words are:

Advise/recommend	Present information, opinions or recommendations to someone to enable that recipient to take action
Amplify	Expand or enlarge upon the meaning of (a statement or quotation)
Analyse	Determine and explain the constituent parts of
Appraise/assess/evaluate	Judge the importance or value of
Assess	See 'appraise'
Clarify	Explain more clearly the meaning of
Comment (critically)	Explain
Compare (with)	Explain similarities and differences between
Contrast	Place in opposition to bring out difference(s)
Criticise	Present the faults in a theory or policy or opinion
Demonstrate	Show by reasoning the truth of
Describe	Present the details and characteristics of
Discuss	Explain the opposing arguments
Distinguish	Specify the differences between
Evaluate	See 'appraise'
Explain/interpret	Set out in detail the meaning of
Illustrate	Use an example - chart, diagram, graph or figure as appropriate - to explain something
Interpret	See 'explain'
Justify	State adequate grounds for
List (and explain)	Itemise (and detail meaning of)
Prove	Show by testing the accuracy of
Recommend	See 'advise'
Reconcile	Make compatible apparently conflicting statements or theories
Relate	Show connections between separate matters
State	Express
Summarise	State briefly the essential points (dispensing with examples and details)
Tabulate	Set out facts or figures in a table

Requirement words which will be avoided

Examiners have been asked to avoid instructions which are imprecise or which may not specifically elicit an answer. The following words will *not* be used.

Consider	As candidates could do this without writing a word
Define	In the sense of stating exactly what a thing is, as CIMA wishes to avoid requiring evidence of rote learning
Examine	As this is what the examiner is doing, not the candidate
Enumerate	'List' is preferred
Identify	
Justify	When the requirement is not 'to state adequate grounds for' but 'to state the advantage of'
List	On its own, without an additional requirement such as 'list and explain'
Outline	As its meaning is imprecise (the addition of the word 'briefly' to any of the suggested action words being more satisfactory)
Review	
Specify	
Trace	

 BPP Publishing

STUDY CHECKLIST

This page is designed to help you chart your progress through the Study Text, including the illustrative questions at the back of it. You can tick off each topic as you study and try questions on it. Insert the dates you complete the chapters and questions in the relevant boxes. You will thus ensure that you are on track to complete your study before the exam.

	Text chapters *Date completed*	**Illustrative questions** *Question numbers*	*Date completed*

PART A: COST ACCOUNTING

1	Cost accounting and cost classification and coding	1
2	Cost behaviour	2
3	Computers and cost accounting	3
4	Dealing with overheads	4
5	Absorption costing and marginal costing compared	5
6	Cost bookkeeping	6
7	Job and batch costing	7,8
8	Contract costing	9
9	Process costing	10
10	Process costing, joint products and by-products	11, 12
11	Service costing	13

PART B: INFORMATION FOR DECISIONS

12	Relevant costing	14
13	Decision making	15,16
14	Breakeven analysis	17,18
15	Limiting factor decision making	19,20

PART C: BUDGETS AND BUDGETARY CONTROL

16	Budgets	21
17	Budgetary control	22

PART D: STANDARD COSTING

18	Standard costing	23
19	Basic variance analysis	24
20	Further variance analysis	25

Part A
Cost accounting

Chapter 1

COST ACCOUNTING AND COST CLASSIFICATION AND CODING

This chapter covers the following topics.

		Syllabus reference	Ability required
1	Introduction to cost accounting	6(a)	Skill
2	Cost accounting and financial accounting	6(a)	Skill
3	Cost classification	6(a)	Skill
4	Cost units and cost centres	6(a)	Skill
5	Cost codes	6(a)	Skill

Introduction

Welcome to *Operational Cost Accounting* and, for those of you who have never met the subject before, welcome to cost accounting. This chapter will introduce the subject to those of you who don't really know what it is (and, in fact, to those of you who do but need your memories refreshing).

In the first section of this chapter, we will examine what cost accounting is and what a cost accountant does. In section 2 we explain why information is analysed differently for cost and financial accounting purposes. We will then examine how costs can be classified and also define cost units and cost centres. These topics, which you covered in Paper 2, are re-examined in detail because much of the rest of the Study Text builds on these foundations.

We end the chapter by discussing a *new topic*, cost coding.

Please don't think that because you may have already covered much of this introductory material you can skip this chapter. An understanding of the areas covered in this chapter is vital before you proceed with any other chapter in this Study Text and you are strongly advised to work through it very carefully. It is particularly important to understand that management relies on the cost accountant. Without the information the cost accountant provides the business cannot be run effectively.

1   INTRODUCTION TO COST ACCOUNTING

What is cost accounting?

1.1   Who can provide the answers to the following questions?

(a) What has the cost of goods produced or services provided been?
(b) What has the cost of operating a department been?
(c) What have revenues been?

1.2   Yes, you've guessed it, the cost accountant.

1.3   Knowing about costs incurred or revenues earned enables management to do the following.

(a) Assess the profitability of a product, a service, a department, or the organisation in total.

(b) Perhaps, set selling prices with some regard for the costs of sale.

(c) Put a value to stocks of goods (raw materials, work in progress, finished goods) that are still held in store at the end of a period, for preparing a balance sheet of the company's assets and liabilities.

1.4 That was quite easy. But who could answer the following questions?

(a) What are the future costs of goods and services likely to be?

(b) How do actual costs compare with planned costs?

(c) What information does management need in order to make sensible decisions about profits and costs?

1.5 Well, you may be surprised, but again it is the cost accountant.

Definition of cost accounting

1.6 The CIMA *Official Terminology* defines cost accounting as: 'The establishment of budgets, standard costs, and actual costs of operations, processes, activities or products; and the analysis of variances, profitability or the social use of funds'.

The changing scope of cost accounting   *11/96*

1.7 Historically cost accounting has dealt with the *accumulation* of historical costs and *charging* of those costs to units of output (answering the questions in 1.1).

1.8 However cost accounting also now provides management with the information it needs to manage the business effectively. Hence cost accounting now also provides the data necessary to help management in *planning, control* and *decision-making*.

1.9 Cost accounting systems are not confined to manufacturing operations. Within manufacturing organisations cost accounting is also applied to service departments such as administration, selling and distribution, and research and development. In addition cost accounting is also used in service industries, government departments and charitable organisations.

Exam focus point

In the exam you may be asked to describe the cost information requirements for a specific organisation. Here are some questions to consider.

(a) What information does the organisation need to be able to plan effectively?

(b) What are the important decisions management will have to take?

(c) What information will indicate to management how the business has performed and how resources are being controlled?

The work of the cost department

1.10 The cost department is responsible for keeping the cost accounting records.

(a) These records should analyse production, administration, marketing costs and so on in such a way as to fulfil all the requirements set out in Paragraph 1.9.

(b) The systems should cater for the production of regular performance statements which are necessary to management for control purposes.

(c) The system should also be capable of analysing the following.

(i) Past costs (for profit measurement, stock valuation)

   (ii)   Present costs (for control, for example by means of comparing current results against the budget)

   (iii)   Future costs (for budgeting and decision making)

Exercise 1

If a company did not have a costing system, what type of information would be unavailable to management?

Solution

(a)   The profitability of individual products, services or jobs.

(b)   The profitability of different departments or operations.

(c)   The cost behaviour of the various items of expenditure in the organisation. This would mean that cost estimation would not be as accurate as it could be.

(d)   The differences between actual results and expected results. With an efficient costing system, such differences can be traced to the manager responsible.

(e)   The level at which to set prices so as to cover costs and generate an acceptable level of profit.

(f)   The effect on profits of increases or decreases in output, or the shutdown of a product line or department.

---

2   COST ACCOUNTING AND FINANCIAL ACCOUNTING

2.1   The financial accounting and cost accounting systems in a business both record the same basic data for income and expenditure, but each set of records may analyse the data in a different way. This is because each system has a different purpose, derived from the uses made of each.

Users of financial accounts

2.2   *Shareholders* use financial accounts to assess:

   (a)   whether their investment is secure; and

   (b)   whether their investment is likely to provide the required income in the form of dividends and/or show an acceptable level of growth (and thus an increasing share price) in the future.

2.3   Shareholders will therefore be interested in using the results to assess whether the business fulfils the above criteria, and whether directors have carried out their stewardship role well. They will be interested in making comparisons of the business's performance over time, and comparisons with other organisations. The financial accounting information has therefore to be presented in a form that can facilitate comparisons; thus financial accounts are prepared in accordance with strict legal guidelines laid down in company law and accounting standards.

2.4   Other users of financial accounts include employees, suppliers, customers and the Inland Revenue.

Users of cost accounts

2.5   As we have seen, management use cost accounts to help them manage their business. Outsiders will not see this information. There are thus no strict rules which govern the way the information should be prepared and presented.

2.6 The fact that management are the primary users of cost accounts, whilst the principal function of financial accounts is to inform outsiders not involved day-to-day with the business, has the following implications.

(a) The cost accounting information may be kept separately from the financial accounting information in two sets of accounts. However an organisation may be able to maintain a single *integrated* set of accounts which contains both cost and financial accounting information (this is more likely with computerisation).

(b) The cost accounting system should be suited to the business's needs. There is no point in having a costing system if its costs outweighs the benefits it provides.

3   COST CLASSIFICATION

3.1 Before any attempt can be made to establish stock valuations and measure profits, plan, make decisions or exercise control, costs must be classified. Classification is the process of arranging items into groups according to their degree of familiarity.

Definition

3.2 '*Cost classification* is the arrangement of items into logical groups, having regard to their nature (subjective classification) or purpose (objective classification). (CIMA *Official Terminology*).

3.3 Classification of costs according to their nature means grouping costs according to whether they are materials, labour or overheads. Each grouping may be subdivided; for example, the materials classification may be subdivided into raw materials, components and consumables. Classifications of costs according to their purposes reflects the uses made of cost accounting information.

(a) Stock valuation and profit measurement
(b) Planning and decision making
(c) Control

Cost classification for stock valuation and profit measurement

Product costs and period costs

3.4 In the United Kingdom, the Statement of Standard Accounting Practice on stocks and work in progress (SSAP 9) requires that, in general, for stock valuation (and hence profit reporting), only *manufacturing* costs should be included in the cost of a product. Cost accountants therefore classify costs as product costs or period costs.

3.5 *Product costs* are 'costs of a finished product built up from its cost elements' (CIMA *Official Terminology*). Such costs are initially identified as part of the value of stock. They become expenses (in the form of cost of goods sold) only when the stock is sold.

3.6 *Period costs* are costs that are deducted as expenses during the current period without ever being included in the value of stock held.

Direct costs and indirect costs (overheads)   *S/98*

3.7 A *direct cost* is a cost that can be traced in full to the product, service or department that is being costed. 'Expenditure which can be economically identified with a specific saleable cost unit'. (CIMA *Official Terminology*)

(a) Direct material costs are the costs of materials that are known to have been used in making and selling a product or even providing a service (unless the materials are used in negligible amounts and/or have a negligible cost, in which case they are grouped under indirect materials).

(b) Direct labour costs are the specific costs of the workforce used to make a product or provide a service. Direct labour costs are established by measuring the time taken for a job, or the time taken in 'direct production work'. Traditionally, direct labour costs have been restricted to wage-earning factory workers, but in recent years, with the development of systems for costing services ('service costing'), the costs of some salaried staff might also be treated as a direct labour cost.

(c) Other direct expenses are those expenses that have been incurred in full as a direct consequence of making a product, providing a service or running a department (depending on whether a product, a service or a department is being costed).

3.8 An *indirect cost* (or *overhead*), on the other hand, is a cost that is incurred in the course of making a product, providing a service or running a department, but which cannot be traced directly and in full to the product, service or department. 'Expenditure on labour, materials or services which cannot be economically identified with a specific saleable cost unit'. (CIMA Official Terminology)

3.9 Examples might be a supervisor's wages (indirect labour cost), cleaning materials (indirect material cost) and buildings insurance (indirect expense).

3.10 Indirect costs are classified as follows.

(a) All indirect material cost, indirect labour cost and indirect expenses *incurred in the factory from receipt of the order until its completion* are included in production (or factory or manufacturing) overhead.

(b) Administration overhead includes all indirect material costs, wages and expenses *incurred in the direction, control and administration of an undertaking*.

(c) All indirect material costs, wages and expenses *incurred in promoting sales and retaining customers* are included in selling overhead.

(d) Distribution overhead includes all indirect material costs, wages and expenses *incurred in making the packed product ready for despatch and delivering it to the customer*.

3.11 Prime cost is another important term. *Prime cost* is often restricted to direct material and direct labour, but may often find that examination questions also include direct expenses in prime cost.

Exam focus point

This last point emphasises the need, as in all exams, to *read the question* very carefully.

Exercise 2

How might the following costs be classified?

(a) Primary packing materials like cartons and boxes
(b) Employees engaged in altering the condition or composition of a product
(c) The hire of tools or equipment for a particular job
(d) Rent and insurance of a factory
(e) Depreciation of office machines
(f) Market research
(g) Wages of despatch clerks
(h) Wages of maintenance staff and stores staff
(i) Cost of glue in box-making
(j) Depreciation of factory buildings

Solution

(a) Direct material cost
(b) Direct labour cost
(c) Direct expense
(d) Production overhead or indirect expense
(e) Administration overhead or indirect expense

(f)   Selling overhead or indirect expense
(g)   Distribution overhead or indirect labour cost
(h)   Indirect labour cost or production overhead
(i)   Indirect materials cost or production overhead
(j)   Indirect expense or production overhead

3.12   A cost may be a direct cost in one cost analysis and an indirect cost in another part. This point is perhaps best illustrated with a simple example.

3.13   The Donkey Oater Racing Stables trains and races two horses, Sancho Panza and Rosinante. Costs for the recent month are as follows.

	£
Salary of the stable manager	1,000
Wages: Special groom to Sancho Panza	80
General stable boy	80
Jockey for both horses: retainer	200
race fees	200
Race entrance fees: Sancho Panza (three races)	150
Rosinante (two races)	100
Hay, straw and so on	600
Depreciation on stable and riding equipment	200
Rent and rates	300
Heating and lighting	100

3.14   (a)   All of the costs listed are direct costs of operating the training and racing stable, with the exception of the various race fees (which are only incurred as and when horses are entered for races).

(b)   The direct costs of keeping one of the horses, Sancho Panza, in the month are the costs of the special groom and race fees. All other costs are one of the following.

(i)   Costs shared with Rosinante such as stable manager's salary, wages of stable boy, jockey's retainer, hay and straw, depreciation, rent and rates, heating and lighting. Some of these costs could be charged directly (for example hay and straw consumed, stable boy's time) if a system for recording the material issued to each horse or time spent with each horse were in operation.

(ii)   Direct costs of the other horse (race fees).

(c)   The direct costs of a race are the entrance fee (£50) and the jockey's fees (£40). Indirect costs would be not only the jockey's retainer, but also the other costs of running the stable.

In conclusion, when classifying a cost as direct or indirect (an overhead), the cost accountant must consider the product or service for which a cost is being established.

Functional costs

3.15   In a 'traditional' costing system for a manufacturing organisation, costs are classified as follows.

(a)   Production or manufacturing costs
(b)   Administration costs
(c)   Marketing, or selling and distribution costs

Classification in this way is known as *classification by function*.

3.16   Many expenses fall comfortably into one or other of these three broad classifications. Manufacturing costs are associated with the factory, selling and distribution costs with the sales, marketing, warehousing and transport departments and administration costs with general office departments (such as accounting and personnel). Other expenses that do not fall fully into one of these classifications might be categorised as 'general overheads' or even listed as a classification on their own (for example research and development costs).

3.17 A commonly found build-up of costs for a product made by a manufacturing organisation is as follows.

	£
Production costs	
Direct material	A
Direct wages	B
Direct expenses	C
Prime cost	A+B+C
Production overheads	D
Full factory cost	A+B+C+D
Administration costs	E
Selling and distribution costs	F
Full cost of sales	A+B+C+D+E+F

Cost classification for decision making

11/95, 5/97

3.18 Decision making is based on the occurrence of future events and hence management require information on expected future costs and revenues. Cost accounting systems are designed to accumulate past costs and revenues for stock valuation and profit measurement and hence future costs and revenues play no part in such a system. Past costs and revenues may, however, provide a close approximation to future costs and revenues and it may therefore be possible to extract decision-making information from them.

Fixed costs and variable costs

3.19 A knowledge of how costs will vary at different levels of activity (or volume) is essential for decision making. The terms *fixed cost* and *variable cost* are generally used to describe how costs react to changes in activity level. A fixed cost is 'The cost which is incurred for a period, and which, within certain output and turnover limits, tends to be unaffected by fluctuations in the levels of activity (output or turnover)' whereas a variable cost is 'Cost which tends to vary with the level of activity' (CIMA *Official Terminology*).

3.20 The distinction between fixed and variable costs lies in whether the amount of costs incurred will rise as the volume of activity increases, or whether the costs will remain the same, regardless of the volume of activity. Some examples are as follows.

(a) Direct material costs will rise as more units of a product are manufactured, and so they are variable costs that vary with the volume of production.

(b) Sales commission is often a fixed percentage of sales turnover, and so is a variable cost that varies with the level of sales (but not with the level of production).

(c) Telephone call charges are likely to increase if the volume of business expands, and so they are a variable overhead cost, varying with the volume of production and sales.

(d) The rental cost of business premises is a constant amount, at least within a stated time period, and so it is a fixed cost that does not vary with the level of activity conducted on the premises.

3.21 Note that costs can be classified as direct costs or indirect costs/overheads, or as fixed or variable costs. These alternative classifications are not, however, mutually exclusive, but are complementary to each other, so that we can find some direct costs that are fixed costs (although most are variable costs) and some overhead costs that are fixed and some overhead costs that are variable.

Exercise 3

Give *three* reasons why direct production labour cost might be regarded as a fixed cost rather than as a variable cost.

Solution

The cost of direct production labour might be regarded as a fixed cost rather than as a variable cost for *three* of the following reasons.

(a) Direct labour may be paid a guaranteed salary, regardless of output.

(b) Production methods may be highly mechanised, with the result that direct labour cost is insignificant and may be approximated to a fixed cost.

(c) A no-redundancy policy may result in labour costs remaining fixed regardless of output.

(d) Union agreements featuring guaranteed manning levels can result in a fixed production labour cost.

Exercise 4

Explain whether you agree with the following statements.

(a) All direct costs are variable.
(b) Variable costs are controllable and fixed costs are not.

Solution

(a) Most direct costs are variable in that the total varies with units produced, hours worked and so on, but it is incorrect to say that all such costs are variable. For example, the manufacture of a new product may require additional working space to be rented, and the rental will not vary with the level of work done. Furthermore, while labour is usually treated as a variable cost, in practice employees' pay is fixed per week, regardless of the volume of output.

(b) It is only true to say that variable costs are controllable and fixed costs are not within a limited range of output. In this range fixed costs will largely be unaffected by changes in output while variable costs will increase or decrease given control decisions. However, in the long run *all* costs are controllable, even to the extent of deciding to close down the factory for good. Conversely, although labour costs are unusually deemed to be variable it is unlikely that a company will dismiss all its employees during a period when output is low, preferring to retain them at a basic wage rather than face the high costs of redundancy payments.

3.22 We will consider fixed and variable costs in more detail in Chapter 2.

Relevant and non-relevant costs

3.23 Costs will either be relevant or non-relevant to any decision that is made.

(a) *Relevant costs* are 'costs appropriate to a specific management decision' (CIMA Official Terminology). Relevant costs (and revenues) will be *changed* by a specific management decision.

(b) *Non-relevant* costs are those that will be unaffected by a decision.

3.24 Relevant costing is considered in more detail in Chapter 12.

Cost classification for control

Controllable and uncontrollable costs

3.25 One of the purposes of cost accounting is to provide control information to management who wish to know whether or not a particular cost item is controllable by means of management action.

(a) A *controllable cost* is 'a cost which can be influenced by its budget holder' (CIMA *Official Terminology*).

(b) An *uncontrollable cost* is a cost that cannot be affected by management within a given time period.

Normal and abnormal costs

3.26   Costs can also be classified by whether they are expected.

(a)   A *normal cost* is a cost which management expected to occur and which is of an expected magnitude.

(b)   An *abnormal cost* is a cost which was not expected or which is larger or smaller than expected. The most common types of normal and abnormal cost arise in process costing, which we cover in Chapters 9 and 10.

3.27   We have included normal and abnormal costs under cost classification for control since such a classification attracts managers' attention and enables them to attempt to control the cost of abnormal events.

Exam focus point

Exam questions may ask you to give *practical examples* of types of cost as well as a definition. Threre are plenty of examples in the paragraphs above and throughout this book (especially in Chapters 2 and 12). If you memorise some of them this will help you to get the distinctions right when you are doing your exam.

---

4   COST UNITS AND COST CENTRES

Cost units

4.1   For all areas of cost accounting, but especially for establishing stock valuations, profits and balance sheet items, the cost accountant must be able to determine the cost of a unit of output. For cost accounting purposes this unit is known as a cost unit.

4.2   A *cost unit* is defined as 'A unit of product or service in relation to which costs are ascertained' (CIMA *Official Terminology*). This means that a cost unit can be anything for which it is possible to ascertain the cost.

4.3   The unit selected must be appropriate to the business, the purpose of the cost ascertainment exercise and the amount of information available. Particular care must be taken in non-manufacturing organisations. Here are some suggestions for cost units for different organisations.

Organisation	*Possible cost unit*
Steelworks	Tonne of steel produced
	Tonne of coke used
Hospital	Patient/day
	Operation
Freight organisation	Tonne/kilometre (ton/mile)
Passenger transport organisation	Passenger/kilometre or mile
Accounting firm	Chargeable hour
Restaurant	Meal served

Composite cost units

4.4   Many of these cost units are what can be called *composite cost units*. A composite cost unit is made up of two parts. For example, a freight transport organisation carries goods over distance.

(a) The volume of goods carried can be measured in tonnes. However, a cost unit of cost per tonne carried does not take account of the distance the goods have been transported (which affects, for example, fuel costs and drivers' wages if paid on a time-rate basis).

(b) If the only cost unit was based on kilometres travelled this would ignore whether the transport capacity was used efficiently, as the cost per kilometre would be the same for transporting a small item on an otherwise empty lorry as a large one on a full lorry.

4.5 Therefore a composite unit, the cost taken to transport one tonne a distance of one kilometre, might be suitable.

4.6 Cost units can also be used as performance indicators, especially in non-profit-making organisations. Consider the National Health Service. The cost per patient per day in two hospitals might be compared to see which was more efficient. However, care should be taken when using indicators like these, as hospitals specialising in different areas may incur quite different costs.

Exercise 5

Suggest suitable cost units which could be used to aid control within the following organisations.

(a) A public transport authority
(b) A hotel with 50 double rooms and 10 single rooms
(c) A hospital
(d) A road haulage business

Solution

(a) (i) Passenger/mile
   (ii) Mile travelled
   (iii) Passenger journey
   (iv) Ticket issued

(b) (i) Guest/night
   (ii) Bed occupied/night
   (iii) Meal supplied

(c) (i) Patient/night
   (ii) Operation
   (iii) Outpatient visit

(d) (i) Tonne/mile
   (ii) Mile

Cost centres

4.7 But how does the cost accountant go about determining the cost of a cost unit?

4.8 To begin with, all costs should be recorded as a direct cost of a cost centre. Even overhead costs are directly traceable to an office or an item of expense and there should be an overhead cost centre to cater for these costs.

4.9 A cost centre is 'A production or service location, function, activity or item of equipment whose costs may be attributed to cost units' (CIMA *Official Terminology*). Each cost centre acts as a collecting place for certain costs before they are analysed further. The total cost of a cost centre may for some purposes be related to the cost units which have passed through the cost centre, or the total cost might be reallocated over other cost centres.

4.10 Suitable cost centres might be as follows.

(a) A *production department* itself, a machine within the department or group of machines, a foreman's work group, a work bench and so on.

(b) *Service departments*, such as the stores, maintenance, production planning and control departments.

(c) *Administration, sales or distribution departments*, such as the personnel, accounting or purchasing departments; a sales region or salesman; or a warehouse or distribution unit.

(d) *Shared costs* (for example rent, rates, electricity or gas bills) may require cost centres of their own, in order to be directly allocated. Shared cost items may be charged to separate, individual cost centres, or they may be grouped into a larger cost centre (for example 'factory occupancy costs', for rents, rates, heating, lighting, building repairs, cleaning and maintenance of a particular factory).

4.11 Charging costs to a cost centre simply involves two steps.

(a) Identifying the cost centre for which an item of expenditure is a direct cost.

(b) Allocating the cost to the cost centre (usually by means of a *cost code*, details of which are given in the next section of this chapter).

Cost centres therefore provide a basis for the collection and further analysis of actual costs. We will look at the next stage of the build-up of the cost of a cost unit in Chapter 4.

5   COST CODES

5.1 We have seen that charging costs to a cost centre involves two steps.

(a) Identifying the cost centre for which an item of expenditure is a direct cost.
(b) Allocating the cost to the cost centre.

5.2 The allocation of the cost to the cost centre is usually by means of a *cost code*.

5.3 In order to provide accurate management information, it is vital that costs are allocated correctly. Each individual cost should therefore be identifiable by its code. This is possible by building up the individual characteristics of the cost into the code.

5.4 The characteristics which are normally identified are as follows.

(a) The nature of the cost (materials, labour, overhead) which is known as a *subjective classification*

(b) The type of cost (direct or indirect and so on)

(c) The cost centre to which the cost should be allocated. This is known as an *objective classification*.

(d) The department which the particular cost centre is in.

Features of a good coding system

5.5 An efficient and effective coding system, whether manual or computerised, should incorporate the following features.

(a) The code must be easy to use and communicate.

(b) Each item should have a unique code.

(c) The coding system must allow for expansion.

(d) If there is a conflict between the ease of using the code by the people involved and its manipulation on a computer, the human interest should dominate.

(e) The code should be flexible so that small changes in a cost's classification can be incorporated without major changes to the coding system itself.

(f)   The coding system should provide a comprehensive system, whereby every recorded item can be suitable coded.

(g)   The coding system should be brief, to save clerical time in writing out codes and to save storage space in computer memory and on computer files. At the same time codes must be long enough to allow for the suitable coding of all items.

(h)   The likelihood of errors going undetected should be minimised.

(i)   There should be a readily available index or reference book of codes.

(j)   Existing codes should be reviewed regularly and out-of-date codes removed.

(k)   Code numbers should be issued from a single central point. Different people should not be allowed to add new codes to the existing list independently.

(l)   The code should be either entirely numeric or entirely alphabetic. In a computerised system, numeric characters are preferable. The use of dots, dashes, colons and so on should be avoided.

(m)   Codes should be uniform (that is, have the same length and the same structure) to assist in the detection of missing characters and to facilitate processing.

(n)   The coding system should avoid problems such as confusion between I and 1, O and 0 (zero), S and 5 and so on.

(o)   The coding system should, if possible, be *significant* (in other words, the actual code should signify something about the item being coded).

(p)   If the code consists of alphabetic characters, it should be derived from the item's description or name (that is, mnemonics should be used).

Types of code

5.6   This is not a study text on computing, so it would be inappropriate to go into great detail on different types of code. However you should be able to write brief comments on some of the main coding methods, as listed below.

(a)   *Sequence (or progressive) codes*

Numbers are given to items in ordinary numerical sequence, so that there is no obvious connection between an item and its code. For example:

000042	2" nails
000043	office stapler
000044	hand wrench

(b)   *Group classification codes*

These are an improvement on simple sequence codes, in that a digit (often the first one) indicates the classification of an item. For example:

4NNNNN	nails
5NNNNN	screws
6NNNNN	bolts

(*Note.* 'N' stands for another digit; 'NNNNN' indicates there are five further digits in the code.)

(c)   *Faceted codes*

These are a refinement of group classification codes, in that each digit of the code gives information about an item. For example:

(i)	The first digit:	1	Nails
		2	Screws
		3	Bolts
			etc...
(ii)	The second digit:	1	Steel
		2	Brass
		3	Copper
			etc...

(iii)   The third digit:

1	50 mm
2	60 mm
3	75 mm
etc...	

A 60mm steel screw would have a code of 212.

(d) *Significant digit codes*

These incorporate some digit(s) which is (are) part of the description of the item being coded. For example:

5000	screws
5050	50 mm screws
5060	60 mm screws
5075	75 mm screws

(e) *Hierarchical codes*

This is a type of faceted code where each digit represents a classification, and each digit further to the right represents a smaller subset than those to the left. For example:

3	=	Screws
31	=	Flat headed screws
32	=	Round headed screws
322	=	Steel (round headed) screws

and so on.

5.7   A coding system does not have to be structured entirely on any one of the above systems - it can mix the various features according to the items which need to be coded. But the system eventually chosen should always be simple to use and understand and it should be flexible (so that it can readily accommodate changes within an organisation, especially expansion).

5.8   For accounting purposes, the coding system most commonly used is a form of hierarchical code. The code will need to show whether an item is an asset (and what sort of an asset) or a liability (and what sort of a liability) and the cost centre to which it is attributable (if the code is to be used for cost accounting).

5.9   When an accounting system is coded in this way, it is called a *chart of accounts*. A simple example of how a chart of accounts can be built up is as follows.

(a) *Outline chart of accounts*

0001 - 0499	Fixed assets
0500 - 0999	Stocks
1000 - 1499	Debtors
1500 - 1999	Prepayments
2000 - 2499	Bank
2500 - 2999	Creditors
3000 - 3499	Accruals
3500 - 3999	Capital and long-term finance
4000 - 4499	Revenue
4500 - 4999	Cost of sales
5000 - 5499	Administration expenses
5500 - 5999	Selling expenses
6000 - 6499	Distribution expenses
6500 - 6999	Finance expenses
7000 - 7499	Depreciation expense

(b) *Detailed chart - fixed assets*

0005	Leasehold premises
0006	Provision for amortisation of lease
7005	Disposal of lease
7006	Amortisation expense
0015	Fixtures

0016	Provision for depreciation of fixtures
7015	Disposal of fixtures
7016	Depreciation expense (fixtures)
0025	Cars
0026	Provision for depreciation of cars
7025	Disposal of cars
7026	Depreciation expense (cars)

(c)   There would follow detailed charts for stocks, debtors, prepayments and so on, but no useful purpose would be served in listing them here.

5.10   If cost accounts are *integrated* with financial accounts, then the code for an item will say where an item should go in both sets of accounts. That is to say, the code will show where in the financial accounts an item should be posted, and to which cost centre it should be allocated.

5.11   The *advantages* of such an integrated system are fairly obvious - items only have to be input into the computer system once, and the computer should be able to reconcile the cost and financial accounts very quickly.

5.12   The *disadvantage* of the system is its complexity - an organisation must be very careful how it sets up its coding system: an error could throw both sets of accounts out, and the system could be rather unwieldy and inflexible.

Example: coding systems

5.13   You are required to formulate a coding system suitable for computer application for an integrated accounting system in a small manufacturing company.

Solution

5.14   A suggested computer-based four-digit numerical coding system is set out below. The codes 1000 - 5999 are for profit and loss accounts and codes 6000 - 9999 are for balance sheet accounts.

	Basic structure	*Code number*	*Allocation*
(a)	First division	1000 - 4999	This range provides for cost accounts and is divided into four main departmental sections with ten cost centre subsections in each department, allowing for a maximum of 99 accounts in each cost centre
	Second division	1000 - 1999	Department 1
		2000 - 2999	Department 2
		3000 - 3999	Department 3
		4000 - 4999	Department 4
	Third division	100 - 999	Facility for ten cost centres in each department
	Fourth division		Breakdown of costs in each cost centre
		01 - 39	direct costs
		40 - 59	variable costs
		60 - 79	fixed costs
		80 - 99	spare capacity
(b)		5000 - 5999	This range provides for:
			(i) revenue accounts;
			(ii) work in progress accounts;
			(iii) finished goods accounts;
			(iv) cost of sales accounts;
			(v) general expenses accounts;
			(vi) profit and loss account

(c)	6000 - 6999	This range provides for individual stores items
(d)	7000 - 7999	This range provides for individual debtor accounts
(e)	8000 - 8999	This range provides for individual creditor accounts
(f)	9000 - 9999	This range is used for other balance sheet accounts including:

(f) continued:
    (i)   stores control account
    (ii) debtors' control account
    (iii) creditors' control account

Account numbers ending in 00 are used to describe the section concerned.

An illustration of the coding of consumable stores might be as follows.

Department 2

Cost centre	1	2	3	4
Consumable stores	2109	2209	2309	2409

5.15   The four-digit codes above indicate the following.

(a)   The first digit, 2, refers to department 2.
(b)   The second digit, 1, 2, 3 or 4, refers to the cost centre which incurred the cost.
(c)   The last two digits, 09, refer to 'materials costs, consumable stores'.

The advantages of a coding system

5.16   (a)   A code is usually briefer than a description, thereby saving clerical time in a manual system and storage space in a computerised system.

      (b)   A code is more precise than a description and therefore reduces ambiguity.

      (c)   Coding facilitates data processing.

Chapter roundup

- Cost accounting has the following purposes.

    o   To accumulate and charge historical costs

    o   To provide management with information for planning, control and decision-making.

- Cost accounting differs from financial accounting primarily because of user needs.

    o   Cost accounts are used by management for their own purposes.

    o   Financial accounts are used by shareholders to monitor the value of their investment and also by third parties such as the Inland Revenue.

- For the purposes of stock valuation and profit measurement costs are classified as product costs or period costs. Product costs are costs identified with goods produced or purchased for resale. Period costs are costs deducted as expenses during the current period.

- A product cost will generally comprise the costs of direct materials, direct labour and direct expenses (a direct cost being a cost that can be traced in full to the product, service or department being costed) and factory (or production or manufacturing) overhead.

- An overhead (or indirect cost) is a cost that is incurred in the course of making a product, providing a service or running a department, but which cannot be traced directly and in full to the product, service or department.

- In a traditional costing system for a manufacturing organisation, costs are often classified by function. This involves classifying costs as production/manufacturing costs, administration costs or marketing/selling and distribution costs.

- For planning and decision-making purposes, costs are classified as fixed or variable. In general, variable costs will rise as the volume of activity increases, fixed costs will not. Many items of expenditure are part-fixed and part-variable and hence are termed semi-fixed or semi-variable.

- For control, costs can be classified as controllable or uncontrollable by management or as normal or abnormal.

- To ascertain the cost of a unit of an organisation's output, costs are allocated to cost centres which are collecting places for costs. Once traced to cost centres, costs can be further analysed into cost units.

- Costs are usually allocated to cost centres by a cost code. We looked at five types of code.

    o   Sequence (or progressive) codes
    o   Group classification codes
    o   Faceted codes
    o   Significant digit codes
    o   Hierarchical codes

Test your knowledge

1   In the current environment, cost accounting deals with nothing more than establishing stock valuations. True or false? (see para 1.8)

2   What does the work of the cost department involve? (1.10)

3   Explain the purposes of cost accounting and financial accounting. (2.1 – 2.6)

4   Distinguish between product costs and period costs. (3.5, 3.6)

5   Distinguish between direct costs and indirect costs. (3.7, 3.8)

6   Define prime cost. (3.11)

7   Functional costs are generally associated with not-for-profit organisations. True or false? (3.15)

8   Distinguish between fixed costs and variable costs. (3.19)

9   A direct cost is always a variable cost. True or false? (3.21)

10   What is a relevant cost? (3.23)

11   What is an abnormal cost? (3.26)

12   What types of cost classification are appropriate for control? (3.25 - 3.27)

13   Suggest ten cost centres. (4.10)

14   What is a significant digit code? (5.6)

Now try illustrative question 1 at the end of the Study Text

Chapter 2

COST BEHAVIOUR

This chapter covers the following topics.

		Syllabus reference	Ability required
1	The importance of understanding cost behaviour	6(a)	Skill
2	Basic principles of cost behaviour	6(a)	Skill
3	Cost behaviour patterns	6(a)	Skill
4	Determining the fixed and variable elements of semi-variable costs	6(a)	Skill
5	The linear assumption of cost behaviour	6(a)	Skill

Introduction

In Chapter 1 we introduced you (or possibly reintroduced you) to the subject of cost accounting and explained, in general terms, what it is and what it does. We then considered the different ways costs can be classified for three different purposes. One of the purposes was decision making. Classification of costs for decision-making purposes requires the division of costs into those whose behaviour is such that they vary directly with changes in activity level (variable costs) and those whose behaviour is such that they do not (fixed costs).

This chapter examines further the division of costs into fixed and variable elements and explains two methods, the scattergraph method and the high-low method, of splitting a cost into these two elements.

We will begin the chapter, however, by looking at why you need to understand cost behaviour and how it impacts on all areas of cost accounting.

As with Chapter 1, you may have covered the basic principles of cost behaviour in your Paper 2 studies. However, because you will need to rely on concepts covered in both this chapter and Chapter 1 in the remainder of the text *and* in future cost and management accounting studies, we have not assumed any prior knowledge and are covering the topic in detail. It is that important!

---

1 THE IMPORTANCE OF UNDERSTANDING COST BEHAVIOUR

1.1 Are the following statements true or false?

(a) 1lb of sugar costs the same now as it did in 1970.

(b) Per kilogram, it costs the same to buy 1 kg of apples as it does to buy 1,000 kgs of apples.

(c) The wage rate of car assembly workers remains unchanged as time passes.

(d) Gas charges have never increased.

(e) If 100 units of electricity are used and the total bill is £100, then 200 units of electricity will cost £200.

(f) A pocket-sized version of a product has never been introduced.

(g) Companies never expand their operations overseas.

1.2 Let us hope that you believed the above statements to be false. If costs always remained unchanged and completely under control and if an organisation's activities remained the same from year to year, there would be no necessity to understand cost behaviour. Yet the conditions described above bear little relationship with reality. Reality is not so simple.

1.3   An understanding of cost behaviour is vital in all areas of cost and management accounting but particularly in the following.

Cost behaviour and decision making   *11/95*

1.4   Conventional cost accounting data collection systems accumulate costs by product to meet the financial accounting requirements of allocating production costs incurred during a period between cost of sales and stock. This type of data collection system is not designed to accumulate product costs for decision-making purposes. Costs derived from the cost accumulation system should not, therefore, be used for decision making.

1.5   An understanding of cost behaviour is thus vital to facilitate an evaluation of different courses of action open to an organisation. Examples of decisions that require information on how costs and revenues vary at different levels of activity include the following.

   (a)   What should the planned activity level be for the next period?

   (b)   Should the selling price be reduced in order to sell more units?

   (c)   Should sales staff be paid by a straight salary, a straight commission or a combination of the two?

   (d)   Should additional plant be purchased so that an expansion of output is possible?

   (e)   Should a particular component be manufactured internally or bought in?

   (f)   Should a contract be undertaken?

1.6   For each of the above decisions, management require estimates of costs at different levels of activity for alternative courses of action. A company might decide to tender for a contract without understanding that the extra work will mean buying a new factory, a factor not taken into account when calculating the tender price. Fulfilling the contract at the tender price is therefore likely to result in an overall loss to the company.

1.7   Management need to understand, for example, that fixed costs do not, *in general*, change as a result of a decision. We will look at this type of cost, and others, in the next section.

Cost behaviour and cost control

1.8   If the accountant does not known the level of costs which should have been incurred as a result of an organisation's activities, how can he or she hope to control costs, there being no benchmark to which the actual costs incurred can be compared?

Cost behaviour and budgeting

1.9   It is unlikely that an accountant could draw up a realistic budget without being aware of cost behaviour. Having established the number of units that can be sold, he or she will be unable to determine the associated costs, if he or she is unaware that the material costs per unit when 10,000 units are produced are less than the material cost per unit when only 5,000 units are produced due to bulk purchase discounts.

2   BASIC PRINCIPLES OF COST BEHAVIOUR

2.1   Although we have established that to plan, budget, control costs and make decisions the accountant must understand cost behaviour, we have yet to define cost behaviour. Cost behaviour is 'The variability of input costs with activity undertaken' (CIMA *Official Terminology*).

2.2   The level of activity (or capacity, output, volume or throughput) refers to the amount of work done, or the number of events that have occurred. Depending on circumstances, the level of activity may refer to the volume of production in a period, the number of items sold, the value of items sold, the number of invoices issued, the number of invoices received, the number of units of electricity consumed, the labour turnover and so on.

2.3   The basic principle of cost behaviour is that as the level of activity rises, costs will usually rise. It will cost more to produce 2,000 units of output than it will cost to produce 1,000 units; it will usually cost more to make five telephone calls than to make one call and so on.

2.4   This principle is common sense. The problem for the accountant, however, is to determine, for each item of cost, the way in which costs rise and by how much as the level of activity increases.

For our purposes here, the level of activity for measuring cost will generally be taken to be the volume of production.

3   COST BEHAVIOUR PATTERNS

Fixed costs   *11/95, 5/98*

3.1   A *fixed cost* is a cost which tends to be unaffected by increases or decreases in the volume of output. Fixed costs are a period charge, in that they relate to a span of time; as the time span increases, so too will the fixed costs (which are sometimes referred to as period costs for this reason).

3.2   A sketch graph of a fixed cost would look like this.

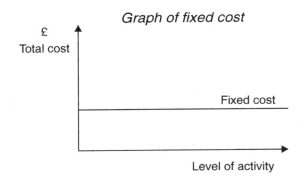

Exam focus point

Exam questions (especially MCQs) may present you with a series of graphs like the ones in this section but without any labels. You would be expected to identify the type of cost depicted by the graphs. Shut your book when you have finished this section and see if you can sketch and label each graph for yourself, and explain why it is the shape it is.

3.3   Examples of a fixed cost would be as follows.

    (a)   The salary of the managing director (per month or per annum)
    (b)   The rent of a single factory building (per month or per annum)
    (c)   Straight line depreciation of a single machine (per month or per annum)

3.4   Note that fixed costs are only constant at all levels of activity within the *relevant range* of activity. The relevant range is the range of activity at which an organisation expects to be operating in the future. It also broadly represents the activity levels at which the organisation has had experience of operating at in the past and for which cost information is available. It can therefore be dangerous to attempt to predict costs at activity levels which are outside the relevant range.

Step costs

3.5   A *step cost* is fixed in nature within certain levels of activity. For example, the depreciation of a machine may be fixed if production remains below 1,000 units per month, but if production exceeds 1,000 units, a second machine may be required, and the cost of depreciation (on two machines) would go up a step.

3.6   A sketch graph of a step cost could look like this.

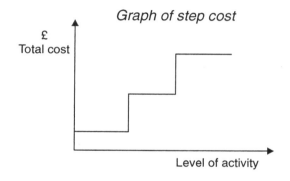

Graph of step cost

£
Total cost

Level of activity

3.7   Other examples of step costs are as follows.

(a)   Rent is a step cost in situations where accommodation requirements increase as output levels get higher.

(b)   Basic pay of employees is nowadays usually fixed, but as output rises, more employees (direct workers, supervisors, managers and so on) are required.

Variable costs   11/95

3.8   A variable cost is a cost which tends to vary directly with the volume of output. The variable cost per unit is the same amount for each unit produced. A constant variable cost per unit implies that the price per unit of material purchased or cost per labour hour worked and so on, is constant, and that the rate of material usage/labour productivity is also constant.

3.9   The following diagram illustrates basic variable cost behaviour.

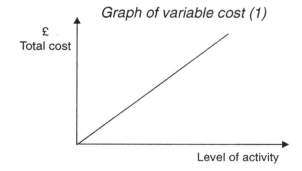

Graph of variable cost (1)

£
Total cost

Level of activity

3.10   The most important variable cost is the cost of raw materials (where there is no discount for bulk purchasing since bulk purchase discounts reduce the cost of purchases). Direct labour costs are, for very important reasons, also classed as a variable cost (even though basic wages are usually fixed).

Sales commission is a variable cost, varying in relation to the volume or value of sales rather than the level of production, and bonus payments for productivity to employees might be variable once a certain level of output is achieved, as the diagram on the following page illustrates. Up to output A, no bonus is earned.

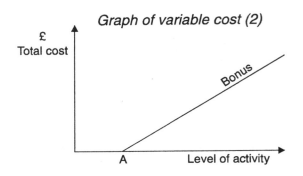

Graph of variable cost (2)

Semi-variable costs (or semi-fixed costs or mixed costs)

3.11 A semi-variable/semi-fixed/mixed cost is 'A cost containing both fixed and variable components and which is thus partly affected by a change in the level of activity' (CIMA *Official Terminology*).

3.12 Examples of these costs include the following.

    (a) *Electricity and gas bills*. There is a standing basic charge plus a charge per unit of consumption.

    (b) *Salesman's salary*. The salesman may earn a monthly basic amount of, say, £600 and then commission of 10% of the value of sales made.

    (c) *Costs of running a car*. The cost is made up of a fixed cost (which includes road tax and insurance) and variable costs (of petrol, oil, repairs and so on) which depend on the number of miles travelled.

Other cost behaviour patterns

3.13 Other cost behaviour patterns may be appropriate to certain cost items. Thus the behaviour pattern of the cost of materials after deduction of bulk purchase discount might be:

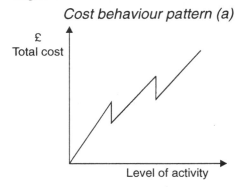

Cost behaviour pattern (a)

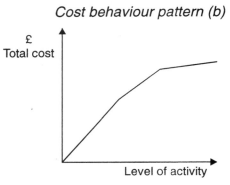

Cost behaviour pattern (b)

depending on:

    (a) whether the bulk purchase discount applies retrospectively to all units purchased as in graph (a); or

    (b) whether the discount applies only to units purchased in excess of a certain quantity. (The earlier units would be paid for at a higher unit cost, as in graph (b).)

3.14   Graph (c) below represents an item of cost which is variable with output up to a certain maximum level of cost; graph (d) represents a cost which is variable with output, subject to a minimum (fixed) charge.

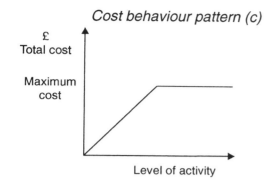

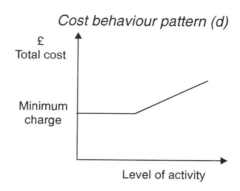

Exercise 1

Leanne Ltd has a fleet of company cars for sales representatives. Running costs have been estimated as follows.

(a)   Cars cost £12,000 when new, and have a guaranteed trade-in value of £6,000 at the end of two years. Depreciation is charged on a straight-line basis.

(b)   Petrol and oil cost 15 pence per mile.

(c)   Tyres cost £300 per set to replace; replacement occurs after 30,000 miles.

(d)   Routine maintenance costs £200 per car (on average) in the first year and £450 in the second year.

(e)   Repairs average £400 per car over two years and are thought to vary with mileage. The average car travels 25,000 miles per annum.

(f)   Tax, insurance, membership of motoring organisations and so on cost £400 per annum per car.

Required

Calculate the average cost per annum of cars which travel 20,000 miles per annum and 30,000 miles per annum.

Solution

Costs should be analysed into fixed, variable and stepped cost items.

(a)   *Fixed costs*

	£ per annum
Depreciation £(12,000 – 6,000) ÷ 2	3,000
Routine maintenance £(200 + 450) ÷ 2	325
Tax, insurance etc	400
	3,725

(b)   *Variable costs*

	Pence per mile
Petrol and oil	15.0
Repairs (£400 ÷ 50,000 miles)	0.8
	15.8

(c)   Step costs are tyre replacement costs, which are £300 at the end of every 30,000 miles.

    (i)   If the car travels less than or exactly 30,000 miles in two years, the tyres will not be changed. Average cost of tyres per annum = £0.

    (ii)   If a car travels more than 30,000 miles and up to (and including) 60,000 miles in two years, there will be one change of tyres in the period. Average cost of tyres per annum = £150 (£300 ÷ 2).

    (iii)   If a car exceeds 60,000 miles in two years (up to 90,000 miles) there will be two tyre changes. Average cost of tyres per annum = £300 (£600 ÷ 2).

The estimated costs per annum of cars travelling 20,000 miles per annum and 30,000 miles per annum would therefore be as follows.

	20,000 miles per annum £	30,000 miles per annum £
Fixed costs	3,725	3,725
Variable costs (15.8p per mile)	3,160	4,740
Tyres	150	150
Cost per annum	7,035	8,615

Cost behaviour and unit costs

3.15   So far we have been considering the behaviour of total costs (such as the total labour cost) as activity levels change. We now need to consider the behaviour of unit costs (such as the labour cost per unit) as activity levels change.

3.16   Suppose, for example, that the variable cost of producing a widget is £5 per unit. It will remain at that cost per unit no matter how many widgets are produced. However if the business's fixed costs are £5,000 then the fixed cost per unit will decrease the more units are produced: if one unit is produced then that one unit will have fixed costs of £5,000 per unit; if 2,500 are produced the fixed cost per unit will be £2; if 5,000 are produced fixed costs per unit will be only £1. Thus as the level of activity increases the fixed cost per unit (and the total cost per unit (fixed cost plus variable cost) will decrease.

3.17   In sketch graph form this may be illustrated as follows.

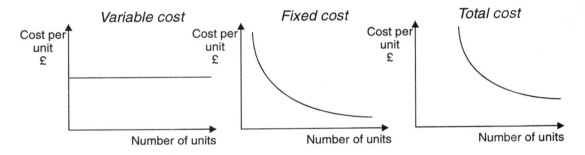

4   **DETERMINING THE FIXED AND VARIABLE ELEMENTS OF SEMI-VARIABLE COSTS**

4.1   It is often possible to assume that within the relevant range of output, costs are either variable, fixed or semi-variable. Step costs are fixed within a certain range, and the cost behaviour patterns shown in Paragraph 3.14 are variable or semi-variable within a certain range.

4.2   For this reason cost accountants usually treat all costs as fixed or variable, and semi-variable costs are divided into their variable element and their fixed element. In fact, estimating cost behaviour to derive figures for fixed and variable costs inevitably involves some approximations and assumptions.

4.3   There are several ways in which fixed cost elements and variable cost elements within semi-variable costs may be estimated. Each method is only an estimate, and can therefore give differing results from the other methods. Moreover the estimates are based on past data and events in the past may not be representative of what happens in the future.

Scattergraph method

4.4   A scattergraph of costs in previous periods can be prepared by plotting data on a graph which has cost on the vertical axis and volume of output on the horizontal axis. A line of best fit can then be drawn through the points so that distances of points above the line equal distances of points below the line.

Scattergraph showing line of best fit

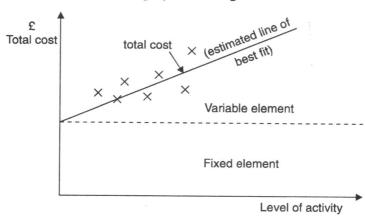

4.5   The fixed cost can be determined by reading the point where the line of best fit cuts the vertical axis. The variable cost per unit can be calculated as (total cost – fixed cost)/number of units, using a point very close to the line of best fit.

Exercise 2

The intersection of the line of best fit on the vertical axis of a scattergraph is £3,750. A point on the line of best fit represents output of 4,500 units at a total cost of £5,100. What is the variable cost per unit?

Solution

Variable cost per unit = £(5,100 – 3,750)/4,500 = £0.30

4.6   This method uses all of the data available. Its principal disadvantage is that the cost line is drawn by visual judgement and thus is a subjective approximation.

High-low method   *11/95, 5/96, 11/96, 5/98*

4.7   To estimate the fixed and variable elements of semi-variable costs, records of costs in previous periods are reviewed and the costs of the following two periods are selected.

(a)   The period with the highest volume of output
(b)   The period with the lowest volume of output

(*Note.* The periods with the highest/lowest output may not be the periods of highest/lowest cost.)

Where inflation makes the costs in each period impossible to compare, costs should be adjusted to the same price level by means of a price level index.

Exam focus point

Note how frequently the high-low method has featured in exam questions, both in MCQs and in Section C questions. Obviously, it is essential that you understand it. Note also that questions may not always specify that the high-low method is to be used: you have to deduce this from the information available.

4.8   The difference between the total cost of the high output and the total cost of the low output will be the variable cost of the difference in output levels as is shown on the following graph, where the difference in cost, £a, is seen to consist entirely of variable costs.

The variable cost per unit may be calculated from this, and the fixed cost may then also be determined.

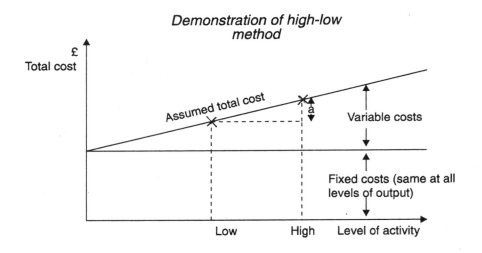

Demonstration of high-low method

Example: the high-low method with inflation

4.9   Crispy Ltd has recorded the following total costs during the last five years.

Year	Output volume Units	Total cost £	Average price level index
19X0	65,000	145,000	100
19X1	80,000	179,200	112
19X2	90,000	209,100	123
19X3	60,000	201,600	144
19X4	75,000	248,000	160

Required

Calculate the total cost that should be expected in 19X5 if output is 85,000 units and the average price level index is 180.

Solution

4.10 (a) Price levels should be adjusted to a common basis, say index level 100, before the variable cost per unit is calculated.

	Output £	Total cost	Cost at price level index = 100 £
High level	90,000 units	209,100	$\times \dfrac{100}{123}$ = 170,000
Low level	60,000 units	201,600	$\times \dfrac{100}{144}$ = 140,000
Variable costs of 30,000 units			30,000

∴ Variable cost per unit = £1

(b) By deducting the variable cost of 90,000 units from the total cost we can determine the fixed costs.

	£
Total cost of 90,000 units (index 100)	170,000
Variable cost of 90,000 units (× £1)	90,000
Fixed costs (index 100)	80,000

(c)   Now we can calculate costs in 19X5 for 85,000 units.

	£
Variable costs (index 100)	85,000
Fixed costs (index 100)	80,000
Total costs (index 100)	165,000

At 19X5 price levels (index 180), total cost $= 165,000 \times \dfrac{180}{100} = £297,000$

Exercise 3

W Ltd has operated a restaurant for the last two years. Revenue and operating costs over the two years have been as follows.

	Year 1 £'000	Year 2 £'000
Revenue	1,348,312	1,514,224
Operating costs		
Food and beverages	698,341	791,919
Wages	349,170	390,477
Other overheads	202,549	216,930

The number of meals served in year 2 showed an 8% increase on the year 1 level of 151,156. An increase of 10% over the year 2 level is budgeted for year 3.

All staff were given hourly rate increases of 6% last year (in year 2). In year 3 hourly increases of 7% are to be budgeted.

The inflation on 'other overheads' last year was 5%, with an inflationary increase of 6% expected in the year ahead.

Food and beverage costs are budgeted to average £5.14 per meal in year 3. This is expected to represent 53% of sales value.

Required

From the information given above, and using the high-low method of cost estimation, determine the budgeted expenditure on wages and other overhead for year 3.

Solution

Wages

We need to discover the variable wages cost, by using the high-low method. There are only two years, so one is taken is 'high' and one as 'low'.

	Year 1	Year 2	Increase
Number of meals	151,156	(× 8%) 163,248	12,092
	£	£	£
Wages cost	349,170	390,477	41,307

We must account for inflation, however, to 'equalise' the two years by adjusting year 1 to year 2 costs. The figure used is the 6% hourly rate increase.

	£	£	£
£349,170 × 106% =	370,120	390,477	20,357

In year 2, the variable wages cost of a meal is $\dfrac{£20,357}{12,092} = £1.68$

	£
Variable wages cost (year 2) (£1.68 × 163,248)	274,257
Fixed wages cost (year 2) (balance)	116,220
Total wages cost (year 2)	390,477

		£
So, in year 3, variable cost =	(163,248 × 110%) meals × £1.68 × 107%	322,800
Fixed cost	£116,220 × 107%	124,355
Total wages cost (year 3)		447,155

Overheads

	Year 1	Year 2	Increase
Number of meals	151,156	163,248	12,092
	£	£	£
Overhead costs	202,549	216,930	14,381
Adjusting year 1 cost to year 2 cost (× 105%)	212,676	216,930	4,254

∴ Variable overhead cost in year 2 is $\dfrac{£4,254}{12,092}$ = £0.352 per meal

	£
∴ In year 2, variable overhead cost (£0.352 × 163,248)	57,463
Fixed overhead cost (balance)	159,467
Total overhead cost (year 2)	216,930

	£
∴ In year 3, variable cost = £0.352 × (163,248 × 110%) meals (W1) × 106%	67,002
Fixed cost = £159,467 × 106%	170,630
Total overhead cost (year 3)	237,632

4.11 The *advantage* of the high-low method is its relative simplicity. Its *disadvantage* is that only two historical cost records from previous periods are used in the cost estimation. unless these two records are a reliable indicator of costs throughout the relevant range of output (which is unlikely), only a loose approximation of fixed and variable costs will be obtained.

5 THE LINEAR ASSUMPTION OF COST BEHAVIOUR

5.1 The previous paragraphs may be summarised as follows.

(a) Individual items of cost may have a cost behaviour pattern with an unusual 'shape', but costs are generally assumed to be fixed, variable or mixed (semi-fixed, semi-variable) within a normal range of output.

(b) The fixed cost and variable cost elements of mixed costs may be estimated, with varying degrees of probable accuracy, by a variety of methods, of which the high-low method is perhaps the simplest to use (but the least accurate in its estimations).

(c) Costs are therefore assumed to rise in a straight line (linear) fashion as the volume of activity increases.

5.2 A worthwhile question to answer at this stage is: are the assumptions above correct? In other words, is it true to say that costs may be divided into a fixed element and a variable cost per unit which is the same for every unit produced? There is a good argument that the variable cost per unit (or the marginal cost per unit in the language of economics), changes with the level of output. Such behaviour could be graphed as follows.

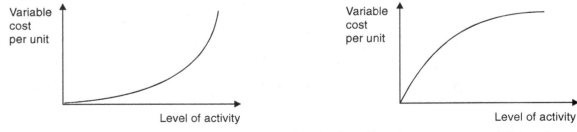

The left hand graph becomes steeper as levels of activity increase, each additional unit of activity adding more to total variable cost than the previous unit, whereas the right hand graph becomes less steep as levels of activity increase, each additional unit adding less to total variable cost than the previous unit.

Exercise 4

Can you think of examples of variable costs which might follow the behaviour patterns depicted in the diagrams above?

Solution

The cost of direct labour where employees are paid a bonus which increases as output levels increase follows the behaviour shown in the left hand graph. The right hand graph shows the behaviour of the cost of direct material where quantity discounts are available.

You may have thought of other examples.

5.3   It is sufficient at this stage to be aware of the difference between the view of the 'economist' and the view of the 'cost accountant' and to understand that the cost accountant justifies his/her linear assumption of cost behaviour for the following reasons.

(a)   It is easier to understand than curvilinear cost behaviour.

(b)   Fixed and variable costs are easier to estimate, and easier to use.

(c)   The assumption of linear costs is only used in practice within normal ranges of output, that is within a 'relevant range of activity'.

5.4   You should therefore bear in mind any assumptions which have been made when estimating cost behaviour patterns so that you use any information about estimated costs with the full knowledge of its possible limitations.

Chapter roundup

- An understanding of cost behaviour is vital for the cost accountant, particularly for cost control, budgeting and decision making.

- Costs which are not affected by the level of activity within the relevant range are fixed costs or period costs.

- Step costs are fixed within a certain range of activity.

- Variable costs increase or decrease with the level of activity, and it is usually assumed that there is a linear relationship between cost and activity.

- Semi-fixed, semi-variable or mixed costs are costs which are part fixed and part variable.

- It is often possible to assume that, within the normal range of output, costs are either variable, fixed or semi-variable.

- The fixed and variable elements of semi-variable costs can be determined by the scattergraph method or the high-low method.

- It is important to establish the time span under consideration in determining cost behaviour patterns. For instance, some fixed costs may become variable in the long run, and, in the very short term, costs which are normally considered to be variable may in fact be fixed.

- Even though fixed costs in total remain constant over a range of activity, the cost per unit will tend to reduce as the level of activity rises because the same fixed cost is being spread over a greater number of units.

Test your knowledge

1   Costs for decision making are taken from the cost accumulation system. True or false? (see para 1.4)

2   Define cost behaviour and level of activity. (2.1, 2.2)

3   Give an example of a fixed cost and a step cost. (3.3, 3.7)

4   What type of cost are electricity bills? (3.12)

5   Describe the high-low method. (4.7, 4.8)

6   Contrast an accountant's and an economist's views of cost behaviour. (5.2, 5.3)

Now try illustrative question 2 at the end of the Study Text

Chapter 3

COMPUTERS AND COST ACCOUNTING

This chapter covers the following topics.

		Syllabus reference	Ability required
1	Information systems and management information systems	6(a)	Skill
2	Cost accounting systems	6(a)	Skill
3	Computerised cost accounting	6(a)	Skill
4	Decision support systems	6(a)	Skill
5	Applications software	6(a)	Skill
6	Spreadsheets	6(a)	Skill
7	Spreadsheets and cost accounting	6(a)	Skill
8	Databases	6(a)	Skill

Introduction

In Chapter 1 we found out what cost accounting is and what a cost accountant does. Of course, not every organisation will have a cost accountant or record costs within a cost accounting system for costing, planning, control and decision-making purposes. This may be because the size of the organisation simply does not warrant it or because there are no statutory requirements to keep detailed cost records. Some small firms therefore only keep traditional financial accounts and prepare cost information in an ad-hoc fashion or not at all. This approach is, however, unsatisfactory for all but the smallest organisations: most firms therefore maintain some form of cost accounting system.

Cost accounting systems range from simple cost analysis systems to computer-based accounting systems incorporating a wide variety of techniques and processes. In this chapter we will begin by considering the place of the cost accounting system within the organisation's overall information system. We will then be looking at cost accounting systems in general and computerised systems in particular, as well as at databases and the relevant applications software which are useful to the cost accountant.

As you work through the remainder of this Study Text keep this chapter constantly in mind. Although you may be preparing costing statements yourself for examination purposes, in practice within your organisation the costing system may be computerised. But, of course, the overriding point to remember is that a manual system is, in essence, exactly the same as a computerised one.

In Chapter 6 we will see how costs are actually recorded in the cost accounting system.

1 INFORMATION SYSTEMS AND MANAGEMENT INFORMATION SYSTEMS

1.1 An organisation is made up of a series of information systems. It is difficult to define an information system since it is really a series of activities or processes.

    (a) Identification of data requirements
    (b) Collection and transcription of data (data capture)
    (c) Data processing
    (d) Communication of processed data to users
    (e) Use of processed data (as information) by users

1.2   Sometimes there are separate information systems for sales, production, personnel, financial and other matters, sometimes there is integration of these sub-systems.

1.3   Information systems can be divided into two broad categories.

(a)   Transaction (or data) processing systems
(b)   Management information systems

Transaction processing systems

1.4   Transaction processing systems could be said to represent the lowest level in a company's use of information systems. They are used for routine tasks in which data items or transactions must be recorded and processed so that operations can continue. Handling sales orders, purchase orders, payroll items and stock records are typical examples.

1.5   Some transaction processing systems have to deal with huge volumes of data, but data processing also occurs on a more modest scale and readily-available applications packages (pre-written and tested software to deal with a particular administrative or commercial task) can be used to deal with routine data processing.

1.6   Although transaction processing does not support the management function of an organisation or perform decision analysis, it is essential to the organisation's daily operation and it provides the foundation upon which a management information system can be built; a sophisticated standard costing system would be of little benefit if the underlying cost analysis performed by the transaction processing system was faulty.

Management information systems

1.7   A management information system (MIS) is defined as 'A collective term for the hardware and software used to drive a database system with the outputs, both to screen and print, being designed to provide easily assimilated information for management' (CIMA *Computing Terminology*). Management information is by no means confined to accounting information, but until relatively recently accounting information systems have been the most formally-constructed and well-developed part of the overall information system of a business enterprise. This is still the case in all but the most advanced organisations.

1.8   An alternative definition of a management information system is 'an information system making use of available resources to provide managers at all levels in all functions with the information from all relevant sources to enable them to make timely and effective decisions for planning, directing and controlling the activities for which they are responsible.'

1.9   A management information system is therefore a system of *disseminating* information which will enable managers to do their job. Since managers must have information, there will always be a management information system in any organisation.

1.10   Most management information systems are not designed, but grow up informally. However, some information systems are specially designed, often because the introduction of computers has forced management to consider its information needs in detail. This is especially the case in large companies.

1.11   Management should try to develop/implement a management information system for their enterprise with care. If they allow the MIS to develop without any formal planning, it will almost certainly be inefficient because data will be obtained and processed in a random and disorganised way and the communication of information will also be random and hit-and-miss.

(a) Some managers will prefer to keep data in their heads and will not commit information to paper. When the manager is absent from work, or is moved to another job, his stand-in or successor will not know as much as he could and should about the work because no information has been recorded to help him.

(b) The organisation will not collect and process all the information that it should, and so valuable information that ought to be available to management will be missing.

(c) Information may be available but not disseminated to the managers who are in a position of authority and so ought to be given it. The information would go to waste because it would not be used. In other words, the wrong people would have the information.

(d) Information is communicated late because the need to communicate it earlier is not understood and appreciated by the data processors.

1.12 The consequences of a poor MIS might be dissatisfaction amongst employees who believe they should be told more, a lack of understanding about what the targets for achievement are and a lack of information about how well the work is being done. Whether a management information system is formally or informally constructed, it should therefore have certain essential characteristics.

(a) The functions of individuals and their areas of responsibility in achieving company objectives should be defined.

(b) Areas of control within the company (eg cost centres, investment centres) should also be clearly defined.

(c) Information required for an area of control should flow to the manager who is responsible for it.

Cost accounting systems

1.13 An organisation's cost accounting system will be part of the overall management information system and will both provide information to assist management in planning, control and decision making and accumulate historical costs to establish stock valuations, profits and balance sheet items.

2 COST ACCOUNTING SYSTEMS

2.1 It is unlikely that, in today's competitive environment, any medium-sized organisation could survive without a cost accounting system. Even in the same industry, however, no two organisations are the same and so no ready-made cost accounting system can suit each and every organisation. Obviously the underlying principles, conventions and objectives of all cost accounting systems are identical but the application of those principles and the methods by which those objectives are pursued will, of course, vary from situation to situation.

2.2 When introducing a cost accounting system the following matters should also be considered.

(a) The information provided by the system should have the following attributes.

    (i)   It should be *relevant*.
    (ii)   It should be *accurate*.
    (iii) It should *inspire confidence*.
    (iv) It should be *timely*.
    (v)   It should be *appropriately communicated*.
    (vi) It should be *cost effective*.

(b) The cost accounting system must have regard for the *production sequence*.

(c) The costing data must identify *specific areas of control* so that each manager may take action on the information relevant to his activity.

(d) The system should take into account the *resources used*.

    (i)   An organisation may use materials with which a high degree of waste will occur or will use materials in bulk so that it may be difficult to measure usage accurately. These matters will affect the system adopted for recording issues of material.

    (ii)   The costing system may have to analyse time worked by labour and time will be influenced by whether workers work individually or in teams, whether the work is repetitive or highly skilled, whether the workers remain in one place or are involved at various stages of the production process and so on.

(e) The system should consider the *relative size* of particular items and should not, for example, provide a detailed analysis of stationery costs. The system should be flexible and capable of adapting to changing conditions.

(f) Most importantly, the *cost of the costing system* must be considered in relation to the size of the organisation and the benefits to be obtained. The system should not be over elaborate but, in considering its cost, the savings which should accrue through the control of materials, labour and production which the system affords should be borne in mind.

(g) The system must be given *periodic and skilled scrutiny* to ensure that sections of it are not obsolescent following change and development in the business.

3 COMPUTERISED COST ACCOUNTING

3.1 In modern cost accounting practice it is extremely common to find that computers play an important part in the collection of cost data and the presentation of cost and management information.

3.2 The most important fact to remember about computerised accounting (whether it is cost accounting or financial accounting) is that, in principle, it is exactly the same as manual accounting.

3.3 Accounting functions retain the same names in a computerised system as in more traditional written records. Computerised accounting still uses the familiar idea of double entry. The principles of working with a computerised cost ledger are exactly what would be expected in the manual methods they replace. The only difference is that the ledger has become 'invisible'. It is now held in a computer-sensible form, ready to be called upon.

3.4 The computer introduces greater efficiency because it is ideally suited for improving the speed and accuracy of entering and posting all the original data. But that is *all* it can do - it can only take over the routine and tedious tasks which would otherwise make the life of an accountant boring. There is no risk of computers taking over the work of the cost accountant!

Advantages of computers

3.5 There are, however, a number of ways in which the use of computers improves the capabilities and capacities of the cost accounting system.

(a) *Volume processing*. Computers can process much larger volumes of data than manual information systems. This means that extensive forecasting and planning models can be developed for very large organisations.

(b) *Speed*. Computers process data very quickly. Cost accountants are therefore able to process more data more swiftly, and so improve the quality and range of the information they provide.

(c) *Up-to-date information*. Before computer technology had widespread use, it would have been fairly typical for monthly control reports to be made available one or two months after the end of the relevant month. For example, control reports for January might not have been available until March or even April. With computers and computer budget models, control data can be available very quickly. For example, control reports for January could be available for management on 1 February. This 'freshness' and up-to-date quality of accounting information improves its usefulness to managers.

(d) *Accuracy*. Computers do not make processing errors, so long as input data is accurate and there are no 'bugs' in the software. With manual accounting systems, computational errors can be all too common!

(e) *Storage capacity*. Computer files are capable of storing large quantities of data cheaply, which can be retrieved quickly when required. This means that more information is available whenever managers want it.

(f) *Complexity/variety*. Computers give cost accountants the ability to provide information that is more complex and more varied.

    (i)   More 'sophisticated' budgeting techniques can be used.

    (ii)   Uncertainty analysis is much more practicable. Cost accountants can provide quick answers to 'what if' questions, for example what would happen if labour productivity fell by 5%, or if wages went up 10%, or materials prices by 8% and so on.

(g) *Accessibility*. Networked systems, make data more widely and readily accessible to managers.

(h) *Presentation of information*. Modern software packages allow for data to be presented in any number of formats (graphs, pie charts, bar charts and so on) and for displays to be interrogated, thereby providing a more flexible and quick service for the cost accountant.

(i) *Calculating ability*. Although cost accounting calculations are, in computer terms, relatively straightforward, computers are ideally suited to doing calculations which are tedious and time-consuming when done manually. The calculations involved in apportioning overheads to cost centres, for example, can take a considerable amount of time if done manually whereas a computer can perform the task almost immediately.

(j) *Decision-making capability*. Computers can test different values or conditions and, depending on the results, take appropriate action. When preparing a cash forecast, for example, a computer can be programmed to allow for any interest payable or receivable on bank balances; a more detailed analysis can therefore be provided, at no extra effort from the cost accountant, leaving him or her time to look at ways of reducing possible overdraft levels, for example.

3.6   This last example illustrates the key to the most effective use of computers for costing purposes; whenever possible they should be used for all routine cost accounting tasks, leaving the cost accountant free to interpret and investigate.

3.7   On the other hand computers do have weaknesses.

(a) *Data invisibility*. Computer data are invisible until printed out or displayed on a VDU. This may cause problems when searching for data outside the established procedure.

(b) *Liability to breakdown*. Due to their considerable power, computers are often given impossible workloads. A computer breakdown can therefore cause major problems - particularly if either a deadline (such as with payroll) or a real-time system (such as production control) are involved.

(c) *Program incomprehensibility*. It may be extremely difficult to amend a program without comprehensive program documentation.

(d) *Information swamping*. Management may be swamped with masses of trivia.

What can a computer do?

3.8 Because the cost of both computer hardware and computer software has fallen so dramatically in recent years, it is now cheaper for a computer to perform a cost accounting task than a cost clerk. Tasks no longer have to be high volume or repetitive to make the introduction of a computer commercially viable; most costing work is now a viable computer application. The following tasks are some of those frequently performed by a computer.

(a) Stock control (including pricing of issues and stock valuations, EOQ and stock control level calculations)

(b) Labour costing

(c) Absorption costing (the analysis of costs to cost centres, apportionment and absorption)

(d) Job, batch and contract costing

(e) Cost bookkeeping (using either integrated or interlocking systems)

(f) Decision making (including the determination of limiting factors) .

(g) Breakeven analysis

(h) Budget preparation (including cash budgets)

(i) Preparation of budgetary control reports (including the calculation of variances)

(j) Standard costing

3.9 Transaction processing systems might carry out cost bookkeeping, labour costing and stock valuations whereas what are known as decision support systems would deal with decision analysis, control reporting and so on.

4   DECISION SUPPORT SYSTEMS

4.1 The term decision support system (DSS) is usually taken to mean flexible and user-friendly computer systems which are designed to produce information in such a way as to help managers to make better decisions. They are now often associated with information 'at the touch of a button' at a manager's personal computer or workstation. DSS can describe a range of systems, from fairly simple information models based on spreadsheets to what are known as expert systems (computer programs which allow users to benefit from expert knowledge and information).

4.2 DSS do not make decisions. The objective is to allow the manager to consider a number of alternatives and evaluate them under a variety of potential conditions.

4.3 A key element in the usefulness of these systems is their ability to function interactively. This is a feature, for example, of spreadsheets, which are described later. Managers using these systems often develop scenarios using earlier results to refine their understanding of the problem and their actions.

4.4 As well as spreadsheets, DSS might include facilities for activity based costing, forecasting, linear programming and regression analysis.

5   APPLICATIONS SOFTWARE

5.1 Great advances have been made in recent years in the development of accounting software. Large companies may still wish to retain in-house expertise in programming and systems development, but a very wide range of PC-based 'off-the-shelf' packages is available to meet the needs of smaller businesses. Many of these packages were originally designed as financial accounting tools, but it is now possible to buy software for almost every application of cost accounting. The more sophisticated packages integrate cost and financial accounting applications.

5.2   The most widely used applications packages relevant to cost accounting are for payroll and stock control. Such packages are unlikely to be designed to do just costing work, however; costing data and reports are often just a by-product.

Payroll applications

5.3   Payroll is an area which particularly lends itself to computerisation. The mechanical and repetitive task of calculating gross pay and deductions for possibly hundreds of employees is one which is exactly suited to electronic processing. As with any other computerised data processing system, to see how a payroll application works, we need to consider the following.

(a)   What data we might expect to be held on file in a payroll system.
(b)   The input, processing and output we might expect to see in the system.

5.4   Payroll files will consist of an individual record for each employee.

(a)   *Standing data* on each employee will include personal details (for example name, employee number, job grade, address), rate of pay and details of deductions (including tax code)

(b)   *Variable (transaction) data* will include gross pay to date, tax to date, pension contributions and so on

5.5   The input into a payroll system will depend on whether it is wages (paid weekly) or salaries (paid monthly) which are being paid - or, of course, a combination of both.

(a)   There are two main inputs into a wages system (a weekly-paid payroll).

(i)   Clock cards or time sheets (sometimes both are used), which normally include details of overtime worked

(ii)   Amount of bonus, or appropriate details if the bonus is calculated by the computer

(b)   Salary systems are similar to those for wages but it is usual for the monthly salary to be generated by the computer from details held on the master file and therefore (with the exception of overtime, bonuses and so on) there is no need for any transaction input. So the inputs for a salary system are just overtime, bonuses and so on (because the basic salary is already on the master file).

5.6   The primary action involved in processing a payroll is calculating an employee's gross pay, calculating and implementing the various deductions in order to find net pay, and then making payment by the appropriate method.

(a)   In the case of wages, this means taking the input data on hours worked and pay details, and calculating the weekly wage due to the employee. The same calculation is carried out every week.

(b)   In the case of salaries, payroll processing might just mean running a master file and paying all the monthly-paid employees the same amount as they received the previous month. This could happen in theory, but in practice there are usually some amendments to make to the monthly pay details, and these are implemented during payroll processing.

5.7   Typical outputs of a payroll system are as follows.

(a)   Payslips
(b)   Payroll (this is often a copy of the payslips)
(c)   Payroll analysis, including analysis of deductions (tax, national insurance and so on) for submission to the tax authorities, and gross pay details for costing purposes
(d)   Coin analysis, cheques, credit transfer forms, as appropriate

(e) In some cases, a disk or tape with payment details, for despatch to the bank and payment through BACS (Bankers Automated Clearing Services). Alternatively the information may be transmitted via the telephone network.

(f) Cost accounting information. Here are two examples.

   (i) *Job costing information of all kinds*. With a well-designed system, time sheet and clock card details can be input to computer accompanied by appropriate codes to identify the jobs, processes or contracts to which they relate. The computer will automatically build up costs on each job and can produce analyses of accumulated costs.

   (ii) *Standard-setting information*. A computer can quickly produce figures for the average and optimum times to complete particular operations. (Again, this assumes an adequate coding system for the time details input.) Labour rate and efficiency variances are an obvious spin-off from this process.

Stock control applications

5.8   Stock control systems vary more widely than perhaps any other. The simplest types involve updating a stock file from movements records. In a manufacturing company it is necessary to distinguish between different categories of stocks (for example raw materials, work in progress, finished goods, consumable stores) and appropriate internal movement documents, such as material requisitions, will be required. In real-time systems it would be possible to give customers up-to-date information on stock availability. By locating stock (say) in another regional warehouse, and bringing it to the customer a better service could be provided. The main features of a simpler stock control system are as follows.

(a) *Inputs* (such as GRNs and despatch notes)

(b) *Outputs* such as details of stock movements (produced every time the system is run), stock balances (produced as required, eg weekly) and stock valuation lists (produced at the end of each accounting period)

(c) The main *file* is the stock ledger. Information held on this file might include stock number, description, standard cost (if appropriate), quantity in stock, bin/bay location and reorder level.

   If summary movements schedules are produced it will also be necessary to maintain the appropriate details on file.

5.9   The stock system is often linked to the purchases and/or sales system, and other inputs/outputs are necessary.

(a) Additional inputs include changes in reorder levels and quantities and notification of despatch to customers.

(b) Additional reports include purchase orders, reorder schedules and production requirements.

5.10 When the sales, purchases, production and stock systems are integrated, data can be input from goods received notes, materials requisition notes, goods returned notes, sales invoices, purchase invoices and so on. This will enable the computer to keep track of quantities of raw materials stocks, work in progress and finished goods stock. If desired, costs can automatically be attributed to stock issues and receipts according to whatever costing system is employed by the company.

Bill of materials

5.11 Many computerised stock control systems have a 'bill of materials' facility. A bill of materials is a specification of the materials and parts required to make a product. This allows assembly records (sometimes called 'explosion records') to be complied, containing details of the various 'assemblies' that make up the final product. A tape deck, for example, may have three main assemblies, the motor mechanism, the electronics and the outer casing. Each individual assembly could be further broken down into its constituent materials and components.

Stock counts

5.12   Finally, it is worth mentioning that it is normal for the results of physical stock counts to be matched against the stock file so that a list of differences can be printed out. This would be done as often as necessary to enable wastage, pilferage, errors and so on to be determined and to allow the stock files to be corrected to bring them back into line with actual quantities on hand.

General purpose applications

5.13   Payroll and stock control applications have specific purposes. A stock control system is used to control stock; it cannot be used to produce a budget. Such applications are used simply to process transactions (thus providing control information).

5.14   The spread of the PC has provided cost accountants with the opportunity to incorporate the use of computers into areas other than transaction processing. General purpose packages are off-the-shelf programs that can be used for processing of a general type, but the computer user can apply the package to a variety of specific uses of his or her own choice. Two examples of general purpose packages are database systems and spreadsheet packages.

6   SPREADSHEETS

What is a spreadsheet?

6.1   A spreadsheet is 'The term commonly used to describe many of the modelling packages available for microcomputers, being loosely derived from the likeness to a "spreadsheet of paper" divided into rows and columns' (CIMA *Computing Terminology*) .

6.2   It can be used to build a *model*, in which data is presented in these rows and columns, and it is up to the model builder to determine what data or information should be presented in it, how it should be presented and how the data should be manipulated by the spreadsheet program. A model represents in mathematical terms the relationships between the significant variables in a business situation.

Modelling

6.3   Later on in this Study Text, you will find a number of topics discussed which relate to budgetary control, decision making and so forth, and a number of forecasting techniques.

6.4   Many of these involve the construction of a model of a real-life situation. That is to say, it is assumed that there are mathematical relationships between a number of variables in the model, which can be used to predict the effect of changes in a variable on future outcomes or other variables.

6.5   When budgets are prepared, it may be the case that some of the factors to consider (for example levels of customer demand, interest rates, the inflation rate and so forth) may vary, and each will have its own effect on the overall profit predicted for the period. For example customer demand for a product may not only be affected by selling price but also by interest rates. Both of these variables have an effect on sales revenue.

6.6   To arrive at a decision as to what price should be charged to maintain a given level of revenue or to increase it, all these factors need to be taken into account. In a manual system, several proforma budgets would need to be prepared taking into account the effect of these different variables.

6.7   It would take an enormous amount of time to prepare these budgets manually. The use of a spreadsheet package, whereby a model is devised and the values of each variable altered at will, speeds up this process as the results are known immediately.

Uses of spreadsheets

6.8   The uses of spreadsheets are really only limited by your imagination, and by the number of rows and columns in the spreadsheet, but some of the more common accounting applications are as follows.

(a)   General ledger
(b)   Inventory records
(c)   Job cost estimates
(d)   Balance sheets
(e)   Cash flow analysis/forecasting
(f)   Market share analysis and planning
(g)   Profit projections
(h)   Profit statements
(i)   Project budgeting and control
(j)   Sales projections and records
(k)   Tax estimation

What all these have in common is that they all involve data processing with numerical, repetitive, time-consuming calculations.

6.9   The great value of spreadsheets, however, derives from their simple format of rows and columns of data.

6.10   The ability of the data users to have direct access themselves to their spreadsheet model via their own personal computer (PC) is also significant. For example, an accountant can construct a cash flow model with a spreadsheet package on the PC in his or her office: he or she can create the model, input the data, manipulate the data and read or print the output direct. He or she will also have fairly instant access to the model whenever it is needed, in just the time it takes to load the model into his or her PC.

The appearance of a spreadsheet

6.11   When a 'blank' spreadsheet is loaded into a computer, the VDU monitor will show lines of empty rows and columns. The rows are usually numbered 1, 2, 3 . . . etc and the columns lettered A, B C . . . etc. Each 'box' in the table - for example, column A row 1, column A row 2, column B row 1 and so on - is referred to as a *cell*. Typically, it will look like this.

	A	B	C	D
1				
2				
3				
4				
5				

6.12   The contents of any cell can be one of the following.

(a)   *Text.* A cell so designated contains words or numerical data (such as a date) that cannot be used in computations.

(b)   *Values.* A value is a number that can be used in a calculation.

(c) *Formulae.* A formula refers to other cells in the spreadsheet, and performs some sort of computation with them. For example, if cell C1 contains the formula $+A1 - B1$ this means that the contents of cell B1 should be subtracted from the contents of cell A1, and the result displayed in cell C1. If the amount in A1 is changed, the amount in C1 will change as well.

How is a spreadsheet used?

6.13 The idea behind a spreadsheet is that the model builder should construct a model, in rows and columns format. The following steps are strongly recommended.

(a) *Input area.* Pick out all the figures in the problem that are subject to change (*variables*) and enter them into the spreadsheet, with clear labels. For example if your problem involves five different figures you might enter the labels in cells A1 to A5 and the figures alongside in cells B1 to B5. This is the *input area* of the spreadsheet.

(b) *Calculation section.* In a different part of the spreadsheet enter the formulae that act upon the figures in the problem. For example if your problem involves multiplying one of your five figures by another and then adding the result to the sum of the other three, you would enter in the first cell (say B7) in your *calculation section* the formula B1*B2, in the second cell the formula SUM (B3:B7). Again labels should be included in column A.

(c) *Output section.* In a large or complex spreadsheet it is good practice to have a separate *output section* for the results of the calculations. For example the result of the calculation SUM (B3:B7) could be a figure that forms part of a budget. The budget would collect together, in a single area of the spreadsheet, the results of numerous calculations like the one in (a) and (b) above.

In practice many spreadsheets are not large enough to warrant a separate output section: in this case the output section will be *combined* with the calculation section. This is the approach used in the example below.

6.14 The value of this approach is that the only cells that need to be changed if the data changes (in next month's budget say) are the cells in the input area. There is far less likelihood that formulae will be accidentally overwritten, destroying the logic of the spreadsheet. This approach makes it easier to change the model and use it again, without having to build a completely new model every time.

Example: constructing a cash flow projection   *S/95*

6.15 Suppose you wanted to set up a simple six-month cash flow projection, in such a way that you could use it to estimate how the projected cash balance figures will change in total when any individual item in the projection is altered. You have the following information.

(a) Sales were £45,000 per month in 19X5, falling to £42,000 in January 19X6. Thereafter they are expected to increase by 3% per month (ie February will be 3% higher than January, and so on).

(b) Debts are collected as follows.

(i)   60% in month following sale.
(ii) 30% in second month after sale.
(iii) 7% in third month after sale.
(iv) 3% remains uncollected.

(c) Purchases are equal to cost of sales, set at 65% of sales.

(d) Overheads were £6,000 per month in 19X5, rising by 5% in 19X6.

(e) Opening cash is an overdraft of £7,500.

(f) Dividends: £10,000 final dividend on 19X5 profits payable in May.

(g)   Capital purchases: plant costing £18,000 will be ordered in January. 20% is payable with order, 70% on delivery in February and the final 10% in May.

Exam focus point

There was a question in the May 1995 exam that first asked candidates to prepare a cash flow forecast, then asked for an explanation of how a spreadsheet could assist in this task.

Headings and layout

6.16   The first job is to put in the various headings that you want on the cash flow projection. At this stage, your screen might look as follows.

	A	B	C	D	E	F	G
1	EXCELLENT PLC						
2	Cash flow projection – six months ending 30 June 19X6						
3		Jan	Feb	Mar	Apr	May	Jun
4		£	£	£	£	£	£
5	Sales						
6	Cash receipts						
7	1 month in arrears						
8	2 months in arrears						
9	3 months in arrears						
10	Total operating receipts						
11							
12	Cash payments						
13	Purchases						
14	Overheads						
15	Total operating payments						
16							
17	Dividends						
18	Capital purchases						
19	Total other payments						
20							
21	Net cash flow						
22	Cash balance b/f						
23	Cash balance c/f						

Inserting formulae

6.17   The next stage is to put in the calculations you want the computer to carry out, expressed as formulae. For example, in cell B10 you want total operating receipts, so you move to cell B10 and put in the formula =SUM(B7:B9). [*Lotus 1-2-3:* @SUM(B7..B9).]

6.18   Look for a moment at cell C7. We are told that sales in January were £42,000 and that 60% of customers settle their accounts one month in arrears. We could insert the formula =B5*0.6 [*Lotus 1-2-3:* +B5*0.6] in the cell and fill in the other cells along the row so that it is replicated in each month. However, consider the effect of a change in payment patterns to a situation where, say, 55% of customer debts are settled after one month. This would necessitate a change to each and every cell in which the 0.6 ratio appears.

6.19   An alternative approach, which makes future changes much simpler to execute, is to put the relevant ratio (here, 60% or 0.6) in a cell *outside* the main table and cross-refer each cell in the main table to that cell. This means that, if the percentage changes, the change need only be reflected in one cell, following which all cells which are dependent on that cell will automatically use the new percentage.

6.20 We will therefore input such values in separate parts of the spreadsheet, as follows. Look at the other assumptions which we have inserted into this part of the spreadsheet.

Note that percentages can either be input in the form 6% or as decimal 0.06. Note especially that negative cash flows must have a minus sign.

	A	B	C	D	E	F
25						
26	*This table contains the key variables for the 19X6 cash flow projections*					
27						
28	Sales growth factor per month		1.03			
29	Purchases as % of sales		-0.65			
30						
31	Debts paid within 1 month		0.6			
32	Debts paid within 2 months		0.3			
33	Debts paid within 3 months		0.07			
34	Bad debts		0.03			
35						
36	Increase in overheads		1.05			
37						
38	Dividends (May)		-10000			
39						
40	Capital purchases		-18000			
41	January		0.2			
42	February		0.7			
43	May		0.1			
44						
45						
46	*This table contains relevant opening balance data as at Jan 19X6*					
47						
48	Monthly sales 19X5		45000			
49	January 1996 sales		42000			
50	Monthly overheads 19X5		-6000			
51	Opening cash		-7500			
52						

6.21 Now we can go back to cell C7 and input =B5*$C$31 [*Lotus 1-2-3:* +B5*C31] and then fill this in across the '1 month in arrears' row. The dollar signs indicate an *absolute cell reference* – one that will not change when we replicate the formulae to other cells. If we assume for the moment that we are copying to cells D7 through to G7 and follow this procedure, the contents of cell D7 would be shown as =C5*$C$31, and so on, as shown below. (Note that, as we have no December sales figure, we will have to deal with cell B7 separately.)

(a) *Formulae*

	A	B	C	D	E	F	G
1	EXCELLENT PLC						
2	Cash flow projection –						
3		Jan	Feb	Mar	Apr	May	Jun
4		£	£	£	£	£	£
5	Sales	42000	42000	42000	42000	42000	42000
6	Cash receipts						
7	1 month in arrears		=B5*$C$31	=C5*$C$31	=D5*$C$31	=E5*$C$31	=F5*$C$31
8	2 months in arrears						
9	3 months in arrears						
10	Total operating receipts						

(b) *Numbers*

	A	B	C	D	E	F	G
1	EXCELLENT PLC						
2	Cash flow projection - six months ending 30 June 19X5						
3		Jan	Feb	Mar	Apr	May	Jun
4		£	£	£	£	£	£
5	Sales	42000	42000	42000	42000	42000	42000
6	Cash receipts						
7	1 month in arrears		25200	25200	25200	25200	25200
8	2 months in arrears						
9	3 months in arrears						
10	Total operating receipts						

6.22 Other formulae required for this projection are as follows.

(a) Cell B5 refers directly to the information we are given - sales of £42,000 in January. We have input this variable in cell C49. The other formulae in row 5 (sales) should reflect the predicted sales growth of 3% per month, as entered in cell C28.

(b) Similar formulae to the one already described for row 7 are required in rows 8 and 9.

(c) Row 10 (total operating receipts) will display simple subtotals, in the form =SUM(B7:B9). [*Lotus 1-2-3:* @SUM(B7..B9).]

(d) Row 13 (purchases) requires a formula based on the data in row 5 (sales) and the value in cell C29 (purchases as a % of sales). This model assumes no changes in stock levels from month to month, and that stocks are sufficiently high to enable this. The formula is B5 ⋆ $C$29. Note that C29 is negative.

(e) Row 15 (total operating payments), like row 10, requires formulae to create subtotals.

(f) Rows 17 and 18 refer to the dividends and capital purchase data input in cells C38 and C40 to 43.

(g) Row 21 (net cash flow) requires a total in the form =B10 + B15 + B21. [*Lotus 1-2-3:* +B10 + B15 + B21.]

(h) Row 22 (balance b/f) requires the contents of the previous month's closing cash figure.

(i) Row 23 (balance b/f) requires the total of the opening cash figure and the net cash flow for the month.

6.23 Once the formulae have been inserted, this is what the spreadsheet would contain. (Remember, formulae are not usually displayed in cells.)

(a) *Formulae*

	A	B	C	D	E	F	G
1	EXCELLENT PLC						
2	Cash flow projection - six i						
3		Jan	Feb	Mar	Apr	May	Jun
4		£	£	£	£	£	£
5	Sales	=C49	=B5*$C$28	=C5*$C$28	=D5*$C$28	=E5*$C$28	=F5*$C$28
6	Cash receipts						
7	1 month in arrears	=$C$48*$C$31	=B5*$C$31	=C5*$C$31	=D5*$C$31	=E5*$C$31	=F5*$C$31
8	2 months in arrears	=$C$48*$C$32	=$C$48*$C$32	=B5*$C$32	=C5*$C$32	=D5*$C$32	=E5*$C$32
9	3 months in arrears	=$C$48*$C$33	=$C$48*$C$33	=$C$48*$C$33	=B5*$C$33	=C5*$C$33	=D5*$C$33
10	Total operating receipts	=SUM(B7:B9)	=SUM(C7:C9)	=SUM(D7:D9)	=SUM(E7:E9)	=SUM(F7:F9)	=SUM(G7:G9)
11							
12	Cash payments						
13	Purchases	=B5*$C$29	=C5*$C$29	=D5*$C$29	=E5*$C$29	=F5*$C$29	=G5*$C$29
14	Overheads	=$C$50	=$C$50*$C$36	=$C$50*$C$36	=$C$50*$C$36	=$C$50*$C$36	=$C$50*$C$36
15	Total operating payments	=SUM(B13:B14)	=SUM(C13:C14)	=SUM(D13:D14)	=SUM(E13:E14)	=SUM(F13:F14)	=SUM(G13:G14)
16							
17	Dividends	0	0	0	0	=C38	0
18	Capital purchases	=C40*C41	=C40*C42	0	0	=C40*C43	0
19	Total other payments	=SUM(B17:B18)	=SUM(C17:C18)	=SUM(D17:D18)	=SUM(E17:E18)	=SUM(F17:F18)	=SUM(G17:G18)
20							
21	Net cash flow	=B10+B15+B19	=C10+C15+C19	=D10+D15+D19	=E10+E15+E19	=F10+F15+F19	=G10+G15+G19
22	Cash balance b/f	=C51	=B23	=C23	=D23	=E23	=F23
23	Cash balance c/f	=SUM(B21:B22)	=SUM(C21:C22)	=SUM(D21:D22)	=SUM(E21:E22)	=SUM(F21:F22)	=SUM(G21:G22)

(b)　*Numbers*

	A	B	C	D	E	F	G
1	EXCELLENT PLC						
2	Cash flow projection – six months ending 30 June 19X6						
3		Jan	Feb	Mar	Apr	May	Jun
4		£	£	£	£	£	£
5	Sales	42000	43260	44558	45895	47271	48690
6	Cash receipts						
7	1 month in arrears	27000	25200	25956	26735	27537	28363
8	2 months in arrears	13500	13500	12600	12978	13367	13768
9	3 months in arrears	3150	3150	3150	2940	3028	3119
10	Total operating receipts	43650	41850	41706	42653	43932	45250
11							
12	Cash payments						
13	Purchases	-27300	-28119	-28963	-29831	-30726	-31648
14	Overheads	-6000	-6300	-6300	-6300	-6300	-6300
15	Total operating payments	-33300	-34419	-35263	-36131	-37026	-37948
16							
17	Dividends					-10000	
18	Capital purchases	-3600	-12600			-1800	
19	Total other payments	-3600	-12600			-11800	
20							
21	Net cash flow	6750	-5169	6443	6521	-4894	7302
22	Cash balance b/f	-7500	-750	-5919	524	7046	2152
23	Cash balance c/f	-750	-5919	524	7046	2152	9454

Sensitivity analysis

6.24　We referred to earlier to the need to design a spreadsheet so that changes in assumptions do not result in major changes to vast ranges of cells. This is why we set up two separate areas of the spreadsheet for 19X6 assumptions and opening balances respectively. Consider each of the following.

(a)　Negotiations with suppliers and gains in productivity have resulted in cost of sales being reduced to 62% of sales.

(b)　The effects of a recession have changed the cash collection profile so that receipts in any month are 50% of prior month sales, 35% of the previous month and 10% of the month before that, with bad debt experience rising to 5%.

(c)　An insurance claim made in 19X5 and successfully settled in December has resulted in the opening cash balance being an overdraft of £3,500.

(d)　Sales growth will only be 2% per month.

6.25　Each of these can be accommodated with no input into the main body of the spreadsheet being necessary at all. The two reference tables are revised as follows.

	A	B	C	D	E	F
25						
26	*This table contains the key variables for the 19X6 cash flow projections*					
27						
28	Sales growth factor per month		1.02			
29	Purchases as % of sales		-0.62			
30						
31	Debts paid within 1 month		0.5			
32	Debts paid within 2 months		0.35			
33	Debts paid within 3 months		0.1			
34	Bad debts		0.05			
35						
36	Increase in overheads		1.05			
37						
38	Dividends (May)		-10000			
39						
40	Capital purchases		-18000			
41	January		0.2			
42	February		0.7			
43	May		0.1			
44						
45						
46	*This table contains relevant opening balance data as at Jan 19X6*					
47						
48	Monthly sales 19X5		45000			
49	January 1996 sales		42000			
50	Monthly overheads 19X5		-6000			
51	Opening cash		-3500			
52						

6.26 The resulting (recalculated) spreadsheet would look like this.

	A	B	C	D	E	F	G
1	**EXCELLENT PLC**						
2	*Cash flow projection - six months ending 30 June 19X6*						
3		Jan	Feb	Mar	Apr	May	Jun
4		£	£	£	£	£	£
5	Sales	42,000	42,840	43,697	44,571	45,462	46,371
6	*Cash receipts*						
7	1 month in arrears	22,500	21,000	21,420	21,848	22,285	22,731
8	2 months in arrears	15,750	15,750	14,700	14,994	15,294	15,600
9	3 months in arrears	4,500	4,500	4,500	4,200	4,284	4,370
10	Total operating receipts	42,750	41,250	40,620	41,042	41,863	42,701
11							
12	*Cash payments*						
13	Purchases	-26,040	-26,561	-27,092	-27,634	-28,187	-28,750
14	Overheads	-6,300	-6,300	-6,300	-6,300	-6,300	-6,300
15	Total operating payments	-32,340	-32,861	-33,392	-33,934	-34,487	-35,050
16							
17	Dividends	0	0	0	0	-10,000	0
18	Capital purchases	-3,600	-12,600	0	0	-1,800	0
19	Total other payments	-3,600	-12,600	0	0	-11,800	0
20							
21	Net cash flow	6,810	-4,211	7,228	7,109	-4,423	7,650
22	Cash balance b/f	-3,500	3,310	-901	6,327	13,436	9,012
23	Cash balance c/f	3,310	-901	6,327	13,436	9,012	16,663
24							

6.27 A great number of such 'what if?' questions can be asked and answered quickly, such as what if sales growth per month is nil, ½%, 1%, 1½%, 2½% or minus 1% and so on? The information obtained should provide management with a better understanding of what the cash flow position in the future might be, and what factors are critical to ensuring that the cash position remains reasonable. It might be found, for example, that the cost of sales must remain less than 67% of sales value, or that sales growth of at least 1½% per month is essential to achieve a satisfactory cash position.

Commands and facilities

6.28   Spreadsheets are versatile tools that can be used for a wide variety of tasks and calculations. The only pre-ordained structure imposed on the end user is the grid of rows and columns. The absence of imposed formats or contents gives the spreadsheet great flexibility and it is this that users find so valuable in decision making.

6.29   Different spreadsheets will offer different facilities, but some of the more basic ones which should feature in all spreadsheet programs are as follows. As you are probably aware from experience, this list is far from exhaustive! Look at the illustration above as you read through.

Facility	Explanation
Database facilities	Data can be sorted alphabetically and numerically and filtered to find particular categories of information. Pivot tables make it possible to rearrange and summarise rows and columns in virtually any way imaginable.
Editing	Data (cells rows or columns) can easily be copied or moved from one part of the spreadsheet to another using a mouse and 'cut and paste' and 'drag and drop' facilities. Data entry is facilitated by intelligent software that can guess, for example, that if you type *Jan 97* in the first cell you are likely to want *Feb 97, Mar 97* and so on in the cells below.
Facilities to rearrange the spreadsheet	You can insert a column or row at a desired spot. For example, you might wish to split 'cash receipts' into 'trade' and 'other'. The insert command facilitates this, and the formulae in the spreadsheet are adjusted automatically.
File commands	Opening, naming, saving, printing and closing the spreadsheet file are the key tasks.
Format	This command controls the way in which headings and data are shown, for example by altering column widths, 'justifying' text and numbers (to indent or have a right-hand justification, etc), changing the number of decimal places displayed, or the font used. You can format the whole spreadsheet, or a specified range of cells.
Graphics facility	Most spreadsheets also contain a graphics facility which enables the presentation of tables of data as graphs or pie charts for example.
Importing and linking	Data can be cut and pasted or imported from other applications such as spreadsheets and word processors. Files can be *dynamically linked* so that if (say) the word processing document is changed then the linked spreadsheet is updated automatically (or *vice versa*).
Macros	Many spreadsheets provide a macro facility. This allows the user to automate a sequence of actions or commands, executing them with the depression of just two pre-defined keys.

Facility	Explanation
Protect facilities	A protect facility ensures that the contents of a specified range of cells (for example the text titles, or a column of base data) cannot be tampered with.

Three-dimensional spreadsheets

6.30   One of the problems with using spreadsheets for financial modelling is that spreadsheets work only in two dimensions (columns and rows). Combining information in three dimensions is difficult. For example, you may wish to produce cost accounting statements for a number of companies in a group, as well as the consolidated results for the group as a whole, analysed over a number of months. In a normal two-dimensional spreadsheet you would have, say, the months across the top as columns, and the income and expenditure information down the side as rows. If there is more than one company involved you have to repeat this two-dimensional design *separately* for each company.

6.31   Modern packages such as Microsoft Excel or Lotus 1-2-3 have a facility that permits working in *three* dimensions, because files consist of workbooks than can contain up to 255 separate sheets. A filing cabinet is perhaps a good analogy, as the user can flip between different sheets stacked in front or behind each other. Cells in one sheet refer to cells in another sheet.

The disadvantages of spreadsheets

6.32   Spreadsheets have disadvantages if they are not properly used, including the following.

(a)   A minor error in the design of a model at any point can affect the validity of data throughout the spreadsheet. Such errors can be very difficult to trace.

(b)   Even if it is properly designed in the first place, it is very easy to corrupt a model by accidentally changing a cell or inputting data in the wrong place.

(c)   It is possible to become over-dependent on them, so that simple one-off tasks that can be done in seconds with a pen and paper are done on a spreadsheet instead. (Similarly most young accountants are dependent on their calculators, and incapable of performing anything but the most simple mental arithmetic.)

(d)   The possibility for experimentation with data is so great that it is possible to lose sight of the original intention of the spreadsheet.

7   SPREADSHEETS AND COST ACCOUNTING   *11/96*

Budgeting

7.1   Budgeting used to be a dreaded task. A great number of numerical manipulations are needed to produce a budget, be it a cash budget or a master budget. Examples which you may have met so far in your studies are, however, far more simple than situations in the real world. Remember, also, that it is highly unlikely that the execution of the steps in the process will be problem free. Because budgeting is an interactive process, budgets may need to be amended many time over; functional budgets will be out of balance with each other and will require modification so that they are compatible. The manual preparation of a master budget and a cash budget in the real world would therefore be daunting. Computers, however, can take the hard work out of budgeting.

Exercise 1

What are the four basic advantages of a computerised system over a manual system which mean that 'computers can take the hard work out of budgeting'?

Solution

(a) A computer has the ability to process a larger volume of data.
(b) A computerised system can process data more rapidly than a manual system.
(c) Computerised systems tend to be more accurate than a manual system.
(d) Computers have the ability to store large volumes of data in a readily accessible form.

7.2 Such advantages make computers ideal both for taking over the manipulation of numbers, and for dealing with the problems associated with changing variables due to the interrelationships between budgets, leaving staff to get involved in the more judgmental aspects of the planning process.

7.3 Budgeting is usually computerised using either a computer program written specifically for the organisation or a commercial spreadsheet package.

7.4 Both methods of computerisation of the budgeting process will involve a mathematical model which represents the real world in terms of financial values. The model will consist of several, or many, interrelated variables, a variable being an item in the model which has a value.

Exam focus point

A question in the November 1996 exam asked how a spreadsheet may be used in the preparation of a *sales* budget. The comprehensive example below should prepare you for questions like this, whatever sort of budget you are asked about. The November 1996 question also asked about the *advantages* of spreadsheets for budgeting: see Exercise 1.

Alternatively you may be asked how spreadsheets could help with some other cost accounting task, such as calculating variances.

Example: a cash budgeting model

7.5 A cash budgeting model would be intended to provide a cash flow plan or target. The model should include all the factors (variables) which have a significant influence on cash flow.

Exercise 2

What variables should typically be included in a cash budgeting model?

Solution

(a) Total sales
(b) Cash sales, perhaps as a percentage of total sales
(c) Credit sales, perhaps as a percentage of total sales
(d) Rate of growth in sales, or seasonal variations in sales
(e) Time taken by debtors to pay what they owe
   (i) Percentage paying one month after invoice
   (ii) Percentage paying two months after invoice
   (iii) Percentage paying three months after invoice
   (iv) Percentage of bad debts
(f) Purchases on credit
   (i) Percentage paid within one month of receipt of invoice
   (ii) Percentage paid within two months of receipt of invoice
(g) Wages and salaries
(h) Other cash expenses
(i) Dividends
(j) Taxation payments
(k) Capital expenditure

7.6 Once the planning model has been constructed, the same model can be used week by week, month after month, or year after year, simply by changing the values of the variables to produce new outputs for cash inflows, cash outflows, net cash flows and cash/bank balance.

7.7 A major advantage of budget models is the ability to evaluate different options and carry out 'what if' analysis. By changing the value of certain variables (for example altering the ratio of cash sales to credit sales, increasing the amount of bad debts or capital expenditure, increasing the annual pay award to the workforce and so on) management are able to assess the effect of potential changes in their environment.

7.8 Computerised models can also incorporate actual results, period by period, and carry out the necessary calculations to produce budgetary control reports.

7.9 The use of a model also allows the budget for the remainder of the year to be adjusted once it is clear that the circumstances on which the budget was originally based have changed.

Example: a model budget

7.10 The management accountant of Edgar Ltd wants to set up a spreadsheet for budgeting purposes. He has already prepared the input section of the spreadsheet which is as shown below.

	A	B	C	D	E	F	G
1							
2	Selling price (£)	24					
3							
4	*Sales forecasts*		*Q1.99*	*Q2.99*	*Q3.99*	*Q4.99*	*Q1.00*
5	Units		126,000	84,000	75,600	117,600	100,800
6							
7	*Stock levels*						
8	Product A - units	31,500					
9	Material X - kg	73,500					
10	Closing stocks percentage		0.25	0.25	0.35	0.35	
11	Fall in material per quarter (kg)	6,300					
12							
13	*Product A unit data*						
14	Material X (kg)	4					
15	Material X (£/kg)	1.6					
16	Direct labour - hours	0.6					
17	Direct labour (£/hour)	3.5					
18							
19	Unit cost (£)	8.5					
20							
21	*Other expenditure*		945,000	1,008,000	987,000	1,050,000	
22	Fixed overhead			1,050,000			
23	Capital expenditure						
24							
25							
26	*Balances b/f*						
27	Debtors	840,000					
28	Bad debts	42,000					
29	Bank balance	462,000					
30	Creditors	201,600					
31	Fixed assets	10,500,000					
32							
33	*Cash flow timing*						
34	Sales revenues						
35	Quarter of sale	0.6					
36	Next quarter	0.38					
37	Bad debts	0.02					
38	Material X						
39	Quarter of purchase	0.7					
40	Next quarter	0.3					
41	Other expenditure						
42	Quarter incurred	1					
43	Next quarter	0					
44							
45	Depreciation rate	0.05					

7.11 This input was derived from the following information which is available for use in the budgeting process for the year to 31 December 1999.

(a) *Sales at selling price per product unit £24*

| | 1999 | | | | 2000 |
	Quarter 1	Quarter 2	Quarter 3	Quarter 4	Quarter 1
Product units	126,000	84,000	75,600	117,600	100,800

(b) *Stock levels*

At 31 December 1998:	Finished product A	31,500 units
	Raw material X	73,500 kg

Closing stocks of finished product A at the end of each quarter are budgeted as a percentage of the sales units of the following quarter as follows.

(i)   At the end of quarters 1 and 2: 25%
(ii)   At the end of quarters 3 and 4: 35%

Closing stock of raw material X is budgeted to fall by 6,300 kg at the end of each quarter in order to reduce holdings by 25,200 kg during 1999.

(c) *Product A unit data*

Material X	4 kg at £1.60 per kg
Direct labour	0.6 hours at £3.50 per hour

(d) *Other quarterly expenditure*

	Quarter 1 £	Quarter 2 £	Quarter 3 £	Quarter 4 £
Fixed overhead	945,000	1,008,000	987,000	1,050,000
Capital expenditure		1,050,000		

(e) *Forecast balances at 31 December 1999*

Debtors	840,000
Bad debts provision	42,000
Bank balance	462,000
Creditors: materials	201,600
Fixed assets (at cost)	10,500,000

(f) *Cash flow timing information*

(i)   Sales revenue: 60% receivable during the quarter of sale, 38% during the next quarter, the balance of 2% being expected bad debts.
(ii)   Material X purchases: 70% payable during the quarter of purchase, the balance of 30% during the next quarter.
(iii) Direct wages, fixed overhead and capital expenditure: 100% payable during the quarter in which they are earned or incurred.

(g) Fixed assets are depreciated on a straight-line basis of 5% per annum, based on the total cost of fixed assets held at any point during a year and assuming nil residual value.

(h) All forecast balances at 31 December 1998 will be received or paid as relevant during the first quarter of 1999.

(i) Stocks of product A are valued on a marginal cost basis for internal budgeting purposes.

Required

(a) Calculate and output the materials purchases budget for each quarter of 1999.

(b) Calculate and output a cash budget for each quarter of 1999.

(c) Calculate and output a budgeted profit and loss account for the year to 31 December 1999.

Solution

7.12 The budgets are given on the next two pages together with the formulae showing how each line is calculated. Spend a little time tracing through the formulae to the relevant inputs, to make sure your understand this (or, better, set up the problem and its solution on a spreadsheet of your own).

#	A	B	C	D	E	F	G	H	I	J	K	L	M
1													
2	Selling price (£)	24						MATERIALS PURCHASES BUDGET					
3	Sales forecasts							Product A	Q1 99	Q2 99	Q3 99	Q4 99	Q1 00
4			Q1 99	Q2 99	Q3 99	Q4 99	Q1 00	Opening stock	-31,500	-21,000	-18,900	-41,160	
5	Units		126,000	84,000	75,600	117,600	100,800	Sales units	126,000	84,000	75,600	117,600	100,800
6								Closing stock	21,000	18,900	41,160	35,280	
7	Stock levels							Production	115,500	81,900	97,860	111,720	
8	Product A - units	31,500						Raw materials					
9	Material X - kg	73,500						Production	462,000	327,600	391,440	446,880	
10	Closing stocks percentage		0.25	0.25	0.35	0.35		Opening stock	-73,500	-67,200	-60,900	-54,600	
11	Fall in material per quarter (kg)	6,300						Closing stock	67,200	60,900	54,600	48,300	
12								Purchases (kg)	455,700	321,300	385,140	440,580	
13	Product A unit data							Cost of purchases (£)	729,120	514,080	616,224	704,928	
14	Material X (kg)	4											
15	Material X (£/kg)	1.6						CASHFLOW					
16	Direct labour - hours	0.6						Receipts					
17	Direct labour (£/hour)	3.5						Q4 1997	798,000				
18								Q1 1999	1,814,400	1,149,120			
19	Unit cost (£)	8.5						Q2 1999		1,209,600	766,080		
20								Q3 1999			1,088,640	689,472	
21	Other expenditure							Q4 1999				1,693,440	
22	Fixed overhead		945,000	1,008,000	987,000	1,050,000		Total income	2,612,400	2,358,720	1,854,720	2,382,912	
23	Capital expenditure			1,050,000									
24								Payments					
25								Creditors					
26	Balances b/f							Q4 1997	201,600				
27	Debtors	840,000						Q1 1999	510,384	218,736			
28	Bad debts	42,000						Q2 1999		359,856	154,224		
29	Bank balance	462,000						Q3 1999			431,357	184,867	
30	Creditors	201,600						Q4 1999				493,450	
31	Fixed assets	10,500,000						Total creditors	711,984	578,592	585,581	678,317	
32								Wages	242,550	171,990	205,506	234,612	
33	Cash flow timing							Overhead	945,000	1,008,000	987,000	1,050,000	
34	Sales revenues							Capital expenditure	0	1,050,000	0	0	
35	Quarter of sale	0.6						Total expenditure	1,899,534	2,808,582	1,778,087	1,962,929	
36	Next quarter	0.38											
37	Bad debts	0.02						Net cash flow	712,866	-449,862	76,633	419,983	
38	Material X							Opening cash balance	462,000	1,174,866	725,004	801,637	
39	Quarter of purchase	0.7						Closing cash balance	1,174,866	725,004	801,637	1,221,620	
40	Next quarter	0.3											
41	Other expenditure							PROFIT AND LOSS ACCOUNT		£	£		
42	Quarter incurred	1						Sales			9,676,800		
43	Next quarter	0						Opening stock		267,750			
44								Production		3,459,330			
45	Depreciation rate	0.05						Closing stock		-299,880			
46								Cost of sales			-3,427,200		
47								Gross profit			6,249,600		
48								Bad debts		193,536			
49								Depreciation		577,500			
50								Fixed overheads		3,990,000	-4,761,036		
51								Net loss			1,488,564		
52													
53													

	H	I	J	K	L	M
1	MATERIALS PURCHASES BUDGET					
2	Product A	Q1 99	Q2 99	Q3 99	Q4 99	Q1 00
3	Opening stock	=-B8	=-I5	=-J5	=-K5	
4	Sales units	=C5	=D5	=E5	=F5	=G5
5	Closing stock	=D5*C10	=E5*D10	=F5*E10	=G5*F10	
6	Production	=SUM(I3:I5)	=SUM(J3:J5)	=SUM(K3:K5)	=SUM(L3:L5)	
7	Raw materials					
8	Production	=I6*B14	=J6*B14	=K6*B14	=L6*B14	
9	Opening stock	=-B9	=-I10	=-J10	=-K10	
10	Closing stock	=B9-B11	=I10-B11	=J10-B11	=K10-B11	
11	Purchases (kg)	=SUM(I8:I10)	=SUM(J8:J10)	=SUM(K8:K10)	=SUM(L8:L10)	
12						
13	Cost of purchases (£)	=I11*B15	=J11*B15	=K11*B15	=L11*B15	
14						
15	CASHFLOW					
16	Receipts					
17	Q4 1997	=B27-B28				
18	Q1 1999	=B2*C5*B35	=B2*C5*B36			
19	Q2 1999		=B2*D5*B35	=B2*D5*B36		
20	Q3 1999			=B2*E5*B35	=B2*E5*B36	
21	Q4 1999				=B2*F5*B35	
22	Total income	=SUM(I17:I21)	=SUM(J17:J21)	=SUM(K17:K21)	=SUM(L17:L21)	
23						
24	Payments					
25	Creditors					
26	Q4 1997	=B30				
27	Q1 1999	=I13*B39	=I13*B40			
28	Q2 1999		=J13*B39	=J13*B40		
29	Q3 1999			=K13*B39	=K13*B40	
30	Q4 1999				=L13*B39	
31	Total creditors	=SUM(I26:I30)	=SUM(J26:J30)	=SUM(K26:K30)	=SUM(L26:L30)	
32	Wages	=I6*B16*B17	=J6*B16*B17	=K6*B16*B17	=L6*B16*B17	
33	Overhead	=C21	=D21	=E21	=F21	
34	Capital expenditure	=C22	=D22	=E22	=F22	
35	Total expenditure	=SUM(I31:I34)	=SUM(J31:J34)	=SUM(K31:K34)	=SUM(L31:L34)	
36						
37	Net cash flow	=I22-I35	=J22-J35	=K22-K35	=L22-L35	
38	Opening cash balance	=B29	=I39	=J39	=K39	
39	Closing cash balance	=SUM(I37:I38)	=SUM(J37:J38)	=SUM(K37:K38)	=SUM(L37:L38)	
40						
41	PROFIT AND LOSS ACCOUNT		£	£		
42	Sales			=SUM(C5:F5)*B2		
43	Opening stock		=B8*B19			
44	Production		=SUM(I6:L6)*B19			
45	Closing stock		=-(L5*B19)			
46	Cost of sales			=-SUM(J43:J45)		
47	Gross profit			=K42+K46		
48	Bad debts		=K42*B37			
49	Depreciation		=(B31+D22)*B45			
50	Fixed overheads		=SUM(C21:F21)			
51				=-SUM(J48:J50)		
52	Net loss			=K47+K51		
53						

Standard costing

7.13 Using traditional systems, standard costs are kept on individual cards with the standard quantities and prices extended and totalled on the card. Problems occur when there is a change in, say, the rate of pay of a grade of labour used in numerous components which are in turn incorporated into numerous assemblies. One price change might require hundreds of amendments, thereby making standard cost revision a lengthy and tedious manual task. The use of a spreadsheet, however, makes changes to standards simple. The spreadsheet automatically reworks the costs of all components, assemblies and finished items on which the particular labour in question work.

7.14 Standard costs can therefore be updated more frequently, making subsequent variance analysis more meaningful and, where standard costs are used in estimating, making prices more realistic. Overall the process becomes more accurate and less administrative work is involved.

Exercise 3

Discuss the possible advantages of the use of computers in materials cost control systems.

Solution

The possible advantages of the use of computers in materials control systems are as follows.

Accuracy
Computers do not make arithmetic errors in calculating management information such as material cost variances and wastage figures. They can be used to make very detailed calculations with complete accuracy, provided the original data input and program contain no errors.

Speed
Computers can update records and calculate figures such as material cost variances much quicker than can be done manually.

Filing and retrieval of data
A computer is capable of rapidly storing and retrieving large volumes of data that would be very cumbersome to handle in a manual system. One entry of data can be used to update and cross-reference a number of records simultaneously.

For instance, data concerning a material purchase can be used to update the stock balance, calculate price variances, adjust the free stock balance and any other updating or cross-referencing that management requires.

Automatic monitoring of stock records
Control levels can be built in to a computerised material stock control system so that the computer produces exception reports to warn management when stocks are reaching levels which are too high or too low, or when they are moving very slowly. Such undesirable stock situations can be overlooked in a manual system, particularly when there is a large number of different stock items to be controlled.

Exercise 4

Suggest information that should be provided to management to assist in maintaining control over material costs.

Solution

The information which should be provided to management to assist in maintaining control over materials cost is as follows.

Materials price reports
Management must be regularly informed of the latest prices being paid for materials. They should be provided with reports on price trends and if a standard costing system is in operation they will also receive information on material price variances.

Material usage rates
The rates of usage of material on each product line should be communicated to management regularly. If a standard costing system is in operation then control will be achieved via the monitoring of material usage variances.

Material wastage reports
A separate wastage report should be provided as soon as possible after material wastage has occurred so that management can take quick correcting action when appropriate.

Stock loss reports
When checks are carried out to verify the physical balance of stock compared with the stock records, a report on any discrepancies should be prepared for management.

Slow-moving and obsolete stock reports
Management must be kept informed of any slow-moving or obsolete stocks so that they can prevent any further purchases being made and can decide what action to take with the stock in hand.

Stock level exception reports
These are reports which are prepared to show management when individual stock items are approaching too high or too low levels. They can then take action to ensure that the situation is remedied.

8 DATABASES
S/97

8.1 A typical accounting application package processes only one sort of data. A payroll file processes only payroll data and a stock file only stock data. An organisation might end up with separate files and processing subsystems for each area of the business. However, in many cases the underlying data used by each application might be the same. A major consequence is that data items are *duplicated* in a number of files (*data redundancy*). They are input more than once (leading to errors and inconsistencies) and held in several files (wasting space). For example, data relating to the hours which an hourly-paid employee has worked on a particular job is relevant both to the payroll system, as the employee's wages will be based on the hours worked, and to the job costing system, as the cost of the employee's time is part of the cost of the job.

8.2   The problem of data redundancy is overcome, partly at least, by an integrated system. An integrated system is a system where one set of data is used for more than one application. In a cost accounting context, it might be possible to integrate parts of the sales ledger, purchase ledger, stock control systems and nominal ledger systems, so that the data input to the sales ledger updates the nominal stock ledger automatically. The diagram below might make this more clear. It deals with stock control, sales order and purchases applications.

(a) Application-specific systems

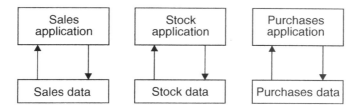

(b) Integrated systems

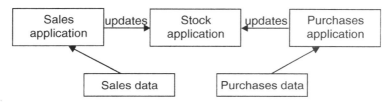

(c) Database

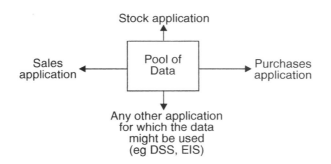

8.3   The integrated systems approach, where different applications update each other, is a half way house between a system based on separate application-specific files and a database approach. Broadly speaking a database is a file of data organised in such a way that it can be used by many applications. Using the example of hours worked given above, the following situations are possible.

(a)   The employee's hours are input twice, once to the payroll application, once to the job costing system, in a non-integrated system of *application-specific files*.

(b)   In an *integrated system*, the data would have been input to the payroll application. The payroll application would have been used to update the job costing application.

(c)   In a *database system* it would only be input once and would be immediately available to both systems.

8.4   A database provides a comprehensive file of data for a number of different users. Each user will have access to the same data, and so a situation cannot exist where different departments each keep their own data files, containing duplicate information but where the information on one file disagrees with the corresponding information on another department's file.

The objectives of a database system

8.5   A database should have four major objectives.

(a)   *It should be shared*. Different users should be able to access the same data in the database for their own processing applications, and at the same time if required. This removes the need for duplicating data on different files.

(b)   *The integrity of the database must be preserved*. This means that one user should not be allowed to alter the data on file so as to spoil the database records for other users. However, users must be able to update the data on file, and so make valid alterations to the data.

(c)   *The database system should provide for the needs of different users*, who each have their own processing requirements and data access methods. In other words, the database should provide for the operational requirements of all its users.

(d)   *The database should be capable of evolving*, both in the short term (it must be kept updated) and in the longer term (it must be able to meet the future data processing needs of users, not just their current needs).

Database management systems

8.6   The database management systems (DBMS) is a complex software system which organises the storage of data in the database in the most appropriate way to facilitate its storage, retrieval and use in different applications. It also provides the link between the user and the data. How a DBMS works is shown in the following diagram.

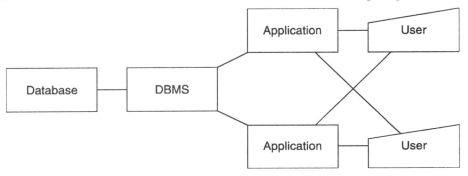

Database administration

8.7   A database administrator will often be appointed to look after the structure, physical storage and security of the data in the best interest of all users. He is responsible for the following.

(a)   Maintaining the database and ensuring there is no duplication of data
(b)   Adding new data (liaising with users, the systems analysts and programmers)
(c)   Maintaining a *data dictionary* which describes the data items
(d)   Maintaining manuals for users describing how to use the facilities of the database
(e)   Overseeing the security of the database
(f)   Ensuring that Data Protection legislation is complied with (in the UK the Data Protection Act 1984, shortly to be replaced by the Data Protection Act 1998)

Database structures

8.8   There are basically three types of database structure.

(a)   *The hierarchical structure*

Many relationships between data are one-to-many or many-to-one relationships. Such relationships can be expressed conveniently in a hierarchy. Each data item is related to only one item above it in the hierarchy, but to any number of data items below it. In a customer database, for example, the hierarchical model might be used to show customers and customer orders. An extract from a parts department database might be structured as follows.

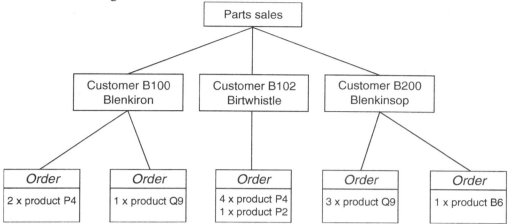

The biggest drawback to the hierarchical data structure is that the user is limited in the number of ways he or she can look for records because the file organisation makes it much easier to search for certain items in the file records than for others.

In the example above, to access an order record it is necessary to specify the customer to which it belongs, which is straightforward. However, let us imagine that you wish to obtain a listing of all customers who have ordered a particular part number. This would require a search of each customer record - a long process.

If the hierarchical model had been structured so that *products* were superior to *orders* and each order contained customer data instead of product data, this would be simpler, but the *first* process would be harder! This asymmetrical character of the hierarchical model makes it unsuitable for many applications, especially where there is not a true hierarchical relationship between the data.

(b) *The network structure*

Life becomes more complicated when we try to express many-to-many relationships. There are two ways of expressing many-to-many relationships. One way of so doing is in a network structure. This is like a hierarchical structure, but any data item may be related to any number of other data items.

(c) *The relational structure*

Another way of expressing many-to-many and one-to-many relationships is the relational data structure. A relational structure organises data elements in a series of two-dimensional tables consisting of rows and columns. A row represents a record, and columns represent part of a record. Returning to the hierarchical model depicted above, we will first consider how it might appear as a *network* model.

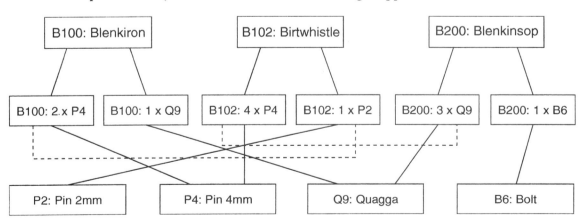

There is still some redundancy of data at the order level, although the problems inherent in the hierarchical model have been eliminated. Taking this a step further, we will consider how the same data might appear in a *relational* model.

Customer table		Product table		Order table		
B100	Blenkiron	B6	Bolt	B100	P4	2
B102	Birtwhistle	P2	Pin 2mm	B100	Q9	1
B200	Blenkinsop	P4	Pin 4mm	B102	P4	4
		Q9	Quagga	B102	P2	1
				B200	Q9	3
				B200	B6	1

The redundant data in the network model (the customer number and part number) have been eliminated. Any data element can be recognised by its record number or field name. The primary key is used to identify a record.

Normalisation

8.9 In a relational database there are a large number of entities, with a large number of relationships between them. However, these relationships can be simplified to the point where all the data for an entity can be regarded as residing in tables, with each column representing an attribute and each row having a key by which it can be uniquely identified. The relationships between these entity types and attributes can be expressed in the form of a table, allowing users of the database management system to extract data in whatever way they want by specifying the relationship or attributes which they want information about.

8.10 A matter of concern for the designer of a database will be what data items should be grouped together in a single record. A variety of ways of grouping data items will be possible, but some will obviously be better than others. Among the objectives in designing a database are the following.

(a) To eliminate unnecessary redundancy (duplication of items).

(b) To reduce the need for restructuring if new types of data arise.

(c) To separate logically distinct aspects of the data so that modifications which concern only one area can be made without affecting other areas.

8.11 To achieve these objectives a step-by-step process of *normalisation* is. Normalisation is a term used in the design of *relational* database systems, to describe the process of reducing complex relationships to a simpler and more regular two-dimensional tabular form.

Using a database

8.12 There are four main operations in using a database.

(a) Creating the database structure, ie the structure of files and records
(b) Entering data on to the database files, and amending/updating it
(c) Retrieving and manipulating the data
(d) Producing reports

Creating a database structure

8.13 Of the four broad operations involved in setting up and using a database, the most crucial is the creation and structure of the database file or files. The files must be structured in such a way that users of the system can *access and process data* in all the ways they want. Unless the files are properly structured, this will not be possible. Before deciding the most appropriate file organisation for a database system, the systems analyst or person creating the database file must first carry out an analysis of all the data for processing and filing, because a full and accurate analysis of data in the system is crucial to the construction of complete and workable database files.

8.14 One approach to data analysis is entity analysis. An *entity* is an item (a person, a job, a business, an activity, a product or stores item etc) about which information is stored. In single application systems (such as a sales ledger system, a payroll system, a purchase ledger system) a record will be made about an entity.

(a) In a sales ledger system, records will be made about customers. A customer is an entity, and all customers can be referred to as an entity set.

(b) Similarly, in a payroll system, records will be made about employees. An employee is an entity, and all employees together can be referred to as an entity set.

8.15 Each record in the file will then be given *attributes*. An attribute is a characteristic or property of an entity.

(a) For a customer, attributes include customer name and address, amounts owing, date of invoices sent and payments received, credit limit and so on.

(b) For a stores item, attributes include stock number, description, quantity, size, colour, supplier, balance in stock, reorder level, reorder quantity and so on.

8.16 The database user must begin by specifying what file or files will be held in the database, what records (entities) and fields (attributes) they will contain, and how many characters will be in each field. The files and fields must be named, and the characteristics of particular fields (for example all-numeric or all-alphabetic fields) should be specified.

Entering and amending data

8.17 When the database structure has been established, the data user can either input data directly or (preferably) import it from existing sources. The data must be kept up-to-date, and so there will be subsequent insertions of new records, deletions of unwanted records and amendments to existing records. In an integrated system, as described earlier, data will continually be fed into the database from other systems such as sales and purchasing.

8.18 Data maintenance functions will allow the same field in every record on file, or all records with certain characteristics, to be amended in the same way by means of a single command. For example, a single command can arrange for all customers on a sales ledger database file whose account type is type 2, say, to have their credit limit raised by 5%.

Exam focus point

A question in the May 1997 exam asked how a database could be used to collect the information required for a variance report. Answers could point out that the database would normally be updated directly with actual data via the posting of accounting transactions. Budget data could be entered manually at the beginning of a period and flexed at the end using the database's data manipulation facilities.

In fact, though, it would be more normal to use a spreadsheet to prepare a variance report. Actual data would be *exported* from the accounting database into the spreadsheet.

If you are very confident of your knowledge there is no reason why you should not challenge the assumptions of an exam question. Don't go out of your way to be argumentative, however, especially if you are not absolutely sure of your knowledge.

Retrieval and manipulation of data

8.19 Data can be retrieved and manipulated in a variety of ways.

(a) Data can be retrieved by specifying the required parameters. For example from a database of employee records, records of all employees in the sales department who have been employed for over 10 years and are paid less than £12,000 pa could be extracted.

(b)   Retrieved data can be sorted on any specified field (for example for employees, sorting might be according to grade, department, age, experience, salary level and so on).

(c)   Some calculations on retrieved data can be carried out - such as calculating totals and average values.

Report production

8.20   Most database packages include a report generator facility which allows the user to design report structures so that information can be presented on screen and printed out in a format which suits the user's requirements and preferences. Report formats can be stored on disk, if similar reports are produced periodically, and called up when required.

Chapter roundup

- Information systems can be divided into two broad categories, transaction (or data) processing systems and management information systems (MIS).

- Computerised cost accounting is exactly the same, in principle, as manual cost accounting.

- Computers have a number of advantages over manual systems.
    - They can process larger volumes of data
    - They can process data very quickly
    - They can provide up-to-date information
    - They are accurate
    - Large quantities of data can be sorted cheaply
    - They can provide more complex and varied information
    - They make data more accessible

- Computers do, however, have weaknesses.
    - Computer data are invisible
    - Computers are liable to breakdown
    - Computer programs can be incomprehensible
    - Managers can be swamped with information

- A decision support system (DSS) is designed to produce information in such a way as to help managers made better decisions.

- The most widely-used applications packages relevant to cost accounting are for payroll and for stock control.

- Databases and spreadsheet packages are particularly useful to cost accountants.

- Spreadsheet models should consist of an *input area* for variables, a *calculation* area for formulae, and an *output* area for the results of the calculations. This approach allows the basic model to be re-used in subsequent periods or for carrying out 'what if?' analyses for decision-making purposes.

- The main operations involved in using a database are as follows.
    - Creating the database structure
    - Entering data onto the database file
    - Retrieving and manipulating the data
    - Producing reports

Test your knowledge

1   Describe an information system. (see para 1.1)

2   What is an MIS? (1.7 - 1.9)

3   List six attributes that cost accounting information should possess. (2.2)

4   Suggest seven advantages of computerised cost accounting systems over manual systems. (3.5)

5   List ten cost accounting tasks frequently performed by a computer. (3.8)

6   What type of cost accounting information can payroll applications software produce? (5.7)

7   List five uses of spreadsheets. (6.8)

8   How do spreadsheets facilitate standard costing? (7.13, 7.14)

9   What are the objectives of a database system? (8.5)

Now try illustrative question 3 at the end of the Study Text

Chapter 4

DEALING WITH OVERHEADS

This chapter covers the following topics.

		Syllabus reference	*Ability required*
1	The problem of overheads	6(a)	Skill
2	Absorption costing	6(a)	Skill
3	Overhead absorption	6(a)	Skill
4	Over and under absorption of overheads	6(a)	Skill
5	Reciprocal servicing	6(a)	Skill
6	Activity based costing	6(a)	Skill

Introduction

In your studies for Paper 2 at Stage 1 you will have learnt how to accumulate the various cost elements which make up total cost. If you have forgotten, the following diagram of an absorption costing cost accumulation system should jog your memory.

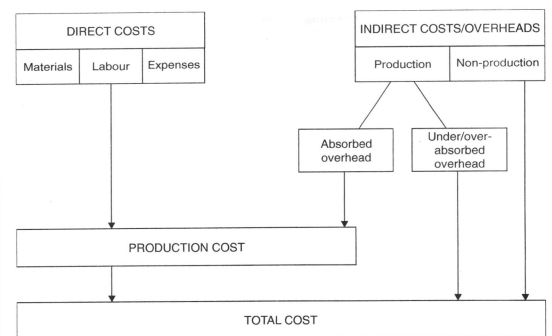

Remember that under a marginal costing system the production overhead absorbed would be variable production overhead only.

The collection and analysis of direct costs was covered in detail at Stage 1 and will be revisited briefly in Chapters 7, 8, 9 and 11 of this Study Text. For Paper 6 we need to concentrate on overheads and so we will be both building on your Stage 1 knowledge and seeing how the techniques which you have already learnt can be applied in more complex situations. We will also look at 'modern approaches to absorption costing' (as stipulated in the syllabus guidance notes). Understanding activity based costing is of particular importance.

1   THE PROBLEM OF OVERHEADS

1.1   Many of the problems in cost accumulation stem from the fact that there are common costs shared by the various products or services provided by an organisation, or by its various departments. These are the indirect costs (overheads) or common processing costs (for joint products).

1.2   If a company manufactures a product, the cost of the product will include the cost of the raw materials and components used in it and the cost of the labour effort required to make it. These are *direct* costs of the product.

1.3   The company would, however, incur many other costs in making the product, which are not directly attributable to a single product, but which are incurred generally in the process of manufacturing a large number of product units. Such costs include factory rent and rates, machine depreciation, supervision costs, the costs of control checks and inspections, design costs, heating and lighting. In some companies, the cost of overheads might greatly exceed the direct costs of production.

1.4   It might seem unreasonable to ignore indirect costs entirely when accumulating the costs of making a product, and yet there cannot be a completely satisfactory way of sharing out indirect costs between the many different items of production which benefit from them. We therefore need to decide whether, when accumulating the costs of an item, the overhead costs should be added to the direct costs of production to arrive at a total product cost.

1.5   There are two principal schools of thought.

(a)   Traditionally, the view has been taken in cost accounting that a fair share of overheads should be added to the cost of units produced. This fair share will include a portion of all production overhead expenditure and possibly administration and marketing overheads too. This is the view embodied in the principles of *absorption costing*.

(b)   Advocates of *marginal costing* take the view that it is sufficient to identify the variable costs of making and selling a product or service. Fixed costs should be dealt with separately and treated as a lump sum cost of the accounting period rather than shared out somehow or other between units produced and sold. Some overhead costs are, however, variable costs which increase as the total level of activity rises. Strictly speaking, therefore, the marginal cost of production and sales should include an amount for variable overheads.

1.6   We will be looking at absorption costing in this chapters. Marginal costing is the subject of the next chapter.

2   ABSORPTION COSTING   *11/96*

2.1   You should have covered absorption costing in your earlier studies. We will therefore summarise the simpler points of the topic but will go into some detail on the more complex areas to refresh your memory.

Exam focus point

There was a lengthy question on cost apportionment in the November 1996 exam. You *must* know the fundamentals of cost accounting if you are to pass your Paper 6 exam. Be sure to do Exercise 1, below, to make sure that your knowledge is up to scratch.

Knowledge brought forward from Paper 2

Absorption costing

- Product costs are built up using absorption costing by a process of allocation, apportionment and overhead absorption.

- *Allocation* is the process by which whole cost items are charged directly to a cost unit or cost centre. Direct costs are allocated directly to cost units.

- Overheads clearly identifiable with cost centres are allocated to those cost centres but costs which cannot be identified with one particular cost centre are allocated to *general overhead cost centres*. The cost of a warehouse security guard would therefore be charged to the warehouse cost centre but heating and lighting costs would be charged to a general overhead cost centre.

- The *first stage of overhead apportionment* is the identification of all overheads as production, service, administration or selling and distribution overheads. Overheads within *general overhead cost centres* therefore have to be shared out (or apportioned) between the other cost centres using a fair basis of apportionment (such as volume of space/floor area occupied by each cost centre for heating and lighting costs).

- The *second stage of overhead apportionment* is to *apportion* the costs of *service cost centres* (both directly allocated and apportioned costs) to production cost centres. One method by which service cost centre costs can be apportioned is to share out the costs of each service cost centre to production cost centres only.

- Costs allocated and apportioned to *administrative and selling and distribution cost* centres are not usually included as part of a product cost (and hence are not included in the value of stock) and *are deducted from the full cost of production* to arrive at the cost of sales.

- The final stage in absorption costing is the *absorption* into product costs (using overhead absorption rates) of the overheads which have been allocated and apportioned to the production cost centres.

Exercise 1

A company is preparing its production overhead budgets and determining the apportionment of those overheads to products. Cost centre expenses and related information have been budgeted as follows.

	Total £	Machine shop A £	Machine shop B £	Assembly £	Canteen £	Maintenance £
Indirect wages	78,560	8,586	9,190	15,674	29,650	15,460
Consumable materials (incl. maintenance)	16,900	6,400	8,700	1,200	600	-
Rent and rates	16,700					
Buildings insurance	2,400					
Power	8,600					
Heat and light	3,400					
Depreciation of machinery	40,200					
Other information:						
Value of machinery	402,000	201,000	179,000	22,000	-	-
Power usage - technical estimates (%)	100	55	40	3	-	2
Direct labour (hours)	35,000	8,000	6,200	20,800	-	-
Machine usage (hours)	25,200	7,200	18,000	-	-	-
Area (sq ft)	45,000	10,000	12,000	15,000	6,000	2,000

Required

Using the direct apportionment to production departments method and bases of apportionment which you consider most appropriate from the information provided, calculate overhead totals for the three production departments.

Solution

	Total £	A £	B £	Assembly £	Canteen £	Maintenance £	Basis of apportionment
Indirect wages	· 78,560	8,586	9,190	15,674	29,650	15,460	Direct
Consumable materials	16,900	6,400	8,700	1,200	600	-	Direct
Rent and rates	16,700	3,711	4,453	5,567	2,227	742	Area
Insurance	2,400	533	640	800	320	107	Area
Power	8,600	4,730	3,440	258	-	172	Usage
Heat and light	3,400	756	907	1,133	453	151	Area
Depreciation	40,200	20,100	17,900	2,200	-	-	Val of mach
	166,760	44,816	45,230	26,832	33,250	16,632	
Reallocate	-	7,600	5,890	19,760	(33,250)	-	Direct labour
Reallocate	-	4,752	11,880	-	-	(16,632)	Mach usage
Totals	166,760	57,168	63,000	46,592	-	-	

3 OVERHEAD ABSORPTION

5/97, 5/98

Use of a predetermined absorption rate

3.1 Overheads are not absorbed on the basis of actual costs but on the basis of estimated or budgeted figures (calculated prior to the beginning of the period) using what is known as an overhead absorption rate. There are a number of reasons for this.

(a) Goods are produced and sold throughout the year, but many actual overheads are not known until the end of the year. It would be inconvenient to wait until the year end in order to decide what overhead costs should be. Unacceptable delays in procedures such as invoicing and estimating, price setting and periodic stock and profit calculations would occur.

(b) An attempt to calculate overhead costs more regularly (such as each month) is possible. The difficulty with this approach would be that actual overheads from month to month would fluctuate randomly; therefore, overhead costs charged to production would depend to a certain extent on random events and changes. For example, only units made in winter would be charged with the heating overhead. Such changes are considered misleading for costing purposes and administratively and clerically inconvenient to deal with.

3.2 Overhead absorption rates, which are defined in CIMA *Official Terminology* as 'A means of attributing overhead to a product or service based, for example, on direct labour hours, direct labour cost or machine hours', are therefore calculated as follows.

(a) Estimate the overhead likely to be incurred during the coming year.

(b) Estimate the total hours, units, or direct costs on which the overhead absorption rates are to be based (activity level).

(c) Divide the estimated overhead by the budgeted activity level to arrive at an absorption rate.

Choosing the appropriate absorption base

Exercise 2

List as many possible bases of absorption (or 'overhead recovery rates') which you can think of.

Solution

(a) A percentage of direct materials cost
(b) A percentage of direct labour cost
(c) A percentage of prime cost
(d) A rate per machine hour
(e) A rate per direct labour hour
(f) A rate per unit
(g) A percentage of factory cost (for administration overhead)
(h) A percentage of sales or factory cost (for selling and distribution overhead)

3.3 The choice of an absorption basis is a matter of judgement and common sense. There are no strict rules or formulae involved. What is required, however, is an absorption basis which realistically reflects the characteristics of a given cost centre and which avoids undue anomalies.

3.4 In theory, each basis of absorption would be possible, but the company should choose a basis for its own costs which seems to be 'fairest'. This choice will be significant in determining the cost of individual products, but the total cost of production overheads is the budgeted overhead expenditure, no matter what basis of absorption is selected. The overhead absorption basis affects the relative share of overhead costs borne by individual products and jobs which is.

Exercise 3

Using the information in and the results of Exercise 1, determine budgeted overhead absorption rates for each of the production departments using bases of absorption which you consider most appropriate from the information provided.

Solution

Absorption rates

Machine shop A: $\dfrac{£57,168}{7,200}$ = £7.94 per machine hour

Machine shop B: $\dfrac{£63,000}{18,000}$ = £3.50 per machine hour

Assembly: $\dfrac{£46,592}{20,800}$ = £2.24 per direct labour hour

---

3.5 We know that the overhead absorption rate is predetermined using figures from the annual budget. If overheads are to be absorbed on the basis of direct labour hours, the overhead absorption rate will be calculated using the total overheads and the number of direct labour hours included in the annual budget.

3.6 Using the predetermined absorption rate, the *actual* cost of production can be established as follows.

	£
Direct materials	X
Direct labour	X
Direct expenses	X
Overheads (based on the predetermined recovery rate)	X
Actual cost of production	X̲

This is the process of overhead absorption. The 'actual' cost of production therefore includes some absorbed overhead, and not a share of actual overhead expenditure.

Exam focus point

In the May 1997 exam, candidates were asked to 'comment critically' on the choice of a particular absorption basis. An understanding of the rationale behind ABC (see later in this chapter) would have helped you to answer this.

Many questions are likely to require you to calculate overhead absorption rates. There were nine marks for doing so in a question in the May 1998 exam.

---

4   OVER AND UNDER ABSORPTION OF OVERHEADS

4.1   The rate of overhead absorption is based on estimates (of both numerator and denominator) and it is quite likely that either one or both of the estimates will not agree with what actually occurs. Actual overheads incurred will probably be either greater than or less than overheads absorbed into the cost of production.

4.2   Over-absorption means that the overheads charged to the cost of sales are greater than the overheads actually incurred. Under-absorption means that insufficient overheads have been included in the cost of sales. The CIMA *Official Terminology* definition of under- or over-absorbed overhead is 'The difference between overhead incurred and overhead absorbed, using an estimated rate, in a given period'.

4.3   Suppose that the budgeted overhead in a production department is £80,000 and the budgeted activity is 40,000 direct labour hours, the overhead recovery rate (using a direct labour hour basis) would be £2 per direct labour hour.

Actual overheads in the period are, say £84,000 and 45,000 direct labour hours are worked.

	£
Overhead incurred (actual)	84,000
Overhead absorbed (45,000 × £2)	90,000
Over absorption of overhead	6,000

4.4   In this example, the cost of produced units or jobs has been charged with £6,000 more than was actually spent and so the cost of production that is recorded will be too high. A favourable adjustment to reconcile the overheads charged to the actual overhead is necessary. The over-absorbed overhead will be written as an adjustment to the profit and loss account at the end of the accounting period to compensate for the excessive overheads charged in product costs.

4.5   Similarly, if overheads absorbed are lower than the amount of overhead incurred, the cost of production (or sales) recorded will be too low. The amount of under absorption will be written as an 'adverse' adjustment to the profit and loss account, to compensate for the under charging of overheads in product costs.

Exercise 4

The total production overhead expenditure of the company in Exercises 1 and 3 was £176,533 and its actual activity was as follows.

	Machine shop A	Machine shop B	Assembly
Direct labour hours	8,200	6,500	21,900
Machine usage hours	7,300	18,700	-

Required

Using the information in and results of Exercises 1 and 3, calculate the under or over absorption of overheads.

Solution

		£	£
Actual expenditure			176,533
Overhead absorbed			
Machine shop A	7,300 hrs × £7.94	57,962	
Machine shop B	18,700 hrs × £3.50	65,450	
Assembly	21,900 hrs × £2.24	49,056	
			172,468
Under-absorbed overhead			4,065

The reasons for under- /over-absorbed overhead   *5/98*

4.6   The overhead absorption rate is predetermined from budget estimates of overhead cost and the expected volume of activity. Under or over recovery of overhead will occur in the following circumstances.

(a)   Actual overhead costs are different from budgeted overheads (an expenditure variance).

(b)   The actual activity level is different from the budgeted activity level (an activity or volume variance).

(c)   Both actual overhead costs and actual activity level are different from the budgeted costs and level.

Exam focus point

Candidates were asked to prepare a statement showing clearly the *causes* of over/under-absorption in the May 1998 exam. The following exercise will give you some practice at this, in case a similar question comes up in the future.

Exercise 5

Elsewhere Ltd has a budgeted production overhead of £180,000 and a budgeted activity of 45,000 machine hours.

Required

Calculate the under-/over-absorbed overhead, and note the reasons for the under-/over-absorption in the following circumstances.

(a)   Actual overheads cost £170,000 and 45,000 machine hours were worked.
(b)   Actual overheads cost £180,000 and 40,000 machine hours were worked.
(c)   Actual overheads cost £170,000 and 40,000 machine hours were worked.

Solution

The overhead recovery rate is £180,000/45,000 = £4 per machine hour.

		£
(a)	Actual overhead	170,000
	Absorbed overhead (45,000 × £4)	180,000
	Over-absorbed overhead	10,000

The reason for the over absorption is that although the actual and budgeted machine hours are the same, actual overheads cost less than expected. There is therefore an expenditure variance.

		£
(b)	Actual overhead	180,000
	Absorbed overhead (40,000 × £4)	160,000
	Under-absorbed overhead	20,000

The reason for the under absorption is that although budgeted and actual overhead costs were the same, fewer machine hours were worked than expected. There is therefore a volume variance.

		£
(c)	Actual overhead	170,000
	Absorbed overhead (40,000 × £4)	160,000
	Under-absorbed overhead	10,000

The reason for the under absorption is a combination of the reasons in (a) and (b) and there are therefore expenditure and volume variances.

5   RECIPROCAL SERVICING   *11/96*

5.1   In Exercise 1 the costs of the canteen were allocated only to production departments, and not to maintenance, even though employees working in maintenance are as likely to use the canteen as anyone else. There are two other methods of service department cost apportionment which apportion the costs of each service department not only to production departments, but also to other service departments which make use of its services.

5.2   Apportionment is a procedure whereby indirect costs are spread fairly between departments. It could therefore be argued that a fair sharing of service department costs is not possible unless consideration is given to the work done by each service department for other service departments, that is unless any *reciprocal services* are taken into account.

5.3   For example, suppose a company has two production and two service departments (stores and maintenance). The following information about activity in the recent costing period is available.

| | Production departments | | Stores | Maintenance |
	A	*B*	*department*	*department*
Overhead costs	£10,030	£8,970	£10,000	£8,000
Cost of material requisitions	£30,000	£50,000	-	£20,000
Maintenance hours needed	8,000	1,000	1,000	-

(a)   If service department overheads were apportioned directly to production departments, the apportionment would be as follows.

| *Service department* | *Basis of apportionment* | *Total cost* | | *A* | | *B* |
		£		£		£
Stores	Material requisitions	10,000	(3/8)	3,750	(5/8)	6,250
Maintenance	Maintenance hours	8,000	(8/9)	7,111	(1/9)	889
		18,000		10,861		7,139
Overheads of departments A and B		19,000		10,030		8,970
		37,000		20,891		16,109

(b)   If, however, recognition is made of the fact that the stores and maintenance department do work for each other, and the basis of apportionment remains the same, we ought to apportion service department costs as follows.

	Dept A	*Dept B*	*Stores*	*Maint-enance*
Stores (100%)	30%	50%	-	20%
Maintenance (100%)	80%	10%	10%	-

This may be done using the repeated distribution method of apportionment or by using algebra. We will demonstrate both methods. You must make sure that you understand them both.

Repeated distribution (continuous allotment) method

5.4

	Production dept A £	Production dept B £	Stores £	Maintenance £
Overhead costs	10,030	8,970	10,000	8,000
First stores apportionment (see note (a))	3,000	5,000	(10,000)	2,000
			0	10,000
First maintenance apportionment	8,000	1,000	1,000	(10,000)
			1,000	0
Second stores apportionment	300	500	(1,000)	200
Second maintenance apportionment	160	20	20	(200)
Third stores apportionment	6	10	(20)	4
Third maintenance apportionment	4	-	-	(4)
	21,500	15,500	0	0

Notes

(a) The first apportionment could have been the costs of maintenance, rather than stores; there is no difference to the final results.

(b) When the repeated distributions bring service department costs down to small numbers (here £4) the final apportionment to production departments is an approximate rounding.

5.5   You should note the difference in the final overhead apportionment to each production department using the different service department apportionment methods. Unless the difference is substantial, the direct apportionment method (the first method we looked at) might be preferred because it is clerically simpler to use. Examination questions should make the choice of the method required reasonably clear to candidates.

Using algebra

5.6   A quicker way, perhaps, of arriving at your conclusions in the example above is to use algebra and simultaneous equations.

5.7   Let us use the same data as the example above.

(a) Let S be the total stores department overhead for apportionment, after it has been apportioned overhead from Maintenance.

(b) Let M be the total of maintenance department overhead after it has been apportioned overhead from Stores.

5.8   We can set up our equations as follows.

$$S = 0.1M + £10,000 \quad (1)$$
$$M = 0.2S + £8,000 \quad (2)$$

5.9   Multiplying (2) by 5 gives us

$$5M = S + £40,000 \quad (3), \text{ which can be rearranged so that}$$
$$S = 5M - £40,000 \quad (4)$$

Subtracting (1) from (4)

$$S = 5M - £40,000 \quad (4)$$
$$S = 0.1M + £10,000 \quad (1)$$
$$0 = 4.9M - £50,000$$

$$M = \frac{£50,000}{4.9} = £10,204$$

Substituting in (1)

$$S = 0.1 \times (£10,204) + £10,000$$
$$S = £11,020$$

5.10 These overheads can be apportioned as follows, using the percentages in Paragraph 5.3(b).

	Production dept A £	Production dept B £	Stores £	Maintenance £
Overhead costs	10,030	8,970	10,000	8,000
Apportion stores total	3,306	5,510	(11,020)	2,204
Apportion maintenance total	8,164	1,020	1,020	(10,204)
	21,500	15,500	-	-

This is the same result as in Paragraph 5.4, using repeated distribution.

5.11 Apportioning service department overheads is only useful if the resulting product costs reflect accurately the amounts expended by service departments. If, however, the apportionment is arbitrary or ill-considered, the absorption of service department costs into product costs may be misleading.

Exercise 6

You are the cost accountant of an industrial concern and have been given the following budgeted information regarding the four cost centres within your organisation.

	Dept 1 £	Dept 2 £	Maintenance dept £	Canteen £	Total £
Indirect labour	60,000	70,000	25,000	15,000	170,000
Consumables	12,000	16,000	3,000	10,000	41,000
Heating and lighting					12,000
Rent and rates					18,000
Depreciation					30,000
Supervision					24,000
Power					20,000
					315,000

You are also given the following information.

	Dept 1	Dept 2	Maintenance dept	Canteen	Total
Floor space in sq. metres	10,000	12,000	5,000	3,000	30,000
Book value of machinery (£)	150,000	120,000	20,000	10,000	300,000
Number of employees	40	30	10		80
Kilowatt hours	4,500	4,000	1,000	500	10,000

You are also told the following.

(a) The canteen staff are outside contractors.

(b) Departments 1 and 2 are production cost centres and the maintenance department and canteen are service cost centres.

Required

(a) Provide an overhead cost statement showing the allocation of overheads and the apportionment of general overheads to the four cost centres, clearly showing the basis of apportionment.

(b) Using the fact that the maintenance department provides 4,000 service hours to department 1, 3,000 service hours to department 2 and 1,000 hours for the canteen, apportion the overheads of the two service departments using the algebraic method.

Solution

(a)

	Basis of apportionment	Dept 1 £	Dept 2 £	Maintenance dept £	Canteen £	Total £
Indirect labour	-	60,000	70,000	25,000	15,000	170,000
Consumables	-	12,000	16,000	3,000	10,000	41,000
Heat and light	Space	4,000	4,800	2,000	1,200	12,000
Rent and rates	Space	6,000	7,200	3,000	1,800	18,000
Depreciation	Book value	15,000	12,000	2,000	1,000	30,000
Supervision	Employees	12,000	9,000	3,000	-	24,000
Power	Kilowatt hrs	9,000	8,000	2,000	1,000	20,000
		118,000	127,000	40,000	30,000	315,000

(b)   Let C = canteen overhead including apportioned maintenance overhead.

Let M = maintenance overhead including apportioned canteen overhead.

$C = 30,000 + \frac{1}{8}M$ (1)

$M = 40,000 + \frac{1}{8}C$ (2)

$8(M - 40,000) = C$ (3) (from (2))

$8(M - 40,000) = 30,000 + \frac{1}{8}M$ (4) (sub (1) into (3))

$8M - 320,000 = 30,000 + \frac{1}{8}M$

$7\frac{7}{8}M = 350,000$

$M = £44,444$

$C = 30,000 + \frac{1}{8}(44,444)$

$C = £35,556$

	Dept 1 £	Dept 2 £	Maintenance £	Canteen £
Overheads	118,000	127,000	40,000	30,000
Apportion maintenance	22,222	16,666	(44,444)	5,556
Apportion canteen	17,778	13,334	4,444	(35,556)
Total	158,000	157,000	-	-

6   ACTIVITY BASED COSTING   *11/96*

The reasons for the development of ABC

6.1   The traditional cost accumulation system which we have been looking at was developed in a time when most organisations produced only a narrow range of products and when overhead costs were only a very small fraction of total costs, direct labour and direct material costs accounting for the largest proportion of the costs. The traditional methods accurately allocate to products the costs of those resources that are used in proportion to the number of units produced of a particular product. Such resources include machine-related costs such as power and lubricants. Errors made in attributing overheads to products were not too significant.

6.2   Nowadays, however, with the advent of advanced manufacturing technology (AMT), overheads are likely to be far more important and in fact direct labour may account for as little as 5% of a product's cost. It therefore now appears difficult to justify the use of direct labour or direct material as the basis for allocating overheads or to believe that errors made in attributing overheads will not be significant and so the demand for more accurate product costs has increased.

6.3   Many resources are used in non-volume related support activities, (which have increased due to AMT) such as setting-up, production scheduling, first item inspection and data processing. These support activities assist the efficient manufacture of a wide range of products and are not, in general, affected by changes in production volume. They tend to vary in the long term according to the range and complexity of the products manufactured rather than the volume of output.

6.4 The wider the range and the more complex the products, the more support services will be required. Consider, for example, factory X which produces 10,000 units of one product, the Alpha, and factory Y which produces 1,000 units each of ten slightly different versions of the Alpha. Support activity costs in the factory Y are likely to be a lot higher than in factory X but the factories produce an identical number of units. Take setting-up. Factory X will only need to set-up once whereas Factory Y will have to set-up the production run at least ten times for the ten different products. Factory Y will therefore incur more set-up costs.

6.5 Traditional costing systems, which assume that all products consume all resources in proportion to their production volumes, tend to allocate too great a proportion of overheads to high volume products (which cause relatively little diversity and hence use fewer support services) and too small a proportion of overheads to low volume products (which cause greater diversity and therefore use more support services). ABC attempts to overcome this problem.

6.6 It is against this background activity based costing, which attempts to overcome this problem, has emerged.

Definition of ABC

6.7 Activity-based costing is defined in CIMA *Official Terminology* as 'An approach to the costing and monitoring of activities which involves tracing resource consumption and costing final output. Resources are assigned to activities and activities to cost objects based on consumption estimates'.

6.8 The major ideas behind activity based costing are as follows.
   (a) Activities cause costs. Activities include ordering, materials handling, machining, assembly, production scheduling and despatching.
   (b) Producing products creates demand for the activities.
   (c) Costs are assigned to a product on the basis of the product's consumption of the activities.

   ABC is defined in CIMA *Official Terminology*, as 'Cost attribution to cost units on the basis of benefit received from indirect activities eg ordering, setting-up, assuring quality'.

Outline of an ABC system   *5/98*

6.9 An ABC system operates as follows.

   (a) *Step 1*
   Identify an organisation's major activities.

   (b) *Step 2*
   Identify the factors which determine the size of the costs of an activity/cause the costs of an activity. These are known as *cost drivers,* defined as 'A factor which causes a change in the cost of an activity' in the CIMA *Official Terminology*. Look at the following examples.

Activity	*Cost driver*
Ordering	Number of orders
Materials handling	Number of production runs
Production scheduling	Number of production runs
Despatching	Number of despatches

   For those costs that vary with production levels in the short term, ABC uses volume-related cost drivers such as labour or machine hours. The cost of oil used as a lubricant on the machines would therefore be added to products on the basis of the number of machine hours, since oil would have to be used for each hour the machine ran.

(c)   *Step 3*

Collect the costs of each activity into what are known as cost pools (equivalent to cost centres under more traditional costing methods).

(d)   *Step 4*

Charge support overheads to products on the basis of their usage of the activity. A product's usage of an activity is measured by the number of the activity's cost driver it generates.

Suppose, for example, that the cost pool for the ordering activity totalled £100,000 and that there were 10,000 orders (the cost driver). Each product would therefore be charged with £10 for each order it required. A batch requiring five orders would therefore be charged with £50.

Example: ABC

6.10   Suppose that Cooplan Ltd manufactures four products, W, X, Y and Z. Output and cost data for the period just ended are as follows.

	Output	Number of production runs in the period	Material cost per unit	Direct labour hours per unit	Machine hours per unit
	Units		£		
W	10	2	20	1	1
X	10	2	80	3	3
Y	100	5	20	1	1
Z	100	5	80	3	3
		14			

Direct labour cost per hour is £5. Overhead costs are as follows.

	£
Short-run variable costs	3,080
Set-up costs	10,920
Expediting and scheduling costs	9,100
Materials handling costs	7,700
	30,800

Required

Calculate product costs using the following approaches.

(a)   Absorption costing
(b)   ABC

Solution

6.11   Using a conventional absorption costing approach and an absorption rate for overheads based on either direct labour hours or machine hours, the product costs would be as follows.

	W	X	Y	Z	Total
	£	£	£	£	£
Direct material	200	800	2,000	8,000	11,000
Direct labour	50	150	500	1,500	2,200
Overheads *	700	2,100	7,000	21,000	30,800
	950	3,050	9,500	30,500	44,000
Units produced	10	10	100	100	
Cost per unit	£95	£305	£95	£305	

* £30,800 ÷ 440 hours = £70 per direct labour or machine hour

Using activity based costing and assuming that the number of production runs is the cost driver for set-up costs, expediting and scheduling costs and materials handling costs and that machine hours are the cost driver for short-run variable costs, unit costs would be as follows.

	W	X	Y	Z	Total
	£	£	£	£	£
Direct material	200	800	2,000	8,000	11,000
Direct labour	50	150	500	1,500	2,200
Short-run variable overheads (W1)	70	210	700	2,100	3,080
Set-up costs (W2)	1,560	1,560	3,900	3,900	10,920
Expediting, scheduling costs (W3)	1,300	1,300	3,250	3,250	9,100
Materials handling costs (W4)	1,100	1,100	2,750	2,750	7,700
	4,280	5,120	13,100	21,500	44,000

	W	X	Y	Z
	£	£	£	£
Units produced	10	10	100	100
Cost per unit	£428	£512	£131	£215

Workings

1	£3,080 ÷ 440 machine hours	=	£7 per machine hour
2	£10,920 ÷ 14 production runs	=	£780 per run
3	£9,100 ÷ 14 production runs	=	£650 per run
4	£7,700 ÷ 14 production runs	=	£550 per run

Summary

Product	Conventional costing Unit cost £	ABC Unit cost £	Difference £
W	95	428	+ 333
X	305	512	+ 207
Y	95	131	+ 36
Z	305	215	− 90

6.12 The figures suggest that the traditional volume-based absorption costing system is flawed.

(a) It under allocates overhead costs to low-volume products (here, W and X with ten units of output) and over allocates overheads to higher-volume products (here Z in particular).

(b) It under allocates overhead costs to less complex products (here W and Y with just one hour of work needed per unit) and over allocates overheads to more complex products (here X and particularly Z).

ABC versus traditional costing methods

6.13 Both absorption costing and ABC systems adopt the two stage allocation process.

Allocation of overheads

6.14 Traditional cost systems allocate overheads to production departments (cost centres) whereas ABC systems assign overheads to each major activity (cost pools). With ABC systems, many activity-based cost pools are established whereas with traditional systems, overheads tend to be pooled by departments. This can result in extensive reapportionments of service department costs to ensure that all overheads are allocated to production departments. ABC establishes separate cost pools for support activities such as despatching. As the costs of these activities are assigned directly to products through cost driver rates, reapportionment of service department costs is avoided.

Part A: Cost accounting

Absorption of overheads

6.15 The principal difference between the two systems is the way in which overheads are absorbed into products. Absorption costing uses usually two absorption bases (labour hours and/or machine hours) to charge overheads to products whereas ABC uses many cost drivers as absorption bases (number of orders, number of dispatches and so on). Absorption rates under ABC should therefore be more closely linked to the causes of overhead costs.

Cost drivers

6.16 The principal idea of ABC is to focus attention on what causes costs to increase, the cost drivers. Just as there are no rules for what to use as the basis for absorbing costs in absorption costing, there are also difficulties in choosing cost drivers.

6.17 Those costs that do vary with production volume, such as power costs, should be traced to products using production volume-related cost drivers as appropriate, such as direct labour hours or direct machine hours.

6.18 Overheads which do not vary with output but with some other activity should be traced to products using transaction-based cost drivers, such as number of production runs and number of orders received.

6.19 Focusing attention on what actually causes overheads and tracing overheads to products on the basis of the usage of the cost drivers ensures that a greater proportion of overheads are product related, whereas traditional costing systems allow overheads to be related to products in rather more arbitrary ways. It is this feature of ABC which produces, it is claimed, greater accuracy.

Exercise 7

A company manufactures two products, L and M, using the same equipment and similar processes. An extract of the production data for these products in one period is shown below.

	L	*M*
Quantity produced (units)	5,000	7,000
Direct labour hours per unit	1	2
Machine hours per unit	3	1
Set-ups in the period	10	40
Orders handled in the period	15	60

Overhead costs	£
Relating to machine activity	220,000
Relating to production run set-ups	20,000
Relating to handling of orders	45,000
	285,000

Required

Calculate the production overheads to be absorbed by one unit of each of the products using the following costing methods.

(a) A traditional costing approach using a direct labour hour rate to absorb overheads

(b) An activity based costing approach, using suitable cost drivers to trace overheads to products

Solution

(a) *Traditional costing approach*

	Direct labour hours
Product L = 5,000 units × 1 hour	5,000
Product M = 7,000 units × 2 hours	14,000
	19,000

∴ Overhead absorption rate		=	$\dfrac{£285,000}{19,000}$
		=	£15 per hour

Overhead absorbed would be as follows.

Product L	1 hour × £15	=	£15 per unit
Product M	2 hours × £15	=	£30 per unit

(b)   *ABC approach*

		Machine hours
Product L	= 5,000 units × 3 hours	15,000
Product M	= 7,000 units × 1 hour	7,000
		22,000

Using ABC the overhead costs are absorbed according to the *cost drivers*.

	£			
Machine-hour driven costs	220,000	÷	22,000 m/c hours	= £10 per m/c hour
Set-up driven costs	20,000	÷	50 set-ups	= £400 per set-up
Order driven costs	45,000	÷	75 orders	= £600 per order

Overhead costs are therefore as follows.

		Product L £		*Product M* £
Machine-driven costs	(15,000 hrs × £10)	150,000	(7,000 hrs × £10)	70,000
Set-up costs	(10 × £400)	4,000	(40 × £400)	16,000
Order handling costs	(15 × £600)	9,000	(60 × £600)	36,000
		163,000		122,000
Units produced		5,000		7,000
Overhead cost per unit		£32.60		£17.43

These figures suggest that product M absorbs an unrealistic amount of overhead using a direct labour hour basis. Overhead absorption should be based on the activities which drive the costs, in this case machine hours, the number of production run set-ups and the number of orders handled for each product.

The merits of activity based costing   *11/96*

6.20   As the above example shows, there is nothing difficult about ABC. Once the necessary information has been obtained it is similar to traditional absorption costing. This simplicity is part of its appeal. Further merits of ABC are as follows.

(a)   Management accounting practice has become distorted by the needs of financial reporting, in particular the need to value stocks, and has not given sufficient priority to the need to provide meaningful product costs. ABC focuses attention on the nature of cost behaviour and attempts to provide meaningful product costs, particularly in an AMT manufacturing environment where overhead costs are a significant proportion of total costs.

(b)   Direct labour costs are a small proportion of conversion costs in AMT production. ABC uses multiple cost drivers to allocate overhead costs to activities and then to products, and does not use what the advocates of ABC would call a meaningless direct labour hour recovery rate or machine hour recovery rate, that associates overhead costs with volume of activity only. Only ABC recognises transaction-based overhead costs that arise out of diversity and complexity of operations.

(c)   The complexity of manufacturing has increased, with wider product ranges, shorter product life cycles, a greater importance being attached to quality and more complex production processes. ABC recognises this complexity with its multiple cost drivers.

(d)   In a more competitive environment, companies must be able to assess product profitability realistically. To do this, they must have a good understanding of what drives overhead costs. ABC gives a meaningful analysis of costs which should provide a suitable basis for product performance measurement in a competitive modern manufacturing environment.

(e) In modern manufacturing systems, overhead functions include a lot of non-factory-floor activities such as product design, quality control, production planning, sales order planning and customer service. ABC is concerned with all overhead costs, including the costs of these functions, and so it takes cost accounting beyond its 'traditional' factory floor boundaries.

(f) ABC is ideally suited to service industries, as we will see in Chapter 11.

Exam focus point

Three questions (in the November 1996, November 1997 and May 1998 exams) have asked about how ABC might be used or might provide useful information for a particular organisation that is currently using absorption costing or marginal costing.

The November 1997 question did not refer specifically to ABC but used the term 'multiple activity bases'.

Criticisms of development ABC

6.21 It has been suggested by critics that activity based costing has some serious flaws.

(a) Some measure of (arbitrary) cost apportionment may still be required at the cost pooling stage for items like rent, rates and building depreciation. If an ABC system has many cost pools the amount of apportionment needed may be greater than ever.

(b) The ability of a single cost driver to explain fully the cost behaviour of all items in its associated pool is questionable.

(c) To have a usable cost driver, a cost must be caused by an activity that is measurable in quantitative terms and which can be related to production output. Some costs might be attributed to customers or market segments rather than to products, but not all costs can be treated in this way. For example, what drives corporate as opposed to product-based advertising (British Airways adverts, for instance) or the cost of the annual external audit?

(d) ABC is sometimes introduced because it is fashionable, not because it will be used by management to provide extra information, to alter production mix or to control non-value added activities for example. If management is not going to use ABC information, an absorption costing system may be simpler to operate.

Chapter roundup

- The traditional approach to dealing with overheads is absorption costing.

- There are three stages in absorption costing: allocation, apportionment and absorption.

- Apportionment has two stages: general overhead apportionment and service department cost apportionment.

- Service department costs can be apportioned to production departments either directly, or using algebra or using the repeated distribution method.

- Overheads are absorbed into products using an appropriate absorption rate based on budgeted costs and budgeted activity levels.

- Under-/over-absorbed overhead occurs when overheads incurred do not equal overheads absorbed.

- An alternative to the traditional methods of accounting for costs is activity based costing. ABC involves the identification of the factors (cost drivers) which cause the costs of an organisation's major activities. Support overheads are charged to products on the basis of their usage of an activity.

- When using ABC, for costs that vary with production levels in the short term, the cost driver will be volume related (labour or machine hours). Overheads that vary with some other activity (and not volume of production) should be traced to products using transaction-based cost drivers such as production runs or number of orders received.

Test your knowledge

1 What is the problem of overheads? (see para 1.4)

2 What are the three steps in calculating overhead absorption rates? (3.2)

3 List three reasons for under-/over-absorbed overhead. (4.6)

4 What two methods of apportioning service department costs take account of the work service departments do for each other? (5.4 - 5.10)

5 What are the basic ideas of ABC? (6.8)

6 What is the advantage of using cost drivers instead of traditional absorption bases?(6.19)

7 What criticisms of ABC have been suggested? (6.21)

Now try illustrative question 4 at the end of the Study Text

Chapter 5

ABSORPTION COSTING AND MARGINAL COSTING COMPARED

This chapter covers the following topics.

		Syllabus reference	Ability required
1	Marginal costing	6(b)	Skill
2	Reconciliations	6(b)	Skill
3	The relative merits of absorption costing and marginal costing	6(b)	Skill

Introduction

The view of those that believe overheads should be incorporated into product costs was considered in Chapter 4. We are now going to examine the viewpoint of those who have the opposite opinion, the supporters of marginal costing.

We will be looking in particular at the differences between absorption costing and marginal costing, the effect on profit of the two methods and their relative merits for management reporting purposes. You encountered the basics of marginal costing in your Paper 2 studies and a brief summary of those basics is included at the beginning of this chapter.

1   MARGINAL COSTING

5/96

Knowledge brought forward from Paper 2

Marginal costing

- Marginal cost = the cost of one unit of a product/service which could be avoided if that unit were not produced/provided = variable cost

- Contribution = sales revenue – variable (marginal) cost of sales

- In marginal costing, *only* variable costs (marginal costs) are charged to the cost of making and selling a product or service. Fixed costs are treated as period costs and are deducted from profit. They are therefore charged in full against the profit of the period in which they are incurred.

- In marginal costing, closing stocks are valued at marginal (variable) production cost whereas, in absorption costing, stocks are valued at their full production cost which includes absorbed fixed production overhead.

- If the opening and closing stock levels differ, the profit reported for the accounting period under the two methods of cost accumulation will be different because the two systems value stock differently.

- In the long run, total profit for a company will be the same whether marginal costing or absorption costing is used because, in the long run, total costs will be the same by either method of accounting. Different accounting conventions merely affect the profit of individual accounting periods.

1.1   For Paper 6, you need to be able to apply the basic principles to more complex situations than those encountered in Paper 2.

Exercise 1

A company makes and sells a single product. At the beginning of period 1, there are no opening stocks of the product, for which the variable production cost is £4 and the sales price £6 per unit. Fixed costs are £2,000 per period, of which £1,500 are fixed production costs. Normal output is 1,500 units per period.

	Period 1 Units	Period 2 Units
Sales	1,200	1,700
Production	1,500	1,400

Required

Prepare profit statements for each period and for the two periods in total using both absorption costing and marginal costing.

Solution

It is important to notice that although production and sales volumes in each period are different (therefore the profit for each period by absorption costing will be different from the profit by marginal costing), over the full period, total production equals sales volume. The total cost of sales is the same and therefore the total profit is the same by either method of accounting. Differences in profit in any one period are merely timing differences which cancel out over a longer period of time.

(a)   *Absorption costing*. The absorption rate for fixed production overhead is £1,500/1,500 units = £1 per unit. The fully absorbed cost per unit = £(4+1) = £5.

		Period 1 £	Period 1 £	Period 2 £	Period 2 £	Total £	Total £
Sales			7,200		10,200		17,400
Production costs							
Variable		6,000		5,600		11,600	
Fixed		1,500		1,400		2,900	
		7,500		7,000		14,500	
Add opening stock b/f	(300×£5)	–		1,500		-	
		7,500		8,500		14,500	
Less closing stock c/f	(300×£5)	1,500		-		-	
Production cost of sales		6,000		8,500		14,500	
Under-absorbed o/hd		-		100		100	
Total costs			6,000		8,600		14,600
Gross profit			1,200		1,600		2,800
Other costs			(500)		(500)		(1,000)
Net profit			700		1,100		1,800

(b)   *Marginal costing*

The marginal cost per unit = £4.

		Period 1 £	Period 1 £	Period 2 £	Period 2 £	Total £	Total £
Sales			7,200		10,200		17,400
Variable production cost		6,000		5,600		11,600	
Add opening stock b/f	(300×£4)	-		1,200		-	
		6,000		6,800		11,600	
Less closing stock c/f	(300×£4)	1,200		-		-	
Variable production cost of sales			4,800		6,800		11,600
Contribution b/f			2,400		3,400		5,800
Contribution c/f			2,400		3,400		5,800
Fixed costs			2,000		2,000		4,000
Profit			400		1,400		1,800

2   RECONCILIATIONS

Reconciling the profit figures given by the two methods 5/96

2.1   The difference in profits reported under marginal costing and absorption costing is due to the different stock valuation methods used.

2.2   Assuming that the fixed overhead absorption rate remains constant, if stock levels *increase* between the beginning and end of a period, *absorption* costing will report the *higher profit* because some of the fixed production overhead incurred during the period will be carried forward in closing stock (which reduces cost of sales) to be set against sales revenue in the following period instead of being written off in full against profit in the period concerned.

2.3   However, if stock levels *decrease, absorption* costing will report the *lower profit* because as well as the fixed overhead incurred, fixed production overhead which had been carried forward in opening stock is released and is also included in cost of sales.

Example: reconciling profits

2.4   The profits reported under absorption costing and marginal costing for period 1 in the example in Exercise 1 would be reconciled as follows.

	£
Marginal costing profit	400
Adjust for fixed overhead in stock:	
Stock increase of 300 units × £1 per unit	300
Absorption costing profit	700

Exercise 2

Reconcile the profits reported under the two systems for period 2 of the example in Exercise 1.

Solution

	£
Marginal costing profit	1,400
Adjust for fixed overhead in stock:	
Stock decrease of 300 units × £1 per unit	(300)
Absorption costing profit	1,100

Reconciling the profit figures for different periods 5/96, 5/98

2.5   As well as being able to reconcile the profits reported for the *same period* using the *different methods*, you must also be able to reconcile the profit figures for *different periods* using the *same method*.

Marginal costing

2.6   Look back at Exercise 1 (solution part (b)). The fixed cost deducted each period is the same and so the change in profit must be due to a change in contribution. But variable cost per unit is the same in each period and hence it must be the change in sales volume which affects contribution and hence profit.

	£
Marginal costing profit for period 1	400
Adjust for affect of change in sales volume on contribution	
Increase in sales volume of 500 units (× £2★)	1,000
Marginal costing profit for period 2	1,400

★ Contribution per unit = £(6 − 4) = £2

Absorption costing

2.7 The change in the sales volume obviously affects the difference between the profits reported in the two periods under absorption costing but the under- or over-absorbed overhead also has to be taken into account.

2.8 We can reconcile the two profit figures in Exercise 1 (solution part (a)) as follows.

	£
Absorption costing profit for period 1	700
Adjust for affect of change in sales volume on profit	
Increase in sales volume of 500 units × £1*	500
Adjust for under-/over-absorbed overhead	
Period 2	(100)
Absorption costing profit for period 2	1,100

* Profit per unit = £(6 – 5) = £1

2.9 The under-absorbed overhead in period 2 makes period 2's profit lower than period 1's and hence it must be deducted from period 1's profit to arrive at period 2's profit.

Exercise 3

Given the fact that October's absorption costing profit is higher than November's and that there was over-absorbed overhead in October and under-absorbed overhead in November and that the number of units sold in November was less than the number sold in October, delete as appropriate + or – in the reconciliation below.

	£
Absorption costing profit for October	X
+ / – Adjustment for affect of change in sales volume on profit	X
+ / – Adjustment for over-absorbed overhead in October	X
+ / – Adjustment for under-absorbed overhead in November	X
Absorption costing profit for November	X

Solution

All three adjustments should be deducted from the profit for October.

The over-absorbed overhead in October made the profit higher than November's and hence it must be deducted to arrive at November's profit. Likewise, the under absorption in November made that month's profit lower than October's and hence it must be deducted from October's.

3 THE RELATIVE MERITS OF ABSORPTION COSTING AND MARGINAL COSTING

3.1 Absorption costing and marginal costing may be compared in three ways.

(a) As costing methods for reporting to management, for the purposes of profit monitoring and control.

(b) As costing methods for reporting profits and inventory values in externally published accounts.

(c) As costing methods for providing information for planning, control and decision making to management.

Exam focus point

All of the techniques and issues raised in this chapter were thoroughly tested in a question in the May 1996 exam. A full question on the topic is perhaps becoming overdue to appear again.

Marginal costing versus absorption costing: reporting to management

3.2   We have already seen that, because of differences in inventory valuations, the reported profit in any period is likely to differ according to the costing method used. Presumably, however, one method might be said to provide a more reliable guide to management about the organisation's profit position.

3.3   With marginal costing, contribution (sales minus variable costs) varies in direct proportion to the volume of units sold. Profits will increase as sales volume rises, by the amount of extra contribution earned. Since fixed cost expenditure does not alter, it can be argued that marginal costing gives an accurate picture of how a firm's cash flows and profits are affected by changes in sales volumes.

3.4   With absorption costing, in contrast, there is no clear relationship between profit and sales volume, and as sales volume rises the total profit will rise by the sum of the gross profit per unit plus the amount of overhead absorbed per unit. Arguably this is a confusing and unsatisfactory method of monitoring profitability.

3.5   If sales volumes are the same from period to period, marginal costing will report the same profit each period (given no change in selling prices or costs). In contrast, using absorption costing, profits can vary with the volume of production, even when the volume of sales is constant. Absorption costing is therefore often criticised because of the possibility of manipulating profit, simply by changing output and inventory levels.

Example: manipulating profits

3.6   GP Ltd budgeted to make and sell 10,000 units of its product in 19X1. The selling price is £10 per unit and the variable cost £4 per unit. Fixed production costs were budgeted at £50,000 for the year.

The company uses absorption costing and budgeted an absorption rate of £5 per unit.

During 19X1, it became apparent that sales demand would only be 8,000 units. The management, concerned about the apparent effect of the low volume of sales on profits, decided to increase production for the year to 15,000 units. Actual fixed costs were still expected to be £50,000 in spite of the significant increase in production volume.

Required

Calculate the profit at an actual sales volume of 8,000 units, using the following methods.

(a)   Absorption costing
(b)   Marginal costing

Solution

3.7   (a)   *Absorption costing*

	£	£
Sales (8,000 × £10)		80,000
Cost of production (15,000 × £9)	135,000	
Less: over-absorbed overhead (5,000 × £5)	(25,000)	
		(110,000)
		(30,000)
Closing stock (7,000 × £9)		63,000
Profit		33,000

(b) *Marginal costing*

	£	£
Sales		80,000
Cost of production (15,000 × £4)	60,000	
Closing stock (7,000 × £4)	28,000	
		32,000
Contribution		48,000
Fixed costs		50,000
Loss		(2,000)

3.8 The difference in profits of £35,000 is explained by the difference in the increase in stock values (7,000 units × £5 of fixed overhead per unit). With absorption costing, the expected profit will be higher than the original budget of (10,000 units × (£10 − 9)) £10,000 simply because £35,000 of fixed overheads will be carried forward in closing stock values.

In contrast, marginal costing would report a contribution of £6 per unit, or £48,000 in total for 8,000 units, which fails to cover the fixed costs of £50,000 by £2,000.

3.9 Dopuch, Birnberg and Demski *(Cost Accounting: Accounting Data for Management's Decisions)* wrote that:

> 'the fact that absorption (profit) may be increased merely by producing in excess of sales can give managers distorted short-term results. There is a story that a tractor firm in the Midwest was left with a large number of unsold units at the end of a period. A manager received a bonus for increasing that period's current (absorption) profit, then left the firm in search of new challenges.'

3.10 This argument in favour of marginal costing is not conclusive, however, because a different situation arises when sales fluctuate from month to month because of seasonal variations in sales demand, but production per month is held constant in order to arrange for an even flow of output (and thereby prevent the cost of idle resources in periods of low demand and overtime in periods of high demand).

Consider the following example.

Example: seasonal variations in sales demand

3.11 Umbrella Ltd budgets to make and sell 3,600 units of its product during 19X2 at a selling price of £5. Production variable costs are £3 per unit and fixed costs for the year are budgeted as £5,400 (divisible equally between the 12 months of the year). Sales demand in the first six months of the year will be only 200 units per month, but demand will double in the second six months to 400 per month. In order to save unnecessary production costs, the company has budgeted to spread production evenly over the year by producing 300 units per month.

Required

Calculate the profits each month using the following costing methods.

(a) Absorption costing
(b) Marginal costing

Solution

3.12 *Absorption costing*

(a) The fixed overhead absorption rate is $\dfrac{£5,400}{3,600 \text{ units}}$ = £1.50 per unit

For each of the first six months of the year, profit per month would be as follows.

	£
Sales (200 units × £5)	1,000
Less full cost of sales (200 units × £4.50)	900
	100
Under-/over-absorbed overhead	0
Profit (£0.50 per unit)	100

For each of the second six months of the year, profit per month would be as follows.

	£
Sales (400 units × £5)	2,000
Less full cost of sales (400 units × £4.50)	1,800
	200
Under-/over-absorbed overhead	0
Profit (£0.50 per unit)	200

Total profit for the year would be 3,600 units × £0.50 = £1,800

(b)   Marginal costing

For each of the first six months of the year, there would be a loss.

	£
Sales (200 units × £5)	1,000
Less variable cost of sales (200 units × £3)	600
Contribution (£2 per unit)	400
Less fixed costs	450
Loss	(50)

For each of the second six months of the year there would be a profit.

	£
Sales (400 units × £5)	2,000
Less variable cost of sales (400 units × £3)	1,200
Contribution (£2 per unit)	800
Less fixed costs	450
Profit	350

Total profit for the year would be £1,800

3.13   In this example it might be argued that in view of the deliberate policy of producing goods for stock in the first half of the year, and selling out of stock in the second half absorption costing would provide a better method of reporting profits month by month. At a profit of £0.50 per unit, total monthly profits double when sales double, which would conform to the expectations of the management of Umbrella Ltd.

3.14   In contrast, marginal costing would report a loss in each of the first six months (which might cause unnecessary concern to management) and a misleadingly large jump into profitability in the second half of the year.

3.15   Other arguments *in favour of absorption costing* for internal profit reporting are as follows.

(a)   Marginal costing fails to recognise the importance of working to full capacity. With absorption costing, the effect of higher production volumes is to reduce unit costs (because the fixed cost per unit is lower) and if sales prices are based on the 'cost-plus' method, the relevance of output capacity to cost, price and sales demand should be apparent.

(b)   Selling prices based on marginal costing might enable the firm to make a contribution on each unit of product it sells, but the total contribution earned might be insufficient to cover all fixed costs.

(c)   In the long run, all costs are variable, and inventory values based on absorption costing will give recognition to these long-run variable costs.

3.16   There are also further arguments *in favour of marginal costing* for internal profit reporting.

(a)   Separating fixed and variable costs helps management to make short-run pricing decisions concerning incremental profits.

(b)   Fixed costs (such as depreciation, rent or salaries) relate to a period of time and should be charged against the revenues of the period in which they are incurred.

(c)   An organisation may make buffer stocks in a period as a precautionary measure, but it does not incur extra fixed costs.

Marginal costing versus absorption costing: external reporting

3.17   It might be argued that absorption costing is preferable to marginal costing in management accounting, in order to be consistent with the requirement of SSAP 9 to include production overhead in inventory values in published accounts. This argument might be especially relevant when a firm has an integrated or combined accounting system for its financial and management accounts.

3.18   The argument is, however, an unimportant one because it is quite easy for a firm to maintain its accounts on a marginal costing basis, and when financial accounts are prepared, to convert its stock values into fully absorbed costs.

Marginal costing versus absorption costing: planning, control and decision-making information

5/96

3.19   It is widely suggested that marginal costing is a better system for providing information for planning, control and decision making. It allows the decision maker much greater flexibility and he/she can see more easily the consequences of, for example, changing volumes of production or regulating sales demand though pricing. It is possible to prepare reports which allow for marginal costing information for decision making, planning and control and absorption costing information for external reporting. Such a report might have the following format.

Production/departmental profit report		£
Sales		X
Less variable cost of sales		X
Contribution		X
Less variable departmental operating costs		X
Contribution to fixed costs of the department		X
Less fixed departmental costs		X
Contribution to company overhead		X
Less pro-rata share of apportioned company overhead		X
Marginal costing profit		X
Adjustment of inventory to absorption costing values		
Opening stock	(X)	
Closing stock	X	
		X or (X)
Absorption costing profit		X

Absorption costing alone would not provide information for budget planning or departmental cost control.

Decision making

3.20   The accounting information required for decision making is different from the accounting information recorded in the books of financial accounts and conventional cost accounts. For cost accounting most UK companies still use absorption costing but this provides totally misleading decision information. For example, suppose that a sales manager has an item of product which he is having difficulty in selling. Its historical full cost is £80, made up of variable costs of £50 and fixed costs of £30. A customer offers £60 for it.

(a) If there is no other customer for the product, £60 would be better than nothing and the product should be sold to improve income and profit by this amount.

(b) If the company has spare production capacity which would otherwise not be used, it would be profitable to continue making more of the same product, if customers are willing to pay £60 for each extra unit made. This is because the additional costs are only £50 so that the profit would be increased marginally by £10 per unit produced.

(c) In absorption costing terms, the product makes a loss of £20, which would discourage the sales manager from accepting a price of £60 from the customer. His decision would be a bad one.

    (i) If the product is not sold for £60, it will presumably be scrapped eventually, so the choice is really between making a loss in absorption costing terms of £20, or a loss of £80 when the stock is written off, whenever this happens.

    (ii) If there is demand for some extra units at £60 each, the absorption costing loss would be £20 per unit, but at the end of the year there would be an additional contribution to overheads and profit of £10 per unit. In terms of absorption costing the under-absorbed overhead would be reduced by £30 (the fixed cost part of the product's full cost) for each extra unit made and sold.

3.21 Absorption costing information about unit profits is therefore irrelevant in short-run decisions in which fixed costs do not change (such as short-run tactical decisions seeking to make the best use of existing facilities). In such circumstances the decision rule is to choose the alternative which maximises contribution.

Summary

3.22 No recommendation of the costing method which should be used can be given. Although any technique can be used for internal purposes, absorption costing must be used for external reporting. An understanding of the behaviour of cost and the implications of contribution is vital for accountants and managers, and the use of marginal costing for planning and decision making is universal (although it is rarely used for cost accumulation).

3.23 It seems, therefore, that there is no ideal costing system. David Allen, in *Back to Basics* (*Management Accounting*, October 1994) cited the following purposes of costing systems.

(a) As an input to financial accounting, for example to arrive at the value at which stock is carried forward on the balance sheet (with a consequent effect on what is shown as profit)

(b) As an input to cost accounting, for example to arrive at the price at which goods are transferred between processes

(c) As a means of measuring performance, for example to compare actual costs with expectations

(d) As a means of directing attention to matters worthy of investigation, for example the cost of a particular activity

(e) In support of a particular decision, for example what selling prices to quote (or, what amounts to the same thing, which business to accept) or whether to make or buy a particular component

These requirements are so different it is not surprising that no costing system seems able to meet all of them. The 'best' method is the one that best suits the purpose for which the information will be used.

Exam focus point

Don't forget about ABC as an alternative method of dealing with overheads. We looked at this in the previous chapter.

If you are a diligent reader of journals such as *Management Accounting* you will often see articles on 'new' methods. These are generally useful for the case studies they provide (which help you to understand the issues in real life organisations), but *ABC is the only new approach that has had any real impact.*

Chapter roundup

- In marginal costing, stocks are valued at variable production cost whereas in absorption costing they are valued at their full production cost.

- Hence, if the opening and closing stock levels differ (assuming that the fixed overhead absorption rate remains constant), the profit reported for the accounting period under the two methods will be different.

- In the long run, however, total profit will be the same whatever method is used.

- Absorption costing and marginal cost profits can be reconciled as follows:

	If stock levels increase	If stock levels decrease
	£	£
Marginal costing profit	X	X
Change in stock level × fixed o/hd absorbed per unit	X	(X)
Absorption costing profit	X	X

- Different periods' profit figures under the two systems can be reconciled as follows:

  o Marginal costing

	£
Marginal costing profit for period 1	X
Adjustment for effect of change in sales volume on contribution	
Increase/(decrease) in sales volume × contribution per unit	X/(X)
Marginal costing profit for period 2	X

  o Absorption costing

	£
Absorption costing profit for period 1	X
Adjustment for effect of change in sales volume on profit:	
Increase/(decrease) in sales volume × profit per unit	X/(X)
Adjustment for under-/over-absorbed overhead in period 1:	
Under-absorbed overhead	X
Over-absorbed overhead	(X)
Adjustment for under-/over-absorbed overhead in period 2:	
Under-absorbed overhead	(X)
Over-absorbed overhead	X
Absorption costing profit for period 2	X

- When reporting to management, absorption costing can be used to manipulate profits by producing in excess of demand. On the other hand, marginal costing can give a misleading impression if demand is seasonal.

- Absorption costing also underlines the need to work to full capacity and cover fixed costs.

- Marginal costing emphasises the fact that fixed costs are period costs, and that a marginal cost of an extra unit is the variable cost.

- Marginal costing is more useful for decision-making, in short-run pricing decisions and situations where extra production will make a positive contribution.

Test your knowledge

1   What is the difference between the valuation of stocks using marginal costing and the valuation using absorption costing? (see 'knowledge brought forward' box)

2   If overheads are under-absorbed in period 2, is the under-absorption added or deducted from period 1's profits in a reconciliation to period 2's profits? (2.9)

3   In what three ways may marginal costing and absorption costing be compared? (3.1)

4   What are the arguments in favour of marginal costing for internal profit reporting? (3.3, 3,5, 3.16)

5   What is business process accounting? (4.3)

Now try illustrative question 5 at the end of the Study Text

Chapter 6

COST BOOKKEEPING

This chapter covers the following topics.

		Syllabus reference	*Ability required*
1	Accounting for costs	6(a)	Skill
2	Interlocking systems	6(a)	Skill
3	Interlocking systems: reconciliation of cost and financial accounts	6(a)	Skill
4	Integrated systems	6(a)	Skill
5	Computerised cost accounting systems	6(a)	Skill

Introduction

Cost accounting systems range from simple analysis systems to computer-based accounting systems incorporating standards, variance analysis and the automatic production of control and operating standards. Despite this, all systems will incorporate a number of common aspects and all records will be maintained using the principles of double entry.

In this chapter we will therefore look at cost bookkeeping. You have no doubt covered double entry bookkeeping and cost bookkeeping forms part of your studies for Paper 2. Some students find cost bookkeeping quite difficult, however (although really, it isn't) and so we are going to go through it in detail.

The overall bookkeeping routine will vary from organisation to organisation but either an interlocking (non-integrated) or an integrated system will be used. We will be looking at each of these systems in detail, seeing how to record costs in them and how the two systems differ.

This chapter covers a lot of ground and discusses a wide variety of techniques. Practice on bookkeeping questions is vital since it is only by doing questions that you will *really* understand how systems of accounts fit together. Make sure therefore you work through the examples given carefully, and also the suggested question at the end of the chapter.

---

1 ACCOUNTING FOR COSTS

1.1 As we explained in Chapter 3, there are no statutory requirements to keep detailed cost records and so some small firms only keep traditional financial accounts and prepare cost information in an ad-hoc fashion. Such an approach is unsatisfactory for all but the smallest organisations, however; most therefore maintain some form of cost accounting system.

1.2 One common aspect of cost accounting systems is that information is kept, not only of the value of *individual* stock items, or the cost of *individual* products or jobs, but also of *total costs*.

Control accounts

1.3 Total costs are included in a control account. This is defined in CIMA *Official Terminology* as 'a ledger account which collects the sum of the postings into the individual accounts which it controls. The balance on the control account should equal the sum of the balances on the individual accounts which are maintained as subsidiary records'.

1.4 Examples of control accounts include the following.

   (a) *Debtors* control account which records the entries into individual sales ledger accounts.

   (b) *Creditors* control account which records the entries into individual purchase ledger control accounts.

   (c) *Materials* control account which records the total cost of invoices received for materials (purchases) and the total cost of materials issued to various departments (ie the sum of the value of all materials requisition notes).

   (d) *Wages* control account which shows how total payroll costs are charged as direct labour costs to work in progress, or as indirect costs to production, administration or selling and distribution overheads.

   (e) *Production overhead control account* which records actual expenditure incurred, and the amount absorbed into individual units, jobs or processes.

   (f) *Work in progress control account* which records the total costs of production (direct materials, direct labour etc) charged to jobs, units or processes and the cost of finished output transferred to the finished goods control account.

1.5 Recording cost transactions using the self-balancing double entry method of a debit and credit entry for each transaction may be achieved in either of the following ways - interlocking (*non-integrated*) systems or *integrated* systems.

Interlocking accounts

1.6 CIMA, in the *Official Terminology*, defines interlocking accounts as 'A system in which the cost accounts are distinct from the financial accounts, the two sets of accounts being kept continuously in agreement by the use of control accounts or reconciled by other means'.

1.7 Separate ledgers are kept for the *cost accounting* function and the *financial accounting* function, which necessitates the reconciliation of the profits produced by the separate profit and loss accounts. The cost accounts use the same basic data (purchases, wages and so on) as the financial accounts, but frequently adopt different bases for matters such as depreciation and stock valuation.

Integrated accounts

1.8 CIMA, in the *Official Terminology*, defines integrated accounts as 'A set of accounting records which provides financial and cost accounts using a common input of data for all accounting purposes'.

1.9 The cost accounting function and the financial accounting function are combined in one system of ledger accounts. The same approach for items such as stock valuation and depreciation will be used and there is no need for a reconciliation between cost accounting profit and financial accounting profit. Financial profit will simply be the cost profit adjusted by non-cost items such as income from investments and charitable donations.

1.10 We shall begin with a description of a system of *interlocking* control accounts where the cost accounts are maintained separately from the financial accounting system.

Exam focus point

Integrated and non-integrated systems, and their reconciliation, is clearly specified as a topic you should study in the syllabus. It has never featured as part of a full question, however, although aspects of cost bookkeeping regularly come up in other contexts such as process costing. When asked whether some areas of the syllabus should receive greater emphasis, the examiner for Paper 6 replied as follows.

'At every sitting of the examination, candidates must demonstrate that they have a thorough understanding of *all aspects of the syllabus*. The intention is therefore to use MCQs and conventional questions to test the majority of topics on the syllabus. To achieve this, the subjects examined in some MCQs are likely to overlap with those in the optional questions so as to ensure that candidates *cannot totally avoid key topic areas*.'

2   INTERLOCKING SYSTEMS

The principal accounts in a system of interlocking accounts

2.1   These are as follows.

   (a)   The resources accounts

   (i)   Materials control account or stores control account
   (ii)   Wages (and salaries) control account
   (iii) Production overhead control account
   (iv)   Administration overhead control account
   (v)   Selling and distribution overhead control account

   (b)   Accounts which record the cost of production items from the start of production work through to cost of sales

   (i)   Work in progress control account
   (ii)   Finished goods control account
   (iii) Cost of sales control account

   (c)   Sales account

   (d)   The costing profit and loss account

   (e)   The under-/over-absorbed overhead account

   (f)   Cost ledger control account (in the cost ledger)

   (g)   Financial ledger control account (in the financial ledger)

How an interlocking system works

2.2   An interlocking system features two ledgers.

   (a)   The *financial* ledger contains asset, liability, revenue, expense and appropriation (such as dividend) accounts. The trial balance of an enterprise is prepared from the financial ledger.

   (b)   The *cost* ledger, on the other hand, is where cost information such as the build-up of work in progress is analysed in more detail.

The financial ledger in an interlocking system

2.3   An interlocking system often works in the following way.

   (a)   All the normal accounting entries that you would expect are made in the financial accounting ledger, for example:

   DEBIT   Wages
   CREDIT   Cash

   The double entry is completed in the financial ledger.

   (b)   The wages data above is also relevant to the preparation of costing information. In many interlocking systems, this data will be passed to the cost ledger. How is this reflected in the financial ledger? A *financial ledger control account* is set up. It is a *memorandum account* and therefore does *not* form part of the double entry in the financial ledger. It merely details the data which will be analysed in further detail in the cost ledger.

The cost ledger in an interlocking system

2.4 The data is transferred to the cost department. How is it treated in the *cost ledger*? We know for example, that wages are a cost item, and will be entered in the cost ledger. Obviously, we need to DEBIT a wages control account in the cost ledger. Where does the CREDIT go? There is no cash account in the cost ledger (cash transactions have nothing to do with cost analysis). Instead the entry is posted to the *cost ledger control account* which is maintained in the cost ledger. This *does* form part of the double entry; it is *not* a memorandum account.

2.5 This cost ledger control account in the cost ledger account completes the costing double entry. In the cost ledger it represents all those accounts in the cost accounting books for which accounts are not maintained (such as cash, creditors, debtors and so on). It therefore does the following.

(a) Makes the cost ledger self-balancing.

(b) Agrees with the memorandum financial ledger control account in the financial ledger.

2.6 (a) So, in the financial ledger we saw

DEBIT   Wages
CREDIT   Cash

In addition the memorandum financial ledger control account is also posted with the wages data. (In other words, there is a debit entry to the memorandum account.)

(b) In the cost ledger, we find

DEBIT   Wages control account
CREDIT   Cost ledger control account

(c) It follows therefore, that the cost ledger control account in the cost ledger should be in agreement with the memorandum financial ledger control account in the financial ledger.

Entries in the cost ledger in an interlocking system

2.7 Control accounts generally play a vital role in interlocking systems.

(a) Control accounts are total accounts. The production overhead control account for example is supported by subsidiary records for actual overhead expenditure and job or process records which show the overheads of individual units or jobs. These must agree with, or reconcile to, the totals in the control account.

(b) The control accounts such as materials, wages, work-in-progress that we will be concerned with only appear in the cost ledger.

2.8 With interlocking accounts (see the flow chart below) the following basic entries are made in the cost ledger.

(a) *Expenditure incurred* (including material purchases, payroll costs etc)

DEBIT   materials, wages or production/administration/sales and distribution overheads control account
CREDIT   cost ledger control account in cost ledger (in place of 'credit cash' or 'credit creditors')

(b) *Direct materials costs* (the cost of materials issued to production)

DEBIT work in progress control account
CREDIT materials control account

(c) *Direct labour costs* (the cost of direct labour time in production)

DEBIT work in progress control account
CREDIT wages control account

(d) *Production overhead absorbed* in the cost of production

DEBIT work in progress control account
CREDIT production overhead control account

The debit side of the work in progress account now contains direct materials and direct labour cost plus absorbed production overhead, in other words factory cost.

(e) *Indirect costs* (materials and labour) incurred

DEBIT production/administration/sales and distribution overhead control account
CREDIT materials/wages control account

(f) *Administration, selling and distribution overheads* absorbed in the cost of sales

DEBIT cost of sales account
CREDIT administration/selling and distribution overheads control account

(g) *Completed work* (the cost of units produced and transferred into finished goods store)

DEBIT finished goods control account
CREDIT work in progress control account

(h) *Cost of sales* (the cost of finished goods sold to customers)

DEBIT cost of sales account
CREDIT finished goods control account

The debit side of the cost of sales account consists of the production cost of goods sold plus the absorbed administration, selling and distribution overhead.

(i) *Sales*

DEBIT cost ledger control account in cost ledger (in place of 'debit cash/debtors')
CREDIT sales account

(j) *Profit* before adjustment for overhead absorption

(i) DEBIT profit and loss account
  CREDIT cost of sales account

(ii) DEBIT sales account
  CREDIT profit and loss account

(k) *Over-absorbed overhead*

DEBIT production/administration/sales and distribution overhead control account
CREDIT under-/over-absorbed overhead account

DEBIT under-/over-absorbed overhead account
CREDIT profit and loss account

(l) Under-absorbed overhead treatment reverses the debits and credits in (k) above.

If there is a profit, the DEBIT for profit in the profit and loss account will have a corresponding CREDIT in the cost ledger control account (in place of 'credit profit and loss reserves').

If there is a loss, the CREDIT in the profit and loss account will have a corresponding DEBIT in the cost ledger control account.

Note that the (a), (b), (c) and so on in the following diagram correspond to the above sections of the paragraph.

A BASIC SYSTEM OF INTERLOCKING ACCOUNTS: COST LEDGER

An approach to interlocking accounts

2.9   Bookkeeping questions involving interlocking accounts will contain a great deal of information. A logical approach is essential.

(a)   Draw up proformas for the necessary cost accounts. (In some questions you will be told which accounts should be used.)

(b)   Enter the opening balances.

(c)   Post materials, wages and costs.

(d)   Calculate overheads absorbed and over/under-absorbed overheads, and post to the relevant accounts.

(e)   Balance off the work in progress account. Generally there will be a balancing figure which you will have to calculate, either the value of closing work-in-progress or the value of completed goods transferred to the finished goods account.

(f)   Balance off the finished goods account. Again there is likely to be a balancing figure, either closing stock or cost of sales.

(g)   Complete the profit and loss account (which will include the balance on the over/under-absorbed overhead account).

Example: interlocking accounts

2.10   You are required to write up the cost ledger accounts of a manufacturing company for the latest accounting period. The following data are relevant.

(a)   There is no stock on hand at the beginning of the period.

(b)   Details of the transactions for the period received from the financial accounts department include the following.

	£
Sales	420,000
Indirect wages:	
production	25,000
administration	15,000
sales and distribution	20,000
Material purchases	101,000
Direct factory wages	153,200
Production overheads	46,500
Selling and distribution expenses	39,500
Administration expenses	32,000

(c)   Other cost data for the period include the following.

Stores issued to production as indirect materials	£15,000
Stores issued to production as direct materials	£77,000
Cost of finished production	£270,200
Cost of goods sold at finished goods stock valuation	£267,700
Standard rate of production overhead absorption	50p per operation hour
Rate of administration overhead absorption	20% of production cost of sales
Rate of sales and distribution overhead absorption	10% of sales revenue
Actual operating hours worked	160,000

Solution

2.11   Ensure that you always make *two* entries for each transaction. You should be able to work through your accounts on completion of the question and mark off each entry twice - once as a debit and once as a credit. Use the information in Paragraph 2.8 to help you complete the question if necessary. Note that the (a), (b), (c) and so on included in each account indicate the account in which corresponding debit and credit entries can be found and *not* the details in Paragraph 2.8.

(a)   COST LEDGER CONTROL (CLC)

	£		£
Sales (i)	420,000	Materials control (b)	101,000
Balance c/d	51,500	Wages control (c)	213,200
		Production overheads (d)	46,500
		Selling expenses (g)	39,500
		Administration expenses (h)	32,000
		Cost P and L account - profit (l)	39,300
	471,500		471,500
		Balance b/d	51,500

(b)   MATERIALS CONTROL

	£		£
CLC - purchases from stores (a)	101,000	Production overhead (d) (indirect materials)	15,000
		WIP issues to production (e)	77,000
		∴Closing stock c/d (balancing item)	9,000
	101,000		101,000
Balance b/d	9,000		

(c)

WAGES CONTROL

	£		£
CLC - total wages (a)	213,200	WIP - direct labour (e)	153,200
		Production overhead (d)	25,000
		Administration overhead (h)	15,000
		Sales and distribution o/head (g)	20,000
	213,200		213,200

(d)

PRODUCTION OVERHEAD CONTROL

	£		£
CLC-production overhead (d)	46,500	WIP overheads absorbed (e)	80,000
Materials control (b)	15,000	(160,000 hrs × 50p per hour)	
Wages control (c)	25,000	Overheads under-absorbed (j)	6,500
		(under-/over-absorbed o/head a/c)	
	86,500		86,500

(e)

WORK IN PROGRESS (WIP)

	£		£
Materials control (b)	77,000	Finished goods - transfer of finished production (f)	270,200
Wages control (c)	153,200		
Production overhead control (d)	80,000	∴ Work in progress at period end c/d	40,000
	310,200		310,200
Balance b/d	40,000		

(f)

FINISHED GOODS

	£		£
WIP - transfer of finished production (e)	270,200	Cost of sales (k)	267,700
		∴ Finished goods in stock at period end c/d	2,500
	270,200		270,200
Balance b/d	2,500		

(g)

SELLING AND DISTRIBUTION OVERHEAD

	£		£
CLC - selling expenses (a)	39,500	Cost of sales account (k) (absorbed overhead) (10% of £420,000)	42,000
Wages control (c)	20,000		
		Under-absorbed overhead (j) (under-/over-absorbed overhead a/c)	17,500
	59,500		59,500

(h)

ADMINISTRATION OVERHEAD

	£		£
CLC - administration expenses (a)	32,000	Cost of sales (k) (20% of £267,700)	53,540
Wages control (c)	15,000		
Over-absorbed overhead (j) (under-/over-absorbed overhead a/c)	6,540		
	53,540		53,540

(i)

SALES

	£		£
Cost profit and loss (l)	420,000	CLC - sales for the period (a)	420,000

(j)

UNDER-/OVER-ABSORBED OVERHEAD

	£		£
Production overhead (d)	6,500	Administration overhead (h)	6,540
Sales etc overhead (g)	17,500	Profit and loss account (l)	
		(balance)	17,460
	24,000		24,000

(k)

COST OF SALES

	£		£
Finished goods (f)	267,700	Profit and loss account (l)	
Administration overhead (h)	53,540	(cost of sales)	363,240
Selling and distribution			
overhead (g)	42,000		
	363,240		363,240

(l)

COST PROFIT AND LOSS

	£		£
Cost of sales (k)	363,240	Sales (i)	420,000
Under-/over-absorbed overhead			
account (j)	17,460		
	380,700		
CLC - profit for the period (a)	39,300		
	420,000		420,000

2.12 Note how a trial balance can be extracted from the cost accounts which include b/d figures. If your trial balance balances you are more than likely to have successfully completed the question.

OPENING TRIAL BALANCE FOR THE FOLLOWING PERIOD

	Dr	Cr
	£	£
Cost ledger control		51,500
Materials stock	9,000	
Work in progress	40,000	
Finished goods stocks	2,500	
	51,500	51,500

Example: interlocking accounts and control accounts

2.13 A second example may help to develop your understanding of control accounts. If you consider that you could follow the solution to the previous example reasonably well, attempt your own solution and compare it with the solution which follows.

2.14 Annie Ltd is a company which operates an interlocking cost accounting system, which is not integrated with the financial accounts. At the beginning of February 19X1, the opening balances in the cost ledger were as follows.

	DR	CR
	£	
Stores ledger control account	36,400	
Work in progress control account	23,000	
Finished goods control account	15,700	
Cost ledger control account		75,100

During February 19X1 the following transactions took place.

	£
Materials purchased	28,700
Materials issued to:	
Production	21,300
Service departments	4,200
Gross factory wages paid	58,900

Of these gross wages, £19,500 were indirect wages.

	£
Production overheads incurred (excluding the items shown above)	1,970
Raw material stocks written off, damaged	1,200
Selling overheads incurred and charged to cost of sales	10,500
Sales	88,000
Material and labour cost of goods sold	52,800

At the end of February 19X1 stocks of work in progress were £7,640 higher than at the beginning of the month. The company operates a marginal costing system.

Required

Prepare the control accounts and costing profit and loss account which would record these transactions in February 19X1.

Solution

2.15   The company operates a marginal costing system and hence production overhead is not included in the value of WIP or finished goods but it treated as a period cost and written off directly to the profit and loss account.

(a)   COST LEDGER CONTROL ACCOUNT (CLC)

	£		£
Sales account (h)	88,000	Opening balance b/f	75,100
Profit and loss account (j)	2,170	Stores ledger control (b)	28,700
Closing balance c/f	85,000	Factory wages control (c)	58,900
		Production overhead control (d)	1,970
		Selling overheads control (g)	10,500
	175,170		175,170
		Opening balance b/f	85,000

(b)   STORES LEDGER CONTROL ACCOUNT

	£		£
Opening balance b/f	36,400	WIP control (e)	21,300
Purchases - CLC (a)	28,700	Production overhead control (d)	4,200
		Profit and loss account (stock written off) (j)	1,200
		Closing balance c/f	38,400
	65,100		65,100
Balance b/f	38,400		

(c)   FACTORY WAGES CONTROL ACCOUNT

	£		£
Gross wages - CLC (a)	58,900	WIP control (balancing figure)(e)	39,400
		Production overhead control (d)	19,500
	58,900		58,900

(d)   PRODUCTION OVERHEAD CONTROL ACCOUNT

	£		£
Stores ledger control (b)	4,200	Profit and loss account	
Factory wages control (c)	19,500	(balancing figure)(j)	25,670
Other costs - CLC (a)	1,970		
	25,670		25,670

(e)   WORK IN PROGRESS (WIP) CONTROL ACCOUNT

	£		£
Opening balance b/f	23,000	Finished goods control (f)	53,060
Stores ledger control (b)	21,300	(balancing figure)	
Factory wages control (c)	39,400	Closing balance c/f	
		(23,000 + 7,640)	30,640
	83,700		83,700
Balance b/f	30,640		

(f)   FINISHED GOODS CONTROL ACCOUNT

	£		£
Opening balance b/f	15,700	Cost of sales (i)	52,800
WIP control (e)	53,060	Closing balance c/f	15,960
	68,760		68,760
Balance b/f	15,960		

(g)   SELLING OVERHEAD CONTROL ACCOUNT

	£		£
CLC (a)	10,500	Cost of sales a/c (i)	10,500

(h)   SALES ACCOUNT

	£		£
Profit and loss a/c (i)	88,000	CLC - sales (a)	88,000

(i)   COST OF SALES ACCOUNT

	£		£
Finished goods control (f)	52,800	Profit and loss a/c (j)	63,300
Selling overhead control (g)	10,500		
	63,300		63,300

(j)   COSTING PROFIT AND LOSS ACCOUNT

	£		£
Cost of sales account (i)	63,300	Sales account (h)	88,000
Production overhead (d)	25,670	Loss (balance) CLC (a)	2,170
Stores ledger control - stock written off (b)	1,200		
	90,170		90,170

TRIAL BALANCE AS AT 28 FEBRUARY 19X1
(not required by the question)

	£	£
Cost ledger control account		85,000
Stores ledger control account	38,400	
Work in progress control account	30,640	
Finished goods control account	15,960	
	85,000	85,000

A broad view of cost control accounts has been given by the previous two examples. It will now be useful to consider some aspects of double entry bookkeeping in more detail, with special reference to accounting for labour and overheads.

Interlocking systems: accounting for labour

2.16 An example now follows to give you some further practice in cost bookkeeping. This question asks you to prepare the journal entries for the transactions. Be prepared to do this in an examination and do not waste time in preparing the 'T' accounts, if you are not requested to do so.

Example: accounting for labour costs

2.17 You are required to prepare the journal entries for the following transactions. Where a debit or credit entry is made to the cost ledger control account, indicate which accounts in the financial books would record the transaction.

(a)   WAGES AND SALARIES FOR THE MONTH OF AUGUST 19X2

	Direct workers £	Indirect production workers £	Admin. staff £	Sales and distribution labour £	Total £
Total wages/salaries:					
Basic pay	20,000	5,000	4,000	8,000	37,000
Overtime premium	1,000	400	-	600	2,000
Bonus	800	200	-	-	1,000
Holiday pay	400	100	100	200	800
Commission	-	-	-	1,000	1,000
	22,200	5,700	4,100	9,800	41,800

	Direct workers £	Indirect production workers £	Admin. staff £	Sales and distribution labour £	Total £
(b) Deductions from pay:					
PAYE	7,000	1,300	800	2,200	11,300
National insurance (social security)	1,200	400	300	600	2,500
	8,200	1,700	1,100	2,800	13,800
(c) Employer's National Insurance contributions	2,000	1,000	1,000	1,500	5,500

(d)   It is known that overtime was worked to deal with a rush order at the specific request of the customer; overtime premium for this job cost £200.

Solution

2.18	Dr £	Cr £
Wages and salaries control account	41,800	
Cost ledger control		41,800

Being the cost of payroll. The financial accounting credit entries would be to PAYE £11,300, employees' National Insurance contributions £2,500 and cash £28,000 and there would be a debit entry to wages expenses of £41,800 which might be analysed further into separate accounts reflecting the categories in (a) above.

Wages and salaries control account	5,500	
Cost ledger control account		5,500

Being employer's National Insurance contributions. In the financial ledger, there would be a debit to wages expense and a credit to employer's national insurance contributions, both of £5,500

Work in progress control account	20,200	
Wages and salaries control account		20,200

Being the cost of direct labour (including overtime premium of £200 as well as direct workers' basic pay)

Production overhead control account	10,700	
Wages and salaries control account		10,700

Being the cost of indirect production labour, including all costs of indirect workers, the indirect costs of direct workers (with £800 of overtime premium) and employer's national insurance contributions for all production workers (£3,000)

	Dr £	Cr £
Administration overhead control account	5,100	
Wages and salaries control account		5,100
Being the cost of administration labour (£4,100 + £1,000)		
Selling and distribution overhead control	11,300	
Wages and salaries control account		11,300
Being the cost of sales and distribution labour		
(£9,800 + £1,500)		

You should remember from your earlier studies that overtime worked at the request of a customer is treated as a direct cost whereas other overtime payments, bonuses and holiday pay are usually treated as overheads. A product should not be forced to bear an extra charge simply because, for example, it happened to be made in overtime hours.

2.19   It is important that you should be able to follow the journal entries clearly. The wages and salaries control account would be as follows.

WAGES AND SALARIES CONTROL A/C

	£		£
CLC (payroll)	41,800	Work in progress	20,200
CLC (Employer's Nat.Ins.)	5,500	Production overhead	10,700
		Admin. overhead	5,100
		Sales and distribution overhead	11,300
	47,300		47,300

Production overhead and notional costs

2.20   The basic ledger entries for overheads were dealt with earlier in this chapter, but a complication may arise if the cost accounts include *notional costs* (Notional costs are 'costs used in product evaluation, decision-making and performance measurement to represent the cost of using resources which have no conventional actual cost' (CIMA *Official Terminology*)). These are charges made in the cost accounts in order to give a more realistic picture of the true cost of an activity. There are two main types of notional cost.

(a)   *Interest on capital.* This represents the nominal cost of capital tied up in production and accounts for the cost of using the capital internally rather than investing it outside the business. The cost accountant makes the charge so that managers are fully aware of the true cost, for example, of holding stocks in the production process. The charge can also help to make the cost of items made with expensive capital equipment more comparable to the cost of items which are not capital-intensive.

(b)   *Nominal rent charge.* This is a nominal charge raised for the use of premises which are owned. This enables a comparison to be made between the cost of production in a factory which is owned and the costs in one which is rented. The nominal rent could be seen as an opportunity cost. The nominal rent charge makes managers more aware of the true cost of occupying the premises.

2.21   Notional interest or nominal rent will not affect profit (except in so far as they may be included in stock values) because a counter-balancing adjustment will be made in the profit and loss account. For example, suppose that nominal rent is £8,000. The accounting entries in the cost ledger would be as follows.

NOMINAL RENT ACCOUNT

	£		£
Profit and loss a/c	8,000	Production overhead	8,000

It may be apparent that £8,000 is added to costs (as production overhead) and a counter-balancing £8,000 is added to costing profit and loss. Nominal rent and notional interest are self-cancelling items.

3   INTERLOCKING SYSTEMS: RECONCILIATION OF COST AND FINANCIAL ACCOUNTS

3.1   When an organisation maintains separate cost accounts and financial accounts, the cost profit will differ from the financial profit because of differences in the revenue and costs that are included in the respective profit and loss accounts. It is an essential accounting function that the cost profit and financial profit are reconciled, and this is effected through a *memorandum reconciliation account*.

3.2   A memorandum reconciliation account, being a memorandum account, is not a part of any double entry system of bookkeeping. It is simply a method by which a record can be made of the differences between the cost accounts and the financial accounts, in order to show why their respective profit figures are different. We are therefore not concerned, in this instance, with 'debits' and 'credits', only with a record of differences.

Differences between the cost accounting profit and financial accounting profit

3.3   There are a number of items which create differences between the cost accounting and financial accounting profit.

(a)   Items appearing in the financial accounts, but *not* in the cost accounts

(i)   Items of income which increase the financial accounts profit, but are excluded from the cost accounts

(1)   Interest or dividends received
(2)   Discounts received (for early settlement of debts)
(3)   Profits on disposal of fixed assets

(ii)   Items of expenditure which reduce the financial accounts profit, but which are excluded from the cost accounts

(1)   Interest paid
(2)   Discounts allowed (for early settlement of debts)
(3)   Losses on disposal of fixed assets
(4)   Losses on investments
(5)   Fines and penalties

(iii)   Items of expenditure which are capitalised as assets in the financial accounts, but are treated as costs in the cost accounts, for example preliminary expenses

(iv)   Appropriation of profit in the financial profit and loss account

(1)   Donations
(2)   Tax
(3)   Dividends paid and proposed
(4)   Transfers to reserves
(5)   Write-off of goodwill, investments and other assets

(b)   Differences between the financial and cost accounts in the calculation of actual overhead costs incurred. If the cost accounts books contain a provision for depreciation account, for example, differences may arise in the choice of the following.

(i)   Depreciation method (straight line method, reducing balance method and so on)

(ii)   The expected life of the equipment

(c)   Items appearing in the cost accounts but not the financial accounts are infrequent, but usually relate to matters such as notional rent and notional interest.

(d)   Valuation of *closing stock* is likely to be made according to different bases for the respective accounts.

(i)   For the financial accounts, the basis of stock valuation will be the lower of cost and net realisable value.

(ii)   For the cost accounts, the basis of stock valuation could be chosen from a variety of possible bases in order to suit management purposes.

Reconciliation of differences in stock valuations

3.4   The reconciliation of differences in stock valuations should be studied carefully. Suppose the financial accounting profit of a company is £10,000, and that the only differences between the financial books and the cost books are the following stock valuations.

	Financial accounts	*Cost accounts*
	£	£
Opening stock of WIP	4,000	5,000
Closing stock of WIP	6,000	7,500
Opening stock of finished goods	12,000	10,000
Closing stock of finished goods	9,000	8,500

3.5   Opening and closing stock value differences will affect profit, and it may be helpful to use the format of a trading account to work out what the effect of a difference is. Consider the following trading account.

TRADING ACCOUNT

	£		£
Opening stock	10	Sales	100
Purchases	80	Closing stock	20
	90		
Gross profit (balancing figure)	30		
	120		120

This account shows the following.

(a)   A higher figure for opening stock reduces profit.
(b)   A higher figure for closing stock increases profit.

3.6   If you are not sure about this point, re-calculate the profit in the following circumstances.

(a)   Opening stock is higher, say £15.
(b)   Closing stock is higher, say £30.

3.7   (a)   Opening stock is higher, say £15.

TRADING ACCOUNT

	£		£
Opening stock	15	Sales	100
Purchases	80	Closing stock	20
	95		
Gross profit	25		
	120		120

(b)   Closing stock is higher, say £30.

TRADING ACCOUNT

	£		£
Opening stock	10	Sales	100
Purchases	80	Closing stock	30
	90		
Gross profit	40		
	130		130

3.8   Let us go back to our example in Paragraph 3.4.

(a)   *Opening stock of WIP*

Cost accounts *stock valuation* £1,000 *higher* ∴ cost accounts *profit* £1,000 *lower.*

(b) *Closing stock of WIP*

Cost accounts *stock valuation* £1,500 *higher* ∴ cost accounts *profit* £1,500 *higher.*

(c) *Opening stock of finished goods*

Cost accounts *stock valuation* £2,000 *lower* ∴ cost accounts *profit* £2,000 *higher.*

(d) *Closing stock of finished goods*

Cost accounts *stock valuation* £500 *lower* ∴ cost accounts *profit* £500 *lower.*

3.9 The reconciliation of profits would be as follows.

	£	£
Financial accounts profit		10,000
Stock valuation adjustments:		
Add: difference in WIP, closing stock	1,500	
difference in finished goods, opening stock	2,000	
		3,500
		13,500
Less: difference in WIP, opening stock	1,000	
difference in finished goods, closing stock	500	
		1,500
Cost accounts profit		12,000

Exercise 1

The valuation of closing stock in JPM's financial accounts is £37,897 whereas in the cost accounts it is £36,322. In a reconciliation of financial accounting profit to cost accounting profit should the difference between these valuations be added to or subtracted from financial accounting profit?

Solution

Deduct the difference from financial accounting profit.

Example: reconciliation of profits in cost accounts and financial accounts

3.10 Hilly Ltd has separate financial and cost accounting systems. Extracts from both sets of accounts for the year ended 30 September 19X2 were as follows.

(a) *Financial accounts*

	Opening stock £	Closing stock £
Stock valuations		
Raw materials	68,000	72,000
Work in progress	14,000	10,000
Finished goods	32,000	41,000

The financial accounting profit and loss account also included the following items.

	£
Debenture interest	10,000
Interest received	1,500
Discounts allowed	4,000
Discounts received	2,000
Net profit (before taxation)	35,000

(b) *Cost accounts*

	Opening stock £	Closing stock £
Stock valuations		
Raw materials	66,000	69,000
Work in progress	16,000	14,000
Finished goods	34,000	40,000

The cost accounting profit and loss account also included the following items.

	£
Notional rent	16,000
Nominal interest on capital employed	20,000
Under-absorbed production overhead	8,000
Over-absorbed selling overhead	2,000

Required

Reconcile the profit reported in the financial accounts with the profit reported in the cost accounts, and calculate the cost accounting profit for the year.

Solution

3.11 There are two areas of possible confusion in this type of problem.

(a) *Cost accounting items.* In this example all of the special items in the cost accounts are self-adjusting, and do not affect the reconciliation of profits.

    (i) *Notional costs* such as nominal rent and notional interest are self-adjusting because the double entry is as follows.

        DEBIT   Overheads (ie increase costs)
        CREDIT   Profit and loss account (ie increase profit to cancel out the extra nominal charge)

        Except insofar as closing stock values are affected, these items should be ignored.

    (ii) *Under- or over-absorbed overhead* is again a self-correcting entry, because it is an adjustment to compensate for the difference between overheads added to product costs and overheads actually incurred. In other words, the overheads absorbed in the cost accounts plus/minus the under-/over-absorbed overheads, should equal the overhead expenditure recorded in the financial accounts.

        For example: (the figures are hypothetical only)

	£
Overheads absorbed	200,000
Over-absorbed overhead	10,000
Cost accounting net cost = overhead incurred	190,000
Financial accounting overheads cost = overhead incurred	190,000
Difference between cost accounts and financial accounts	0

(b) *Stock valuations*

    (i) If the value of opening stocks is higher in the financial accounts than in the cost accounts, the effect is to make the financial accounting profit smaller than the cost accounting profit. The reconciliation adjustment is therefore to *add* the stock difference to the financial accounting profit to reach the cost accounting profit.

    (ii) If the value of closing stocks is higher in the financial accounts than in the cost accounts, the effect is to make the financial accounting profit higher than the cost accounting profit, therefore the stock difference should be *subtracted* from the financial accounting profit to reach the cost accounting profit.

3.12 In this solution, opening and closing stocks are shown separately, and the three stock categories are also shown; therefore 6 (2×3) adjustments for stocks are made. It would be quicker to do a single calculation to adjust for total stock changes, but this method is not recommended in a solution to an examination question (unless the question itself appears to encourage a 'short-cut' solution).

3.13   MEMORANDUM RECONCILIATION ACCOUNT

	£	£	£
Financial accounting profit			35,000
Adjustments for items appearing in the financial accounts, but not in the cost accounts:			
Debenture interest	10,000		
Discounts allowed	4,000		
		14,000	
Discounts received	(2,000)		
Interest received	(1,500)		
		(3,500)	
Net extra charges against financial accounting profit			10,500
			45,500
Adjustments for items charged in the cost accounts, but not in the financial accounts			0
			45,500
Stock differences			
Raw materials opening stock (68,000 – 66,000)		2,000	
Raw materials closing stock (72,000 – 69,000)		(3,000)	
Work in progress opening stock (14,000 – 16,000)		(2,000)	
Work in progress closing stock (10,000 – 14,000)		4,000	
Finished goods opening stock (32,000 – 34,000)		(2,000)	
Finished goods closing stock (41,000 – 40,000)		(1,000)	
			(2,000)
Cost accounting profit			43,500

Exercise 2

Elsewhere Ltd's profit for the year ended 30 April 19X2 as shown in the financial accounts is £16,540. For the same period the cost accounts show a profit of £6,967

Inspection of the two sets of accounts has revealed the following.

Stock type		Financial accounts £	Cost accounts £
Raw materials - opening stock	*329*	5,191	4,862
Raw materials - closing stock	*– 81*	5,478	5,397
WIP - opening stock	*– 12*	8,898	8,910
WIP - closing stock	*123*	7,990	8,113
Finished goods - opening stock	*– 157*	12,566	12,723
Finished goods - closing stock	*– 16*	12,714	12,730

Items in the financial accounts but not in the cost accounts included the following.

	£
Profit on sale of lorry	3,521
Interest received	750
Dividend received	5,520

Required

Reconcile the financial profit to the cost profit.

6749
218
6967

Solution

MEMORANDUM RECONCILIATION ACCOUNT

	£	£
Financial accounting profit		16,540
Adjustments for items appearing in the financial accounts, but not in the cost accounts:		
Profit on sale of lorry	(3,521)	
Interest received	(750)	
Dividend received	(5,520)	
		(9,791)
Adjustment for items appearing in the cost accounts, but not in the financial accounts.		0
Stock differences		
Raw materials - opening stock (5,191 – 4,862)	329	
Raw materials - closing stock (5,478 – 5,397)	(81)	
WIP - opening stock (8,898 – 8,910)	(12)	
WIP - closing stock (7,990 – 8,113)	123	
Finished goods - opening stock (12,566 – 12,723)	(157)	
Finished goods - closing stock (12,714 – 12,730)	16	
		218
Cost accounting profit		6,967

4   INTEGRATED SYSTEMS

4.1   With a system of integrated accounts (see flow chart), the financial and cost accounts are combined in one set of self-balancing ledger accounts. This eliminates the need to operate cost ledger and financial ledger control accounts and reconcile the respective cost and financial profits.

With interlocking accounts a separate cost ledger is maintained. With integrated accounts there is no separate cost ledger. Just remember that there is *no* 'c' in 'integrated'.

4.2   Note the following points about integrated accounts.

(a)   To facilitate the control of costs, and assist with management information, the same classifications used in the cost ledger of an interlocking system are also used in an integrated system.

(b)   All transactions normally excluded from a cost ledger are included in an integrated ledger.

(c)   Additional ledger accounts required by an integrated system over and above those in the cost ledger of an interlocking system are as follows.

(i)   Control accounts for debtors and creditors
(ii)   Bank account
(iii)   Fixed assets accounts, subdivided into categories of assets
(iv)   Other assets and liabilities accounts
(v)   Share capital account, retained profit account and other reserve accounts

(d)   There is no cost ledger control account, because this appears in a system of interlocking accounts only as a substitute for accounts such as debtors, creditors and cash.

A BASIC SYSTEM OF INTEGRATED ACCOUNTS

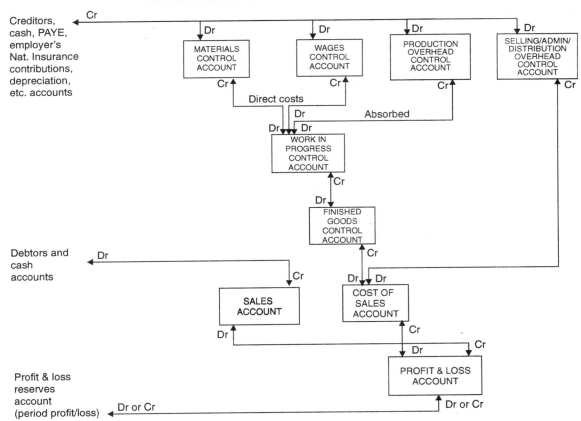

(*Note.* The same simplifications which were made in the chart for interlocking accounts have also been made here.)

4.3   Refer back to the earlier examples of interlocking accounts entries and try to identify the differences which would appear in a set of integrated accounts.

The advantages and disadvantages of integrated accounts

4.4   The advantage of integrated accounts over separate systems for cost and financial accounting is the saving in administration effort. Only one set of accounts needs to be maintained, instead of two, and the possible confusion arising from having two sets of accounts with different figures for stock values and profits and so on does not exist.

4.5   The disadvantage of integrated accounts is that one set of accounts is expected to fulfil two different purposes.

(a)   Stewardship of the business and external reporting
(b)   Provision of internal management information

At times, these different purposes may conflict; for example, the valuation of stocks will conform to the requirements of SSAP 9, whereas the cost accountants might have preferred, given their own choice, to value closing stocks at, say, marginal cost or replacement cost.

4.6   In addition, the cost-coding of expenditures, to serve both financial accounting and cost accounting purposes, will be more complex and a double purpose coding system (with longer numerical cost codes) will probably have to be used.

4.7   The way in which integrated accounts actually work is perhaps best explained by means of an example.

Example: integrated accounts

4.8 Using the notes given below for the month of October 19X2, with respect to Spooky Ltd, you are required to do the following.

(a) Write up the integrated accounts.
(b) Prepare a trading profit and loss account for October 19X2.
(c) Compile a trial balance as at 31 October 19X2.

Notes

(a) *Balances as at 1 October 19X2*

	£'000
Land and buildings	250
Plant, machinery and other fixed assets	320
Provision for depreciation: land and buildings	20
plant etc	170
Raw material stores	30
Work in progress	20
Finished goods	60
Bank (overdraft)	50
Debtors	74
Creditors	85
Share capital	100
Share premium20	
Profit and loss reserve (credit balance)	290
Creditors for income tax and National Insurance	19

(b) *Transactions for the month of October 19X2*

	£'000
Materials received from suppliers and invoiced	40
Materials issued to production	32
Materials issued to production service departments	8
Materials issued to administrative departments	2

	Gross wages £'000	PAYE & Nat. insurance £'000	£'000
Direct wages	33	8	25
Production indirect wages	7	1	6
Administrative staff wages and salaries	10	3	7
Selling staff wages and salaries	10	3	7
	60	15	45

Expenses for:	production overhead (cash paid)	15
	administration overhead (cash paid)	8
	selling overhead (cash paid)	20
Depreciation:	buildings: (assume all this is production overhead)	2
	plant and machinery	35
	office equipment, administrative departments	5

	£'000
Production overhead absorbed	75
Production completed and transferred to finished goods stores	150
Production cost of goods sold	196
Employer's contribution, national insurance:	
production	2
administration	1
selling	1
Sales in October, all on credit	278
Cash paid to: creditor for national insurance and PAYE	19
creditors	45
Cash received from debtors	290

Administration and selling overheads are treated as a period charge
No fixed assets were bought or sold in the month.

This example ignores dividends (and taxation).

Solution

4.9 In a set of integrated accounts, there is no cost ledger control account. Instead of this account, we have all the accounts which appear in a normal system of financial accounting such as debtors, creditors, bank (and cash), fixed asset accounts, provision for depreciation accounts, share capital, share premium and profit and loss reserves, discounts allowed and received, interest and dividends.

4.10 An especially tricky area is wages, and you may come across two methods of accounting for these.

   (a) *First method.* The wages may be recorded in a single wages and salaries account. The entries in this account would be as follows.

   (i) DEBIT   wages and salaries account
        CREDIT   bank account, income tax account and National Insurance account (employees' contributions)

   (ii) DEBIT   work in progress account, production overhead account, administration overhead account and sales and distribution overhead account
        CREDIT   wages and salaries account

   (iii) Employer's national insurance contributions might be shown as follows.

        DEBIT   production, administration or sales distribution overhead account
        CREDIT   national insurance account

   (b) *Second method.* Two wages accounts might be used: a wages payable account, to record the gross payable costs, and a wages control account, which would be used to analyse the wages into direct (WIP) cost and indirect (overhead account) costs. The accounting entries would be as follows.

   (i) DEBIT   wages payable account
        CREDIT   bank account, income tax account and National Insurance account (employees' contributions)

   The amount of the transaction should be the wages payable in the accounting period.

   (ii) DEBIT   wages control account
        CREDIT   wages payable account

   The amount of the transaction should be the wages chargeable to the period. There may be a closing balance on the wages payable account, for accrued wages at the end of the period, that is, for work done but not yet paid for. This would be a closing credit balance.

   (iii) DEBIT   work in progress account, production administration or selling and distribution overhead accounts
        CREDIT   wages control account

   (iv) Employer's National Insurance contributions might be accounted for in several ways, as follows.

        DEBIT   (1) production, administration or selling and distribution overhead accounts
              or   (2) wages control account
          or even   (3) wages payable account
        CREDIT   national insurance account

An examination question may give you some indication as to the appropriate entries required, otherwise you must select your own method. It is helpful to be aware, however, that variations in the accounting procedures for wages costs do occur, and you should be 'ready for anything' which might arise. In this solution, the first method will be used.

4.11 (a)

RAW MATERIALS STORES ACCOUNT

	£'000		£'000
Balance b/f	30	Work in progress (d)	32
Creditors (n)	40	Production overhead (c)	8
		Administration overhead (g)	2
		Balance c/f	28
	70		70
Balance b/f	28		

(b)

WAGES AND SALARIES ACCOUNT

	£'000		£'000
Bank (l)	45	Work in progress (d)	33
Creditors for PAYE		Production overhead (c)	7
and national insurance (o)	15	Administration overhead (g)	10
		Selling overhead (h)	10
	60		60

(c)

PRODUCTION OVERHEAD ACCOUNT

	£'000		£'000
Raw materials stores (a)	8	Work in progress (d)	75
Wages and salaries (b)	7		
Bank (expenses) (l)	15		
Creditor for PAYE and			
national insurance (o)	2		
Depreciation: buildings (q)	2		
Depreciation: plant etc (s)	35		
Over-absorbed overhead (i)	6		
	75		75

(d)

WORK IN PROGRESS ACCOUNT

	£'000		£'000
Balance b/f	20	Finished goods (e)	150
Raw materials stores (a)	32		
Wages and salaries (b)	33		
Production overhead (c)	75	Balance c/f	10
	160		160
Balance b/f	10		

(e)

FINISHED GOODS ACCOUNT

	£'000		£'000
Balance b/f	60	Cost of sales (f)	196
Work in progress (d)	150	Balance c/f	14
	210		210
Balance b/f	14		

(f)

COST OF SALES ACCOUNT

	£'000		£'000
Finished goods (e)	196	Profit and loss account (k)	196

The administration and selling overheads have been written straight to the trading and profit and loss account, (k).

(g)

ADMINISTRATION OVERHEAD ACCOUNT

	£'000		£'000
Raw materials stores (a)	2	Profit and loss account (k)	26
Wages and salaries (b)	10		
Bank (expenses) (l)	8		
Creditor for PAYE and			
national insurance (o)	1		
Depreciation (s)	5		
	26		26

(h)

SELLING OVERHEAD ACCOUNT

	£'000		£'000
Wages and salaries (b)	10	Profit and loss account (k)	31
Bank (expenses) (l)	20		
Creditor for PAYE and national insurance (o)	1		
	31		31

(i)

UNDER-/OVER-ABSORBED OVERHEAD ACCOUNT

	£'000		£'000
Profit and loss account (k)	6	Production overhead account (c)	6

(j)

SALES ACCOUNT

	£'000		£'000
Profit and loss account (k)	278	Debtors (m)	278

(k)

TRADING AND PROFIT AND LOSS ACCOUNT

	£'000		£'000
Cost of sales (f)	196	Sales (j)	278
Gross profit c/d	82		
	278		278
Administration overhead (g)	26	Gross profit b/d	82
Selling overhead (h)	31	Over-absorbed overhead (i)	6
Profit and loss reserves (v)	31		
	88		88

(l)

CASH AND BANK ACCOUNT

	£'000		£'000
Debtors (m)	290	Balance b/f	50
		Wages and salaries (b)	45
		Production overhead (c)	15
		Administration overhead (g)	8
		Selling overhead (h)	20
		Creditor for PAYE and national insurance (o)	19
		Creditors (n)	45
		Balance c/f (surplus)	88
	290		290
Balance b/f	88		

(m)

DEBTORS ACCOUNT

	£'000		£'000
Balance b/f	74	Bank (l)	290
Sales (j)	278	Balance c/f	62
	352		352
Balance b/f	62		

(n)

CREDITORS ACCOUNT

	£'000		£'000
Bank (l)	45	Balance b/f	85
Balance c/f	80	Raw materials stores (a)	40
	125		125
		Balance b/f	80

(o)   CREDITOR FOR PAYE AND NATIONAL INSURANCE

	£'000		£'000
Bank (l)	19	Balance b/f	19
		Wages and salaries (b)	15
Balance c/f	19	Employer's contributions:	
		Production overhead (c)	2
		Administration overhead (g)	1
		Selling overhead (h)	1
	38		38
		Balance b/f	19

(p)   LAND AND BUILDINGS ACCOUNT

	£'000		£'000
Balance b/f	250	Balance c/f	250

(q)   PROVISION FOR DEPRECIATION: LAND AND BUILDINGS

	£'000		£'000
Balance c/f	22	Balance b/f	20
		Production overhead (c)	2
	22		22
		Balance b/f	22

(r)   PLANT, MACHINERY AND OTHER FIXED ASSETS

	£'000		£'000
Balance b/f	320	Balance c/f	320

(s)   PROVISION FOR DEPRECIATION: PLANT ETC

	£'000		£'000
Balance c/f	210	Balance b/f	170
		Production overhead (c)	35
		Administration overhead (g)	5
	210		210
		Balance b/f	210

(t)   SHARE CAPITAL ACCOUNT

	£'000		£'000
Balance c/f	100	Balance b/f	100

(u)   SHARE PREMIUM ACCOUNT

	£'000		£'000
Balance c/f	20	Balance b/f	20

(v)   PROFIT AND LOSS RESERVES

	£'000		£'000
Balance c/f	321	Balance b/f	290
		Profit and loss account (k)	31
	321		321
		Balance b/f	321

The trial balance as at 31 October 19X2 is as follows.

	DR £'000		CR £'000
Raw materials stores (a)	28	Creditors (n)	80
Work in progress (d)	10	Creditor for national insurance	
Finished goods (e)	14	and PAYE (o)	19
Cash and bank (l)	88	Provision for depreciation:	
Debtors (m)	62	Land and buildings (q)	22
Land and buildings (p)	250	Plant etc (s)	210
Plant etc (r)	320	Share capital (t)	100
		Share premium (u)	20
		Profit and loss reserves (v)	321
	772		772

Exercise 3

In the absence of the accountant you have been asked to prepare a month's cost accounts for Liverpool Ltd, a company which operates a costing system which is fully integrated with the financial accounts. The cost clerk has provided you with the following information.

(a)   Balances at beginning of month

	£
Stores ledger control account	24,175
Work in progress control account	19,210
Finished goods control account	34,164
Creditors control account	15,187
Prepayments of production overheads brought forward from previous month	2,100

(b)   Information relating to events during the month

	£
Materials purchased	76,150
Materials issued from stores	29,630
Gross wages paid: direct workers	15,236
indirect workers	4,232
Recorded non-productive time of direct workers	5,230
Payments to creditors	58,320
Selling and distribution overheads incurred	5,240
Other production overheads incurred but not yet paid for	14,200
Sales	75,400
Cost of finished goods sold	59,830
Cost of goods completed and transferred into finished goods store during the month	62,130

(c)   Balances at end of month

	£
Physical stock value of work in progress at month end	24,800

(d)   The production overhead absorption rate is 150% of direct wages.

Required

Prepare the following accounts for the month.

(a)   Stores ledger control account
(b)   Work in progress control account
(c)   Finished goods control account
(d)   Production overhead control account
(e)   Creditors control account
(f)   Profit and loss account

Solution

(a)   STORES LEDGER CONTROL ACCOUNT

	£		£
Opening balance b/f	24,175	Work in progress control	
Creditors control		(materials issued)	29,630
(materials purchased)	76,150	Closing stock c/f	70,695
	100,325		100,325

(b)   WORK IN PROGRESS CONTROL ACCOUNT

	£		£
Opening balance b/f	19,210	Finished goods control	
Stores ledger account		(cost of goods transferred)	62,130
(materials issued)	29,630	Closing stock c/f	24,800
Wages control			
(direct wages)	15,236		
Production overhead control			
(overhead absorbed			
15,236 × 150%)	22,854		
	86,930		86,930

(c)   FINISHED GOODS CONTROL ACCOUNT

	£		£
Opening balance b/f	34,164	Profit and loss account	
Work in progress control		(cost of sales)	59,830
(cost of goods completed)	62,130	Closing stock c/f	36,464
	96,294		96,294

(d)   PRODUCTION OVERHEAD CONTROL ACCOUNT

	£		£
Prepayments b/f	2,100	Work in progress control	
Wages control (idle time		(overheads absorbed)	22,854
of direct workers)	5,230	Prepayment c/f (bal)	2,908
Wages control (indirect			
workers wages)	4,232		
Creditors control (other			
overheads incurred)	14,200		
	25,762		25,762

(e)   CREDITORS CONTROL ACCOUNT

	£		£
Cash account (payments)	58,320	Opening balance b/f	15,187
Creditors c/f	47,217	Stores ledger control	
		(materials purchased)	76,150
		Production overhead control	
		(other overheads)	14,200
	105,537		105,537

(f)   PROFIT AND LOSS ACCOUNT

	£		£
Finished goods control		Sales	75,400
(cost of goods sold)	59,830		
Gross profit c/f	15,570		
	75,400		75,400
Selling and distribution		Gross profit b/f	15,570
overheads	5,240		
Net profit c/f	10,330		
	15,570		15,570

5   COMPUTERISED COST ACCOUNTING SYSTEMS

5.1   Computers have swept away the principal objection to integrated systems, that of one set of accounts being expected to fulfil two different purposes. An efficient coding system can make it possible for transactions to be recorded just once but the same basic data to be analysed for both cost accounting and financial accounting purposes. If you can't remember the features of an efficient coding system look back at Section 5 in Chapter 1.

5.2   An article by Rod Newing in *Management Accounting* in September 1996 highlighted the following advantages of unified systems.

(a)   Simplification of design

(b)   Elimination of control accounts and reconciliations

(c)   Immediate updating of all appropriate ledger accounts when a transaction is processed

(d)   Elimination of unnecessary entries, for example matching of invoices with accruals removing the need for reversing entries

(e)   Elimination of time-consuming period-end procedures

(f)   Linking of sales and purchases, or combination of sales and purchases into a single trading account

Chapter roundup

- There are two types of cost accounting system - interlocking (non-integrated) and integrated.

- Interlocking systems contain separate cost accounting and financial accounting ledgers. A memorandum financial ledger control account is set up in the financial ledger. It does not form part of the double entry but merely details the data which will be analysed in further detail in the cost ledger.

- A cost ledger control account is maintained in the cost ledger to complete the costing double entry. It represents the financial ledger accounts which are not maintained in the cost ledger (such as cash, debtors and creditors).

- Control accounts play a vital role in cost accounting systems.

- When an organisation operates an interlocking accounts system, it is necessary to reconcile the cost accounting profit with the financial accounting profit. Items which create differences between the cost accounting and financial accounting profits include the following.
  - Stock valuations (opening and closing)
  - Profits and losses on disposal of fixed assets
  - Interest paid and received
  - Appropriation of profit

- Integrated accounts combine both financial and cost accounts in one system of ledger accounts. A reconciliation between cost and financial profits is not necessary with an integrated system.

- The advantage of integrated accounts is that only one set of accounts needs to be maintained. The disadvantage is that one set of accounts is expected to fulfil two purposes: stewardship of the business/external reporting and provision of internal management information.

Test your knowledge

1   List the principal accounts in an interlocking system. (see para 2.1)

2   What is the purpose of the cost ledger control account in the cost ledger? (2.4-2.6)

3   What is the double entry for the following?
   (a)   Production overhead absorbed in the cost of production (2.8(d))
   (b)   Completed work transferred to finished goods store (2.8(g))

4   List ten items which might appear in a reconciliation of cost accounting profit and financial accounting profit. (3.3)

5   What are the advantages and disadvantages of integrated accounts? (4.4 - 4.6)

Now try illustrative question 6 at the end of the Study Text

Chapter 7

JOB AND BATCH COSTING

This chapter covers the following topics.

		Syllabus reference	*Ability required*
1	Job costing	6(a)	Skill
2	Batch costing	6(a)	Skill

Introduction

In Chapter 4 we learnt how to accumulate costs in order to determine the cost of a product produced/service provided by an organisation and in Chapter 6 we saw how to record costs in a cost accounting system using double entry cost bookkeeping and control accounts. The procedures covered in these two chapters are, however, generalised and are unlikely to be used by most organisations in exactly the way we have looked at them. What actually happens in 'real life' is that the procedures are incorporated into a costing method.

A costing method is a method of costing which is designed to suit the way goods are processed or manufactured or the way that services are provided. Each organisation's costing method will therefore have unique features, but it is more than likely that costing methods of firms in the same line of business will have features in common. On the other hand, organisations involved in completely different activities, such as hospitals and car part manufacturers, will use very different costing methods.

The principal costing methods are job and batch costing, contract costing, process costing, service and output costing. We will be looking at each of these methods in Chapters 7 - 11.

We start with job and batch costing. Job, batch and contract costing (the subject of Chapter 8) are all types of *specific order costing*, defined in CIMA *Official Terminology* as 'The basic cost accounting method applicable where work consists of separate contracts, jobs or batches'.

Knowledge brought forward from Paper 2

Job costing and batch costing

- A job is a cost unit which consists of a single order or contract. The features of job costing are as follows.
    - o   Work is undertaken to customers' special requirements.
    - o   Each order is of short duration.
    - o   Jobs move through processes and operations as a continuously identifiable unit.
    - o   Each job usually differs in one or more respects from every other job and therefore a separate record must be maintained to show the details of a particular job.

- Job costs are collected on a job cost sheet/card.

- Rectification costs (costs of rectifying substandard work) can be either charged as a direct cost of the job concerned if *not* a frequent occurrence or treated as production overhead if regarded as a normal part of the work carried out generally.

- In general, the procedures for costing a batch (a cost unit which consists of a separate, readily identifiable group of units) are very similar to those for costing jobs. The batch is treated as a job during production. Once the batch is completed, the cost per unit is calculated as total batch cost ÷ number of units in the batch.

1   JOB COSTING   5/96, 5/98

Procedure for the performance of jobs

1.1   The normal procedure which is adopted in jobbing concerns involves the following.

   (a)   The prospective customer approaches the supplier and indicates the requirements of the job.

   (b)   A responsible official sees the prospective customer and agrees with him the precise details of the items to be supplied, for example the quantity, quality, size and colour of the goods, the date of delivery and any special requirements.

   (c)   The *estimating department* of the organisation then prepares an *estimate* for the job. This will include the cost of the materials to be used (detailed on a bill of materials), the wages expected to be paid, the appropriate amount for factory, administration, selling and distribution overhead, the cost where appropriate of additional equipment needed specially for the job, and finally the supplier's profit margin. The total of these items will represent the quoted selling price.

Collection of job costs

1.2   The collection of information for costing and pricing jobs involves two stages.

   (a)   The preparation of an estimated job cost and hence an estimated quotation price.

   (b)   As the job processes, the posting to a job account in the work in progress ledger (and possibly to a job cost card in a manual system) of actual costs as information is gathered.

Exercise 1

What details would you expect to see recorded on a job cost sheet/card?

Solution

   (a)   Job number (also known as works order number)
   (b)   Description of work
   (c)   Customer's name and address
   (d)   Expected delivery date
   (e)   Details of estimated and actual materials usage and cost
   (f)   Details of estimated and actual labour hours and cost
   (g)   Estimated and actual overheads cost
   (h)   Selling price
   (i)   Date delivered
   (j)   Delivery note number
   (k)   Invoice number

1.3   Information for each cost element can be gathered as follows.

   (a)   *Direct material cost*

   The *estimated* cost will be calculated by valuing all items on the bill of materials. Materials that have to be specially purchased for the job in question will need to be priced by the purchasing department.

   The *actual* cost of materials used will be calculated by valuing materials issues notes for those issues from store for the job and/or from invoices for materials specially purchased. All documentation should indicate the job number to which it relates.

   Note that it is possible that different valuation bases may be used to value stock items for the estimate (perhaps replacement cost) and in the ledger accounts (perhaps FIFO or weighted average).

   (b)   *Direct labour cost*

   The *estimated* labour time requirement will be calculated from past experience of similar types of work or work study engineers may prepare estimates following detailed specifications. Labour rates will need to take account of any increases, overtime and bonuses.

The *actual* labour hours will be available from either time sheets or job tickets/cards, using job numbers where appropriate to indicate the time spent on each job. The actual labour cost will be calculated using the hours information and current labour rates (plus bonuses, overtime payments and so on).

(c) *Direct expenses*

The *estimated* cost of any expenses likely to be incurred can be obtained from a supplier. Invoices for *actual* direct expenses incurred can be charged to the job cost card or the job account in the work in progress ledger.

(d) *Production overheads*

The *estimated production overheads* to be included in the job cost will be calculated from overhead absorption rates in operation and the estimate of the basis of the absorption rate (for example, direct labour hours). This assumes the job estimate is to include overheads (in a competitive environment management may feel that if overheads are to be incurred irrespective of whether or not the job is taken on, the minimum estimated quotation price should be based on variable costs only).

The *actual production overhead* to be included in the job cost will be calculated from the overhead absorption rate and the actual results (such as labour hours coded to the job in question). Inaccurate overhead absorption rates can seriously harm an organisation; if jobs are over priced, customers will go elsewhere and if jobs are under priced revenue will fail to cover costs.

(e) *Administration, selling and distribution overheads*

The organisation may absorb non-production overheads using any one of a variety of methods (percentage on full production cost, for example) and estimates of these costs and the actual costs should be included in the estimated and actual job cost.

If, for example, an outside haulage contractor will be required for delivery of the job to the customer, then an estimate of this cost should be obtained and the invoice value charged to the ledger once the cost has been incurred.

Exercise 2

Can you think of a costing technique which might be particularly appropriate for attributing *non-production overheads* to jobs?

Solution

Activity based costing

Work in progress

1.4   At the year end, work in progress is simply the sum of the costs incurred on incomplete work (provided that the costs are lower than the net realisable value of the customer order).

Pricing the job

1.5   The estimated profit will depend on the particular circumstance of the job and organisation in question. In competitive situations the profit may be small but if the organisation is sure of securing the job the margin may be greater. In general terms, the profit earned on each job should conform to the requirements of the organisation's overall business plan.

1.6   The final price quoted will, of course, be affected by what competitors charge and what the customer will be willing to pay.

Exam focus point

Part of a question in the May 1998 exam asked candidates to prepare a quotation for a job.

Job costing and computerisation

1.7 Job cost sheets exist in manual systems, but it is increasingly likely that in large organisations the job costing system will be computerised, using accounting software specifically designed to deal with job costing requirements. A computerised job accounting system is likely to contain the following features.

(a) Every job will be given a *job code number*, which will determine how the data relating to the job is stored.

(b) A separate set of codes will be given for the *type of costs* that any job is likely to incur. Thus, 'direct wages', say, will have the same code whichever job they are allocated to.

(c) In a sophisticated system, costs can be analysed both by *job* (for example all costs related to Job 456), but also by *type* (for example direct wages incurred on all jobs). It is thus easy to perform control analysis and to make comparisons between jobs.

(d) A job costing system might have facilities built into it which incorporate other factors relating to the performance of the job. In complex jobs, sophisticated planning techniques might be employed to ensure that the job is performed in the minimum time possible: time management features may be incorporated into job costing software.

Exam focus point

In an article on specific order costing (*Management Accounting*, February 1996), the examiner for Paper 6 explained how the details recorded on a cost sheet would be incorporated into a computer system:

'Each of these items would in computer language be a separate field on the record used for the customer order. In fact, these fields record summary information and may therefore be described as forming the header record. Each of these header records will be supported by a number of transaction records. These will record separately each item of material used and its cost, each amount of labour time and its cost, and the overhead and other costs incurred. The sum of these transaction records at any time will be programmed to equal the value of the corresponding field on the header record. This means that the header record shows the total cost of the customer order analysed by cost category, and if further analysis is required this can be obtained from the transaction records.'

Example: job costing

1.8 In order to identify the costs incurred in carrying out a range of work to customer specification in its factory, a company has a job costing system. This system identifies costs directly with a job where this is possible and reasonable. In addition, production overhead costs are absorbed into the cost of jobs at the end of each month, at an actual rate per direct labour hour for each of the two production departments and the company absorbs non-production overheads at a rate of 5% of production cost per job.

One of the jobs carried out in the factory during the month just ended was Job No 123. The following information has been collected relating specifically to this job.

(a) 400 kilos of Material Y were issued from stores to Department A.

(b) 76 direct labour hours were worked in Department A at a basic wage of £4.50 per hour. Six of these hours were classified as overtime at a premium of 50%.

(c) 300 kilos of Material Z were issued from stores to Department B.

(d) Department B returned 30 kilos of material Z to the storeroom, being excess to requirements for the job.

(e) 110 direct labour hours were worked in Department B at a basic wage of £4.00 per hour. 30 of these hours were classified as overtime at a premium of 50%. All overtime worked in Department B in the month is a result of the request of a customer for early completion of another job which had been originally scheduled for completion in the month following.

(f) Department B discovered defects in some of the work, which was returned to Department A for rectification. Three labour hours were worked in Department A on rectification (these are additional to the 76 direct labour hours in Department A noted above). Such rectification is regarded as a normal part of the work carried out generally in the department.

(g) Department B damaged five kilos of material Z which then had to be disposed of. Such losses of material are not expected to occur.

(h) Total costs incurred during the month on all jobs in the two production departments were as follows.

	Department A £	Department B £
Direct materials issued from stores (note (i))	6,500	13,730
Direct materials returned to stores	135	275
Direct labour, at basic wage rate (note (ii))	9,090	11,200
Indirect labour, at basic wage rate	2,420	2,960
Overtime premium	450	120
Lubricants and cleaning compounds	520	680
Maintenance	720	510
Other	1,200	2,150

Notes

(i) This includes, in Department B, the scrapped Material Z. This was the only material scrapped in the month.

(ii) All direct labour in Department A is paid a basic wage of £4.50 per hour, and in Department B £4.00 per hour. Department A direct labour includes a total of 20 hours spent on rectification work.

(i) Materials are priced at the end of each month on a weighted average basis. Relevant information of material stock movements during the month, for Material Y and Z, is as follows.

	Material Y	Material Z
Opening stock	1,050 kilos (value £529.75)	6,970 kilos (value £9,946.50)
Purchases	600 kilos at £0.50 per kilo 500 kilos at £0.50 per kilo 400 kilos at £0.52 per kilo	16,000 kilos at £1.46 per kilo
Issues from stores	1,430 kilos	8,100 kilos
Returns to stores	-	30 kilos

Required

Prepare a list of the costs that should be assigned to Job No 123. Provide an explanation of your treatment of each item.

Solution

1.9 *Job 123: Costs*

Materials	£	Explanation
Material Y (W1)	202.00	The question states that this specifically relates to Job No 123.
Material Z (W2)	391.50	As above. The figure takes account of the fact that of the 300 kilos initially issued to the job, 30 kilos were returned and are therefore not included. The lost five kilos are discussed in W2.

Labour

Department A 76 hrs × £4.50 per hr	342.00	As material Y
Department B 110 hrs × £4 per hr	440.00	As material Y. (Overtime is not a consideration at this stage.) In neither the case of dept A or dept B was the overtime worked specifically at the request of the Job 123 customer and so the overtime premium should not be a direct cost of Job 123.

Overheads

Department A 76 hrs × £2.70 per hour (W3)	205.20	The explanation of items included in overheads, and the calculation of absorption rates, are shown at W3.
Department B 110 hrs × £2.25 per hour (W3)	247.50	
Non-production		
5% × £1,828.20	91.41	5% of the total of materials, labour and production overheads.

Workings

1 *Cost of material Y issued to Job 123*

This is priced at the month-end weighted average.

	kg	£
Balance b/f	1,050	529.75
plus, at 50p per kg	600	300.00
plus, at 50p per kg	500	250.00
plus, at 52p per kg	400	208.00
	2,550	1,287.75

Hence weighted average is $\dfrac{£1,287.75}{2,550 \text{ kg}} = 50\frac{1}{2}$ p per kg

So cost of stock issued
to Job 123 is
$$400 \text{ kg} \times 50\frac{1}{2}\text{p per kg}$$
$$= \underline{\underline{£202}}$$

2 *Cost of material Z issued to Job 123*

Also priced at the month-end weighted average

	kg	£
Balance b/f	6,970	9,946.50
plus, at £1.46 per kg	16,000	23,360.00
	22,970	33,306.50

Hence weighted average is $\dfrac{£33,306.50}{22,970} = £1.45$ per kg

So cost of stock issued to
Job 123 is
$$(300-30)\text{kg} \times £1.45 \text{ per kg}$$
$$= £391.50$$

It is assumed that the five kilos damaged in Department B will be charged to Job 123, just as any adverse material usage would be charged to the job in hand. An alternative approach would be to regard the loss of the five kilos as an exceptional item and charge it as an overhead cost to an appropriate overhead cost centre (eg abnormal wastage in Department B).

3   *Rates of overhead absorption*

(a)   *Departmental costs*

Department	A £	B £	Explanation
Rectification work 20 hrs × £4.50 per hr	90	-	Rectification is *normal* and part of work carried out *generally* in the dept.
Indirect labour	2,420	2,960	Their time is not allocated to any particular job, but all jobs benefit indirectly.
Overtime premium	450	-	The inclusion of over-time premium in over-heads ensures that all jobs bear the same direct wage rate, regardless of whether they were performed in what is classified as overtime, or not. All overtime in Dept B, however, is specifically attributable to another job because the over-time was incurred at the specific request of the customer for the job.
Lubricants	520	680	Each job benefits from these in a general way.
Maintenance	720	510	
Other	1,200	2,150	
	5,400	6,300	

(b)   *Departmental direct labour hours*

	A	B
	£9,090	11,200
	£4.50 / hr	£4 / hr
Hours worked	2,020 hrs	2,800 hrs
Less Rectification work	(20) hrs	-
Direct labour hrs	2,000 hrs	2,800 hrs

Rectification work — Included in overheads

Hence absorption rates = $\dfrac{£5,400}{2,000 \text{ hrs}}$ $\dfrac{£6,300}{2,800 \text{ hrs}}$

= £2.70 per hr   £2.25 per hr

Exercise 3

Discuss briefly how information concerning the cost of individual jobs could be used.

Solution

The cost of an individual job can be used in four principal ways.

(a)   The costs may be *used to establish a price* which the customer should be charged for the job, in situations where the customer agrees to pay a price based on 'actual cost plus'. Because the job's share of fixed and variable production overhead has been included in the cost (in addition to, of course, the direct costs of the job), a selling price set in excess of total costs will ensure that all expenses have been covered, provided of course that the organisation works at budgeted capacity.

(b)   The information may be *used in budgeting for future periods*. If the work to customer specification forms any sort of a pattern, an analysis of previous years' jobs will provide a useful basis for the production of future periods' work.

(c)   Job costs can be *used for control purposes*. If an estimated cost for a job is produced, actual costs can be compared with estimate. Excess costs can be investigated with a view to control action.

(d)   In cases where a customer is quoted a firm price before a job begins, actual job costs can be *used to measure the actual profit or loss on each job*.

Job costing for internal services

1.10   It is possible to use a job costing system to control the costs of an internal service department, such as the maintenance department or the printing department. If a job costing system is used it is possible to charge the user departments for the cost of specific jobs carried out, rather than apportioning the total costs of these service departments to the user departments using an arbitrarily determined apportionment basis.

1.11   An internal job costing system for service departments will have the following advantages.

(a)   *Realistic apportionment.* The identification of expenses with jobs and the subsequent charging of these to the department(s) responsible means that costs are borne by those who incurred them.

(b)   *Increased responsibility and awareness.* User departments will be aware that they are charged for the specific services used and may be more careful to use the facility more efficiently. They will also appreciate the true cost of the facilities that they are using and can take decisions accordingly.

(c)   *Control of service department costs.* The service department may be restricted to charging a standard cost to user departments for specific jobs carried out or time spent. It will then be possible to measure the efficiency or inefficiency of the service department by recording the difference between the standard charges and the actual expenditure.

(d)   *Budget information.* This information will ease the budgeting process, as the purpose and cost of service department expenditure can be separately identified.

2   BATCH COSTING   *5/96*

2.1   Costs are collected for batches in much the same way as they are collected for jobs.

Example: batch costing

2.2   A company manufactures widgets to order and has the following budgeted overheads for the year, based on normal activity levels.

Department	Budgeted Overheads £	Budgeted activity
Welding	6,000	1,500 labour hours
Assembly	10,000	1,000 labour hours

Selling and administrative overheads are 20% of factory cost. An order for 250 widgets type X128, made as Batch 5997, incurred the following costs.

Materials	£12,000
Labour	100 hours welding shop at £2.50/hour
	200 hours assembly shop at £1/hour

£500 was paid for the hire of special X-ray equipment for testing the welds.

Required

Calculate the cost per unit for Batch 5997.

Solution

2.3   The first step is to calculate the overhead absorption rate for the production departments.

$$\text{Welding} = \frac{£6,000}{1,500} = £4 \text{ per labour hour}$$

$$\text{Assembly} = \frac{£10,000}{1,000} = £10 \text{ per labour hour}$$

Total cost - Batch no 5997

		£	£
Direct material			12,000
Direct expense			500
Direct labour	100 × 2.50 =	250	
	200 × 1.00 =	200	
			450
Prime cost			12,950
Overheads	100 × 4 =	400	
	200 × 10 =	2,000	
			2,400
Factory cost			15,350
Selling and administrative cost (20% of factory cost)			3,070
Total cost			18,420

$$\text{Cost per unit} = \frac{£18,420}{250} = £73.68$$

Exercise 4

The management of a company manufacturing electrical components is considering introducing an historical batch costing system into their factory.

Required

(a)   Outline the information and procedures required in order to obtain the actual direct material cost of each batch of components manufactured.

(b)   Identify the elements which could make up a direct operative's gross wage and for each element explain, with supporting reasons, whether it should be regarded as part of the prime cost of the components manufactured.

Solution

(a)   The necessary information and procedures are set out below.

(i)   A *batch card* must be set up for each batch, carrying a unique identifying number. This card will be used to collect information on the costs of the batch.

        (ii)   Quantities of materials issued to each batch should be documented by some form of *materials requisition document*. This will be a record of materials issued from stores. A similar document should be used to record materials returned to stores.

        (iii)   The materials issued from stores need to be priced in some way. One method is to maintain a *perpetual inventory system* on stores ledger accounts. The cards would be updated for material receipts from goods inward notes, which would have to be priced at actual cost. The materials requisition document would be the source for updating the cards for material issues. A decision would have to be taken on the basis for pricing such issues; possible bases include LIFO, FIFO and average cost.

  (b)   Elements included in an operative's gross wage are basic wage, overtime earnings, shift premium, and bonus payments.

        (i)   *Basic wage* is remuneration for the operative's ordinary working hours. To the extent that these hours are occupied directly with manufacturing, the related wage should be regarded as prime cost, since it can be directly related to particular components. Any wage in respect of idle time or time spent on non-manufacturing activities is not part of prime cost.

        (ii)   *Overtime earnings* frequently arise because a company is seeking to increase production. The amount of overtime premium should be spread over production generally rather than charged solely to those units produced during the overtime hours. The basic wage earned during overtime hours should be treated as in (i) above: it should be regarded as prime cost if it is related to time spent on manufacturing activities.

        (iii)   *Shift premium* would not normally be related to specific units of production and so should not be regarded as prime cost. Even if it could be so related, the same argument as for overtime premium would suggest that it should be spread over all units produced.

        (iv)   *Bonus payments* arising under a piece work scheme can usually be related very easily to specific units of production and are therefore part of prime cost. Other bonus payments, for example payments under a group bonus scheme, are not traceable in the same way and should be regarded as overhead.

Chapter roundup

- Job costing is the costing method used where each cost unit is separately identifiable. The work is undertaken to customers' special requirements, is of comparatively short duration, is usually carried out within a factory or workshop and moves through processes and operations as a continuously identifiable unit.

- Costs for each job are collected on a job cost sheet or job card in a manual system or in a job account in the work in progress ledger in a computerised system.

  o   Material costs for each job are determined from material requisition notes.

  o   Labour times on each job are recorded on a job ticket, which is then costed and recorded on the job cost sheet. Some labour costs, such as overtime premium or the cost of rectifying sub-standard output, might be charged either directly to a job or else as an overhead cost, depending on the circumstances in which the costs have arisen.

  o   Overhead is absorbed into the cost of jobs using the predetermined overhead absorption rates.

- Job costing can be used to control the costs of an internal service department.

- Batch costing is similar to job costing in that each batch of similar articles is separately identifiable. The cost per unit manufactured in a batch is the total batch cost divided by the number of units in the batch.

Test your knowledge

1   What are the two stages in the collection of information for costing and pricing jobs? (see para 1.2)

2   How are the overheads to be included in the job cost calculated? (1.3)

3   What are the likely features of a computerised job accounting system? (1.7)

4   What are the advantages of an internal job costing system for service departments? (1.12)

5   How is the cost per unit in batch costing calculated? (2.3)

Now try illustrative questions 7 and 8 at the end of the Study Text

Chapter 8

CONTRACT COSTING

This chapter covers the following topics.

		Syllabus reference	Ability required
1	Introduction to contract costing	6(a)	Skill
2	Recording contract costs	6(a)	Skill
3	Contract accounts	6(a)	Skill
4	Retention monies and progress payments	6(a)	Skill
5	Profits on contracts	6(a)	Skill
6	Losses on incomplete contracts	6(a)	Skill
7	Disclosure of long-term contracts in financial accounts	6(a)	Skill

Introduction

Imagine trying to build up job costs on a job ticket in the way described in the previous chapter during the excavation of the tunnel under the English Channel or the construction of a skyscraper. It would be impossible. In industries such as building and construction work, civil engineering and shipbuilding, job costing is not usually appropriate. Contract costing is.

A contract is a cost unit or cost centre which is charged with the direct costs of production and an apportionment of head office overheads. Contract costing is the name given to a method of job costing where the job to be carried out is of such magnitude that a formal contract is made between the customer and supplier. It applies where work is undertaken to customers' special requirements and each order is of long duration (compared with the time to which job costing applies). The work is usually constructional and *in general* the method is similar to job costing, although there are, of course, a few differences.

A key topic in contract costing is the recognition of profits or losses. We will demonstrate how profits to be accounted for are calculated (based on work completed and the prudence concept). Losses by contrast are accounted for in full as soon as they are recognised.

You may have already encountered contract costing during your financial accounting studies of SSAP 9. Section 7 will look at how the cost accounting treatment of contracts interacts with SSAP 9.

1   INTRODUCTION TO CONTRACT COSTING   S/96, S/97, S/98

Features of contract costing

1.1   (a)   A formal contract is made between customer and supplier.

(b)   Work is undertaken to customers' special requirements.

(c)   The work is for a relatively long duration. Large jobs may take a long time to complete, perhaps two or three years. Even when a contract is completed within less than twelve months, it is quite possible that the work may have begun during one financial year and ended during the supplier's next financial year; therefore the profit on the contract will relate to more than one accounting period.

(d)   The work is frequently constructional in nature.

(e)   The method of costing is similar to job costing.

(f)   The work is frequently based on site.

(g)   It is not unusual for a site to have its own cashier and time-keeper.

The CIMA defines contract costing in the *Official Terminology* as 'A form of specific order costing: attribution of costs to individual contracts'.

1.2   The problems which may arise in contract costing are as follows.

(a)   *Identifying direct costs:* because of the large size of the job, many cost items which are usually thought of as production overhead are charged as direct costs of the contract (for example supervision, hire of plant, depreciation or loss in value of plant which is owned, sub-contractors' fees or charges and so on).

(b)   *Low indirect costs:* because many costs normally classed as overheads are charged as direct costs of a contract, the absorption rate for overheads should only apply a share of the cost of those cost items which are not already direct costs. For most contracts the only item of indirect cost would be a charge for head office expenses.

(c)   *Difficulties of cost control:* because of the size of some contracts and some sites, there are often cost control problems (material usage and losses, pilferage, labour supervision and utilisation, damage to and loss of plant and tools, vandalism and so on).

(d)   *Dividing the profit between different accounting periods:* when a contract covers two or more accounting periods, how should the profit (or loss) on the contract be divided between the periods?

1.3   We can begin to address these problems by looking at the way in which contract costs are recorded.

Exam focus point

There was a comprehensive question on contract costing in May 1996, covering most of the topics in this chapter. This was not well answered, according to the examiner's comments, and another question followed in May 1997. Contract costing has also featured in MCQs.

Besides having a good understanding of contract costing you also need to be able to explain the differences between it and other methods such as job or batch costing and process costing.

---

2   RECORDING CONTRACT COSTS   5/96

Direct materials

2.1   The direct materials used on a contract may be obtained from the company's central stores or they may be delivered direct to the site by the company's suppliers. In both cases carefully prepared documentation must ensure that the correct contract is charged with the correct materials. A materials requisition note would record the movement of materials from stores; the supplier's invoice supported by a goods received note would document the cost of materials delivered direct to site.

2.2   Materials issued from a central store or delivered by a supplier are often in excess of the quantities actually required. The surplus quantities are eventually returned to store, a material returns note prepared and the cost of the materials credited to the contract account.

2.3   At the end of an accounting period, a contract may be incomplete and if this is the case, there will probably be materials on site which have not yet been used. (Indeed some of them may never be used, but eventually returned to store.) Materials on site at the end of an accounting period should be carried forward as 'closing stock of materials on site' and brought forward as opening stock at the beginning of the next accounting period.

Direct labour

2.4   Since all the work done by direct labour on a contract site is spent exclusively on a single contract, the direct labour cost of the contract should be easily identified from the wages sheets. If some employees work on several contracts at the same time, perhaps travelling from one site to another, their time spent on each contract will have to be recorded on time sheets, and each contract charged with the cost of these recorded hours. The cost of supervision, which is usually a production overhead in job costing, will be a direct cost of a contract.

Subcontractors

2.5   On large contracts, much work may be done by subcontractors. The invoices of subcontractors will be treated as a direct expense of the contract, although if the invoiced amounts are small, it may be more convenient to account for them as 'direct materials' rather than as direct expenses.

The cost of plant

2.6   A feature of most contract work is the amount of plant used. Plant used on a contract may be owned by the company, or hired from a plant hire firm.

Exercise 1

If plant is hired from a plant hire firm, how should the cost be treated?

Solution

If the plant is hired, the cost will be a direct expense of the contract.

2.7   If the plant is owned by the company, a variety of accounting methods may be employed.

Method one: charging depreciation

2.8   The contract may be charged depreciation on the plant, on a straight line or reducing balance basis. For example if a company has some plant which cost £10,000 and which is depreciated at 10% per annum straight line (to a residual value of nil) and a contract makes use of the plant for six months, a depreciation charge of £500 would be made against the contract.

2.9   The disadvantage of this apparently simple method of costing for plant is that the contract site foreman is not made directly responsible and accountable for the actual plant in his charge. The foreman must be responsible for receipt of the plant, returning the plant after it has been used and proper care of the plant whilst it is being used.

Method two: charging the contract with current book value

2.10   A more common method of costing for plant is to charge the contract with the current book value of the plant.

DEBIT   Contract account

CREDIT   Plant account (fixed asset account) - with the value of the plant net of depreciation

At the end of an accounting period, the contract account is credited with the written down value of the equipment.

CREDIT   Contract account (plant written down value) carried forward as an opening balance at the start of the next period.

When plant is returned from the site to head office (or transferred to another contract site), the contract account is credited with the written down value of the plant.

DEBIT   Plant account (or another contract account)
CREDIT   Contract account (written down value)

2.11   A numerical example will help to illustrate this method. Contract number 123 obtained some plant and loose tools from central store on 1 January 19X2. The book value of the plant was £100,000 and the book value of the loose tools was £8,000. On 1 October 19X2, some plant was removed from the site: this plant had a written down value on 1 October of £20,000. At 31 December 19X2, the plant remaining on site had a written down value of £60,000 and the loose tools had a written down value of £5,000.

CONTRACT 123 ACCOUNT

	£		£
1 January 19X2		*1 October 19X2*	
Plant issued to site	100,000	Plant transferred	20,000
Loose tools issued to site	8,000	*31 December 19X2*	
		Plant value c/f	60,000
		Loose tools value c/f	5,000
		Depreciation (bal fig)	23,000
	108,000		108,000

The difference between the values on the debit and the credit sides of the account (£20,000 for plant and £3,000 for loose tools) is the depreciation cost of the equipment for the year.

Method three: using a plant account

2.12   A third method of accounting for plant costs is to open a *plant account*, which is debited with the depreciation costs and the running costs (repairs, fuel and so on) of the equipment. A notional hire charge is then made to contracts using the plant, at a rate of £x per day.

For example suppose that a company owns some equipment which is depreciated at the rate of £100 per month. Running costs in May 19X3 are £300. The plant is used on 20 days in the month, 12 days on Contract X and 8 days on Contract Y. The accounting entries would be as follows.

PLANT ACCOUNT

	£		£
Depreciation	100	Contract X (hire for 12 days)	240
Running costs	300	Contract Y (hire for 8 days)	160
	400		400

CONTRACT X

	£		£
Plant account (notional hire)	240		

CONTRACT Y

	£		£
Plant account (notional hire)	160		

Overhead costs

2.13   Overhead costs are added periodically (for example at the end of an accounting period) and are based on predetermined overhead absorption rates for the period. You may come across examples where a share of head office general costs is absorbed as an overhead cost to the contract, but this should not happen if the contract is unfinished at the end of the period, because only *production* overheads should be included in the value of any closing work in progress.

3   CONTRACT ACCOUNTS

3.1   The account for a contract is a job account, or work in progress account, and is a record of the direct materials, direct labour, direct expenses and overhead charges on the contract. If we ignore, for the moment, profits on a part-finished contract, a typical contract account might appear as shown below. Check the items in the account carefully, and notice how the cost (or value) of the work done emerges as work in progress.

On an unfinished contract, where no profits are taken mid-way through the contract, this cost of work in progress is carried forward as a closing stock balance.

Example: a contract account

3.2
CONTRACT 794 - LUTTERBINS HOLIDAY CAMP

	£		£
Book value of plant on site b/d	14,300	Materials returned to stores or	
Materials requisition from stores	15,247	transferred to other sites	2,100
Materials and equipment purchased	36,300	Proceeds from sale of materials	
Maintenance and operating costs		on site and jobbing work for	
of plant and vehicles	14,444	other customers	600
Hire charges for plant and		Book value of plant transferred	4,800
vehicles not owned	6,500	Materials on site c/d	7,194
Tools and consumables	8,570	Book value of plant on site c/d	6,640
Direct wages	23,890		21,334
Supervisors' and engineers' salaries			
(proportion relating to time spent		Cost of work done c/d	
on the contract)	13,000	(balancing item)	139,917
Other site expenses	12,000		
Overheads (apportioned perhaps on			
the basis of direct labour hours)	17,000		
	161,251		161,251
Materials on site b/d	7,194		
Book value of plant on site b/d	6,640		
Cost of work done b/d	139,917		

4   RETENTION MONIES AND PROGRESS PAYMENTS

Progress payments

4.1   Because a contract price may run into millions of pounds, a customer is likely to be required under the terms of the contract to make progress payments to the contractor throughout the course of the work so that the contractor does not suffer from significant cash flow problems.

4.2   The amount of the payments will be based on the value of work done (as a proportion of the contract price). This value is known as the *value certified* and will be assessed by an architect or surveyor (for a building contract) or qualified engineer in his certificate. A certificate provides confirmation that work to a certain value has been completed, and that some payment to the contractor is now due. The amount of the payment will be calculated as follows.

The value of work done and certified by the architect or engineer
minus   a retention (see below)
minus   the payments made to date
equals   payment due.

4.3   Thus, if an architect's certificate assesses the value of work done on a contract to be £125,000 and if the retention is 10%, and if £92,000 has already been paid in progress payments the current payment will be:

£125,000 – £12,500 – £92,000 = £20,500

4.4 When progress payments are received from the customer, the accounting entry is as follows.

DEBIT   Bank (or cost ledger control account)
CREDIT   Cash received on account, or contractee account.

Retention monies

4.5 A customer is unlikely to want to pay the full amount of the value certified in case the contractor fails to complete the work or it later turns out that some of the work is of an unacceptable standard. There is therefore often a retention (usually between 2% and 10% of the certified value). Retention monies are released when the contract is fully completed and accepted by the customer. Until then the retention is regarded by the contractor as a debtor.

5   PROFITS ON CONTRACTS   5/96, 5/97

5.1 You may have noticed that the progress payments do not necessarily give rise to profit immediately because of retentions. Let us now turn our attention to how profits are calculated on contracts.

Profits on contracts completed in one accounting period

5.2 If a contract is started and completed in the same accounting period, the calculation of the profit is straightforward, sales minus the cost of the contract. Suppose that a contract, No 6548, has the following costs.

	£
Direct materials (less returns)	40,000
Direct labour	35,000
Direct expenses	8,000
Plant costs	6,000
Overhead	11,000
	100,000

The work began on 1 February 19X3 and was completed on 15 November 19X3 in the contractor's same accounting year.

The contract price was £120,000 and on 20 November the inspecting engineer issued the final certificate of work done. At that date the customer had already paid £90,000 and the remaining £30,000 was still outstanding at the end of the contractor's accounting period. The accounts would appear as follows.

CONTRACT 6548 ACCOUNT

	£		£
Materials less returns	40,000	Cost of sales (P&L)	100,000
Labour	35,000		
Expenses	8,000		
Plant cost	6,000		
Overhead	11,000		
	100,000		100,000

WORK CERTIFIED ACCOUNT

	£		£
Turnover (P&L)	120,000	Contractee account	120,000
	120,000		120,000

CONTRACTEE (CUSTOMER) ACCOUNT

	£		£
Contract a/c - value of work certified	120,000	Cash	90,000
		Balance c/f (debtor in balance sheet)	30,000
	120,000		120,000

The profit on the contract will, in this case, be treated in the profit and loss account as follows.

	£
Turnover	120,000
Cost of sales	100,000
	20,000

Taking profits on incomplete contracts

5.3 A more difficult problem emerges when a contract is incomplete at the end of an accounting period. The contractor may have spent considerable sums of money on the work, and received substantial progress payments, and even if the work is not finished, the contractor will want to claim some profit on the work done so far.

5.4 To make this point clearer, suppose that a company starts four new contracts in its accounting year to 31 December 19X1, but at the end of the year, none of them has been completed. All of the contracts are eventually completed in the first few months of 19X2 and they make profits of £40,000, £50,000, £60,000 and £70,000 respectively, £220,000 in total. If profits are not taken until the contracts are finished, the company would make no profits at all in 19X1, when most of the work was done, and £220,000 in 19X2. Such violent fluctuations in profitability would be confusing not only to the company's management, but also to shareholders and the investing public at large.

5.5 The problem arises because contracts are for long-term work, and it is a well-established practice that some profits should be taken in an accounting period, even if the contract is incomplete. Let us look at an example.

5.6 Suppose that contract 246 is started on 1 July 19X2. Costs to 31 December 19X2, when the company's accounting year ends, are derived from the following information.

	£
Direct materials issued from store	18,000
Materials returned to store	400
Direct labour	15,500
Plant issued, at book value 1 July 19X2	32,000
Written-down value of plant 31 December 19X2	24,000
Materials on site, 31 December 19X2	1,600
Overhead costs	2,000

As at 31 December, certificates had been issued for work valued at £50,000 and the contractee had made progress payments of £45,000. The company has calculated that more work has been done since the last certificates were issued, and that the cost of work done but not yet certified is £8,000. The final contract price is £82,000 and the estimated total cost of the contract is £64,000.

The contract account would be prepared as follows.

CONTRACT 246 ACCOUNT

	£	£		£
Materials	18,000		Value of plant c/d	24,000
Less returns	400		Materials on site c/d	1,600
		17,600	Cost of work done not	
Labour		15,500	certified c/d	8,000
Plant issued at book value		32,000	Cost of work certified	33,500
Overheads		2,000		
		67,100		67,100

WORK CERTIFIED ACCOUNT

	£		£
Turnover (P&L)	50,000	Contractee account	50,000
	50,000		50,000

CONTRACTEE ACCOUNT

	£		£
Work certified account	50,000	Cash (progress payment)	45,000
		Balance c/f	5,000
	50,000		50,000

5.7 *Points to note*

(a) The work done, but not yet certified, must be valued at cost, and not at the value of the unissued certificates. It would be imprudent to suppose that the work has been done to the complete satisfaction of the architect or engineer, who may not issue certificates until further work is done.

(b) We have ignored retentions here.

Estimating the size of the profit

5.8 The method of calculating profit on an incomplete contract may vary, and you should check any examination question carefully to find out whether a specific method is stated in the text of the question. The concept of prudence should be applied, and it is suggested that the following guidelines be followed for calculating profit on an incomplete contract.

5.9 If the contract is in its early stages, no profit should be taken. Profit should only be taken when the outcome of the contract can be assessed with reasonable accuracy. The value for sales must therefore be exactly the same as the cost of work certified to date.

5.10 If the contract is in its later stages, you will normally be able to calculate profit as a proportion of total estimated profit in the following way.

(a) *Calculate total anticipated profit*

In the example about contract 246 above, this is calculated as follows.

	£	£
Contract price		82,000
Costs incurred (£ (33,500 + 8,000))	41,500	
Estimated costs to complete		
(£(64,000 – 41,500))	22,500	
		64,000
Estimated contract profit		18,000

(b) *Estimate degree of completion*

This estimated contract profit is the profit that the organisation expects to earn once the contract is complete but since it is not yet complete it would be wrong to recognise all of the profit at the end of the current accounting period. The degree of completion of the contract must therefore be estimated. The estimation can be based on sales value or costs.

(i) Using sales value, degree of completion $= \dfrac{\text{value of work certified}}{\text{contract price}} \times 100\%$

$= \dfrac{50,000}{82,000} \times 100\% = 61\%$

(ii) Using costs, degree of completion $= \dfrac{\text{cost of work done}}{\text{estimated total costs}} \times 100\%$

$= \dfrac{41,500}{64,000} \times 100\% = 65\%$

The two bases produce different degrees of completion; it does not matter which is used *providing* the basis is used consistently.

(c)   *Calculate the profit earned to date*

We can now calculate the profit earned to date.

(i)   Based on sales value: £18,000 × 61% = £10,980
(ii)   Based on cost: £18,000 × 65% = £11,700

(d)   *Complete the profit and loss account entries*

	£
Value certified = Turnover	50,000
Profit ((c) (i))	10,980
Cost of sales	39,020

	£
Costs incurred	41,500
Cost of sales	39,020
Work in progress	2,480

You will see how to account for this work in progress in Paragraph 7.3.

5.11   The above approach was possible because you were given future costs to complete the contract. If in the exam you are *not* given future costs, the following approach can be used.

			£
Value certified	=	Turnover	50,000
Cost of work certified	=	Cost of sales	(33,500)
Profit			16,500
Cost incurred			41,500
Cost of sales			33,500
Work in progress (cost of work done not certified)			8,000

5.12   Only using this method will cost of sales automatically equal cost of work certified. In any event some would argue that taking profit as value certified – cost of work certified is imprudent; the profit figure should be a more conservative figure (say $^2/_3$ or ¾ of £16,500). If a more conservative figure is used, turnover and cost of sales will be less than £50,000 and £33,500 respectively. Work in progress will be greater than £8,000; it will thus include not only costs of work done not certified, but also a proportion of the cost of work certified.

5.13   A loss on the contract may be foreseen. The method of dealing with losses is covered in the next section.

Exercise 2

Landy Stroyers plc is a construction company. Data relating to one of its contracts, XYZ, for the year to 31 December 19X2, at which point it was 70% complete, are as follows.

	£'000
Value of work certified to 31 December 19X1	500
Cost of work certified to 31 December 19X1	360
Plant on site b/f at 1 January 19X2	30
Materials on site b/f at 1 January 19X2	10
Cost of contract to 1 January 19X2 b/f	370
Materials issued from store	190
Sub-contractors' costs	200
Wages and salaries	200
Overheads absorbed by contract in 19X2	100
Plant on site c/f at 31 December 19X2	15
Materials on site c/f at 31 December 19X2	5
Value of work certified to 31 December 19X2	1,200
Cost of work certified to 31 December 19X2	950
Contract price	1,700
Costs to complete	300

No profit has been taken on the contract prior to 19X2. There are no retentions.

Required

(a)   Calculate the total cumulative cost of contract XYZ to the end of December 19X2.

(b)   Calculate the gross profit for the contract.

(c)   Estimate the size of the profit which should be taken in the period using sales value as a basis.

Solution

(a)

CONTRACT ACCOUNT

	£'000		£'000	£'000
Cost of contract b/f	370	Plant on site c/f		15
Plant on site b/f	30	Materials on site c/f		5
Materials on site b/f	10	Cost of work certified	950	
Materials from stores	190	Cost of work not certified (bal)	130	
Sub-contractors' costs	200	Cost of contract c/f		1,080
Wages and salaries	200			
Overheads	100			
	1,100			1,100

(b)

	£,000	£,000
Contract price		1,700
Costs incurred	1,080	
Costs to complete	300	
		1,380
Estimated contract profit		320

(c)   Profit = £320,000 × $\dfrac{1{,}200}{1{,}700}$ = £225,882

(This would correspond to the following turnover, cost of sales, and work in progress carried down at 31 December 19X2.

	£
Value certified = Turnover	1,200,000
Profit	225,882
Cost of sales	974,118

	£
Cost incurred	1,080,000
Cost of sales	974,118
Work in progress	105,882)

---

6   LOSSES ON INCOMPLETE CONTRACTS   *S/96, S/97*

6.1   At the end of an accounting period, it may be that instead of finding that the contract is profitable, a loss is expected. When this occurs, the total expected loss should be taken into account as soon as it is recognised, even though the contract is not yet complete. The contract account should be credited with the anticipated future loss (the total loss expected to arise over the entire life of the contract – loss to date) and the profit and loss account debited with the total expected loss (final cost of contract – full contract price).

6.2   The same accounting procedure would be followed on completed contracts, as well as incomplete contracts, but it is essential that the full amount of the loss on the total contract, if foreseeable, should be charged against company profits at the earliest opportunity, even if a contract is incomplete. This means that in the next accounting period, the contract should break even, making neither a profit nor a loss, because the full loss has already been charged to the profit and loss account.

Example: loss on contract

6.3   Contract 257 was begun on 22 March 19X3. By 31 December 19X3, the end of the contractor's accounting year, costs incurred were as follows.

	£
Materials issued	24,000
Materials on site, 31 December	2,000
Labour	36,000
Plant issued to site 22 March	40,000
Written-down value of plant, 31 December	28,000
Overheads	6,000

The contract is expected to end in February 19X4 and at 31 December 19X3, the cost accountant estimated that the final cost of the contract would be £95,000. The full contract price is £90,000. Work certified at 31 December was valued at £72,000. The contractee has made progress payments up to 31 December of £63,000.

Required

Prepare the contract account.

Solution

6.4   CONTRACT 257 ACCOUNT

	£		£
Materials issued	24,000	Materials on site c/f	2,000
Labour	36,000	Plant at written-down value, c/f	28,000
Plant issued, written-down value	40,000	Cost of work c/d (balancing figure)	76,000
Overheads	6,000		
	106,000		106,000
Cost of work done, b/d	76,000	Cost of sales (P&L)	77,000
Anticipated future loss★	1,000		
	77,000		77,000

★ The total estimated loss on the contract is £5,000 (£90,000 – £95,000). Of this amount £4,000 has been lost in the current period (£76,000 – £72,000) and so £1,000 is anticipated as arising in the future: in the next period the company will invoice £18,000 (£90,000 – £72,000) and will incur costs of £19,000 (£95,000 – £76,000). This is taken as a loss in the current period.

The loss is posted via postings of £72,000 to turnover and £77,000 to cost of sales (£5,000 net).

Exercise 3

Jibby Ltd's year end is 30 April. At 30 April 19X4 costs of £43,750 have been incurred on contract N53. The value of work certified at the period end is £38,615. The contract price is £57,500 but it is anticipated that the final costs at 30 September 19X4, when the contract is expected to end, will be £63,111.

Required

(a)   Prepare the contract account.
(b)   Calculate the figures for turnover and cost of sales for the period to 30 April 19X4.

Solution

(a)   CONTRACT N53

	£		£
Cost of work done b/d	43,750	Cost of sales (P&L)	44,226
Anticipated future loss	*476		
	44,226		44,226

*£[(63,111 – 57,500) – (43,750 – 38,615)] = £476.

(b)   Turnover = £38,615

      Cost of sales = £44,226

---

7   DISCLOSURE OF LONG-TERM CONTRACTS IN FINANCIAL ACCOUNTS

5/96, 5/97

7.1   There is a *Statement of standard accounting practice*, SSAP 9, first issued in 1975 but revised in 1988, relating to stocks and long-term contracts. The statement defines how stocks and work in progress should be valued in the financial accounts, and makes particular reference to long-term contract work in progress and profits. Although there is no requirement that cost accounting procedures should be the same as financial accounting procedures and standards, it is generally thought that conformity between the financial accounts and the cost accounts is desirable in contract costing.

7.2   SSAP 9 makes the following requirements with relation to the profit and loss account.

(a)   The profit and loss account will contain turnover and related costs deemed to accrue to the contract over the period, so that the profit and loss account reflects the net profit on the contract taken in the period.

(b)   The profit taken needs to reflect the proportion of the work carried out at the accounting date, and to take account of any known inequalities of profitability at the various stages of a contract.

(c)   Where the outcome of a contract cannot be reasonably assessed before its completion, no profits should be taken on the incomplete contract.

(d)   The amount of profit taken to the profit and loss account for an incomplete contract should be judged with prudence.

(e)   If it is expected that there will be a loss on the contract as a whole, provision needs to be made for the whole of the loss as soon as it is recognised (in accordance with the prudence concept). The amount of the loss should be deducted from the amounts for long-term contracts included under stocks, and where a credit balance results, it should be disclosed separately under creditors or provisions for liabilities and charges.

7.3   SSAP 9 requires that balances relating to long-term contracts are split into two elements so that the following disclosures can be made in the balance sheet.

(a)   Work done on long-term contracts not yet recognised in the profit and loss account is calculated as the difference between:

(i)   cost of work done and
(ii) cost of sales.

If cost of work done > cost of sales, the balance is disclosed under 'stocks' as long-term contract balances (a type of work in progress).

If cost of sales > cost of work done, the balance is disclosed under 'creditors' or 'provisions for liabilities and charges'.

(b)   There will also be a *difference* between:

(i)	amounts recognised as turnover and	X
(ii)	progress payments received	(X)
		X

If amounts recognised as turnover > progress payments received, the balance is disclosed under debtors as 'amounts recoverable on long-term contracts'.

If progress payments received > amounts recognised as turnover, the balance will be offset against any 'stocks' balance (with any remaining balance being disclosed within creditors).

Example: disclosure of long-term contract balances

7.4   Contract 139 was begun on 1 April 19X2 and has cost £150,000 by the end of December 19X2 when the company's accounting year ends. The cost of work certified to date is £142,000 and the value of work certified is £175,000. The contractee retains 10% of the value of work certified and has made progress payments of £157,500 by the end of December. The contract price is £290,000 and total contract costs are expected to be £260,000.

It has been decided that the calculation of the profit on the contract attributable to the year ended 31 December 19X2 should be based on sales value.

Required

Determine the balance sheet disclosures for contract 139.

Solution

7.5   We begin by calculating the P & L account entries.

	£	£
Contract price		290,000
Costs incurred	150,000	
Estimated costs to complete	110,000	
		260,000
Estimated contract profit		30,000

$$\text{Degree of completion} = \frac{175,000}{290,000} \times 100\% = 60\%$$

Profit attributable to year ended 31 December 19X2 = £30,000 × 60% = £18,000.

Profit and loss account entries are as follows.

	£
Turnover	175,000
Cost of sales (balance)	157,000
Profit	18,000

7.6   Remember that we need to calculate two balance sheet disclosure elements.

(a)   *Costs related to the contract not allocated to cost of sales*

	£
Cost of work done	150,000
Cost of sales	157,000
	7,000

This will be disclosed under provisions for liabilities and charges or creditors.

The figure of £7,000 can be reconciled as follows.

	£'000
Value certified	175
Cost of work certified	(142)
Apparent profit to date	33
Profit recognised	(18)
Cost of work not certified	(8)
	7

(b)   *Amounts recoverable on long-term contracts*

	£
Amount recognised on turnover	175,000
Progress payments received	(157,500)
	17,500

This will be recognised in debtors

Don't forget that the retention of 10% should also be shown in debtors.

Exercise 4

Reconcile the figure of £2,480 calculated in Paragraph 5.13.

Solution

	£
Value certified	50,000
Cost of work certified	(33,500)
Apparent profit	16,500
Profit recognised	(10,980)
Cost of work not certified	(8,000)
Work in progress	(2,480)

Exercise 5

Look back at the example which begins in Paragraph 6.2. Calculate the balance sheet disclosures at 31 December 19X3.

Solution

CONTRACTEE ACCOUNT

	£		£
Work certified	72,000	Cash	63,000
		Balance c/f	9,000
	72,000		72,000
Balance b/f	9,000		

Work done not allocated to cost of sales	£
Cost of work done	76,000
Cost of sales	77,000
	(1,000)

This credit balance should be disclosed separately under creditors or provision for liabilities and charges.

Amounts recoverable on long-term contracts	£
Amounts recognised as turnover	72,000
Less progress payments	(63,000)
	9,000

The value of plant on site (£28,000) and materials on site (£2,000) would also be included in the company's balance sheet as at 31 December 19X3.

Contract costing and computers

7.7   The recording of contract costing transactions within a computerised system is similar to that for job and batch costing transactions. Contract costing is more complex, however, and details of the valuation certificates, progress payments and retentions also need to be recorded.

Chapter roundup

- Contract costing is a form of job costing which applies where the job is on a large scale and for a long duration. The majority of costs relating to a contract are direct costs.

- Contract costs are collected in a contract account.

- A customer is likely to be required to make progress payments which are calculated as the value of work done and certified by the architect or engineer minus a retention minus the payments made to date.

- The long duration of a contract usually means that an estimate must be made of the profit earned on each incomplete contract at the end of the accounting period. There are several different ways of calculating contract profits, but the overriding consideration must be the application of the prudence concept.

- If a loss is expected on a contract, the total expected loss should be taken into account as soon as it is recognised, even if the contract is not complete.

- SSAP 9 requires the following disclosures in the balance sheet.

  o Work done on long-term contracts which has yet to be recognised in the profit and loss account (cost of work done – cost of sales) should be disclosed under 'stocks' as 'long-term contract balances' (but should be disclosed under provisions for liabilities and charges if negative).

  o The difference between (a) 'amounts recognised as turnover' and (b) 'progress payments received' will be recognised in debtors as 'amounts recoverable on long-term contracts' if (a) > (b), but will either be offset against the stock balance mentioned above if (b) > (a) or disclosed under creditors.

Test your knowledge

1   List the features of contract costing. (see para 1.1)

2   How would you account for plant depreciation in contract accounts? (2.8 - 2.11)

3   How is the amount of a progress payment calculated? (4.2)

4   What are retention monies? (4.5)

5   How much profit should be taken on a contract in the early stages? (5.9)

6   How would you account for a loss on an incomplete contract? (6.1)

7   What requirements does SSAP 9 make with relation to the profit and loss account? (7.2)

8   If progress payments received are greater than amounts recognised as turnover, is the difference recognised in debtors or offset against 'long-term contracts balance' in stock? (7.3)

Now try illustrative question 9 at the end of the Study Text

Chapter 9

PROCESS COSTING

This chapter covers the following topics.

		Syllabus reference	Ability required
1	Introduction to process costing	6(a)	Skill
2	The basics of process costing	6(a)	Skill
3	Losses in process	6(a)	Skill
4	Valuing closing work in progress	6(a)	Skill
5	Valuing opening work in progress: FIFO method	6(a)	Skill
6	Valuing opening work in progress: weighted average cost method	6(a)	Skill
7	Accounting for both changes in stock levels and losses	6(a)	Skill
8	Identification of losses/gains at different stages in the process	6(a)	Skill
9	Output costing	6(a)	Skill

Introduction

In this and the next two chapters we are going to turn our attention to process costing/continuous operation costing which is defined in CIMA *Official Terminology* as 'The costing method applicable where goods or services result from a sequence of continuous or repetitive operations or processes. Costs are averaged over the units produced during the period'.

The main subdivisions of this costing method are process costing (which we will look at in this chapter and Chapter 10) and service/function costing (covered in Chapter 11). Output costing, a form of process costing, is also considered briefly at the end of this chapter.

You have covered some aspects of process costing in your Paper 2 studies (although you did not have to deal with opening work in progress, for example).

1 INTRODUCTION TO PROCESS COSTING   5/97

1.1 Process costing is used where it is not possible to identify separate units of production, or jobs, usually because of the continuous nature of the production processes involved. It is common (but not essential) to identify process costing with continuous production such as oil refining, or the manufacture of soap, paint, textiles, paper, foods and drinks, many chemicals and so on. Process costing may also be associated with the continuous production of large volumes of low-cost items, such as cans or tins.

1.2 The features of process costing which make it different from specific order costing are as follows.

(a) The output of one process is the input to a subsequent process until a completed product is produced.

(b) The continuous nature of production in many processes means that there will usually be closing work in progress which must be valued. In process costing it is not possible to build up cost records of the cost per unit of output or the cost per unit of closing stock because production in progress is an indistinguishable homogeneous mass.

(c) There is often a *loss in process* due to spoilage, wastage, evaporation and so on.

(d) Output from production may be a single product, but there may also be a by-product (or by-products) and/or joint products.

1.3 The aim of this chapter is to describe how cost accountants keep a set of accounts to record the costs of production in a processing industry. The aim of the set of accounts is to derive a cost, or valuation, for output and closing stock. This basically straightforward aim is complicated in practice by the following problems.

(a) Establishing a system of accounting for loss, and the scrap value of loss, which will give a realistic and 'fair' valuation for units of output

(b) Deciding on a method of valuation for closing work in progress

(c) Valuing output when there is opening work in progress at the start of a period

(d) Establishing a cost for joint products when two or more products are produced together from common input and the same process

The first three problems will be dealt with in this chapter and the fourth in the next.

Exam focus point

When asked the depth to which process costing would be examined, the examiner replied as follows:

'Candidates should be able to deal with opening and closing work in process; losses (which may be either fully or partially complete) with no value, a scrap value or a disposal cost; joint products; by-products and the further processing decision. Some or all of these issues may be included in a single question.'

Process costing is likely to be examined at every exam sitting either as an MCQ, or as a longer question, or both.

---

2   THE BASICS OF PROCESS COSTING

2.1 Where a series of separate processes is required to manufacture the finished product, the output of one process becomes the input to the next until the final output is made in the final process. For example, if two processes are required the accounts would look like this.

PROCESS 1 ACCOUNT

	Units	£		Units	£
Direct materials	1,000	50,000	Output to process 2	1,000	90,000
Direct labour		20,000			
Production overhead		20,000			
	1,000	90,000		1,000	90,000

PROCESS 2 ACCOUNT

	Units	£		Units	£
Materials from process 1	1,000	90,000	Output to finished goods	1,500	150,000
Added materials	500	30,000			
Direct labour		15,000			
Production overhead		15,000			
	1,500	150,000		1,500	150,000

2.2 Note that direct labour and production overhead may be treated together in an examination question as 'conversion cost'.

2.3 *Added* materials, labour and overhead in process 2 are added gradually throughout the process. Materials from process 1, in contrast, will often be introduced in full at the start of process 2.

2.4 The 'units' columns in the process accounts are for memorandum purposes only and help you to ensure that you do not miss out any entries.

Framework for dealing with process costing

2.5 Process costing is centred around four key stages. The exact work done at each stage will depend on whether there are normal losses, scrap, opening and closing stock etc.

(a) *Determine output and losses*

This stage involves

 (i)   determining expected output;
 (ii) calculating normal loss and abnormal loss and gain;
 (iii) calculating equivalent units if there is closing or opening work in progress.

(b) *Calculate cost per unit of output, losses and WIP*

This stage involves calculating cost per unit or cost per equivalent unit.

(c) *Calculate total cost of output, losses and WIP*

In some examples this will be straightforward; however in cases where there is closing and/or opening work-in-progress a *statement of evaluation* will have to be prepared.

(d) *Complete accounts*

This stage involves

 (i) completing the process account;
 (ii) writing up the other accounts required by the question such as abnormal loss/gain accounts, scrap accounts etc.

3   LOSSES IN PROCESS

3.1 Losses during processing can happen through evaporation of liquids, wastage, or rejected units, and so the quantity of materials output from a process might be less than the quantities input. How would any losses be costed?

Three different ways of costing losses

3.2 Suppose that input to a process consists of 100 litres of material. Total process costs are £85,652. What is the cost per litre if output is as follows?

(a) 92 litres
(b) 98 litres

Base cost per unit on output

3.3 One way of costing the output is to say that the cost per unit should be based on actual units produced (output), so that any lost units have no cost at all.

		Cost per unit		
(a)	If output is 92 litres	$\frac{£85,652}{92}$	=	£931 per litre
(b)	If output is 98 litres	$\frac{£85,652}{98}$	=	£874 per litre

You should see that the cost per litre varies according to the actual loss in the period. This means that if some loss in process is unavoidable, and if the amount of loss varies a little from period to period, this approach to costing will result in fluctuations in unit costs.

It might be more satisfactory to take a longer-term view of loss, and calculate average unit costs on the basis of average loss over a longer period of time. This would give greater stability and consistency to unit costs of production between one period (such as one month) and the next.

Base cost per unit on input

3.4 A second way of costing the output is to say that lost units have a cost, which should be charged to the P & L account whenever they occur. The cost per unit would then be based on units of *input* rather than units of output.

		Cost per unit £		Cost of output £		Cost of loss £
(a)	If output is 92 litres	$\frac{£85,652}{100}$	856.52	(× 92) 78,799.84		(× 8) 6,852.16
(b)	If output is 98 litres	$\frac{£85,652}{100}$	856.52	(× 98) 83,938.96		(× 2) 1,713.04

The cost of the loss would be written off directly to the P & L account.

The main drawback to this method of costing is that if some loss in processing is unavoidable and to be expected, there would be some cost of production unavoidably written off to the P & L account in every period, and this is an unsatisfactory method of costing.

Differentiate between expected and unexpected losses

3.5 The third method of costing loss (described below) is a compromise system, which is based on the following view.

(a) If some loss is to be expected, it should not be given a cost.
(b) If there is some loss that 'shouldn't happen', it ought to be given a cost.

Normal loss and abnormal loss/gain   5/95

3.6 The average or expected loss is referred to as *normal loss*. This is given no cost.

3.7 When actual loss exceeds normal loss, the difference is called *abnormal loss* which is given a cost.

3.8 When actual loss is less than normal loss, we keep normal loss unchanged, and treat the difference between actual and normal loss as an *abnormal gain*. This is given a 'cost', which is debited rather than credited to the process cost account: it is a 'negative' cost and so an item of gain.

3.9 Normal loss, abnormal loss and abnormal gain can be illustrated using the previous example. The cost per unit should be based on expected output, which is input minus normal loss. Let's suppose that normal loss is 5% of input.

3.10 If actual output is 92 litres, the stages are as follows.

(a) *Determine output and losses*

Normal output is 95 litres, and so there is an abnormal loss of 3 litres.

(b) *Calculate cost per unit of output, losses and WIP*

$$\text{Cost per unit} = \frac{£85,652}{(100-5)\text{ litres}} = \frac{£85,652}{95} = £901.60 \text{ per litre}$$

(c) *Calculate total cost of output and losses*

	£
Cost of output (92 × £901.60)	82,947.20
Normal loss	0.00
Abnormal loss (3 litres × £901.60)	2,704.80
	85,652.00

(d) *Complete accounts*

The process account and abnormal loss account would be:

PROCESS ACCOUNT

	Units	£		Units	£
Cost of materials, labour and overhead	100	85,652	Finished goods	92	82,947.20
			Normal loss	5	0.00
			Abnormal loss	3	2,704.80
	100	85,652		100	85,652.00

ABNORMAL LOSS A/C

	£		£
Process a/c	2704.80	P & L account	2704.80

3.11 If actual output is 98 litres, the stages are as follows.

(a) *Determine output and losses*

Normal output is 95 litres, and normal loss is 5 litres, therefore there is an abnormal gain of (98 – 95) = 3 litres.

(b) *Calculate cost per unit of output and losses*

This will be £901.60 as above.

(c) *Calculate total cost of output and losses*

	£
Cost of output (98 × £901.60)	88,356.80
Normal loss	0.00
	88,356.80
Abnormal gain (3 litres × £901.60)	(2,704.80)
	85,652.00

(d) *Complete accounts*

The process account and abnormal gain account would be:

PROCESS ACCOUNT

	Units	£		Units	£
Cost of materials, labour and overhead	100	85,652.00	Finished goods	98	88,356.80
Abnormal gain	3	2,704.80	Normal loss	5	0.00
	103	88,356.80		103	88,356.80

ABNORMAL GAIN A/C

	£		£
P & L account	2704.80	Process a/c	2704.80

Exercise 1

3,000 units of material are input to a process. Process costs are as follows.

Material	£11,700
Conversion costs	£6,300

Output is 2,000 units. Normal loss is 20% of input.

Required

Prepare a process account and the appropriate abnormal loss/gain account.

Solution

(a) *Determine output and losses*

We are told that output is 2,000 units.

Normal loss = 20% × 3,000 = 600 units

Abnormal loss = (3,000 − 600) − 2,000 = 400 units

(b) *Calculate cost per unit of output and losses*

$$\text{Cost per unit} = \frac{\pounds(11,700 + 6,300)}{2,400} = \pounds 7.50$$

(c) *Calculate total cost of output and losses*

		£
Output	(2,000 × £7.50)	15,000
Normal loss		0
Abnormal loss	(400 × £7.50)	3,000
		18,000

(d) *Complete accounts*

PROCESS ACCOUNT

	Units	£		Units	£
Material	3,000	11,700	Output	2,000	15,000
Conversion costs		6,300	Normal loss	600	
			Abnormal loss	400	3,000
	3,000	18,000		3,000	18,000

ABNORMAL LOSS ACCOUNT

	£		£
Process a/c	3,000	P&L account	3,000

Scrap value of loss

3.12 Loss or spoilage may have a scrap value. When loss or spoilage is sold as scrap ('Discarded material having some value' (CIMA *Official Terminology*)), there are two ways of accounting for the income.

(a) Add the revenue from the scrap sales to total sales revenue in the period.

(b) Subtract the sales revenue from the scrap from the costs of production and the cost of abnormal loss in the period.

One of the complexities of process costing is that although it might seem simpler to adopt method (a), it is more usual to adopt method (b).

3.13 If a distinction is made between normal loss and abnormal loss/gain the accounting treatment of scrap in process costing is as follows.

(a) The scrap value of normal loss will probably be deducted from the cost of materials in the process. This is done in the cost accounts themselves by crediting the scrap value of normal loss to the process account.

(b) The scrap value of *abnormal loss (or abnormal gain)* will probably be set off against its cost, in an abnormal loss (abnormal gain) account, and only the balance on the account will be written to the P & L account at the end of the period.

3.14 As the exercise that follows will show, accounting for scrap fits into our process costing framework as follows:

(a) *Determine output and losses*

This stage is important, as the scrap value of normal losses will be accounted for differently.

(b) *Calculate costs of output and losses*

(c)   To do this we must first *separate* the scrap value of normal loss from abnormal loss. *Then* we will subtract the scrap value of normal loss from the cost of the process and divide by the expected output to determine cost per unit, and subsequently total costs.

(d)   *Complete accounts*

In the process account the units of *normal loss* will be costed at their *scrap value*. The units of *abnormal loss/gain* will be costed at the cost per unit calculated in (b).

The other relevant accounting entries are as follows.

(i)   For normal losses

DEBIT   Scrap account
CREDIT   Process account

with the scrap value of normal loss.

(ii)   For abnormal losses

DEBIT   Scrap account
CREDIT   Abnormal loss account

with the scrap value of abnormal loss.

For abnormal gains

DEBIT   Abnormal gain account
CREDIT   Scrap account

with the scrap value of abnormal gain.

(iii)   Complete scrap account

DEBIT   Cash received
CREDIT   Scrap account

with cash received from sale of actual scrap.

Exercise 2

Nan Ltd has a factory which operates two production processes. Normal spoilage in each process is 10%, and scrapped units out of process 1 sell for 50p per unit whereas scrapped units out of process 2 sell for £3. Output from process 1 is transferred to process 2: output from process 2 is finished output ready for sale.

Relevant information about costs for period 5 are as follows.

	Process 1		Process 2	
	Units	£	Units	£
Input materials	2,000	£8,100		
Transferred to process 2	1,750			
Materials from process 1			1,750	
Added materials			1,250	£1,900
Labour and overheads		£10,000		£22,000
Output to finished goods			2,800	

Required

Prepare the following cost accounts.

(a)   Process 1
(b)   Process 2
(c)   Abnormal loss
(d)   Abnormal gain
(e)   Scrap

Solution

(a)   *Process 1*

(i)   *Determine output and losses*

The normal loss is 10% of 2000 units = 200 units, and the actual loss is (2000 - 1750) = 250 units. This means that there is abnormal loss of 50 units.

Actual output	1,750 units
Abnormal loss	50 units
Expected output (90% of 2,000)	1,800 units

(ii) *Calculate cost per unit of output and losses*

(1) The total value of scrap is 250 units at 50p per unit = £125. We must split this between the scrap value of normal loss and the scrap value of abnormal loss.

	£
Normal loss	100
Abnormal loss	25
Total scrap (250 units × 50p)	125

(2) The scrap value of normal loss is first deducted from the materials cost in the process, in order to calculate the output cost per unit and then credited to the process account as a 'value' for normal loss. The cost per unit in process 1 is calculated as follows.

	Total cost £		Cost per expected unit of output £
Materials	8,100		
Less normal loss scrap value *	100		
	8,000	(÷ 1,800)	4.44
Labour and overhead	10,000	(÷ 1,800)	5.56
Total	18,000	(÷ 1,800)	10.00

* It is usual to set this scrap value of normal loss against the cost of materials.

(iii) *Calculate total cost of output and losses*

		£
Output	(1,750 units × £10.00)	17,500
Normal loss	(200 units × £0.50)	100
Abnormal loss	(50 units × £10.00)	500
		18,100

(iv) *Complete accounts*

Now we can put the process 1 account together.

PROCESS 1 ACCOUNT

	Units	£		Units	£
Materials	2,000	8,100	Output to process 2*	1,750	17,500
Labour and overhead		10,000	Normal loss (scrap a/c)	200	100
			Abnormal loss a/c*	50	500
	2,000	18,100		2,000	18,100

* At £10 per unit.

(b) *Process 2*

(i) *Determine output and losses*

The normal loss is 10% of the units processed = 10% of (1,750 (from process 1) + 1,250) = 300 units. The actual loss is (3,000 - 2,800) = 200 units, so that there is abnormal gain of 100 units. These are *deducted* from actual output in arriving at the number of expected units (normal output) in the period.

Expected units of output

	Units
Actual output	2,800
Abnormal gain	(100)
Expected output (90% of 3,000)	2,700

(ii) *Calculate cost per unit of output and losses*

(1) The total value of scrap is 200 units at £3 per unit = £600. We must split this between the scrap value of normal loss and the scrap value of abnormal gain. Abnormal gain's scrap value is 'negative'.

		£
Normal loss scrap value	300 units × £3	900
Abnormal gain scrap value	100 units × £3	(300)
Scrap value of actual loss	200 units × £3	600

(2) The scrap value of normal loss is first deducted from the cost of materials in the process, in order to calculate a cost per unit of output, and then credited to the process account as a 'value' for normal loss. The cost per unit in process 2 is calculated as follows.

	Total cost £		Cost per expected unit of output £
Materials:			
Transferred from process 1	17,500		
Added in process 2	1,900		
	19,400		
Less scrap value of normal loss	900		
	18,500	(÷ 2,700)	6.85
Labour and overhead	22,000	(÷ 2,700)	8.15
	40,500	(÷ 2,700)	15.00

(iii) *Calculate total cost of output and losses*

		£
Output	(2,800 × £15.00)	42,000
Normal loss	(300 units × £3.00)	900
		42,900
Abnormal gain	(100 units × £15.00)	(1,500)
		41,400

(iv) *Complete accounts*

PROCESS 2 ACCOUNT

	Units	£		Units	£
From process 1	1,750	17,500	Finished output	2,800	42,000
Added materials	1,250	1,900			
Labour and overhead		22,000	Normal loss (scrap a/c)	300	900
	3,000	41,400			
Abnormal gain a/c	100	1,500			
	3,100	42,900		3,100	42,900

(c) and (d)

Abnormal loss and abnormal gain accounts

For each process, one or the other of these accounts will record three items.

(i) The cost/value of the abnormal loss/gain. This is the corresponding entry to the entry in the process account.

(ii) The scrap value of the abnormal loss or gain, to set off against it.

(iii) A balancing figure, which is written to the P&L account as an adjustment to the profit figure.

ABNORMAL LOSS ACCOUNT

	£		£
Process 1	500	Scrap a/c (scrap value of abnormal loss)	25
		Profit and Loss a/c (balance)	475
	500		500

ABNORMAL GAIN ACCOUNT

	£		£
Scrap a/c (scrap value of abnormal gain units)	300	Process 2	1,500
Profit & Loss a/c (balance)	1,200		
	1,500		1,500

(e)   *Scrap account*

This is credited with the cash value of actual units scrapped. The other entries in the account should all be identifiable as corresponding entries to those in the process accounts, and abnormal loss and abnormal gain accounts.

SCRAP ACCOUNT

	£		£
Normal loss:		Cash: sale of	
Process 1 (200 × 50p)	100	process 1 scrap (250 × 50p)	125
Process 2 (300 × £3)	900	Cash: sale of	
Abnormal loss a/c	25	process 2 scrap (200 × £3)	600
		Abnormal gain a/c	300
	1,025		1,025

Exercise 3

Look back at Exercise 1. Suppose the units of loss could be sold for £1 each. Prepare appropriate accounts.

Solution

(a)   *Determine output and losses*

Actual output	2,000 units
Abnormal loss	400 units
Expected output	2,400 units

(b)   *Calculate cost per unit of output and losses*

	£
Scrap value of normal loss	600
Scrap value of abnormal loss	400
Total scrap (1,000 units × £1)	1,000

(c)   *Calculate total cost of output and losses*

		£
Output	(2,000 × £7.25)	14,500
Normal loss	(600 × £1.00)	600
Abnormal loss	(400 × £7.25)	2,900
		18,000

$$\text{Cost per expected unit} = \frac{£\big((11,700 - 600) + 6,300\big)}{2,400} = £7.25$$

(d)   *Complete accounts*

PROCESS ACCOUNT

	Units	£		Units	£
Material	3,000	11,700	Output	2,000	14,500
Conversion costs		6,300	Normal loss	600	600
			Abnormal loss	400	2,900
	3,000	18,000		3,000	18,000

ABNORMAL LOSS ACCOUNT

	£		£
Process a/c	2,900	Scrap a/c	400
		P&L a/c	2,500
	2,900		2,900

SCRAP ACCOUNT

	£		£
Normal loss	600	Cash	1,000
Abnormal loss	400		
	1,000		1,000

Losses with a disposal cost

3.15 As well as being able to deal with questions in which scrap or loss units are worthless or have a scrap value, you must also be able to deal with losses which have a disposal cost.

3.16 The basic calculations required in such circumstances are as follows.

(a) Increase the process costs by the cost of disposing of the units of normal loss and use the resulting cost per unit to value good output and abnormal loss/gain.

(b) The normal loss is given no value in the process account.

(c) Include the disposal costs of normal loss on the debit side of the process account.

(d) Include the disposal costs of abnormal loss in the abnormal loss account and hence in the transfer of the cost of abnormal loss to the profit and loss account.

3.17 Suppose that input to a process was 1,000 units at a cost of £4,500. Normal loss is 10% and there are no opening and closing stocks. Actual output was 860 units and loss units had to be disposed of at a cost of £0.90 per unit.

Normal loss = 10% × 1,000 = 100 units

∴ Abnormal loss = 900 − 860 = 40 units

$$\text{Cost per unit} = \frac{£4,500 + (100 \times £0.90)}{900} = £5.10$$

3.18 The relevant accounts would be as follows.

PROCESS ACCOUNT

	Units	£		Units	£
Cost of input	1,000	4,500	Output	860	4,386
Disposal cost of			Normal loss	100	-
normal loss		90	Abnormal loss	40	204
	1,000	4,590		1,000	4,590

ABNORMAL LOSS ACCOUNT

	£		£
Process a/c	204	Profit and loss a/c	240
Disposal cost (40 × £0.90)	36		
	240		240

4   VALUING CLOSING WORK IN PROGRESS   5/95

4.1   Suppose that we have the following account for Process 2 for period 13.

PROCESS ACCOUNT

	Units	£			£
Transfers from process 1	500	10,000			
Materials	500	6,200	Finished goods	800	?
Labour and overhead		2,850	Closing WIP	200	?
	1,000	19,050		1,000	19,050

How do we value the finished goods and closing work in process?

4.2   With any form of process costing involving closing WIP, we have to apportion costs between output and closing WIP. To apportion costs 'fairly' we make use of the concept of *equivalent units of production*.

Equivalent units   5/98

4.3   Equivalent units are defined in the CIMA *Official Terminology* as follows: 'Notional whole units representing uncompleted work. Used to apportion costs between work in process and completed output'.

4.4   We will assume that in the example above the degree of completion is as follows.

   (a)   *Direct materials*. These are added in full at the start of processing, and so any closing WIP will have 100% of their direct material content. (This is not always the case in practice. Materials might be added gradually throughout the process, in which case closing stock will only be a certain percentage complete as to material content. We will look at this later in the chapter.)

   (b)   *Direct labour and production overhead* (also known as '*conversion costs*'). These are usually assumed to be incurred at an even rate through the production process, so that when we refer to a unit that is 50% complete, we mean that it is half complete for labour and overhead, although it might be 100% complete for materials.

4.5   Let us also assume that the closing WIP is 100% complete for materials and 25% complete for labour and overhead.

4.6   How would we now put a value to the finished output and the closing WIP?

In stage (a) of our framework, we have been told what output and losses are. However we also need to calculate *equivalent units*.

STATEMENT OF EQUIVALENT UNITS

		Materials		*Labour and overhead*	
	Total units	*Degree of completion*	*Equivalent units*	*Degree of completion*	*Equivalent units*
Finished output	800	100%	800	100%	800
Closing WIP	200	100%	200	25%	50
	1,000		1,000		850

4.7   In stage (b) the important figure is average cost per equivalent unit. This can be calculated as follows.

STATEMENT OF COSTS PER EQUIVALENT UNIT

	Materials	*Labour and overhead*
Costs incurred in the period	£6,200	£2,850
Equivalent units of work done	1,000	850
Cost per equivalent unit (approx)	£6.20	£3.3529

4.8   To calculate total costs for stage (c), we prepare a statement of evaluation to show how the costs should be apportioned between finished output and closing WIP.

STATEMENT OF EVALUATION

		Materials			*Labour and overheads*		
		Cost of			*Cost of*		
Item	*Equivalent units*	*equivalent units*	*Cost*	*Equivalent units*	*equivalent units*	*Cost*	*Total cost*
		£	£		£	£	£
Finished output	800	6.20	4,960	800	3.3529	2,682	7,642
Closing WIP	200	6.20	1,240	50	3.3529	168	1,408
	1,000		6,200	850		2,850	9,050

4.9   The process account (work in progress, or work in process account) would be shown as follows.

PROCESS ACCOUNT

	Units	£		Units	£
Materials	1,000	6,200	Finished goods	800	7,642
Labour overhead		2,850	Closing WIP	200	1,408
	1,000	9,050		1,000	9,050

4.10   In the next section we are going to be looking at how to value opening work in progress, for which there are two methods.

Exam focus point

In the May 1998 exam, a question on equivalent units used the terms 'material - equivalent units' and 'conversion - equivalent units'. Don't let this terminology confuse you: the figures required are the same as the ones calculated above.

---

5   VALUING OPENING WORK IN PROGRESS: FIFO METHOD

5.1   Opening work in progress is partly complete at the beginning of a period and is valued at the cost incurred to date. In our previous example, closing stock of 200 units at the end of period 13 would be carried forward as opening stock, value £1,408, at the beginning of period 14.

5.2   It therefore follows that the work required to complete units of opening stock is 100% minus the work done in the previous period. For example, if 100 units of opening stock are 70% complete at the beginning of June 19X2, the equivalent units of production would be as follows.

Equivalent units in previous period	(May 19X2) (70%)	=	70
Equivalent units to complete work in current period	(June 19X2) (30%)	=	30
Total work done			100

5.3   The FIFO method of valuation deals with production on a first in, first out basis. The assumption is that the first units completed in any period are the units of opening stock that were held at the beginning of the period. The characteristics of FIFO are best explained with an example.

Example: WIP and FIFO

5.4   Suppose that information relating to process 1 of a two-stage production process is as follows, for August 19X2.

Opening stock 500 units: degree of completion		60%
cost to date		£2,800

Costs incurred in August 19X2	£
Direct materials (2,500 units introduced)	13,200
Direct labour	6,600
Production overhead	6,600
	26,400

Closing stock 300 units: degree of completion	80%

There was no loss in the process.

Required

Prepare the process 1 account for August 19X2.

5.5   As the term implies, first in, first out means that in August 19X2 the first units completed were the units of opening stock.

Opening stocks:	work done to date =	60%
	plus work done in August 19X2 =	40%

The cost of the work done up to 1 August 19X2 is known to be £2,800, so that the cost of the units completed will be £2,800 plus the cost of completing the final 40% of the work on the units in August 19X2.

5.6   Once the opening stock has been completed, all other finished output in August 19X2 will be work started as well as finished in the month.

	Units
Total output in August 19X2 ★	2,700
Less opening stock, completed first	500
Work started and finished in August 19X2	2,200

(★ Opening stock plus units introduced minus closing stock = 500 + 2,500 – 300)

5.7   What we are doing here is taking the total output of 2,700 units, and saying that we must *divide* it into two parts as follows.

(a)   The opening stock, which was first in and so must be first out.
(b)   The rest of the units, which were 100% worked in the period.

Dividing finished output into two parts in this way is a necessary feature of the FIFO valuation method.

5.8   Continuing the example, closing stock of 300 units will be started in August 19X2, but not completed.

The total cost of output to process 2 during August 19X2 will be as follows.

		£
Opening stock	cost brought forward	2,800 (60%)
	plus cost incurred during August 19X2,	
	to complete	x (40%)
		2,800 + x
Fully worked 2,200 units		y
Total cost of output to process 2, FIFO basis		2,800 + x + y

Equivalent units will again be used as the basis for apportioning *costs incurred during August 19X2*. Be sure that you understand the treatment of 'opening stock units completed', and can relate the calculations to the principles of FIFO valuation.

(a) *Determine output and losses*

STATEMENT OF EQUIVALENT UNITS

	Total units		Equivalent units of production in August 19X2
Opening stock units completed	500	(40%)	200
Fully worked units	2,200	(100%)	2,200
Output to process 2	2,700		2,400
Closing WIP	300	(80%)	240
	3,000		2,640

(b) *Calculate cost per unit of output and losses*

STATEMENT OF COSTS PER EQUIVALENT UNIT

$$\frac{\text{Cost incurred}}{\text{equivalent units}} = \frac{£26,400}{2,640}$$

Cost per equivalent unit   =   £10

Note that costs incurred do *not* include the costs brought forward in opening WIP.

(c) *Calculate total costs of output, losses and WIP*

STATEMENT OF EVALUATION

	Equivalent units	Valuation £
Opening stock, work done in August 19X2	200	2,000
Fully worked units	2,200	22,000
Closing WIP	240	2,400
	2,640	26,400

The total value of the completed opening stock will be £2,800 (brought forward) plus £2,000 added in August before completion = £4,800.

(d) *Complete accounts*

PROCESS 1 ACCOUNT

	Units	£		Units	£
Opening stock	500	2,800	Output to process 2:		
Direct materials	2,500	13,200	Opening stock completed	500	4,800
Direct labour		6,600	Fully worked units	2,200	22,000
Production o'hd		6,600		2,700	26,800
			Closing WIP	300	2,400
	3,000	29,200		3,000	29,200

(e) Look back to the beginning of Paragraph 5.8. We now know that the value of x is £(4,800 – 2,800) = £2,000 and the value of y is £22,000.

Attempt the following exercise yourself before reading further.

Exercise 4

The following information relates to process 3 of a three-stage production process for the month of January 19X4.

Opening stock

300 units complete as to:		£
materials from process 2	100%	4,400
added materials	90%	1,150
labour	80%	540
production overhead	80%	810
		6,900

In January 19X4, a further 1,800 units were transferred from process 2 at a valuation of £27,000. Added materials amounted to £6,600 and direct labour to £3,270. Production overhead is absorbed at the rate of 150% of direct labour cost. Closing stock at 31 January 19X4 amounted to 450 units, complete as to:

process 2 materials	100%
added materials	60%
labour and overhead	50%

Required

Prepare the process 3 account for January 19X4 using FIFO valuation principles.

Solution

(a)   STATEMENT OF EQUIVALENT UNITS

	Total units	Process 2 materials	Added materials		Conversion costs
Opening stock	300	0	(10%)	30 (20%)	60
Fully worked units *	1,350	1,350		1,350	1,350
Output to finished goods	1,650	1,350		1,380	1,410
Closing stock	450	450	(60%)	270 (50%)	225
	2,100	1,800		1,650	1,635

* Transfers from process 2, minus closing stock.

(b)   STATEMENT OF COSTS PER EQUIVALENT UNIT

	Total cost £	Equivalent units	Cost per equivalent unit £
Process 2 materials	27,000	1,800	15.00
Added materials	6,600	1,650	4.00
Direct labour	3,270	1,635	2.00
Production overhead (150% of £3,270)	4,905	1,635	3.00
			24.00

(c)   STATEMENT OF EVALUATION

	Process 2 materials £		Additional materials £		Labour £		Overhead £	Total £
Opening stock cost b/f	4,400		1,150		540		810	6,900
Added in Jan 19X4	-	(30x£4)	120	(60x£2)	120	(60x£3)	180	420
	4,400		1,270		660		990	7,320
Fully worked units	20,250		5,400		2,700		4,050	32,400
Output to finished goods	24,650		6,670		3,360		5,040	39,720
Closing stock (450x£15)	6,750	(270x£4)	1,080	(225x£2)	450	(225x£3)	675	8,955
	31,400		7,750		3,810		5,715	48,675

(d)   PROCESS 3 ACCOUNT

	Units	£		Units	£
Opening stock b/f	300	6,900	Finished goods a/c	1,650	39,720
Process 2 a/c	1,800	27,000			
Stores a/c		6,600			
Wages a/c		3,270			
Production o'hd a/c		4,905	Closing stock c/f	450	8,955
	2,100	48,675		2,100	48,675

Previous process costs

5.9   A common mistake made by students is to forget to include the costs of the previous process as an input cost in a subsequent process when dealing with production that passes through a number of processes (such as in Paragraph 1.4).

5.10   Note that the costs of the previous process (Process 1 in Paragraph 1.4) are combined together into a single cost of input in Process 2 and that we always assume that the transfers into Process 2 are 100% complete with respect to Process 1 costs. The cost of any additional materials added in Process 2 is treated separately from Process 1 costs.

6   VALUING OPENING WORK IN PROGRESS: WEIGHTED AVERAGE COST METHOD

6.1   An alternative to FIFO is the weighted average cost method of stock valuation which calculates a weighted average cost of units produced from both opening stock and units introduced in the current period.

By this method no distinction is made between units of opening stock and new units introduced to the process during the accounting period. The cost of opening stock is added to costs incurred during the period, and completed units of opening stock are each given a value of one full equivalent unit of production.

Example: weighted average cost method

6.2   Magpie Ltd produces an item which is manufactured in two consecutive processes. Information relating to process 2 during September 19X3 is as follows.

Opening stock 800 units		
Degree of completion:		£
process 1 materials	100%	4,700
added materials	40%	600
conversion costs	30%	1,000
		6,300

During September 19X3, 3,000 units were transferred from process 1 at a valuation of £18,100. Added materials cost £9,600 and conversion costs were £11,800.

Closing stock at 30 September 19X3 amounted to 1,000 units which were 100% complete with respect to process 1 materials and 60% complete with respect to added materials. Conversion cost work was 40% complete.

Magpie Ltd uses a weighted average cost system for the valuation of output and closing stock.

Required

Prepare the process 2 account for September 19X3.

Solution

6.3   (a)   Opening stock units count as a full equivalent unit of production when the weighted average cost system is applied. Closing stock equivalent units are assessed in the usual way.

STATEMENT OF EQUIVALENT UNITS

	Total units		Process 1 material	Added material		Conversion costs
Opening stock	800	(100%)	800	800		800
Fully worked units *	2,000	(100%)	2,000	2,000		2,000
Output to finished goods	2,800		2,800	2,800		2,800
Closing stock	1,000	(100%)	1,000	(60%) 600	(40%)	400
	3,800		3,800	3,400		3,200

(* 3,000 units from process 1 minus closing stock of 1,000 units)

(b)   The cost of opening stock is added to costs incurred in September 19X3, and a cost per equivalent unit is then calculated.

STATEMENT OF COSTS PER EQUIVALENT UNIT

	Process 1 material £	Added materials £	Conversion costs £
Opening stock	4,700	600	1,000
Added in September 19X3	18,100	9,600	11,800
Total cost	22,800	10,200	12,800
Equivalent units	3,800 units	3,400 units	3,200 units
Cost per equivalent unit	£6	£3	£4

(c) STATEMENT OF EVALUATION

	Process 1 material £	Added materials £	Conversion costs £	Total cost £
Output to finished goods				
(2,800 units)	16,800	8,400	11,200	36,400
Closing stock	6,000	1,800	1,600	9,400
				45,800

(d) PROCESS 2 ACCOUNT

	Units	£		Units	£
Opening stock b/f	800	6,300	Finished goods a/c	2,800	36,400
Process 1 a/c	3,000	18,100			
Added materials		9,600			
Conversion costs		11,800	Closing stock c/f	1,000	9,400
	3,800	45,800		3,800	45,800

7   ACCOUNTING FOR BOTH CHANGES IN STOCK LEVELS AND LOSSES

7.1   The previous paragraphs have dealt separately with the following.

(a) The treatment of loss and scrap

(b) The use of equivalent units as a basis for apportioning costs between units of output and units of closing stock

We must now look at a situation where both problems occur together, that is there is opening and closing stock in process, and also losses occurring during the process. We shall begin with an example where loss has no scrap value.

7.2   The rules are as follows.

(a) Costs should be divided between finished output, closing stock and abnormal loss/gain using equivalent units as a basis of apportionment.

(b) Units of abnormal loss/gain are often taken to be one full equivalent unit each, and are valued on this basis.

(c) Abnormal loss units are an addition to the total equivalent units produced but abnormal gain units are subtracted in arriving at the total number of equivalent units produced.

(d) Units of normal loss are valued at zero equivalent units.

Example: changes in stock level and losses

7.3   The following data has been collected.

Opening stock	none
Input units	2,800 units
Cost of input	£16,695
Normal loss	10%; nil scrap value
Output to finished goods	2,000 units
Closing stock	450 units, 70% complete
Total loss	350 units

Required

Prepare the process account for the period.

Solution

7.4   (a)   STATEMENT OF EQUIVALENT UNITS

	Total units		Equivalent units of work done this period
Completely worked units	2,000	(× 100%)	2,000
Closing stock	450	(× 70%)	315
Normal loss	280		0
Abnormal loss	70	(× 100%)	70
	2,800		2,385

(b)   STATEMENT OF COST PER EQUIVALENT UNIT

$$\frac{\text{Costs incurred}}{\text{Equivalent units of work done}} = \frac{16,695}{2,385}$$

Cost per equivalent unit   =   £7

(c)   STATEMENT OF EVALUATION

	Equivalent units	£
Completely worked units	2,000	14,000
Closing stock	315	2,205
Abnormal loss	70	490
	2,385	16,695

(d)   PROCESS ACCOUNT

	Units	£		Units	£
Opening stock	-	-	Normal loss	280	0
Input costs	2,800	16,695	Finished goods a/c	2,000	14,000
			Abnormal loss a/c	70	490
			Closing stock c/d	450	2,205
	2,800	16,695		2,800	16,695

Example: more changes in stock level and losses

7.5   Consider the following information.

	Units	Degree of completion		Cost
		Materials	*Conversion cost*	*£*
Opening stock	700 units	100%	30%	6,400
Closing stock	300 units	100%	40%	
Costs of input:				
direct materials	4,000 units			£30,400
conversion costs				£16,440

Normal loss: 5% of input during the period
Output to next process: 4,300 units

Required

Prepare the process account for the period, using the FIFO method of valuation.

Solution

7.6 (a) (i) Total loss   =   opening stock plus input minus (output plus closing stock)

=   700 + 4,000 – (4,300 + 300)

=   100 units

Normal loss   =   200 units (5% of 4,000)

Abnormal gain =   100 units (200 –100)

Units of abnormal gain are subtracted in arriving at the total of equivalent units of production in the period.

(ii)   STATEMENT OF EQUIVALENT UNITS

	Total units		Materials		Equivalent units Conversion costs
Opening stock completed	700	(0%)	0	(70%)	490
Fully worked units	3,600		3,600		3,600
Output to next process	4,300		3,600		4,090
Normal loss	200		0		0
Closing stock	300	(100%)	300	(40%)	120
	4,800		3,900		4,210
Abnormal gain	(100)		(100)		(100)
Equivalent units	4,700		3,800		4,110

(b) STATEMENT OF COSTS PER EQUIVALENT UNIT

	Materials	Conversion costs
Costs incurred during the period	£30,400	£16,440
Equivalent units of production	3,800 units	4,110 units
Cost per equivalent unit	£8	£4

(c) STATEMENT OF EVALUATION

	Materials Units	£	Conversion costs Units	£	Total £
Opening stock b/f					6,400
Work this period	0	0	490	1,960	1,960
					8,360
Fully worked units	3,600	28,800	3,600	14,400	43,200
Closing stock	300	2,400	120	480	2,880
Abnormal gain	(100)	(800)	(100)	(400)	(1,200)
	3,800	30,400	4,110	16,440	53,240

(d)   PROCESS ACCOUNT

	Units	£		Units	£
Opening stock	700	6,400	Normal loss	200	0
Direct materials	4,000	30,400	Output to next process:		
Conversion costs		16,440	Opening stock completed	700	8,360
	4,700	53,240	Fully worked units	3,600	43,200
Abnormal gain	100	1,200	Closing stock	300	2,880
	4,800	54,440		4,800	54,440

Changes in stock levels, loss and scrap

7.7 When loss has a scrap value, the accounting procedures are the same as those previously described, and changes in stock levels during a period do not affect these procedures in any way. However, if the equivalent units are a different percentage (of the total units) for materials, labour and overhead, it is a convention that the scrap value of normal loss is deducted from the cost of materials before a cost per equivalent unit is calculated. This point will be illustrated in the following example.

Example: stock, loss and scrap

7.8 The following information relates to process 2 of a three-stage production process for period 8.

Material input from process 1	5,000 units at £1.85 per unit
Material added	£2,245
Labour	£4,320
Overhead	£3,090
Number of units scrapped	800 units

Opening stock was 600 units, complete as to:

		£
material from process 1	100%, cost	945
material added	60%, cost	180
labour	30%, cost	405
overhead	30%, cost	135
		1,665

Work in progress at period end 1,000 units
Complete as to:

material from process 1	100%
material added	75%
labour	40%
overhead	20%

Normal loss is taken as 10% of input during the period. Scrap value of any loss is 50p per unit.

Required

Prepare the process account and the abnormal loss account.

Solution

7.9 Normal loss is 10% of 5,000 units = 500 units. The normal loss on the opening stock of 600 units was accounted for in the previous period, period 7, and should not be calculated a second time in period 8.

(a) (i)

Input	Units	
Opening stock		600
Input materials		5,000
		5,600
Output		
Opening stock completed	600	
Normal loss	500	
Abnormal loss (800 – 500)	300	
Closing stock	1,000	
		2,400
Units started and finished in period 8		3,200

(ii) STATEMENT OF EQUIVALENT UNITS

		Equivalent units			
	Total units	*Process 1 material*	*Added material*	*Labour*	*Overhead*
Normal loss	500	0	0	0	0
Abnormal loss	300	300	300	300	300
Opening stock completed	600	0	240	420	420
Fully worked units	3,200	3,200	3,200	3,200	3,200
Closing stock	1,000	1,000	750	400	200
	5,600	4,500	4,490	4,320	4,120

(b)   STATEMENT OF COST PER EQUIVALENT UNIT

	Total £	Equivalent units	Cost per equivalent unit £
Item of cost			
Material from process 1	* 9,000	4,500	2.00
Added material	2,245	4,490	0.50
Labour	4,320	4,320	1.00
Overhead	3,090	4,120	0.75

* (5,000 units × £1.85 less scrap value of normal loss = £9,250 − £250 = £9,000)

It is a convention that the scrap value of normal loss should be deducted from the cost of materials and more specifically, where appropriate, from the cost of materials input from the previous process.

(c)   STATEMENT OF EVALUATION

	Opening stock completed £	Fully worked units £	Abnormal loss £	Closing stock £
Material from process 1 (at £2)	0	6,400	600	2,000
Added material (at £0.50)	120	1,600	150	375
Labour (at £1)	420	3,200	300	400
Overhead (at £0.75)	315	2,400	225	150
	855	13,600	1,275	2,925

The cost of work to complete the opening stock was £855 in period 8. Period 7 costs were £1,665. Total costs of these units were therefore £(855 + 1,665) = £2,520.

(d)   (i)   PROCESS 2 ACCOUNT - PERIOD 8

	Units	£		Units	£
Opening stock	600	1,665	Normal loss (scrap a/c)	500	250
Material from process 1	5,000	9,250	Abnormal loss a/c	300	1,275
Added materials		2,245	Process 3:		
Labour		4,320	Opening stock finished	600	2,520
Overhead		3,090	Other units	3,200	13,600
			Closing stock c/d	1,000	2,925
	5,600	20,570		5,600	20,570

(ii)   ABNORMAL LOSS ACCOUNT

	£		£
Process 2 a/c	1,275	Scrap a/c (300 units × 50p)	150
		Profit and loss account	1,125
	1,275		1,275

7.10   Where stocks are valued, not on a FIFO basis, but on a *weighted average basis*, the value of opening stock is added to the costs in period 8, and completed units of opening stock are each given a value of one full equivalent unit of production.

In the previous example, the cost per equivalent unit would have been as follows.

STATEMENT OF COST PER EQUIVALENT UNIT

	Process 1 material £	Added material £	Labour £	Overhead £
Period 8 costs	9,000(net)	2,245	4,320	3,090
Value of opening stock	945	180	405	135
	9,945	2,425	4,725	3,225
Equivalent units (opening stock finished = 600 equivalent units)	5,100	4,850	4,500	4,300
Costs per equivalent unit	£1.95	£0.50	£1.05	£0.75

Total cost per equivalent unit = £4.25

Evaluation would be as follows.

STATEMENT OF EVALUATION

			£
(a)	Output to finished goods	3,800 units × £4.25	16,150
(b)	Abnormal loss	300 units × £4.25	1,275
(c)	Closing stock	(1,000 × £1.95 plus 750 × £0.50 plus 400 × £1.05 plus 200 × £0.75)	2,895
			20,320

When the scrap value of normal loss is added (£250) the total values on the credit side of the process account will again be £20,570.

Which to use - FIFO or weighted average

7.11 FIFO stock valuation is more common than the weighted average method, and should be used unless an indication is given to the contrary. You may find that you are presented with limited information about the opening stock, which forces you to use either the FIFO or the weighted average method. The rules are as follows.

(a) If you are told the *degree of completion* of each element in opening stock, but not the value of each cost element, then you must use the FIFO method.

(b) If you are given the value of each cost element in opening stock, but not given the degree of completion of each cost element, then you must use the weighted average method.

8 IDENTIFICATION OF LOSSES/GAINS AT DIFFERENT STAGES IN THE PROCESS

8.1 In our previous examples, we have assumed that loss occurs at the completion of processing, so that units of abnormal loss or abnormal gain count as a full equivalent unit of production. It may be, however, that units are rejected as scrap or 'loss' at an inspection stage before the completion of processing. When this occurs, units of abnormal loss should count as a proportion of an equivalent unit, according to the volume of work done and materials added up to the point of inspection. An example may help as an illustration.

Example: incomplete rejected items

8.2 Koffee Ltd is a manufacturer of processed goods, and the following information relates to process 2 during September 19X2.

During the month 1,600 units were transferred from process 1, at a valuation of £10,000. Other costs in process 2 were as follows.

Added materials	£4,650
Labour and overhead	£2,920

Units are inspected in process 2 when added materials are 50% complete and conversion cost 30% complete. No losses are normally expected, but during September 19X2, actual loss at the inspection stage was 200 units, which were sold as scrap for £2 each.

The company uses a FIFO method of stock valuation.

Required

Prepare the process 2 account and abnormal loss account for September 19X2.

Solution

8.3   (a)   The equivalent units of work done this period are as follows.

STATEMENT OF EQUIVALENT UNITS

Item	Total units	Process 1 material	Equivalent units Added material	Conversion costs
Units from process 1	1,600			
Abnormal loss	(200)	200	(50%) 100	(30%) 60
Fully worked units, Sept 19X2	1,400	1,400	1,400	1,400
		1,600	1,500	1,460

(b)   STATEMENT OF COST PER EQUIVALENT UNIT

Costs incurred, Sept 19X2	£10,000	£4,650	£2,920
Equivalent units	1,600	1,500	1,460
Cost per equivalent unit	£6.25	£3.10	£2

(c)   STATEMENT OF EVALUATION

	Process 1 material £	Added material £	Conversion cost £	Total £
Fully worked units	8,750	4,340	2,800	15,890
Abnormal loss	1,250	310	120	1,680
	10,000	4,650	2,920	17,570

The only difference between this example and earlier examples is that abnormal loss has been valued at less than one equivalent unit, for added materials and conversion costs.

(d)   PROCESS 2 ACCOUNT

	Units	£		Units	£
Process 1 output	1,600	10,000	*Output*		
Added materials	-	4,650	Good units	1,400	15,890
Labour and overhead	-	2,920	Abnormal loss	200	1,680
	1,600	17,570		1,600	17,570

(e)   ABNORMAL LOSS ACCOUNT

	£		£
Process 2 account	1,680	Cash (sale of scrap)	400
		Profit and loss a/c	1,280
	1,680		1,680

9   OUTPUT COSTING

9.1   This method of costing is used by organisations who produce just one product in a single process. An example of such a process is a quarry from which just one product (chalk, slate and so on) is extracted.

9.2   It is a very simple method of costing. Since there is only one product and one cost centre there is no point in making complex calculations and the cost of a unit of production (perhaps a tonne of chalk) is therefore ascertained by collecting and analysing all the relevant costs and then dividing each cost by the total production to find the unit cost.

Exam focus point

Process costing seems to give students problems. The examiner actually described candidates' performance on the process costing question in the May 1995 exam as a disaster. So we make no apologies for covering all aspects of the subject in detail rather than assuming any prior knowledge. There are lots of exercises and examples in this chapter. Make sure you have worked through them carefully since question practice is the only way of learning how to apply the various rules to different situations.

Chapter roundup

- Process costing is based on a set of quite rigid rules which, once learnt, enable you to deal with any process costing situation. We have summarised these rules below.

- The four key stages of process costing are as follows.
  - o Determining output, losses and equivalent units
  - o Calculating cost per unit of output, losses and WIP
  - o Calculating total cost of output, losses and WIP
  - o Completing process accounts, and other relevant accounts

- Losses may occur in process. If a certain level of loss is expected, this is known as *normal loss*. If losses are greater than expected, the extra loss is *abnormal loss*. If losses are less than expected, the difference is known as *abnormal gain*.

- It is conventional for the scrap value of normal loss to be deducted from the cost of materials before a cost per equivalent unit is calculated. Units of normal loss are valued at their scrap value in the process account.

- Abnormal losses and gains never affect the cost of good units of production. The scrap value of abnormal losses is not credited to the process account, and abnormal loss and gain units carry the same full cost as a good unit of production.

- When units are partly completed at the end of a period (and hence there is closing work in progress), it is necessary to calculate the equivalent units of production in order to determine the cost of a completed unit.

- Account can be taken of opening work in progress using either the FIFO method or the weighted average cost method.
  - o The basic assumption of the FIFO method is that the first units completed in any period are the units of opening stock held at the beginning of the period.
  - o In the weighted average method, no distinction is made between units of opening stock and new units introduced to the process during the period. The cost of opening stock is added to costs incurred during the period, and units of opening stock are each given a value of one full equivalent unit of production.

- If there is opening and closing WIP, losses during the process and the loss has no scrap value the following rules should be followed.
  - o Costs should be divided between finished output, closing stock and abnormal loss/gain using equivalent units as a basis of apportionment.
  - o Units of abnormal loss/gain are often taken to be one full equivalent unit each, and are valued on this basis.
  - o Abnormal loss units are an addition to the total equivalent units produced but abnormal gain units are subtracted in arriving at the total number of equivalent units produced.

- When loss has a scrap value and the equivalent units are a different percentage (of the total units) for materials, labour and overhead, it is conventional that the scrap value of normal loss is deducted from the cost of materials before a cost per equivalent unit is calculated.

- If units are rejected as scrap or 'loss' at an inspection stage before the completion of processing, units of abnormal loss should count as a proportion of an equivalent unit, according to the volume of work done and materials added up to the point of inspection.

- Output costing is a simple form of process costing and is used by organisations which produce only one product in a single process.

- The next chapter will continue the study of process costing and it is vital that you are happy with everything covered in this chapter before you move on.

Test your knowledge

1 What is conversion cost? (see para 2.2)

2 Distinguish between the ways in which normal loss and abnormal loss are valued. (3.6, 3.7)

3 What is the normal method of dealing with the scrap value of abnormal loss or gain? (3.13)

4 What is an equivalent unit? (4.3)

5 What three 'statements' are usually prepared when answering a process costing question? (4.6-4.8)

6 Distinguish between the FIFO and weighted average cost methods of valuing opening WIP. (5.3,6.1)

7 What are the rules for dealing with situations in which there is opening and closing WIP and losses? (7.2)

8 Unless given an indication to the contrary, which method of valuing opening WIP should be used? (7.11)

9 How is a unit cost calculated in output costing? (9.2)

Now try illustrative question 10 at the end of the Study Text

Chapter 10

PROCESS COSTING, JOINT PRODUCTS AND BY-PRODUCTS

This chapter covers the following topics.

		Syllabus reference	*Ability required*
1	Contrasting joint products and by-products	6(a)	Skill
2	Problems in accounting for joint products	6(a)	Skill
3	Apportioning common costs to joint products	6(a)	Skill
4	Joint products in process accounts	6(a)	Skill
5	The further processing decision	6(a)	Skill
6	Costing by-products	6(a)	Skill
7	By-products, waste and evaporation losses	6(a)	Skill

Introduction

You should now be aware of the most simple and the more complex areas of process costing. In this chapter we are going to turn our attention to the methods of accounting for joint products and by-products which arise as a result of a continuous process. We encountered joint products and by-products very briefly in Paper 2 (you should have learnt what they are) but your study of the topic for Paper 6 goes a lot further.

We will begin by looking at why joint products warrant their own chapter (basically because of the difficulties inherent in costing them and because of what is known as the 'further processing decision'). We will then examine the ways in which both joint and by-products can be costed and look at how they are integrated into process accounting. We will also consider the further processing decision: should part-finished output be sold or processed further?

---

1   CONTRASTING JOINT PRODUCTS AND BY-PRODUCTS   5/98

1.1   *Joint products* are defined in CIMA *Official Terminology* as 'Two or more products separated in processing, each having a sufficiently high saleable value to merit recognition as a main product'.

1.2   Joint products are two or more products which are output from the same processing operation, but which are indistinguishable from each other (that is, they are the same commonly processed materials) up to their point of separation. Joint products have a substantial sales value (or a substantial sales value after further, separate processing has been carried out to make them ready for sale). Often they require further processing before they are ready for sale.

1.3   Joint products arise, for example, in the oil refining industry where diesel fuel, petrol, paraffin and lubricants are all produced from the same process.

1.4   A *by-product* is defined in CIMA *Official Terminology* as 'Output of some value produced incidentally in manufacturing something else (main product)'.

1.5   A by-product is a product which is similarly produced at the same time and from the same common process as the 'main product' or joint products. The distinguishing feature of a by-product is its relatively low sales value in comparison to the main product. In the timber industry, for example, by-products include sawdust, small offcuts and bark.

1.6   As indicated already, the difference between joint products and by-products is their relative sales value. But where is the dividing line? What exactly separates a joint product from a by-product?

The answer lies in management attitudes to their products, which in turn is reflected in the cost accounting system.

(a)   A *joint product* is regarded as an important saleable item, and so it should be separately costed. The profitability of each joint product should be assessed in the cost accounts.

(b)   A *by-product* is not important as a saleable item, and whatever revenue it earns is a 'bonus' for the organisation. It is not worth the trouble of measuring costs for by-products, because of their relative insignificance. It is therefore equally irrelevant to consider a by-product's profitability. The only question is how to account for the 'bonus' net revenue that a by-product earns.

2   PROBLEMS IN ACCOUNTING FOR JOINT PRODUCTS

2.1   Joint products are not separately identifiable until a certain stage is reached in the processing operations. This stage is the 'split-off point', sometimes referred to as the separation point. Costs incurred prior to this point of separation are *common* or *joint costs*, and these need to be allocated (apportioned) in some manner to each of the joint products. In the following sketched example, there are two different split-off points.

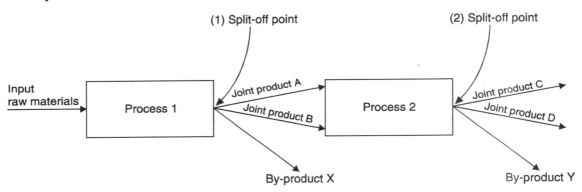

2.2   The special problems in accounting for joint products are basically of two different sorts.

(a)   How common costs should be apportioned between products, in order to put a value to closing stocks and to the cost of sale (and profit) for each product.

(b)   Whether it is more profitable to sell a joint product at one stage of processing, or to process the product further and sell it at a later stage.

We will return to the second problem in Section 6 of this chapter. Let us for now consider the first problem.

3   APPORTIONING COMMON COSTS TO JOINT PRODUCTS   *5/95, 11/97*

3.1   The problem of costing for joint products concerns *common costs*, that is those common processing costs shared between the units of eventual output up to their 'split-off point'. Some method needs to be devised for sharing the common costs between the individual joint products for the following reasons.

(a)   To put a value to closing stocks of each joint product.

(b)   To record the costs and therefore the profit from each joint product. This is of limited value however, because the costs and therefore profit from one joint product are influenced by the share of costs assigned to the other joint products. Management decisions would be based on the apparent relative profitability of the products which has arisen due to the arbitrary apportionment of the joint costs.

(c) Perhaps to assist in pricing decisions.

3.2 Here are some examples of the common costs problem.

(a) How to spread the common costs of oil refining between the joint products made (petrol, naphtha, kerosene and so on).

(b) How to spread the common costs of running the telephone network between telephone calls in peak rate times and cheap rate times, or between local calls and long-distance calls.

3.3 Various methods that might be used to establish a basis for apportioning or allocating common costs to each product are as follows.

(a) Physical measurement

(b) Relative sales value apportionment method 1; sales value at split-off point

(c) Relative sales value apportionment method 2; sales value of end product less further processing costs after split-off point

(d) A weighted average method

Exam focus point

Question 2 (a compulsory question) in the November 1997 exam covered almost all examinable aspects of process costing and joint and by-products, and offered six easy marks for explanation. You can find this question in the BPP *Practice & Revision Kit* for Paper 6.

Dealing with common costs: physical measurement

3.4 With physical measurement, the common cost is apportioned to the joint products on the basis of the proportion that the output of each product bears by weight or volume to the total output. An example of this would be the case where two products, product 1 and product 2, incur common costs to the point of separation of £3,000 and the output of each product is 600 tons and 1,200 tons respectively.

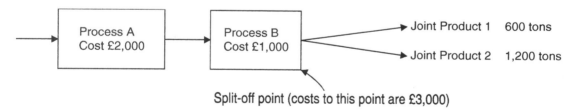

Product 1 sells for £4 per ton and product 2 for £2 per ton.

The division of the common costs (£3,000) between product 1 and product 2 could be based on the tonnage of output.

	Product 1		*Product 2*	*Total*
Output	600 tons	+	1,200 tons	1,800 tons
Proportion of common cost	$\dfrac{600}{1,800}$		$\dfrac{1,200}{1,800}$	
	£		£	£
Apportioned cost	1,000		2,000	3,000
Sales	2,400		2,400	4,800
Profit	1,400		400	1,800
Profit/sales ratio	58.3%		16.7%	37.5%

3.5 This method is unsuitable where the products separate during the processes into different states, for example where one product is a gas and another is a liquid. Furthermore, this method does not take into account the relative income-earning potentials of the individual products, with the result that one product might appear very profitable and another appear to be incurring losses.

Dealing with common costs: sales value at split-off point

3.6 With relative sales value apportionment of common cost, the cost is allocated according to the product's ability to produce income. This method is most widely used because the assumption that some profit margin should be attained for all products under normal marketing conditions is satisfied. The common cost is apportioned to each product in the proportion that the sales value of that product bears to the sales value of the total output from the particular processes concerned. Using the previous example where the sales price per unit is £4 for product 1 and £2 for product 2.

(a)	Common costs of processes to split-off point	£3,000
(b)	Sales value of product 1 at £4 per ton	£2,400
(c)	Sales value of product 2 at £2 per ton	£2,400

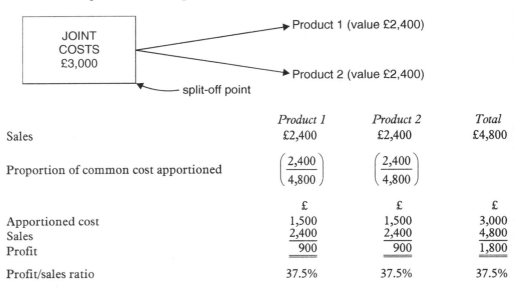

	Product 1	Product 2	Total
Sales	£2,400	£2,400	£4,800
Proportion of common cost apportioned	$\left(\frac{2,400}{4,800}\right)$	$\left(\frac{2,400}{4,800}\right)$	
	£	£	£
Apportioned cost	1,500	1,500	3,000
Sales	2,400	2,400	4,800
Profit	900	900	1,800
Profit/sales ratio	37.5%	37.5%	37.5%

3.7 A comparison of the gross profit margin resulting from the application of the above methods for allocating common costs will illustrate the greater acceptability of the relative sales value apportionment method. Physical measurement gives a higher profit margin to product 1, not necessarily because product 1 is highly profitable, but because it has been given a smaller share of common costs.

Dealing with common costs: sales value minus further processing costs

3.8 Joint products may have no known market value at the point of separation, because they need further separate processing to make them ready for sale. The allocation of common product costs should be done as follows.

(a) Ideally, by determining a relative sales value at the split off point for each product.

(b) If a relative sales value cannot be found, by taking the final sales value of the joint products, deducting further processing costs of each product from its sales value, and using the resulting residual sales value as a basis for allocation. This residual sales value is sometimes referred to as the notional or proxy sales value of a joint product.

Example: sales value minus further processing costs

3.9 JT Ltd has a factory where four products are originated in a common process.

During period 4, the costs of the common process were £16,000. Output was as follows.

	Units made	Units sold	Sales value per unit
Product P1	600		
Product Q1	400		
Product R	500	400	£7
Product S	600	450	£10

Products P1 and Q1 are further processed, separately, to make end-products P2 and Q2.

	Units processed	Units sold	Cost of further processing	Sales value per unit
Product P1/P2	600	600	£1,000	£10 (P2)
Product Q1/Q2	400	300	£2,500	£20 (Q2)

Required

Calculate the costs of each joint product and the profit from each of them in period 4. There were no opening stocks.

Solution

3.10 (a) It is helpful to begin a solution to joint product problems with a diagram of the process.

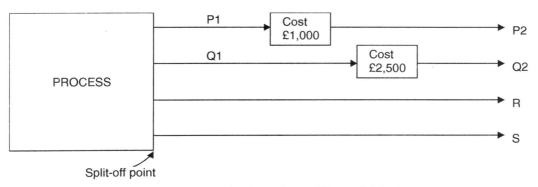

(b) Next we calculate the assumed sales values of P1 and Q1.

	P2 £	Q2 £
Sales value of production	6,000	8,000
Less further processing costs	1,000	2,500
Assumed sales value, P1, Q1	5,000 (P1)	5,500 (Q1)

(c) Now we can apply sales values to apportion common costs.

Joint product	Sales value of production £	%	Apportionment of common costs £
P1	5,000	25	4,000
Q1	5,500	27 1/2	4,400
R	3,500	17 1/2	2,800
S	6,000	30	4,800
	20,000	100	16,000

(d)   We can now draw up the profit statement.

	P1/2 £	Q1/2 £	R £	S £	Total £
Common costs	4,000	4,400	2,800	4,800	16,000
Further processing	1,000	2,500	-	-	3,500
Cost of production	5,000	6,900	2,800	4,800	19,500
Less closing stock	0	1,725	560	1,200	3,485
Cost of sales	5,000	5,175	2,240	3,600	16,015
Sales	6,000	6,000	2,800	4,500	19,300
Profit	1,000	825	560	900	3,285
Profit/sales ratio	17%	14%	20%	20%	17%

Exercise 1

Calculate the profit for the period and the value of closing stocks if common costs are apportioned using the units method.

Solution

Joint product	Units produced	%	Apportionment of common costs £
P1	600	28.6	4,576
Q1	400	19.0	3,040
R	500	23.8	3,808
S	600	28.6	4,576
	2,100	100.0	16,000

Profit statement

	P1/2 £	Q1/2 £	R £	S £	Total £
Common costs of production	4,576	3,040	3,808	4,576	16,000
Further processing	1,000	2,500	-	-	3,500
Cost of production	5,576	5,540	3,808	4,576	19,500
Less closing stock	0	1,385	762	1,144	3,291
Cost of sales	5,576	4,155	3,046	3,432	16,209
Sales	6,000	6,000	2,800	4,500	19,300
Profit/(loss)	424	1,845	(246)	1,068	3,091
Profit/sales ratio	7%	31%	-	24%	16%

Dealing with common costs: weighted average method

3.11   The weighted average method of common cost apportionment is a development of the units method of apportionment. Since units of joint product may not be comparable in physical resemblance or physical weight (they may be gases, liquids or solids) units of each joint product may be multiplied by a weighting factor, and 'weighted units' would provide a basis for apportioning the common costs.

Exam focus point

The examiner has confirmed that candidates should be able to use the weighting method of apportioning common costs to joint products.

Example: weighted average method

3.12   MG Ltd manufactures four products which emerge from a joint processing operation. In April 19X3, the costs of the joint production process were as follows.

	£
Direct materials	24,000
Direct labour	2,000
	26,000

Production overheads are added using an absorption rate of 400% of direct labour costs. Output from the process during April 19X3 was as follows.

Joint product	Output
D	600 litres
W	400 litres
F	400 kilograms
G	500 kilograms

Units of output of D, W, F and G and to be given weightings of 3, 5, 8 and 3 respectively for apportioning common costs.

Required

Apportion the joint costs.

Solution

3.13   Total costs are £26,000 for direct cost plus £8,000 overhead. The costs would be £34,000, apportioned as follows.

Joint product	Output Units	Weighting	Weighted units
D	600	3	1,800
E	400	5	2,000
F	400	8	3,200
G	500	3	1,500
			8,500

The costs are therefore apportioned at a rate of £34,000/8,500 = £4 per weighted unit.

Joint product	Apportionment of common cost £
D	7,200
E	8,000
F	12,800
G	6,000
	34,000

4   JOINT PRODUCTS IN PROCESS ACCOUNTS   5/95

4.1   The following example will illustrate how joint products are incorporated into process accounts.

Example: joint products and process accounts

4.2   Three joint products are manufactured in a common process, which consists of two consecutive stages. Output from process 1 is transferred to process 2, and output from process 2 consists of the three joint products, Alpha, Beta and Gamma. All joint products are sold as soon as they are produced.

Data for period 2 of 19X6 are as follows.

	Process 1	*Process 2*
Opening and closing stock	None	None
Direct material		
(30,000 units at £2 per unit)	£60,000	-
Conversion costs	£76,500	£226,200
Normal loss	10% of input	10% of input
Scrap value of normal loss	£0.50 per unit	£2 per unit
Output	26,000 units	10,000 units of Alpha
		7,000 units of Beta
		6,000 units of Gamma

Selling prices are £18 per unit of Alpha, £20 per unit of Beta and £30 per unit of Gamma.

Required

(a) Prepare the Process 1 account.
(b) Prepare the Process 2 account using the sales value method of apportionment.
(c) Prepare a profit statement for the joint products.

Solution

4.3 (a) *Process 1 equivalent units*

	Total units	*Equivalent units*
Output to process 2	26,000	26,000
Normal loss	3,000	0
Abnormal loss (balance)	1,000	1,000
	30,000	27,000

Costs of process 1

	£
Direct materials	60,000
Conversion costs	76,500
	136,500
Less scrap value of normal loss (3,000 × £0.50)	1,500
	135,000

Cost per equivalent unit $\dfrac{£135,000}{27,000} = £5$

PROCESS 1 ACCOUNT

	Units	£		Units	£
Direct materials	30,000	60,000	Output to process 2		
Conversion costs		76,500	(26,000 × £5)	26,000	130,000
			Normal loss (scrap value)	3,000	1,500
			Abnormal loss a/c	1,000	
			(1,000 × £5)		5,000
	30,000	136,500		30,000	136,500

(b) *Process 2 equivalent units*

	Total units	*Equivalent units*
Units of Alpha produced	10,000	10,000
Units of Beta produced	7,000	7,000
Units of Gamma produced	6,000	6,000
Normal loss (10% of 26,000)	2,600	0
Abnormal loss (balance)	400	400
	26,000	23,400

Costs of process 2

	£
Material costs - from process 1	130,000
Conversion costs	226,200
	356,200
Less scrap value of normal loss (2,600 × £2)	5,200
	351,000

Cost per equivalent unit $\dfrac{£351,000}{23,400} = £15$

Cost of good output $(10,000 + 7,000 + 6,000) = 23,000$ units $\times £15 = £345,000$

The sales value of joint products, and the apportionment of the output costs of £345,000, is as follows.

	Sales value		Costs (process 2)
	£	%	£
Alpha (10,000 × £18)	180,000	36	124,200
Beta (7,000 × £20)	140,000	28	96,600
Gamma (6,000 × £30)	180,000	36	124,200
	500,000	100	345,000

PROCESS 2 ACCOUNT

	£		£
Process 1 materials	130,000	Finished goods accounts	
Conversion costs	226,200	- Alpha	124,200
		- Beta	96,600
		- Gamma	124,200
		Normal loss (scrap value)	5,200
		Abnormal loss a/c	6,000
	356,200		356,200

(c)   PROFIT STATEMENT

	Alpha	Beta	Gamma
	£'000	£'000	£'000
Sales	180.0	140.0	180.0
Costs	124.2	96.6	124.2
Profit	55.8	43.4	55.8
Profit/ sales ratio	31%	31%	31%

Exercise 2

Prepare the Process 2 account and a profit statement for the joint products in the above example using the units basis of apportionment.

Solution

PROCESS 2 ACCOUNT

	£		£
Process 1 materials	130,000	Finished goods accounts	
Conversion costs	226,200	- Alpha (10,000 × £15)	150,000
		- Beta (7,000 × £15)	105,000
		- Gamma (6,000 × £15)	90,000
		Normal loss (scrap value)	5,200
		Abnormal loss a/c (400 × £15)	6,000
	356,200		356,200

PROFIT STATEMENT

	Alpha	Beta	Gamma
	£'000	£'000	£'000
Sales	180	140	180
Costs	150	105	90
Profit	30	35	90
Profit/ sales ratio	16.7%	25%	50%

---

5   THE FURTHER PROCESSING DECISION   *5/95*

5.1   It was stated earlier in Paragraph 2.2(b) that a different type of problem with joint products occurs when there is a choice between selling part-finished output or processing it further. This decision problem is best explained by a simple example.

Example: further processing

5.2   Alice Ltd manufactures two joint products, A and B. The costs of common processing are £15,000 per batch, and output per batch is 100 units of A and 150 units of B. The sales value of A at split-off point is £90 per unit, and the sales value of B is £60 per unit. An opportunity exists to process product A further, at an extra cost of £2,000 per batch, to produce product C. One unit of joint product A is sufficient to make one unit of C which has a sales value of £120 per unit.

Should the company sell product A, or should it process A and sell product C?

Solution

5.3

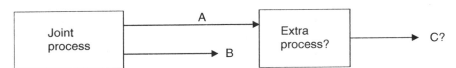

The problem is resolved on the basis that product C should be sold if the sales value of C minus its further processing costs exceeds the sales value of A.

	£
Sales value of C, per batch (100 × £120)	12,000
Sales value of A, per batch (100 × £90)	9,000
Incremental revenue from further processing	3,000
Further processing cost	2,000
Benefit from further processing in order to sell C	1,000 per batch

5.4   If the further processing cost had exceeded the incremental revenue from further processing, it would have been unprofitable to make and sell C. It is worth noting that the apportionment of joint processing costs between A and B is irrelevant to the decision, because the total extra profit from making C will be £1,000 per batch whichever method is used.

Exercise 3

PCC Ltd produces two joint products, Pee and Cee, from the same process. Joint processing costs of £150,000 are incurred up to split-off point, when 100,000 units of Pee and 50,000 units of Cee are produced. The selling prices at split-off point are £1.25 per unit for Pee and £2.00 per unit for Cee.

The units of Pee could be processed further to produce 60,000 units of a new chemical, Peeplus, but at an extra fixed cost of £20,000 and variable cost of 30p per unit of input. The selling price of Peeplus would be £3.25 per unit.

Required

Ascertain whether the company should sell Pee or Peeplus.

Solution

The only relevant costs/incomes are those which compare selling Pee against selling Peeplus. Every other cost is irrelevant: they will be incurred regardless of what the decision is.

	Pee			Peeplus
Selling price per unit	£1.25			£3.25
	£		£	£
Total sales	125,000			195,000
Post-separation processing costs	-	Fixed	20,000	
	-	Variable	30,000	50,000
Sales minus post-separation (further processing) costs	125,000			145,000

It is £20,000 more profitable to convert Pee into Peeplus.

6   COSTING BY-PRODUCTS   5/95

6.1   A by-product is a supplementary or secondary product (arising as the result of a process) whose value is small relative to that of the principal product. Nevertheless the by-product has some commercial value and its accounting treatment usually consists of one of the following.

(a)   Income (minus any post-separation further processing or selling costs) from the sale of the by-product may be added to sales of the main product, thereby increasing sales turnover for the period.

(b)   The sales of the by-product may be treated as a separate, incidental source of income against which are set only post-separation costs (if any) of the by-product. The revenue would be recorded in the profit and loss account as 'other income'.

(c)   The sales income of the by-product may be deducted from the cost of production or cost of sales of the main product.

(d)   The net realisable value of the by-product may be deducted from the cost of production of the main product. The net realisable value is the final saleable value of the by-product minus any post-separation costs. Any closing stock valuation of the main product or joint products would therefore be reduced.

The choice of method (a), (b), (c) or (d) will be influenced by the circumstances of production and ease of calculation, as much as by conceptual correctness. The method you are most likely to come across in examinations is method (d). An example will help to clarify the distinction between the different methods.

Example: methods of accounting for by-products

6.2   During November 19X3, Splatter Ltd recorded the following results.

Opening stock	main product P, nil
	by-product Z, nil
Cost of production	£120,000

Sales of the main product amounted to 90% of output during the period, and 10% of production was held as closing stock at 30 November.

Sales revenue from the main product during November 19X2 was £150,000.

A by-product Z is produced, and output had a net sales value of £1,000. Of this output, £700 was sold during the month, and £300 was still in stock at 30 November.

Required

Calculate the profit for November using the four methods of accounting for by-products.

Solution

6.3   The four methods of accounting for by-products are shown below.

(a)   *Income from by-product added to sales of the main product*

	£	£
Sales of main product (£150,000 + £700)		150,700
Opening stock	0	
Cost of production	120,000	
	120,000	
Less closing stock (10%)	12,000	
Cost of sales		108,000
Profit, main product		42,700

The closing stock of the by-product has no recorded value in the cost accounts.

(b) *By-product income treated as a separate source of income*

	£	£
Sales, main product		150,000
Opening stock	0	
Cost of production	120,000	
	120,000	
Closing stock (10%)	12,000	
Cost of sales, main product		108,000
Profit, main product		42,000
Other income		700
Total profit		42,700

The closing stock of the by-product again has no value in the cost accounts.

(c) *Sales income of the by-product deducted from the cost of production in the period*

	£	£
Sales, main product		150,000
Opening stock	0	
Cost of production (120,000 – 700)	119,300	
	119,300	
Less closing stock (10%)	11,930	
Cost of sales		107,370
Profit, main product		42,630

Although the profit is different from the figure in (a) and (b), the by-product closing stock again has no value.

(d) *Net realisable value of the by-product deducted from the cost of production in the period*

	£	£
Sales, main product		150,000
Opening stock	0	
Cost of production (120,000 – 1,000)	119,000	
	119,000	
Less closing stock (10%)	11,900	
Cost of sales		107,100
Profit, main product		42,900

As with the other three methods, closing stock of the by-product has no value in the books of accounting, but the value of the closing stock (£300) has been used to reduce the cost of production, and in this respect it has been allowed for in deriving the cost of sales and the profit for the period.

Exercise 4

Randolph Ltd manufactures two joint products, J and K, in a common process. A by-product X is also produced. Data for the month of December 19X2 were as follows.

Opening stocks	nil	
Costs of processing	direct materials	£25,500
	direct labour	£10,000

Production overheads are absorbed at the rate of 300% of direct labour costs.

		Production Units	Sales Units
Output and sales consisted of:	product J	8,000	7,000
	product K	8,000	6,000
	by-product X	1,000	1,000

The sales value per unit of J, K and X is £4, £6 and £0.50 respectively. The saleable value of the by-product is deducted from process costs before apportioning costs to each joint product. Costs of the common processing are apportioned between product J and product K on the basis of sales value of production.

Required

Calculate the profit for December 19X2. Analyse this profit by individual products.

Solution

The sales value of production was £80,000.

	£	
Product J (8,000 × £4)	32,000	(40%)
Product K (8,000 × £6)	48,000	(60%)
	80,000	

The costs of production were as follows.	£
Direct materials	25,500
Direct labour	10,000
Overhead (300% of £10,000)	30,000
	65,500
Less sales value of by-product (1,000 × 50p)	500
Net production costs	65,000

The profit statement would appear as follows (nil opening stocks).

		Product J		Product K	Total
		£		£	£
Production costs	(40%)	26,000	(60%)	39,000	65,000
Less closing stock	(1,000 units)	3,250	(2,000 units)	9,750	13,000
Cost of sales		22,750		29,250	52,000
Sales	(7,000 units)	28,000	(6,000 units)	36,000	64,000
Profit		5,250		6,750	12,000

7   BY-PRODUCTS, WASTE AND EVAPORATION LOSSES   *S/95, S/98*

7.1   Our final example shows how waste and losses can be incorporated into a question.

Example: waste and losses

7.2   The relevant data for process 3 of the manufacturing operations of Kie plc, a chemical company, in period 6 are as follows.

Opening and closing stocks	Nil
Materials transferred from process 2	20,000 litres at £5 per litre
Conversion costs	£67,000

Output

Finished production	12,500 litres
By-product	3,000 litres
Waste	2,500 litres

Wasted units are the same chemical as finished output, except that they have been polluted during the process. They must be disposed of at a cost of £2 per litre.

The by-product is packed at a further cost of £2 per litre. Its selling price is £3 per litre. The net realisable value of the by-product produced in a period is credited to the process 3 account during that period. During period 6, 2,000 litres of by-product were sold.

The normal output from the process per 1,000 litres of input is as follows.

Finished production	700 litres
By-product	150 litres
Waste	100 litres
Loss through evaporation	50 litres

Required

Prepare the process 3 account, the by-product account, the waste account and the abnormal loss/gain account for period 6.

Solution

7.3   There are two types of loss in this example: evaporation and waste. In each case it is necessary to distinguish between normal waste loss and normal evaporation loss on the one hand, and abnormal loss or gain on the other.

Another point to note about normal waste is that instead of having a scrap value to be credited to the process account, it has a disposal cost. The disposal cost of normal waste is *debited* to the process account.

(a)   *Equivalent units of production*

	Litres	Equivalent units
Finished output	12,500	12,500
By-product	3,000	0
Normal waste (20 × 100)	2,000	0
Abnormal waste (2,500 – 2,000)	500	500
Normal loss through evaporation (20 × 50)	1,000	0
Abnormal loss (balance)-evaporation	1,000	1,000
Total input units	20,000	14,000

(b)   *Costs of production*

	£
Materials from process 2	100,000
Conversion costs	67,000
Normal waste: disposal costs (2,000 × £2)	4,000
	171,000
Less net realisable value of by-product ★(3,000 litres × £1)	3,000
	168,000

★ Units sold are irrelevant, given the wording of the question.

(c)   *Cost per equivalent unit* = £168,000 ÷ 14,000 = £12

PROCESS 3 ACCOUNT

	£		£
Process 2 materials	100,000	By-product: net realisable value	3,000
Conversion costs	67,000	Finished production	
Normal waste disposal costs	4,000	(12,500 × £12)	150,000
		Abnormal loss - evaporation	
		(1,000 × £12)	12,000
		Abnormal loss - waste	
		(500 × £12)	6,000
	171,000		171,000

BY - PRODUCT ACCOUNT

	£		£
Cash or CLC		Cash or CLC	
(packing costs, 2,000 × £2)	4,000	(sales of 2,000 litres)	6,000
Process account		Closing stock (1,000 litres)	
(3,000 litres × £1)	3,000	(balancing figure)	1,000
	7,000		7,000

It is assumed that the unsold by-product has not yet been packed. (*Tutorial note.* The closing stock, if not yet packed, is valued at its net realisable value.)

NORMAL WASTE ACCOUNT

	£		£
Cash or CLC		Process 3 account	
(Disposal costs paid for)	4,000	(Disposal cost of normal waste)	4,000

Normal waste disposal costs are 2,000 litres × £2

ABNORMAL LOSS (WASTE) ACCOUNT

	£		£
Cash or CLC		Profit and loss account	7,000
(Disposal costs 500 litres × £2)	1,000		
Process a/c (abnormal loss of			
waste)	6,000		
	7,000		7,000

ABNORMAL LOSS (EVAPORATION) ACCOUNT

	£		£
Process account (1,000 × £12)	12,000	Profit and loss account	12,000

Chapter roundup

- Joint products are two or more products separated in a process, each of which has a significant value compared to the other. A by-product is an incidental product from a process which has an insignificant value compared to the main product(s).

- The point at which joint and by-products become separately identifiable is known as the split-off point or separation point. Costs incurred up to this point are called common costs or joint costs.

- There are four basic methods of apportioning common costs, each of which can produce significantly different results. These methods are as follows.

  o Physical measurement

  o Relative sales value apportionment method; sales value at split-off point

  o Relative sales value apportionment method; sales value of end product less further processing costs after split-off point

  o Weighted average method

- The relative sales value method is most widely used because (ignoring the effect of further processing costs) it assumes that all products achieve the same profit margin.

- The decision as to whether to process a product further is made by comparing the resulting increase in sales value with the costs incurred in further processing.

- The most common method of accounting for by-products is to deduct the net realisable value of the by-product from the cost of the main products.

Test your knowledge

1   What is the difference between a joint product and a by-product? (see paras 1.1, 1.4)

2   What is meant by the term 'split-off' point? (2.1)

3   Name three methods of apportioning common costs to joint products. (3.3)

4   How would you decide whether to process a product further or to sell it at the split-off point? (5.3)

5   Describe four methods of accounting for by-products. (6.1)

Now try illustrative questions 11 and 12 at the end of the Study Text

Chapter 11

SERVICE COSTING

This chapter covers the following topics.

		Syllabus reference	Ability required
1	Service industry costing	6(a)	Skill
2	Service department costing	6(a)	Skill
3	Job costing and services	6(a)	Skill

Introduction

At last! The final costing method! This chapter looks at service costing, which is concerned with establishing the costs, not of items of production, but of services rendered. It is used by organisations operating in a service industry that wish to cost their services, and by organisations wishing to establish the cost of services carried out by some of their own departments.

1   SERVICE INDUSTRY COSTING   11/95, 11/96

What are service organisations?

1.1   Service organisations do not make or sell tangible goods. Profit-seeking service organisations include accountancy firms, law firms, management consultants, transport companies, banks, insurance companies and hotels. Almost all non-profit-making organisations - hospitals, schools, libraries and so on - are also service organisations.

1.2   Service costing differs from the other costing methods (product costing methods) for a number of reasons.

(a)   With many services, the cost of direct materials consumed will be relatively small compared to the labour, direct expenses and overheads cost. In product costing the direct materials are often a greater proportion of the total cost.

(b)   The output of most service organisations is often intangible and hence difficult to define. A unit cost is therefore difficult to calculate.

(c)   The service industry includes such a wide range of organisations which provide such different services and have such different cost structures that costing will vary considerably from one to another.

Service/function costing is defined in CIMA *Official Terminology* as 'Cost accounting for services or functions, eg canteens, maintenance, personnel. These may be referred to as service centres, departments or functions'. Service costing is also known as operations costing.

1.3   Specific characteristics of services are *intangibility, simultaneity, perishability* and *heterogeneity.* Consider a haircut.

(a)   A haircut is *intangible* in itself, and the performance of the service comprises many other intangible factors, like the music in the salon, the personality of the hairdresser, the quality of the coffee.

(b) The production and consumption of a haircut are *simultaneous,* and therefore it cannot be inspected for quality in advance, nor can it be returned if it is not what was required.

(c) Haircuts are *perishable,* that is, they cannot be stored. You cannot buy them in bulk, and the hairdresser cannot do them in advance and keep them stocked away in case of heavy demand. The incidence of work in progress in service organisations is less frequent than in other types of organisation.

(d) A haircut is *heterogeneous* and so the exact service received will vary each time: not only will two hairdressers cut hair differently, but a hairdresser will not consistently deliver the same standard of haircut.

1.4   Tom Sheridan, in his article 'Costing in the service sector' (*Management Accounting*, May 1996) expands on these differences between service costing and product costing.

> 'Britain has a powerful service economy but nonetheless costing has only become a talking point in the service sector in the last decade. The service sector is wide-ranging. It not only covers a whole variety of business areas but also includes the head office administrative element of manufacturing companies...
>
> In theory costing should be easier in the service sector: there are no stocks or work-in-progress to be valued while, secondly, being a Johnny-come-lately in costing, it has been possible to ... take advantage of the new concepts ... Not a few new businesses in the service sector have been able to introduce ABC or incorporate ABC concepts, right from the start without going through the trauma and expense of dismantling their previous costing systems.
>
> But there are disadvantages too. The products are so subjective. Simultaneity and perishability are also key factors. One cannot build for stock. A lawyer without clients loses billable time for ever, a hotel with rooms unoccupied or an airline with seats unsold cannot recoup the costs after the event...
>
> If management's bottom-line objective is - as it usually is - cost management through cost understanding and traceability, the task is not made any easier because in most service industries one is dealing with intangibles. Everything is intangible. You cannot touch the product as you can in manufacturing. So, how do you measure it? How does one define a product or service? How does one cost IT? Everything seems to be an overhead and therefore, try as one will, one cannot get away from that bugbear of the management accountant's life - allocations ...
>
> A key to unravelling the complexities is to take an ABC approach ...'

Unit cost measures

1.5   We mentioned above that the output of most service organisations is difficult to define. This is a particular problem with service costing: the difficulty in defining a realistic cost unit that represents a suitable measure of the service provided. Frequently, a composite cost unit may be deemed more appropriate if the service is a function of two activity variables. Hotels, for example, may use the 'occupied bed-night' as an appropriate unit for cost ascertainment and control. You may remember that we discussed such cost units in Chapter 1.

1.6   Typical cost units used by companies operating in a service industry are shown below.

Service	*Cost unit*
Road, rail and air transport services	Passenger/mile or kilometre, ton/mile, tonne/kilometre
Hotels	Occupied bed-night
Education	Full-time student
Hospitals	Patient
Catering establishments	Meal served

1.7   Each organisation will need to ascertain the cost unit most appropriate to its activities. If a number of organisations within an industry use a common cost unit, valuable comparisons can be made between similar establishments. This is particularly applicable to hospitals, educational establishments and local authorities. Unit costs are also useful control measures as we shall see in the examples that follow.

1.8   Whatever cost unit is decided upon, the calculation of a cost per unit is as follows.

$$\text{Cost per unit} = \frac{\text{Total costs for period}}{\text{Number of service units in the period}}$$

1.9   The following examples will illustrate the principles involved in service industry costing and the further considerations to bear in mind when costing services.

Exam focus point

Service costing featured in full-length questions in the November 1995 and November 1996 exams. The November 1995 question provided a list of the costs a consultancy business had incurred in its first twelve months and asked students to calculate various rates such as an hourly rate for productive client work. The November 1996 question was about a hotel and asked students to allocate costs between different services (restaurant, bar etc) and calculate rates such as 'cost per guest-night'.

Example: costing an educational establishment

1.10   A university offers a range of degree courses. The university organisation structure consists of three faculties each with a number of teaching departments. In addition, there is a university administrative/management function and a central services function.

(a)   The following cost information is available for the year ended 30 June 19X3.

   (i)   *Occupancy costs*
   Total £1,500,000

   Such costs are apportioned on the basis of area used which is as follows.

	Square metres
Faculties	7,500
Teaching departments	20,000
Administration/management	7,000
Central services	3,000

   (ii)   *Administrative/management costs*
   Direct costs: £1,775,000
   Indirect costs: an apportionment of occupancy costs

   Direct and indirect costs are charged to degree courses on a percentage basis.

   (iii)   *Faculty costs*
   Direct costs: £700,000
   Indirect costs: an apportionment of occupancy costs and central service costs

   Direct and indirect costs are charged to teaching departments.

   (iv)   *Teaching departments*
   Direct costs: £5,525,000
   Indirect costs: an apportionment of occupancy costs and central service costs plus all faculty costs

   Direct and indirect costs are charged to degree courses on a percentage basis.

   (v)   *Central services*
   Direct costs: £1,000,000
   Indirect costs: an apportionment of occupancy costs

(b)   Direct and indirect costs of central services have, in previous years, been charged to users on a percentage basis. A study has now been completed which has estimated what user areas would have paid external suppliers for the same services on an individual basis. For the year ended 30 June 19X3, the apportionment of the central services cost is to be recalculated in a manner which recognises the cost savings achieved by using the central services facilities instead of using external service companies. This is to be done by apportioning the overall savings to user areas in proportion to their share of the estimated external costs.

The estimated external costs of service provision are as follows.	£'000
Faculties	240
Teaching departments	800
Degree courses:	
Business studies	32
Mechanical engineering	48
Catering studies	32
All other degrees	448
	1,600

(c) Additional data relating to the degree courses is as follows.

		Degree course	
	Business studies	*Mechanical engineering*	*Catering studies*
Number of graduates	80	50	120
Apportioned costs (as % of totals)			
Teaching departments	3.0%	2.5%	7%
Administration/management	2.5%	5.0%	4%

Central services are to be apportioned as detailed in (b) above.

The total number of undergraduates from the university in the year to 30 June 19X3 was 2,500.

Required

(a) Calculate the average cost per undergraduate for the year ended 30 June 19X3 and discuss the relevance of this information to the university management.

(b) Calculate the average cost per undergraduate for each of the degrees in business studies, mechanical engineering and catering studies, showing all relevant cost analysis.

(c) Suggest reasons for any differences in the average cost per undergraduate from one degree to another, and discuss briefly the usefulness of such information to the university management.

Solution

1.11 (a) The average cost per undergraduate is as follows.

	Total costs for university £'000
Occupancy	1,500
Admin/management	1,775
Faculty	700
Teaching departments	5,525
Central services	1,000
	10,500
Number of undergraduates	2,500
Average cost per undergraduate for year ended 30 June 19X3	£4,200

The average cost per undergraduate is not particularly relevant for the university management. It is a figure that can be monitored from year to year. If it becomes too high then control action needs to be taken to bring costs down.

(b) Average cost per undergraduate for each course is as follows.

	Business studies £	Mechanical engineering £	Catering studies £
Teaching department costs (W1 and using % in question)	241,590	201,325	563,710
Admin/management costs (W1 and using % in question)	51,375	102,750	82,200
Central services (W2)	22,400	33,600	22,400
	315,365	337,675	668,310
Number of undergraduates	80	50	120
Average cost per undergraduate for year ended 30 June 19X3	£3,942	£6,754	£5,569

Workings

1   Cost allocation and apportionment

Cost item	Basis of apportionment	Teaching departments £'000	Admin/ management £'000	Central services £'000	Faculties £'000
Direct costs	allocation	5,525	1,775	1,000	700
Occupancy costs	area used	800	280	120	300
Central services reapportioned	(W2)	560	-	(1,120)	168
Faculty costs reallocated	allocation	1,168	-	-	(1,168)
		8,053	2,055		

2   Apportioning savings to user areas on the basis given in the question gives the same result as apportioning internal costs in proportion to the external costs.

	External costs £'000	Apportionment of internal central service costs £'000
Faculties	240	168.0
Teaching	800	560.0
Degree courses:		
Business studies	32	22.4
Mechanical engineering	48	33.6
Catering studies	32	22.4
All other degrees	448	313.6
	1,600	1,120.0

(c) *Possible reasons for the differences in the average cost per undergraduate.*

(i)   Some of the courses may require lecturers of greater skill, who command higher rates of pay.

(ii)   Teaching methods may be different on the various courses. Some may be split into small groups, each needing a separate tutor. Others may be taught by one lecturer in a large group, or two or more lecturers simultaneously.

(iii) Teaching aids in use will vary from course to course. Both mechanical engineering and catering studies require specialist equipment.

(iv)   Some courses may take longer to complete than others.

(v)   Some courses may feature intensive one-to-one tuition as a matter of routine, whereas others will operate on the basis of seminars or lectures.

(vi)   Management and administration charges will vary from course to course. Catering studies is likely to require extensive space for kitchens.

(vii) The students for each course may be drawn from different years. The overall size of each year may be different.

Usefulness of the information

(i)   The information on the average cost per graduate from one degree to another is far more useful than that about the average cost per graduate for the year. Although there is little control information to be gained from comparing the average cost per graduate for one degree with that of another, the monitoring of the cost per graduate for each degree course on a year by year basis will prove useful. Such information will allow an assessment of how well the costs relating to particular disciplines are being controlled.

(ii)   Consideration should be given to the costs actually included in the analysis. The management should consider whether unavoidable costs (costs which would not be avoided if the degree course ceased) should be incorporated.

(iii) The information may prove more useful if it is used in conjunction with qualitative information such as pass rates and student satisfaction with the course.

Exercise 1

Briefly describe cost units that are appropriate to a transport business.

Solution

The cost unit is the basic measure of control in an organisation, used to monitor cost and activity levels. The cost unit selected must be measurable and appropriate for the type of cost and activity. Possible cost units which could be suggested are as follows.

Cost per kilometre

(a)   Variable cost per kilometre

(b)   Fixed cost per kilometre

      This is not particularly useful for control purposes because it will tend to vary with the kilometres run.

(c)   Total cost of each vehicle per kilometre

(d)   Maintenance cost of each vehicle per kilometre

Cost per tonne-kilometre

This can be more useful than a cost per kilometre for control purposes, because it combines the distance travelled and the load carried, both of which affect cost.

Cost per operating hour

Once again, many costs can be related to this cost unit, including the following.

(a)   Total cost of each vehicle per operating hour
(b)   Variable costs per operating hour
(c)   Fixed costs per operating hour

Exercise 2

Mary Manor Hotel has 80 rooms and these are all either double or twin-bedded rooms offered for either holiday accommodation or for private hire for conferences and company gatherings.

In addition the hotel has a recreation area offering swimming pool, sauna and so on. This area is for the use of all residents with some days being available for paying outside customers.

The restaurant is highly regarded and widely recommended. This is used by the guests and is also open to the general public.

Required

Discuss the possible features of an accounting information system that might be used in this organisation.

Solution

The accounting information system that might be used in this organisation would require the following features.

(a) The hotel should be divided into a number of responsibility centres, with one manager responsible for the performance of each centre. Examples of such centres could be rooms, recreation area and restaurant.

(b) The costing system must be capable of identifying the costs and revenues to be allocated to each responsibility centre.

(c) The system must also include a fair method of apportioning those costs and revenues which cannot be directly allocated to a specific centre.

(d) Each responsibility centre would have a detailed budget against which the actual results would be compared for management control purposes.

(e) The information system must be capable of providing rapid feedback of information to managers so that prompt control action can be taken where appropriate.

(f) Key control measures should also be used, perhaps with standard targets set in advance. Examples include the following.

    (i) Cost per bed per night
    (ii) Cost per sauna hour
    (iii) Cost per meal in the restaurant

These control measures would also provide the basic information from which a pricing decision can be made.

Charging customers for services

1.12 The procedure for charging customers for services is similar to that which applies in job costing. A mark up will be added to the cost per unit to give a selling price which will provide the required level of profit.

1.13 The choice of the cost unit by the organisation is important to ensure that an equitable charge is made to the users of the service.

1.14 Consider a transport company which has the choice between the following cost units.

(a) Cost per tonne
(b) Cost per kilometre
(c) Cost per tonne kilometre

1.15 The cost unit based on tonne kilometres will be by far the most equitable since it will take account of both the distance travelled and the tonnage carried.

2   SERVICE DEPARTMENT COSTING

2.1 Service department costing is used to establish a specific cost for an 'internal service' which is a service provided by one department for another, rather than sold externally to customers. Service departments therefore include canteens and data processing departments.

The purposes of service department costing

2.2 Service department costing will be a waste of time unless it has a purpose, and it has two basic purposes.

(a) *To control the costs and efficiency in the service department.*

If we establish a distribution cost per tonne/km, a canteen cost per employee, a maintenance cost per machine hour, job cost per repair, or a mainframe computer operating cost per hour, we can do the following in order to establish control measures.

(i)   Compare actual costs against a target or standard

(ii) Compare actual costs in the current period against actual costs in previous periods

(b) *To control the costs of the user departments, and prevent the unnecessary use of services.*

If the costs of services are charged to the user departments in such a way that the charges reflect the use actually made by each user department of the service department's services then the following will occur.

(i)   The overhead costs of user departments will be established more accurately. Some service department variable costs might be identified as costs which are directly attributable to the user department.

(ii) If the service department's charges for a user department are high, the user department might be encouraged to consider whether it is making an excessively costly and wasteful use of the service department's service.

(iii) The user department might decide that it can obtain a similar service at a lower cost from an external service company and so the service department will have priced itself out of the market. This is clearly not satisfactory from the point of view of the organisation as a whole.

2.3   Service costing also provides a *fairer basis* for charging service costs to user departments, instead of charging service costs as overheads on a broad direct labour hour basis, or similar arbitrary apportionment basis. This is because service costs are related more directly to *use*.

2.4   Two examples may be given.

(a) If repair costs in a factory are costed as jobs with each bit of repair work being given a job number and costed accordingly, repair costs can be charged to the departments on the basis of repair jobs actually undertaken, instead of on a more generalised basis, such as apportionment according to machine hour capacity in each department. Departments with high repair costs could then consider their high incidence of repairs, the age and reliability of their machines, or the skills of the machine operators.

(b) If mainframe computer costs are charged to a user department on the basis of a cost per hour, the user department would make the following assessment.

(i)   Whether it was getting good value from its use of the mainframe computer.

(ii) Whether it might be better to hire the service of a computer bureau, or perhaps install a stand-alone microcomputer system in the department.

The bases for charging service costs to user departments

2.5   The 'cost' of support services charged to user departments could be based on any of the following.

(a) No charge at all
(b) Total actual cost
(c) Standard absorption cost
(d) Variable cost
(e) Opportunity cost

No charge at all

2.6   If service costs are not charged directly to the user departments, they will be either:

(a) apportioned on a more arbitrary basis between production departments, in a system of absorption costing; or

(b) charged against profit as a period charge in a system of marginal costing,

without any attempt to recognise that some departments might be using services more than others.

Total actual cost

2.7   By this method, the total costs of the service department are accumulated over a period of time. No distinction is made between fixed and variable costs in the department.

The charge to the user departments will then be:

$$\frac{\text{Total actual cost}}{\text{Total activity (eg hours worked)}} \times \text{work done for user department}$$

2.8   For example, a distribution department might charge production departments for road haulage (carriage inwards). If actual distribution costs are £200,000 per month and 400,000 tonne/miles are delivered, the charge to the production departments would be £0.50 per tonne mile.

2.9   This method might be suitable in the following circumstances.

(a)   If it is difficult to separate fixed and variable costs
(b)   If it is difficult to establish standard costs

2.10   There are several problems with this method.

(a)   If actual service costs are charged to user departments, then user departments will be charged for any overspending and inefficiency in the service departments. The user departments 'suffer' from poor cost control in the service departments.

(b)   If the service department is not working at full capacity, the charge per unit of service would be higher than if the department is more busy. This might discourage user departments from using the service, to avoid high service charges.

(c)   The fluctuating charges which can result from the use of actual costs would make it difficult for the user departments to plan and control costs.

Standard absorption cost

2.11   By this method, the charge to user departments for support services is based on a standard, predetermined cost for the service. This service cost will consist of variable costs plus a share of fixed costs for the service department.

2.12   Standard cost has an advantage over actual cost. Standard cost is based on:

$$\frac{\text{Standard total costs}}{\text{Standard (budgeted) service activity}}$$

The user departments would therefore *not* be penalised for either of the following.

(a)   Overspending and inefficiency in the service departments
(b)   Under-capacity in the service department

2.13   There are, however, two problems with using standard absorption costs as a basis for charging for services.

(a)   It is necessary to review the standard cost regularly and frequently, so that user departments do not get a false impression of the cost of the service.

(b)   There is a problem in deciding what the standard activity level ought to be.

Variable cost

2.14   By this method of charging, support services are costed at marginal or variable cost only. This could be either standard or actual variable cost.

The advantage of this method is that user departments are charged for the extra costs incurred by using more of the service, which would help to provide better costing information within a system of marginal costing.

2.15 There are a number of weaknesses or problems with this system.

 (a) The user departments would be under a false impression as to the true full cost of the service that they are using, because they would be charged with just the marginal costs.

 (b) If actual variable costs are used, there would be no control of overspending and inefficiency in the service department because the service department would simply 'pass on' its overspending in higher charges to the user department.

 (c) If standard variable costs are used it will be necessary to revise the standard regularly.

Opportunity cost

2.16 This method would be appropriate where the service department is working at full capacity and is also providing services outside the company. This means that profit is forgone every time the service department provides a service internally, which should be reflected in an opportunity cost charge.

 The main problem associated with this method is that it is difficult to establish the opportunity cost.

Exercise 3

Identify three different reasons for the charging of service department costs to user departments and comment on the charging methods which may be relevant in the case of maintenance, computer services, and health, safety and welfare service departments.

Solution

Service department costs are charged to user departments for the following reasons.

 (a) User departments which use most of the services are made responsible for them.

 (b) Service costs are included in production costs, where appropriate. Overheads related to production are included in many stock valuations.

 (c) The 'true' cost of each user department is known to management.

 (d) User departments are encouraged to use the service (if they are being charged for it) as opposed to external contractors.

Maintenance might be easy to allocate, especially if machines are in definite locations, and there is a distinct chain of responsibility. Maintenance costs could be charged out in the budget as part of production overhead at a predetermined rate, or in an activity based costing system. This would be for budgetary purposes only. In practice, during the budget period, maintenance jobs could be charged out on an individual basis, directly to user departments.

Computer services cost could be charged on the basis of computer time for normal processing, and any computer projects which are directly attributable to user departments could be charged directly. Some estimate would be needed of any system enhancements required during the year.

Health, safety and welfare department's costs could be allocated to user departments on the basis of employee numbers in the case of nursing care, or floor space in the case of fire prevention equipment, alarm systems and so forth.

---

3 JOB COSTING AND SERVICES   *11/95*

3.1 Service costing is one of the subdivisions of continuous operation costing and as such should theoretically be applied when the services result from a sequence of continuous or repetitive operations or processes. Service costing is therefore ideal for catering establishments, road, rail and air transport services and hotels. However, just because an organisation provides a service, it does not mean that service costing should automatically be applied.

3.2   Remember that job costing applies where work is undertaken to customers' special requirements. An organisation may therefore be working in the service sector but may supply one-off services which meet particular customers' special requirements; in such a situation job costing may be more appropriate than service costing. For example, a consultancy business, although part of the service sector, could use job costing. Each job could be given a separate number. Time sheets could be used to record and analyse consultants' time, showing the time spent against each job number as well as, for example, travelling time and mileage. Other costs such as stationery could be charged direct to each job as necessary.

3.3   As we explained in Chapter 7, job costing can also be used for costing internal services.

Exam focus point

Job costing was the appropriate option to suggest and explain in the November 1995 question about how a firm of consultants should charge its clients. This is a good example of the need to avoid pigeon-holing your knowledge: service costing questions could also test you on, say, job costing (Chapter 7), or relevant costing (Chapter 12) and *vice versa*.

Chapter roundup

- Service costing can be used by companies operating in a service industry or by companies wishing to establish the cost of services carried out by some of their departments.

- Service costing for internal services adds to the administrative burdens of an organisation because it costs time and money. The benefits of the system should therefore exceed the costs of its operation.

- Not all service departments can be costed using the approach laid out in this chapter. For example, it would be difficult to work out a job cost or service unit cost for the accounting department, personnel department or general administration work at head office. These service costs would be charged as general overheads and then apportioned between user departments on a suitable basis.

- A problem faced in both service costing situations is the selection of an appropriate cost unit. The unit will often be a two-part one, such as the tonne/kilometre. Whatever cost unit is decided upon, the calculation of a cost per unit will be the total costs for the period divided by the number of service units in the period.

- Service costing differs from process costing in that it does not operate within rigid rules. You will therefore have to use your common sense in service cost analysis situations.

Test your knowledge

1   Suggest three reasons why service costing differs from other costing methods. (see para 1.2)

2   How is the cost per unit calculated? (1.8)

3   What are the two basic purposes of service department costing? (2.2)

4   List the five bases for charging service costs to user departments. (2.5)

5   Describe three weaknesses of using variable cost as a method of charging service department costs to user departments. (2.15)

Now try illustrative question 13 at the end of the Study Text

Part B
Information for decisions

Chapter 12

RELEVANT COSTING

This chapter covers the following topics.

		Syllabus reference	Ability required
1	Relevant and non-relevant costs	6(a),(b)	Skill
2	Some rules for identifying relevant costs	6(b)	Skill
3	The relevant cost of scarce resources	6(b)	Skill
4	Relevant costs and minimum pricing	6(b)	Skill
5	The assumptions in relevant costing	6(b)	Skill
6	Qualitative factors in decision making	6(b)	Skill

Introduction

This chapter heralds the beginning of the second part of this Study Text. The subject of this part is decision-making information and each of the four chapters will look at different aspects of the subject.

So what is a decision? Arising from the existence of a choice about what to do, a decision is the selection of the choice that seems best from those available. As a management accountant you may make decisions, but your principal role will be in providing management information. Your job is to present that information to the decision makers to help them to reach their decision, and to make recommendations and give advice and suggestions to the decision maker.

Decision-making information is unlike the accounting information recorded in the financial accounts and/or conventional cost accounts. Its provision relies on the application of the principles of marginal costing (which you covered in Chapter 5), a knowledge of cost behaviour (which was the topic of Chapter 2), and relevant costing, which is the subject of this chapter.

1 RELEVANT AND NON-RELEVANT COSTS

5/95, 11/97

Relevant costs

1.1 The costs which should be used for decision making are often referred to as *relevant costs*. In its *Official Terminology*, the CIMA defines relevant costs as 'Costs appropriate to a specific management decision'.

Exam focus point

Relevant costing appears to be one of the examiner's favourite topics and so, although it is in the syllabus for Paper 2, we will cover the basics again. The examiner commented in his report on the November 1995 exam that 'candidates' knowledge in this area was very superficial' so you would be well advised to work through this chapter very carefully.

1.2 A relevant cost is a future, incremental cash flow.

(a) Relevant costs are *future costs*.

(i)   A decision is about the future; it cannot alter what has been done already. A cost that has been incurred in the past is totally irrelevant to any decision that is being made 'now'.

(ii)   Costs that have been incurred include not only costs that have already been paid, but also costs that are the subject of legally binding contracts, even if payments due under the contract have not yet been made. (These are known as *committed costs*.)

(b) Relevant costs are *cash flows*.

(i)   It is assumed that decisions are taken which will maximise the 'satisfaction' of a company's owners, and although the time value of money affects the worth of cash flows from a project over a longer period, all short-run decisions are assumed to improve the owner's satisfaction if they increase net cash inflows.

> 'The decision rule will be to accept opportunities that increase the value of future cash resources and to reject those that decrease it.'   (Arnold)

(ii)   Only cash flow information is required.

This means that costs or charges which do not reflect additional cash spending should be ignored for the purpose of decision making. These include the following.

(1)   Depreciation, as a fixed overhead incurred.

(2)   Notional rent or interest, as a fixed overhead incurred.

(3)   All overheads absorbed. Fixed overhead absorption is always irrelevant since it is overheads to be incurred which affect decisions. (Confusingly, variable overhead costs are usually relevant because they should be incurred at the same rate that they are absorbed.)

(c) Relevant costs are *incremental costs*.

(i)   A relevant cost is one which arises as a direct consequence of a decision. Thus, only costs which will differ under some or all of the available opportunities should be considered; relevant costs are therefore sometimes referred to as incremental costs.

(ii)   For example, if an employee is expected to have no other work to do during the next week, but will be paid his basic wage (of, say, £100 per week) for attending work and doing nothing, his manager might decide to give him a job which earns only £40. The net gain is £40 and the £100 is irrelevant to the decision because although it is a future cash flow, it will be incurred anyway whether the employee is given work or not.

Differential costs, avoidable costs and opportunity costs   5/97

1.3   Other terms are used to describe relevant costs.

(a) *Differential costs* are relevant costs which are simply the additional costs incurred as a consequence of a decision. Sometimes the term 'differential costs' is used to compare the differences in cost between *two* alternative courses of action, while 'incremental costs' is used to state the relevant costs when *three or more* options are compared. The CIMA *Official Terminology* makes no distinction and defines both as 'The difference in total cost between alternatives; calculated to assist decision-making'.

(b) *Avoidable costs* is a term usually associated with shutdown or disinvestment decisions, but it can be applied to control decisions too. They are defined as 'The specific costs of an activity or sector of a business which would be avoided if that activity or sector did not exist' (CIMA *Official Terminology*).

(c) *Opportunity costs* (the benefit forgone by choosing one opportunity instead of the next best alternative) is another term for relevant costs. CIMA provide the following definition: 'The value of a benefit sacrificed when one course of action is chosen, in preference to an alternative course of action' (*Official Terminology*).

Exercise 1

An information technology consultancy firm has been asked to do an urgent job by a client, for which a price of £2,500 has been offered. The job would require the following.

(a) 30 hours' work from one member of staff, who is paid on an hourly basis, at a rate of £20 per hour, but who would normally be employed on work for clients where the charge-out rate is £45 per hour. No other member of staff is able to do the member of staff in question's work.

(b) The use of 5 hours of mainframe computer time, which the firm normally charges out to external users at a rate of £50 per hour. Mainframe computer time is currently used 24 hours a day, 7 days a week.

(c) Supplies and incidental expenses of £200.

Required

Calculate the opportunity cost of the job.

Solution

The opportunity cost of the job would be calculated as follows.

	£
Labour (30 hours × £45)	1,350
Computer time opportunity cost (5 hours × £50)	250
Supplies and expenses	200
	1,800

The opportunity cost of labour and computer time is the normal charge-out rate of £45 and £50 per hour respectively.

Non-relevant costs   *11/97*

1.4 A number of terms are used to describe costs that are *irrelevant* for decision making because they are either not future cash flows or they are costs which will be incurred anyway, regardless of the decision that is taken.

Sunk costs

1.5 A *sunk cost* ('A past cost not directly relevant in decision-making' (CIMA *Official Terminology*)) is used to describe the cost of an asset which has already been acquired and which can continue to serve its present purpose, but which has no significant realisable value and no income value from any other alternative purpose. Examples of sunk costs include the following.

(a) *Dedicated fixed assets.* Suppose a company purchased an item of computer equipment two years ago for £20,000. It has been depreciated to a net book value of £7,000 already, but in fact it already has no resale value because of developments in computer technology. The equipment can be used for its existing purpose for at least another year, but the company is considering whether or not to purchase more modern equipment with additional facilities and so scrap the existing equipment now.

In terms of decision making and relevant costs the existing equipment, which initially cost £20,000 but now has a net book value of £7,000, is a sunk cost. The money has been spent and the asset has no alternative use. 'Writing off' the asset and incurring a 'paper' loss on disposal of £7,000 would be irrelevant to the decision under consideration.

(b) *Development costs already incurred.* Suppose that a company has spent £250,000 in developing a new service for customers, but the marketing department's most recent findings are that the service might not gain customer acceptance and could be a commercial failure. The decision whether or not to abandon the development of the new service would have to be taken, but the £250,000 spent so far should be ignored by the decision makers because they are sunk costs.

Committed costs

1.6   A *committed cost* is a future cash outflow that will be incurred anyway, whatever decision is taken now about alternative opportunities. Committed costs may exist because of contracts already entered into by the organisation, which it cannot get out of.

Notional costs

1.7   A *notional cost* or *imputed cost* is a hypothetical accounting cost to reflect the use of a benefit for which no actual cash expense is incurred. Examples in cost accounting systems include the following.

(a)   Notional rent, such as that charged to a subsidiary, cost centre or profit centre of an organisation for the use of accommodation which the organisation owns.

(b)   Notional interest charges on capital employed, sometimes made against a profit centre or cost centre.

The CIMA *Official Terminology* definition is 'A cost used in product evaluation, decision-making and performance measurement to represent the cost of using resources which have no conventional 'actual cost'.

Historical costs

1.8   Although *historical costs* are irrelevant for decision making, historical cost data will often provide the best available basis for predicting *future* costs.

Fixed and variable costs   *11/95*

1.9   Unless you are given an indication to the contrary, you should assume the following.

(a)   Variable costs will be relevant costs.
(b)   Fixed costs are irrelevant to a decision.

This need not be the case, however, and you should analyse variable and fixed cost data carefully. Do not forget that 'fixed' costs may only be fixed in the short term.

Attributable costs

1.10   The concept of *attributable costs* was developed by Shillinglaw who argued that for many decisions, the assumption that fixed costs will remain unchanged is invalid. He distinguished between two types of fixed cost: divisible fixed costs and indivisible fixed costs.

'A fixed cost is 'divisible' if significant shifts in the volume of activity will require increases or permit decreases in the total amount of that cost. Thus, if a factory has 20 turret lathes, lathes depreciation is a divisible fixed cost. If it has one turret lathe, then depreciation is an indivisible fixed cost. It will be immediately apparent that this would be a reasonable definition of short-run variable costs if the word 'significant' were deleted. This is not accidental because a divisible fixed cost is variable with respect to volume if the volume increment is large enough and the time horizon is long enough.'

1.11   (a)   A divisible fixed cost is therefore a cost with a behaviour pattern which is a step cost.

(b)   The example of lathe depreciation is used to show the concept of divisibility, but for decision-making purposes, of course, depreciation cannot be a relevant cost. A similar argument, however, would apply to 20 employees in a factory who are each paid a fixed weekly wage, or fixed monthly salary.

1.12   Shillinglaw argued for the concept of *attributable cost*. 'Attributable cost is the cost per unit that could be avoided, on the average, if a product or function were discontinued entirely without changing the supporting organisation structure.' It should consist of the following.

(a) Short-run variable costs

(b) Divisible fixed costs

(c) Indivisible traceable costs (fixed costs which are indivisible, but which can be traced directly to the product or function, a departmental manager's salary being an indivisible traceable cost of the department because if the department were to shut down, the manager would no longer be required, or paid for)

Contribution theory

1.13 Contribution theory provides a basis for the provision of information for decision making. Managers who are making a decision should focus on those costs and revenues that will change as a result of the decision. Since fixed costs will often remain unaltered it is, as we have discussed, usually the variable costs that are the relevant costs. Revenues will also alter when activity levels change.

1.14 Contribution theory is based on marginal costing principles. Contribution is the difference between sales revenue and variable cost. By focusing on changes in contribution, managers can identify the net incremental effect of a particular decision. Allowance can then be made for any steps in fixed costs in order to appreciate the overall financial impact of the decision.

Direct and indirect costs

1.15 Direct and indirect costs may be relevant or non-relevant, depending on the situation in question. Direct labour, for example, may be paid regardless of whether or not a particular product is manufactured. On the other hand, additional direct labour may be required and the cost of this would be a relevant cost.

2   SOME RULES FOR IDENTIFYING RELEVANT COSTS

The relevant cost of materials   *5/95, 11/97*

2.1 The *relevant* cost of raw materials is generally their *current replacement cost.*

The exception to this rule occurs *if materials have already been purchased but will not be replaced.* The relevant cost of using them will then be the higher of the following.

(a) Their current resale value
(b) The value they would obtain if they were put to an alternative use

If the materials have no resale value and no other possible use, then the relevant cost of using them for the opportunity under consideration would be nil.

You should test your knowledge of the relevant cost of materials by attempting the following exercise.

Exercise 2

Darwin Ltd has been approached by a customer who would like a special job to be done for him, and who is willing to pay £22,000 for it. The job would require the following materials.

Material	Total units required	Units already in stock	Book value of units in stock £/unit	Realisable value £/unit	Replacement cost £/unit
A	1,000	0	-	-	6.00
B	1,000	600	2.00	2.50	5.00
C	1,000	700	3.00	2.50	4.00
D	200	200	4.00	6.00	9.00

Material B is used regularly by Darwin Ltd, and if units of B are required for this job, they would need to be replaced to meet other production demand.

Materials C and D are in stock as the result of previous over buying, and they have a restricted use. No other use could be found for material C, but the units of material D could be used in another job as substitute for 300 units of material E, which currently costs £5 per unit (and of which the company has no units in stock at the moment).

Required

Calculate the relevant costs of material for deciding whether or not to accept the contract.

Solution

(a) *Material A* is not yet owned. It would have to be bought in full at the replacement cost of £6 per unit.

(b) *Material B* is used regularly by the company. There are existing stocks (600 units) but if these are used on the contract under review a further 600 units would be bought to replace them. Relevant costs are therefore 1,000 units at the replacement cost of £5 per unit.

(c) 1,000 units of *material C* are needed and 700 are already in stock. If used for the contract, a further 300 units must be bought at £4 each. The existing stocks of 700 will not be replaced. If they are used for the contract, they could not be sold at £2.50 each. The realisable value of these 700 units is an opportunity cost of sales revenue forgone.

(d) The required units of *material D* are already in stock and will not be replaced. There is an opportunity cost of using D in the contract because there are alternative opportunities either to sell the existing stocks for £6 per unit (£1,200 in total) or avoid other purchases (of material E), which would cost 300 x £5 = £1,500. Since substitution for E is more beneficial, £1,500 is the opportunity cost.

(e) *Summary of relevant costs*

	£
Material A (1,000 × £6)	6,000
Material B (1,000 × £5)	5,000
Material C (300 × £4) plus (700 × £2.50)	2,950
Material D	1,500
Total	15,450

The relevant cost of using machines

2.2 Using machinery will involve some incremental costs, *user costs*. These include repair costs arising from use, hire charges and any fall in resale value of owned assets which results from their use. Depreciation is *not* a relevant cost.

Example: user costs

2.3 Sydney Ltd is considering whether to undertake some contract work for a customer. The machinery required for the contract would be as follows.

(a) A special cutting machine will have to be hired for three months for the work (the length of the contract). Hire charges for this machine are £75 per month, with a minimum hire charge of £300.

(b) All other machinery required in the production for the contract has already been purchased by the organisation on hire purchase terms. The monthly hire purchase payments for this machinery are £500. This consists of £450 for capital repayment and £50 as an interest charge. The last hire purchase payment is to be made in two months' time. The cash price of this machinery was £9,000 two years ago. It is being depreciated on a straight line basis at the rate of £200 per month. However, it still has a useful life which will enable it to be operated for another 36 months.

The machinery is highly specialised and is unlikely to be required for other, more profitable jobs over the period during which the contract work would be carried out. Although there is no immediate market for selling this machine, it is expected that a customer might be found in the future. It is further estimated that the machine would lose £200 in its eventual sale value if it is used for the contract work.

Required

Calculate the relevant cost of machinery for the contract.

Solution

2.4 (a) The cutting machine will incur an incremental cost of £300, the minimum hire charge.

(b) The historical cost of the other machinery is irrelevant as a past cost; depreciation is irrelevant as a non-cash cost; and future hire purchase repayments are irrelevant because they are committed costs. The only relevant cost is the loss of resale value of the machinery, estimated at £200 through use. This user cost will not arise until the machinery is eventually resold and the £200 should be discounted to allow for the time value of money. However, discounting is ignored here.

(c) *Summary of relevant costs*

	£
Incremental hire costs	300
User cost of other machinery	200
	500

Exercise 3

A machine which originally cost £12,000 has an estimated life of ten years and is depreciated at the rate of £1,200 a year. It has been unused for some time, however, as expected production orders did not materialise.

A special order has now been received which would require the use of the machine for two months.

The current net realisable value of the machine is £8,000. If it is used for the job, its value is expected to fall to £7,500. The net book value of the machine is £8,400.

Routine maintenance of the machine currently costs £40 a month. With use, the cost of maintenance and repairs would increase to £60 a month.

Required

Determine the cost of using the machine for the order.

Solution

	£
Loss in net realisable value of the machine through using it on the order £(8,000 – 7,500)	500
Costs in excess of existing routine maintenance costs £(120 – 80)	40
Total marginal user cost	540

The loss in net realisable value by using the machine is, strictly speaking, a little higher than £500. The £7,500 future realisable value should be discounted to a present value amount, and the loss in value through use would be the difference between £8,000 and this discounted amount.

Capital expenditure, depreciation and relevant costs

2.5 The historical cost of equipment that has already been purchased is not a relevant cost for decision-making; nor is depreciation. However when the equipment has not been purchased yet, and the decision would involve such a purchase, the situation is different.

2.6 The relevant cost of machinery whose purchase would be a consequence of a decision can be measured in either of two ways, both of which involve discounted cash flow (DCF) techniques, covered briefly in your earlier studies.

(a) The cost of the purchase can be treated as an initial cash outlay of an investment project at time 0 and the relevant costs and benefits of the decision can be assessed over the full life of the project.

(b)   Alternatively, the equipment cost can be converted into an annual charge, which incorporates both the capital cost and a notional interest charge over the expected life of the equipment.

2.7   Method (a) is the simple application of DCF principles to an investment appraisal situation. We will, however, have a look at method (b) here. Where a decision involves the purchase of a capital item, its relevant cost on an *annualised basis*, assuming a nil residual value at the end of the item's operational life, is as follows.

$$\frac{\text{Capital cost}}{\text{Annuity factor}}$$

The annuity factor is the DCF present value of £1 per annum for the life of the equipment at the appropriate cost of capital (interest rate). A table of these factors is at the end of this text.

Example: annualised relevant cost of a capital item

2.8   Timothy Ltd has to decide whether to appoint a new salesperson to its sales force. It has been estimated that the products that the appointee would sell earn a contribution equal to 30% of sales price.

The salary and direct running costs and expenses of the salesperson would total £30,000 a year. In addition, there would be associated capital equipment costs of £20,000. The equipment would have a life of four years and no residual value.

The equipment will be depreciated on a straight line basis over four years.

The company's cost of capital is 15%.

Required

Calculate the minimum extra annual sales revenue that a salesperson would have to achieve in the first year in order to justify the appointment (on a financial basis).

Solution

2.9   The depreciation charge should be ignored.

An annualised charge, which is stated in terms of £ at year 0 (that is, 'now'), for the equipment is as follows.

$$\frac{\text{Capital cost}}{\text{Annuity factor for 4 years at 15\%}} = \frac{£20,000}{2.855} = £7,005$$

This annualised charge for each of four years is a relevant cost which provides for both the purchase cost of the equipment and financing costs. It is now comparable (in time) with the £30,000 salary.

	£
Annualised cost of equipment	7,005
Other direct costs of salesperson	30,000
Annual contribution required to break even	37,005

Annual sales revenue required to break even = £37,005 $\times \dfrac{100}{30}$ = £123,350

3   THE RELEVANT COST OF SCARCE RESOURCES   *5/95, 11/97*

3.1   When a decision maker is faced with an opportunity which would call for the use of a scarce resource (a resource such as materials or labour which is in short supply), the total incremental cost of using the resource will be higher than the direct cash cost of purchasing it. This is because the resource could be used for other purposes, and so by using it in one way, the benefits obtainable from using it another way must be forgone.

3.2   A numerical example may help to clarify this point. Suppose that a customer has asked whether your company would be willing to undertake a contract for him. The work would involve the use of certain equipment for five hours and its running costs would be £2 per hour. However, your company faces heavy demand for usage of the equipment which earns a contribution of £7 per hour from this other work. If the contract is undertaken, some of this work would have to be forgone.

3.3   The contribution obtainable from putting the scarce resource to its alternative use is its opportunity cost (sometimes referred to as its 'internal' opportunity cost). Quite simply, since the equipment can earn £7 per hour in an alternative use, the contract under consideration should also be expected to earn at least the same amount. This can be accounted for by charging the £7 per hour as an opportunity cost to the contract and the total relevant cost of 5 hours of equipment time would be as follows.

	£
Running costs (5 × £2)	10
Internal opportunity cost (5 × £7)	35
Relevant cost	45

It is important to notice that the variable running costs of the equipment are included in the total relevant cost.

3.4   A rule for identifying the relevant cost of a scarce resource is that the *total relevant cost* of the resource consists of the following.

(a)   The *contribution/incremental profit forgone* from the next-best opportunity for using the scarce resource *and*

(b)   The *variable cost* of the scarce resource, that is, the cash expenditure to purchase the resource

3.5   Try to identify the relevant costs of labour and overheads in the following example.

Example: relevant costs of labour and variable overheads

3.6   Gloria Ltd has been offered £21,000 by a prospective customer to make some purpose-built equipment. The extra costs of the machine would be £3,000 for materials. There would also be a requirement for 2,000 labour hours. Labour wages are £4 per hour, variable overhead is £2 per hour and fixed overhead is absorbed at the rate of £4 per hour.

Labour, however, is in limited supply, and if the job is accepted, men would have to be diverted from other work which is expected to earn a contribution of £5 per hour towards fixed overheads and profit.

Required

Assess whether the contract should be undertaken.

Solution

3.7   The relevant costs of the scarce resource, labour, are the sum of the following.

(a)   The variable costs of the labour and associated variable overheads
(b)   The contribution forgone from not being able to put it to its alternative use

Fixed costs are ignored because there is no incremental fixed cost expenditure.

		£
Materials		3,000
Labour (2,000 hours at £4 per hour)		8,000
Variable overhead (2,000 hours at £2 per hour)		4,000
		15,000
Opportunity cost:		
Contribution forgone from other work (2,000 hours × £5 per hour)		10,000
Total costs		25,000
Revenue		21,000
Net loss on contract		(4,000)

The contract should not be undertaken.

3.8   It is worth thinking carefully about labour costs. The labour force will be paid £8,000 for 2,000 hours work, and variable overheads of £4,000 will be incurred no matter whether the men are employed on the new job or on other work. Relevant costs are future cash flows arising as a direct consequence of a decision, and the decision here will not affect the total wages paid. If this money is going to be spent anyway, should it not therefore be ignored as an irrelevant cost?

3.9   The answer to this crucial question is 'no'. The labour wages and variable overheads are relevant costs even though they will be incurred whatever happens. The reason for this is that the other work earns a contribution of £5 per hour *after having covered* labour and variable overhead costs. Work on the purpose-built equipment ought therefore to do at least the same.

3.10 If we can suppose that the other work costs, say, £1 per hour in materials, the contribution of £5 per hour would mean that this other work earned £5 contribution after covering the variable costs of materials (£1), labour (£4) and variable overheads (£2) so that revenue would be £12 per hour worked.

	£	£
(Hypothetical) revenue per hour		12
(Hypothetical) materials cost per hour	1	
Labour cost per hour	4	
Variable overhead cost per hour	2	
Variable costs per hour in total		7
Contribution per hour		5

(a)   In the 2,000 hours of labour time we are thinking of diverting to the purpose-built equipment, the contribution forgone from other work would be £10,000 after covering labour and variable overhead costs, as follows.

	£	£
Revenue (2,000 × £12)		24,000
Variable costs:		
Materials (2,000 × £1)	2,000	
Labour (2,000 × £4)	8,000	
Variable overhead (2,000 × £2)	4,000	
		14,000
Contribution		10,000

(b)   In 2,000 hours on the other contract, to make the purpose-built equipment, contribution measured in similar terms would be calculated as follows.

	£	£
Contract revenue		21,000
Variable costs:		
Materials	3,000	
Labour	8,000	
Variable overhead	4,000	
		15,000
Contribution		6,000

(c)   Since the other work earns a great contribution by £4,000, it is more profitable. The option to make the purpose-built equipment should be rejected.

4   RELEVANT COSTS AND MINIMUM PRICING   *5/95*

4.1   The minimum price for a one-off product or service contract is its total relevant costs: this is the price at which the company would make no incremental profit and no incremental loss from undertaking the work, but would just achieve an incremental cost breakeven point. The following example will illustrate the technique.

Exam focus point

There was a minimum pricing problem in the May 1995 exam. Candidates were asked to prepare a cost estimate using an opportunity cost approach and suggest the minimum price that should be quoted. In particular, candidates were asked to *give reasons* for their valuation of items in the estimate, once again emphasising the crucial need to understand and be able to explain the theory *in words* as well as numbers.

Example: relevant costs and minimum price

4.2   Minimax Ltd has just completed production of an item of special equipment for a customer, only to be notified that this customer has now gone into liquidation.

After much effort, the sales manager has been able to interest a potential buyer who might buy the machine if certain conversion work could first be carried out.

(a)   The sales price of the machine to the original buyer had been fixed at £138,600 and had included an estimated normal profit mark-up of 10% on total costs. The costs incurred in the manufacture of the machine were as follows.

	£
Direct materials	49,000
Direct labour	36,000
Variable overhead	9,000
Fixed production overhead	24,000
Fixed sales and distribution overhead	8,000
	126,000

(b)   If the machine is converted, the production manager estimates that the cost of the extra work required would be as follows.

Direct materials (at cost) £9,600
Direct labour
  Department X: 6 workers for 4 weeks at £210 per worker per week
  Department Y: 2 workers for 4 weeks at £160 per worker per week

(c)   Variable overhead would be 20% of direct labour cost, and fixed production overhead would be absorbed as follows.

Department X: 83.33% of direct labour cost
Department Y: 25% of direct labour cost

(d)   Additional information is available as follows.

(i)   In the original machine, there are three types of material.

(1)   Type A could be sold for scrap for £8,000.

(2)   Type B could be sold for scrap for £2,400 but it would take 120 hours of casual labour paid at £3.50 per hour to put it into a condition in which it would be suitable for sale.

(3)   Type C would need to be scrapped, at a cost to Minimax Ltd of £1,100.

(ii)   The direct materials required for the conversion are already in stock. If not needed for the conversion they would be used in the production of another machine in place of materials that would otherwise need to be purchased, and that would currently cost £8,800.

(iii)   The conversion work would be carried out in two departments, X and Y. Department X is currently extremely busy and working at full capacity; it is estimated that its contribution to fixed overhead and profits is £2.50 per £1 of labour.

Department Y, on the other hand, is short of work but for organisational reasons its labour force, which at the moment has a workload of only 40% of its standard capacity, cannot be reduced below its current level of eight employees, all of whom are paid a wage of £160 per week.

(iv) The designs and specifications of the original machine could be sold to an overseas customer for £4,500 if the machine is scrapped.

(v) If conversion work is undertaken, a temporary supervisor would need to be employed for four weeks at a total cost of £1,500. It is normal company practice to charge supervision costs to fixed overhead.

(vi) The original customer has already paid a non-returnable deposit to Minimax Ltd of 12.5% of the selling price.

Required

Calculate the minimum price that Minimax Ltd should accept from the new customer for the converted machine. Explain clearly how you have reached this figure.

Solution

4.3 The minimum price is the price which reflects the relevant costs (opportunity costs) of the work. These are established as follows.

(a) Past costs are not relevant, and the £126,000 of cost incurred should be excluded from the minimum price calculation. It is necessary, however, to consider the alternative use of the direct materials which would be forgone if the conversion work is carried out.

	£
Type A	
Revenue from sales as scrap (note (i))	8,000
Type B	
Revenue from sales as scrap,	
minus the additional cash costs necessary to	
prepare it for sale (£2,400 – (120 × £3.50)) (note (i))	1,980
Type C	
Cost of disposal if the machine is not converted	
(a negative opportunity cost) (note (ii))	(1,100)
Total opportunity cost of materials types A, B and C	8,880

By agreeing to the conversion of the machine, Minimax Ltd would therefore lose a net revenue of £8,880 from the alternative use of these materials.

Notes

(i) Scrap sales would be lost if the conversion work goes ahead.
(ii) These costs would be incurred unless the work goes ahead.

(b) The cost of additional direct materials for conversion is £9,600, but this is an historical cost. The relevant cost of these materials is the £8,800 which would be spent on new purchases if the conversion is carried out. If the conversion work goes ahead, the materials in stock would be unavailable for production of the other machine mentioned in item (d)(ii) of the question and so the extra purchases of £8,800 would then be needed.

(c) Direct labour in departments X and Y is a fixed cost and the labour force will be paid regardless of the work they do or do not do. The cost of labour for conversion in department Y is not a relevant cost because the work could be done without any extra cost to the company.

In department X, however, acceptance of the conversion work would oblige the company to divert production from other profitable jobs. The minimum contribution required from using department X labour must be sufficient to cover the cost of the labour and variable overheads and then make an additional £2.50 in contribution per direct labour hour.

Department X: costs for direct labour hours spent on conversion

6 workers × 4 weeks × £210 =	£5,040
Variable overhead cost £5,040 × 20% =	£1,008
Contribution forgone by diverting labour from other work £2.50 per £1 of labour cost = £5,040 × 250% =	£12,600

(d) Variable overheads in department Y are relevant costs because they will only be incurred if production work is carried out. (It is assumed that if the workforce is idle, no variable overheads would be incurred.)

Department Y   20% of (2 workers × 4 weeks × £160) = £256

(e) If the machine is converted, the company cannot sell the designs and specifications to the overseas company. £4,500 is a relevant (opportunity) cost of accepting the conversion order.

(f) Fixed overheads, being mainly unchanged regardless of what the company decides to do, should be ignored because they are not relevant (incremental) costs. The additional cost of supervision should, however, be included as a relevant cost of the order because the £1,500 will not be spent unless the conversion work is done.

(g) The non-refundable deposit received should be ignored and should not be deducted in the calculation of the minimum price. Just as costs incurred in the past are not relevant to a current decision about what to do in the future, revenues collected in the past are also irrelevant.

4.4   Estimate of minimum price for the converted machine

	£	£
Opportunity cost of using the direct materials		
types A, B and C		8,880
Opportunity cost of additional materials for conversion		8,800
Opportunity cost of work in department X		
Labour	5,040	
Variable overhead	1,008	
Contribution forgone	12,600	
		18,648
Opportunity cost: sale of designs and specifications		4,500
Incremental costs:		
Variable production overheads in department Y		256
Fixed production overheads (additional supervision)		1,500
Minimum price		42,584

5   THE ASSUMPTIONS IN RELEVANT COSTING

5.1   Relevant costs are future costs. Whenever anyone tries to predict what will happen in the future, the predictions could well be wrong. Cost accountants have to make the best forecasts of relevant income and costs that they can, and at the same time recognise the assumptions on which their estimates are based. A variety of assumptions will be made, and you ought to be aware of them.

Exam focus point

In particular, if you make an assumption in answering an examination question and you are not sure that the examiner or marker will appreciate or recognise the assumption you are making, you should explain it in narrative in your solution.

5.2   Some of the assumptions that are typically made in relevant costing are as follows.

(a) *Cost behaviour patterns* are *known*; if a department closes down, for example, the attributable fixed cost savings would be known.

Similarly, if a factory increases its capacity significantly, any change in fixed cost expenditure or in the variable cost per unit would also be known. This is not necessarily so, and it is always important to question assumptions of this nature. Thus, if you are told in an examination question that a factory intends to increase production by 50%, and you are invited to assume in your number work that fixed costs and unit variable costs would be unaffected, it is important to challenge this assumption as a footnote to your solution, making the following points.

(i)   Is it clear that the factory could handle such a large increase in output?

(ii)   If so, fixed costs would probably change dramatically, and there might also be a shift in unit variable costs.

(b)   The *amount of fixed costs, unit variable costs, sales price and sales demand are known with certainty*. However, it is possible to apply risk and uncertainty analysis to decisions and so recognise that what will happen in the future is not certain. You will cover such techniques in your later studies.

(c)   *The objective of decision making in the short run is to maximise 'satisfaction'*, which is often regarded as 'short-term profit'. However, there are many qualitative factors or financial considerations, other than those of profit, which may influence a final decision: again a footnote may be called for.

(d)   *The information on which a decision is based is complete and reliable.*

6   QUALITATIVE FACTORS IN DECISION MAKING

6.1   Qualitative factors in decision making are factors which might influence the eventual decisions but which have not been quantified in terms of relevant income or costs. They may stem from two sources.

(a)   Non-financial objectives

(b)   Factors which might be quantifiable in money terms, but which have not been quantified, perhaps because there is insufficient information to make reliable estimates

Examples of qualitative factors

6.2   Qualitative factors in decision making will vary with the circumstances and nature of the opportunity being considered. Here are some examples.

(a)   The *availability of cash*. An opportunity may be profitable, but there must be sufficient cash to finance any purchases of equipment and build-up of working capital. If cash is not available, new sources of funds (for example an overdraft or loan) must be sought.

(b)   *Inflation*. The effect of inflation on the prices of various items may need to be considered, especially where a fixed price contract is involved in the decision: if the income from an opportunity is fixed by contract, but the costs might increase with inflation, the contract's profitability would be over-stated unless inflation is taken into account.

(c)   *Employees*. Any decision involving the shutdown of a plant, creation of a new work shift, or changes in work procedures or location will require acceptance by employees, and ought to have regard to employee welfare.

(d)   *Customers*. Decisions about new products or product closures, the quality of output or after-sales service will inevitably affect customer loyalty and customer demand. It is also important to remember that a decision involving one product may have repercussions on customer attitudes towards a range of products. For example, a company which sells a range of garden tools and equipment under a single brand name should consider the effects on demand for the entire brand range if one product (for example a garden rake) is deleted, or a new product of poor quality is added.

(e) *Competitors*. In a competitive market, some decisions may stimulate a response from rival companies. For example, the decision to reduce selling prices in order to raise demand may not be successful if all competitors take similar action.

(f) *Timing factors*

    (i) There might be a choice in deciding when to take up an opportunity. The choice would not be 'accept or reject'; there would be three choices.

        (1) Accept an opportunity now.
        (2) Do not accept the opportunity now, but wait before doing so.
        (3) Reject the opportunity.

    (ii) There might also be choice about the following.

        (1) If a department is shut down, will the closure be permanent, or temporary? Temporary closure may be a viable proposition during a period of slack demand.

        (2) If a decision is taken to sell goods at a low price where the contribution earned will be relatively small, it is important to consider the duration of the low price promotion. If it is a long-term feature of selling, and if demand for the product increases, the company's total contribution may sink to a level where it fails even to cover fixed costs.

(g) *Suppliers*. Some decisions will affect suppliers, whose long-term goodwill maybe damaged by a decision to close a product line temporarily. Decisions to change the specifications for purchased components, or change stockholding policies so as to create patchy, uneven demand might also put a strain on suppliers. In some cases, where a company is the supplier's main customer, a decision to reduce demand or delay payments for goods received might drive the supplier out of business.

(h) *Feasibility*. A proposal may look good in outline, but technical experts or departmental managers may have some reservations about their ability to carry it out. For example, a decision may be required to buy some computer equipment, but the departmental manager might have reservations about the willingness of his staff to accept the proposal, the possibility of implementing the scheme by the planned date, and even whether the proposed scheme will actually do the job intended.

(i) *Flexibility and internal control*. Decisions to subcontract work, or to enter into a long-term contract have the disadvantages of inflexibility and lack of controllability. Where requirements may be changeable, it would be preferable to build flexibility into the organisation of operations.

(j) *Unquantified opportunity costs*. Even where no opportunity costs are specified, it is probable that other opportunities would be available for using the resources to earn profit. It may be useful to qualify a recommendation by stating that a given project would appear to be viable on the assumption that there are no other more profitable opportunities available.

(k) *Political pressures*. Some large companies may suffer political pressures applied by the government to influence their investment or disinvestment decisions.

(l) *Legal constraints*. A decision might occasionally be rejected because of doubts about the legality of the proposed action.

Chapter roundup

- Relevant costs are *future, incremental cash flows*.

- An opportunity cost is the benefit forgone by choosing one opportunity instead of the next best alternative.

- Non-relevant costs include sunk costs, committed costs, notional costs and historical costs.

- The relevant cost of raw materials is their current replacement cost unless the materials have been purchased and will not be replaced, in which case their relevant cost is the higher of their current resale value and the value they would obtain if they were put to an alternative use.

- The relevant costs of using machinery are called user costs.

- The relevant cost of capital expenditure can be measured using either traditional DCF appraisal techniques or on an annualised basis.

- The relevant cost of a scarce resource is the sum of the contribution/incremental profit forgone from the next best opportunity for using the scarce resource and the variable cost of the scarce resource.

- The minimum price for a one-off product or service contract is its total relevant costs.

- There are a number of assumptions typically made in relevant costing
  - Cost behaviour patterns are known
  - The amount of fixed costs, unit variable costs, sales price and sales demand are known with certainty
  - The objective is to maximise satisfaction (short-term profit)
  - The information on which a decision is based is complete and reliable

- Qualitative factors in decision making include the following.
  - The availability of cash
  - Inflation
  - Employees
  - Customers
  - Competitors
  - Timing factors
  - Suppliers
  - Feasibility
  - Flexibility and internal control
  - Unquantified opportunity costs
  - Political pressures
  - Legal constraints

Test your knowledge

1   Distinguish between incremental costs and differential costs. (1.3)

2   What is a committed cost? (1.6)

3   What is an attributable cost? (1.12)

4   What are user costs? (2.2)

5   How is the cost of a capital item annualised? (2.7)

6   How is the total relevant cost of a scarce resource calculated? (3.4)

7   State some assumptions commonly made in relevant costing. (5.2)

8   List some qualitative factors which may be relevant to decision making. (6.2)

Now try illustrative question 14 at the end of the Study Text

Chapter 13

DECISION MAKING

This chapter covers the following topics.

		Syllabus reference	Ability required
1	Shutdown problems	6(b)	Skill
2	Make or buy decisions	6(b)	Skill
3	Accepting or rejecting orders	6(b)	Skill
4	Factors to consider when making pricing decisions	6(b)	Knowledge
5	Approaches to pricing	6(b)	Knowledge

Introduction

This chapter continues our look at the provision of information for decisions and the use of relevant costing and examines two types of decision, decisions about alternatives and pricing decisions.

Decisions about alternatives are based on two principal ideas: there is either a choice between doing A *or* B, or there is a choice between doing or not doing A. You will need to apply relevant costing concepts so don't attempt to begin working through this chapter until you are 100% happy with everything in Chapter 12. (We looked at very straightforward decision making at Stage 1 and so the concepts and techniques covered will not be entirely new to you.)

Pricing decisions, which we will be looking at in the second part of the chapter, must of course have some regard for cost: the selling price of a product must exceed its average unit cost of sale in order to make a profit. However, pricing decisions must also recognise the importance of a whole range of other factors which can be grouped under the general heading of demand.

- The selling price will influence demand. At higher selling prices, the demand for (most) products is lower.

- Demand in turn should influence the choice of price, with a price being chosen that enables the organisation to maximise its profits, maximise sales revenue, increase market share or achieve whatever other objective it might have. The strength of demand depends in turn not only on price, but also on factors such as competitors, the life cycle of the product, branding, advertising and other forms of sales promotion and selling effort, and the quality of the product or service.

Pricing decisions may be influenced by longer-term strategic considerations or by short-term tactical or operational factors. The price of a product or service may vary over its life cycle, from its initial launch on the market until its eventual withdrawal. Cost is therefore just one factor to be taken into account in the pricing decision.

---

1 SHUTDOWN PROBLEMS

5/98

1.1 Shutdown or discontinuance problems involve decisions about the following.

(a) Whether or not to close down a product line, department or other activity, either because it is making losses or because it is too expensive to run.

(b) If the decision is to shut down, whether the closure should be permanent or temporary.

1.2 In practice, shutdown decisions may often involve longer-term considerations, and some account must be taken of capital expenditures and revenues.

(a) A shutdown should result in savings in operating costs for a number of periods into the future.

(b) Closure will probably release unwanted fixed assets for sale. Some assets might have a small scrap value, but other assets, in particular property, might have a substantial sale value.

(c) Employees affected by the closure must be made redundant or relocated, perhaps after retraining, or else offered early retirement. There will be lump sum payments involved which must be taken into account in the financial arithmetic.

For example, suppose that the closure of a regional office would result in annual savings of £100,000, fixed assets could be sold off to earn income of £2 million, but redundancy payments would be £3 million. The shutdown decision would involve an assessment of the net capital cost of closure (£1 million) against the annual benefits (£100,000 pa).

1.3 It is possible, however, for shutdown problems to be simplified into short-run decisions by making one of the following assumptions.

(a) Fixed asset sales and redundancy costs would be negligible.

(b) Income from fixed asset sales would match redundancy costs and so these capital items would be self-cancelling.

In such circumstances the financial aspect of shutdown decisions would be based on short-run relevant costs.

Example: adding or deleting products

1.4 A company manufactures three products, Pawns, Rooks and Bishops. The present net annual income from these is:

	Pawns £	Rooks £	Bishops £	Total £
Sales	50,000	40,000	60,000	150,000
Variable costs	30,000	25,000	35,000	90,000
Contribution	20,000	15,000	25,000	60,000
Fixed costs	17,000	18,000	20,000	55,000
Profit/loss	3,000	(3,000)	5,000	5,000

The company is concerned about its poor profit performance, and is considering whether or not to cease selling Rooks. It is felt that selling prices cannot be raised or reduced without adversely affecting net income. £5,000 of the fixed costs of Rooks are direct fixed costs which would be saved if production ceased. All other fixed costs, it is considered, would remain the same.

1.5 By stopping production of Rooks, the consequences would be a £10,000 fall in profits:

	£
Loss of contribution	(15,000)
Savings in fixed costs	5,000
Incremental loss	(10,000)

1.6 Suppose, however, it were possible to use the resources realised by stopping production of Rooks and switch to producing a new item, Crowners, which would sell for £50,000 and incur variable costs of £30,000 and extra direct fixed costs of £6,000. A new decision is now required:

	Rooks	Crowners
	£	£
Sales	40,000	50,000
Less variable costs	25,000	30,000
	15,000	20,000
Less direct fixed costs	5,000	6,000
Contribution to shared fixed costs and profit	10,000	14,000

It would be more profitable to shut down production of Rooks and switch resources to making Crowners, in order to boost profits by £4,000 to £9,000.

Qualitative factors

1.7   As usual the decision is not merely a matter of choosing the best financial option. Qualitative factors related to the impact on employees, customers, competitors and suppliers must once more be considered.

Exercise 1

A company's product range includes product F, on which the following data (relating to a year's production) are available.

	£
Revenue	200,000
Materials cost	157,000
Machine power cost	14,000
Overheads: type A	28,000
type B	56,000

Type A overheads would be avoided if production of product F ceased, but type B overheads would not be. Both types of overheads are absorbed in direct proportion to machine power cost, and that cost is a purely variable cost.

Required

Determine whether production of product F should be ended.

Solution

	£	£
Revenue		200,000
Less: materials cost	157,000	
machine power cost	14,000	
type A overheads	28,000	
		199,000
Contribution		1,000

Production of product F should be continued, because it makes a contribution of £1,000 a year.

1.8   You may consider by now that you understand the basic principles of selecting relevant costs for 'decision accounting' and it may therefore be useful at this stage to test your understanding with a more advanced example. Attempt your own solution before reading on.

Example: shutdown decisions

1.9   Ayeco Ltd, with a head office in Ayetown, has three manufacturing units. One is in Beetown, the second in Ceetown and the third in Deetown. The company manufactures and sells an air-conditioner under the brand-name of Ayecool at a price of £200. It is unable to utilise fully its manufacturing capacity.

Summarised profit and loss statements for the year are shown below.

	Beetown £'000	Ceetown £'000	Deetown £'000	Total £'000
Costs				
Direct materials	200	800	400	1,400
Direct wages	200	900	350	1,450
Production overhead:				
variable	50	300	150	500
fixed	200	600	300	1,100
Sub-total	650	2,600	1,200	4,450
Selling overhead:				
variable	25	200	100	325
fixed	75	250	150	475
Administration overhead	100	450	200	750
Sub-total	850	3,500	1,650	6,000
Head office costs	50	200	100	350
Total	900	3,700	1,750	6,350
Profit	100	300	250	650
Sales	1,000	4,000	2,000	7,000

The management of the company has to decide whether or not to renew the lease of the property at Beetown, which expires next year. The company has been offered an extension to the lease at an additional cost of £50,000 per annum. This situation concerning the lease has been known for some time, so the accountant has collected relevant information to aid the decision. It is estimated that the cost of closing down Beetown would be offset by the surplus obtained by the sale of plant, machinery and stocks.

If Ayeco Ltd does not renew the lease of the Beetown property it has two alternatives.

(a) Accept an offer from Zeeco Ltd, a competitor, to take over the manufacture and sales in Beetown area and pay to Ayeco Ltd a commission of £3 for each unit sold.

(b) Transfer the output at present made in Beetown to either Ceetown or Deetown. Each of these units has sufficient plant capacity to undertake the Beetown output but additional costs in supervision, salaries, storage and maintenance would be incurred. These additional costs are estimated as amounting yearly to £250,000 at Ceetown and to £200,000 at Deetown.

If the Beetown sales are transferred to either Ceetown or Deetown, it is estimated that additional transport costs would be incurred in delivering to customers in the region of Beetown, and that these would amount to £15 per unit and £20 per unit respectively.

Required

Present a statement to the board of directors of Ayeco Ltd to show the estimated annual profit which would arise from the following alternative courses of action.

(a) Continuing production at all three sites
(b) Closing down production at Beetown and accepting the offer from Zeeco Ltd
(c) Transferring Beetown sales to Ceetown
(d) Transferring Beetown sales to Deetown

Comment on your statement, indicating any problems which may arise from the various decisions which the board may decide to take.

Solution

1.10 The main difficulty in answering this question is to decide what happens to fixed cost expenditure if the Beetown factory is closed, and what would be the variable costs of production and sales at Ceetown or Deetown if work was transferred from Beetown.

1.11 It should be assumed that the direct fixed costs of the Beetown factory will be saved when shutdown occurs. These costs will include rent, depreciation of machinery, salaries of administrative staff and so on and it is therefore probably correct to assume that savings on shutdown will include all fixed costs charged to Beetown with the exception of the apportioned head office costs.

1.12 The variable cost of production at Ceetown or Deetown is more tricky, because the variable cost/sales ratio and the contribution/sales ratio differs at each factory.

	Beetown %	Ceetown %	Deetown %
Direct materials/sales	20.0	20.0	20.0
Direct wages/sales	20.0	22.5	17.5
Variable production overhead/sales	5.0	7.5	7.5
Variable selling overhead/sales	2.5	5.0	5.0
Total variable costs/sales	47.5	55.0	50.0
Contribution/sales	52.5	45.0	50.0

1.13 Labour appears to be less efficient at Ceetown and more efficient at Deetown, but variable overheads are more costly at both Ceetown and Deetown than at Beetown. It is probably reasonably accurate to assume that the variable cost/sales ratio of work transferred from Beetown will change to the ratio which is current at the factory to which the work is transferred. Transport costs would then be added as an additional cost item.

1.14 *Statement of estimated annual profit*

Option 1. Continuing production at all three sites

	£
Profit before rent increase on lease	650,000
Increase in annual cost of lease	50,000
Revised estimate of annual profit	600,000

Option 2. Accepting the offer from Zeeco Ltd.

	£	£
Current estimate of total profit		650,000
Less revenue lost from closing Beetown	(1,000,000)	
Direct costs saved at Beetown	850,000	
	(150,000)	
Commission from Zeeco Ltd* (5,000 × £3)	15,000	
Net loss from closure		(135,000)
Revised estimate of total profit		515,000

* Number of units = £1,000,000 ÷ £200 per unit = 5,000 units.

Option 3. Transfer work to Ceetown

	£	£	£
Current estimate of total profit			650,000
Direct costs saved by closing Beetown		850,000	
Extra costs at Ceetown			
Variable costs (55% of £1,000,000)	(550,000)		
Extra costs of supervision etc	(250,000)		
Extra costs of transport (5,000 units × £15)	(75,000)		
		(875,000)	
Net extra costs of transfer			(25,000)
Revised estimate of total profit			625,000

Option 4. Transfer work to Deetown

	£	£	£
Current estimate of total profit			650,000
Direct costs saved by closing Beetown		850,000	
Extra costs at Deetown			
Variable costs (50% of £1,000,000)	(500,000)		
Extra costs of supervision etc	(200,000)		
Extra costs of transport (5,000 units × £20)	(100,000)		
		(800,000)	
Net savings from transfer			50,000
Revised estimate of total profit			700,000

Conclusion

The preferred option should be to transfer production from Beetown to Deetown, since profits would rise to £700,000, and would be £75,000 higher than profits obtainable from the next most profitable option (option 3).

Comments on the example

1.15 The previous example illustrates how accounting information for decision making can often be presented in a concise form, without the need to reproduce a complete table of revenues, costs and profits for each option. You should study the presentation of the figures above, and note how they show only the relevant costs or benefits arising as a direct consequence of each decision option.

1.16 The eventual management decision may not be to transfer to Deetown, because other qualitative factors might influence the final decision. These would include the following.

(a) Concern for employees at Beetown and the wish to avoid redundancies.

(b) Problems in recruiting additional staff at Deetown: the required labour might not be readily available.

(c) The possibility that the extra workload at Deetown might reduce labour efficiency there, making costs of production higher than those estimated in the statement.

(d) Difficulties in assembling and organising a transport fleet might persuade management to reject options 3 and 4.

Exam focus point

The May 1998 exam featured a discontinuance question involving four products. Candidates had to prepare a statement showing the results of continuing to produce the products, then do a second statement showing what would happen if one of the products were discontinued and the volume of production of another were increased, and finally reconcile the two statements. Then they had to comment on any non-financial matters that should be considered.

When to close

1.17 As well as being able to deal with 'whether to close' situations you must also be able to handle 'when to close' situations.

Example: when to close

1.18 Daisy Ltd currently publish, print and distribute a range of catalogues and instruction manuals. The management have now decided to discontinue printing and distribution and concentrate solely on publishing. Stem Ltd will print and distribute the range of catalogues and instruction manuals on behalf of Daisy Ltd commencing either at 30

June 19X0 or 30 November 19X0. Stem Ltd will receive £65,000 per month for a contract which will commence either at 30 June 19X0 or 30 November 19X0.

The results of Daisy Ltd for a typical month are as follows.

	Publishing £'000	Printing £'000	Distribution £'000
Salaries and wages	28.0	18.0	4.0
Materials and supplies	5.5	31.0	1.1
Occupancy costs	7.0	8.5	1.2
Depreciation	0.8	4.2	0.7

Other information has been gathered relating to the possible closure proposals.

(a) Two specialist staff from printing will be retained at their present salary of £1,500 each per month in order to fulfil a link function with Stem Ltd. One further staff member will be transferred to publishing to fill a staff vacancy through staff turnover, anticipated in July. This staff member will be paid at his present salary of £1,400 per month which is £100 more than that of the staff member who is expected to leave. On closure all other printing and distribution staff will be made redundant and paid an average of two months redundancy pay.

(b) The printing department has a supply of materials (already paid for) which cost £18,000 and which will be sold to Stem Ltd for £10,000 if closure takes place on 30 June 19X0. Otherwise the material will be used as part of the July 19X0 printing requirements. The distribution department has a contract to purchase pallets at a cost of £500 per month for July and August 19X0. A cancellation clause allows for non-delivery of the pallets for July and August for a one-off payment of £300. Non-delivery for August only will require a payment of £100. If the pallets are taken from the supplier, Stem Ltd has agreed to purchase them at a price of £380 for each month's supply which is available. Pallet costs are included in the distribution material and supplies cost stated for a typical month.

(c) Company expenditure on apportioned occupancy costs to printing and distribution will be reduced by 15% per month if printing and distribution departments are closed. At present, 30% of printing and 25% of distribution occupancy costs are directly attributable costs which are avoidable on closure, whilst the remainder are apportioned costs.

(d) Closure of the printing and distribution departments will make it possible to sub-let part of the building for a monthly fee of £2,500 when space is available.

(e) Printing plant and machinery has an estimated net book value of £48,000 at 30 June 19X0. It is anticipated that it will be sold at a loss of £21,000 on 30 June 19X0. If sold on 30 November 19X0 the prospective buyer will pay £25,000.

(f) The net book value of distribution vehicles at 30 June 19X0 is estimated as £80,000. They could be sold to the original supplier at £48,000 on 30 June 19X0. The original supplier would purchase the vehicles on 30 November 19X0 for a price of £44,000.

Required

Using the above information, prepare a summary to show whether Daisy Ltd should close the printing and distribution departments on financial grounds on 30 June 19X0 or on 30 November 19X0. Explanatory notes and calculations should be shown.

Solution

1.19

		Handover 30.6.X0 £	Handover 30.11.X0 £	Difference £
Relevant inflows				
Stocks (W2)		10,000		10,000
Pallet sale (W3)		380		380
Rent	(5 × £2,500)	12,500		12,500
Fixed asset sales				
Printing		27,000	25,000	2,000
Distribution		48,000	44,000	4,000
Total inflows		97,880	69,000	28,880
Relevant outflows				
Salaries and wages (W1)		15,500	110,000	(94,500)
Materials and supplies (W2)			142,500	(142,500)
Pallets (W3)		600		600
Occupancy costs (W4)				
Apportioned		29,112	34,250	(5,138)
Direct			14,250	(14,250)
Stem fee	(5 × £65,000)	325,000		325,000
Total outflows		370,212	301,000	69,212
Net inflow/(outflow)		(272,332)	(232,000)	(40,332)

The operation should be kept open until 30.11.19X0.

Workings

1   *Salaries and wages*

	Printing £	Distribution £	Total £
Costs if 30.6.X0 handover			
2 × £1,500 × 5 months	15,000	-	15,000
£100 × 5 months		500	500
			15,500
Costs if 30.11.X0 handover			
5 months usual costs	90,000	20,000	110,000

2   *Stocks*

The £18,000 cost of production is a sunk cost from previous periods. Therefore only the income is recorded. Also, the £10,000 income could be seen as one of the opportunity costs of continuing production.

			£
Therefore materials costs are	printing:	(£31,000 × 5 – £18,000) =	137,000
	distribution:	(£1,100 × 5) =	5,500
			142,500

3   *Pallets*

The alternative flows can be estimated as follows.

	£
Take both deliveries	
Payment (2 × £500) =	1,000
Resale (2 × £380) =	760
Net flow	240
Take one delivery (ie July)	
Payment	500
Cancellation fee (August)	100
	600
Sale to Stem	380
Net flow	220
Take no deliveries	
Cancellation fee	£300

Only the July delivery should be taken.

4   *Site costs*

	Printing £	Distribution £	Total £
Total occupancy costs (5 months)	42,500	6,000	48,500
of which directly attributable (30%/25%)	(12,750)	(1,500)	(14,250)
∴ Apportioned costs	29,750	4,500	34,250
Reduction in apportioned costs (15%)	(4,463)	(675)	(5,138)
Apportioned costs after closure	25,287	3,825	29,112

2   MAKE OR BUY DECISIONS

11/96

2.1   A make or buy problem involves a decision by an organisation about whether it should make a product or whether it should pay another organisation to do so. Examples of make or buy decisions would be:

(a)   whether a company should manufacture its own components, or else buy the components from an outside supplier;

(b)   whether a construction company should do some work with its own employees, or whether it should sub-contract the work to another company;

(c)   whether a *service* should be carried out by an internal department or whether an external organisation should be employed.

2.2   The 'make' option should give management more direct control over the work, but the 'buy' option often has the benefit that the external organisation has a specialist skill and expertise in the work. Make or buy decisions should certainly not be based exclusively on cost considerations.

Example: make or buy and no limiting factors

2.3   Starfish Ltd makes four components, W, X, Y and Z, for which costs in the forthcoming year are expected to be as follows

	W	X	Y	Z
Production (units)	1,000	2,000	4,000	3,000
Unit marginal costs	£	£	£	£
Direct materials	4	5	2	4
Direct labour	8	9	4	6
Variable production overheads	2	3	1	2
	14	17	7	12

Directly attributable fixed costs per annum and committed fixed costs are as follows.

	£
Incurred as a direct consequence of making W	1,000
Incurred as a direct consequence of making X	5,000
Incurred as a direct consequence of making Y	6,000
Incurred as a direct consequence of making Z	8,000
Other fixed costs (committed)	30,000
	50,000

A sub-contractor has offered to supply units of W, X, Y and Z for £12, £21, £10 and £14 respectively.

Required

Decide whether Starfish Ltd should make or buy the components.

Solution

2.4 The relevant costs are the differential costs between making and buying, and they consist of differences in unit variable costs plus differences in directly attributable fixed costs.

	W	X	Y	Z
	£	£	£	£
Unit variable cost of making	14	17	7	12
Unit variable cost of buying	12	21	10	14
	(2)	4	3	2
Annual requirements (units)	1,000	2,000	4,000	3,000
	£	£	£	£
Extra variable cost of buying (per annum)	(2,000)	8,000	12,000	6,000
Fixed costs saved by buying	(1,000)	(5,000)	(6,000)	(8,000)
Extra total cost of buying	(3,000)	3,000	6,000	(2,000)

2.5 The company would save £3,000 pa by sub-contracting component W (where the purchase cost would be less than the marginal cost per unit to make internally) and would save £2,000 pa by sub-contracting component Z (because of the saving in fixed costs of £8,000).

In this example, relevant costs are the variable costs of in-house manufacture, the variable costs of sub-contracted units, and the saving in fixed costs.

Further considerations

2.6 Important further considerations would be as follows.

(a) If components W and Z are sub-contracted, the company will have spare capacity. How should that spare capacity be profitably used? Are there hidden benefits to be obtained from sub-contracting? Would the company's workforce resent the loss of work to an outside sub-contractor, and might such a decision cause an industrial dispute?

(b) Would the sub-contractor be reliable with delivery times, and would he supply components of the same quality as those manufactured internally?

(c) Does the company wish to be flexible and maintain better control over operations by making everything itself?

(d) Are the estimates of fixed cost savings reliable? In the case of Product W, buying is clearly cheaper than making in-house. In the case of product Z, the decision to buy rather than make would only be financially beneficial if it is feasible that the fixed cost savings of £8,000 will really be 'delivered' by management. All too often in practice, promised savings fail to materialise!

3 ACCEPTING OR REJECTING ORDERS

3.1 An order will probably be accepted if it increases contribution and profit, and rejected if it reduces profit. Examination questions may set problems relating to the acceptance or rejection of a special order.

Example: accepting or rejecting orders

3.2 Holdup Ltd makes a single product which sells for £20, and for which there is great demand. It has a variable cost of £12, made up as follows.

	£
Direct material	4
Direct labour (2 hrs)	6
Variable overhead	2
	12

The labour force is currently working at full capacity producing a product that earns a contribution of £4 per labour hour. A customer has approached the company with a request for the manufacture of a special order for which he is willing to pay £5,500.

The costs of the order would be £2,000 for direct materials, and 500 labour hours will be required.

Required

Decide whether the order should be accepted.

Solution

3.3 (a) Labour is a limiting factor. By accepting the order, work would have to be diverted away from the standard product, and contribution will be lost, that is, there is an opportunity cost of accepting the new order, which is the contribution forgone by being unable to make the standard product.

(b) Direct labour pay costs £3 per hour, but it is also usually assumed that variable production overhead varies with hours worked, and must therefore be spent in addition to the wages cost of the 500 hours.

(c)

	£	£
Value of order		5,500
Cost of order		
Direct materials	2,000	
Direct labour (500 hrs × £3)	1,500	
Variable overhead (500 hrs × £1)	500	
Opportunity cost (500 hrs × £4) (Contribution forgone)	2,000	
Relevant cost of the order		6,000
Loss incurred by accepting the order		(500)

The order should not be accepted. In other words, although accepting the order would earn a contribution of £1,500 (£5,500 − £4,000), the lost production of the standard product would reduce contribution earned elsewhere by £2,000.

4   FACTORS TO CONSIDER WHEN MAKING PRICING DECISIONS   *11/96*

4.1 We have seen how the concept of relevant costs can be used as the starting point for setting a minimum price but cost is only one of the factors to bear in mind when setting a price.

The organisation's objectives

4.2 We generally assume that an organisation's objective is to maximise profit. However alternative objectives are possible, for example increased market share, maximisation of sales revenue, to be known as a supplier of luxury goods or to provide a service to the community. The organisation's pricing policy will reflect whatever objective it chooses. The maximisation of sales revenue, for example, is most likely if either prices are very low so that volumes are high or if prices are exceptionally high (although volumes will, of course, be low).

The market in which the organisation operates

4.3 If the organisation is operating under conditions of perfect competition (many buyers and many sellers all dealing in an identical product), neither producer nor user has any market power and both must accept the prevailing market price.

4.4 If the organisation is in the position of a monopolist (one seller who dominates many buyers), it can use its market power to set a profit-maximising price.

4.5   Most of British industry can be described as an oligopoly (relatively few competitive companies dominate the market). Whilst each large firm has the ability to influence market prices, the unpredictable reaction from the other giants makes the final industry price difficult to determine.

Demand

4.6   You should remember from your Stage 1 *Economic Environment* studies that most organisations face a downward-sloping demand curve (the higher the price, the lower the demand). Economic theory suggests that the volume of demand for a good in the *market as a whole* is influenced by variables such as the following.

(a)   Price of the good
(b)   Price of other goods
(c)   Size and distribution of household income
(d)   Tastes and fashion
(e)   Expectations
(f)   Obsolescence

4.7   The volume of demand for one organisation's goods rather than another's is influenced by three principal factors: product life cycle, quality and marketing.

(a)   *Product life cycle.* Most products pass through the following phases.

(i)   *Introduction,* where a new product takes time to find acceptance by would-be purchasers and there is little demand.

(ii)   *Growth,* when the product gains market acceptance, sales start to rise and costs (and therefore prices) fall. Demand continually increases.

(iii)   *Maturity,* when demand reaches a stable level.

(iv)   *Decline.* Demand eventually falls off, because of obsolescence, changes in fashion, the availability of superior alternatives and so on.

Different versions of the same product may have different life cycles, and consumers are often aware of this. For example, the prospective buyer of a new car is more likely to purchase a recently introduced Ford than a Vauxhall that has been on the market for several years, even if there is nothing to choose in terms of quality and price.

(b)   *Quality.* One firm's product may be perceived to be better quality than another's, and may in some cases actually be so, if it uses sturdier materials, goes faster or does whatever it is meant to do in a 'better' way. Other things being equal, the better quality good will be more in demand than other versions.

(c)   *Marketing.* You may be familiar with the 'four Ps' of the marketing mix, all of which influence demand for a firm's goods.

(i)   Price
(ii)   Product
(iii)   Place
(iv)   Promotion

Price elasticity of demand

4.8   The price an organisation charges will be affected by whether demand for an item is *elastic* (a small change in the price produces a large change in the quantity demanded) or *inelastic* (a small change in the price produces only a small change in the quantity demanded).

Costs

4.9   An organisation has to decide whether a price should be based on fully absorbed cost or marginal cost.

Competition

4.10   When competitors sell exactly the same product in the same market, price differences are likely to have a significant effect on demand. For example, the price of petrol at filling stations in a local area will be much the same. If it was not, customers would go to the cheapest place. When organisations sell similar products which are not exactly identical, or where the geographical location of the sales point is of some significance, there is more scope for charging different prices.

Inflation

4.11   An organisation should recognise the effects of inflation on its pricing decisions. When its costs are rising, it must try to ensure that its prices are increased sufficiently and regularly enough to make an adequate profit (in the case of a profit-making concern) or to cover its costs (in the case of non-profit-making organisations, where it is only necessary to break even).

Legislation

4.12   Certain organisations have their prices controlled by legislation or regulatory bodies.

Availability of substitutes

4.13   When an organisation is making a pricing decision it must take into account products/services that customers could switch to if they were not happy with the price set. For example, coach transport organisations have to consider the ability of customers to switch to travelling with British Rail.

4.14   There are, of course, other factors which organisations should consider when setting prices but those we have listed should make it clear that cost is only one of many factors which influence the pricing decision.

Exam focus point

Many questions that are mainly concerned with testing your knowledge of other aspects of cost accounting may include a requirement to suggest what price should be charged, or a requirement to calculate the *sales* in a period (critically dependent on price, of course). Don't forget the many factors that need to be considered if you are asked to make comments in your answer.

---

5   APPROACHES TO PRICING

5.1   You will be looking at various approaches to pricing in your studies for Paper 10 but a brief summary of the principal ones is useful at this point.

Full cost plus pricing

5.2   A traditional approach to pricing products is full cost plus pricing, whereby the sales price is determined by calculating the full cost of the product and adding a percentage mark-up for profit.

5.3   A business might have an idea of the percentage profit margin it would like to earn and so might decide on an average profit mark-up as a general guideline for pricing decisions. This would be particularly useful for businesses that carry out a large amount of contract work or jobbing work, for which individual job or contract prices must be quoted regularly to prospective customers.

5.4   However, the percentage profit mark-up does not have to be fixed, but can be varied to suit the circumstances. In particular, the percentage mark-up can be varied to suit demand conditions in the market.

5.5   The full cost plus approach to pricing is commonly used in practice, but varying the size of the profit mark-up gives the pricing decisions much-needed flexibility so as to adapt to demand conditions.

5.6   The main disadvantage of this approach to pricing is fails to recognise that since demand may be determined by price, there will be a profit-maximising combination of price and demand. A cost plus based approach to pricing will be most unlikely to arrive at the profit-maximising price. Full cost plus pricing also fails to allow for competition and opportunity costs. It can also be too inflexible if a business is tendering for a contract.

5.7   The *advantages* of full cost plus pricing are as follows.

   (a)   Since the size of the profit margin can be varied at management's discretion, a decision based on a price in excess of full cost should ensure that a company working at normal capacity will cover all its fixed costs and make a profit. Companies may benefit from cost plus pricing in the following circumstances.

      (i)   When they carry out large contracts which must make a sufficient profit margin to cover a fair share of fixed costs

      (ii)   If they must justify their prices to potential customers (for example for government contracts)

      (iii) If they find it difficult to estimate expected demand at different sales prices

   (b)   It is a simple, quick and cheap method of pricing which can be delegated to junior managers. This may be particularly important with jobbing work where many prices must be decided and quoted each day.

Marginal cost plus pricing

5.8   Instead of pricing products or services by adding a profit margin on to *full* cost, a business might add a profit margin on to *marginal* cost (either the marginal cost of production or else the marginal cost of sales). This is sometimes called *mark-up pricing*.

5.9   The *advantages* of a marginal cost plus approach to pricing are as follows.

   (a)   It is a simple and easy method to use.

   (b)   The mark-up can be varied, and so provided that a rigid mark-up is not used, mark-up pricing can be adjusted to reflect demand conditions.

   (c)   It draws management attention to contribution and the effects of higher or lower sales volumes on profit. In this way, it helps to create a better awareness of the concepts and implications of marginal costing and breakeven analysis. For example, if a product costs £10 a unit and a mark-up of 150% is added to reach a price of £25 a unit, management should be clearly aware that every additional £1 of sales revenue would add 60p to contribution and profit.

   (d)   Mark-up pricing is convenient where there is a readily identifiable basic variable cost. Retail industries are the most obvious example, and it is quite common for the prices of goods in shops to be fixed by adding a mark-up (20% or $33^{1}/_{3}\%$, say) to the purchase cost. For example, a department store might buy in items of pottery at £3 each, add a mark-up of one third and resell the items at £4.

5.10   The main *disadvantages* of marginal cost plus pricing are as follows.

   (a)   Although the size of the mark-up can be varied in accordance with demand conditions, it is not a method of pricing which ensures that sufficient attention is paid to demand conditions, competitors' prices and profit maximisation.

(b) It ignores fixed overheads in the pricing decision, but the price must be high enough to ensure that a profit is made after covering fixed costs. Pricing decisions cannot ignore fixed costs altogether.

Minimum pricing

5.11 We looked at this approach in Chapter 12. A minimum price is the price that would have to be charged so that the following costs are just covered.

(a) The incremental costs of producing and selling the item

(b) The opportunity costs of the resources consumed in making and selling the item

A minimum price would leave the business no better or worse off in financial terms than if it did not sell the item.

5.12 Two essential points about a minimum price are as follows.

(a) It is based on relevant costs.

(b) It is unlikely that a minimum price would actually be charged because if it were, it would not provide the business with any incremental profit. However, the minimum price for an item shows the following.

   (i)   An absolute minimum below which the price should not be set.

   (ii) The incremental profit that would be obtained from any price that is actually charged in excess of the minimum. For example, if the minimum price is £200 and the actual price charged is £240, the incremental profit on the sale would be £40.

5.13 If there are no scarce resources and a company has spare capacity, the minimum price of a product is the incremental cost of making it. Any price in excess of this minimum would provide an incremental contribution towards profit.

5.14 If there are scarce resources and a company makes more than one product, minimum prices must include an allowance for the opportunity cost of using the scarce resources to make and sell the product (instead of using the resources on the next most profitable product).

Exercise 2

Ship Ltd has recently shut down its London factory which used to make cushions, although all the stocks of raw materials and machinery are still there awaiting disposal. A former customer has just asked whether he could be supplied with one last delivery of 500 cushions. You ascertain the following facts.

(a) There is sufficient covering material in stock. This originally cost £400 but has a disposal value of £190.

(b) There is sufficient stuffing in stock. This originally cost £350. It was to have been shipped to the Bristol factory at a cost of £80. The Bristol factory would currently expect to pay £500 for this quantity.

(c) Labour costs would be £450.

(d) A supervisor could be spared from the Bristol factory for the week needed to produce the cushions. His normal wage is £160 and his rail fare and hotel bill in London would amount to £135.

(e) Before the factory was closed, fixed overheads were absorbed at 200% of direct labour cost.

Required

Calculate the minimum price that could be quoted.

Solution

The minimum price is estimated from the relevant costs of producing the cushions.

	£
Covering material: the opportunity cost of this material is its scrap value of £190, the original cost being irrelevant because it is a historical cost, not a future cash flow	190
Stuffing : the opportunity cost of the stuffing is the savings forgone by not sending it to Bristol, net of the transport costs of getting it to Bristol £(500 – 80)	420
Labour: incremental cost	450
Supervisor's expenses: incremental expense item	135
Minimum price	1,195

The supervisor's basic wage and the overheads are irrelevant to the decision because these are costs that would be incurred anyway, even if the cushions were not produced.

Pricing decisions and demand

5.15   Price theory or demand theory, which you will have come across in your previous studies of economics, is based on the idea that a connection can be made between price, quantity demanded and sold, and total revenue. Demand varies with price, and so if an estimate can be made of demand at different price levels, it should be possible to derive either a profit-maximising price or a revenue-maximising price.

The theory of demand cannot be applied in practice, however, unless realistic estimates of demand at different price levels can be made.

5.16   In practice, businesses might not make estimates of demand at different price levels, but they might still make pricing decisions on the basis of demand conditions and competition in the market.

Chapter roundup

- Shutdown problems involve decisions about whether or not to close down a product line, department or other activity and, if the decision is to shut down, when it should be shut down and/or whether the closure should be permanent or temporary. The basis of the decision is an assessment of short-run relevant costs. Qualitative factors such as concern for employees need to be considered as well.

- A make or buy problem involves a decision by an organisation about whether it should make a product or whether it should pay another organisation to do so. If the situation involves no scarce resources, the relevant costs of the decision will be the differential costs between the two options. Qualitative factors to consider include subcontractor reliability and workforce resentment.

- An order should usually be accepted if it increases contribution and profit and rejected if it reduces contribution and profit.

- When setting prices an organisation should consider the following.
  - o   Its objectives
  - o   The market in which it operates
  - o   Demand
  - o   The product life cycle
  - o   Quality
  - o   Marketing
  - o   Price elasticity of demand
  - o   Cost
  - o   Competition
  - o   Inflation
  - o   Legislation
  - o   The availability of substitutes.

- In full cost pricing the sales price is determined by calculating the full cost of the product and adding a percentage mark-up for profit.

- Marginal cost plus pricing, sometimes called mark-up pricing, involves adding a profit margin on to the marginal cost of production or the marginal cost of sales.

- A price charged under minimum pricing would cover the incremental costs of producing and selling the item and the opportunity costs of the resources consumed making and selling the item.

- It would leave the business no better or worse off than if it did not sell the item. The minimum price is based on relevant costs.

- These cost-based approaches to pricing have many weaknesses, the most important of which is that they do not recognise demand factors. In practice businesses seem to use the cost-based approach as the basis for their pricing decisions, with adjustments to allow for demand factors.

- Prices must cover costs, including overheads. Only very occasionally should a price be set at a small margin above the minimum price. A cost plus approach might be taken as a starting point for pricing but the size of the profit mark-up must be flexible, to allow for market conditions. Ideally, however, prices should be decided only after an assessment has been made of the likely demand at different price levels.

Test your knowledge

1   How are shutdown problems simplified into short-run decisions? (see para 1.3)

2   Suggest four qualitative factors to be borne in mind when making a shutdown decision. (1.16)

3   What are the relevant costs of a make or buy decision with no scarce resources? (2.4)

4   Suggest four further considerations when making a make or buy decision. (2.6)

5   What are the four stages of a product life cycle? (4.7)

6   What is elastic demand? (4.8)

7   What are the advantages of full cost plus pricing? (5.7)

Now try illustrative questions 15 and 16 at the end of the Study Text

Chapter 14

BREAKEVEN ANALYSIS

This chapter covers the following topics.

		Syllabus reference	*Ability required*
1	Breakeven analysis and breakeven point	6(b)	Skill
2	The C/S ratio	6(b)	Skill
3	The margin of safety	6(b)	Skill
4	Target profits	6(b)	Skill
5	Decisions to change sales price or costs	6(b)	Skill
6	Breakeven analysis and sales mix decisions	6(b)	Knowledge
7	Breakeven charts, contribution charts and profit/volume charts	6(b)	Skill
8	Sensitivity analysis	6(b)	Skill
9	Limitations of breakeven analysis	6(b)	Skill
10	Spreadsheets and breakeven analysis	6(a), (b)	Skill

Introduction

Think back to Chapter 1. Do you remember the questions to which we said the cost accountant should be able to provide answers? One of them was 'What information does management need in order to make sensible decisions about profits and costs?'. You should by now realise that the cost accountant needs estimates of fixed and variable costs, and revenues, at various output levels. The cost accountant, to be able to provide such information, must be fully aware of cost behaviour because, to be able to estimate costs, he/she must know what a particular cost will do given particular conditions.

An understanding of cost behaviour is not, however, all that you may need to know. The application of breakeven analysis, which is based on the cost behaviour principles and marginal costing ideas that we covered in Chapters 2 and 5, is sometimes necessary so that the appropriate decision-making information can be provided. We are going to cover breakeven analysis in this chapter.

---

1 BREAKEVEN ANALYSIS AND BREAKEVEN POINT   *11/95, 5/96*

1.1 Breakeven analysis is an application of marginal costing techniques. It is sometimes called cost-volume-profit (CVP) analysis. By using marginal costing techniques, it is possible to ascertain the contribution per unit. The total contribution from all sales during a period is then compared with the fixed costs for that period; any excess or deficiency of contribution over fixed costs represents the profit or loss respectively for the period.

1.2 The management of an organisation usually wishes to know not only the profit likely to be made if the aimed-for production and sales for the year are achieved, but also 'The level of activity at which there is neither profit nor loss' (the *breakeven point* as defined in CIMA *Official Terminology*) and the amount by which actual sales can fall below anticipated sales without a loss being incurred.

1.3 The breakeven point (BEP) can be calculated arithmetically. The number of *units* needed to be sold in order to break even will be the total fixed costs divided by the contribution per unit. This is because the contribution required to break even must be an amount which exactly equals the amount of fixed costs.

$$\text{Breakeven point} = \frac{\text{Total fixed costs}}{\text{Contribution per unit}} = \frac{\text{Contribution required to break even}}{\text{Contribution per unit}}$$

$$= \text{Number of units of sale required to break even.}$$

Example: breakeven point

1.4 | | |
|---|---|
| Expected sales | 10,000 units at £8 = £80,000 |
| Variable cost | £5 per unit |
| Fixed costs | £21,000 |

Required

Compute the breakeven point.

Solution

1.5
The contribution per unit is £(8–5)	=	£3
Contribution required to break even	=	fixed costs = £21,000
Breakeven point (BEP)	=	21,000 ÷ 3
	=	7,000 units
In revenue, BEP	=	(7,000 × £8) = £56,000

Sales above £56,000 will result in profit of £3 per unit of additional sales. Sales below £56,000 will mean a loss of £3 per unit for each unit by which sales fall short of 7,000 units. In other words, profit will improve or worsen by the amount of contribution per unit.

	7,000 units £		7,001 units £
Revenue	56,000		56,008
Less variable costs	35,000		35,005
Contribution	21,000		21,003
Less fixed costs	21,000		21,000
Profit	0	(= breakeven)	3

2   THE C/S RATIO   11/95, 5/96

2.1 An alternative way of calculating the breakeven point to give an answer in terms of sales revenue is as follows.

$$\frac{\text{Required contribution = Fixed costs}}{\text{C/S ratio}} = \text{Sales revenue at breakeven point}$$

(The C/S (contribution/sales) ratio is also sometimes called a profit/volume or P/V ratio).

2.2 In the example in Paragraph 1.4 the C/S ratio = $\dfrac{£3}{£8}$ = 37.5%

Breakeyen is where sales revenue = $\dfrac{£21,000}{37.5\%}$

$$= £56,000$$

At a price of £8 per unit, this represents 7,000 units of sales.

The contribution/sales ratio is a measure of how much contribution is earned from each £1 of sales. The C/S ratio of 37.5% in the above example means that for every £1 of sales, a contribution of 37.5p is earned. Thus, in order to earn a total contribution of £21,000 and if contribution increases by 37.5p per £1 of sales, sales must be:

$$\frac{£1}{37.5p} = 21,000 = £56,000$$

Exercise 1

The C/S ratio of product G is 24%. GB Ltd, the manufacturer of product G, wishes to make a contribution of £100,000 towards fixed costs. How many units of product G must be sold if the selling price is £1 per unit?

Solution

$$\frac{\text{Required contribution}}{\text{C / S ratio}} = \frac{£100,000}{24\%} = £416,667$$

Exam focus point

The examiner has confirmed that candidates may be required to deal with calculations involving a number of products with different C/S ratios. However, the relevant type of breakeven chart (see Section 7), known as the 'multi-product breakeven chart', will *not* be examined.

---

3   THE MARGIN OF SAFETY   *11/96*

3.1   In budgeting, the *margin of safety* is a measure by which the budgeted volume of sales is compared with the volume of sales required to break even. It is the difference in units between the budgeted sales volume and the breakeven sales volume and it is sometimes expressed as a percentage of the budgeted sales volume. (It may also be expressed as the difference between the budgeted sales revenue and breakeven sales revenue, expressed as a percentage of the budgeted sales revenue.)

Example: margin of safety

3.2   Mal de Mer Ltd makes and sells a product which has a variable cost of £30 and which sells for £40. Budgeted fixed costs are £70,000 and budgeted sales are 8,000 units.

Required

Calculate the breakeven point and the margin of safety.

Solution

3.3   (a)   Breakeven point $\quad = \dfrac{\text{Total fixed costs}}{\text{Contribution per unit}} = \dfrac{£70,000}{£(40-30)}$

$$= 7,000 \text{ units}$$

(b)   Margin of safety $\quad = 8,000 - 7,000 \text{ units} = 1,000 \text{ units}$

which may be expressed as $\quad \dfrac{1,000 \text{ units}}{8,000 \text{ units}} \times 100\% = 12\tfrac{1}{2}\% \text{ of budget}$

(c)   The margin of safety indicates to management that actual sales can fall short of budget by 1,000 units or 12½% before the breakeven point is reached and no profit at all is made.

4   TARGET PROFITS   *11/95, 11/96, 11/97*

4.1   (a)   At the breakeven point, sales revenue equals total costs and there is no profit.

$$S = V + F$$

where S = Sales revenue
        V = Total variable costs
        F = Total fixed costs

(b)   Subtracting   V from each side of the equation, we get:

$$S - V = F, \text{ that is, total contribution = fixed costs.}$$

Example: breakeven arithmetic

4.2   Butterfingers Ltd makes a product which has a variable cost of £7 per unit.

Required

If fixed costs are £63,000 per annum, calculate the selling price per unit if the company wishes to break even with a sales volume of 12,000 units.

Solution

4.3
			£
Contribution required to break even (= Fixed costs)	=	£63,000	
Volume of sales	=	12,000 units	
Required contribution per unit (S – V)	=	£63,000 ÷ 12,000 =	5.25
Variable cost per unit (V)	=		7.00
Required sales price per unit (S)	=		12.25

4.4   A similar formula may be applied where a company wishes to achieve a certain profit during a period. To achieve this profit, sales must cover all costs and leave the required profit, that is:

$$S = V + F + P, \text{ where}$$
$$P = \text{required profit}$$

Subtracting V from each side of the equation, we get:

$$S - V = F + P, \text{ so}$$
$$\text{Total contribution required} = F + P$$

Example: target profits (1)

4.5   Riding Breeches Ltd makes and sells a single product, for which variable costs are as follows.

	£
Direct materials	10
Direct labour	8
Variable production overhead	6
	24

The sales price is £30 per unit, and fixed costs per annum are £68,000. The company wishes to make a profit of £16,000 per annum.

Required

Determine the sales required to achieve this profit.

Solution

4.6
Required contribution	=	fixed costs + profit
	=	£68,000 + £16,000 = £84,000

Required sales can be calculated in one of two ways.

(a) $\dfrac{\text{Required contribution}}{\text{Contribution per unit}} = \dfrac{£84,000}{£(30 - 24)}$

$$= 14,000 \text{ units, or } £420,000 \text{ in revenue}$$

(b) $\dfrac{\text{Required contribution}}{\text{C/S ratio}}$ $=$ $\dfrac{£84,000}{20\%}$

$=$ £420,000 of revenue, or 14,000 units.

Exercise 2

Seven League Boots Ltd wishes to sell 14,000 units of its product, which has a variable cost of £15 to make and sell. Fixed costs are £47,000 and the required profit is £23,000.

Required

Calculate the sales price per unit.

Solution

Required contribution	=	fixed costs plus profit
	=	£47,000 + £23,000
	=	£70,000
Required sales		14,000 units
Required contribution per unit sold		£5
Variable cost per unit		£15
Required sales price per unit		£20

Example: target profits (2)

4.7 Tripod Ltd makes and sells three products, X, Y and Z. The selling price per unit and costs are as follows.

	X	Y	Z
Selling price per unit	£80	£50	£70
Variable cost per unit	£50	£10	£20

Fixed costs per month = £160,000

The maximum sales demand per month is 2,000 units of each product and the minimum sales demand is 1,000 of each.

Required

(a) Comment on the potential profitability of the company.

(b) Suppose that there is a fixed demand for X and Y of 1,500 units per month, which will not be exceeded, but for which firm orders have been received. Determine how many units of Z would have to be sold to achieve a profit of at least £25,000 per month.

Solution

4.8 (a) When there is no indication about whether marginal or absorption costing is in use, it is simpler (and more informative too) to assess profitability with contribution analysis and marginal costing. This is the requirement in part (a) of the problem. The obvious analysis to make is a calculation of the worst possible and best possible results.

	Best possible			Worst possible		
	Sales units	Contrib'n per unit	Total cont'n	Sales units	Contrib'n per unit	Total cont'n
		£	£		£	£
X	2,000	30	60,000	1,000	30	30,000
Y	2,000	40	80,000	1,000	40	40,000
Z	2,000	50	100,000	1,000	50	50,000
Total contribution			240,000			120,000
Fixed costs			160,000			160,000
Profit/(loss)			80,000			(40,000)

The company's potential profitability ranges from a profit of £80,000 to a loss of £40,000 per month.

(b) The second part of the problem is a variation of a 'target profit' calculation.

	£	£
Required (minimum) profit per month		25,000
Fixed costs per month		160,000
Required contribution per month		185,000
Contribution to be earned from:		
product X 1,500 × £30	45,000	
product Y 1,500 × £40	60,000	
		105,000
Contribution required from product Z		80,000
Contribution per unit of Z		£50
Minimum required sales of Z per month in units		1,600

Exam focus point

The calculations illustrated throughout this chapter feature regularly in MCQs. The calculation of target profits, for instance, came up in the November 1997 exam.

---

5 DECISIONS TO CHANGE SALES PRICE OR COSTS

5.1 You may come across a problem in which you will be expected to offer advice as to the effect of altering the selling price, variable cost per unit or fixed cost. These problems are slight variations on basic breakeven arithmetic, and some examples will be used to illustrate typical questions.

Example: change in selling price

5.2 Baker Ltd bake and sell a single type of cake. The variable cost of production is 15p and the current sales price is 25p. Fixed costs are £2,600 per month, and the annual profit for the company at current sales volume is £36,000. The volume of sales demand is constant throughout the year.

The sales manager wishes to raise the sales price to 29p per cake, but considers that a price rise will result in some loss of sales.

Required

Ascertain the minimum volume of sales required each month to justify a rise in price to 29p.

Solution

5.3 The minimum volume of demand which would justify a price of 29p is one which would leave total profit at least the same as before, ie £3,000 per month. Required profit should be converted into required contribution, as follows.

	£
Monthly fixed costs	2,600
Monthly profit, minimum required	3,000
Current monthly contribution	5,600
Contribution per unit (25p − 15p)	10p
Current monthly sales	56,000 cakes

The minimum volume of sales required after the price rise will be an amount which earns a contribution of £5,600 per month, no worse than at the moment. The contribution per cake at a sales price of 29p would be 14p.

$$\text{Required sales} = \frac{\text{required contribution}}{\text{contribution per unit}} = \frac{£5,600}{14p} = 40,000 \text{ cakes per month}$$

Example: change in production costs

5.4 Bun Ltd makes a product which has a variable production cost of £8 and a variable sales cost of £2 per unit. Fixed costs are £40,000 per annum, the sales price per unit is £18, and the current volume of output and sales is 6,000 units.

The company is considering whether to hire a machine to improve production. Annual hire costs would be £10,000 and it is expected that the variable cost of production would fall to £6 per unit.

Required

(a) Determine the number of units that must be produced and sold to achieve the same profit as is currently earned, if the machine is hired.

(b) Calculate the annual profit with the machine if output and sales remain at 6,000 units per annum.

Solution

5.5 The current unit contribution is £(18 − (8+2)) = £8

		£
(a)	Current contribution (6,000 × £8)	48,000
	Less current fixed costs	40,000
	Current profit	8,000

With the new machine fixed costs will go up by £10,000 to £50,000 per annum. The variable cost per unit will fall to £(6 + 2) = £8, and the contribution per unit will be £10.

	£
Required profit (as currently earned)	8,000
Fixed costs	50,000
Required contribution	58,000
Contribution per unit	£10
Sales required to earn £8,000 profit	5,800 units

(b) *If sales are 6,000 units*

	£	£
Sales (6,000 × £18)		108,000
Variable costs: production (6,000 × £6)	36,000	
sales (6,000 × £2)	12,000	
		48,000
Contribution (6,000 × £10)		60,000
Less fixed costs		50,000
Profit		10,000

Sales price and sales volume

5.6 It may be clear by now that, given no change in fixed costs, total profit is maximised when the total contribution is at its maximum. Total contribution in turn depends on the unit contribution and on the sales volume.

5.7 An increase in the sales price will increase unit contribution, but sales volume is likely to fall because fewer customers will be prepared to pay the higher price. A decrease in sales price will reduce the unit contribution, but sales volume may increase because the goods on offer are now cheaper. The optimum combination of sales price and sales volume is arguably the one which maximises total contribution.

Example: profit maximisation

5.8 Caro Ltd has developed a new product which is about to be launched on to the market. The variable cost of sales of the product is £12 per unit. The marketing department has estimated that at a sales price of £20, annual demand would be 10,000 units.

However, if the sales price is set above £20, sales demand would fall by 500 units for each 50p increase above £20. Similarly, if the price is set below £20, demand would increase by 500 units for each 50p stepped reduction in price below £20.

Required

Determine the price which would maximise Caro Ltd's profit in the next year.

Solution

5.9 At a price of £20 per unit, the unit contribution would be £(20 − 12) = £8. Each 50p increase (or decrease) in price would raise (or lower) the unit contribution by 50p. The total contribution is calculated at each sales price by multiplying the unit contribution by the expected sales volume.

	Unit price	*Unit contribution*	*Sales volume*	*Total contribution*
	£	£	Units	£
	20.00	8.00	10,000	80,000
(a)	*Reduce price*			
	19.50	7.50	10,500	78,750
	19.00	7.00	11,000	77,000
(b)	*Increase price*			
	20.50	8.50	9,500	80,750
	21.00	9.00	9,000	81,000
	21.50	9.50	8,500	80,750
	22.00	10.00	8,000	80,000
	22.50	10.50	7,500	78,750

The total contribution would be maximised, and therefore profit maximised, at a sales price of £21 per unit, and sales demand of 9,000 units.

6 BREAKEVEN ANALYSIS AND SALES MIX DECISIONS

6.1 The cost accountant may need to provide information to enable management to make sales mix decisions. You are *not* required to be able to quantify the effects on profit of a change in sales mix from that originally budgeted but you must be able to explain the effects of different sales mixes. One way of doing this is to consider breakeven points for different sales mixes. Consider the following example.

6.2 JM Ltd makes and sells two products, the J and the M. The budgeted selling price of the J is £60 and that of the M, £72. Variable costs associated with producing and selling the J are £30 and, with the M, £60. Annual fixed production and selling costs of JM Ltd are £3,369,600.

JM Ltd has two production/sales options. The J and the M can be sold either in the ratio two Js to three Ms or in the ratio one J to two Ms.

6.3 We can decide on the optimal mix by looking at breakeven points. We need to begin by determining contribution per unit.

	J	*M*
	£ per unit	£ per unit
Selling price	60	72
Variable cost	30	60
Contribution	30	12

Mix 1

Contribution per 5 units sold = (£30 × 2) + (£12 × 3) = £96

Breakeven point = $\dfrac{£3,369,600}{£96}$ = 35,100 sets of five units

Breakeven point:	*J*		*M*	
in units	(35,100 × 2)	70,200	(35,100 × 3)	105,300
in £	(× £60)	£4,212,000	(× £72)	£7,581,600

'Total' breakeven point = £11,793,600

Mix 2

Contribution per 3 units sold = (£30 × 1) + (£12 × 2) = £54

Breakeven point = $\dfrac{£3,369,600}{£54}$ = 62,400 sets of three units.

Breakeven point:	*J*		*M*	
in units	(62,400 × 1)	62,400	(62,400 × 2)	124,800
in £	(× £60)	£3,744,000	(× £72)	£8,985,600

'Total' breakeven point = £12,729,600

6.4 Ignoring commercial considerations, mix 1 is preferable to mix 2. This is because it results in a lower level of sales to break even (because of the higher average contribution per unit sold). The average contribution for mix 1 is £19.20 (£96 ÷ 5). In mix 2 it is £18 (£54 ÷ 3). Mix 1 contains a higher proportion (40% as opposed to $33^{1}/3$%) of the more profitable product.

Exercise 3

TIM Ltd produces and sells two products, the MK and the KL. The company expects to sell 1 MK for every 2 KLs and have monthly sales revenue of £150,000. The MK has a C/S ratio of 20% whereas the KL has a C/S ratio of 40%. Budgeted monthly fixed costs are £30,000.

Required

Calculate the budgeted breakeven sales revenue.

Solution

Average C/S ratio = $\dfrac{(20\% \times 1) + (40\% \times 2)}{3}$ = $33^{1}/3$%

Sales revenue at the breakeven point = $\dfrac{\text{fixed costs}}{\text{C / S ratio}}$ = $\dfrac{£30,000}{0.333}$

= £90,000

---

7   BREAKEVEN CHARTS, CONTRIBUTION CHARTS AND PROFIT/VOLUME CHARTS

Breakeven charts   *11/95*

7.1 The breakeven point can also be determined graphically using a breakeven chart which is defined in CIMA *Official Terminology* as 'A chart which indicates approximate profit or loss at different levels of sales volume within a limited range'. The way to prepare it is as follows.

(a) Show on the horizontal axis the sales/output in units and on the vertical axis values for sales revenue and costs.

(b) Draw the *sales line*, which starts at the origin (zero sales volume = zero sales revenue) and ends at the point which signifies the expected sales.

(c) Draw the *fixed costs* line which runs above and parallel to the horizontal axis, at a point on the vertical axis denoting the total fixed costs.

(d) Draw the *total costs line*, which starts at the point where the fixed costs line meets the vertical axis (at zero output), and ends at the point which represents, on the horizontal axis, the anticipated sales in units, and on the vertical axis the sum of the total variable cost of those units plus the total fixed costs.

(e) *Confirm the chart is accurate* by checking points on the graph correspond to values calculated arithmetically.

7.2 The breakeven point is the intersection of the sales line and the total costs line. By projecting the lines horizontally and vertically from this point to the appropriate axes, it is possible to read off the breakeven point in sales units and sales value.

7.3 The number of units represented on the chart by the distance between the breakeven point and the expected (or budgeted) sales, in units, indicates the margin of safety.

7.4 You must be able to draw all of the charts described in the following paragraphs.

Example: a breakeven chart

7.5 The budgeted annual output of a factory is 120,000 units. The fixed overheads amount to £40,000 and the variable costs are 50p per unit. At a sales price is £1 per unit all 120,000 units are sold.

Required

Construct a breakeven chart showing the current breakeven point and profit earned up to the present budgeted capacity.

Solution

7.6 We begin by calculating the profit at the budgeted annual output.

	£
Sales (120,000 units)	120,000
Variable costs	60,000
Contribution	60,000
Fixed costs	40,000
Profit	20,000

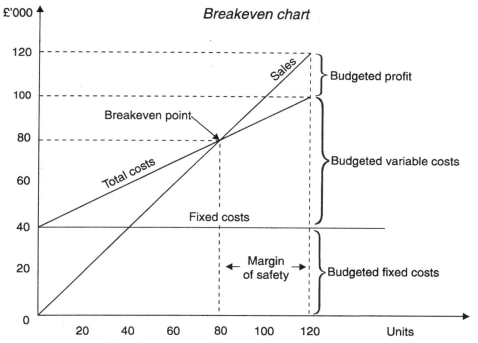

The components of the chart are as follows.

(a) The vertical axis represents money (costs and revenue) and the horizontal axis represents the level of activity (production and sales). The chart should cover the relevant ranges on both axes and should of course be clearly labelled.

(b) The sales line is drawn by plotting two points and joining them up.

   (i) At zero sales, revenue is nil.
   (ii) At the budgeted output and sales of 120,000 units, revenue is £120,000.

(c) The fixed costs are represented by a straight line parallel to the horizontal axis (in our example, at £40,000).

(d) The variable costs are added 'on top of fixed costs, to give total costs. It is assumed that fixed costs are the same in total and variable costs are the same per unit at all levels of output.

   The line of total costs is therefore a straight line and only two points need to be plotted and joined up. Perhaps the two most convenient points to plot are total costs at zero output, and total costs at the budgeted output and sales.

   (i) At zero output, costs are equal to the amount of fixed costs only, £40,000, since there are no variable costs.

   (ii) At the budgeted output of 120,000 units, costs are £100,000.

	£
Fixed costs	40,000
Variable costs 120,000 × 50p	60,000
Total costs	100,000

(e) The breakeven point is where total costs are matched exactly by total revenue. From the chart, this can be seen to occur at output and sales of 80,000 units, when revenue and costs are both £80,000. This breakeven point can be proved mathematically as:

$$\frac{\text{required contribution} = \text{fixed costs}}{\text{contribution per unit}} = \frac{£40,000}{50\text{p per unit}} = 80,000 \text{ units}$$

7.7 The margin of safety can be seen on the chart as the difference between the budgeted level of activity and the breakeven level.

The value of breakeven charts

7.8   Breakeven charts may be helpful to management in planning the production and marketing of individual products, or the entire product range of their company.

(a)   A chart gives a visual display of how much output needs to be sold to make a profit and what the likelihood would be of making a loss if actual sales fell short of the budgeted expectations.

(b)   Extending the chart beyond the break-even point will enable management to see the profits made if more units are sold.

(c)   The chart can be used to compare actual figures to budgeted, this year's figures to last year's or for sensitivity analysis (see below).

7.9   However it is important to realise the following.

(a)   A breakeven chart is a means of showing, in 'picture' form, the cost-volume-profit 'arithmetic' of sales revenues, fixed costs and variable costs. In practice, management is more likely to use the arithmetical techniques of breakeven analysis without bothering to draw charts as a visual aid.

(b)   Although the cost line starts at zero output and can be extended to costs at very high volumes of output and sales, cost accountants would claim that the estimates of fixed plus variable costs are not accurate over the entire range of output, but only within a *'relevant' range* (or 'normal range') of output. It is generally assumed that this relevant range will include the breakeven point and the budgeted output and so, for all practical purposes, the breakeven chart is accurate enough.

Contribution (or contribution breakeven) charts   *11/96, 5/98*

7.10   As an alternative to drawing the fixed cost line first, it is possible to start with that for variable costs. This is known as a contribution chart and is defined in CIMA *Official Terminology* as 'a graph showing the effect on contribution and on overall profit of changes in sales volume or value.'

7.11   To produce this chart, the variable costs line is plotted joining up zero output (where variable costs are zero) and variable costs at the budgeted output.

7.12   Total costs are then plotted by joining fixed costs at zero output (where fixed costs = total costs) with fixed plus variable costs at the budgeted output.

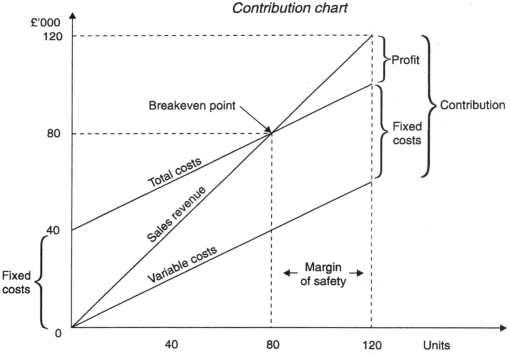

Contribution chart

7.13 One of the advantages of the contribution chart is that is shows clearly the contribution for different levels of production (indicated here at 120,000 units, the budgeted level of output) as the 'wedge' shape between the sales revenue line and the variable costs line. At the breakeven point, the contribution equals fixed costs exactly. At levels of output above the breakeven point, the contribution is larger, and not only covers fixed costs, but also leaves a profit. Below the breakeven point, the loss is the amount by which contribution fails to cover fixed costs.

Exam focus point

Make sure you can draw a contribution breakeven chart and identify and explain the significance of each of its components. This was worth ten marks (one fifth of the way to a pass) in the November 1996 and May 1998 exams.

The P/V chart

7.14 The P/V (profit-volume) chart is a variation of the breakeven chart which provides a simple illustration of the relationship of costs and profit to sales, and of the margin of safety. The CIMA *Official Terminology* provides the same definition for both this type of chart and a contribution chart. A P/V chart is constructed as follows (look at the chart in the example that follows as you read the explanation).

(a) 'P' is on the y axis

   (i) 'P' actually comprises not only 'profit' but *contribution* to profit (in monetary value), extending above and below the x axis with a zero point at the intersection of the two axes.

   (ii) The negative section below the x axis represents fixed costs. This means that at zero production, the firm is incurring a loss equal to the fixed costs.

(b) 'V' is on the x axis and comprises either *volume* of *sales* or value of sales (revenue). Note that the x axis is at the *centre*, not the bottom of the page.

(c) The profit-volume line is a straight line.

   (i) Its starting point (at zero production) is the intercept on the y axis representing the level of fixed costs.

   (ii) Its gradient is contribution/unit (or the C/S ratio if sales value is used rather than units).

   (iii) The P/V line will cut the x axis at the breakeven point of sales volume.

   (iv) Any point on the P/V line above the x axis represents the profit to the firm (as measured on the vertical axis) for that particular level of sales.

7.15 Let's draws a P/V chart for our example. At sales of 120,000 units, total contribution will be $120,000 \times £(1 - 0.5) = £60,000$ and total profit will be £20,000.

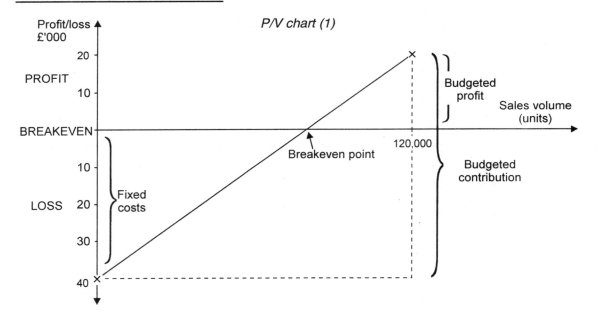

The advantage of the P/V chart

7.16 The P/V chart shows clearly the effect on profit and breakeven point of any changes in selling price, variable cost, fixed cost and/or sales demand.

7.17 If the budgeted selling price of the product in our example is increased to £1.20, with the result that demand drops to 105,000 units despite additional fixed costs of £10,000 being spent on advertising, we could add a line representing this situation to our P/V chart.

7.18 At sales of 105,000 units, contribution will be 105,000 × £(1.20 − 0.50) = £73,500 and total profit will be £23,500 (fixed costs being £50,000).

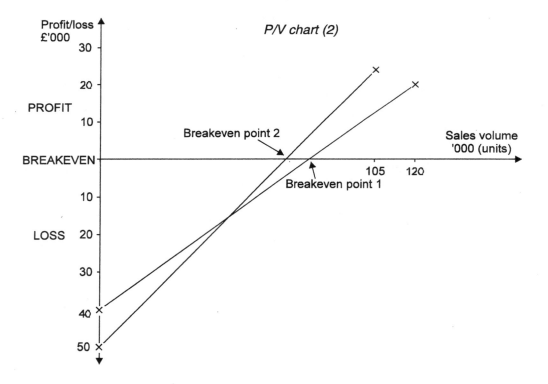

7.19 The diagram shows that if the selling price is increased, the breakeven point occurs at a lower level of sales revenue (71,429 units instead of 80,000 units), although this is not a particularly large increase when viewed in the context of the projected sales volume. It is also possible to see that for sales above 50,000 units, the profit achieved will be higher (and the loss achieved lower) if the price is £1.20. For sales volumes below 50,000 units the first option will yield lower losses.

7.20   The P/V chart is the clearest way of presenting such information; two conventional breakeven charts on one set of axes would be very confusing.

Exam focus point

The examiner has confirmed that candidates *may* be expected to draw P/V charts which incorporate changes to variables.

The economist's breakeven chart

7.21   The charts we have looked at so far are based on the accountant's linear assumption of cost behaviour. The economist's cost line is, however, curvilinear (as explained in Chapter 2) and hence the economist's breakeven chart (as shown below) differs from the accountant's.

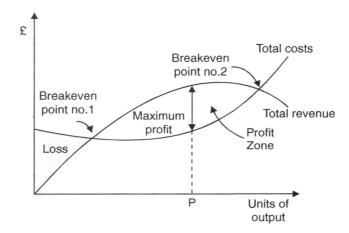

7.22   Note the following points.

   (a)   The total revenue line is *curvilinear* because to increase the number of units sold the selling price has to be reduced. The line therefore increases at a decreasing rate and eventually begins to decline as the benefits of increased sales volume are outweighed by the adverse effect of price reductions.

   (b)   The total costs line shows *economies of scale* at first (unit costs decrease as output increases), but then turns upwards as *diminishing returns* set in.

   (c)   The shape of the total costs and total revenue lines means that there are *two* breakeven points. At the second, decreasing total revenue equals increasing total costs. The first is similar to the single breakeven point shown on an accountant's breakeven chart.

   (d)   Profits are maximised at point P, where there is the greatest vertical difference between the total cost and total revenue curves.

7.23   The accountant's breakeven chart is not intended to provide an accurate representation of total costs and total revenue behaviour in all ranges of output but rather to represent behaviour over the range of output in which the firm expects to be operating in the future (relevant range). Within the relevant range (usually the levels at which the firm has had experience of operating in the past and for which cost information is available), the economist's and accountant's charts are not too different. The two types of chart are superimposed below.

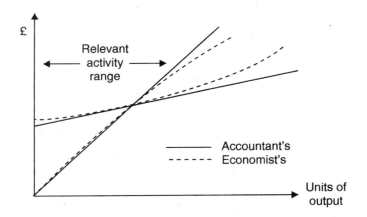

8   SENSITIVITY ANALYSIS

8.1   Sensitivity analysis is a term used to describe any technique whereby factors involved in a situation (such as sales volume, sales price per unit, material costs or labour costs) are varied one at a time and the effect on a particular outcome determined. The objective is to identify sensitive factors - those that have most influence on outcomes - so that they can be further analysed before a final decision is taken.

8.2   Sensitivity analysis can be applied to many areas of management accounting including breakeven analysis.

Breakeven charts and sensitivity analysis

8.3   Breakeven charts can be used in a form of sensitivity analysis to show variations in the possible sales price, variable costs or fixed costs and the resulting affects on the breakeven point and the margin of safety. Suppose that a company sells a product which has a variable cost of £2 per unit. Fixed costs are £15,000. It has been estimated that if the sales price is set at £4.40 per unit, the expected sales volume would be 7,500 units; whereas if the sales price is lower, at £4 per unit, the expected sales volume would be 10,000 units.

Required

Draw a breakeven chart to show the budgeted profit, the breakeven point and the margin of safety at each of the possible sales prices.

Solution

8.4

Workings	*Sales price £4.40 per unit* £		*Sales price £4 per unit* £
Fixed costs	15,000		15,000
Variable costs (7,500 × £2.00)	15,000	(10,000 × £2.00)	20,000
Total costs	30,000		35,000
Budgeted revenue (7,500 × £4.40)	33,000	(10,000 × £4.00)	40,000

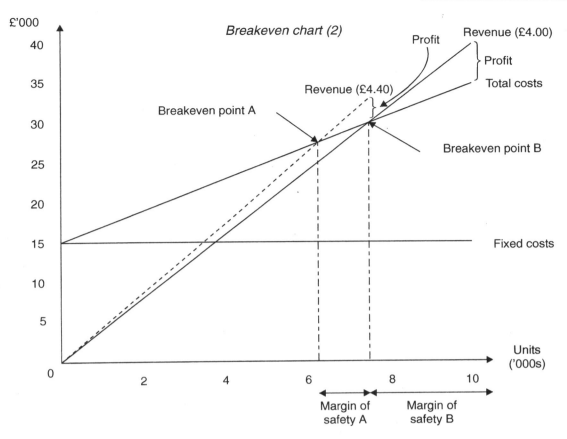

(a)   Breakeven point A is the breakeven point at a sales price of £4.40 per unit, which is 6,250 units or £27,500 in costs and revenues.

$$(\text{check: } \frac{\text{required contribution to break even}}{\text{contribution per unit}} = \frac{£15,000}{£2.40 \text{ per unit}} = 6,250 \text{ units})$$

The margin of safety (A) is 7,500 units − 6,250 units = 1,250 units or 16.7% of expected sales.

(b)   Breakeven point B is the breakeven point at a sales price of £4 per unit which is 7,500 units or £30,000 in costs and revenues.

$$(\text{check: } \frac{\text{required contribution to break even}}{\text{contribution per unit}} = \frac{£15,000}{£2 \text{ per unit}} = 7,500 \text{ units})$$

The margin of safety (B) = 10,000 units − 7,500 units = 2,500 units or 25% of expected sales.

8.5   Since a price of £4 per unit gives a higher expected profit and a wider margin of safety, this price will probably be preferred even though the breakeven point is higher than at a sales price of £4.40 per unit.

Sensitivity analysis and the P/V chart

8.6   Just as breakeven charts can be used to show how variations in sales price, variable costs and fixed costs affect the breakeven point and the margin of safety, so too can P/V charts. Two circumstances can be considered.

(a)   *Fixed cost changes* do not alter the slope of the P/V line but change the point of intersection and therefore the breakeven point.

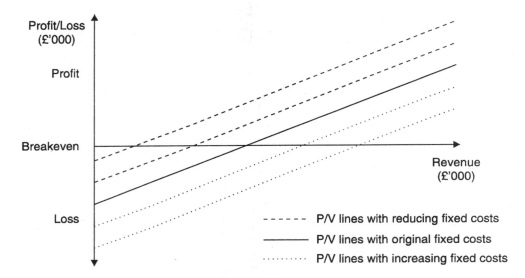

Such a diagram shows how the breakeven point and the level of profit or loss at different levels of revenue will change depending on the level of fixed costs.

(b) *Variable cost and sales price changes* alter the slope of the line and hence the breakeven point and the profit or loss.

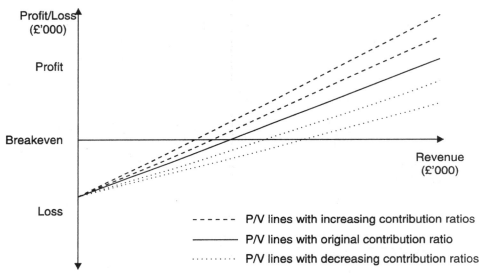

Such a diagram shows how the breakeven point and the level of profit or loss at different levels of revenue will change depending on the contribution ratio.

8.7 Suppose the budgeted selling price of the product in our example is increased to £1.20, with the result that demand drops to 105,000 units despite additional fixed costs of £10,000 being spent on advertising. We could add a line representing this situation to P/V chart (1).

8.8 At a sales level of 105,000 units, contribution will be $105,000 \times £(1.20 - 0.50) = £73,500$ and total profit will be £23,500 (fixed costs being £50,000).

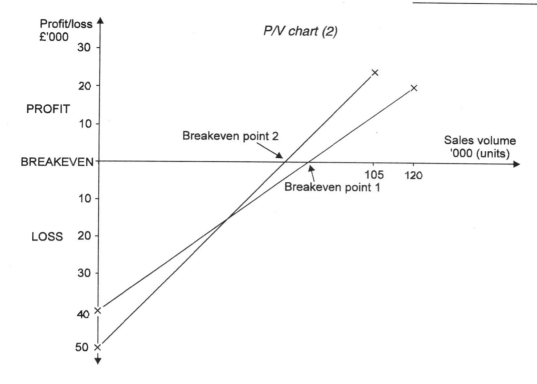

8.9   The diagram shows that if the selling price is increased, the breakeven point occurs at a lower level of sales revenue (71,429 units instead of 80,000 units), although this is not a particularly large increase when viewed in the context of the projected sales volume. It is also possible to see that for sales above 50,000 units, the profit achieved will be higher (and the loss achieved lower) if the price is £1.20. For sales volumes below 50,000 units the first option will yield lower losses.

8.10 Changes in the variable cost per unit or in fixed costs at certain activity levels can also be easily incorporated into a P/V chart. The profit or loss at each point where the cost structure changes should be calculated and plotted on the graph so that the profit/volume line becomes a series of straight lines.

8.11 For example, suppose that in our original example, at sales levels in excess of 120,000 units the variable cost per unit increases to £0.60 (perhaps because of overtime premiums that are incurred when production exceeds a certain level). At sales of 130,000 units, contribution would therefore be $130,000 \times £(1 - 0.60) = £52,000$ and total profit would be £12,000.

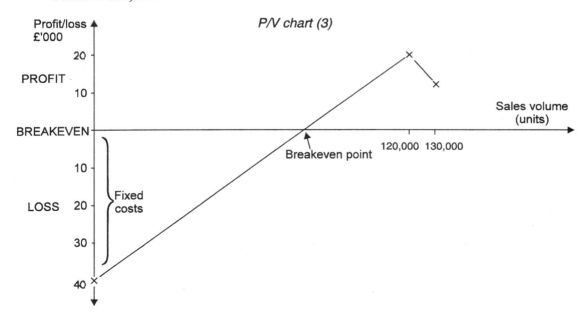

9   LIMITATIONS OF BREAKEVEN ANALYSIS

9.1   Traditionally, before PCs and spreadsheets became widespread, textbooks set out the major limitations of breakeven analysis as follows.

(a) A breakeven chart can only apply to one single product or a single mix (fixed proportions) of a group of products. This restricts its usefulness.

(b) It is assumed that fixed costs are the same in total and variable costs are the same per unit at all levels of output. This assumption is a great simplification.

     (i) Fixed costs will change if output falls or increases substantially (most fixed costs are step costs).

     (ii) The variable cost per unit will decrease where economies of scale are made at higher output volumes, and the variable cost per unit will also eventually rise where diseconomies of scale begin to appear at higher volumes of output (for example the extra cost of labour in overtime working).

It is important to remember that although a breakeven chart is drawn on the assumption that fixed costs and the variable cost per unit are constant, this is only correct within a normal range or relevant range of output. It is generally assumed that both the budgeted output and also the breakeven point of sales lie within this relevant range.

It is also important to remember that a breakeven chart aids short-term decision-making; over the long term inflation may make a difference.

(c) It is assumed that sales prices will be constant at all levels of activity. This may not be true, especially at higher volumes of output, where the price may have to be reduced to win the extra sales.

(d) Production and sales are assumed to be the same and therefore the consequences of any increase in stock levels (when production volumes exceed sales) or 'de-stocking' (when sales volumes exceed production levels) are ignored.

(e) Uncertainty in the estimates of fixed costs and unit variable costs is often ignored in breakeven analysis, and some costs (for example mixed costs and step costs) are not always easily categorised or divided into fixed and variable.

9.2   Many of these limitations can now easily be overcome, however, and breakeven analysis is a useful technique for managers in planning sales prices, the desired sales mix, and profitability. Breakeven charts are 'decorative' in the sense that they provide a graphical representation of breakeven arithmetic but this is highly useful for decision makers who trust *you* to get the figures right and who are guided by other less tangible factors, as well as the numbers.

10   SPREADSHEETS AND BREAKEVEN ANALYSIS

10.1   Because breakeven analysis is based on a number of straightforward mathematical equations, spreadsheet models can be easily built.

10.2   For example, suppose an organisation wanted to know what the *sales level* would have to be at three different *fixed cost levels* and three different *variable cost levels* to reach three different *profit levels*.

10.3   A computer can calculate the twenty-seven different sales levels quickly, without error, using a spreadsheet model as shown below.

10.4   Any values for fixed costs, variable costs or profit can be inserted and the computer will calculate the required sales level.

	A	B	C	D	E
1	Fixed costs	Variable costs as a % of sales	Sales revenue needed to earn a profit of:		
2			£10,000	£20,000	£30,000
3	£		£	£	£
4	20,000	40%	50,000	66,667	83,333
5	20,000	45%	54,545	72,727	90,909
6	20,000	50%	60,000	80,000	100,000
7	30,000	40%	66,667	83,333	100,000
8	30,000	45%	72,727	90,909	109,091
9	30,000	50%	80,000	100,000	120,000
10	40,000	40%	83,333	100,000	116,667
11	40,000	45%	90,909	109,091	127,273
12	40,000	50%	100,000	120,000	140,000
13					

Exercise 4

Cell C5 contains the following formula.

=(A5+10000)/(1-B5)

Explain this.

Solution

Remember the basic pattern, and you will never go far wrong.

$$\frac{\underset{\underline{(V)}}{S}}{\underset{\underline{(F)}}{\overset{C}{}}}$$
$$P$$

If V = (0.45 * S), then C = ((1 - 0.45) * S). So, S = (C/(1 - 0.45))

Also, C = (F + P).

If C = ((1 - 0.45) * S), and C = (F + P), then S = ((F + P)/(1 − 0.45))

If you cannot follow this, you are not up to scratch with your understanding of breakeven analysis and you need to do some more work.

10.5   In addition to speed and convenience, computers allow a more sophisticated approach to breakeven analysis than is covered in this chapter. Spreadsheet models could incorporate multiple cost drivers, non-linear relationships and various sales mixes. Moreover, analysis need not be restricted to the relevant range.

Exam focus point

In the light of the above, bear in mind when you are answering exam questions that the assumptions listed in Section 9 are necessary so that the analysis is simple enough to allow breakeven models to be constructed *manually*. Computer models, if carefully built, allow most assumptions to be dropped and a vast array of different scenarios to be investigated with merely a few keystrokes.

Chapter roundup

- Breakeven analysis has a number of purposes.

    o   To provide information to management about cost behaviour for routine planning and 'one-off' decision making

    o   To determine what volume of sales is needed at any given budgeted sales price in order to break even

    o   To identify the 'risk' in the budget by measuring the margin of safety

    o   To calculate the effects on profit of changes in variable costs, C/S ratios, sales price and volume, product mix, and so on.

- Make sure that you understand how to calculate the following.

    o   The breakeven point

    o   The C/S ratio

    o   The margin of safety and target profits

- You should be able to apply the principles of breakeven analysis both to decisions about whether to change sales prices or costs and to problems of profit maximisation.

- You should also be able to construct breakeven, contribution and profit/volume charts.

- *Do not forget* that breakeven analysis does have limitations.

    o   It is only valid within a 'relevant range' of output volumes

    o   It measures profitability, but does not consider the volume of capital employed to achieve such profits, and so ignores return on capital employed

    o   It does not take account of uncertain or intangible factors such as political and economic developments or customer perceptions.

- *Forget* any limitations related to the time and effort required to do the calculations: these are nil or negligible if a computer is used.

Test your knowledge

1   What is the formula for calculating the breakeven point in terms of the number of units required to break even? (see para 1.3)

2   Give the formula which uses the C/S ratio to calculate the breakeven point. (2.1)

3   What is the margin of safety? (3.1)

4   What is the 'relevant range' on a breakeven chart? (7.9)

5   What is a profit/volume chart? (7.14)

6   What is the advantage of P/V charts? (7.16)

7   What are the 'limitations' of breakeven charts and breakeven analysis? (9.1)

8   How can these limitations be overcome? (10.3 – 10.5)

Now try illustrative questions 17 and 18 at the end of the Study Text

Chapter 15

LIMITING FACTOR DECISION MAKING

This chapter covers the following topics.

		Syllabus reference	Ability required
1	Limiting factors	6(b)	Knowledge
2	Decisions involving one limiting factor	6(b)	Knowledge
3	Decisions involving one limiting factor and limited sales demand	6(b)	Knowledge
4	Make or buy decisions and scarce resources	6(b)	Knowledge
5	Limiting factors and shadow prices	6(b)	Knowledge
6	Using limiting factor analysis	6(b)	Knowledge

Introduction

From your study of economics you should be aware of the concept of a scare resource, which is a resource of which there is a limited supply. Once a scarce resource affects the ability of an organisation to earn profits a scarce resource becomes known as a limiting factor.

If faced with a limiting factor an organisation's volume of output and sales will be constrained; management therefore have to make a decision about what product mix (or mix of services) to provide in order to maximise profits with the available capacity.

The cost accountant assists in this type of decision by applying what is known as limiting factor analysis to provide the appropriate information. Limiting factor analysis, like breakeven analysis, involves the application of marginal costing techniques.

1 LIMITING FACTORS

1.1 The CIMA *Official Terminology* defines a limiting factor or a key factor as 'Anything which limits the activity of an entity. An entity seeks to optimise the benefit it obtains from the limiting factor'.

Exam focus point

You may remember limiting factor analysis from your Paper 2 studies but since it is ideal examination question material we are going to look at the topic from basics (especially since the examiner commented in his November 1995 examination report that many candidates were unable to perform the technique).

1.2 The limiting factor may change from time to time for the same entity or product. Thus when raw materials are in short supply, performance or profit may be expressed in terms of 'per kilo of material' (that is, for example, profit is £4.50 per kilo of raw material used), or in a restricted skilled labour market, as 'per skilled labour hour'. Alternatively, the limiting factor may be one critical process in a chain of processes.

1.3 It is worth noting that a limiting factor, if there is one, ought to be identified when the annual budget is being prepared since the budget will have to be based on what is achievable given the available resources. As such, limiting factor decisions are actually more in the nature of routine rather than ad hoc decisions.

1.4 An organisation might be faced with just one limiting factor (other than maximum sales demand) but there might also be several scarce resources, with two or more of them putting an effective limit on the level of activity that can be achieved.

1.5 Examples of limiting factors are as follows.

(a) *Sales*. There may be a limit to sales demand.

(b) *Labour*. The limit may be either in terms of total quantity or of particular skills. Either way, there will be insufficient labour to produce enough to satisfy sales demand.

(c) *Materials*. There may be insufficient available materials to produce enough units to satisfy sales demand.

(d) *Manufacturing capacity*. There may not be sufficient machine capacity for the production required to meet sales demand.

(e) *Financial resources*. There may not be enough cash to pay for the necessary production.

1.6 If sales demand is the factor which restricts greater production output, profit will be maximised by making exactly the amount required for sales (and no more) provided that each product sold earns a positive contribution.

If labour supply, materials availability, machine capacity or cash availability limits production to less than the volume which could be sold, management is faced with the problem of deciding what to produce and what should not be produced because there are insufficient resources to make everything.

1.7 It is assumed in limiting factor analysis that management would select a product mix or service mix that would maximise profit and that profit is maximised when contribution is maximised (given no change in fixed cost expenditure incurred). In other words, marginal costing ideas are applied.

(a) *Contribution* will be *maximised* by earning the *biggest possible contribution per unit of limiting factor*.

Thus if grade A labour is the limiting factor, contribution will be maximised by earning the biggest contribution per hour of grade A labour worked. Similarly, if machine time is in short supply, profit will be maximised by earning the biggest contribution per machine hour worked.

(b) The limiting factor decision therefore involves the determination of the *contribution earned per unit of scarce resource* by each different product.

(c) If the sales demand is limited, the profit-maximising decision will be to produce the top-ranked product(s) up to the sales demand unit.

In limiting factor decisions, we generally assume that fixed costs are the same whatever production mix is selected, so that the only relevant costs are variable costs.

2   DECISIONS INVOLVING ONE LIMITING FACTOR   *5/97, 11/97*

2.1 When there is just one limiting factor, the technique for establishing the contribution-maximising product mix or service mix is to rank the products or services in order of contribution-earning ability per unit of limiting factor. Here are a series of examples to illustrate both the technique and the further considerations involved.

Exam focus point

If there is *more than one* limiting factor, other techniques are available. You will study these for Paper 7, *Management Science Applications*.

Example: limiting factor (1)

2.2   Sausage Ltd makes two products, the Mash and the Sauce. Unit variable costs are as follows.

	Mash	*Sauce*
	£	£
Direct materials	1	3
Direct labour (£3 per hour)	6	3
Variable overhead	1	1
	8	7

The sales price per unit is £14 per Mash and £11 per Sauce. During July 19X2 the available direct labour is limited to 8,000 hours. Sales demand in July is expected to be as follows.

Mash   3,000 units
Sauce   5,000 units

Required

Determine the production budget that will maximise profit, assuming that fixed costs per month are £20,000 and that there are no opening stock of finished goods or work in progress.

Solution

2.3   (a)   The first step in the solution is to confirm that the limiting factor is something other than sales demand.

	Mash	*Sauces*	*Total*
Labour hours per unit	2 hrs	1 hr	
Sales demand	3,000 units	5,000 units	
Labour hours needed	6,000 hrs	5,000 hrs	11,000 hrs
Labour hours available			8,000 hrs
Shortfall			3,000 hrs

Labour is the limiting factor on production.

(b)   The second step is to identify the contribution earned by each product per unit of scarce resource, that is, per labour hour worked.

	Mash	*Sauce*
	£	£
Sales price	14	11
Variable cost	8	7
Unit contribution	6	4
Labour hours per unit	2 hrs	1 hr
Contribution per labour hour (= per unit of limiting factor)	£3	£4

Although Mashes have a higher unit contribution than Sauces, two Sauces can be made in the time it takes to make one Mash. Because labour is in short supply it is more profitable to make Sauces than Mashes.

(c)   The final stage in the solution is to work out the budgeted production and sales. Sufficient Sauces will be made to meet the full sales demand, and the remaining labour hours available will then be used to make Mashes.

(i)

Product	*Demand*	*Hours required*	*Hours available*	*Priority for manufacture*
Sauces	5,000	5,000	5,000	1st
Mashes	3,000	6,000	3,000 (bal)	2nd
		11,000	8,000	

(ii)

Product	Units	Hours needed	Contribution per unit £	Total
Sauces	5,000	5,000	4	20,000
Mashes (balance)	1,500	3,000	6	9,000
		8,000		29,000
Less fixed costs				20,000
Profit				9,000

(d) Note that it is *not* more profitable to begin by making as many units as possible of the product with the bigger unit contribution. We could make 3,000 units of Mash (£6 per unit) in 6,000 hours and 2,000 units of Sauce (£4 per unit) in the remaining 2,000 hours. However, contribution would be £(3,000 × £6) plus £(2,000 × £4) = £26,000, and profit would be only £6,000. Unit contribution is not the correct way to decide priorities, because it take *two* hours to earn £6 from a Mash and *one* hour to earn £4 from a Sauce. Sauces make more profitable use of the scarce resource, labour hours.

Example: limiting factor (2)

2.4 Rugby Ltd makes three products, grumpits, widgets and splodgets, for which there is unlimited sales demand at the budgeted sales price of each. A grumpit takes 5 hours to make, has a variable cost of £24 and a sales price of £39. A widget takes 3 hours to make, has a variable cost of £18 and a sales price of £30. A splodget takes 2 hours to make, has a variable cost of £10 and a sales price of £20. All three products use the same type of labour, which is in restricted supply.

Required

Determine which product should be made in order to maximise profits.

Solution

2.5 There is no limitation on sales demand, but labour is in restricted supply, and so to determine the profit-maximising production mix, we must rank the products in order of contribution-earning capability per labour hour.

	Grumpits £	Widgets £	Splodgets £
Sales price	39	30	20
Variable costs	24	18	10
Contribution	15	12	10
Hours per unit	5 hrs	3 hrs	2 hrs
Contribution per labour hour	£3	£4	£5

The ranking is   1st Splodgets

2nd Widgets

3rd Grumpits

Although grumpits have the highest unit contribution, splodgets are more profitable because they make the greatest contribution in each scarce hour of labour time worked.

15 splodgets (earning a contribution of 15 × £10 = £150) can be made in 30 hours. In 30 hours it would only be possible to make 10 widgets (earning a contribution of 10 × £12 = £120), or alternatively 6 grumpits (earning a contribution of 6 × £15 = £90).

Opportunity costs

2.6 An alternative way of looking at the above problem is to think in terms of the opportunity cost, the best alternative foregone.

2.7 In the example above, if splodgets are to be made, this would mean they have been produced in preference to grumpits and widgets. Widgets have a higher contribution per unit of scarce resource (labour), than grumpits. Therefore the opportunity cost associated with producing splodgets is £4 per labour hour (the value of the contribution foregone from producing the best alternative (widgets)). This cost is incorporated into splodgets' production costs as follows.

	Splodgets
	£
Selling price per unit	<u>20</u>
Variable costs	10
Opportunity cost of labour (£4 × 2 hours)	<u>8</u>
	<u>18</u>
Net benefit	<u>2</u>

This net benefit can be reconciled with the calculation of contribution per labour hour.

	£
Splodget contribution per labour hour	5
Widget contribution per labour hour	<u>4</u>
	<u>1</u>

Splodgets take two hours to make, the benefit per splodget = 2 × £1 = £2

2.8   Alternatively, if grumpits or widgets are chosen, the best alternative foregone is the splodget, which has a contribution of £5 per labour hour.

2.9   Using the same technique as above.

		Grumpits	*Widgets*
		£	£
Selling price		<u>39</u>	<u>30</u>
Variable costs		24	18
Opportunity costs	(5 hrs × £5)	25	
	(3 hrs × £5)		<u>15</u>
		<u>49</u>	<u>33</u>
Net benefit		<u>(10)</u>	<u>(3)</u>

Both grumpits and widgets have negative net benefits; by contrast splodgets have positive net benefits. Therefore splodgets are the most profitable product to produce.

Exam focus point

In general in the exam most problems will have the following characteristics.

(a)   A finite number of products are considered.
(b)   Each product uses the same resources in different quantities.
(c)   No other uses of the resources are considered.

In these circumstances the limiting factor method should be used.

The opportunity cost method should be used in circumstances where products use different resources, and the choice of products is not a finite number.

Exercise

Harvey Ltd is currently preparing its budget for the year ending 30 September 19X2. The company manufactures and sells three products, Beta, Delta and Gamma.

The unit selling price and cost structure of each product is budgeted as follows.

	Beta £	Delta £	Gamma £
Selling price	100	124	32
Variable costs:			
Labour	24	48	6
Materials	26	7	8
Overhead	10	5	6
	60	60	20
Contribution per unit	40	64	12

Direct labour rate is budgeted at £6 per hour, and fixed costs at £1,300,000 per annum. The company has a maximum production capacity of 228,000 direct labour hours.

A meeting of the board of directors has been convened to discuss the budget and to resolve the problem as to the quantity of each product which should be made and sold. The sales director presented the results of a recent market survey which reveals that market demand for the company's products will be as follows.

Product	Units
Beta	24,000
Delta	12,000
Gamma	60,000

The production director proposes that since Gamma only contributes £12 per unit, the product should no longer be produced, and the surplus capacity transferred to produce additional quantities of Beta and Delta. The sales director does not agree with the proposal. Gamma is considered necessary to complement the product range and to maintain customer goodwill. If Gamma is not offered, the sales director believes that sales of Beta and Delta will be seriously affected. After further discussion the board decided that a minimum of 10,000 units of each product should be produced. The remaining production capacity would then be allocated so as to achieve the maximum profit possible.

Required

Prepare a budget statement which clearly shows the maximum profit which could be achieved in the year ending 30 September 19X2.

Solution

First we need to ascertain whether labour hours are a scarce resource.

	Units demanded	Labour hours per unit	Total labour hours
Beta	24,000	4 (£24/£6)	96,000
Delta	12,000	8 (£48/£6)	96,000
Gamma	60,000	1 (£6/£6)	60,000
			252,000

Since only 228,000 hours are available we need to establish which product earns the greatest contribution per labour hour.

	Beta	Delta	Gamma
Contribution	40	64	12
Labour hours	4	8	1
Contribution per labour hour	£10	£8	£12
Ranking	2nd	3rd	1st

The optimum production plan must take into account the requirement that 10,000 units of each product are produced, and then allocate the remaining hours according to the above ranking.

		Hours
Beta	10,000 units × 4 hours	40,000
Delta	10,000 units × 8 hours	80,000
Gamma	10,000 units × 1 hour	10,000
		130,000
Gamma	50,000 units × 1 hour (full demand)	50,000
Beta	12,000 units × 4 hours (balance)	48,000
		228,000

BUDGET STATEMENT

Contribution	£
Beta (22,000 units × £40)	880,000
Delta (10,000 units × £64)	640,000
Gamma (60,000 units × £12)	720,000
	2,240,000
Fixed costs	1,300,000
Profit	940,000

3   DECISIONS INVOLVING ONE LIMITING FACTOR AND LIMITED SALES DEMAND   *11/95, 5/97*

3.1   Although you will not be asked to deal with situations where two factors are *actually* limiting, you may be asked to deal with situations where two limiting factors (and also demand) are *potentially* limiting. The approach in these situations is to find out which factor (if any) prevents the business from fulfilling maximum demand. Products will be ranked in terms of contribution-earning ability per unit of the limiting factor, if one of the factors is limiting.

Example: limited sales demand

3.2   Lucky Ltd manufactures and sells three products, X, Y and Z, for which budgeted sales demand, unit selling prices and unit variable costs are as follows.

		X		Y		Z	
Budgeted sales demand		550 units		500 units		400 units	
		£	£	£	£	£	£
Unit sales price			16		18		14
Variable costs:	materials	8		6		2	
	labour	4		6		9	
			12		12		11
Unit contribution			4		6		3

The company has existing stocks of 250 units of X and 200 units of Z, which it is quite willing to use up to meet sales demand.

All three products use the same direct materials and the same type of direct labour. In the next year, the available supply of materials will be restricted to £4,800 (at cost) and the available supply of labour to £6,600 (at cost).

Required

Determine what product mix and sales mix would maximise the company's profits in the next year.

Solution and discussion

3.3   There appear to be two scarce resources, direct materials and direct labour. However, this is not certain, and because there is a limited sales demand as well, it might be that there is:

(a)   no limiting factor at all, except sales demand, that is none of the resources are scarce; or

(b)   only one scarce resource that prevents the full potential sales demand being achieved.

3.4   When faced with a problem of this kind, you should begin by establishing how many scarce resources there are, and if there are any, which one or which ones are they?

In this example we have:

	X Units	Y Units	Z Units
Budgeted sales	550	500	400
Stock in hand	250	0	200
Minimum production to meet demand	300	500	200

	Minimum production to meet sales demand Units	Required materials at cost £	Required labour at cost £
X	300	2,400	1,200
Y	500	3,000	3,000
Z	200	400	1,800
Total required		5,800	6,000
Total available		4,800	6,600
(Shortfall)/Surplus		(1,000)	600

Materials are a limiting factor, but labour is not.

3.5 The next step is to rank X, Y and Z in order of contribution earned per £1 of direct materials consumed.

	X £	Y £	Z £
Unit contribution	4	6	3
Cost of materials	8	6	2
Contribution per £1 materials	£0.50	£1.00	£1.50
Ranking	3rd	2nd	1st

Z should be manufactured up to the limit where units produced plus units in stock will meet sales demand, then Y second and X third, until all the available materials are used up.

Ranking	Product	Sales demand less units in stock Units	Production quantity Units		Materials cost £
1st	Z	200	200	(× £2)	400
2nd	Y	500	500	(× £6)	3,000
3rd	X	300	175	(× £8)	*1,400
			Total available		4,800

* Balancing amount using up total available.

3.6 The profit-maximising budget is as follows.

	X Units	Y Units	Z Units
Opening stock	250	0	200
Add production	175	500	200
Sales	425	500	400

	X £	Y £	Z £	Total £
Revenue	6,800	9,000	5,600	21,400
Variable costs	5,100	6,000	4,400	15,500
Contribution	1,700	3,000	1,200	5,900

4 MAKE OR BUY DECISIONS AND SCARCE RESOURCES 11/95

4.1 A company might want to do more things than it has the resources for, and so its choice would be:

(a) to make the best use of the resources it has got, and ignore the opportunities to buy help from outside;

(b)   to combine internal resources with buying externally so as to do more and increase profitability further.

4.2   Buying help from outside is justifiable if it adds to profits. However, a further decision is then how to split the work between internal and external effort. What parts of the work should be given to suppliers or sub-contractors so as to maximise profitability?

4.3   In a situation where a company must sub-contract work to make up a shortfall in its own in-house capabilities, its total costs will be minimised if those units bought have the lowest extra variable cost of buying per unit of scarce resource saved by buying of all the products in question.

This basic principle can be illustrated with a simple example.

Example: make or buy decision with scarce resources

4.4   Seaman Ltd manufactures three components, S, A and T using the same machines for each. The budget for the next year calls for the production and assembly of 4,000 of each component. The variable production cost per unit of the final product is:

	Machine hours	Variable cost £
1 unit of S	3	20
1 unit of A	2	36
1 unit of T	4	24
Assembly		20
		100

Only 24,000 hours of machine time will be available during the year, and a sub-contractor has quoted the following unit prices for supplying components: S £29; A £40; T £34.

Required

Advise Seaman Ltd.

Discussion and solution

4.5   The company's budget calls for 36,000 hours of machine time, if all the components are to be produced in-house. Only 24,000 hours are available, and so there is a shortfall of 12,000 hours of machine time, which is therefore a limiting factor. The shortage can be overcome by subcontracting the equivalent of 12,000 machine hours' output to the subcontractor.

The assembly costs are not relevant costs because they are unaffected by the decision.

4.6   *Incorrect conclusion:* The company should minimise its internal costs first, and sub-contract what it cannot make itself. In this example, the temptation might be to decide that the variable cost of making each product is:

Product	Variable cost £	Machine hours per unit	Variable cost per machine hour £
S	20	3	6.67
A	36	2	18.00
T	24	4	6.00

and so in-house production would be cheapest by concentrating on T first, then S and finally A, giving a production and buying schedule as follows:

Product		Units	Hours		Variable costs £
Make:	T	4,000	16,000		96,000
	S	2,666	8,000	(balance)	53,320
			24,000		149,320
Buy:	S	1,334		(× £29)	38,686
	A	4,000		(× £40)	160,000
Total costs (excluding assembly)					348,006

4.7 *This is not the cheapest option.* Costs can be reduced still further by minimising the extra variable costs of sub-contracting per unit of scarce resource saved (that is, per machine hour saved).

	S £	A £	T £
Variable cost of making	20	36	24
Variable cost of buying	29	40	34
Extra variable cost of buying	9	4	10
Machine hours saved by buying	3 hrs	2 hrs	4 hrs
Extra variable cost of buying per hour saved	£3	£2	£2.50

4.8 *Correct conclusion:* it is cheaper to buy A than to buy T and it is most expensive to buy S. The priority for *making* the components in-house will be in the reverse order: S, then T, then A. There are enough machine hours to make all 4,000 units of S (12,000 hours) and to produce 3,000 units of T (another 12,000 hours). 12,000 hours' production of T and A must be sub-contracted.

The cost-minimising and so profit-maximising make and buy schedule is as follows:

	Component	Machine hours used/saved	Number of units	Unit variable cost £	Total variable cost £
Make:	S	12,000	4,000	20	80,000
	T	12,000	3,000	24	72,000
		24,000			152,000
Buy:	T	4,000	1,000	34	34,000
	A	8,000	4,000	40	160,000
500		12,000			
Total variable cost of components, excluding assembly costs					346,000

5 LIMITING FACTORS AND SHADOW PRICES

S/97

5.1 Whenever there are limiting factors, there will be opportunity costs. As we have seen, these are the benefits forgone by using a limiting factor in one way instead of in the next most profitable way.

5.2 For example, suppose that a company manufactures two items X and Y, which earn a contribution of £24 and £18 per unit respectively. Product X requires 4 machine hours per unit, and product Y 2 hours. Only 5,000 machine hours are available, and potential sales demand is for 1,000 units each of X and Y.

5.3 Machine hours would be a limiting factor, and with X earning £6 per hour and Y earning £9 per hour, the profit-maximising decision would be as follows.

	Units	Hours	Contribution £
Y	1,000	2,000	18,000
X (balance)	750	3,000	18,000
		5,000	36,000

Priority is given to Y because the opportunity cost of making Y instead of more units of X is £6 per hour (X's contribution per machine hour), and since Y earns £9 per hour, the incremental benefit of making Y instead of X would be £3 per hour.

5.4   If extra machine hours could be made available, more units of X (up to 1,000) would be made, and an extra contribution of £6 per hour could be earned. Similarly, if fewer machine hours were available, the decision would be to make fewer units of X and to keep production of Y at 1,000 units, and so the loss of machine hours would cost the company £6 per hour in lost contribution. This £6 per hour, the marginal contribution-earning potential of the limiting factor at the profit-maximising output level, is referred to as the *shadow price* (or *dual price)* of the limiting factor.

5.5   The shadow price of a resource is its *internal opportunity cost.* This is the marginal contribution towards fixed costs and profit that can be earned for each unit of the limiting factor that is available.

6   USING LIMITING FACTOR ANALYSIS   *11/95*

6.1   Limiting factor analysis provides us with a profit-maximising product mix, within the assumptions made. It is important to remember, however, that other considerations, so far not considered in our examples, might entirely alter the decision reached.

6.2   Look back at the example beginning in Paragraph 2.4 and consider the following points.

(a)   *Price increases.* Can the sales price of either product be raised, thereby increasing unit contribution, and the contribution per labour hour, without reducing sales demand? Since sales demand is apparently unlimited, it would be reasonable to suspect that both products are underpriced.

(b)   *Interdependence of sales.* To what extent are sales of each product interdependent? For example, a manufacturer of knives and forks could not expect to cease production of knives without affecting sales demand for the forks.

(c)   *Effect on fixed costs.* Would a decision to cease production of widgets really have no effect on fixed costs? The assumption that fixed costs are unaffected by limiting factor decisions is not always valid, and closure of either the widgets or splodgets production line might result in fixed cost savings (for example a reduction in premises costs, production planning costs, product design costs, or equipment depreciation).

Qualitative factors

6.3   When a decision is being made, qualitative factors should also be borne in mind.

(a)   *Demand.* Will the decision reached (perhaps to make and sell just one product rather than two) have a harmful effect on customer loyalty and sales demand?

(b)   *Long-term effects.* Is the decision going to affect the long-term as well as the short-term plans of the organisation? If a particular product is not produced, or produced at a level below sales demand, is it likely that competitors will take over vacated markets? Labour skilled in the manufacture of the product may be lost and a decision to reopen or expand production of the product in the future may not be possible.

(c)   *Labour.* If labour is a limiting factor, is it because the skills required are difficult to obtain, perhaps because the organisation is using very old-fashioned production methods, or is the organisation a high-tech newcomer in a low-tech area? Or perhaps the conditions of work are so unappealing the people simply do not want to work for the organisation.

(d)   *Other limiting factors.* The same sort of questions should be asked whatever the limiting factor. If machine hours are in short supply is this because more machines are needed, or newer, more reliable and efficient machines? If materials are in short supply, what are competitors doing? Have they found an equivalent or better substitute? Is it time to redesign the product?

Assumptions in limiting factor analysis

6.4   In the examples covered in the chapter, certain assumptions were made. If any of the assumptions are not valid, then the profit-maximising decision might be different. These assumptions are as follows.

(a)   *Fixed costs will be the same* regardless of the decision that is taken, and so the profit-maximising and contribution-maximising output level will be the same.

This will not necessarily be true, since some fixed costs might be directly attributable to a product or service. A decision to reduce or cease altogether activity on a product or service might therefore result in some fixed cost savings, which would have to be taken into account.

(b)   *The unit variable cost is constant*, regardless of the output quantity of a product or service. This implies the following.

(i)   The price of resources will be unchanged regardless of quantity; for example, there will be no bulk purchase discount of raw materials.

(ii)   Efficiency and productivity levels will be unchanged; regardless of output quantity the direct labour productivity, the machine time per unit, and the materials consumption per unit will remain the same.

(c)   *The estimates of sales demand* for each product, and the *resources required* to make each product, *are known with certainty*.

In the example in Paragraph 3.2, there were estimates of the maximum sales demand for each of 3 products, and these estimates were used to establish the profit-maximising product mix. Suppose the estimates were wrong? The product mix finally chosen would then either mean that some sales demand of the most profitable item would be unsatisfied, or that production would exceed sales demand, leaving some stock unsold. Clearly, once a profit-maximising output decision is reached, management will have to keep their decision under continual review, and adjust their decision as appropriate in the light of actual results.

(d)   *Units of output are divisible*, and a profit-maximising solution might include fractions of units as the optimum output level.

Where fractional answers are not realistic, some rounding of the figures will be necessary.

6.5   Given that these basic assumptions usually apply, a suitable adjustment will have to be made for any problem involving a limiting factor where one (or more) of the assumptions is invalid.

Practical difficulties with using limiting factor analysis

6.6   Difficulties with applying limiting factor analysis in practice include the following.

(a)   It may be difficult to identify which resources are likely to be in short supply and what the amount of their availability will be.

Estimates of future availability will inevitably be prone to inaccuracy and any such inaccuracies will invalidate the profit-maximising product mix derived from the use of the technique.

(b)   It is by no means certain that management make product mix decisions which are profit-maximising. They may be more concerned to develop a production/sales plan which:

(i)   is realistic;
(ii)   is acceptable to the individual managers throughout the organisation;
(iii)   is acceptable to the rest of the workforce; and
(iv)   promises a 'satisfactory' profit and accounting return.

In other words, management might look for a *satisfactory* product mix which achieves a satisfactory return, sales turnover and market share whilst at the same time plans operations and targets of achievement which employees can accept as realistic, not too demanding and unreasonable, and not too threatening to their job security.

If a 'satisfactory' output decision is adopted, the product mix or service mix recommended by the technique will inevitably be 'watered down', amended or ignored.

Exam focus point

An examination problem might present you with a situation in which there is a limiting factor, without specifically stating that this is so, and you will have the task of recognising what the situation is. You may be given a hint with the wording of the question.

(a) 'It is possible that the main raw material used in manufacturing the products will be difficult to obtain in the next year.'

(b) 'The company employs a fixed number of employees who work a maximum overtime of eight hours on top of the basic 36 hour week. The company has also agreed that no more staff will be recruited next year.'

In (a) there is a hint that raw materials might be a limiting factor. In (b), perhaps less obviously, a maximum limit is placed on the available labour hours, and so the possibility should occur to you that perhaps labour is a limiting factor.

If you suspect the existence of a limiting factor, some quick computations should confirm your suspicions.

(a) Calculate the amount of the scarce resource (material quantities, labour hours, machine hours and so on) needed to meet the potential sales demand.

(b) Calculate the amount of the scarce resource available (for example number of employees multiplied by maximum working hours per employee).

(c) Compare the two figures. Obviously, if the resources needed exceed the resources available, there is a limiting factor on output and sales.

Chapter roundup

- A scarce resource is a resource of which there is a limited supply.

- Once a scarce resource affects the ability of an organisation to earn profits, a scarce resource becomes known as a limiting factor.

- If sales demand is the factor which restricts greater production output, profit will be maximised by making exactly the amount required for sales (and no more), provided that each product earns a positive contribution.

- If resources are limiting factors, contribution will be maximised by earning the biggest possible contribution per unit of limiting factor.

- Where there is just one limiting factor, the technique for establishing the contribution-maximising product or service mix is to rank the products or services in order of contribution-earning ability per unit of limiting factor.

- Where there is a maximum potential sales demand for an organisation's products or services, they should still be ranked in order of contribution-earning ability per unit of the limiting factor. The contribution-maximising decision, however, will be to produce the top-ranked products (or to provide the top-ranked services) up to the sales demand limit.

- In a situation where an organisation must subcontract work to make up a shortfall in its own in-house capabilities, its total costs will be minimised if the units bought have the lowest extra variable cost of buying per unit of scarce resource saved by buying.

- The shadow price or dual price of a limiting factor is its marginal contribution-earning potential at the profit-maximising output level.

- Practical problems can occur when using the technique in practice.

- Qualitative factors, such as effect on customer goodwill, ability to restart production and reasons for a resource being a limiting factor, should also be borne in mind in product mix decisions.

- Various assumptions are made in limiting factor analysis.
  o Fixed costs remain the same regardless of the decision taken
  o Unit variable cost is constant regardless of the decision taken
  o Estimates of sales demand and resources required are known with certainty
  o Units of output are divisible

- If you suspect the existence of a limiting factor, calculate the amount of the scarce resource needed to meet potential sales demand, calculate the amount of the scarce resource available and then compare the two figures.

Test your knowledge

1 What is a limiting factor? (see intro and para 1.1)

2 Provide four examples of limiting factors. (1.5)

3 Marginal costing ideas are applied in limiting factor analysis. True or false? (1.7)

4 What are the relevant costs in limiting factor decisions? (1.7)

5 What is the technique for establishing the optimal product mix when faced with one limiting factor? (2.1)

6 How does the technique differ if there is also a limit to sales demand? (3.1)

7 How is the profit-maximising product mix determined in a make or buy decision involving scarce resources? (4.3)

8 List four assumptions made in limiting factor analysis. (6.4)

Now try illustrative questions 19 and 20 at the end of the Study Text

Part C
Budgets and budgetary control

Chapter 16

BUDGETS

This chapter covers the following topics.

		Syllabus reference	*Ability required*
1	Budgetary planning and control systems	6(c)	Skill
2	The preparation of budgets	6(c)	Skill
3	The sales budget	6(c)	Skill
4	Production and related budgets	6(c)	Skill
5	Cash budgets	6(c)	Skill
6	The master budget	6(c)	Skill
7	Monitoring procedures	6(c)	Skill

Introduction

This chapter begins a new topic, budgeting. You will meet the topic at all stages of your future examination studies and so it is vital that you get a firm grasp of it now.

You may recognise much of this chapter from your cost accounting studies for Paper 2; you have already covered most of the topics in this chapter at a basic level and so we have included a couple of deemed knowledge boxes on the most straightforward areas.

The chapter begins by explaining the reasons for operating a budgetary planning and control system and then explains some of the key terms and techniques associated with budgeting.

You should have already covered budget preparation (including the preparation of cash budgets) but we will look at some more complex examples. The culmination of the budgeting process is, as you probably remember from Paper 2, the master budget, and an example of master budget preparation is included in Section 6.

Section 7 explains how the budgeting process does not stop once the master budget has been prepared but is a constant task of the cost accountant.

Lastly we shall look at how management attitudes can affect the budgeting process, and how the cost accountant should respond to management requirements.

Chapter 17 builds on the general awareness of budgeting which you will have gained in this chapter and considers the control function of budgets.

---

1 BUDGETARY PLANNING AND CONTROL SYSTEMS

1.1 The budget is 'a quantitative statement for a defined period of time, which may include planned revenues, expenses, assets, liabilities and cash flows. A budget provides a focus for the organisation, aids the co-ordination of activities and facilitates planning' (CIMA *Official Terminology*).

1.2 There is, however, little point in an organisation simply preparing a budget for the sake of preparing a budget. A beautifully laid out budgeted profit and loss account filed in the cost accountant's file and never looked at again is worthless. The organisation should gain from both the actual preparation process and from the budget once it has been prepared.

1.3   Budgets are therefore not prepared in isolation and then filed away but are the concrete components of what is known as the budgetary planning and control system. A budgetary planning and control system is essentially a system for ensuring *communication, coordination* and *control* within an organisation. Communication, coordination and control are general objectives: more information is provided by an inspection of the specific objectives of a budgetary planning and control system.

(a)   *To ensure the achievement of the organisation's objectives*

Objectives for the organisation as a whole, and for individual departments and operations within the organisation, are set. Quantified expressions of these objectives are then drawn up as targets to be achieved within the timescale of the budget plan.

(b)   *To compel planning*

This is probably the most important feature of a budgetary planning and control system. Planning forces management to look ahead, to set out detailed plans for achieving the targets for each department, operation and (ideally) each manager and to anticipate problems. It thus prevents management from relying on ad hoc or uncoordinated planning which may be detrimental to the performance of the organisation.

(c)   *To communicate ideas and plans*

A formal system is necessary to ensure that each person affected by the plans is aware of what he or she is supposed to be doing. Communication might be one-way, with managers giving orders to subordinates, or there might be a two-way dialogue and exchange of ideas.

(d)   *To coordinate activities*

The activities of different departments or sub-units of the organisation need to be coordinated to ensure maximum integration of effort towards common goals. This concept of coordination implies, for example, that the purchasing department should base its budget on production requirements and that the production budget should in turn be based on sales expectations. Although straightforward in concept, coordination is remarkably difficult to achieve, and there is often 'sub-optimality' and conflict between departmental plans in the budget so that the efforts of each department are not fully integrated into a combined plan to achieve the company's best targets.

(e)   *To provide a framework for responsibility accounting*

Budgetary planning and control systems require that managers of budget centres are made responsible for the achievement of budget targets for the operations under their personal control.

(f)   *To establish a system of control*

A budget is a yardstick against which actual performance is measured and assessed. Control over actual performance is provided by the comparisons of actual results against the budget plan. Departures from budget can then be investigated and the reasons for the departures can be divided into controllable and uncontrollable factors.

(g)   *To motivate employees to improve their performance*

The interest and commitment of employees can be retained via a system of feedback of actual results, which lets them know how well or badly they are performing. The identification of controllable reasons for departures from budget with managers responsible provides an incentive for improving future performance.

The benefits of budgeting

1.4   Provided the budgetary control system is carefully planned, controlled and co-ordinated, the objectives detailed above should be realised and translated into benefits (although, of course, such benefits will not appear overnight).

1.5   Despite the simple definition of a budget, its preparation and subsequent use provide the basis for a system which should have far-reaching implications for the organisation concerned.

2   THE PREPARATION OF BUDGETS

2.1   Having seen why organisations prepare budgets, we will now turn our attention to the mechanics of budget preparation. We will begin by defining and explaining a number of terms.

Planning

2.2   Planning is described in the *Official Terminology* as 'The establishment of objectives, and the formulation, evaluation and selection of the policies, strategies, tactics and action required to achieve them. Planning comprises long-term/strategic planning, and short-term operation planning. The latter is usually for a period of one year'.

The overall planning process therefore covers both the long and short term.

(a)   Strategic planning covers periods longer than one year and involves 'The formulation, evaluation and selection of strategies for the purpose of preparing a long-term plan of action to attain objectives. Also known as corporate planning and long range planning' (CIMA *Official Terminology*).

(b)   Budgetary planning or short-term tactical planning involves preparing detailed plans, which generally cover one year, for an organisation's functions, activities and departments. Budgetary planning works within the framework set by the strategic plans and converts those strategic plans into action.

(c)   Operation planning is planning on a very short-term or day-to-day basis and is concerned with planning how an organisation's resources will be used. Operation planning works within the framework set by the budgetary plans and converts the budgetary plans into action.

The budget period

2.3   The budget period is 'The period for which a budget is prepared and used, which may then been sub-divided into control periods' (CIMA *Official Terminology*). Except for capital expenditure budgets, the budget period is commonly the accounting year (sub-divided into 12 or 13 control periods).

The budget manual

2.4   The budget manual is a collection of instructions governing the responsibilities of persons and the procedures, forms and records relating to the preparation and use of budgetary data.

A budget manual may contain the following.

(a)   An *explanation of the objectives of the budgetary process*

(i)   The purpose of budgetary planning and control

(ii)   The objectives of the various stages of the budgetary process

(iii) The importance of budgets in the long-term planning and administration of the enterprise

(b)   *Organisational structures*

(i)   An organisation chart
(ii)   A list of individuals holding budget responsibilities

(c)   *Principal budgets*

(i)   An outline of each
(ii)   The relationship between them

(d) *Administrative details of budget preparation*

  (i)   Membership, and terms of reference of the budget committee
  (ii)   The sequence in which budgets are to be prepared
  (iii) A timetable

(e) *Procedural matters*

  (i)   Specimen forms and instructions for completing them
  (ii)   Specimen reports
  (iii) Account codes (or a chart of accounts)
  (iv)   The name of the budget officer to whom enquiries must be sent

The responsibility for preparing budgets

2.5   Managers responsible for preparing budgets should ideally be the managers (and their subordinates) who are responsible for carrying out the budget, selling goods or services and authorising expenditure.

  (a) The sales manager should draft the sales budget and selling overhead cost centre budgets.

  (b) The purchasing manager should draft the material purchases budget.

  (c) The production manager should draft the direct production cost budgets.

  (d) Various cost centre managers should prepare the individual production, administration and distribution cost centre budgets for their own cost centre.

  (e) The cost accountant will analyse the budgeted overheads to determine the overhead absorption rates for the next budget period.

Budget committee

2.6   The coordination and administration of budgets is usually the responsibility of a budget committee (with the managing director as chairman). The budget committee is assisted by a budget officer who is usually an accountant. Every part of the organisation should be represented on the committee, so there should be a representative from sales, production, marketing and so on. Functions of the budget committee include the following.

  (a) *Coordination* of the preparation of budgets, which includes the issue of the budget manual

  (b) *Issuing of timetables* for the preparation of functional budgets

  (c) *Allocation of responsibilities* for the preparation of functional budgets

  (d) *Provision of information* to assist in the preparation of budgets

  (e) *Communication of final budgets* to the appropriate managers

  (f) *Comparison* of actual results with budget and the investigation of variances

  (g) *Continuous assessment* of the budgeting and planning process, in order to improve the planning and control function

Budget preparation

2.7   Let us now look at the steps involved in the preparation of a budget. The procedures will differ from organisation to organisation, but the step-by-step approach described in this chapter is indicative of the steps followed by many organisations. The preparation of a budget may take weeks or months, and the budget committee may meet several times before the master budget is finally agreed.

You may not be familiar with the term departmental/functional budget. We therefore reproduce below the CIMA *Official Terminology* definition.

'A budget of income and/or expenditure applicable to a particular function.

A function may refer to a department or a process. Functional budgets frequently include:

- production cost budget (based on a forecast of production and plant utilisation);
- marketing cost budget, sales budget;
- personnel budget;
- purchasing budget;
- research and development budget.'

The principal budget factor

2.8 The first task in the budgetary process is to identify the *principal budget factor*. This is also known as the *key* budget factor or *limiting* budget factor.

2.9 For example, a company's sales department might estimate that it could sell 1,000 units of product X, which would require 5,000 hours of grade A labour to produce. If there are no units of product X already in stock, and only 4,000 hours of grade A labour available in the budget period, then the company would be unable to sell 1,000 units of X because of the shortage of labour hours. Grade A labour would be a limiting budget factor.

2.10 The company's management must choose one of the following options.

(a) Reduce budgeted sales by 20%.

(b) Try to increase the availability of grade A labour by 1,000 hours (25%) by recruitment or overtime working.

(c) Try to sub-contract the production of 1,000 units to another manufacturer, but still profit on the transaction.

2.11 The principal budget factor is usually sales demand: a company is usually restricted from making and selling more of its products because there would be no sales demand for the increased output at a price which would be acceptable/profitable to the company. The principal budget factor may also be machine capacity, distribution and selling resources, the availability of key raw materials or the availability of cash.

2.12 Once this factor is defined then the rest of the budget can be prepared. For example, if sales are the principal budget factor then the production manager can only prepare his budget after the sales budget is complete. Management may not know what the limiting budget factor is until a draft budget has been attempted. The first draft budget will therefore usually begin with the preparation of a draft sales budget.

Knowledge brought forward from Paper 2

Steps in the preparation of a budget

- Identification of *principal/key/limiting budget factor* (the factor (usually sales) which prevents an organisation from expanding at present beyond a certain point, for which the budget is usually the first to be prepared)

- Preparation of a *sales budget* (in units and in sales value for each product, based on a sales forecast)

- Preparation of a *production budget* (calculated as sales ± budgeted change in finished goods stock, in units)

- Preparation of a *finished goods stock budget* (to determine the planned change in finished goods stock levels)

- Preparation of *budgets for production resources*

    o Materials usage
    o Machine usage
    o Labour

- Preparation of a *raw materials stock budget* (to determine the planned change in raw materials stock levels)

- Preparation of a *raw materials purchases budget* (calculated as usage ± budgeted change in raw materials stock)

- Preparation of *overhead cost budgets* (such as production, administration, selling and distribution and R&D)

- Calculation of *overhead absorption rates* (if absorption costing is used)

- Preparation of a *cash budget* (and others as required, *capital expenditure* and *working capital* budgets)

- Preparation of a *master budget* (budgeted P&L account and budgeted balance sheet)

2.13   Remember that it is unlikely that the execution of the above steps will be problem-free. The budgets must be reviewed in relation to one another. Such a review may indicate that some budgets are out of balance with others and need modifying so that they will be compatible with other conditions, constraints and plans. The budget officer must identify such inconsistencies and bring them to the attention of the manager concerned.

2.14   Alternatively, there may have been a change in one of the organisational policies, such as a change in selling prices, which will need to be incorporated into the budget. The revision of one budget may lead to the revision of all budgets. This process must continue until all budgets are acceptable.

2.15   If such changes are made manually, the process can be very time consuming and costly. Computer spreadsheets, as we discussed in Chapter 3, can help immensely.

Exercise 1

A company that manufactures and sells a range of products, with sales potential limited by market share, is considering introducing a system of budgeting.

Required

(a)   List (in order of preparation) the functional budgets that need to be prepared.

(b)   State which budgets the master budget will comprise.

(c)   Consider how the work outlined in (a) and (b) can be coordinated in order for the budgeting process to be successful.

Solution

(a) The sequence of budget preparation will be roughly as follows.

    (i) Sales budget

    (The market share limits demand and so sales is the principal budget factor. All other activities will depend upon this forecast.)

    (ii) Finished goods stock budget (in units)

    (iii) Production budget (in units)

    (iv) Production resources budgets (materials, machine hours, labour)

    (v) Overhead budgets for production, administration, selling and distribution, research and development and so on

Other budgets required will be the capital expenditure budget, the working capital budget (debtors and creditors) and, very importantly, the cash budget.

(b) The master budget is the summary of all the functional budgets. It often includes a summary profit and loss account and balance sheet.

(c) Procedures for preparing budgets can be contained in a budget manual which shows which budgets must be prepared when and by whom, what each functional budget should contain and detailed directions on how to prepare budgets including, for example, expected price increases, rates of interest, rates of depreciation and so on.

The formulation of budgets can be coordinated by a budget committee comprising the senior executives of the departments responsible for carrying out the budgets: sales, production, purchasing, personnel and so on.

The budgeting process may also be assisted by the use of a spreadsheet/computer budgeting package.

3 THE SALES BUDGET

3.1 We have already established that, for many organisations, the principal budget factor is sales volume. The sales budget is therefore often the primary budget from which the majority of the other budgets are derived.

3.2 Before the sales budget can be prepared a sales forecast has to be made. A forecast is an estimate of what is likely to occur in the future. The forecast becomes the budget once management have accepted it as the objective or target. Sales forecasting is complex and difficult and involves the consideration of a number of factors.

(a) Past sales patterns
(b) The economic environment
(c) Results of market research
(d) Anticipated advertising during the budget period
(e) Competition
(f) Changing consumer taste
(g) New legislation
(h) Distribution and quality of sales outlets and personnel
(i) Pricing policies and discounts offered
(j) Legislation
(k) Environmental factors

3.3 On the basis of the sales forecast and the production capacity of the organisation, a sales budget will be prepared. This may be subdivided, possible subdivisions being by product, by sales area, by management responsibility and so on.

3.4 Once the sales budget has been agreed, related budgets can be prepared.

4 PRODUCTION AND RELATED BUDGETS

4.1 If the principal budget factor was production capacity then the production budget would be the first to be prepared. To assess whether production is the principal budget factor, the production capacity available must be determined. This should take into account the following factors.

(a) *Available labour,* including idle time, overtime and standard output rates per hour

(b) *Availability of raw materials* including allowances for losses during production

(c) *Maximum machine hours available,* including expected idle time and expected output rates per machine hour

It is, however, normally sales volume that is the constraint and therefore the production budget is prepared after the sales budget and the finished goods stock budget.

4.2 The production budget will show the quantities and costs for each product and product group and will tie in with the sales and stock budgets. This co-ordinating process is likely to show any shortfalls or excesses in capacity at various times over the budget period.

4.3 If there is likely to be a shortfall then consideration should be given to overtime, subcontracting, machine hire, new sources of raw materials or some other way of increasing output. A significant shortfall means that production capacity is, in fact, the limiting factor.

4.4 If capacity exceeds sales volume for a length of time then consideration should be given to product diversification, a reduction in selling price (if demand is price elastic) and so on.

4.5 Once the production budget has been finalised, the labour, materials and machine budgets can be drawn up. These budgets will be based on budgeted activity levels, existing stock positions and projected labour and material costs.

Example: the preparation of the production budget and direct labour budget

4.6 Landy Ltd manufactures two products, A and B, and is preparing its budget for 19X3. Both products are made by the same grade of labour, grade Q. The company currently holds 800 units of A and 1,200 units of B in stock, but 250 of these units of B have just been discovered to have deteriorated in quality, and must therefore be scrapped. Budgeted sales of A are 3,000 units and of B 4,000 units, provided that the company maintains finished goods stocks at a level equal to three months' sales.

Grade Q labour was originally expected to produce one unit of A in two hours and one unit of B in three hours, at an hourly rate of £2.50 per hour. In discussions with trade union negotiators, however, it has been agreed that the hourly wage rate should be raised by 50p per hour, provided that the times to produce A and B are reduced by 20%.

Required

Prepare the production budget and direct labour budget for 19X3.

Solution

4.7 The expected time to produce a unit of A will now be 80% of 2 hours = 1.6 hours, and the time for a unit of B will be 2.4 hours. The hourly wage rate will be £3, so that the direct labour cost will be £4.80 for A and £7.20 for B (thus achieving a saving for the company of 20p per unit of A produced and 30p per unit of B).

(a) *Production budget*

		Product A			*Product B*	
		Units	Units		Units	Units
Budgeted sales			3,000			4,000
Closing stocks	($^3/_{12}$ of 3,000)	750		($^3/_{12}$ of 4,000)	1,000	
Opening stocks (minus stocks scrapped)		800			950	
(Decrease)/increase in stocks			(50)			50
Production			2,950			4,050

(b) *Direct labour budget*

	Grade Q Hours	Cost £
2,950 units of product A	4,720	14,160
4,050 units of product B	9,720	29,160
Total	14,440	43,320

It is assumed that there will be no idle time among grade Q labour which, if it existed, would have to be paid for at the rate of £3 per hour.

The standard hour

4.8 A useful concept in budgeting for labour requirements is the standard hour or standard minute which is 'The amount of work achievable at standard efficiency levels in an hour or minute' (CIMA *Official Terminology*), expressed in terms of a standard unit of work done in a standard period of time. For example, budgeted output of different products or jobs in a period could be converted into standard hours of production, and a labour budget constructed accordingly.

4.9 Standard hours are particularly useful when management wants to monitor the production levels of a variety of dissimilar units. For example product A may take five hours to produce and product B, seven hours. If four units of each product are produced, instead of saying that total output is eight units, we could state the production level as $(4 \times 5) + (4 \times 7)$ standard hours = 48 standard hours.

Example: direct labour budget based on standard hours

4.10 Truro Ltd manufactures a single product, Q, with a single grade of labour. Its sales budget and finished goods stock budget for period 3 of 19X6 are as follows.

Sales	700 units
Opening stocks, finished goods	50 units
Closing stocks, finished goods	70 units

The goods are inspected only when production work is completed, and it is budgeted that 10% of finished work will be scrapped.

The standard direct labour hour content of product Q is three hours. The budgeted productivity ratio for direct labour is only 80% (which means that labour is only working at 80% efficiency).

The company employs 18 direct operatives, who are expected to average 144 working hours each in period 3.

Required

(a) Prepare a production budget.

(b) Prepare a direct labour budget.

(c) Comment on the problem that your direct labour budget reveals, and suggest how this problem might be overcome.

Solution

4.11 (a) *Production budget*

	Units
Sales	700
Add closing stock	70
	770
Less opening stock	50
Production required of 'good' output	720
Wastage rate	10%
Total production required	$720 \times \dfrac{100 \, *}{90} = 800$ units

(* Note that the required adjustment is 100/90, not 110/100, since the waste is assumed to be 10% of total production, not 10% of good production.)

(b) Now we can prepare the direct labour budget.

Standard hours per unit	3
Total standard hours required = 800 units × 3 hours	2,400 hours
Productivity ratio	80%

Actual hours required $2,400 \times \dfrac{100}{80} = 3,000 \text{ hours}$

(c) If we look at the direct labour budget against the information provided, we can identify the problem.

	Hours
Budgeted hours available (18 operatives × 144 hours)	2,592
Actual hours required	3,000
Shortfall in labour hours	408

The (draft) budget indicates that there will not be enough direct labour hours to meet the production requirements. This problem might be overcome in one, or a combination, of the following ways.

(i) Reduce the closing stock requirement below 70 units. This would reduce the number of production units required.

(ii) Persuade the workforce to do some overtime working.

(iii) Perhaps recruit more direct labour if long-term prospects are for higher production volumes.

(iv) Discuss with the workforce (or their union representatives) the following possibilities.

(1) Improve the productivity ratio, and so reduce the number of hours required to produce the output.

(2) If possible, reduce the wastage rate below 10%.

Example: the material purchases budget

4.12 Tremor Ltd manufactures two products, S and T, which use the same raw materials, D and E. One unit of S uses 3 litres of D and 4 kilograms of E. One unit of T uses 5 litres of D and 2 kilograms of E. A litre of D is expected to cost £3 and a kilogram of E £7.

Budgeted sales for 19X2 are 8,000 units of S and 6,000 units of T; finished goods in stock at 1 January 19X2 are 1,500 units of S and 300 units of T, and the company plans to hold stocks of 600 units of each product at 31 December 19X2.

Stocks of raw material are 6,000 litres of D and 2,800 kilograms of E at 1 January, and the company plans to hold 5,000 litres and 3,500 kilograms respectively at 31 December 19X2.

The warehouse and stores managers have suggested that a provision should be made for damages and deterioration of items held in store, as follows.

Product S :	loss of 50 units
Product T :	loss of 100 units
Material D :	loss of 500 litres
Material E :	loss of 200 kilograms

Required

Prepare a material purchases budget for the year 19X2.

Solution

4.13 To calculate material purchase requirements, it is first of all necessary to calculate the budgeted production volumes and material usage requirements.

	Product S		Product T	
	Units	Units	Units	Units
Sales		8,000		6,000
Provision for losses		50		100
Closing stock	600		600	
Opening stock	1,500		300	
(Decrease)/increase in stock		(900)		300
Production budget		7,150		6,400

	Material D		Material E	
	Litres	Litres	Kg	Kg
Usage requirements				
To produce 7,150 units of S		21,450		28,600
To produce 6,400 units of T		32,000		12,800
Usage budget		53,450		41,400
Provision for losses		500		200
		53,950		41,600
Closing stock	5,000		3,500	
Opening stock	6,000		2,800	
(Decrease)/increase in stock		(1,000)		700
Material purchases budget		52,950		42,300

	Material D	Material E
Cost per unit	£3 per litre	£7 per kg
Cost of material purchases	£158,850	£296,100
Total purchases cost	£454,950	

Using stock control formulae in budget preparation

4.14 In the previous example, you were simply told the stock levels. In an exam, however, you may also be required to use stock control formulae to determine stock levels.

Knowledge brought forward from Paper 2

Stock control formulae

- Reorder level = maximum usage × maximum lead time

- Minimum level = reorder level − (average usage × average lead time)

- Maximum level = reorder level + reorder quantity − (minimum usage × minimum lead time)

- Economic order quantity (EOQ) = $\sqrt{\dfrac{2CoD}{Ch}}$

Exercise 2

The following information relates to material R.

Cost per kg = £100

Cost of ordering, per order = £500

Annual cost of holding 1 kg of R, as a % of cost = 10%

	Maximum	Average	Minimum
Usage each week (kgs)	3,500	2,800	2,000
Lead time (wks)	5 wks	2 wks	?

A year consists of 48 weeks.

Calculate the following.

(a)   The reorder level
(b)   The EOQ
(c)   The minimum level

Solution

(a)   Reorder level   = maximum usage × maximum lead time
                         = 3,500 × 5 = 17,500 kgs

(b) $EOQ = \sqrt{\dfrac{2CoD}{Ch}} = \sqrt{\dfrac{2 \times £500 \times (2,800 \times 48)}{£100 \times 10\%}} = 3,666$ kgs

(c)   Minimum level   = reorder level – (average usage × average lead time)
                         = 17,500 – (2,800 × 2)
                         = 11,900 kgs

4.15   Now work through the following example which incorporates stock control formulae into a budgeting question.

Example: budgets and stock control formulae

4.16   The following data relate to the JIP, the product produced by Giring Ltd.

Budgeted data

	1 October to 1 December 19X5			1 January to 31 March 19X6		
Sales division	1	2	3	1	2	3
Sales of JIP (£'000)	54	342	228	60	360	240
Stocks of JIP						
opening (units)	90	320	260	100	350	250
maximum (units)	150	500	350	150	500	350

Standard cost data

Direct materials	Me1	10 kgs at £3 per kilo
	Me2	5 kgs at £2 per kilo
Direct wages	S	5 hours at £4 per hour
	SS	2 hours at £5 per hour

Production overhead is absorbed as a labour hour rate, that is £12 per hour in respect of S and £10 per hour in respect of SS.

Administration and selling overhead is recovered at 20% of production cost.

Profit is calculated at 10% of selling price.

Direct materials data

	Materials	
	Me1	Me2
Maximum consumption per week (kgs)	3,600	1,800
Minimum consumption per week (kgs)	2,400	1,200
Reorder quantity (kgs)	20,000	12,000
Stock at 30 September 19X5 (kgs)	24,500	13,650
Stock at 31 December 19X5 (kgs)	23,000	14,400
Lead time from suppliers (weeks)		
Maximum	6	5
Minimum	4	3

A major sales campaign is planned in the budget period beginning 1 April 19X6. In anticipation of an increase in sales, an advertising campaign will commence in the previous quarter. The production director has requested that stocks of raw materials be increased to maximum level by 1 April 19X6 and the sales director has requested that stocks of finished goods be increased to maximum level by 1 April 19X6.

Required

Prepare the following budgets for the three months ending 31 March 19X6.

(a) Production
(b) Purchases
(c) Production cost

Solution

4.17 *Working:* Calculation of standard cost and profit per unit

			£ per unit
Direct materials	Me1		30
	Me2		10
Direct wages	S		20
	SS		10
Production overhead	S - 5 hours × £12		60
	SS - 2 hours × £10		20
Total production cost			150
Administration and selling overhead - 20%			30
			180
Profit - 10% of selling price			20
Selling price			200

(a) *Product JIP - Production Budget for three months ending 31 March 19X6*

			Units	Units
Sales units	- Division 1		300	
	- Division 2		1,800	
	- Division 3		1,200	
				3,300
Add required closing stock	- Division 1		150	
	- Division 2		500	
	- Division 3		350	
				1,000
				4,300
Less opening stock	- Division 1		100	
	- Division 2		350	
	- Division 3		250	
				700
Required production				3,600

(b) Maximum stock = reorder level + reorder quantity – (minimum usage × minimum lead time)

		Me1 kgs	*Me2* kgs
Reorder level = Maximum usage × Maximum lead time			
	Me1 = 3,600 × 6	21,600	
	Me2 = 1,800 × 5		9,000
Reorder quantity		20,000	12,000
		41,600	21,000
Minimum usage × minimum lead time			
	Me1 = 2,400 × 4	9,600	
	Me2 = 1,200 × 3		3,600
Maximum stocks		32,000	17,400

Direct materials - Purchases budget for the three months ending 31 March 19X6

	Me1 kgs	*Me2* kgs
Required closing stocks (maximum level)	32,000	17,400
Production requirements		
Me1 3,600 × 10kg	36,000	
Me2 3,600 × 5kg		18,000
	68,000	35,400
Less opening stock 31 December 19X5	23,000	14,400
Purchases	45,000	21,000
× standard price (£3/£2)	£135,000	£42,000

(c)   *Production cost budget for the three months ending 31 March 19X6*

		£'000	£'000
Direct materials	- Me1 3,600 × £30	108	
	- Me2 3,600 × £10	36	
			144
Direct wages	- S 3,600 × £20	72	
	- SS 3,600 × £10	36	
			108
Production overhead	- S 3,600 × £60	216	
	- SS 3,600 × £20	72	
			288
Total production cost			540

Non-production overheads

4.18   We have seen that an increasing proportion of overheads are not directly related to the volume of production such as administration and research and development.

4.19   Key decisions in the budgeting process for these costs will include the following.

(a)   Deciding which fixed costs are committed (will be incurred no matter what) and which fixed costs will depend on management decisions.

(b)   Deciding what factors will influence the level of variable costs. Administration costs for example will be partly governed by the number of orders received.

5   CASH BUDGETS   *5/95, 5/96, 5/98*

The usefulness of cash budgets

5.1   The cash budget is one of the most important planning tools that an organisation can use. It shows the cash effect of all plans made within the budgetary process and hence its preparation can lead to a modification of budgets if it shows that there are insufficient cash resources to finance the planned operations.

5.2   It can also give management an indication of potential problems that could arise and allows them the opportunity to take action to avoid such problems. A cash budget can show four positions. Management will need to take appropriate action depending on the potential position.

Cash position		Appropriate management action
Short-term surplus	(a)	Pay creditors early to obtain discount
	(b)	Attempt to increase sales by increasing debtors and stocks
	(c)	Make short-term investments
Short-term deficit	(a)	Increase creditors
	(b)	Reduce debtors
	(c)	Arrange an overdraft
Long-term surplus	(a)	Make long-term investments
	(b)	Expand
	(c)	Diversify
	(d)	Replace/update fixed assets
Long-term deficit	(a)	Raise long-term finance (such as via issue of share capital)
	(b)	Consider shutdown/disinvestment opportunities

5.3 A cash budgeting question in an examination could ask you to recommend appropriate action for management to take once you have prepared the cash budget. Ensure your advice takes account both of whether there is a surplus or deficit and whether the position is long or short term.

Exam focus point

Cash budgeting appears to be a favourite topic of the examiner, having been examined in May 1995 and May 1996. Although you covered cash budgeting in Paper 2 the examiner advised that 'future candidates should ensure that they feel competent in the use of [these] more advanced aspects of budget preparation', which we cover in this Section.

For instance, cash budgets may require you to calculate the interest to be received or paid on closing balances. The examiner has commented as follows.

'This could simply require candidates to calculate interest to be received or paid based on the closing balance or average balance of the previous period and incorporate the receipt or payment in the cash budget. Alternatively it could require them to make a decision as to whether to pay suppliers to obtain a discount and thus lose interest receivable/pay interest or take the normal credit period before settling with creditors. These are two possible scenarios, but they are not an exhaustive list.'

What to include in a cash budget

5.4 A cash budget is prepared to show the expected receipts of cash and payments of cash during a budget period.

5.5 Receipts of cash may come from:
(a) cash sales;
(b) payments by debtors (credit sales);
(c) the sale of fixed assets;
(d) the issue of new shares or loan stock and less formalised loans;
(e) the receipt of interest and dividends from investments outside the business.

Remember that bad debts will *never be received in cash* and doubtful debts may not be received so you have to adjust if necessary for such items.

5.6 Although all the receipts in Paragraph 5.5 would affect a cash budget they would not all appear in the profit and loss account.

(a) The issue of new shares or loan stock is a balance sheet item.

(b) The cash received from an asset affects the balance sheet, and the profit or loss on the sale of an asset, which appears in the profit and loss account, is not the cash received but the difference between cash received and the written down value of the asset at the time of sale.

5.7   Payments of cash may be for:

(a)   purchase of stocks;
(b)   payroll costs or other expenses;
(c)   purchase of capital items;
(d)   payment of interest, dividends or taxation.

5.8   Not all payments are profit and loss account items. The purchase of capital equipment and the payment of VAT affect the balance sheet. Some costs in the profit and loss account such as profit or loss on sale of fixed assets or depreciation are not cash items but are costs derived from accounting conventions.

5.9   In addition, the timing of cash receipts and payments may not coincide with the recording of profit and loss account transactions. For example, a dividend might be declared in the results for 19X6 and shown in the profit and loss account for that year, but paid in 19X7.

5.10   Cash budgets are most effective if they are treated as *rolling budgets*. Rolling budgets involve a process of continuous budgeting whereby regularly each period (week, month, quarter) a new future period is added to the budget whilst the earliest period is deleted. In this way the budget is constantly revised to reflect the most up to date position. We will be looking at rolling budgets in more detail in Chapter 17.

Knowledge brought forward from Paper 2

Steps in the preparation of a cash budget

- Set up a proforma cash budget.

		Month 1	Month 2	Month 3
		£	£	£
Cash receipts:	Receipts from debtors	X	X	X
	Loan etc	X	X	X
		X	X	X
Cash payments:	Payments to creditors	X	X	X
	Wages etc	X	X	X
		X	X	X
Opening balance		X	X	X
Net cash flow (receipts - payments)		X	X	X
Closing balance		X	X	X

- Enter the figures that can be entered straightaway (receipts or payments that you are told occur in a specific month)

- Sort out cash receipts from debtors.

  ° Establish budgeted sales month by month.
  ° Establish the length of credit period taken by debtors.

$$\text{Debtors collection period (no of days credit)} = \frac{\text{average (or year - end) debtors during period}}{\text{total credit sales in period}} \times \text{no of days in period}$$

  ° Hence determine when budgeted sales revenue will be received as cash (by considering cash receipts from total debtors, ignoring any provision for doubtful debts).

  ° Establish when opening debtors will pay.

- Establish when any other cash income will be received.

- Sort out cash payments to creditors.

  ° Establish production quantities and materials usage quantities each month.

  ° Establish materials stock changes and hence the quantity and cost of materials purchases each month.

  ° Establish the length of credit period taken from suppliers.

$$\text{Creditors payment period} \atop \text{(no of days credit)} = \frac{\text{average (or year - end) creditors during period}}{\text{total purchases on credit in period}} \times \text{no of days in period}$$

- ° Hence calculate when cash payments to suppliers will be made and when the amount due to opening creditors will be paid.
- Establish when any other cash payments (excluding non-cash items such as depreciation) will be made.

Example: profit and loss account and cash budget

5.11 Penny Ltd operates a retail business. Purchases are sold at cost plus 33¹/₃%.

(a)

	Budgeted sales in month £	Labour cost in month £	Expenses incurred in month £
January	40,000	3,000	4,000
February	60,000	3,000	6,000
March	160,000	5,000	7,000
April	120,000	4,000	7,000

(b) It is management policy to have sufficient stock in hand at the end of each month to meet half of next month's sales demand.

(c) Creditors for materials and expenses are paid in the month after the purchases are made/expenses incurred. Labour is paid in full by the end of each month. Labour costs and expenses are treated as period costs in the P & L account.

(d) Expenses include a monthly depreciation charge of £2,000.

(e) (i) 75% of sales are for cash.
    (ii) 25% of sales are on one month's credit.

(f) The company will buy equipment costing £18,000 for cash in February and will pay a dividend of £20,000 in March. The opening cash balance at 1 February is £1,000.

Required

(a) Prepare a cash budget for February and March.
(b) Prepare a profit and loss account for February and March.

Solution

5.12 (a) CASH BUDGET

	February £	March £
Receipts		
Receipts from sales	55,000 (W1)	135,000 (W2)
Payments		
Trade creditors	37,500 (W3)	82,500 (W3)
Expense creditors	2,000 (W4)	4,000 (W4)
Labour	3,000	5,000
Equipment purchase	18,000	-
Dividend	–	20,000
Total payments	60,500	111,500
Receipts less payments	(5,500)	23,500
Opening cash balance b/f	1,000	(4,500)★
Closing cash balance c/f	(4,500)★	19,000

Workings

			£
1	Receipts in February	75% of Feb sales (75% × £60,000)	45,000
		25% of Jan sales (25% × £40,000)	10,000
			55,000

			£
2	Receipts in March	75% of Mar sales (75% × £160,000)	120,000
		25% of Feb sales (25% × £60,000)	15,000
			135,000

3	*Purchases*		*January*		*February*
			£		£
	For Jan sales	(50% of £30,000)	15,000		
	For Feb sales	(50% of £45,000)	22,500	(50% of £45,000)	22,500
	For Mar sales		–	(50% of £120,000)	60,000
			37,500		82,500

These purchases are paid for in February and March.

4   *Expenses*

Cash expenses in January (£4,000 – £2,000) and February (£6,000 – £2,000) are paid in February and March respectively. Depreciation is not a cash item.

(b)   PROFIT AND LOSS ACCOUNT

	February		*March*	
	£	£	£	£
Sales		60,000		160,000
Cost of purchases (75%)		45,000		120,000
Gross profit		15,000		40,000
Less: Labour	3,000		5,000	
Expenses	6,000		7,000	
		9,000		12,000
Net profit		6,000		28,000

5.13   Note the following.

(a)   The asterisks show that the cash balance at the end of February is carried forward as the opening cash balance for March.

(b)   The fact that profits are made in February and March disguises the fact that there is a cash shortfall at the end of February.

(c)   Steps should be taken either to ensure that an overdraft facility is available for the cash shortage at the end of February, or to defer certain payments so that the overdraft is avoided.

(d)   Some payments must be made on due dates (payroll, taxation and so on) but it is possible that other payments can be delayed, depending on the requirements of the business and/or the goodwill of suppliers.

Cash budgets and an opening balance sheet

5.14   You might be given a cash budget question in which you are required to analyse an opening balance sheet to decide how many outstanding debtors will pay what they owe in the first few months of the cash budget period, and how many outstanding creditors must be paid.

Example: cash budgets and opening balance sheet

5.15   A balance sheet as at 31 December 19X4 shows the following details.

Debtors	£150,000
Trade creditors	£60,000

You are given the following information.

(a) Debtors are allowed two months to pay.

(b) $1\frac{1}{2}$ months' credit is taken from trade creditors.

(c) Sales and materials purchases were both made at an even monthly rate throughout 19X4.

Required

Ascertain the months of 19X5 in which the debtors will eventually pay and the creditors will be paid.

5.16 (a) Since debtors take two months to pay, the £150,000 of debtors in the balance sheet represents credit sales in November and December 19X4, who will pay in January and February 19X5 respectively. Since sales in 19X4 were at an equal monthly rate, the cash budget should plan for receipts of £75,000 each month in January and February from the debtors in the opening balance sheet.

(b) Similarly, since creditors are paid after $1\frac{1}{2}$ months, the balance sheet creditors will be paid in January and the first half of February 19X5, which means that budgeted payments will be as follows.

	£
In January (purchases in 2nd half of November and 1st half of December 19X4)	40,000
In February (purchases in 2nd half of December 19X4)	20,000
Total creditors in the balance sheet	60,000

(The balance sheet creditors of £60,000 represent $1\frac{1}{2}$ months' purchases, so that purchases in 19X4 must be £40,000 per month, which is £20,000 per half month.)

5.17 Bad debts and provisions for doubtful debts may complicate the calculation of cash received from credit customers. Suppose that Wolf Ltd had debtors on 1 January 19X4 and 31 December 19X4 as follows.

	1 Jan	*31 Dec*
	£	£
Debtors in total	36,000	42,000
Less provision for doubtful debts	(6,000)	(10,000)
Debtors reported in balance sheet	30,000	32,000

During 19X4 the value of sales amounted to £200,000 and the provision for doubtful debts was increased by £4,000 (from £6,000 to £10,000).

What was the amount of cash received from customers in 19X4?

5.18 The cash receipts are calculated from the total debtors, ignoring the provision for doubtful debts. The provision is made just in case some customers default on payment but they have not defaulted yet.

	£
Debtors at the beginning of the year	36,000
Sales during the year	200,000
	236,000
Debtors at the end of the year	(42,000)
Cash received during the year	194,000

5.19 A further problem may arise if a business plans to build up or reduce its stock level over the budget period. This makes it more difficult to calculate amounts paid to suppliers.

Example: calculating the amounts paid to suppliers

5.20 At 31 December 19X5 ESP Ltd held stocks which cost £60,000. The period of credit allowed by suppliers is one month and trade creditors at 31 December 19X5 amounted to £30,000. It is company policy to hold stocks equal to the cost of sales in the next two months and, until the end of 19X5, the monthly cost of sales was £30,000.

From 1 January 19X6 the company expects to increase its monthly sales by 20%. The policy on stock levels will remain unchanged, and suppliers will continue to allow one month's credit.

Required

Calculate the cash payments to trade creditors each month in 19X6.

Solution

5.21 (a) We must first calculate the volume of purchases each month. In January 19X6 the stock levels must be increased from £60,000 to 120% of £60,000 = £72,000 (ie two months' cost of sales at the new volume of sales). In addition, monthly consumption of stocks will rise 20% from £30,000 to £36,000.

	£
In January, purchases must be as follows.	
Value of stock required at 31 January	72,000
Stock used up/sold in January	36,000
Total stock needed	108,000
Value of stock as at 1 January	(60,000)
Purchases required in January	48,000

Purchases from February onwards must then be enough to replace the stocks used up (£36,000 per month).

(b) Having calculated purchases, we can now establish when payments will be made, allowing for one month's credit from suppliers.

Month of purchase	Cost of purchases £	Month of payment
December 19X5 (opening balance sheet)	30,000	January
January 19X6	48,000	February
February	36,000	March
March	36,000	April

Monthly payments of £36,000 become regularly established from March 19X6 onwards.

Exercise 3

If ABC Ltd's annual sales are £100,000 and the contribution/sales ratio is 35%, calculate the variable cost of sales.

Solution

£100,000 × 65% = £650,000

Exercise 4

Universe Ltd is to begin trading on 1 January 19X3. Management have budgeted the following sales revenue for January to June 19X3.

Jan	Feb	Mar	April	May	June
£13,000	£17,000	£10,000	£11,000	£5,000	£20,000

It is expected that most sales will be on credit (5% of total sales being for cash). To encourage early payment the company will offer a discount scheme. A discount of 5% will be offered on all cash sales and on all credit sales where payment is made within 1 week of sale.

Of the credit sales, 30% are expected to take the discount. (Assume that all debtors who take the discount pay in the month of sale although this is not entirely true). Of the remainder of credit sales, 75% are expected to pay in the month following sale and the remainder in the month after.

Bad debts are expected to be 2% of total credit sales.

Required

Calculate the amounts budgeted to be recovered in each of the months from January to June 19X3.

Solution

	Jan £	Feb £	Mar £	Apr £	May £	Jun £
Sales	13,000	17,000	10,000	11,000	5,000	20,000
Cash sales (5%)	(650)	(850)	(500)	(550)	(250)	(1,000)
Gross credit sales	12,350	16,150	9,500	10,450	4,750	19,000
Bad debts (2%)	(247)	(323)	(190)	(209)	(95)	(380)
Net credit sales	12,103	15,827	9,310	10,241	4,655	18,620
Credit sales with discount (30%)	(3,631)	(4,748)	(2,793)	(3,072)	(1,397)	(5,586)
Other credit sales	8,472	11,079	6,517	7,169	3,258	13,034
Total sales with discount (cash & credit)	4,281	5,598	3,293	3,622	1,647	6,586
Discount (5%)	(241)	280	165	181	82	329
	4,067	5,318	3,128	3,441	1,565	6,257
Other credit sales	8,472	11,079	6,517	7,169	3,258	13,034
Receipts (75%)		6,354	8,309	4,888	5,377	2,444
(25%)			2,118	2,770	1,629	1,792
	-	6,354	10,427	7,658	7,006	4,236
Total sales with discount	4,067	5,318	3,128	3,441	1,565	6,257
Other credit sales	-	6,354	10,427	7,658	7,006	4,236
Total receipts	4,067	11,672	13,555	11,099	8,571	10,493

Exam focus point

You will be expected to be capable of dealing with cash budget problems for your examination and to interpret the budget you prepare. Another example and an exercise are therefore included for careful study.

Example: a month by month cash budget

5.22 From the following information which relates to Bovary Ltd you are required to prepare a month by month cash budget for the second half of 19X5 and to append such brief comments as you consider might be helpful to management.

(a) The company's only product, a vest, sells at £40 and has a variable cost of £26 made up as follows.

Material £20   Labour £4   Overhead £2

(b) Fixed costs of £6,000 per month are paid on the 28th of each month.

(c) Quantities sold/to be sold on credit

May	June	July	Aug	Sept	Oct	Nov	Dec
1,000	1,200	1,400	1,600	1,800	2,000	2,200	2,600

(d) Production quantities

May	June	July	Aug	Sept	Oct	Nov	Dec
1,200	1,400	1,600	2,000	2,400	2,600	2,400	2,200

(e) Cash sales at a discount of 5% are expected to average 100 units a month.

(f) Customers are expected to settle their accounts by the end of the second month following sale.

(g) Suppliers of material are paid two months after the material is used in production.

(h) Wages are paid in the same month as they are incurred.

(i) 70% of the variable overhead is paid in the month of production, the remainder in the following month.

(j)   Corporation tax of £18,000 is to be paid in October.

(k)   A new delivery vehicle was bought in June. It cost £8,000 and is to be paid for in August. The old vehicle was sold for £600, the buyer undertaking to pay in July.

(l)   The company is expected to be £3,000 overdrawn at the bank at 30 June 19X5.

(m) No increases or decreases in raw materials, work in progress or finished goods are planned over the period.

(n)   No price increases or cost increases are expected in the period.

Solution

5.23   Cash budget for July 1 to December 31 19X5

	July £	Aug £	Sept £	Oct £	Nov £	Dec £	Total £
Receipts							
Credit sales	40,000	48,000	56,000	64,000	72,000	80,000	360,000
Cash sales	3,800	3,800	3,800	3,800	3,800	3,800	22,800
Sale of vehicle	600	-	-	-	-	-	600
	44,400	51,800	59,800	67,800	75,800	83,800	383,400
Payments							
Materials	24,000	28,000	32,000	40,000	48,000	52,000	224,000
Labour	6,400	8,000	9,600	10,400	9,600	8,800	52,800
Variable overhead (W)	3,080	3,760	4,560	5,080	4,920	4,520	25,920
Fixed costs	6,000	6,000	6,000	6,000	6,000	6,000	36,000
Corporation tax				18,000			18,000
Purchase of vehicle		8,000					8,000
	39,480	53,760	52,160	79,480	68,520	71,320	364,720
Receipts less payments	4,920	(1,960)	7,640	(11,680)	7,280	12,480	18,680
Balance b/f	(3,000)	1,920	(40)	7,600	(4,080)	3,200	(3,000)
Balance c/f	1,920	(40)	7,600	(4,080)	3,200	15,680	15,680

Working

Variable overhead

	June £	July £	Aug £	Sept £	Oct £	Nov £	Dec £
Variable overhead production cost	2,800	3,200	4,000	4,800	5,200	4,800	4,400
70% paid in month		2,240	2,800	3,360	3,640	3,360	3,080
30% in following month		840	960	1,200	1,440	1,560	1,440
		3,080	3,760	4,560	5,080	4,920	4,520

Comments

(a)   There will be a small overdraft at the end of August but a much larger one at the end of October. It may be possible to delay payments to suppliers for longer than two months or to reduce purchases of materials or reduce the volume of production by running down existing stock levels.

(b)   If neither of these courses is possible, the company may need to negotiate overdraft facilities with its bank. Note that if payments are all made at the beginning of a month and receipts are all at the end of a month any overdraft limit arrangement on the basis of budgeted month-end balances will not be large enough. In October, for example, the overdraft *could* at some point be as large as £(7,600 – 67,800) = £60,200. The detail, and not just the final balances, must be studied carefully.

(c)   The cash deficit is only temporary and by the end of December there will be a comfortable surplus. The use to which this cash will be put should ideally be planned in advance.

Exercise 5

You are presented with the following budgeted cash flow data for your organisation for the period November 19X1 to June 19X2. It has been extracted from functional budgets that have already been prepared.

	Nov X1	Dec X1	Jan X2	Feb X2	Mar X2	Apr X2	May X2	June X2
	£	£	£	£	£	£	£	£
Sales	80,000	100,000	110,000	130,000	140,000	150,000	160,000	180,000
Purchases	40,000	60,000	80,000	90,000	110,000	130,000	140,000	150,000
Wages	10,000	12,000	16,000	20,000	24,000	28,000	32,000	36,000
Overheads	10,000	10,000	15,000	15,000	15,000	20,000	20,000	20,000
Dividends		20,000						40,000
Capital expenditure			30,000			40,000		

You are also told the following.

(a) Sales are 40%, cash 60% credit. Credit sales are paid two months after the month of sale.

(b) Purchases are paid the month following purchase.

(c) 75% of wages are paid in the current month and 25% the following month.

(d) Overheads are paid the month after they are incurred.

(e) Dividends are paid three months after they are declared.

(f) Capital expenditure is paid two months after it is incurred.

(g) The opening cash balance is £15,000.

The managing director is pleased with the above figures as they show sales will have increased by more than 100% in the period under review. In order to achieve this he has arranged a bank overdraft with a ceiling of £50,000 to accommodate the increased stock levels and wage bill for overtime worked.

Required

(a) Prepare a cash budget for the six-month period January to June 19X2.

(b) Comment upon your results in the light of your managing director's comments and offer advice.

Solution

(a)

	January	February	March	April	May	June
	£	£	£	£	£	£
Cash receipts						
Cash sales	44,000	52,000	56,000	60,000	64,000	72,000
Credit sales	48,000	60,000	66,000	78,000	84,000	90,000
	92,000	112,000	122,000	138,000	148,000	162,000
Cash payments						
Purchases	60,000	80,000	90,000	110,000	130,000	140,000
Wages						
75%	12,000	15,000	18,000	21,000	24,000	27,000
25%	3,000	4,000	5,000	6,000	7,000	8,000
Overheads	10,000	15,000	15,000	15,000	20,000	20,000
Dividends			20,000			
Capital expenditure			30,000			40,000
	85,000	114,000	178,000	152,000	181,000	235,000
b/f	15,000	22,000	20,000	(36,000)	(50,000)	(83,000)
Net cash flow	7,000	(2,000)	(56,000)	(14,000)	(33,000)	(73,000)
c/f	22,000	20,000	(36,000)	(50,000)	(83,000)	(156,000)

(b) The overdraft arrangements are quite inadequate to service the cash needs of the business over the six-month period. If the figures are realistic then action should be taken now to avoid difficulties in the near future. The following are possible courses of action.

(i)   Activities could be curtailed.

(ii) Other sources of cash could be explored, for example a long-term loan to finance the capital expenditure and a factoring arrangement to provide cash due from debtors more quickly.

(iii) Efforts to increase the speed of debt collection could be made.

(iv) Payments to creditors could be delayed.

(v)   The dividend payments could be postponed (the figures indicate that this is a small company, possibly owner-managed).

(vi) Staff might be persuaded to work at a lower rate in return for, say, an annual bonus or a profit-sharing agreement.

(vii) Extra staff might be taken on to reduce the amount of overtime paid.

(viii) The stockholding policy should be reviewed; it may be possible to meet demand from current production and minimise cash tied up in stocks.

5.24   You have probably been working carefully through these examples and exercises using a calculator. It will no doubt have made you appreciate the usefulness of spreadsheets in budget preparation (as discussed in Chapter 3).

6   THE MASTER BUDGET   *11/96*

6.1   When all the functional budgets and the cash budget have been prepared, they are summarised and a budgeted profit and loss account and budgeted balance sheet prepared. These provide the overall picture of the planned performance for the budget period.

Example: a master budget

6.2   Ionesco Ltd produces two products, Abs and Surds. The budget for the forthcoming year to 31 March 19X8 is to be prepared. Expectations for the forthcoming year include the following.

(a)   IONESCO LTD
      BALANCE SHEET AS AT 1 APRIL 19X7

	£	£
Fixed assets		
Land and buildings		45,000
Plant and equipment at cost	187,000	
Less accumulated depreciation	75,000	
		112,000
Current assets		
Raw materials	7,650	
Finished goods	23,600	
Debtors	19,500	
Cash	4,300	
	55,050	
Current liabilities		
Creditors	6,800	
		48,250
		205,250
Financed by		
Share capital		150,000
Retained profit		55,250
		205,250

(b) *Finished products*

The sales director has estimated the following.

		Abs	*Surds*
(i)	Demand for the company's products	4,500 units	4,000 units
(ii)	Selling price per unit	£32	£44
(iii)	Closing stock of finished products at 31 March 19X8	400 units	1,200 units
(iv)	Opening stock of finished products at 1 April 19X7	900 units	200 units
(v)	Unit cost of this opening stock	£20	£28
(vi)	Amount of plant capacity required for each unit of product		
	Machining	15 min	24 min
	Assembling	12 min	18 min
(vii)	Raw material content per unit of each product		
	Material A	1.5 kilos	0.5 kilos
	Material B	2.0 kilos	4.0 kilos
(viii)	Direct labour hours required per unit of each product	6 hours	9 hours

Finished goods are valued on a FIFO basis at full production cost.

(c) *Raw materials*

		Material A	*Material B*
(i)	Closing stock requirement in kilos at 31 March 19X8	600	1,000
(ii)	Opening stock at 1 April 19X7 in kilos	1,100	6,000
(iii)	Budgeted cost of raw materials per kilo	£1.50	£1.00

Actual costs per kilo of opening stocks are as budgeted cost for the coming year.

(d) *Direct labour*

The standard wage rate of direct labour is £1.60 per hour.

(e) *Production overhead*

Production overhead is absorbed on the basis of machining hours, with separate absorption rates for each department. The following overheads are anticipated in the production cost centre budgets.

	Machining department £	*Assembling department* £
Supervisors' salaries	10,000	9,150
Power	4,400	2,000
Maintenance and running costs	2,100	2,000
Consumables	3,400	500
General expenses	19,600	5,000
	39,500	18,650

Depreciation is taken at 5% straight line on plant and equipment. A machine costing the company £20,000 is due to be installed on 1 October 19X7 in the machining department, which already has machinery installed to the value of £100,000 (at cost). Land worth £180,000 is to be acquired in December 19X7.

(f) *Selling and administration expenses*

	£
Sales commissions and salaries	14,300
Travelling and distribution	3,500
Office salaries	10,100
General administration expenses	2,500
	30,400

(g) There is no opening or closing work in progress and inflation should be ignored.

(h) Budgeted cash flows are as follows.

	Quarter 1	Quarter 2	Quarter 3	Quarter 4
Receipts from customers	70,000	100,000	100,000	40,000
Payments:				
Materials	7,000	9,000	10,000	5,000
Wages	33,000	20,000	11,000	15,000
Other costs and expenses	10,000	100,000	205,000	5,000

Required

Prepare the following for the year ended 31 March 19X8 for Ionesco Ltd.

(a) Sales budget
(b) Production budget (in quantities)
(c) Plant utilisation budget
(d) Direct materials usage budget
(e) Direct labour budget
(f) Production overhead budget
(g) Computation of the production cost per unit for each product
(h) Direct materials purchases budget
(i) Cost of goods sold budget
(j) Cash budget
(k) A master budget consisting of a budgeted profit and loss account and balance sheet

Solution

6.3 (a) *Sales budget*

	Market demand	Selling price	Sales value
	Units	£	£
Abs	4,500	32.00	144,000
Surbs	4,000	44.00	176,000
			320,000

(b) *Production budget*

	Abs	Surds
	Units	Units
Sales requirement	4,500	4,000
(Decrease)/increase in finished goods stock	(500)	1,000
Production requirement	4,000	5,000

(c) *Plant utilisation budget*

Product	Units	Machining Hours per unit	Machining Total hours	Assembling Hours per unit	Assembling Total hours
Abs	4,000	0.25	1,000	0.20	800
Surds	5,000	0.40	2,000	0.30	1,500
			3,000		2,300

(d) *Direct materials usage budget*

	Material A	Material B
	kg	kg
Required for production:		
Abs: 4,000 × 1.5 kilos	6,000	-
4,000 × 2.0 kilos	-	8,000
Surds: 5,000 × 0.5 kilos	2,500	-
5,000 × 4.0 kilos	-	20,000
Material usage	8,500	28,000
Unit cost	£1.50 per kilo	£1.00 per kilo
Cost of materials used	£12,750	£28,000

(e) *Direct labour budget*

Product	Production Units	Hours required per unit	Total hours	Rate per hour £	Cost £
Abs	4,000	6	24,000	1.60	38,400
Surds	5,000	9	45,000	1.60	72,000
				Total direct wages	110,400

(f) *Production overhead budget*

	Machining dept £	Assembling dept £
Production overhead allocated and apportioned (excluding depreciation)	39,500	18,650
Depreciation costs		
(i) Existing plant		
(5% of £100,000 in machining)	5,000	
(5% of £87,000 in assembly)		4,350
(ii) Proposed plant		
(5% of $^6/_{12}$ × £20,000)	500	
Total production overhead	45,000	23,000
Total machine hours (see (c))	3,000 hrs	2,300 hrs
Absorption rate per machine hour	£15	£10

(g) *Cost of production*

			Abs £		Surds £
Direct material	A	1.5 kg × £1.50	2.25	0.5 kg × £1.50	0.75
	B	2.0 kg × £1.00	2.00	4.0 kg × £1.00	4.00
Direct labour		6 hrs × £1.60	9.60	9 hrs × £1.60	14.40
Production overhead					
Machining department		15 mins at £15 per hr	3.75	24 min at £15 per hr	6.00
Assembling department		12 mins at £10 per hr	2.00	18 mins at £10 per hr	3.00
Production cost per unit			19.60		28.15

(h) *Direct material purchases budget*

	A kg	B kg
Closing stock required	600	1,000
Production requirements	8,500	28,000
	9,100	29,000
Less opening stock	1,100	6,000
Purchase requirements	8,000	23,000
Cost per unit	£1.50	£1.00
Purchase costs	£12,000	£23,000

(i) *Cost of goods sold budget* (Using FIFO)

	Abs Units	£	Surds Units	£
Opening stocks	900 (× £20.00)	18,000	200 (× £28.00)	5,600
Cost of production	4,000 (× £19.60)	78,400	5,000 (× £28.15)	140,750
	4,900	96,400	5,200	146,350
Less closing stocks	400 (× £19.60)	7,840	1,200 (× £28.15)	33,780
Cost of sales	4,500	88,560	4,000	112,570

Notes
(i) The cost of sales of Abs = 900 units at £20 each plus 3,600 units at £19.60 each.
(ii) The cost of sales of Surds = 200 units at £28 each plus 3,800 units at £28.15 each.

(j) *Cash budget for year to 31.3.X8*

	Quarter 1 £	Quarter 2 £	Quarter 3 £	Quarter 4 £	Total £
Receipts	70,000	100,000	100,000	40,000	310,000
Payments					
Materials	7,000	9,000	10,000	5,000	31,000
Labour	33,000	20,000	11,000	15,000	79,000
Other costs and expenses	10,000	100,000	205,000	5,000	320,000
	50,000	129,000	226,000	25,000	430,000
Receipts less payments	20,000	(29,000)	(126,000)	15,000	(120,000)
Opening cash balance b/f	4,300	24,300	(4,700)	(130,700)	4,300
Closing cash balance c/f	24,300	(4,700)	(130,700)	(115,700)	(115,700)

(k) MASTER BUDGET

Budgeted profit and loss account for year to 31.3.X8

	Abs £	Surds £	Total £
Sales	144,000	176,000	320,000
Less cost of sales	88,560	112,570	201,130
Gross profit	55,440	63,430	118,870
Less selling and administration			30,400
Net profit			88,470

Note. There will be no under-/over-absorbed production overhead in the budgeted profit and loss account.

Budgeted balance sheet at 31.3.X8

	£	£	£
Fixed assets			
Land and buildings (W1)			225,000
Plant and equipment at cost (W2)		207,000	
Less accumulated depreciation (W3)		84,850	
			122,150
			347,150
Current assets			
Raw materials (W4)		1,900	
Finished goods (W5)		41,620	
Debtors (W6)		29,500	
		73,020	
Current liabilities			
Creditors (W7)	10,750		
Bank overdraft (W8)	115,700		
		126,450	
Net current liabilities			(53,430)
			293,720
Financed by			
Share capital			150,000
Retained profit (W9)			143,720
			293,720

Workings

1

	£
Opening balance at 1.4.X7	45,000
Addition	180,000
Cost at 31.3.X8	225,000

2

	£
Opening balance at 1.4.X7	187,000
Addition	20,000
Cost at 31.3.X8	207,000

3

	£
Opening balance at 1.4.X7	75,000
Addition in period	5,000
((f)(i) and (ii) of solution)	4,350
	500
Accumulated depreciation at 31.3.X8	84,850

4

	A	B	Total
Closing stock (kgs)	600	1,000	
Cost per kg	× £1.50	× £1.00	
Value of closing stock	£900	£100	£1,900

5

	Abs	Surds	Total
Closing stock (units)	400	1,200	
Cost per unit ((g) of solution)	× £19.60	× £28.15	
	£7,840	£33,780	£41,620

6

	£
Opening balance	19,500
Sales ((a) of solution)	320,000
Receipts (from cash budget)	(310,000)
Closing balance	29,500

7

	£	£
Opening balance at 1.4.X7		6,800
Land	180,000	
Machine	20,000	
Labour	110,400	
Production overhead	39,500	
	18,650	
		58,150
Materials	12,000	
	23,000	
		35,000
Expenses		30,400
		433,950
		440,750
Cash payments (from cash budget)		(430,000)
Closing balance at 31.3.X8		10,750

8   From cash budget £115,700 overdrawn

9

	£
Retained profit b/f	55,250
Profit for year	88,470
Retained profit c/f	143,720

7   MONITORING PROCEDURES

7.1   The budgeting process does not stop once the budgets have been agreed. Actual results should be compared on a regular basis with the budgeted results. The frequency with which such comparisons are made depends very much on the organisation's circumstances and the sophistication of its control systems but it should occur at least monthly. Management should receive a report detailing the differences and should investigate the reasons for the differences. If the differences are within the control of management, corrective action should be taken to bring the reasons for the difference under control and to ensure that such inefficiencies do not occur in the future. We will look at this procedure in more detail in the next chapter.

7.2   The differences may have occurred, however, because the budget was unrealistic to begin with or because the actual conditions did not reflect those anticipated (or could have possibly been anticipated). This would therefore invalidate the remainder of the budget.

7.3 Because the original budget was unrealistic or because of changes in anticipated conditions, the budget committee may need to reappraise the organisation's future plans and may need to adjust the budget to take account of such changes. The revised budget then represents a revised statement of formal operating plans for the remaining portion of the budget period.

7.4 The important point to note is that the budgetary process does not end for the current year once the budget period has begun: budgeting should be seen as a continuous and dynamic process.

Chapter roundup

- The objectives of a budgetary planning and control system are as follows.
    - To ensure the achievement of the organisation's objectives
    - To compel planning
    - To communicate ideas and plans
    - To coordinate activities
    - To provide a framework for responsibility accounting
    - To establish a system of control
    - To motivate employees to improve their performance

- A budget is a quantified plan of action for a forthcoming accounting period.

- The budget manual is a collection of instructions governing the responsibilities of persons and the procedures, forms and records relating to the preparation and use of budgetary data.

- Managers responsible for preparing budgets should ideally be the managers responsible for carrying out the budget.

- The budget committee is the coordinating body in the preparation and administration of budgets.

- The principal budget factor should be identified at the beginning of the budgetary process, and the budget for this is prepared before all the others.

- Once prepared, the subsidiary budgets must be reviewed to ensure they are consistent with one another.

- Cash budgets show the expected receipts and payments during a budget period and are a vital management control tool.

- The master budget is a summary of the functional (subsidiary) budgets and cash budget and includes a budgeted profit and loss account and a budgeted balance sheet.

- The budgeting process does not end for the forthcoming year once the budget period has begun: budgeting should be seen as a continuous and dynamic process.

Test your knowledge

1 What are the aims of a system of budgetary planning and control? (see para 1.3)

2 What are the functions of a budget committee? (2.6)

3 What is meant by the term *principal budget factor*? (2.8, 2.9)

4 What is the difference between a forecast and a budget? (3.2)

5 Explain the concept of the standard hour. (4.8)

6 How is the reorder level calculated? (4.14)

7 What is possible appropriate management action if a cash budget shows a long-term surplus? (5.2)

Now try illustrative question 21 at the end of the Study Text

Chapter 17

BUDGETARY CONTROL

This chapter covers the following topics.

		Syllabus reference	Ability required
1	Fixed and flexible budgets	6(c)	Skill
2	Preparing flexible budgets	6(c)	Skill
3	Flexible budgets and budgetary control	6(c)	Skill
4	Budget centres and budgetary control reports	6(c)	Skill
5	Feedback and feedforward control mechanisms	6(c)	Skill
6	Forecasting and budgets	6(c)	Skill
7	Alternative budgeting systems	6(c)	Skill
8	Motivation and budget information	6(c)	Skill

Introduction

You should now be able to prepare functional budgets and a master budget and have a firm grasp of the budgeting process. This chapter continues the budgeting theme and looks at budgetary control and, in the last section of the chapter, alternative budgeting systems.

Budgetary control is basically the comparison of actual results with budgeted results. Variances are calculated to identify the differences between actual and budgeted results and these differences are reported to management so that appropriate action can be taken.

Such a system relies upon a system of flexible (as opposed to fixed) budgets. Flexible budgets are vital for both planning and control and this chapter shows how they are constructed and their use in the overall budgetary control process. The topic should be familiar to you from your Paper 2 studies and so we will be concentrating on just the most complex areas.

We will also be looking at feedback and feedforward control mechanisms. These are quite technical-sounding terms for, as you will see, material which you have actually already covered.

Other topics covered briefly in this chapter include the difference between a budget and a forecast and alternative approaches (to those we have covered so far) to budgeting.

This chapter concludes our study of budgeting. You will, however, come across variances, which are mentioned in relation to flexible budgets in this Chapter, in Chapter 19. Chapter 18 begins a new part and looks at standard costing.

1 FIXED AND FLEXIBLE BUDGETS
11/96

1.1 The master budget prepared before the beginning of the budget period is known as the *fixed* budget. By the term 'fixed', we do not mean that the budget is kept unchanged. Revisions to a fixed master budget will be made if the situation so demands. The term 'fixed' means the following.

(a) The budget is prepared on the basis of an estimated volume of production and an estimated volume of sales, but no plans are made for the event that actual volumes of production and sales may differ from budgeted volumes.

(b) When actual volumes of production and sales during a control period (month or four weeks or quarter) are achieved, a fixed budget is not adjusted (in retrospect) to the new levels of activity.

1.2   A flexible budget is 'A budget which, by recognising different cost behaviour patterns, is designed to change as volume of output changes' (CIMA *Official Terminology*). Flexible budgets may be used in one of two ways.

    (a)   *At the planning stage*. For example, suppose that a company expects to sell 10,000 units of output during the next year. A master budget (the fixed budget) would be prepared on the basis of these expected volumes. However, if the company thinks that output and sales might be as low as 8,000 units or as high as 12,000 units, it may prepare *contingency* flexible budgets, at volumes of, say 8,000, 9,000, 11,000 and 12,000 units. There are a number of advantages of planning with flexible budgets.

        (i)   It is possible to find out well in advance the costs of lay-off pay, idle time and so on if output falls short of budget.

        (ii)   Management can decide whether it would be possible to find alternative uses for spare capacity if output falls short of budget. (Could employees be asked to overhaul their own machines instead of paying for an outside contractor?)

        (iii)   An estimate of the costs of overtime, subcontracting work or extra machine hire if sales volume exceeds the fixed budget estimate can be made. From this, it can be established whether there is a limiting factor which would prevent high volumes of output and sales being achieved.

    (b)   *Retrospectively*. At the end of each control period, flexible budgets can be used to compare actual results achieved with what results should have been under the circumstances. Flexible budgets are an essential factor in budgetary control.

        (i)   Management needs to know about how good or bad actual performance has been. To provide a measure of performance, there must be a yardstick (budget/standard) against which actual performance can be measured.

        (ii)   Every business is dynamic, and actual volumes of output cannot be expected to conform exactly to the fixed budget. Comparing actual costs directly with the fixed budget costs is meaningless.

        (iii)   For useful control information, it is necessary to compare actual results at the actual level of activity achieved against the results that should have been expected at this level of activity, which are shown by the flexible budget.

2   PREPARING FLEXIBLE BUDGETS   *11/96*

> **Knowledge brought forward from Paper 2**
>
> *The preparation of flexible budgets*
>
> - The first step in the preparation of a flexible budget is the determination of cost behaviour patterns, which means deciding whether costs are fixed, variable or semi-variable.
>
> - Fixed costs will remain constant as activity levels change.
>
> - For non-fixed costs, divide each cost figure by the related activity level. If the cost is a linear variable cost, the cost per unit will remain constant. If the cost is a semi-variable cost, the unit rate will reduce as activity levels increase.
>
> - Split semi-variable costs into their fixed and variable components using the high-low method or the scattergraph method.
>
> - Calculate the budget cost allowance for each cost item as budget cost allowance = budgeted fixed cost* + (number of units produced/sold × variable cost per unit)**.
>
>   * nil for totally variable cost   ** nil for fixed cost

Example: fixed and flexible budgets

2.1   Suppose that Gemma Ltd expects production and sales during the next year to be 90% of the company's output capacity, that is, 9,000 units of a single product. Cost estimates will be made using the high-low method (which we looked at in Chapter 2) and the following historical records of cost.

	Units of output/sales	Cost of sales
	9,800	£44,400
	7,700	£38,100

The company's management is not certain that the estimate of sales is correct, and has asked for flexible budgets to be prepared at output and sales levels of 8,000 and 10,000 units. The sales price per unit has been fixed at £5.

Required

Prepare appropriate budgets.

Solution

2.2 If we assume that within the range 8,000 to 10,000 units of sales, all costs are fixed, variable or mixed (in other words there are no stepped costs, material discounts, overtime premiums, bonus payments and so on) the fixed and flexible budgets would be based on the estimate of fixed and variable cost.

		£
Total cost of 9,800 units	=	44,400
Total cost of 7,700 units	=	38,100
Variable cost of 2,100 units	=	6,300

The variable cost per unit is £3.

		£
Total cost of 9,800 units	=	44,400
Variable cost of 9,800 units (9,800 × £3)	=	29,400
Fixed costs (all levels of output and sales)	=	15,000

2.3 The fixed budgets and flexible budgets can now be prepared as follows.

	Flexible budget 8,000 units £	Fixed budget 9,000 units £	Flexible budget 10,000 units £
Sales (× £5)	40,000	45,000	50,000
Variable costs (× £3)	24,000	27,000	30,000
Contribution	16,000	18,000	20,000
Fixed costs	15,000	15,000	15,000
Profit	1,000	3,000	5,000

The need for flexible budgets

2.4 We have seen that flexible budgets may be prepared in order to plan for variations in the level of activity above or below the level set in the fixed budget. It has been suggested, however, that since many cost items in modern industry are fixed costs, the value of flexible budgets in planning is dwindling.

(a) In many manufacturing industries, plant costs (depreciation, rent and so on) are a very large proportion of total costs, and these tend to be fixed costs.

(b) Wage costs also tend to be fixed, because employees are generally guaranteed a basic wage for a working week of an agreed number of hours.

(c) With the growth of service industries, labour (wages or fixed salaries) and overheads will account for most of the costs of a business, and direct materials will be a relatively small proportion of total costs.

2.5 Flexible budgets are nevertheless necessary, and even if they are not used at the planning stage, they must be used for budgetary control variance analysis.

3   FLEXIBLE BUDGETS AND BUDGETARY CONTROL

3.1   The CIMA *Official Terminology* defines budgetary control as 'The establishment of budgets relating the responsibilities of executives to the requirements of a policy, and the continuous comparison of actual with budgeted results, either to secure by individual action the objectives of that policy or to provide a basis for its revision'.

3.2   In other words, individual managers are held responsible for investigating differences between budgeted and actual results, and are then expected to take corrective action or amend the plan in the light of actual events.

3.3   It is therefore vital to ensure that valid comparisons are being made. Consider the following example.

3.4   Penny Ltd manufactures a single product, the Darcy. Budgeted results and actual results for May 19X6 are as follows.

	Budget	*Actual*	*Variance*	
Production and sales of the Darcy (units)	7,500	8,200		
	£	£	£	
Sales revenue	75,000	81,000	6,000	(F)
Direct materials	22,500	23,500	1,000	(A)
Direct labour	15,000	15,500	500	(A)
Production overhead	22,500	22,800	300	(A)
Administration overhead	10,000	11,000	1,000	(A)
	70,000	72,800	2,800	(A)
Profit	5,000	8,200	3,200	(F)

Note. (F) denotes a favourable variance and (A) an unfavourable or adverse variance.

3.5   In this example, the variances are meaningless for the purposes of control. All costs were higher than budgeted but the volume of output was also higher; it is to be expected that actual variable costs would be greater those included in the fixed budget. However, it is not possible to tell how much of the increase is due to poor cost control and how much is due to the increase in activity.

3.6   Similarly it is not possible to tell how much of the increase in sales revenue is due to the increase in activity. Some of the difference may be due to a difference between budgeted and actual selling price but we are unable to tell from the analysis above.

3.7   For control purposes we need to know the answers to questions such as the following.

(a)   Were actual costs higher than they should have been to produce and sell 8,200 Darcys?

(b)   Was actual revenue satisfactory from the sale of 8,200 Darcys?

3.8   Instead of comparing actual results with a fixed budget which is based on a different level of activity to that actually achieved, the correct approach to budgetary control is to compare actual results with a budget which has been flexed to the actual activity level achieved.

3.9   Suppose that we have the following estimates of the behaviour of Penny Ltd's costs.

(a)   Direct materials and direct labour are variable costs.

(b)   Production overhead is a semi-variable cost, the budgeted cost for an activity level of 10,000 units being £25,000.

(c)   Administration overhead is a fixed cost.

(d) Selling prices are constant at all levels of sales.

3.10 The budgetary control analysis should therefore be as follows.

	Fixed budget	*Flexible budget*	*Actual results*	*Variance*
Production and sales (units)	7,500	8,200	8,200	
	£	£	£	£
Sales revenue	75,000	82,000 (W1)	81,000	1,000 (A)
Direct materials	22,500	24,600 (W2)	23,500	1,100 (F)
Direct labour	15,000	16,400 (W3)	15,500	900 (F)
Production overhead	22,500	23,200 (W4)	22,800	400 (F)
Administration overhead	10,000	10,000 (W5)	11,000	1,000 (A)
	70,000	74,200	72,800	1,400 (F)
Profit	5,000	7,800	8,200	400 (F)

Workings

1 Selling price per unit = £75,000 ÷ 7,500 = £10 per unit
   Flexible budget sales revenue = £10 × 8,200 = £82,000

2 Direct materials cost per unit = £22,500 ÷ 7,500 = £3
   Budget cost allowance = £3 × 8,200 = £24,600

3 Direct labour cost per unit = £15,000 ÷ 7,500 = £2
   Budget cost allowance = £2 × 8,200 = £16,400

4 Variable production overhead cost per unit
   = £(25,000 − 22,500)/(10,000 − 7,500)
   = £2,500/2,500 = £1 per unit
   ∴ Fixed production overhead cost = £22,500 − (7,500 × £1) = £15,000
   ∴ Budget cost allowance = £15,000 + (8,200 × £1) = £23,200

5 Administration overhead is a fixed cost and hence budget cost allowance = £10,000

3.11 (a) In selling 8,200 units, the expected profit should have been, not the fixed budget profit of £5,000, but the flexible budget profit of £7,800. Instead actual profit was £8,200 ie £400 more than we should have expected.

One of the reasons for this improvement is that, given output and sales of 8,200 units, the cost of resources (material, labour etc) was £1,400 lower than expected. Profit was therefore increased by £1,400 because costs were less than expected. (A comparison of the fixed budget and the actual costs in Paragraph 3.4 appeared to indicate that costs were not being controlled since all of the variances were adverse).

In Chapter 19 you will see how these total cost variances can be analysed to reveal how much of the variance is due to lower resource prices and how much is due to efficient resource usage.

(b) The sales revenue was, however, £1,000 less than expected because a lower price was charged than budgeted.

We know this because flexing the budget has eliminated the effect of changes in the volume sold, which is the only other factor that can affect sales revenue. In Chapter 20 you will learn that this variance of £1,000 (A) is known as a selling price variance.

The lower selling price could have been caused by the increase in the volume sold (to sell the additional 700 units the selling price had to fall below £10 per unit). We do not know if this is the case but without flexing the budget we could not know that a different selling price to that budgeted had been charged. Our initial analysis in Paragraph 3.4 had appeared to indicate that sales revenue was ahead of budget.

3.12   The difference of £400 between the flexible budget profit of £7,800 at a production level of 8,200 units and the actual profit of £8,200 is due to the net effect of cost savings of £1,400 and lower than expected sales revenue (by £1,000).

3.13   The difference between the original budgeted profit of £5,000 and the actual profit of £8,200 is the total of the following.

   (a)   The savings in resource costs/lower than expected sales revenue (as indicated by the difference between the flexible budget and the actual results)

   (b)   The effect of producing and selling 8,200 units instead of 7,500 units (as indicated by the difference between the fixed budget and the flexible budget).

   We can analyse the difference caused by actual sales volume being 700 units greater than budgeted sales volume as follows.

	£	£
Sales revenue increased by		7,000
Costs increased by:		
Direct materials	2,100	
Direct labour	1,400	
Production overhead	700	
Administration overhead	-	
		(4,200)
Profit increased by		2,800

3.14   A full variance analysis statement would be as follows.

	£	£
Fixed budget profit		5,000
Variances		
Sales volume	2,800 (F)	
Selling price	1,000 (A)	
Direct materials cost	1,100 (F)	
Direct labour cost	900 (F)	
Production overhead cost	400 (F)	
Administration overhead cost	1,000 (A)	
		3,200 (F)
Actual profit		8,200

3.15   If management believes that any of the variances are large enough to justify it, they will investigate the reasons for their occurrence to see whether any corrective action is necessary. We will look at this process in more detail in Chapter 20.

Exercise 1

Flower Ltd budgeted to sell 200 units and produced the following budget.

	£	£
Sales		71,400
Variable costs		
Labour	31,600	
Material	12,600	
		44,200
Contribution		27,200
Fixed costs		18,900
Profit		8,300

Actual sales turned out to be 230 units, which were sold for £69,000. Actual expenditure on labour was £27,000 and on material £24,000. Fixed costs totalled £10,000.

Required

Prepare a flexible budget that will be useful for management control purposes.

Solution

	Budget 200 units £	Per unit £	Flexed budget 230 units	Actual 230 units £	Variance
Sales	71,400	357	82,110	69,000	13,110 (A)
Variable costs					
Labour	31,600	158	36,340	27,000	9,340 (F)
Material	12,600	63	14,490	24,000	9,510 (A)
	44,200	221	50,830	51,000	
Contribution	27,200	136	31,280	18,000	13,280 (A)
Fixed costs	18,900		18,900	10,000	8,900 (F)
Profit	8,300		12,380	8,000	4,380 (A)

Preparing a flexible budget - absorption costing

3.16   In a flexible budget, the aim is to decide what total costs (and profit) should be at differing levels of output and sales. Since fixed costs are the same at all levels of output (within a normal or relevant range of activity), only variable costs and revenues vary with increases or decreases in the level of activity.

3.17   Although fixed costs *incurred* do not change as the level of activity increases or decreases, the amount of fixed costs *absorbed* will vary. This is because the fixed overhead absorption rate is pre-determined at the start of the budget period, and is based on the expected level of activity in the *fixed* budget.

Exam focus point

The examiner has confirmed that candidates *could* be asked to prepare a flexible budget on an absorption costing basis.

3.18   Suppose that a company, which has an absorption costing system, budgets for fixed production overhead of £4,000 and output/sales of 1,000 units. The overhead absorption rate will therefore be £4 per unit. If the company decides to prepare a fixed master budget and also flexible budgets at output levels of 900 units and 1,100 units, the overhead costs in the budget would be as follows.

	Flexible budget 900 units £	Fixed budget 1,000 units £	Flexible budget 1,100 units £
Overhead cost of production (× £4 per unit) - absorbed	3,600	4,000	4,400
(Under-)/over-absorbed overhead	(400)	-	400
Overhead incurred	4,000	4,000	4,000

Exercise 2

Butler Ltd manufactures a single product, with a variable manufacturing cost of £24 per unit and a selling price of £40 per unit. Fixed production overheads are £180,000 per period. The normal level of output in each period is 30,000 units, so that an overhead absorption rate of £6 per unit is applied. Any under- or over-absorbed overhead is written off to the profit and loss account in the period in which it arises. We will assume that no other expenses are incurred. In each of two periods, 1 and 2, the volumes of production and sales were as follows.

	Period 1	Period 2
	Units	Units
Opening stock b/f	10,000	22,000
Production	35,000	26,000
	45,000	48,000
Closing stock c/f	22,000	10,000
Sales	23,000	38,000

Required

Use flexible budgeting techniques to calculate the company's manufacturing and trading results for periods 1 and 2 and explain the difference in profit between period 1 and period 2.

Solution

	Period 1	Period 2
Production	35,000 units	26,000 units
	£	£
Overheads absorbed (× £6)	210,000	156,000
Overheads incurred	180,000	180,000
Over-/(under)-absorbed overhead	30,000	(24,000)

Manufacturing and trading results

	Period 1		Period 2	
	£	£	£	£
Sales		920,000		1,520,000
Opening stock (at £30 per unit)	300,000		660,000	
Production (at £30 per unit)	1,050,000		780,000	
	1,350,000		1,440,000	
Closing stock (at £30)	660,000		300,000	
Cost of sales		690,000		1,140,000
		230,000		380,000
Over-/(under)-absorbed overhead		30,000		(24,000)
		260,000		356,000

The difference in profit is £96,000. This is explained as follows.

	£
Difference in profit due to sales volume (15,000 units × £(40 − 30) per unit)	150,000
Difference in profit due to under-/over absorption of overheads	(54,000)
	96,000

Flexible budgets, control and computers

3.19   The production of flexible budget control reports is an area in which computers can provide invaluable assistance to the cost accountant, calculating flexed budget figures using fixed budget and actual results data and hence providing detailed variance analysis. For control information to be of any value it must be produced quickly: speed is one of the many advantages of computers.

4   BUDGET CENTRES AND BUDGETARY CONTROL REPORTS

4.1   Budgetary control is based around a system of budget centres, a *budget centre* being defined in CIMA *Official Terminology* as 'A centre for which an individual budget is drawn up'. Each budget centre will have its own budget and a manager will be responsible for managing the budget centre and ensuring that the budget is met.

Budgetary control reports

4.2   If the budget holders (managers of budget centres) are to attempt to meet budgets they must receive regular budgetary control reports so that they can monitor the budget centre's operations and take any necessary control action.

5   FEEDBACK AND FEEDFORWARD CONTROL MECHANISMS   *5/95, 5/98*

Feedback

5.1   The term 'feedback' is used to describe both the process of reporting back control information to management and the control information itself. In a business organisation, it is information produced from within the organisation (management control reports) with the purpose of helping management and other employees with control decisions.

(a)   *Single loop feedback*, normally expressed as feedback, is the feedback of relatively small variations between actual and plan in order that corrective action can bring performance in line with planned results. This implies that the existing plans will not change. This type of feedback is associated with budgetary control and standard costing.

(b)   *Double loop feedback*, also known as higher level feedback, ensures that plans, budgets, organisational structures and the control systems themselves are revised to meet changes in conditions.

(c)   Feedback will most often be *negative:* targets were missed and this was *not* what was required. It may, however, be *positive:* targets were missed, but other targets were hit which were better than those we were aiming at. Negative feedback would result in control action to get back onto target. Positive feedback means that the target should be moved.

Feedforward control

5.2   Most control systems make use of a comparison between results of the current period (historical costs) and the planned results. Past events are therefore used as a means of controlling or adjusting future activity.

5.3   Consider, however, a *cash budget*. This is used to identify likely peaks and troughs in cash balances, and if it seems probably, say, that a higher overdraft facility will be needed later in the year, control action will be taken in advance of the actual need, to make sure that the facility will be available. This is an example of *feedforward control*, that is, control based on comparing original targets or actual results with a *forecast* of future results.

5.4   The 'information revolution', which has arisen from computer technology, management information systems theory and the growing use of quantitative techniques has widened the scope for the use of this control technique. Forecasting models can be constructed which enable regular revised forecasts to be prepared about what is now likely to happen in view of changes in key variables (such as sales demand, wage rates and so on). We will be looking at forecasting later in this chapter.

5.5   If regular forecasts are prepared, managers will have both the current forecast and the original plan to guide their action. The original plan may or may not be achievable in view of the changing circumstances. The current forecast indicates what is expected to happen in view of these circumstances.

5.6   Control comparisons which are then possible are as follows.

(a)   *Current forecast versus plan.* What action must be taken to get back to the plan, given the differences between the current forecast and the plan? Is any control action worthwhile?

(b)   If control action is planned, the current forecast will need to be amended to take account of the effects of the control action and a *revised forecast* prepared.

(c)   The next comparison should then be *revised forecast versus plan* to determine whether the plan is now expected to be achieved.

(d) A comparison between the *original current forecast* and the *revised forecast* will show what the expected effect of the control action will be.

(e) At the end of a control period, actual results will be analysed and two comparisons may be made.

   (i) *Actual results versus the revised forecast*

   Why did differences between the two occur?

   (ii) *Actual results so far in the year versus the plan*

   How close are actual results to the plan?

(f) At the same time, a *new current forecast* should be prepared, and the cycle of comparisons and control action may begin again.

It is in this way that costs are constantly controlled and monitored.

Exam focus point

The May 1998 exam included a question that asked how a cash budget might be used for feedback and feedforward control. In feedback terms, a comparison of what was meant to happen with what actually happened might help to explain, say, an unexpectedly high interest charge for a certain period. The use of cash budgets for feedforward control is explained above.

---

6 FORECASTING AND BUDGETS

6.1 It has been said that budgeting is more a test of forecasting skill than anything else and there is a certain amount of truth in such a comment. Forecasts need to be made of sales volumes and prices, wage rates and earnings, material availability's and prices, rates of inflation, the cost of bought-in services and the cost of overhead items such as power. However, it is *not* sufficient to simply add a percentage to last year's budget in the hope of achieving a realistic forecast.

6.2 A forecast is an estimate of what might happen in the future. It is a best estimate, based on certain assumptions about the conditions that are expected to apply. A budget, in contrast, is a plan of what the organisation is aiming to achieve and what it has set as a target. A budget should be realistic and so it will be based to some extent on forecasts prepared. In formulating a budget, however, management will be trying to establish some control over the conditions that will apply in the future.

6.3 When a budget is set it will, for a short time, be the same as the forecasts. As actual events progress and the situation develops and changes, however, new forecasts might be prepared that differ from the budget targets. Management might be able to take control action to bring forecasts back into line with the budget; alternatively, management will have to accept that the budget will not be achieved, or it will be exceeded, depending on what the current forecasts indicate.

7 ALTERNATIVE BUDGETING SYSTEMS

Incremental budgeting

7.1 Before the annual budget is prepared, a base should be chosen from which the process will begin. The traditional approach is to base the budget on the current year's results plus an extra amount for estimated growth or inflation next year. This approach is known as incremental budgeting since it is concerned mainly with the increments in costs and revenues which will occur in the coming period.

7.2 Incremental budgeting is a reasonable procedure if current operations are as effective, efficient and economical as they can be. It is appropriate for budgeting for costs such as staff salaries, which may be estimated on the basis of current salaries plus an increment for inflation and are hence administratively fairly easy to prepare. It is also used for budgeting for expenditure which is not linked to activity level (usually that associated with non-operating functions such as research and development expenditure).

7.3   In general, however, it is an inefficient form of budgeting as it encourages slack and wasteful spending to creep into budgets. Past inefficiencies are perpetuated since the relationship between costs, benefits and objectives are rarely subjected to close scrutiny.

7.4   To ensure that inefficiencies are not concealed, alternative approaches to budgeting have been developed. One such approach is zero base budgeting.

Zero base budgeting

7.5   Zero base budgeting was very well defined in an article in *Management Accounting* by Anthony R Morden.

> 'Zero-base budgeting is a formalised system of budgeting for the activities of an enterprise *as if each activity were being performed for the first time*, ie from a zero base. Essentially, a number of alternative levels of provision for each activity are identified, costed and evaluated in terms of the benefits to be obtained from them.
>
> ZBB is based on the belief that management should be required to justify *existing* activities in exactly the same way as new proposals. Thus, established activities will have to be compared with alternative applications of the resources that they would use during the budgetary planning period. Implicit in ZBB therefore, is the concept of opportunity cost.
>
> Zero-based budgeting takes away the *implied right* of existing activities to receive a continued allocation of resources.'

Rolling budgets

7.6   If management need the chance to revise their plans (perhaps because it is suspected that a new competitor will enter the market at the beginning of the year, the effect of which cannot be quantified when the budget is set or perhaps because inflation is very high or is expected to rise or fall by a large amount during the course of the year) management may decide to introduce a system of rolling budgets (also called continuous budgets).

7.7   Rolling budgets are an attempt to prepare targets and plans which are more realistic and certain, particularly with a regard to price levels, by shortening the period between preparing budgets.

7.8   Instead of preparing a *periodic budget* annually for the full budget period, there would be budgets every one, two, three or four months (three to six, or even twelve budgets each year). Each of these budgets would plan for the next twelve months so that the current budget is extended by an extra period as the current period ends: hence the name rolling budgets.

7.9   Suppose, for example, that a rolling budget is prepared every three months. The first three months of the budget period would be planned in great detail, and the remaining nine months in lesser detail, because of the greater uncertainty about the longer-term future.

If a first continuous budget is prepared for January to March in detail and April to December in less detail, a new budget will be prepared towards the end of March, planning April to June in detail and July to March in less detail. Four rolling budgets would be prepared every 12 months on this 3 and 9 month basis, requiring, inevitably, greater administrative effort.

The detail in the first three months would be principally important for the following.

(a) Planning working capital and short-term resources (cash, materials, labour and so on).

(b) Control: the budget for each control period should provide a more reliable yardstick for comparison with actual results.

7.10 The higher cost and effort required for rolling budgets would be justified by more accurate planning. The main advantage is that whereas a twelve-month budget (periodic budget) becomes outdated when there is rapid inflation or major changes in market conditions, a rolling budget system allows for more frequent reassessments and revisions in the light of inflationary trends and other events.

If annual budgets are formulated by adding an allowance for inflation to last year's figures, there is a danger that the annual rate of inflation will be over-estimated so that the budgets will be too high and thus encourage overspending by departments. In contrast, quarterly budgets prepared on a rolling basis are likely to predict inflation rates more accurately because shorter-term forecasts are used.

Exercise 3

What advantages and disadvantages of rolling budgets can you think of?

Solution

The advantages are as follows.

(a) They reduce the element of uncertainty in budgeting. If a high rate of inflation or major changes in market conditions or any other change is likely which cannot be quantified with accuracy, rolling budgets concentrate detailed planning and control on short-term prospects where the degree of uncertainty is much smaller.

(b) They force managers to reassess the budget regularly, and to produce budgets which are up to date in the light of current events and expectations.

(c) Planning and control will be based on a recent plan instead of a fixed annual budget that might have been made many months ago and which is no longer realistic.

(d) There is always a budget which extends for several months ahead. For example, if rolling budgets are prepared quarterly there will always be a budget extending for the next 9 to 12 months. If rolling budgets are prepared monthly there will always be a budget for the next 11 to 12 months. This is not the case when fixed annual budgets are used.

The disadvantages of rolling budgets can be a deterrent to using them.

(a) A system of rolling budgets calls for the routine preparation of a new budget at regular intervals during the course of the one financial year. This involves more time, effort and money in budget preparation.

(b) Frequent budgeting might have an off-putting effect on managers who doubt the value of preparing one budget after another at regular intervals, even when there are major differences between the figures in one budget and the next.

---

8   MOTIVATION AND BUDGET INFORMATION

8.1 The attitude of managers towards the budget control information they receive might reduce the information's effectiveness. The sorts of attitude that might be found are as follows.

(a) Budget reports could well be seen as having a relatively low priority in the list of management tasks to be seen to. Managers might take the view that they have more pressing jobs on hand than looking at routine control reports.

(b) Managers might resent budget control information; they may see it as part of a system of trying to find fault with their work. This resentment is likely to be particularly strong when budgets or standards are imposed on managers without allowing them to participate in the budget-setting process. When managers resent control reports, they are likely to adopt a hostile and defensive attitude.

(c) If budgets are seen as pressure devices to push managers into doing better, control reports will be resented.

(d) Managers may not understand the information in the budget control reports, because they are unfamiliar with accounting terminology or principles.

(e) Managers might have a false sense of what their objectives should be. A production manager, for example, might consider it more important to maintain quality standards regardless of cost, and a service department manager might similarly think that his department must maintain a certain level of service, regardless of expense. They would then dismiss adverse expenditure variances as inevitable and unavoidable.

(f) If there are flaws in the system of recording actual costs, managers will dismiss budget control information as unreliable.

(g) Budget control information might be received weeks after the end of the period to which it relates, in which case managers might regard it as out-of-date and no longer useful.

(h) In not-for-profit organisations such as charities, managers may be more concerned with non-quantifiable objectives such as help given, and may regard control reports as irrelevant to the *real* purposes of the organisation.

8.2 It is therefore obvious that accountants and senior management should try to develop and implement budgeting systems that are acceptable to the budget holders and produce positive effects.

8.3 Argyris has discovered in his research that budgets are often considered as pressure devices and are used as part of a management policing system which leads to the budgeting system having a demotivating effect - the opposite to that intended. To foster motivation, acceptance by the managers concerned of their budgets and of the levels of performance contained in the budgets is vital.

The cost accountant and motivation

8.4 It is questionable whether performance measurements, and a control system based on these measurements, can ever motivate managers properly towards achieving the organisation's goals.

(a) No accounting measures of performance can provide a comprehensive assessment of what a person has achieved for the organisation.

> 'The measurement system is not perfect and while some measured behaviours have organisational significance, others do not; in which case, the relationship between the performance measurement process and the reward system can conceivably encourage a concern with what is measured, regardless of organisational relevance.' (Hopwood)

(b) An accounting system cannot even fully reflect the *economic* aspects of performance.

(c) It is usually impossible to segregate the *controllable* component of performance from the uncontrollable component in formal performance measures. This gives rise to 'unfairness' in performance evaluation.

(d) Accounting reports tend to concentrate on short-term achievements, to the exclusion of the long-term effects.

(e) Many accounting reports try to serve several different purposes, and in trying to satisfy several needs actually satisfy none properly.

8.5 The cost accountant does not have the authority to do much on his or her own to improve hostile or apathetic attitudes to control information. There has to be support, either from senior management or from cost and profit centre managers themselves. However, the accountant can do quite a lot to improve and then maintain the standard of a budgetary control reporting system.

(a) Senior management can offer support by doing the following.

(i) Making sure that a system of responsibility accounting is adopted within the organisation, and that individual managers are fully aware of what their areas of responsibility are, and how they will be held accountable for results in these areas.

(ii) Allowing managers to have a say in formulating their budgets or standards. The 'participative approach' in budgeting should reduce hostility to control reporting.

(iii) Offering incentives (for example bonuses) to managers who meet budget targets.

(iv) Regarding budgetary control information as a 'tool' for managers to use constructively, not a way of apportioning blame and punishing managers who fail to achieve a target or standard.

(b) Cost centre/profit centre managers should accept their responsibilities. Ideally, they ought to be aware of the benefits of a budgetary control system and welcome the feedback of control information. If necessary, in-house training courses in the budgetary control system could be held to encourage a collective, cooperative and positive attitude amongst managers.

(c) The cost accountant should improve (or maintain) the quality of the budgetary control system by doing the following.

(i) Developing a working relationship with operational managers, for example going out to meet them and discussing the control reports, instead of sitting in isolation in the accounting office, divorced from contact with the people to whom he or she sends the control reports.

(ii) Explaining the meaning of budgets and control reports. Explanations can be provided in a budget manual, but managers have to be encouraged to read and use the manual if the message is to get across this way.

(iii) Trying to make sure that actual costs are recorded accurately at the point of data capture.

(iv) Trying to ensure that budgets are up-to-date, either by having a system of rolling budgets, or else by updating budgets or standards as necessary, and also ensuring that standards are 'fair' so that control information is realistic.

(v) Mailing reports useful to the reader.

Budget reports

8.6 The cost accountant must produce information in a form that best suits management if the information is to have a positive motivational effect. The following criteria should be applied.

(a) Reports should be *clear*.

(b) Reports should be *to the point* using the principle of reporting by exception.

(c) Reports should be *relevant* to the reader; clear distinctions should be drawn if possible between directly attributable costs over which a manager should have influence, and apportioned or fixed costs which are unavoidable or uncontrollable.

(d) *Significant variances* should be highlighted for investigation.

(e) Accounting jargon should be kept to a minimum.

(f) Reports should be *timely,* which means they must be produced in good time to allow the individual to take control action before any adverse results get much worse.

Chapter roundup

- Fixed budgets remain unchanged regardless of the level of activity; flexible budgets are designed to flex with the level of activity.

- A prerequisite of flexible budgeting is a knowledge of cost behaviour.

- The preparation of a flexible budget is based upon the calculation of a budget cost allowance for each cost item.

  Budget cost allowance = budgeted fixed cost* + (number of units produced/sold × variable cost per unit)**

  * nil for totally variable cost
  ** nil for fixed cost

- Comparison of a fixed budget with the actual results for a different level of activity is of little use for control purposes. Flexible budgets should be used to show what cost and revenues should have been for the actual level of activity.

- The differences between the components of a flexible budget and actual results are known as budget variances.

- Budgetary control is based around a system of budget centres.

- Feedback is both the process of reporting back control information to management and the control information itself. It can be positive or negative.

- Feedforward control is control based on comparing original targets or actual results with a forecast of future results.

- Alternative budgeting systems include ZBB and rolling budgets.

Test your knowledge

1   Distinguish between a fixed budget and a flexible budget. (see paras 1.1, 1.2)

2   Describe the uses of a flexible budget in planning and as a retrospective control measure. (1.2)

3   What is the correct approach to budgetary control? (3.8)

4   What is a budget centre? (4.1)

5   What is single loop feedback? (5.1)

6   What is the difference between a forecast and a budget? (6.2)

7   What is ZBB? (7.5)

8   What is a rolling budget? (7.8)

Now try illustrative question 22 at the end of the Study Text

Part D
Standard costing

Chapter 18

STANDARD COSTING

This chapter covers the following topics.

		Syllabus reference	Ability required
1	The uses of standard costing	6(d)	Skill
2	Setting standards	6(d)	Skill
3	Standards: their evolution and continuous improvement	6(d)	Skill
4	Long-term changes in standards	6(d)	Skill
5	Budgets and standards compared	6(d)	Skill

Introduction

Just as there are standards for most things in our daily lives (cleanliness in hamburger restaurants, educational achievement of nine-year olds, number of underground trains running on time) there are standards for the costs of units of products and units of services rendered in a commercial organisation. Moreover, just as the standards in our daily lives are not always met, the standards for the costs of units of products and services rendered are not always met. We will not, however, be considering the cleanliness of hamburger restaurants in this chapter but we will be looking at standard costs and standard costing.

Standard costing was covered at an elementary level in Paper 2, simply as an introduction to the technique of variance analysis. We obviously look at the topic in more depth for your Paper 6 studies.

In the next chapter we will see how standard costing forms the basis of variance analysis, the vital management control tool which we looked at briefly in the previous chapter.

1 THE USES OF STANDARD COSTING

1.1 A *standard cost* is a carefully predetermined estimated unit cost. It is usually a standard cost per unit of production or per unit of service rendered but it is also possible to have a standard cost per routine task completed, or a standard cost per £1 of sale. A standard cost per unit of production may include administration, selling and distribution costs, but in many organisations, the assessment of standards is confined to production costs only.

1.2 The CIMA *Official Terminology* definition of standard costing is 'A control technique which compares standard costs and revenues with actual results to obtain variances which are used to stimulate improved performance'.

1.3 *Standard costing* is the preparation of standard costs to be used in the following circumstances.

(a) To assist in *setting budgets* and *evaluating managerial performance*.

(b) To act as a *control device* by establishing standards, highlighting (via variance analysis) activities that do not conform to plan and thus alerting management to those areas that may be out of control and in need of corrective action.

(c) To enable the principle of *'management by exception'* to be practised. A standard cost, when established, is an average expected unit cost. Because it is only an average, actual results will vary to some extent above and below the average. Variances should only be reported where the difference between actual and standard is significant.

(d)   To *provide a prediction of future costs* to be used in decision-making situations.

(e)   To *value stocks and cost production* for cost accounting purposes. It is an alternative method of valuation to methods like FIFO, LIFO or replacement costing.

(f)   To *motivate staff and management* by the provision of challenging targets.

(g)   To *provide guidance on improvement of efficiency*.

1.4   Although the use of standard costs to simplify the keeping of cost accounting records should not be overlooked, we will be concentrating on the control and variance analysis aspect of standard costing.

Variances

1.5   Standard costing involves the establishment of predetermined estimates of the costs of products or services, the collection of actual costs and the comparison of the actual results with the predetermined estimates. The predetermined costs are known as standard costs and the difference between standard and actual is known as a *variance*. The process by which the total difference between standard and actual results is analysed is known as *variance analysis*.

When standard costing is used

1.6   Although standard costing can be used in a variety of costing situations (batch and mass production, process manufacture, jobbing manufacture (where there is standardisation of parts) and service industries (if a realistic cost unit can be established)), the greatest benefit from its use can be gained if there is a degree of repetition in the production process. It is therefore most suited to mass production and repetitive assembly work. However, a standard cost can be calculated per task if there is a similarity of tasks. In this way standard costing can be used by some service organisations.

2   SETTING STANDARDS

2.1   A standard cost implies that a standard or target exists for every single element that contributes to the product: the types, usage and prices of materials and parts, the grades, rates of pay and times for the labour involved, the production methods, tools and so on. The standard cost for each part of the product is recorded on a standard cost card, an example of which is given below.

STANDARD COST CARD				
Product: the Splodget, No 12345				
	Cost	*Requirement*	£	£
Direct materials				
A	£2.00 per kg	6 kgs	12.00	
B	£3.00 per kg	2 kgs	6.00	
C	£4.00 per litre	1 litre	4.00	
Others			2.00	
				24.00
Direct labour				
Grade I	£4.00 per hour	3 hrs	12.00	
Grade II	£5.40 per hour	5 hrs	27.00	
				39.00
Variable production overheads	£1.00 per hour	8 hrs		8.00
Fixed production overheads	£3.00 per hour	8 hrs		24.00
Standard full cost of production				95.00

2.2 Standard costs may be used in both marginal and absorption costing systems. The card illustrated has been prepared under an absorption costing system, with selling and administration costs excluded from the standard.

2.3 The responsibility for setting standard costs should be shared between managers able to provide the necessary information about levels of expected efficiency, prices and overhead costs. Standard costs are usually revised once a year (to allow for the new overheads budget, inflation in prices, and any changes in expected efficiency of materials usage or of labour).

Setting standards for materials costs

2.4 Direct materials costs per unit of raw material will be estimated by the purchasing department from their knowledge of the following.

(a) Purchase contracts already agreed
(b) Pricing discussions with regular suppliers
(c) Quotations and estimates from potential suppliers
(d) The forecast movement of prices in the market
(e) The availability of bulk purchase discounts
(f) Material quality required

2.5 A few problems can, however, arise.

(a) The standard cost ought to include an allowance for *bulk purchase discounts*, if these are available on all or some of the purchases, and it may have to be a weighted average price of the differing prices charged for the same product by alternative suppliers.

(b) A decision must be taken as to how to deal with *price inflation*.

2.6 Suppose that a material costs £10 per kilogram at the moment, and during the course of the next 12 months, it is expected to go up in price by 20% to £12 per kilogram. What standard price should be selected: the current price of £10 per kilogram or the average expected price for the year, which might be, for example, £11 per kilogram? Either would be possible, but neither would be entirely satisfactory.

(a) If the current price were used in the standard, the reported price variance would become adverse as soon as prices go up, which might be very early in the year. If prices go up gradually rather than in one big jump, it would be difficult to select an appropriate time for revising the standard.

(b) If an estimated mid-year price were used, price variances should be favourable in the first half of the year and adverse in the second half, again assuming that prices go up gradually. Management could only really check that in any month, the price variance did not become excessively adverse (or favourable) and that the price variance switched from being favourable to adverse around month six or seven and not sooner.

2.7 Standard costing for materials is therefore more difficult in times of inflation but it is still worthwhile.

(a) Usage and efficiency variances will still be meaningful.

(b) Inflation is measurable: there is no reason why its effects cannot be removed from the variances reported.

(c) Standard costs can be revised, so long as this is not done too frequently.

Setting standards for labour costs

2.8 Direct labour rates per hour will be set by reference to the payroll and to any agreements on pay rises and/or bonuses with trade union representatives of the employees.

(a) A separate hourly rate or weekly wage will be set for each different labour grade/type of employee.

(b) An average hourly rate will be applied for each grade (even though individual rates of pay may vary according to age and experience).

Setting standards for material usage and labour efficiency

2.9 To estimate the materials required to make each product (material usage) and also the labour hours required (labour efficiency), technical specifications must be prepared for each product by production experts (either in the production department or the work study department). Material usage and labour efficiency standards are known as performance standards.

(a) The *standard product specification* for materials must list the quantities required of each material in the product. These standard input quantities must be made known to the operators in the production department (so that control action by management to deal with excess material wastage will be understood by them).

(b) The *standard operation sheet* for labour will specify the expected hours required by each grade of labour in each department to make one unit of product. These standard times must be carefully set and must be understood by the labour force. Where necessary, standard procedures or operating methods should be stated.

Types of standard   *5/96*

2.10 The setting of standards raises the problem of how demanding the standard should be. Should the standard represent a perfect performance or an easily attainable performance. There are four types of standard.

Ideal standard

2.11 These are based on perfect operating conditions: no wastage, no spoilage, no inefficiencies, no idle time, no breakdowns. Variances from ideal standards are useful for pinpointing areas where a close examination may result in large savings, but they are likely to have an unfavourable motivational impact because reported variances will always be adverse. Employees will often feel that the goals are unattainable and not work so hard.

Attainable standard

2.12 These are based on the hope that a standard amount of work will be carried out efficiently, machines properly operated or materials properly used. Some allowance is made for wastage and inefficiencies. If well-set they provide a useful psychological incentive by giving employees a realistic, but challenging target of efficiency. The consent and co-operation of employees involved in improving the standard are required.

Current standard

2.13 There are standards based on current working conditions (current wastage, current inefficiencies). The disadvantage of current standards is that they do not attempt to improve on current levels of efficiency.

Basic standard

2.14 These are standards which are kept unaltered over a long period of time, and may be out of date. They are used to show changes in efficiency or performance over a long period of time. Basic standards are perhaps the least useful and least common type of standard in use.

2.15 Ideal standards, attainable standards and current standards each have their supporters and it is by no means clear which of them is preferable.

(a) Variances from ideal standards are useful for pinpointing areas where a close examination might result in large cost savings.

(b) It has been argued from experience that ideal standards provide an incentive to greater efficiency even though the standard cannot be achieved.

(c) Ideal standards cannot be achieved and so there will always be adverse variances. If the standards are used for budgeting, an allowance will have to be included for these 'inefficiencies'.

(d) Current standards or attainable standards are a better basis for budgeting, because they represent the level of productivity which management will wish to plan for.

Exam focus point

Six marks were available in the May 1996 exam for explaining the difference between attainable standards and ideal standards. However, it would not have been quite enough simply to churn out the information above, word for word, because candidates were specifically asked to *use the information in the question* when giving their answers. It is always a good idea to show the examiner that you have read and understood the question, whether you are specifically asked to do so or not.

Setting standards for overheads

2.16 The overhead absorption rate is usually based on the number of direct labour hours and so the standard overhead cost per unit is usually calculated as follows.

Standard labour hours per unit × standard absorption rate per hour

The standard absorption rate per hour is the same as the predetermined overhead absorption rate as calculated for an absorption costing system.

2.17 The standard absorption rate will depend on the planned production volume for a period. Production volume will depend on two factors.

(a) Production capacity (or 'volume capacity') measured perhaps in standard hours of output, which in turn reflects production direct labour hours. We looked at standard hours in Chapter 16.

(b) Efficiency of working, by labour or machines, allowing for rest time and contingency allowances.

2.18 Suppose that a department has a work force of ten men, each of whom works a 36 hour week to make standard units, and each unit has a standard time of two hours to make. The expected efficiency of the work-force is 125%.

(a) Budgeted capacity, in direct labour hours, would be 10 × 36 = 360 production hours per week.

(b) Budgeted efficiency is 125% so that the work-force should take only 1 hour of actual production time to produce 1.25 standard hours of output.

(c) This means in our example that budgeted output is 360 production hours × 125% = 450 standard hours of output per week. At 2 standard hours per unit, this represents production activity or volume of 225 units of output per week.

Exercise 1

Output, capacity and efficiency are inter-related items, and you should check your understanding of them by attempting a quick answer to the following problem.

ABC Ltd carries out routine office work in a sales order processing department, and all tasks in the department have been given standard times. There are 40 clerks in the department who work on average 140 hours per month each. The efficiency ratio of the department is 110%.

Required

Calculate the budgeted output in the department.

Solution

Capacity	=	40 × 140 = 5,600 hours per month
Efficiency	=	110%
Budgeted output	=	5,600 × 110% = 6,160 standard hours of work per month

Capacity levels

2.19 Capacity levels are needed to establish a standard absorption rate for production overhead, when standard absorption costing is used. Any one of three capacity levels might be used for budgeting.

(a) *Full capacity.* This is 'output (expressed in standard hours) that could be achieved if sales orders, supplies and workforce were available for all installed workplaces' (CIMA *Official Terminology*). This is the theoretical capacity, assuming continuous production without any stoppages due to factors such as machine downtime, supply shortages or labour shortages. Full capacity would be associated with ideal standards.

(b) *Practical capacity.* This is 'full capacity less an allowance for known unavoidable volume losses' (CIMA *Official Terminology*). Some stoppages are unavoidable, such as maintenance time for machines, and resetting time between jobs, some machine breakdowns and so on. Practical capacity is below full capacity, and would be associated with attainable standards.

(c) *Budgeted capacity.* This is 'standard hours planned for the period, taking into account budgeted sales, supplies, workforce availability and efficiency expected' (CIMA *Official Terminology*). This capacity is therefore the capacity (labour hours, machine hours) needed to produce the budgeted output, and would be associated with *current standards*, which relate to current conditions but may not be representative of normal practical capacity over a longer period of time.

2.20 *Idle capacity* would be defined as the practical capacity in a period less the budgeted capacity measured in standard hours of output. It represents unused capacity that ought to be available, but which is not needed because the budgeted volume is lower than the practicable volume that could be achieved.

2.21 Capacity ratios can be calculated. They provide similar information to variances.

Exercise 2

Given the following information, calculate an idle capacity ratio, a production volume ratio and an efficiency ratio and explain their meanings.

Full capacity	10,000 standard hours	Standard hours produced	6,500
Practical capacity	8,000 standard hours	Actual hours worked	7,000
Budgeted capacity	7500 standard hours		

Solution

$$\text{Idle capacity ratio} = \frac{\text{Practical capacity} - \text{budgeted capacity}}{\text{Practical capacity}} \times 100\%$$

$$= \frac{8,000 - 7,500}{8,000} \times 100\% = 6.25\%.$$

This means that 6.25% of practical capacity will be unused because budgeted volume is lower than the volume that could be achieved.

Production volume ratio $= \dfrac{\text{Standard hours produced}}{\text{Budgeted capacity}} \times 100\%$

$= \dfrac{6,500}{7,500} \times 100\% = 86^2/_3\%$

This means actual output was only $86^2/_3\%$ of budgeted output.

Efficiency ratio $= \dfrac{\text{Standard hours produced}}{\text{Actual hours worked}} \times 100\% = \dfrac{6,500}{7,000} \times 100\% = 92.86\%$

This means that the labour force were working at 92.86% efficiency.

Setting standards for selling price and margin

2.22 As well as standard costs, standard selling prices and standard margins can be set. The standard selling price will depend on a number of factors including the following.

(a) Anticipated market demand
(b) Competing products
(c) Manufacturing costs
(d) Inflation estimates

2.23 The standard sales margin is the difference between the standard cost and the standard selling price.

Exercise 3

(a) Describe the possible problems which could arise when setting standards.

(b) List possible advantages of standard costing.

Solution

(a) (i) Deciding how to incorporate inflation into planned unit costs.

(ii) Agreeing a short-term labour efficiency standard (current, attainable or ideal).

(iii) Deciding on the quality of materials to be used (a better quality of material will cost more, but perhaps reduce material wastage).

(iv) Deciding on the appropriate mix of component materials, where some change in the mix is possible (for example in the manufacture of foods and drink).

(v) Estimating materials prices where seasonal price variations or bulk purchase discounts may be significant.

(vi) Finding sufficient time to construct accurate standards. Standard setting can be a time-consuming process.

(vii) Incurring the cost of setting up and maintaining a system for establishing standards.

(viii) Dealing with possible behavioural problems. Managers responsible for the achievement of standards might resist the use of a standard costing control system for fear of being blamed for any adverse variances.

(b) (i) Carefully planned standards are an aid to more accurate budgeting.

(ii) Standard costs provide a yardstick against which actual costs can be measured.

(iii) The setting of standards involves determining the best materials and methods which may lead to economies.

(iv) A target of efficiency is set for employees to reach and cost consciousness is stimulated.

(v) Variances can be calculated which enable the principle of 'management by exception' to be operated. Only the variances which exceed acceptable tolerance limits need to be investigated by management with a view to control action.

(vi) Standard costs and variance analysis can provide a way of motivating managers to achieve better performance. However, care must be taken to distinguish between controllable and non-controllable costs in variance reporting.

3   STANDARDS: THEIR EVOLUTION AND CONTINUOUS IMPROVEMENT

Evolution

3.1   When an organisation introduces a system of standard costing, it is quite possible that the standards initially set will not be the most accurate reflection of what occurs 'on average'. As with most things, however, 'practice makes perfect' (or practice makes better at least!). Initial standards may need substantial revision in the early period of a standard costing system's life. A standard therefore needs to evolve over a couple of accounting periods before it can be used as a useful measure for control purposes.

Continuous improvement

3.2   The evolution of standards does not, however, stop after a couple of accounting periods. Standards must be continuously improved to ensure that they do mirror what is currently happening and that they are the most accurate 'average'. The improvement can come from two sources.

Improvement of standard setting process

3.3   Standard setting procedures may be refined and increased to enable more accurate standards to be set.

(a) Work study methods may, for example, be established within the organisation. These enable accurate estimates of labour time to be made.

(b) The introduction of computerised information systems provides more reliable standards. In their 1989 research study *Cost Control into the 1990s: A Survey of Standard Costing and Budgeting Practices in the UK*, Puxty and Lyall found that the introduction of information technology had radically changed the standard costing system of a number of companies. Some companies had previously applied standard costing to their material costs only. Computerisation had allowed them to extend the system to labour and overheads too.

Revision of standards

3.4   In practice standard costs are usually revised once a year to allow for the new overheads budget, inflation in prices and wage rates, and any changes in expected efficiency of material usage, labour or machinery. Puxty and Lyall's research study showed that most organisations revise their standards annually. Some revise them more frequently than this: about 7% revise them quarterly.

3.5   Some argue that standards should be revised as soon as there is any change in the basis upon which they were set. Clearly, for example, if a standard is based on the cost of a material that is no longer available or the use of equipment which has been replaced, it is meaningless to compare actual performance using the new material and equipment with the old standard.

3.6   Coates, Rickwood and Stacey in their book *Management Accounting in Practice* put forward the following reasons for revising standards.

'(a) Manufacturing methods are *significantly* changed due to plant layout, machinery alterations, change in product design, use of different materials, etc.

(b) The relationship of normal capacity and actual activity is *significantly* out of balance.

(c) The disparity between the standard and expected performance is *so significant* that the standard as a measurement loses its value.

(d) An existing standard is discovered to be incorrectly set and a *significant* difference exists.'

(JB Coates, CP Rickwood, RJ Stacey, *Management Accounting in Practice,* CIMA)

3.7 Others contend that frequent changes in standards renders them ineffective as motivators and measures of performance, since it will be perceived that target setters are constantly 'moving the goal posts'. It has also been argued that frequent changes are too time-consuming from the point of view of administration, although the introduction of computer systems renders this objection less forceful. Coates et al. concede the following point.

'Revisions should be *held to a minimum,* despite the fact that standards may not be precise, in order to provide for relative comparisons between operating periods and/or versus budget.'

3.8 The most suitable approach would therefore appear to be a policy of revising the standards whenever changes of a permanent and reasonably long-term nature occur, but not in response to temporary 'blips' in price or efficiency.

4 LONG-TERM CHANGES IN STANDARDS

4.1 Although standards are developed from past and current information, they should reflect technical and current factors expected for the period in which the standards are to be applied. Management should not think that once standards are set they will remain useful for ever. Standards must evolve over an organisation's life to reflect its changing methods and processes. Out-of-date standards will produce variances that are illogical bases for planning, control, decision making or performance evaluation. Current operational performance cannot be compared to out-of-date standards.

'Labour and material usage standards normally are set by the industrial engineering department. Material price normally is considered the responsibility of purchasing. Similarly, the labour rates are set by the personnel department. As the production processes change (improve), past standards become less than realistic, and should be revised. It is the responsibility of departments that originally created the standard to inform the accounting department about the need for revising the standards.

But, unfortunately, some managers prefer to keep the old standards because the new improved production process makes their performance look better with old standards.'

(LU Tatikonda, 'Production Managers Need a Course in Cost Accounting', *Management Accounting* (June 1987), published by Institute of Management Accountants, Montvale, N J)

4.2 Consider a computer manufacturer. Suppose that the standard price for computer chips was set in 1990 and not changed until 1993. In the three-year period, however, the price of chips would have dramatically decreased. Consistently favourable material price variances would have been reported. It should have been noticed by management that the standard was not appropriate for evaluating the purchasing manager's performance, inventory valuation or decision making on product pricing. The price reductions occurring since the standard was set would render the standard obsolete and worthless.

4.3 The advent of advanced manufacturing technology also has an impact on the meaning and relevance of standards. It is quite possible that, with advanced manufacturing technology, variable overheads are incurred in relation to machine time rather than labour time, and standard costs should reflect this where appropriate.

4.4 With CADCAM (computer-aided design/computer aided manufacture) systems for example, the planning of manufacturing requirements can be computerised, with the useful spin-off that standard costs can also be constructed by computer, thus saving administrative time and expense while providing far more accurate standards.

Are variances useful?

4.5   It is therefore vital that current, up-to-date standards are used that reflect the relevant technical and operational expectations for the period in which the standards are to be applied.

4.6   Some commentators have argued traditional variance analysis is unhelpful and potentially misleading in the modern organisation, and can make managers focus their attention on the wrong issues. Here are just two examples.

   (a)   *Efficiency variance.* Traditional variance analysis emphasises adverse efficiency variances should be avoided, which means that managers should try to prevent idle time and to keep up production. In a total quality management environment, just in time may be used (JIT being defined in CIMA *Official Terminology* as 'A system whose objective is to produce or procure products as they are required by a customer or for use, rather than for stock.') In these circumstances, manufacturing to eliminate idle time could result in the manufacture of unwanted products that must be held in store and might eventually be scrapped. Efficiency variances could focus management attention on the wrong problems.

   (b)   *Materials price variance.* In a JIT environment the key issues in materials purchasing are supplier reliability, materials quality, and delivery in small order quantities. Purchasing managers should not be shopping around every month looking for the cheapest price. Many JIT systems depend on long-term contractual links with suppliers, which means that material price variances are not relevant for management control purposes.

5   BUDGETS AND STANDARDS COMPARED   *5/95, 5/97*

5.1   A budget is a quantified monetary plan for a future period, which mangers will try to achieve. Its major function lies in communicating plans and coordinating activities within an organisation.

   A standard is a carefully predetermined quantity target which can be achieved in certain conditions.

5.2   Budgets and standards are similar in the following ways.

   (a)   They both involve looking to the future and forecasting what is likely to happen given a certain set of circumstances.

   (b)   They are both used for control purposes. A budget aids control by setting financial targets or limits for a forthcoming period. Actual achievements or expenditures are then compared with the budgets and action is taken to correct any variances where necessary. A standard also achieves control by comparison of actual results against a predetermined target.

5.3   As well as being similar, budgets and standards are interrelated. For example, a standard unit production cost can act as the basis for a production cost budget. The unit cost is multiplied by the budgeted activity level to arrive at the budgeted expenditure on production costs.

5.4   There are, however, important differences between budgets and standards.

   (a)   A budget gives the planned total aggregate costs for a function or cost centre whereas a standard shows the unit resource usage for a single task, for example the standard labour hours for a single unit of production.

   (b)   The use of standards is limited to situations where repetitive actions are performed and output can be measured. Budgets can be prepared for all functions, even where output cannot be measured.

   (c)   A standard need not be expressed in monetary terms. For example, a standard rate of output can be determined for control purposes without the need to put a financial value on it. In contrast, a budget is expressed in money terms.

In summary, budgets and standards are very similar and interrelated, but there are important differences between them.

Exam focus point

In the May 1995 exam candidates were asked to explain why budgetary control might be preferred to standard costing in a non-manufacturing environment. (You should be able to answer this if you try to recall the four essential characteristics of a *service*). In May 1997, on the other hand, candidates were asked to explain the difference between the two and describe when it might be beneficial to operate both systems.

Chapter roundup

- A standard is a predetermined unit of cost for stock valuation, budgeting and control.

- A standard cost card shows full details of the standard cost of each product.

- The standard for each type of cost (labour, material and so on) is made up of a standard resource price and a standard resource usage.

- Performance standards are used to set efficiency targets. There are four types: ideal, attainable, current and basic.

- Capacity levels are needed to establish a standard absorption rate for production overheads. Any one of full capacity, practical capacity or budgeted capacity might be used for budgeting.

- Standards should reflect technical and other factors expected for the period in which the standards are to be applied.

- Remember (from Chapter 3) that computers in general and spreadsheets in particular are very useful in standard costing.

Test your knowledge

1   In what circumstances is standard costing used? (see para 1.2)

2   What problems might occur in setting standard prices for materials? (2.5)

3   There are four types of performance standard in standard costs. Which is the most short term of the four? Which is most suitable as a long-term standard? (2.10 - 2.15)

4   What are the motivational implications of (a) ideal and (b) attainable standards? (2.11 - 2.12)

5   What is the difference between full capacity and practical capacity? (2.19)

6   Suggest four reasons why standards may need revising.(3.6)

7   Provide two examples which show why standard costing can cause managers to focus their attention on the wrong issues. (4.6)

8   List three differences between budgets and standards. (5.4)

Now try illustrative question 23 at the end of the Study Text

Chapter 19

BASIC VARIANCE ANALYSIS

This chapter covers the following topics.

		Syllabus reference	Ability required
1	Variances	6(d)	Skill
2	Direct material cost variances	6(d)	Skill
3	Direct labour cost variances	6(d)	Skill
4	Variable production overhead variances	6(d)	Skill
5	Fixed production overhead variances	6(d)	Skill
6	The reasons for cost variances	6(d)	Skill
7	The significance of cost variances	6(d)	Skill

Introduction

The actual results achieved by an organisation during a reporting period (week, month, quarter, year) will, more than likely, be different from the expected results (the expected results being the standard costs and revenues which we looked at in the previous chapter). Such differences may occur between individual items, such as the cost of labour and the volume of sales, and between the total expected profit/contribution and the total actual profit/contribution.

Management will have spent considerable time and trouble setting standards. Actual results have differed from the standards. The wise manager will consider the differences that have occurred and use the results of his considerations to assist him in his attempts to attain the standards. The wise manager will use variance analysis as a method of control.

In your studies for Paper 2 you will have covered direct material cost variances, direct labour cost variances and total fixed and variable overhead variances. Because students often find variance analysis quite difficult (although, really, it isn't) we are going to go over direct material cost and direct labour cost variances again in detail.

We will then go on to look at fixed and variable overhead variances. You covered fixed and variable overhead total variances in Paper 2, but we will go a stage further and sub-divide these variances.

In Chapter 20 we will build on the basics set down in this chapter by introducing sales variances, and discussing how information should be presented.

The final chapters of this Study Text are therefore vitally important. Make sure that you understand everything covered in each chapter before moving on.

---

1 VARIANCES

1.1 A variance is the 'Difference between planned, budgeted, or standard cost and actual cost; and similarly for revenue' (CIMA *Official Terminology*). The process by which the *total* difference between standard and actual results is analysed is known as variance analysis which is defined in CIMA *Official Terminology* as 'The evaluation of performance by means of variances whose timely reporting should maximise the opportunity for managerial action'. When actual results are better than expected results, we have a favourable variance (F). If, on the other hand, actual results are worse than expected results, we have an adverse variance (A).

1.2 Variances can be divided into three main groups: variable cost variances, sales variances and fixed production overhead variances. In the remainder of this chapter we will consider, in detail, variable cost variances and fixed production overhead variances.

Exam focus point

Variance analysis is a highly-examinable topic and has been included as part or all of a section B or C question *and* examined in the MCQ section in all sittings of the paper. You must be able to calculate variances and understand what your calculations show. Do not simply learn how to calculate the variances by heart, however. Understand the concepts behind the calculations. This includes understanding the need to take account of extra information, such as unavoidable idle time, and thus produce 'realistic' variances. In his report on the May 1995 exam the examiner advised 'that variance analysis in an important aspect of management accounting and that [students] should ensure that they are fully conversant with standard costing systems and variance analysis'.

---

2 DIRECT MATERIAL COST VARIANCES   5/95, 11/95, 6/96

2.1 The direct material total variance (the difference between what the output actually cost and what it should have cost, in terms of material) can be divided into two sub-variances.

(a) *The direct material price variance*

This is the difference between the standard cost and the actual cost for the *actual* quantity of material used or purchased. In other words, it is the difference between what the material did cost and what it should have cost.

(b) *The direct material usage variance*

This is the difference between the standard quantity of materials that *should* have been used for the number of units *actually* produced, and the actual quantity of materials used, valued at the *standard* cost per unit of material. In other words, it is the difference between how much material should have been used and how much material was used, valued at standard cost.

Example: direct material variances

2.2 Product X has a standard direct material cost as follows.

10 kilograms of material Y at £10 per kilogram = £100 per unit of X.

During period 4, 1,000 units of X were manufactured, using 11,700 kilograms of material Y which cost £98,600.

Required

Calculate the following variances.

(a) The direct material total variance
(b) The direct material price variance
(c) The direct material usage variance

Solution

2.3 (a) *The direct material total variance*

This is the difference between what 1,000 units should have cost and what they did cost.

	£
1,000 units should have cost (× £100)	100,000
but did cost	98,600
Direct material total variance	1,400 (F)

The variance is favourable because the units cost less than they should have cost.

Now we can break down the direct material total variance into its two constituent parts: the direct material price variance and the direct material usage variance.

(b) *The direct material price variance*

This is the difference between what 11,700 kgs should have cost and what 11,700 kgs did cost.

	£
11,700 kgs of Y should have cost (× £10)	117,000
but did cost	98,600
Material Y price variance	18,400 (F)

The variance is favourable because the material cost less than it should have.

(c) *The direct material usage variance*

This is the difference between how many kilograms of Y should have been used to produce 1,000 units of X and how many kilograms were used, valued at the standard cost per kilogram.

1,000 units should have used (× 10 kgs)	10,000 kgs
but did use	11,700 kgs
Usage variance in kgs	1,700 kgs (A)
× standard cost per kilogram	× £10
Usage variance in £	£17,000 (A)

The variance is adverse because more material than should have been used was used.

(d) *Summary*

	£
Price variance	18,400 (F)
Usage variance	17,000 (A)
Total variance	1,400 (A)

Materials variances and opening and closing stock

5/96

2.4 Suppose that a company uses raw material P in production, and that this raw material has a standard price of £3 per metre. During one month 6,000 metres are bought for £18,600, and 5,000 metres are used in production. At the end of the month, stock will have been increased by 1,000 metres. In variance analysis, the problem is to decide the material price variance. Should it be calculated on the basis of materials purchased (6,000 metres) or on the basis of materials used (5,000 metres)?

2.5 The answer to this problem depends on how closing stocks of the raw materials will be valued.

(a) If they are valued at *standard cost*, (1,000 units at £3 per unit) the price variance is calculated on material *purchases* in the period.

(b) If they are valued at actual cost *(FIFO)* (1,000 units at £3.10 per unit) the price variance is calculated on materials *used in production* in the period.

2.6 A full standard costing system is usually in operation and therefore the price variance is usually calculated on purchases in the period. The variance on the full 6,000 metres will be written off to the costing profit and loss account, even though only 5,000 metres are included in the cost of production.

2.7 There are two main advantages in extracting the material price variance at the time of receipt.

(a) If variances are extracted at the time of receipt they will be brought to the attention of managers *earlier* than if they are extracted as the material is used. If it is necessary to correct any variances then management action can be more timely.

(b) Since variances are extracted at the time of receipt, *all stocks will be valued at standard price*. This is administratively easier and it means that all issues from stocks can be made at standard price. If stocks are held at actual cost it is necessary to calculate a separate price variance on each batch as it is issued. Since issues are usually made in a number of small batches this can be a time-consuming task, especially with a manual system.

The disadvantage is that the timing of the reporting of the price variances is arbitrary, which may cause difficulties when comparing performance in different periods or when extracting trends.

2.8 The price variance would be calculated as follows.

	£
6,000 metres of material P purchased should cost (× £3)	18,000
but did cost	18,600
Price variance	600 (A)

3   DIRECT LABOUR COST VARIANCES   *S/95, 11/95*

3.1 The calculation of direct labour variances is very similar to the calculation of direct material variances.

The *direct labour total variance* (the difference between what the output should have cost and what it did cost, in terms of labour) can be divided into two sub-variances.

(a) *The direct labour rate variance*

This is similar to the direct material price variance. If is the difference between the standard cost and the actual cost for the actual number of hours paid for.

In other words, it is the difference between what the labour did cost and what it should have cost.

(b) *The direct labour efficiency variance*

This is similar to the direct material usage variance. It is the difference between the hours that *should* have been worked for the number of units *actually* produced, and the actual number of hours worked, valued at the standard rate per hour.

In other words, it is the difference between how many hours should have been worked and how many hours were worked, valued at the standard rate per hour.

Example: direct labour variances

3.2 The standard direct labour cost of product X is as follows.

2 hours of grade Z labour at £5 per hour = £10 per unit of product X.

During period 4, 1,000 units of product X were made, and the direct labour cost of grade Z labour was £8,900 for 2,300 hours of work.

Required

Calculate the following variances.

(a) The direct labour total variance
(b) The direct labour rate variance
(c) The direct labour efficiency (productivity) variance

Solution

3.3 (a) *The direct labour total variance*

This is the difference between what 1,000 units should have cost and what they did cost.

	£
1,000 units should have cost (× £10)	10,000
but did cost	8,900
Direct labour total variance	1,100 (F)

The variance is favourable because the units cost less than they should have done.

Again we can split this total variance into two parts.

(b) *The direct labour rate variance*

This is the difference between what 2,300 hours should have cost and what 2,300 hours did cost.

	£
2,300 hours of work should have cost (× £5 per hr)	11,500
but did cost	8,900
Direct labour rate variance	2,600 (F)

The variance is favourable because the labour cost less than it should have cost.

(c) *The direct labour efficiency variance*

1,000 units of X should have taken (× 2 hrs)	2,000 hrs
but did take	2,300 hrs
Efficiency variance in hours	300 hrs (A)
× standard rate per hour	× £5
Efficiency variance in £	£1,500 (A)

The variance is adverse because more hours were worked than should have been worked.

(d) *Summary*

	£
Rate variance	2,600 (F)
Efficiency variance	1,500 (A)
Total variance	1,100 (F)

Idle time variance

3.4 A company may operate a costing system in which any idle time is recorded. Idle time may be caused by machine breakdowns or not having work to give to employees, perhaps because of bottlenecks in production or a shortage of orders from customers. When idle time occurs, the labour force is still paid wages for time at work, but no actual work is done. Time paid for without any work being done is unproductive and therefore inefficient. In variance analysis, idle time is an adverse efficiency variance.

3.5 When idle time is recorded separately, it is helpful to provide control information which identifies the cost of idle time separately, and in variance analysis, there will be an idle time variance as a separate part of the total labour efficiency variance. The remaining efficiency variance will then relate only to the productivity of the labour force during the hours spent *actively* working.

Example: labour variances with idle time

3.6 During period 5, 1,500 units of product X were made and the cost of grade Z labour was £17,500 for 3,080 hours. During the period, however, there as a shortage of customer orders and 100 hours were recorded as idle time.

Required

Calculate the following variances.

(a) The direct labour total variance
(b) The direct labour rate variance
(c) The idle time variance
(d) The direct labour efficiency variance

Solution

3.7   (a)   *The direct labour total variance*

	£
1,500 units of product X should have cost (× £10)	15,000
but did cost	17,500
Direct labour total variance	2,500 (A)

Actual cost is greater than standard cost. The variance is therefore adverse.

(b)   *The direct labour rate variance*

The rate variance is a comparison of what the hours paid should have cost and what they did cost.

	£
3,080 hours of grade Z labour should have cost (× £5)	15,400
but did cost	17,500
Direct labour rate variance	2,100 (A)

Actual cost is greater than standard cost. The variance is therefore adverse.

(c)   *The idle time variance*

The idle time variance is the hours of idle time, valued at the standard rate per hour.

Idle time variance = 100 hours (A) × £5 = £500 (A)

Idle time is *always* an adverse variance.

(d)   *The direct labour efficiency variance*

The efficiency variance considers the hours actively worked (the difference between hours paid for and idle time hours). In our example, there were (3,080 – 100) = 2,980 hours when the labour force was not idle. The variance is calculated by taking the amount of output produced (1,500 units of product X) and comparing the time it should have taken to make them, with the actual time spent *actively* making them (2,980 hours). Once again, the variance in hours is valued at the standard rate per labour hour.

1,500 units of product X should take (× 2hrs)	3,000 hrs
but did take (3,080 – 100)	2,980 hrs
Direct labour efficiency variance in hours	20 hrs (F)
× standard rate per hour	× £5
Direct labour efficiency variance in £	£100 (F)

(e)   *Summary*

	£
Direct labour rate variance	2,100 (A)
Idle time variance	500 (A)
Direct labour efficiency variance	100 (F)
Direct labour total variance	2,500 (A)

3.8   Remember that, if idle time is recorded, the actual hours used in the efficiency variance calculation are the hours *worked* and not the hours paid for.

Exercise 1

Growler Ltd is planning to make 100,000 units per period of product AA. Each unit of AA should require 2 hours to produce, with labour being paid £11 per hour. Attainable work hours are less than clock hours, so 250,000 hours have been budgeted in the period.

Actual data for the period was:

Units produced	120,000
Direct labour cost	£3,200,000
Clock hours	280,000

Required

Calculate the following variances.

(a)   Labour rate variance
(b)   Labour efficiency variance
(c)   Idle time variance

Solution

The question is similar to part of a *Cost Accounting and Quantitative Methods* question in May 1996. The examiner reported most candidates failed to appreciate the significance of the information about attainable work hours as compared with clock hours, and thus failed to calculate a realistic efficiency variance.

The information means that clock hours have to be multiplied by $\frac{200,000}{250,000}$ (80%) in order to

arrive at a realistic efficiency variance.

(a)   *Labour rate variance*

	£'000	
280,000 hours should have cost (× £11)	3,080	
but did cost	3,200	
Labour rate variance	120	(A)

(b)   *Labour efficiency variance*

120,000 units should have taken (× 2 hours)	240,000	hrs
but did take (280,000 × 80%)	224,000	hrs
	16,000	hrs (F)
	× £11	
Labour efficiency variance	£176,000	(F)

(c)   *Idle time variance*

280,000 × 20%	56,000	hrs
	× £11	
	£616,000	(A)

4   VARIABLE PRODUCTION OVERHEAD VARIANCES   5/95, 11/95

4.1   Suppose that the variable production overhead cost of product X is as follows.

2 hours at £1.50 = £3 per unit

During period 6, 400 units of product X were made. The labour force worked 820 hours, of which 60 hours were recorded as idle time. The variable overhead cost was £1,230.

Calculate the following variances.

(a)   The variable overhead total variance
(b)   The variable production overhead expenditure variance
(c)   The variable production overhead efficiency variance

4.2   Since this example relates to variable production costs, the total variance is based on actual units of production. (If the overhead had been a variable selling cost, the variance would be based on sales volumes.)

	£	
400 units of product X should cost (× £3)	1,200	
but did cost	1,230	
Variable production overhead total variance	30	(A)

4.3   In many variance reporting systems, the variance analysis goes no further, and expenditure and efficiency variances are not calculated. However, the adverse variance of £30 may be explained as the sum of two factors.

(a)   The hourly rate of spending on variable production overheads was higher than it should have been, that is there is an expenditure variance.

(b)   The labour force worked inefficiently, and took longer to make the output than it should have done. This means that spending on variable production overhead was higher than it should have been, in other words there is an efficiency (productivity) variance. The variable production overhead efficiency variance is exactly the same, in hours, as the direct labour efficiency variance, and occurs for the same reasons.

4.4   It is usually assumed that variable overheads are incurred during active working hours, but are not incurred during idle time (for example the machines are not running, therefore power is not being consumed, and no direct materials are being used). This means in our example that although the labour force was paid for 820 hours, they were actively working for only 760 of those hours and so variable production overhead spending occurred during 760 hours.

4.5   (a)   *The variable production overhead expenditure variance*

This is the difference between the amount of variable production overhead that should have been incurred in the actual hours actively worked, and the actual amount of variable production overhead incurred.

	£
760 hours of variable production overhead should cost (× £1.50)	1,140
but did cost	1,230
Variable production overhead expenditure variance	90 (A)

(b)   *The variable production overhead efficiency variance*

If you already know the direct labour efficiency variance, the variable production overhead efficiency variance is exactly the same in hours, but priced at the variable production overhead rate per hour. In our example, the efficiency variance would be as follows.

400 units of product X should take (× 2hrs)	800 hrs
but did take (active hours)	760 hrs
Variable production overhead efficiency variance in hours	40 hrs (F)
× standard rate per hour	× £1.50
Variable production overhead efficiency variance in £	£60 (F)

(c)   *Summary*

	£
Variable production overhead expenditure variance	90 (A)
Variable production overhead efficiency variance	60 (F)
Variable production overhead total variance	30 (A)

5   FIXED PRODUCTION OVERHEAD VARIANCES   *5/95, 11/95, 11/96, 5/98*

5.1   Textbooks vary in their treatment of fixed production overhead variances. What follows accords with the treatment in the 1996 CIMA *Official Terminology* and in the widely-respected work of Colin Drury, *Management and Cost Accounting*, (1992).

5.2   You may have noticed that the method of calculating cost variances for variable cost items is essentially the same for labour, materials and variable overheads. Fixed production overhead variances are very different. In an absorption costing system, they are an attempt to explain the under- or over-absorption of fixed production overheads in production costs.

5.3   The fixed production overhead total variance may be broken down into two parts as usual.

(a)   An expenditure variance
(b)   A volume variance

5.4   The fixed production overhead volume variance sometimes causes confusion and may need more explanation. The most important point is that the volume variance applies to fixed production overhead costs only and not to variable production overheads.

(a)   Variable production overheads incurred change with the volume of activity. Thus, if the budget is to work for 300 hours and variable production overheads are incurred and absorbed at a rate of £6 per hour, the variable production overhead budget will be £1,800. If, however, actual hours worked turn out to be only 200 hours, the variable production overhead absorbed will be £1,200, but the expected expenditure will also be £1,200, so that there will be no under- or over-absorption of production overhead because of volume changes.

(b) Fixed production overheads are different because the level of expenditure does not change as the number of hours worked varies. Thus if the budget is to work for 300 hours and fixed production overheads are budgeted to be £2,400, the fixed production overhead absorption rate will be £8 per hour. Now if actual hours worked are only 200 hours, the fixed production overhead absorbed will be £1,600, whereas expected expenditure will be unchanged at £2,400. There is an under absorption of £800 because of the volume variance of 100 hours shortfall multiplied by the absorption rate of £8 per hour.

5.5 You will find it easier to calculate and understand fixed production overhead variances if you keep in mind the whole time the fact that you are trying to explain the reasons for any under- or over-absorbed production overhead. Remember that the absorption rate is calculated as follows.

$$\text{Overhead absorption rate} = \frac{\text{budgeted fixed production overhead}}{\text{budgeted level of activity}}$$

5.6 If either the numerator or the denominator or both in the absorption rate calculation are incorrect then we will have under- or over-absorbed production overhead.

(a) The fixed production overhead *expenditure variance* measures the under or over absorption caused by the actual *production overhead expenditure* being different from budget, that is the numerator being incorrect.

(b) The fixed production overhead *volume variance* measures the under or over absorption caused by the *actual production or hours of activity* being different from the budgeted production or budgeted number of hours used in calculating the absorption rate.

How to calculate the variances

5.7 (a) *Fixed production overhead total variance*

This is the difference between fixed production overhead incurred and fixed production overhead absorbed. In other words, it is the under- or over-absorbed fixed production overhead.

(b) *Fixed production overhead expenditure variance*

This is the difference between the budgeted fixed production overhead expenditure and actual fixed production overhead expenditure.

(c) *Fixed production overhead volume variance*

This is the difference between actual and budgeted production/volume multiplied by the standard absorption rate per *unit*.

5.8 You should now be ready to work through an example to demonstrate these fixed overhead variances.

Example: fixed production overhead variances

5.9 1,000 units of product X are budgeted to be produced during period 7. The expected time to produce a unit of X is two hours, and the budgeted fixed production overhead is £20,000. The standard fixed production overhead cost per unit of product X will therefore be as follows.

$$2 \text{ hours at } \left(\frac{20,000}{2 \times 1,000} \right) \text{ per hour (ie £10)} = £20 \text{ per unit}$$

Actual fixed production overhead expenditure in period 7 turns out to be £20,450. The labour force manages to produce 1,100 units of product X in 2,200 hours of work.

Required

Calculate the following variances.

(a) The fixed production overhead total variance
(b) The fixed production overhead expenditure variance
(c) The fixed production overhead volume variance

Solution

5.10 (a) *Fixed production overhead total variance*

	£
Fixed production overhead incurred	20,450
Fixed production overhead absorbed (1,100 units × £20 per unit)	22,000
Fixed production overhead total variance	1,550 (F)

This gives us the total under-/over-absorbed overhead.

The variance is favourable because more overheads were absorbed than budgeted.

(b) *Fixed production overhead expenditure variance*

	£
Budgeted fixed production overhead expenditure	20,000
Actual fixed production overhead expenditure	20,450
Fixed production overhead expenditure variance	450 (A)

The variance is adverse because actual expenditure was greater than budgeted expenditure.

(c) *Fixed production overhead volume variance*

The production volume achieved was greater than expected. The fixed overhead volume variance measures the difference at the standard rate.

	£
Actual production at standard rate (1,100 × £20 per unit)	22,000
Budgeted production at standard rate (1,000 × £20 per unit)	20,000
Fixed production overhead volume variance	2,000 (F)

The variance is favourable because output was greater than expected.

5.11 Do not worry if you find fixed production overhead variances more difficult to grasp than the other variances we have covered. Most students do. Read over this section again and then try the following exercise.

Exercise 2

Brain Ltd produces and sells one product only, the Blob, the standard cost for one unit being as follows.

	£
Direct material A - 10 kilograms at £20 per kg	200
Direct material B - 5 litres at £6 per litre	30
Direct wages - 5 litres at £6 per hour	30
Fixed production overhead	50
Total standard cost	310

The fixed overhead included in the standard cost is based on an expected monthly output of 900 units.

During April 19X3 the actual results were as follows.

Production	800 units
Material A	7,800 kg used, costing £159,900
Material B	4,300 litres used, costing £23,650
Direct wages	4,200 hours worked for £24,150
Fixed production overhead	£47,000

Required

(a) Calculate price and usage variances for each material.
(b) Calculate labour rate and efficiency variances.
(c) Calculate fixed production overhead expenditure and volume variances

Solution

(a)   *Price variance - A*

	£
7,800 kgs should have cost (× £20)	156,000
but did cost	159,900
Price variance	3,900 (A)

Usage variance - A

800 units should have used (× 10 kgs)	8,000 kgs
but did use	7,800 kgs
Usage variance in kgs	200 kgs (F)
× standard cost per kilogram	× £20
Usage variance in £	£4,000 (F)

Price variance - B

	£
4,300 litres should have cost (× £6)	25,800
but did cost	23,650
Price variance	2,150 (F)

Usage variance - B

800 units should have used (× 5 l)	4,000 l
but did use	4,300 l
Usage variance in litres	300 (A)
× standard cost per litre	× £6
Usage variance in £	£1,800 (A)

(b)   *Labour rate variance*

	£
4,200 hours should have cost (× £6)	25,200
but did cost	24,150
Rate variance	1,050 (F)

Labour efficiency variance

800 units should have taken (× 5 hrs)	4,000 hrs
but did take	4,200 hrs
Efficiency variance in hours	200 hrs (A)
× standard rate per hour	× £6
Efficiency variance in £	£1,200 (A)

(c)   *Fixed overhead expenditure variance*

	£
Budgeted expenditure (£50 × 900)	45,000
Actual expenditure	47,000
Expenditure variance	2,000 (A)

Fixed overhead volume variance

	£
Budgeted production at standard rate (900 × £50)	45,000
Actual production at standard rate (800 × £50)	40,000
Volume variance	5,000 (A)

Exercise 3

Which of the capacity variances which we looked at in Chapter 18 provide information similar to that provided by the following variances?

(a)   Labour efficiency variance
(b)   Overhead volume variance
(c)   Variable overhead efficiency variance

Solution

(a)   Efficiency ratio
(b)   Production volume ratio
(c)   Efficiency ratio

6   THE REASONS FOR COST VARIANCES   5/97, 5/98

6.1   There are many possible reasons for cost variances arising, including efficiencies and inefficiencies of operations, errors in standard setting and changes in exchange rates. There now follows a list of a few possible causes of cost variances.

Variance	*Favourable*	*Adverse*
(a) Material price	Unforeseen discounts received Greater care taken in purchasing Change in material standard	Price increase Careless purchasing Change in material standard
(b) Material usage	Material used of higher quality than standard More effective use made of material Errors in allocating material to jobs	Defective material Excessive waste Theft Stricter quality control Errors in allocating material to jobs
(c) Labour rate	Use of apprentices or other workers at a rate of pay lower than standard	Wage rate increase Use of higher grade labour
(d) Idle time	*The idle time variance is always adverse.*	Machine breakdown Non-availability of material Illness or injury to worker
(e) Labour efficiency	Output produced more quickly than expected, ie actual output in excess of standard output set for same number of hours because of work motivation, better quality of equipment or materials, or better methods Errors in allocating time to jobs	Lost time in excess of standard allowed Output lower than standard set because of deliberate restriction, lack of training, or sub-standard material used Errors in allocating time to jobs
(f) Overhead expenditure	Savings in costs incurred More economical use of services	Increase in cost of services used Excessive use of services Change in type of services used
(g) Overhead volume	Production or level of activity greater than budgeted	Production or level of activity less than budgeted

Exam focus point

This is not an exhaustive list and in an examination question you should review the information given and use your imagination and common sense to suggest possible reasons for variances.

7   THE SIGNIFICANCE OF COST VARIANCES

7.1   Once variances have been calculated management are faced with three options.

(a) They can investigate every reported variance. This would be extremely time consuming and expensive and could lead to investigations which result in no improvement to operations even if the cause of the variance was determined.

(b) Alternatively, management could do nothing with the reported variances, making a mockery of the supposed control function arising from variance analysis.

(c) The best option lies somewhere between the two extremes.

7.2 There are a number of factors which can be taken into account when deciding whether or not a variance should be investigated.

Materiality

7.3 A standard cost is really only an *average* expected cost and is not a rigid specification. Small variations either side of this average are therefore bound to occur. The problem is to decide whether a variation from standard should be considered significant and worthy of investigation. Tolerance limits can be set and only variances which exceed such limits would require investigating.

Controllability

7.4 Controllability must also influence the decision about whether to investigate. If there is a general worldwide increase in the price of a raw material there is nothing that can be done internally to control the effect of this. If a central decision is made to award all employees a 10% increase in salary, staff costs in division A will increase by this amount and the variance is not controllable by division A's manager. Uncontrollable variances call for a change in the plan, not an investigation into the past.

The type of standard being used

7.5 The efficiency variance reported in any control period, whether for materials or labour, will depend on the efficiency level set. If, for example, an ideal standard is used, variances will always be adverse.

7.6 A similar problem arises if average price levels are used as standards. If inflation exists, favourable price variances are likely to be reported at the beginning of a period, to be offset by adverse price variances later in the period as inflation pushes prices up.

Interdependence between variances   *5/98*

7.7 Quite possibly, individual variances should not be looked at in isolation. One variance might be inter-related with another, and much of it might have occurred only because the other, inter-related, variance occurred too.

7.8 When two variances are interdependent (interrelated) one will usually be adverse and the other one favourable. Here are some examples.

Materials price and usage

7.9 It may be decided to purchase cheaper materials for a job in order to obtain a favourable price variance, possibly with the consequence that materials wastage is higher and an adverse usage variance occurs. If the cheaper materials are more difficult to handle, there might be some adverse labour efficiency variance too.

If a decision is made to purchase more expensive materials, which perhaps have a longer service life, the price variance will be adverse but the usage variance might be favourable.

Labour rate and efficiency

7.10 If employees in a workforce are paid higher rates for experience and skill, using a highly skilled team to do some work would incur an adverse rate variance, but should also obtain a favourable efficiency variance. In contrast, a favourable rate variance might indicate a larger-than-expected proportion of inexperienced workers in the workforce, which could result in an adverse labour efficiency variance, and perhaps poor materials handling and high rates of rejects too (adverse materials usage variance).

Costs of investigation

7.11   The costs of an investigation should be weighed against the benefits of correcting the cause of a variance.

7.12   Although you are not expected to have a detailed knowledge of the significance of variances (you will encounter the topic in Paper 10), you should now realise that the operation of a standard costing system goes beyond the simple calculation of variances.

Chapter roundup

- Variances measure the difference between actual results and expected results.

- The direct material total variance can be subdivided into the direct material *price* variance and the direct material *usage* variance.

- Direct material price variances are extracted at the time of *receipt* of the materials, *not* the time of usage.

- The direct labour total variance can be subdivided into the direct labour *rate* variance and the direct labour *efficiency* variance.

- If idle time arises, it is usual to calculate a separate idle time variance, and to base the calculation of the efficiency variance on active hours (when labour actually worked) only. It is always an adverse variance.

- The variable production overhead total variance can be subdivided into the variable production overhead *expenditure* variance and the variable production overhead *efficiency* variance (based on active hours).

- The fixed production overhead total variance can be subdivided into an *expenditure* variance and a *volume* variance.

- Ensure that you can provide possible reasons for cost variances.

- Materiality, controllability, type of standard being used and the interdependence of variances should be taken into account when assessing the significance of reported variances.

Test your knowledge

1   Which two variances subdivide the direct material total variance? (see para 2.1)

2   What are the two main advantages in calculating the material price variance at the time of receipt of materials? (2.7)

3   What does the direct labour rate variance mean? (3.1)

4   Idle time is a favourable efficiency variance. True or false? (3.4)

5   Suggest two reasons for an adverse variable overhead variance. (4,3)

6   Why is the calculation of fixed overhead variances different from that of variable overhead variances? (5.4)

7   Give three possible causes of an adverse material usage variance. (6.1)

8   What problem arises if average price levels are used as standards and inflation exists? (7.6)

9   What is the interdependence of variances? (7.7)

Now try illustrative question 24 at the end of the Study Text

Chapter 20

FURTHER VARIANCE ANALYSIS

This chapter covers the following topics.

		Syllabus reference	Ability required
1	Sales variances	6(d)	Skill
2	Operating statements	6(d)	Skill
3	Variances in a standard marginal costing system	6(d)	Skill
4	Deriving actual data from standard cost details and variances	6(d)	Skill
5	Standard cost bookkeeping	6(d)	Skill

Introduction

The objective of the process of cost variance analysis, which we looked at in the previous chapter, is to assist management in the control of costs. Costs are, however, only one factor which contribute to the achievement of planned profit. Sales are another important factor and sales variances can be calculated to aid management's control of their business. We will therefore begin this chapter by examining sales variances (which are new to you, since they were not covered in Paper 2).

Having discussed the variances you need to know about, we will be looking in Section 2 at the ways in which variances should be presented to management to aid their control of the organisation.

We then consider in Section 3 how marginal cost variances differ from absorption cost variances and how marginal costing information should be presented.

Finally we will examine two further topics which regularly arise both in the multi choice section of paper 6 and also as part of longer questions. Firstly we will consider how actual data can be derived from standard cost details and variances. Questions of this sort are popular with the examiner because effectively they mean carrying out variance analysis backwards and hence are a good test of understanding. Secondly we will look at standard cost bookkeeping which is, as the name suggests, the method of incorporating variances into cost bookkeeping (which you may remember was the topic of Chapter 6). You covered standard cost bookkeeping for Paper 2 but, don't worry, we are going through it again in detail in case you've forgotten how to do it.

1 SALES VARIANCES

5/97, 11/97

Selling price variance

1.1 The selling price variance is a measure of the effect on expected profit of a different selling price to standard selling price. It is calculated as the difference between what the sales revenue should have been for the actual quantity sold, and what it was.

1.2 Suppose that the standard selling price of product X is £15. Actual sales in 19X3 were 2,000 units at £15.30 per unit. The selling price variance is calculated as follows.

	£
Sales revenue from 2,000 units should have been (× £15)	30,000
but was (× £15.30)	30,600
Selling price variance	600 (F)

The variance is favourable because the price was higher than expected.

Sales volume profit variance

1.3   The sales volume profit variance is the difference between the actual units sold and the budgeted quantity, valued at the standard profit per unit. In other words, it measures the increase or decrease in standard profit as a result of the sales volume being higher or lower than budgeted.

1.4   Suppose that a company budgets to sell 8,000 units of product J for £12 per unit. The standard full cost per unit is £7. Actual sales were 7,700 units, at £12.50 per unit.

The sales volume profit variance is calculated as follows.

Budgeted sales volume	8,000 units
Actual sales volume	7,700 units
Sales volume variance in units	300 units (A)
× standard profit per unit (£(12–7))	× £5
Sales volume variance	£1,500 (A)

The variance is adverse because actual sales were less than budgeted.

Example: sales variances

1.5   Jasper Ltd has the following budget and actual figures for 19X4.

	Budget	*Actual*
Sales units	600	620
Selling price per unit	£30	£29

Standard full cost of production = £28 per unit.

Required

Calculate the selling price variance and the sales volume profit variance.

Solution

1.6   The selling price variance is calculated as follows.

	£
Sales revenue for 620 units should have been (× £30)	18,600
but was (× £29)	17,980
Selling price variance	620 (A)

1.7   The sales volume profit variance is calculated as follows.

Budgeted sales volume	600 units
Actual sales volume	620 units
Sales volume variance in units	20 units (F)
× standard profit per unit (£(30 – 28))	× £2
Sales volume variance	£40 (F)

The significance of sales variances

1.8   The connection between sales price and sales volume variances is perhaps an obvious one. A reduction in the sales price might stimulate bigger sales demand, so that an adverse sales price variance might be counterbalanced by a favourable sales volume variance. Similarly, a price rise would give a favourable price variance, but possibly at the cost of a fall in demand and an adverse sales volume variance.

1.9   It is therefore important in analysing an unfavourable variance that the overall consequence should be considered, that is, has there been a counterbalancing favourable variance as a direct result of the unfavourable one?

1.10 Because cost accountants analyse total variances into component elements (materials price and usage, labour rate, idle time, efficiency, and so on) they should not lose sight of the overall 'integrated' picture of events, and any interdependence between variances should be reported whenever it is suspected to have occurred.

2   OPERATING STATEMENTS

5/97, 5/98

> **Exam focus point**
>
> Sales variances are liable to come up both as part of a longer question or as MCQs.

2.1 So far, we have considered how variances are calculated without considering how they combine to reconcile the difference between budgeted profit and actual profit during a period. This reconciliation is usually presented as a report to senior management at the end of each control period. The report is called an operating statement or statement of variances. The CIMA *Official Terminology* definition of an operating statement is 'A regular report for management of actual cost, and revenue, as appropriate. Usually compares actual with budget and shows variances'.

2.2 An extensive example will now be introduced, both to revise the variance calculations already described, and also to show how to combine them into an operating statement.

Example: variances and operating statements

2.3 Sydney Ltd manufactures one product, and the entire product is sold as soon as it is produced. There are no opening or closing stocks and work in progress is negligible. The company operates a standard costing system and analysis of variances is made every month. The standard cost card for the product, a boomerang, is as follows.

STANDARD COST CARD - BOOMERANG

		£
Direct materials	0.5 kilos at £4 per kilo	2.00
Direct wages	2 hours at £2.00 per hour	4.00
Variable overheads	2 hours at £0.30 per hour	0.60
Fixed overhead	2 hours at £3.70 per hour	7.40
Standard cost		14.00
Standard profit		6.00
Standing selling price		20.00

Selling and administration expenses are not included in the standard cost, and are deducted from profit as a period charge.

Budgeted output for the month of June 19X7 was 5,100 units. Actual results for June 19X7 were as follows.

Production of 4,850 units was sold for £95,600.
Materials consumed in production amounted to 2,300 kgs at a total cost of £9,800.
Labour hours paid for amounted to 8,500 hours at a cost of £16,800.
Actual operating hours amounted to 8,000 hours.
Variable overheads amounted to £2,600.
Fixed overheads amounted to £42,300.
Selling and administration expenses amounted to £18,000.

Required

Calculate all variances and prepare an operating statement for the month ended 30 June 19X7.

Solution

			£
2.4	(a)	2,300 kg of material should cost (× £4)	9,200
		but did cost	9,800
		Material price variance	600 (A)

(b) 4,850 boomerangs should use (× 0.5 kgs)   2,425 kg

		£
but did use		2,300 kg
Material usage variance in kgs		125 kg (F)
× standard cost per kg		× £4
Material usage variance in £		£ 500 (F)

	£
(c) 8,500 hours of labour should cost (× £2)	17,000
but did cost	16,800
Labour rate variance	200 (F)

(d) 4,850 boomerangs should take (× 2 hrs)	9,700 hrs
but did take (active hours)	8,000 hrs
Labour efficiency variance in hours	1,700 hrs (F)
× standard cost per hour	× £2
Labour efficiency variance in £	£3,400 (F)

(e) Idle time variance 500 hours (A) × £2   £1,000 (A)

	£
(f) 8,000 hours incurring variable o/hd expenditure should cost (× £0.30)	2,400
but did cost	2,600
Variable overhead expenditure variance	200 (A)

(g) Variable overhead efficiency variance is the same as the
labour efficiency variance:

	£
1,700 hours (F) × £0.30 per hour	£ 510 (F)

	£
(h) Budgeted fixed overhead (5,100 units × 2 hrs × £3.70)	37,740
Actual fixed overhead	42,300
Fixed overhead expenditure variance	4,560 (A)

	£
(i) Actual production at standard rate (4,850 units × £7.40)	35,890
Budgeted production at standard rate (5,100 units × £7.40)	37,740
Fixed overhead volume variance	1,850 (A)

	£
(j) Revenue from 4,850 boomerangs should be (× £20)	97,000
but was	95,600
Selling price variance	1,400 (A)

(k) Budgeted sales volume	5,100 units
Actual sales volume	4,850 units
Sales volume profit variance in units	250 units
× standard profit per unit	× £6 (A)
Sales volume profit variance in £	£1,500 (A)

2.5 There are several ways in which an operating statement may be presented. Perhaps the most common format is one which reconciles budgeted profit to actual profit. In this example, sales and administration costs will be introduced at the end of the statement, so that we shall begin with 'budgeted profit before sales and administration costs'.

2.6 Sales variances are reported first, and the total of the budgeted profit and the two sales variances results in a figure for 'actual sales minus the standard cost of sales' as follows.

	£	£
Budgeted profit, before sales and administration costs		
(5,100 units × £6 profit)		30,600
Selling price variance	1,400 (A)	
Sales volume profit variance	1,500 (A)	
		2,900 (A)
		27,700
Actual sales (£95,600) less the standard cost of sales (4,850 × £14)		

2.7 The cost variances are then reported, and an actual profit (before sales and administration costs) calculated. Sales and administration costs are then deducted to reach the actual profit for June 19X7.

SYDNEY LTD - OPERATING STATEMENT JUNE 19X7

		£	£
Budgeted profit before sales and administration costs			30,600
Sales variances:	price	1,400 (A)	
	volume	1,500 (A)	
			2,900 (A)
Actual sales minus the standard cost of sales			27,700

Cost variances	(F)	(A)	
	£	£	
Material price		600	
Material usage	500		
Labour rate	200		
Labour efficiency	3,400		
Labour idle time		1,000	
Variable overhead expenditure		200	
Variable overhead efficiency	510		
Fixed overhead expenditure		4,560	
Fixed overhead volume		1,850	
	4,610	8,210	3,600 (A)
Actual profit before sales and administration costs			24,100
Sales and administration costs			18,000
Actual profit, June 19X7			6,100

Check	£	£
Sales		95,600
Materials	9,800	
Labour	16,800	
Variable overhead	2,600	
Fixed overhead	42,300	
Sales and administration	18,000	
		89,500
Actual profit		6,100

2.8 As mentioned earlier, there are several ways in which an operating statement can be presented. Another way is to reconcile the actual sales minus the standard cost of sales with the actual profit. In other words, only the cost variances are shown on the face of the operating statement.

3   VARIANCES IN A STANDARD MARGINAL COSTING SYSTEM   *11/96*

3.1 In all of the examples we have worked through so far, a system of standard absorption costing has been in operation. If an organisation uses standard marginal costing instead of standard absorption costing, there will be two differences in the way the variances are calculated.

   (a) In marginal costing, fixed costs are not absorbed into product costs and so there are no fixed cost variances to explain any under or over absorption of overheads. There will, therefore, be *no fixed overhead volume variance*. There will be a fixed overhead expenditure variance which is calculated in exactly the same way as for absorption costing systems.

(b) The sales volume variance will be valued at standard *contribution* margin (sales price per unit minus variable costs of sale per unit), *not* standard *profit* margin.

Example: marginal costing operating statement

3.2 Returning once again to the example of Sydney Ltd, the variances in a system of standard marginal costing would be as follows.

(a) There is no fixed overhead volume variance.

(b) The standard contribution per unit of boomerang is £(20 – 6.60) = £13.40, therefore the sales volume contribution variance of 250 units (A) is valued at (× £13.40) = £3,350 (A).

3.3 The other variances are unchanged. However, this operating statement differs from an absorption costing operating statement in that:

(a) fixed production costs are added back to budgeted profit before sales and administration costs to give budgeted contribution;

(b) sales variances are added to/deducted from budgeted contribution to give actual sales minus the standard *variable* cost of sales (and *not* actual sales minus the standard cost of sales);

(c) variable cost variances alone are added/subtracted to arrive at actual contribution (a line which is not paralleled on the absorption cost statement);

(d) budgeted fixed production overhead is adjusted by the fixed overhead expenditure variance to give actual fixed production overhead. This is deducted from actual contribution to arrive at actual profit before sales and administration costs.

3.4 Therefore an operating statement might appear as follows.

SYDNEY LTD - OPERATING STATEMENT JUNE 19X7

	£	£	£
Budgeted profit before sales and administration costs			30,600
Budgeted fixed production costs			37,740
Budgeted contribution			68,340
Sales variances: volume		3,350 (A)	
price		1,400 (A)	
			4,750 (A)
Actual sales (£95,600) minus the standard variable cost of sales			63,590
(4,850 × £6.60)			

	(F)	(A)	
	£	£	
Variable cost variances			
Material price		600	
Material usage	500		
Labour rate	200		
Labour efficiency	3,400		
Labour idle time		1,000	
Variable overhead expenditure		200	
Variable overhead efficiency	510		
	4,610	1,800	
			2,810 (F)
Actual contribution			66,400
Budgeted fixed production overhead		37,740	
Expenditure variance		4,560 (A)	
Actual fixed production overhead			42,300
Actual profit before sales and administration costs			24,100
Sales and administration costs			18,000
Actual profit			6,100

Note. The profit here is the same on the profit calculated by standard absorption costing because there were no changes in stock levels. Absorption costing and marginal costing do not always produce an identical profit figure.

Exercise 1

MilBri Limited, a manufacturing firm, operates a standard marginal costing system. It makes a single product, LI, using a single raw material AN.

Standard costs relating to LI have been calculated as follows.

Standard cost schedule - LI	*Per unit* *£*
Direct material, AN, 100 kg at £5 per kg	500
Direct labour, 10 hours at £8 per hour	80
Variable production overhead, 10 hours at £2 per hour	20
	600

The standard selling price of a LI is £900 and MilBri produce 1,020 units a month.

During December 19X0, 1,000 units of LI were produced. Relevant details of this production are as follows.

Direct material AN
90,000 kgs costing £720,000 were bought and used.

Direct labour
8,200 hours were worked during the month and total wages were £63,000.

Variable production overhead
The actual cost for the month was £25,000.

Stocks of the direct material AN are valued at the standard price of £5 per kg.

Each LI was sold for £975.

Required

Calculate the following for the month of December 19X0.

(a)   Variable production cost variance

(b)   Direct labour cost variance, analysed into rate and efficiency variances

(c)   Direct material cost variance, analysed into price and usage variances

(d)   Variable production overhead variance, analysed into expenditure and efficiency variances

(e)   Selling price variance

(f)   Sales volume contribution variance

Solution

(a)   This is simply a 'total' variance.

	£
1,000 units should have cost (× £600)	600,000
but did cost (W)	808,000
Variable production cost variance	208,000 (A)

(b)   *Direct labour cost variances*

	£
8,200 hours should cost (× £8)	65,600
but did cost	63,000
Direct labour rate variance	2,600 (F)

1,000 units should take (× 10 hours)	10,000 hrs
but did take	8,200 hrs
Direct labour efficiency variance in hrs	1,800 hrs (F)
× standard rate per hour	× £8
Direct labour efficiency variance in £	£14,400 (F)

Summary	£
Rate	2,600 (F)
Efficiency	14,400 (F)
Total	17,000 (F)

(c) *Direct material cost variances*

	£
90,000 kg should cost (× £5)	450,000
but did cost	720,000
Direct material price variance	270,000 (A)

1,000 units should use (× 100 kg)	100,000 kg
but did use	90,000 kg
Direct material usage variance in kgs	10,000 kg (F)
× standard cost per kg	× £5
Direct material usage variance in £	£50,000 (F)

Summary	£
Price	270,000 (A)
Usage	50,000 (F)
Total	220,000 (A)

(d) *Variable production overhead variances*

	£
8,200 hours incurring o/hd should cost (× £2)	16,400
but did cost	25,000
Variable production overhead expenditure variance	8,600 (A)

Efficiency variance in hrs (from (b))	1,800 hrs (F)
× standard rate per hour	× £2
Variable production overhead efficiency variance	£3,600 (F)

Summary	£
Expenditure	8,600 (A)
Efficiency	3,600 (F)
Total	5,000 (A)

(e) *Selling price variance*

	£
Revenue from 1,000 units should have been (× £900)	900,000
but was (× £975)	975,000
Selling price variance	75,000 (F)

(f) *Sales volume contribution variance*

Budgeted sales	1,020 units
Actual sales	1,000 units
Sales volume variance in units	20 units (A)
× standard contribution margin (£(900 − 600))	× £300
Sales volume contribution variance in £	£6,000 (A)

Workings

	£
Direct material	720,000
Total wages	63,000
Variable production overhead	25,000
	808,000

4   DERIVING ACTUAL DATA FROM STANDARD COST DETAILS AND VARIANCES

5/95, 5/97

Exam focus point

The majority of examination questions provide you with data about actual results and you have to calculate variances. One way in which the examiner can test your understanding of the topic, however, is to provide information about variances from which you have to 'work backwards' to determine the actual results. This section should equip you to deal with such questions.

Example: working backwards

4.1   The standard cost card for the trough, one of the products made by Pig Ltd, is as follows.

	£
Direct material 16 kgs × £6 per kg	96
Direct labour 6 hours × £12 per hour	72
Fixed production overhead 6 hours × £14 per hour	84
	252

Pig Ltd reported the following variances in control period 13 in relation to the trough.

Direct material price: £18,840 favourable
Direct material usage: £480 adverse
Direct labour rate: £10,598 adverse
Direct labour efficiency: £8,478 favourable
Fixed production overhead expenditure: £14,192 adverse
Fixed production overhead volume: £11,592 favourable

Actual fixed production overhead cost £200,000 and direct wages, £171,320. Pig Ltd paid £5.50 for each kg of direct material. There was no opening or closing stocks of the material.

Required

Calculate the following.

(a)   Budgeted output
(b)   Actual output
(c)   Actual hours worked
(d)   Average actual wage rate per hour
(e)   Actual number of kilograms purchased and used

Solution

4.2   (a)   Let budgeted output = q

Fixed production overhead expenditure variance = budgeted overhead – actual overhead = £(84q – 200,000) = £14,192 (A)

$$\therefore 84q - 200,000 = -14,192$$
$$84q = -14,192 + 200,000$$
$$q = 185,808 \div 84$$
$$\therefore q = 2,212 \text{ units}$$

(b)

	£
Total direct wages cost	171,320
Adjust for variances:	
labour rate	(10,598)
labour efficiency	8,478
Standard direct wages cost	169,200

∴ Actual output   = Total standard cost ÷ unit standard cost
= £169,200 ÷ £72
= 2,350 units

(c)

		£
Total direct wages cost		171,320.0
Less rate variance		(10,598.0)
Standard rate for actual hours		160,722.0
÷ standard rate per hour		÷ £12.0
Actual hours worked		13,393.5 hrs

(d)   Average actual wage rate per hour = actual wages/actual hours = £171,320/13,393.5 = £12.79 per hour.

(e)   Number of kgs purchased and used = x

	£
x kgs should have cost (× £6)	6.0x
but did cost (× £5.50)	5.5x
Direct material price variance	0.5x

∴   £0.5x = £18,840
∴   x = 37,680 kgs

Exercise 2

The standard material content of one unit of product A is 10kgs of material X which should cost £10 per kilogram. In June 19X4, 5,750 units of product A were produced and there was an adverse material usage variance of £1,500.

Required

Calculate the quantity of material X used in June 19X4.

Solution

Let the quantity of material X used = Y

5750 units should have used (× 10kgs)	57,500 kgs
but did use	Y kgs
Usage variance in kgs	(Y − 57,500) kgs
× standard price per kg	× £10
Usage variance in £	£1,500 (A)

∴ 10(Y − 57,500) = 1,500
        Y − 57,500 = 150
∴   Y = 57,650 kgs

---

5   STANDARD COST BOOKKEEPING   *11/95, 5/96*

5.1   Now that you know how to calculate variances you need to be able to incorporate them into a cost bookkeeping system. We looked at cost bookkeeping in detail in Chapter 6. Glance back at the chapter if you need to remind yourself of the main principles.

5.2   Don't be put off by the sound of standard cost bookkeeping. It is no more complicated than the bookkeeping you have looked at so far. It is simply an extension of the basic system and is used when an organisation runs a standard costing system.

5.3   The general principle in standard cost bookkeeping is that cost variances should be recorded as *early as possible*. They are recorded in the relevant account where they arise and the appropriate double entry is taken to a variance account. Examples are as follows.

(a)   *Material price variances* are apparent when materials are purchased, and they are therefore recorded in the *stores account*. If a price variance is adverse, we should credit the stores account and debit a variance account with the amount of the variance.

(b)   *Material usage variances* do not occur until output is actually produced in the factory, and they are therefore recorded in the *work in progress account*. If a usage variance is favourable, we should debit the work in progress account and credit a variance account with the value of the variance.

5.4 There are some possible variations in accounting method between one company's system and others, especially in the method of recording overhead variances, but the following are the basic principles.

(a) The material price variance is recorded in the stores control account.

(b) The labour rate variance is recorded in the wages control account.

(c) The following variances are recorded in the work in progress account.

    (i)   Material usage variance
    (ii)   Idle time variance
    (iii) Labour efficiency variance
    (iv) Variable overhead efficiency variance

(d) The production overhead expenditure variance will be recorded in the production overhead control account.

(e) The production overhead volume variance may be recorded in the fixed production overhead account. (*Note.* Alternatively, you may find the volume variance recorded in the work in progress account.)

(f) Sales variances do *not* appear in the books of account. Sales are recorded in the sales account at actual invoiced value.

(g) The balance of variances in the variance account at the end of a period may be written off to the profit and loss account.

Exercise 3

What double entry would record a favourable labour rate variance?

Solution

Dr   Wages control account
Cr   Variance account

5.5 The actual process is best demonstrated with an example. Work carefully through the one which follows, ensuring that you know how the various variances are recorded.

Example: cost bookkeeping and variances

5.6 Zed operates an integrated accounting system and prepares its final accounts monthly. You are provided with the following information.

Balances as at 1 October

	£'000
Issued share capital	1,500
Profit and loss balance	460
Freehold buildings	1,000
Plant and machinery, at cost	500
Plant and machinery: depreciation provision	300
Motor vehicles, at cost	240
Motor vehicles: depreciation provision	80
10% debentures	240
Creditors (materials)	144
Creditors (expenses)	36
Stock - raw materials	520
Wages payable	40
Debtors	246
Bank	162
Stock - finished goods	132

Data for the month of October

Materials purchased	400,000 kgs at £4.90 per kg
Issued to production	328,000 kgs
Paid to creditors	£1,800,000
Direct wages incurred	225,000 hours at £4.20 per hour
Direct wages paid	£920,000
Production overhead incurred on credit	£1,490,000
Expense creditors paid	£1,900,000
Cash received from debtors	£4,800,000
Sales	£4,875,000
Plant and machinery purchased for cash on 1 October	£100,000
Administration and selling o/hd incurred on credit	£895,000
Production and sales	39,000 units

Additional data

Debenture interest	payable monthly
Depreciation provision	plant and machinery, 20% pa on cost
	motor vehicles, 25% pa on cost
Stocks of raw materials and finished goods	maintained at standard

The operation of motor vehicles is regarded as a cost of selling

Standard data

Direct material price	£5.00 per kg
Direct material usage	8 kgs per unit
Direct wages	£4.00 per hour
Direct labour	6 hours per unit
Production overhead	absorbed at 150% of direct wages
Gross profit	calculated at one-sixth of selling price
Budgeted output	10,000 units per week

Required

(a) Calculate the appropriate variances for October. You are not required to calculate sales variances.

(b) Show the following ledger accounts for October.

    (i)   Stores ledger control account
    (ii)   Direct wages control account
    (iii)   Production overhead control account
    (iv)   Administration and selling overhead control account
    (v)   Work in progress control account
    (vi)   Finished goods control account
    (vii)   Cost of sales control account
    (viii) Sales account
    (ix)   Variances account
    (x)   Profit and loss account

Solution

5.7   (a)   We will begin by determining the standard unit cost.

Standard cost per unit	£
Direct materials (8 kgs × £5)	40
Direct labour (6 hrs × £4)	24
Production overhead (150% × £24)	36
	100

Direct material price variance	£'000
400,000 kgs should cost (× £5)	2,000
but did cost (400,000 × £4.90)	1,960
	40 (F)

Direct material usage variance

39,000 units should use (× 8)	312,000 kgs
but did use	328,000 kgs
Variance in units	16,000 kgs (A)
× standard price per unit	× £5
	£80,000 (A)

Direct labour rate variance

	£'000
225,000 hours should cost (× £4)	900
but did cost (225,000 × £4.20)	945
	45 (A)

Direct labour efficiency variance

39,000 units should take (× 6 hrs)	234,000 hrs
but did take	225,000 hrs
Variance in hours	9,000 hrs (F)
× standard cost per hour	× £4
	£36,000 (F)

Production overhead expenditure variance

	£'000	£'000
Budgeted expenditure (10,000 × 4 wks × £36)		1,440
Actual expenditure		
Incurred on credit	1,490	
Depreciation (20% × 1/12 × £(500 + 100))	10	
		1,500
		60 (A)

Note. Operation of motor cars is a cost of selling and therefore not included in production overhead.

Production overhead volume variance

	£'000
Actual production at standard rate (39,000 × £36)	1,404
Budgeted production at standard rate (10,000 × 4 wks × £36)	1,440
	36 (A)

(b) (i)   STORES LEDGER CONTROL ACCOUNT

	£'000		£'000
Balance b/f	520	Work in progress	
Creditors		(328,000 × £5)	1,640
(400,000 × £4.90)	1,960	Balance c/d	880
Material price variance	40		
	2,520		2,520
Balance b/d	880		

Notes

(1)   Materials are issued from store at standard price.
(2)   The material price variance is recorded in this account.

(ii)   DIRECT WAGES CONTROL ACCOUNT

	£'000		£'000
Bank	920	Balance b/f	40
Balance c/d	65	Work in progress	
		(225,000 hrs × £4)	900
		Labour rate variance	45
	985		985
		Balance b/d	65

Notes

(1) Labour hours are costed to production at the standard rate per hour.
(2) The labour rate variance is recorded in this account.

(iii)

PRODUCTION OVERHEAD CONTROL ACCOUNT

	£'000		£'000
Creditors	1,490	Work in progress	
Depreciation on plant		(39,000 × £36)	1,404
and machinery	10	*Production overhead*	
		expenditure variance	60
		Production overhead	
		volume variance	36
	1,500		1,500

Notes

(1) Production is charged with the standard rate for the hours actively worked.

(2) The production overhead expenditure variance is shown in this account

(3) In this example, the volume variance is shown in the overhead account.

(iv)

ADMIN AND SELLING OVERHEAD CONTROL ACCOUNT

	£'000		£'000
Creditors	895	Profit and loss	900
Motor vehicle depreciation	5		
	900		900

(v)

WORK IN PROGRESS CONTROL ACCOUNT

	£'000		£'000
Stores ledger	1,640	Finished goods	
Direct wages	900	(39,000 × £100)	3,900
Production overhead	1,404	*Direct material usage*	
Direct labour		*variance*	80
efficiency variance	36		
	3,980		3,980

Notes

(1) Output is valued at standard production cost.
(2) The efficiency variances appear in this account.

(vi)

FINISHED GOODS CONTROL ACCOUNT

	£'000		£'000
Balance b/f	132	Cost of sales	3,900
Work in progress	3,900	Balance c/d	132
	4,032		4,032
Balance b/d	132		

(vii)

COST OF SALES CONTROL ACCOUNT

	£'000		£'000
Finished goods	3,900	Profit and loss	3,900

(viii)

SALES ACCOUNT

	£'000		£'000
Profit and loss	4,875	Bank/debtors	4,875

(ix)

VARIANCES ACCOUNT

	£'000		£'000
Wages (labour rate)	45	Stores (material price)	40
Production (expenditure)	60	WIP (labour efficiency)	36
Production (volume)	36	Profit and loss account	145
WIP (material usage)	80		
	221		221

Exam focus point

The variances are recorded in a variances account as part of the double entry system. The balance on the account at the end of the period is written off to the profit and loss account. Sometimes a separate account is used for each variance, but the double entry principles would be the same. In an examination you should prepare a separate account for each variance unless you are instructed otherwise.

(x)

PROFIT AND LOSS ACCOUNT

	£'000		£'000
Cost of sales	3,900	Sales	4,875
Administration and selling	900	Loss for month	72
Debenture interest	2		
Variances	145		
	4,947		4,947

5.8   As well as preparing ledger accounts you must also be able to prepare journal entries

Example: journal entries

5.9   Suppose that 4 kgs of material A are required to make one unit of product JPM, each kilogram costing £10. It takes direct labour 5 hours to make one unit of product JPM. The labour force is paid £4.50 per hour.

During the period the following results were recorded.

Material A: 8,200 kgs purchased on credit ★	£95,000
Material A: kgs issued to production★	8,200 kgs
Units of product JPM produced★	1,600
Direct labour hours worked★	10,000
Cost of direct labour★	£32,000

Required

(a)   Calculate the following variances for the period.

  (i)   Material price variance
  (ii)   Material usage variance
  (iii)   Labour rate variance
  (iv)   Labour efficiency variance

(b)   Prepare journal entries for the transactions marked ★ above, together with the variances calculated in (a).

Note

You should make the following assumptions.

  (i)   An integrated accounting system is maintained.
  (ii)   The raw material account is maintained at standard cost.
  (iii)   Work in progress is debited with the standard cost of direct labour.
  (iv)   The finished goods account is maintained at standard cost.
  (v)   There are no opening or closing stocks of work in progress.

Solution

				£
5.10	(a)	(i)	8,200 kgs should cost (× £10)	82,000
			but did cost	95,000
			Material price variance	13,000 (A)
		(ii)	1,600 units of JPM should use (× 4 kgs)	6,400 kgs
			but did use	8,200 kgs
			Usage variance in kgs	1,800 kgs (A)
			× standard cost per kg	× £10
			Material usage variance	£18,000 (A)

(iii)

		£
10,000 hours should cost (× £4.50)		45,000
but did cost		32,000
Labour rate variance		13,000 (F)

(iv)

	£
1,600 units of JPM should take (× 5 hrs)	8,000 hrs
but did take	10,000 hrs
Efficiency variance in hrs	2,000 hrs (A)
× standard rate per hour	× £4.50
Labour efficiency variance	£9,000 (A)

(b) (i)

	£	£
Stores ledger control account (8,200 kgs × £10)	82,000	
Material price variance	13,000	
Creditors		95,000

The purchase of materials on credit

(ii)

	£	£
Work in progress control account	82,000	
Stores ledger control account		82,000

The issue of material A to production

(iii)

	£	£
Material usage variance	18,000	
Work in progress control account		18,000

The bookkeeping of the material A usage variance

(iv)

	£	£
Work in progress control account (10,000 hrs × £4.50)	45,000	
Direct labour control account		32,000
Direct labour rate variance		13,000

The charging of labour to work in progress

(v)

	£	£
Direct labour efficiency variance	9,000	
Work in progress control account		9,000

The bookkeeping of the labour efficiency variance

(vi)

	£	£
Finished goods control account (1,600 × £62.50 (W))	100,000	
Work in progress control account		100,000

The transfer of finished goods from work in progress

Working

Standard cost of product JPM

	£
Material A (4 kgs × £10)	40.00
Direct labour (5 hrs × £4.50)	22.50
	62.50

Exercise 4

A company uses raw material J in production. The standard price for material J is £3 per metre. During the month 6,000 metres were purchased for £18,600, of which 5,000 metres were issued to production.

Required

Show the journal entries to record the above transactions in integrated accounts in the following separate circumstances.

(a) When raw material stock is valued at standard cost, that is the direct materials price variance is extracted on receipt.

(b) When raw materials stock is valued at actual cost, that is the direct materials price variance is extracted as the materials are used.

Solution

(a)

	£	£
Raw material stock (6,000 × £3)	18,000	
Direct material price variance	600	
Creditors		18,600

Purchase on credit of 6,000 metres of material J

	£	£
Work in progress (5,000 × £3)	15,000	
Raw material stock		15,000

Issue to production of 5,000 metres of J

(b)

	£	£
Raw material stock	18,600	
Creditors		18,600

Purchase on credit of 6,000 metres of material J

	£	£
Work in progress	15,000	
Direct material price variance (5,000 × £(3.10 – 3.00))	500	
Raw material stock		15,500

Issue to production of 5,000 metres of material J

Note that in both cases the material is charged to work in progress at standard price. In (b) the price variance is extracted only on the material which has been used up, the stock being valued at actual cost.

The advantages of standard cost bookkeeping

5.11 There are a number of advantages of using standard costing as opposed to recording actual transactions and comparing them with budgets as part of a system of budgetary control.

(a) Stock and work in progress is valued at standard cost which *removes* the *valuation/pricing disadvantages* inherent in using LIFO, FIFO or one of the average cost bases. All that is needed is a record of movements in the quantity of stock; the value of stock may be obtained simply by multiplying the physical stock by the standard cost per unit. This saves both clerical time and costs. Stock valuations based on standard costs may be included in externally published financial statements provided that the standard costs used are current and attainable.

(b) Variances are *automatically highlighted*, they do not actually have to be calculated.

(c) If the cost bookkeeping system is integrated with the financial accounts bookkeeping system, any *reconciliation problems are avoided*; managers may take variances more seriously if they are included in the financial accounts.

Chapter roundup

- The selling price variance measures the effect on profit of a different selling price to standard selling price.

- The sales volume profit variance measures the effect on profit of sales volume being different to budgeted volume.

- Operating statements show how the combination of variances reconcile budgeted profit and actual profit.

- There are two main differences between the variances calculated in an absorption costing system and the variances calculated in a marginal costing system.

    o   In a marginal costing system the only fixed overhead variance is an expenditure variance

    o   The sales volume variance is valued at standard contribution margin, not standard profit margin.

- Ensure that you are able to derive actual data from standard cost details and variances.

- The general principle in standard cost bookkeeping is that cost variances should be recorded as early as possible. They are recorded in the relevant account in which they arise and the appropriate double entry is taken to a variance account.

Test your knowledge

1   What is the sales volume profit variance? (see para 1.3)

2   In which specific ways do variances in a standard marginal costing system differ from those in a standard absorption costing system? (3.1)

3   The material usage variance is recorded in the stock control account. True or false? (5.4)

4   How are sales variances recorded in books of account? (5.4)

Now try illustrative question 25 at the end of the Study Text

Appendices

APPENDIX 1: PREPARATION AND PRESENTATION OF REPORTS TO MANAGEMENT

1   REPORTS TO MANAGEMENT

1.1   The examiner has indicated that questions on the syllabus section *Information for Decisions* could require wholly written answers and it is therefore possible that you will be asked to prepare a report. You will lose valuable marks if you do not present your answer in the format requested. You should therefore read carefully through this appendix if you are at all unsure of the correct approach to report writing.

2   GENERAL PRINCIPLES OF REPORT WRITING

2.1   The purpose of reports and their subject matter vary widely, but there are certain generally-accepted principles of report writing that can be applied to most types of report, both in practice and (allowing for the falseness of the situation and the limited information available) in exams

(a)   *Identification of report user, report writer and date.* Reports should indicate in a clear place, to whom they are directed, who has written them and the date of their preparation.

(b)   *Subject matter/title.* This description should be as short as possible whilst being explicit at the same time.

(c)   *Confidentiality.* If the report is confidential this fact must be printed at the top of the report and possibly on every page.

(d)   *Contents page.* If the report is extensive, it should open with a list of contents by section, paragraph number, or whatever is most helpful. This will rarely be necessary in an exam, but will often be helpful in practice in your job.

(e)   *Terms of reference.* If it is not sufficiently clear from the report's title/subject description, the introductory section of the report should explain why the report has been written and the terms of reference. As noted above the terms of reference will explain not only the purpose of the report but also any restrictions on its scope.

When timescale is important, this should be specified in the terms of reference. For example, the board of directors might call for a report so that they can take a decision by a certain cut-off date, perhaps whether to put in a tender for a major contract and if so at what price, in a situation where a customer has invited tenders which must be submitted by a certain date.

(f)   *Sources of information.* In practice a report will often draw on a variety of sources for its information, and these sources should be acknowledged in the report. Alternatively, if the report is based on primary research, the nature of the fact-finding should be explained, perhaps in an appendix to the report.

(g)   *Sections.* Wherever it is helpful for clarity the main body of the report should be divided into sections. The sections should have a logical sequence, and each section should ideally have a clear heading. These headings (or sub-headings) should if possible be standardised when reports are produced regularly. Paragraphs should be numbered, for ease of reference. Each paragraph should be concerned with one basic idea.

(h) *Appendices*. To keep the main body of the report short enough to hold the reader's interest, detailed explanations, charts and tables of figures should be put into appendices. The main body of the report should make cross-references to the appendices in appropriate places.

In an examination, you will need to do the calculations first, before you start to write your report, and you should state in your solution that your workings would be incorporated into an appendix to the report. Your report can then refer to the appendix, and the marker will know what you mean.

(i) *Summary of recommendations*. A report will usually contain conclusions or recommendations about the course of action to be taken by the report user. These conclusions or recommendations should perhaps be stated at the beginning of the report (after the introduction and statement of terms of reference). The main body of the report should then follow, in its logically-progressive sections, and should lead the report user through the considerations that led the report writer to these conclusions.

The conclusions or recommendations should then be re-stated at the end of the main body of the report.

Any assumptions, forecasts or conjectures should not be passed off as fact but signalled as such by using phrases like 'It is assumed that...', 'The probable result...'.

(j) *Prominence of important items*. The most significant items in a report should be given prominence.

(k) *Report summaries*. Long reports should be summarised in brief. However, as suggested already it is better to keep the main report itself brief, with the detail in appendices: then a report summary would not be necessary.

(l) *Implications for management*. Reference should be made where appropriate to costs, savings and other benefits that might accrue, and to any other implications for management in the report's recommendations (implications for staff recruitment, training or redundancies and so on).

(m) *Completeness*. A report should be logically complete and should not overlook any item or consideration so that its recommendations are called into question.

3   STYLE

3.1   As should be clear from the comments above, there are certain stylistic requirements in the writing of reports, formal or informal.

(a) *Objectivity and balance*. Even in a report designed to persuade as well as inform, subjective value-judgements and emotions should be kept out of the content and style as far as possible: the bias, if recognised, can undermine the credibility of the report and its recommendations. Emotive words or words otherwise loaded should be avoided.

In formal reports, it is usually better to use *impersonal constructions* rather than 'I', or 'we', which carry personal and possibly subjective associations. In other words, first person subjects should be replaced with third person:

I/we found that...

It became clear that...
(Your name) found that...
Investigation revealed that...

(b) Colloquialisms and abbreviated forms should be avoided in formal written English: colloquial (informal) 'I've', 'don't' and so on should be replaced by 'I have' and 'do not'. You should not use expressions like 'the staff will be a bit cheesed off' (or worse!): formal phrases should be used, such as 'will be demotivated'. If you need to refer to any of the ubiquitous acronyms that plague cost and management accounting (ABC, JIT and the rest), write it in full the first time: 'Activity Based Costing (ABC)', 'Just In Time (JIT)'.

(c) *Ease of understanding*. This will involve avoiding technical language and complex sentence structures for non-technical users. The material will have to be logically organised, especially if it is leading up to a conclusion or recommendation; relevant themes should be signalled by appropriate headings for scanning. The layout of the report should display data clearly and attractively. Figures and diagrams should be used with discretion, and it might be helpful to highlight key figures within large tables.

3.2   Various display techniques may be used to make the content of a report easy to identify and digest. For example, the relative importance of points should be signalled, each point should be referenced, and the body of text should be broken up to be easy on the eye. These things may be achieved as follows.

(a) *Headings*. Spaced out or enlarged capitals may be used for the main title. Important headings, say of sections of the report, may be in CAPITALS. <u>Underlining</u> or *italics* may be used for subheadings.

(b) *References*. Each section or point in a formal report should have a code for easy identification and reference.

I, II, III, IV, V etc A, B, C, D, E etc	may be used to reference main section headings.
1, 2, 3, 4, 5 etc	may be used to reference subsections.
(a), (b), (c) etc (i), (ii), (iii) etc	may be used to reference points and subpoints, with appropriate indentation.

Alternatively a 'decimal' system may be used, like the Dewey Decimal Classification System used in libraries:

1	<u>Heading 1</u>
1.1	Subheading 1
1.1.1	Point 1
1.1.2	Point 2
1.2	Subheading 2 etc.

(c) *Spacing*. Intelligent use of spacing separates headings from the body of the text for easy scanning, and also makes a large block more attractive and 'digestible'.

3.3   Reports should be written in ordinary clear English. Technical terms should be avoided except in reports to technical people. Care should be given to the choice of words - some words have a slangy or emotive meaning or other special associations, and such words should be avoided if possible. Spelling and grammatical mistakes should be avoided and care should be taken with punctuation. These give the report user a poor initial impression of the report writer's ability and might undermine his confidence in the content of the report. Figures should not be confusing. If the report includes large tables of figures, key figures should be highlighted.

4   CHECKLIST FOR REPORT WRITING

4.1   The following checklist for report writing indicates many of the factors that should be considered.

(a) *Purpose or terms of reference*

   (i)   What is the report being written about?

   (ii)   Why is it needed?

   (iii)   What effect might the report have if its findings or recommendations are acted upon?

   (iv)   Who are the report users? How much do they know already?

   (v)   What is wanted - a definite recommendation or less specific advice?

   (vi)   What previous reports have there been on the subject, what did they find or recommend, and what action was taken on these findings, or recommendations?

(b) *Information in the report*

   (i)   What is the source of each item of information in the report?

   (ii)   How old is the information?

(iii) What period does the report cover - a month, a year?

(iv) How can the accuracy of the information be checked and verified? To what extent might it be subject to error?

(c) *Preparing the report*

(i) Who is responsible for preparing the report?

(ii) How long will it take to prepare?

(iii) How is the information in the report put together (for numerical information, what computations are carried out on the source data to arrive at the figures in the report?)

(iv) How many copies of the report should be prepared and to whom should they be sent?

(d) *Usefulness of the report*

(i) What use will the report be in its present form? What action is it intended to trigger?

(ii) How will each recipient of the report use it for his or her own purposes?

(iii) Does the report meet the requirements of the terms of reference?

5 RECOMMENDED FORMAT FOR THE EXAM

5.1 Most of the CIMA model solutions to the new syllabus Specimen Papers use some variant of the following format for reports.

REPORT

To: Board of Directors

From: Cost Accountant   **Date:**

Subject: Report Format

Body of report

Signed: Cost Accountant

5.2 Note that the date is always set to the right in CIMA solutions and is always left blank. The word 'Re' is sometimes used in place of 'Subject'. CIMA model solutions *always* include 'Signed' at the bottom, and although you might think this is somewhat superfluous information (you have already said who the report is from) we recommend that you follow this style. Do not sign your own name, however! Do not draw a box round your report: we have only done this to make our example stand out. Use underlining (with a ruler) to distinguish headings.

6 WRITING THE REPORT

Who are you?

6.1 Get into role: sometimes you are the cost accountant of the firm described, sometimes you are the finance director (and therefore a board member yourself). In an exam context this will not have much impact on the *substance* of your answer, but it will affect the style of your writing to some extent. Take care over the use of the first personal pronoun ('I'/'We'). Think about the extent of your personal influence over the people you are reporting to.

Who is the report for?

6.2   Take note also of who you are writing to. This may affect the technical language you can use and the style of the report.

Structure your report

6.3   Follow the requirements. Questions are usually very specific about the points to be addressed in your report. If you are asked to comment on four matters, (a) to (d), then it makes sense to structure your report around four sections, headed as appropriate.

Figures and workings

6.4   If you are asked to analyse figures, think carefully about how the analysis can most usefully be presented. This is difficult because your time will be limited and you will be worrying about getting the calculations right. Do not assume that the way information is laid out in the question is the way you should lay it out in your answer: it is sometimes helpful to set figures side by side that are presented in separate tables in the question. It is sometimes helpful to lay out in columns information that is given to you in rows, or vice versa. Sometimes it can be revealing to regroup data in some way.

APPENDIX 2: CUMULATIVE PRESENT VALUE TABLE

This table shows the present value of £1 per annum, receivable or payable at the end of each year for *n* years.

Periods (n)	Discount rates (r)									
	1%	2%	3%	4%	5%	6%	7%	8%	9%	10%
1	0.990	0.980	0.971	0.962	0.952	0.943	0.935	0.926	0.917	0.909
2	1.970	1.942	1.913	1.886	1.859	1.833	1.808	1.783	1.759	1.736
3	2.941	2.884	2.829	2.775	2.723	2.673	2.624	2.577	2.531	2.487
4	3.902	3.808	3.717	3.630	3.546	3.465	3.387	3.312	3.240	3.170
5	4.853	4.713	4.580	4.452	4.329	4.212	4.100	3.993	3.890	3.791
6	5.795	5.601	5.417	5.242	5.076	4.917	4.767	4.623	4.486	4.355
7	6.728	6.472	6.230	6.002	5.786	5.582	5.389	5.206	5.033	4.868
8	7.652	7.325	7.020	6.733	6.463	6.210	5.971	5.747	5.535	5.335
9	8.566	8.162	7.786	7.435	7.108	6.802	6.515	6.247	5.995	5.759
10	9.471	8.983	8.530	8.111	7.722	7.360	7.024	6.710	6.418	6.145
11	10.368	9.787	9.253	8.760	8.306	7.887	7.499	7.139	6.805	6.495
12	11.255	10.575	9.954	9.385	8.863	8.384	7.943	7.536	7.161	6.814
13	12.134	11.348	10.635	9.986	9.394	8.853	8.358	7.904	7.487	7.103
14	13.004	12.106	11.296	10.563	9.899	9.295	8.745	8.244	7.786	7.367
15	13.865	12.849	11.938	11.118	10.380	9.712	9.108	8.559	8.061	7.606

Periods (n)	Discount rates (r)									
	11%	12%	13%	14%	15%	16%	17%	18%	19%	20%
1	0.901	0.893	0.885	0.877	0.870	0.862	0.855	0.847	0.840	0.833
2	1.713	1.690	1.668	1.647	1.626	1.605	1.585	1.566	1.547	1.528
3	2.444	2.402	2.361	2.322	2.283	2.246	2.210	2.174	2.140	2.106
4	3.102	3.037	2.974	2.914	2.855	2.798	2.743	2.690	2.639	2.589
5	3.696	3.605	3.517	3.433	3.352	3.274	3.199	3.127	3.058	2.991
6	4.231	4.111	3.998	3.889	3.784	3.685	3.589	3.498	3.410	3.326
7	4.712	4.564	4.423	4.288	4.160	4.039	3.922	3.812	3.706	3.605
8	5.146	4.968	4.799	4.639	4.487	4.344	4.207	4.078	3.954	3.837
9	5.537	5.328	5.132	4.946	4.772	4.607	4.451	4.303	4.163	4.031
10	5.889	5.650	5.426	5.216	5.019	4.833	4.659	4.494	4.339	4.192
11	6.207	5.938	5.687	5.453	5.234	5.029	4.836	4.656	4.486	4.327
12	6.492	6.194	5.918	5.660	5.421	5.197	4.988	4.793	4.611	4.439
13	6.750	6.424	6.122	5.842	5.583	5.342	5.118	4.910	4.715	4.533
14	6.982	6.628	6.302	6.002	5.724	5.468	5.229	5.008	4.802	4.611
15	7.191	6.811	6.462	6.142	5.847	5.575	5.324	5.092	4.876	4.675

Multiple choice questions and suggested solutions

The following data are to be used for questions 1 and 2 below.

Budgeted and actual data for Korman and Gowan Ltd for the year to 31 December 19X1 is as follows.

	Budget	Actual
Fixed production overhead		
Department P	£78,000	£81,000
Department Q	£114,000	£112,000
Direct labour hours		
Department P	1,500	1,000
Department Q	8,000	10,000
Machine hours		
Department P	2,500	2,000
Department Q	500	600

Fixed production overhead is absorbed on a machine hour basis in Department P and a direct labour hour basis in Department Q.

1   In the year to 31 December 19X1, absorbed fixed production overhead was

   A £194,500   B £199,600   C £200,665   D £204,900   E £209,400

2   Fixed overhead in the year was

   A   under-absorbed by £1,000
   B   over-absorbed by £7,600
   C   over-absorbed by £11,900
   D   over-absorbed by £12,900
   E   under-absorbed by £11,900

3   Houseboxes Ltd uses a standard costing system, and values all its stocks of raw materials at standard price. Stocks are issued to work in progress at standard price. Data for July 19X2 are as follows.

Opening stock	Nil
Goods received	400 units of Material X
Goods subsequently issued to production	300 units of Material X
Standard price per unit of X	£2.00
Actual price per unit of X	£2.50

The cost accounting entry for the material price variance would be

A	Debit	Price variance account	£150
	Credit	Stores account	£150
B	Debit	Stores account	£150
	Credit	Price variance account	£150
C	Debit	Price variance account	£200
	Credit	Stores account	£200
D	Debit	Stores account	£200
	Credit	Price variance account	£200
E	Debit	Stores account	£600
	Credit	Price variance account	£600

4   Kane Furniture Ltd maintains separate cost and financial accounts. The cost accounts do *not* include fixed asset records. The profit in the financial accounts for the year ended 31 December 19X1 was £40,000.

The following information is also available for the year, showing the differences between the cost accounts and the financial accounts.

(a) Opening stocks:	financial accounts	£26,000
	cost accounts	£21,000
(b) Closing stocks:	financial accounts	£23,000
	cost accounts	£19,000

(c) The company received dividends of £2,500.

(d) A machine with a net book value of £7,000 was sold for £3,000 during the year.

The profit recorded in the cost accounts was

A £37,500   **B** £39,500   **C** £40,500   **D** £41,000   **E** £42,500

5   Brixon Mortar plc began a major construction contract on 1 January 19X1, which is expected to take eight years to complete. Cost data for the second year of the contract work, 19X2, include the following.

	Accrued at 31.12.X1 £	Prepayment 31.12.X1 £	Cash paid in 19X2 £	Accrued at 31.12.X2 £
Site wages	15,000	-	400,000	22,000
Contract expenses	-	8,000	200,000	5,000

What are the costs for site wages and contract expenses for the contract in 19X2?

A £566,000   **B** £580,000   **C** £604,000   **D** £620,000   **E** £407,000

The following data are to be used for questions 6, 7 and 8 below.

Dringweed, an agricultural fertiliser, is manufactured in a single continuous process. Opening stock on 1 March was 200 units, which were valued at £30,095, which consists of £25,200 in materials cost and £4,895 in conversion cost. This was 100% complete as to materials and 25% complete as to conversion cost. 1,200 units were added to production during March, and these had a materials cost of £168,000. Closing stock of 200 units on 31 March was 100% complete as to materials and 50% complete as to conversion cost. Conversion costs during March were £158,125. There was no loss in process

6   What were the equivalent units of production in March?

	Materials	Conversion costs
A	1,400 units	1,350 units
B	1,200 units	1,100 units
C	1,200 units	1,150 units
D	1,200 units	1,250 units
E	1,250 units	1,200 units

7   Using the FIFO method of stock valuation, what was the cost of finished goods completed during March?

A £315,570   **B** £335,095   **C** £341,845   **D** £349,985   **E** £266,500

8   Using the weighted average method of stock valuation, what was the value of closing stock of work in process at 31 March?

A £40,140   **B** £40,650   **C** £47,020   **D** £52,680   **E** £27,600

The following data are to be used for questions 9, 10 and 11 below.

Actual sales of a retail company, Markup Ltd, for November and December 19X1, together with budgeted monthly sales for January - June 19X2, are shown below.

		Sales	
		£	
19X1	November	160,000	(actual)
	December	210,000	(actual)
19X2	January	80,000	
	February	60,000	
	March	100,000	
	April	90,000	
	May	120,000	
	June	150,000	

The company sells food products with a very short shelf life, and so it carries no stocks of goods beyond the end of any day. All goods purchased on any day are resold during the day.

The purchase price of the goods for Markup Ltd is 75% of their retail price. Purchases are on 1½ months' credit. Sales are 50% for cash and 50% on credit. One half of credit customers pay after 1 month and the other half pay after 2 months.

There are no bad debts. Sales and purchases occur at an even rate throughout each month.

9   What are the budgeted cash receipts in February 19X2?

A £77,500   **B** £102,500   **C** £132,500   **D** £175,000   **E** £105,200

10   What are the budgeted cash receipts in the six month period January - June 19X2?

A £600,000   **B** £615,000   **C** £625,000   **D** £640,000   **E** £692,500

11   What are the budgeted cash payments to suppliers in the six month period January - June 19X2?

A £450,000   **B** £495,000   **C** £430,000   **D** £680,000   **E** £510,000

12   Hake and Legge Ltd manufactures Product T and uses a standard costing system. Closing stocks of direct materials are valued at actual cost. Data for the production of product T in June include the following.

Direct materials used (material V)	21,600 kg of material
Cost of direct materials used	£128,304
Direct materials price variance (material V)	£1,296 (F)
Direct materials usage variance (material V)	£2,880 (A)

4,800 units of Product T were manufactured in June.

What is the standard direct materials cost of Product T?

A   4.6 kg of V at £5.88 per kg
B   4.5 kg of V at £5.94 per kg
C   4.5 kg of V at £6.00 per kg
D   4.4 kg of V at £6.00 per kg
E   4.4 kg of V at £5.94 per kg

The following data are to be used for questions 13, 14, 15, and 16 below.

Hitchin Parts Ltd, which manufactures a single product, used the following standard cost for the year 19X2.

	£ per unit
Direct materials	4
Direct labour	6
Variable production overhead	1
Fixed production overhead	6
	17
Standard selling price	20
Standard profit	3

Actual results in 19X2, when actual sales were 16,000 units, included the following.

	£
Direct materials cost variance	1,700(A)
Direct labour cost variance	1,200(F)
Variable production overhead total variance	600(F)
Fixed production overhead total variance	9,000(F)
Fixed production overhead expenditure variance	3,000(A)
Selling price variance	2,700(A)
Sales volume profit variance	4,500(F)

There were no opening stocks in 19X2, and no closing stocks of direct materials or work in progress. Closing stocks of finished goods were budgeted to be nil. Actual closing stocks are valued at standard full cost.

13 What was the budgeted profit in 19X2?

  A £43,500   **B** £47,325   **C** £48,000   **D** £52,500   **E** £29,000

14 What was the actual profit in 19X2?

  A £45,400   **B** £51,400   **C** £54,400   **D** £58,900   **E** £45,300

15 What was the value of closing stocks at the end of 19X2?

  A £5,500   **B** £8,500   **C** £11,000   **D** £17,000   **E** £16,000

16 What were actual sales revenue and actual fixed overhead expenditure in 19X2?

	Sales revenue	Fixed overhead expenditure
A	£317,300	£81,000
B	£317,300	£90,000
C	£317,300	£99,000
D	£322,700	£99,000
E	£320,000	£87,000

*The following data are to be used for questions **17** and **18** below.*

The accountant of Katten Mousse plc has calculated the company's breakeven point from the following data.

	£
Selling price per unit	6.00
Variable production cost per unit	1.20
Variable selling cost per unit	0.40
Fixed production cost per unit, based on a budgeted 10,000 units pa	4.00
Fixed selling costs per unit, based on budgeted 10,000 units pa	0.80

17 What is the company's breakeven point?

  A 8,333 units   **B** 9,091 units   **C** 10,000 units   **D** 10,900 units   **E** 10,909 units

18 It is now expected that the variable production cost per unit and the selling price per unit will each increase by 10%, and fixed production costs will rise by 25%.

What will the breakeven point now be, to the nearest whole unit?

A 9,470 units **B** 11,885 units **C** 12,295 units **D** 12,397 units **E** 11,880 units

The following data are to be used for questions 19 and 20 below.

Square Wheels Ltd, a small transport company, operates with just two vehicles, and has produced the following forecast for next year.

Operating kilometres	60,000
	£
Total wages cost	40,000
Total vehicle running costs	48,000
Other costs (all fixed)	24,000
Revenue	120,000

Revenue and vehicle running costs vary with operating kilometres.

19 The breakeven point for the year, in operating kilometres, is

A 45,000   **B** 50,000   **C** 53,333   **D** 54,000   **E** 53,000

20 If the forecast were to be only 55,000 kilometres, and wages were reduced to £32,000, the breakeven point in operating kilometres would be

A 41,250   **B** 42,778   **C** 44,000   **D** 46,667   **E** 47,000

21 Scorsatz Okker Ltd has a machine which it purchased two years ago for £15,000, and which now has a net book value of £5,000. Perry Striker, the company's chief executive, is wondering whether to use the machine for a one-year project. If not used, it would have no other use, and although it could be sold, there would be a loss on disposal of £2,000. If used for the project, the machine would have a one-year life, after which it would have no resale value, but would cost £1,500 to dispose of. The variable operating costs of the machine would be £6,000 for the year.

In deciding whether to go ahead with the one-year project, and ignoring interest costs, the relevant costs of the machine would be

A £9,000   **B** £9,500   **C** £6,000   **D** £12,500   **E** £10,500

22 Finnish Inline Ltd manufactures component Q and end product T. One unit of Q goes into the manufacture of one unit of T. Budgeted manufacturing costs are as follows.

	Component Q	Product T
	£	£
Component Q	-	10
Raw materials	2	2
Direct labour	4	8
Variable overhead	1	2
Fixed overhead	3	6
	10	28
Sales price		35
Profit		7

Direct labour is a variable cost. The company is working at full capacity, and can only just produce enough units of component Q to meet the demand for product T.

An outside customer asks Finnish Inline Ltd to sell it 3,000 units of component Q. If the company agrees, it will incur additional inspection and testing costs of £3,000.

What is the minimum price per unit of Q that Finnish Inline would have to charge if it agreed to supply the customer, so as not to suffer any drop in profits?

A £17   **B** £21   **C** £24   **D** £31   **E** £36

23 Homard Vantage Ltd manufactures four components, W, X, Y and Z, using the same machines for each. Unit production costs, for components produced in-house, are as follows.

	W	X	Y	Z
	£	£	£	£
Direct materials	5	2	6	3
Direct labour	15	6	9	8
Variable overhead	8	6	9	4
Production overhead	16	12	18	8
	44	26	42	23
Budgeted production requirements (units)	4,500	6,000	4,000	9,000

Variable overheads are incurred at the rate of £2 per machine hour. Direct labour is a fixed cost, and the unit costs above represent an apportionment of this cost.

Only 54,000 hours of machine time will be available during the year, and a subcontractor who has short-term excess capacity has quoted the following unit prices for supplying components in the next budget period.

W	£41
X	£23
Y	£42
Z	£20

Which component should be purchased externally so as to minimise total costs in the budget period?

A   Component W
B   Component X
C   Component Y
D   Component Z
E   Both components W and X

24 Rhodes Hides Ltd manufactures three joint products, W, X and Y in a common process. The cost and production data for March is as follows.

	£
Opening stock	40,000
Direct materials input	80,000
Conversion costs	100,000
Closing stock	20,000

Output and sales were as follows.

	Production Units	Sales Units	Sales price per unit £
W	20,000	15,000	4
X	20,000	15,000	6
Y	40,000	50,000	3

If costs are apportioned between joint products on a market value basis, what was the cost per unit of product X in March?

A £2.50   **B** £3.00   **C** £3.75   **D** £4.00   **E** £1.875

25   Harrop Lane Ltd manufactures two products by passing materials through two consecutive processes. Results for June were as follows.

Process 1   Input materials at £1.50 per kg: £9,000
Conversion costs: £5,850
Output to Process 2: 5,500 kgs
Defective production (scrapped on completion): 500 kgs

Process 2   Conversion costs: £14,675
Output: Joint Product X: 2,500 kgs, sales price £16 per kg
Joint Product Y: 2,500 kgs, sales price £8 per kg
By-product Z: 500 kgs, sales price £2 per kg

There were no opening or closing stocks in either process. Normal loss is 10% in Process 1 and nil in Process 2. Joint product costs are apportioned on a sales value basis. By-product income is credited to the process account. All output of Z was sold in June.

Taking profit as the difference between sales and full production costs, what was the profit per kilo of Joint Product X in June, to two decimal places?

A £8.05   **B** £8.32   **C** £8.39   **D** £8.72   **E** £4.16

26   Pitt Head Ltd produces a single product and currently uses absorption costing for its internal management accounting reports. The fixed production overhead absorption rate is £34 per unit. Opening stocks for the year were 100 units, and closing stocks were 180 units. Cole Meinschaft, the company's management accountant, is considering a switch to marginal costing as the stock valuation basis.

If marginal costing were used, the management accounting profit for the year, compared with the profit calculated by the absorption costing method, would then be:

A £6,120 lower
B £3,400 lower
C £2,720 lower
D £3,400 higher
E £2,720 higher

The following data are to be used for questions 27 and 28 below.

Gould and Silver plc purchases a basic commodity and then refines it for resale. Budgeted sales of the refined product are as follows.

	March	April	May	June
Sales in kg	9,000	9,000	8,000	7,000

Other relevant data are as follows.

(a)   The basic raw material cost is £3 per kg purchased.

(b)   Material losses are 10% of finished output.

(c)   Material suppliers are paid 20% in the month of purchase and 80% in the month following purchase.

(d)   The target month-end raw material stock level is 5,000 kg plus 25% of the raw materials required for next month's budgeted production.

(e)   The target month-end stock level for finished goods is 6,000 kg plus 25% of next month's budgeted sales.

27   What are the budgeted raw material purchases for April?

A 8,500 kg   **B** 9,350 kg   **C** 9,444.25 kg   **D** 9,831.25 kg   **E** 9,625 kg

28   What are the budgeted payments in April to suppliers of raw material?

   A £26,550   **B** £27,305   **C** £27,990   **D** £29,205   **E** £28,050

29   Which of the following factors affect cash flow, but are not included in the profit and loss account?

   Factor
   1   Funds from the issue of share capital
   2   Revaluation of a fixed asset
   3   Decrease in the level of trade debtors
   4   Repayment of a bank loan

   A   Factors 1 and 4 only
   B   Factors 2 and 4 only
   C   Factors 1, 2 and 3 only
   D   Factors 1, 3 and 4 only
   E   Factors 1, 2, 3 and 4

30   What is an attainable standard?

   A   A standard which is established for use in the short term, relating to currently attainable conditions

   B   A standard established for use over a long period, which is used as the basis for developing a current standard

   C   A standard which can be attained under ideal conditions, and which gives no allowance for waste, machine breakdowns and other inefficiencies

   D   A standard which represents reasonably achievable future performance, giving some allowance for normal waste, machine breakdowns and other inefficiencies

   E   None of these

1   D

	Department P	Department Q
Budgeted overhead expenditure	£78,000	£114,000
Budgeted activity	2,500 machine hrs	8,000 direct labour hrs
Absorption rate	£31.20 per machine hr	£14.25 per direct labour hr

	£
Overhead absorbed:	
Department P (2,000 machine hrs × £31.20)	62,400
Department Q (10,000 labour hours × £14.25)	142,500
Total overhead absorbed	204,900

2   C

	£
Overhead absorbed (see 1 above)	204,900
Overhead incurred (81,000 + 112,000)	193,000
Over-absorbed overhead	11,900

3   C

STORES ACCOUNT

	£		£
Creditors (400 × £2.50)	1,000	WIP (300 × £2)	600
		Price variance a/c (balance,	
		or 400 × £0.50)	200
		Closing stock c/fwd (100 × £2)	200
	1,000		1,000

PRICE VARIANCE

	£
Stores a/c	200

4   E

	£
Profit in the financial accounts	40,000
Stock valuation differences	
Cost accounts opening stock lower in value by	5,000
Cost accounts closing stock lower in value by	(4,000)
	41,000
Items in the financial accounts and not in the cost accounts	
Dividends received	(2,500)
Loss on sale of machine	4,000
Cost accounting profit	42,500

5   D   This is a problem which calls for sorting out accruals and prepayments.

	Site wages £	Contract expenses £	Total £
Cash paid in 19X2	400,000	200,000	
less accruals at 31.12.X1	(15,000)	-	
add prepayments at 31.12.X1	-	8,000	
	385,000	208,000	
add accruals at 31.12.X1	22,000	5,000	
Chargeable to the contract for 19X2	407,000	213,000	620,000

6   D

		Equivalent units	
	Total units	Materials	Conversion costs
Opening stock: work already done	200	200	50
Opening stock: to complete in March		0	150
Other finished work	1,000	1,000	1,000
Closing stock	200	200	100
	1,400	1,200	1,250

Equivalent units of work done in March:

Materials	1,200
Conversion costs	1,250

7   A

	Materials	Conversion cost	Total
Costs incurred in March	£168,000	£158,125	
Equivalent units of work in March	1,200	1,250	
Cost per equivalent unit	£140	£126.50	£266.50

Cost of finished goods produced:

	£
Opening stock (200 units) value b/f	30,095
Cost to complete (150 × £126.50)	18,975
	49,070
Cost of other units produced in March (1,000 units · £266.50)	266,500
Total cost of finished goods produced	315,570

8   A   Using weighted average costing, the equivalent units would be calculated as follows.

	Materials Units	Conversion costs Units
Finished goods	1,200	1,200
Closing stock	200	100 (50%)
	1,400	1,300
	£	£
Cost	25,200	4,895
	168,000	158,125
	193,200	163,020
Cost per equivalent unit	£138	£125.40

Value of closing stock

	£
200 units of materials × £138	27,600
100 units of conversion cost × £125.40	12,540
	40,140

9   B

	£
50% of sales in February (cash sales)	30,000
25% of sales in January	20,000
25% of sales in December	52,500
	102,500

10   D   The quickest method of calculation is to take opening debtors plus sales minus closing debtors.

	£'000
Debtors at 1 January 19X1 (25% of 160 + 50% of 210)	145
Sales in January - June (80 + 60 + 100 + 90 + 120 + 150)	600
	745
Debtors at 30 June 19X2 (25% of 120 + 50% of 150)	105
Cash receipts in January - June	640

11   E   There are no stocks, and so purchases in any period will relate to sales in the same period. Since 1½ months' credit is taken, the payments in the January - June period will be for the following purchases.

$^1/_2$ of November 19X0 purchases
Purchases in December - April
$^1/_2$ of May 19X1 purchases

This is (in £'000) 75% × (80 + 210 + 80 + 60 + 100 + 90 + 60) = 510, that is £510,000

12   D   Since stocks are valued at actual cost, the raw materials price variance is calculated on materials quantities used (rather than quantities purchased).

	£
21,600 kg of V did cost	128,304
Price variance	1,296 (F)
21,600 kg of V should cost	129,600

Standard cost per kg of V = £6.

Usage variance is £2,880 (A).

	Kg
Usage variance in kg (£2,880 ÷ £6)	480 (A)
4,800 units of T did use	21,600
4,800 units of T should use	21,120

Standard usage per unit of T = 4.4 kg

13   A

Actual sales	16,000 units
Sales volume profit variance, in £	£4,500 (F)
Sales volume profit variance, in units (÷ £3)	1,500 units (F)
Budgeted sales (16,000 − 1,500)	14,500 units
Budgeted profit per unit	£3
Budgeted profit in total	£43,500

14   C

	£	£
Budgeted profit		43,500
Selling price variance		2,700 (A)
Sales volume profit variance		4,500 (F)
		45,300
Variances		
Direct materials cost	1,700 (A)	
Direct labour cost	1,200 (F)	
Variable overhead cost	600 (F)	
Fixed overhead cost	9,000 (F)	
		9,100 (F)
Actual profit		54,400

15   B

	£
Total fixed overhead variance	9,000 (F)
Fixed overhead expenditure variance	3,000 (A)
Difference = fixed overhead volume variance	12,000 (F)

This represents the difference between budgeted and actual production in units, multiplied by the standard fixed overhead rate per unit = 12,000 ÷ 6 = 2,000 units (F).

Budgeted production	14,500 units
Difference from budget	2,000 units (F)
Actual production	16,500 units

Since sales were 16,000 units, closing stocks must be 500 units, valued at (× £17) £8,500.

16   B

	£
Profit margin on 16,000 units should be (× £3)	48,000
Selling price variance	2,700 (A)
Actual profit margin	45,300

Actual sales revenue = £45,300 + (16,000 × £17) = £317,300

			£
There were 14,500 units in the budget.			
Budgeted fixed overhead (× £6)			87,000
Fixed overhead expenditure variance			3,000 (A)
Actual fixed overhead expenditure			90,000

17   E

	£
Budgeted fixed costs (10,000 ☐ £4) + (10,000 ☐ £0.80)	£48,000
Unit contribution £(6 – 1.20 – 0.40)	£4.40
Breakeven point (£48,000 ÷ £4.40)	10,909 units

18   B

	£
Selling costs are unchanged (both variable and fixed)	
New sales price £(6 × 1.1)	6.60
New variable cost per unit £(1.20 × 1.1) + £0.40	1.72
New unit contribution	4.88

New fixed costs (40,000 × 1.25) + 8,000	£58,000
New breakeven point (58,000 ÷ £4.88)	11,885 units

19   C   The wording of the question indicates that only vehicle running costs are variable costs. Wages are fixed cost items.

	£
Revenue	120,000
Variable costs	48,000
Contribution	72,000
Contribution per kilometre	£1.20

$$\text{Breakeven point} = \frac{\text{Fixed costs}}{\text{Contribution per km}} = \frac{£64,000}{£1.20 \text{ per km}} = 53,333 \text{ km}$$

20   D   Fixed costs now reduced to (£32,000 + £24,000) = £56,000

$$\text{Breakeven point} \frac{£56,000}{£1.20 \text{ per km}} = 46,667 \text{ km}$$

The change in the forecast operating distance has no relevance for the breakeven point.

21   E   The company would lose the opportunity to sell the machine now, and would instead incur disposal costs in one year. These are both relevant costs.

	£	
Variable operating costs	6,000	
Current disposal value of machine (opportunity cost)	3,000	(5,000–2,000)
Disposal cost in one year's time	1,500	
	10,500	

22   C

	£
Contribution forgone from lost sales of T (3,000 × £(35 – 2 – 8 – 2))	69,000
Incremental inspection and testing costs	3,000
	72,000

Minimum price (÷ 3,000 units) = £24

23   B   To produce the budgeted quantity of each component would need 18,000 hours of in-house machine time for each component, which is exactly the amount of the shortfall.

	W	X	Y	Z
	£	£	£	£
Unit variable cost	13	8	15	7
External purchase cost	41	23	42	20
Difference in cost	28	15	27	13
	÷ 4	÷ 3	÷ 4½	÷ 2
Difference per machine hour	£7	£5	£6	£6.50
Priority for external purchase	4th	1st	2nd	3rd

24   C

	£
Opening stock	40,000
Materials	80,000
Conversion costs	100,000
	220,000
Closing stock	20,000
Cost of production	200,000

Production costs are apportioned on the sales value of units produced.

Product	Units produced	Sales value £	Apportion- ment of costs £	Cost per unit £
W	20,000	80,000 (2)	50,000	2.500
X	20,000	120,000 (3)	75,000	3.750
Y	40,000	120,000 (3)	75,000	1.875
			200,000	

25   B

Process 1	Kgs
Input	6,000
Normal loss (10%)	600
Expected output (equivalent units)	5,400

Cost per expected unit of output (£14,850 ÷ 5,400) = £2.75

Total cost of output transferred to Process 2 (× 5,500) = £15,125

Process 2 costs	£
Transfers from Process 1	15,125
Conversion costs	14,675
	29,800
less: by-product revenue (500 × £2)	1,000
	28,800

Product	Kgs	Sales value £	Apportioned costs £	Profit £	Profit per kg £
X	2,500	40,000	(2) 19,200	20,800	8.32
Y	2,500	20,000	(1) 9,600	10,400	4.16
		60,000	28,800		

26   C   If marginal costing is used to value stock instead of absorption costing, then the difference in profits will be equal to the change in stock volume multiplied by the fixed production overhead absorption rate:

80 units × £34 = £2,720

Since closing stocks are higher than opening stocks, the marginal costing profit will be lower than the absorption costing profit. This is because the marginal costing profit does not 'benefit' from an increase in the amount of fixed production overheads taken to stock (rather than to the profit and loss account).

27   B   Raw material requirements depend on the level of production, which in turn depends on sales and finished goods stock requirements.

	February kg	March kg	April kg	May kg
Required finished stock				
Base stock	6,000	6,000	6,000	6,000
+ 25% of next month's sales	2,250	2,250	2,000	1,750
= Required stock at month end	8,250	8,250	8,000	7,750
+ Sales		9,000	9,000	8,000
		17,250	17,000	15,750
– opening stock		8,250	8,250	8,000
= Finished production required		9,000	8,750	7,750
+ 10% for losses				
= Raw material required for production		9,900	9,625	8,525

Now that the requirements for production are known, raw material stock requirements must be taken into account to determine the level of purchases.

	February kg	March kg	April kg
Required material stock			
Base stock	5,000	5,000.00	5,000.00
+ 25% of material required for next month's production	2,475	2,406.25	2,131.25
= Required closing material stock	7,475	7,406.25	7,131.25
+ Production requirements		9,900.00	9,625.00
		17,306.25	16,756.25
– Opening material stock		7,475.00	7,406.25
= Required purchases		9,831.25	9,350.00

28   D   We can use the purchases figures calculated in the previous solution.

	March	April
Purchases	9,831.25 kg	9,350 kg
× £3 per kg	£29,493.75	£28,050

Therefore, budgeted payments to suppliers in April are:

	£
80% × March purchases =	23,595
20% × April purchases =	5,610
	29,205

29   D   None of the factors would be included in the profit and loss account, and factor 2 is the only one which does not affect cash flow. The revaluation of a fixed asset would be shown as an increase in reserves, but there will be no cash movement until the asset is sold.

30   D   The CIMA defines an attainable standard as one which relates to reasonable attainable future performance and objectives. Option D is therefore correct. The other options are different types of standard:

Option A describes a current standard.
Option B describes a basic standard.
Option C describes an ideal standard.

Illustrative questions and suggested solutions

Questions with time and mark allocations indicate examination-standard questions.

1   CLASSIFICATION AND CODING

(a) Distinguish between classification and coding of costs.

(b) What are the major requirements for a practical coding system?

2   REGIMENT OF THE LINE LTD

Regiment of the Line Ltd operates two factories, one in Wolverhampton and the other in Gunnersbury.

The Grenadier factory at Wolverhampton is producing output in excess of sales demand, and it will be necessary to reduce output in the next period from the current 90% level of activity (11,700 units) to 75%.

The Fusilier factory at Gunnersbury is also currently working at 90% level of activity (8,100 units of a different product) but due to heavy sales demand, it is intended to increase output to 115%.

You are given the following information about cost and revenue.

Grenadier factory at Wolverhampton

	Level of activity		
	80%	90%	100%
	£	£	£
Direct materials	72,800	81,900	91,000
Direct labour	62,400	70,200	78,000
Production overhead	59,200	63,100	67,000
Sales	208,000	234,000	260,000

Fusilier factory at Gunnersbury

	Level of activity				
	80%	90%	100%	105%	110%
	£	£	£	£	£
Direct materials	79,200	89,100	99,000	102,825	106,650
Direct labour	57,600	64,800	72,000	76,500	81,000
Production overhead	49,800	53,400	57,000	58,800	60,600
Sales	216,000	243,000	270,000	283,500	297,000

REQUIREMENT:

Prepare a statement to show the expected marginal costs, contribution and profit for each factory at the proposed level of activity.

3   COST CENTRES AND UNITS   *45 mins*

(a) (i) Explain the terms 'cost centre' and 'cost unit'.

    (ii) Suggest suitable cost units which may be used to aid control within the following organisations.

        (1) A hospital
        (2) A road haulage business
        (3) A hotel with forty double rooms and five single rooms
        (4) A public transport authority.   **10 Marks**

(b) A medium-sized company with 600 employees produces and sells twenty different products within the 'car care' product range (for example car shampoos, polishes, touch-up paints and so on), the ultimate consumers being owners or operators of motor cars. Annual sales total £15 million and distribution is through three channels of distribution (wholesalers, retail traders and garages). There are 22 salesmen employed by the company.

Technically, the company is regarded as efficient but administratively it is backward because little money has been spent on office procedures and systems. However, the company now has the opportunity to use a computer for two, but only two, of the following tasks.

    (i)   Payroll preparation and gross pay analysis, currently done on two keyboard accounting machines

    (ii)   Stores records and stores control for materials and finished goods, currently done manually

    (iii)   Sales analysis by value per salesman, currently done manually

REQUIREMENT:

As the cost accountant, write a brief report to the managing director suggesting which two of the three tasks should be transferred to the computer, stating the reasons for your recommendations and also stating the reason(s) for excluding the other task.   **15 Marks**

Total Marks = 25

4   SPREADDEM FAIRLEY LTD   *54 mins*

Spreaddem Fairley Ltd has five cost centres.

(a)   Machining department

(b)   Assembly department

(c)   Finishing department

(d)   Stores department

(e)   Building occupancy - this cost centre is charged with all costs relating to the use of the building

In the cost accounting treatment of the costs of these cost centres, the total costs of building occupancy are apportioned before the stores department costs are apportioned.

Costs incurred during Period 7 of the current year were as follows.

(a)

Allocated costs	*Total* £	*Machining* £	*Assembly* £	*Finishing* £	*Stores* £
Indirect materials	2,800	500	1,700	600	-
Indirect wages	46,600	11,000	21,900	6,700	7,000
Power	2,000	1,500	400	100	-
Maintenance	2,600	1,900	600	100	-
Other expenses	900	300	100	200	300
	54,900	15,200	24,700	7,700	7,300

(b)

Other costs	£
Rent	3,000
Rates	800
Lighting and heating	200
Plant and equipment depreciation	19,800
Insurance on plant and equipment	1,980
Insurance on building	200
Company pension scheme	28,000
Factory administration	12,500
Contract costs of cleaning factory buildings	1,400
Building repairs	400
	68,280

(c)

General information	*Machining*	*Assembly*	*Finishing*	*Stores*
Area occupied (square metres)	3,000	4,000	2,000	1,000
Plant and equipment at cost (£'000)	1,400	380	150	50
Number of employees	100	350	150	25
Direct labour hours	24,000	80,000	35,000	-
Direct wages (£)	24,000	89,400	36,000	-
Number of stores requisitions	556	1,164	270	-

REQUIREMENTS:

(a) Prepare an overhead analysis sheet showing the basis of apportionments made (calculated to the nearest £). **15 Marks**

(b) Calculate an overhead absorption rate based on direct labour hours for the assembly department and the finishing department. **4 Marks**

(c) State brief reasons for your choice of the basis of apportionment for each overhead item or group of items. **6 Marks**

(d) State what information you would have preferred to use in apportioning the costs for any of the overhead items, instead of the information given in this question. **5 Marks**

Total Marks = 30

5   **A COMPANY** *45 mins*

A company manufactures a single product with the following variable costs per unit.

	£
Direct materials	7.00
Direct labour	5.50
Manufacturing overhead	2.00

The selling price of the product is £36.00 per unit. Fixed manufacturing costs are expected to be £1,340,000 for a period. Fixed non-manufacturing costs are expected to be £875,000. Fixed manufacturing costs can be analysed as follows.

Production department		Service department	General factory
1	2		
£380,000	£465,000	£265,000	£230,000

'General factory' costs represent space costs, for example rates, lighting and heating. Space utilisation is as follows.

	%
Production department 1	40
Production department 2	50
Service department	10

60% of service department costs are labour related and the remaining 40% machine related.

Normal production department activity is as follows.

	Direct labour hours	Machine hours	Production Units
Department 1	80,000	2,400	120,000
Department 2	100,000	2,400	120,000

Fixed manufacturing overheads are absorbed at a predetermined rate per unit of production for each production department, based upon normal activity.

REQUIREMENTS:

(a) Prepare a profit statement for a period using the full absorption costing system described above and showing each element of cost separately. Costs for the period were as per expectation, except for additional expenditure of £20,000 on fixed manufacturing overhead in production department 1. Production and sales were 116,000 and 114,000 units respectively for the period. **14 Marks**

(b) Prepare a profit statement for the period using marginal costing principles instead. **5 Marks**

(c) Contrast the general effect on profit of using absorption and marginal costing system respectively. (Use the figures calculated in (a) and (b) above to illustrate your answer.) **6 Marks**

Total Marks = 25

6   CAPET   *45 mins*

(a) The cost accountant and the financial accountant of Capet Ltd have each completed their final accounts for the year. Shown below are the manufacturing, trading and profit and loss accounts, together with a statement reconciling the cost and financial profits.

REQUIREMENTS:

Show the following accounts in the cost ledger.

(i)   Raw materials
(ii)   Work in progress
(iii) Finished goods
(iv)   Profit and loss

MANUFACTURING ACCOUNT
FOR THE YEAR ENDED 31 DECEMBER 19X1

	£'000	£'000
Raw materials		
Opening stock	110	
Purchases	640	
	750	
Less returns	(20)	
	730	
Closing stock	(130)	
		600
Direct wages		
Paid	220	
Accrued	20	
		240
Prime cost		840
Production expenses		162
Work in progress		
Opening stock	25	
Closing stock	(27)	
		(2)
Cost of goods manufactured		1,000

TRADING, PROFIT AND LOSS ACCOUNT
FOR THE YEAR ENDED 31 DECEMBER 19X1

	£'000	£'000
Sales	1,530	
Less returns	(30)	
		1,500
Cost of finished goods sold		
Opening stock	82	
Cost of goods manufactured	1,000	
	1,082	
Less closing stock	(72)	
		(1,010)
Gross profit		490
Discount received		10
		500
Administration expenses	200	
Sales expenses	70	
Discount allowed	20	
Debenture interest	10	
		(300)
Net profit for the year		200

RECONCILIATION STATEMENT	£'000	£'000	£'000
Profit shown in the financial accounts			200
Items not shown in the cost accounts			
Discount allowed		20	
Debenture interest		10	
Sales expenses		70	
Discount received		(10)	
			90
			290
Difference in stock valuation			
Opening stock, raw materials	7		
Opening stock, finished goods	9		
Closing stock, raw materials	15		
		31	
Closing stock, work in progress	(5)		
Opening stock, work in progress	(3)		
Closing stock, finished goods	(4)		
		(12)	
			19
Profit shown in the cost accounts			309

Notes

Production overhead is absorbed at a rate of two thirds of wages.

Administration overhead is written off in the period in which incurred.

20 Marks

(b) Discuss briefly the reasons for including in a cost accounting system notional interest on capital locked up in stock and its treatment in preparing a reconciliation of cost and financial profits. **5 Marks**

Total Marks = 25

7 BATCH COSTING

A printing firm is proposing offering a leaflet advertising service to local traders.

The following costs have been estimated for a batch of 10,000 leaflets.

Setting up machine	6 hours at £10 per hour
Artwork	£20 per batch
Paper	£1.80 per 100 sheets
Other printing materials	£15
Direct labour cost	4 hours at £6 per hour

Fixed overheads allocated to this side of the business are £1,000 per annum and recovered on the basis of orders received, which are expected to be two per week for 50 weeks in the year.

The management requires 25% profit on selling price.

REQUIREMENTS:

(a) Calculate a price to be quoted per 1,000 leaflets for batches of 2,000, 5,000, 10,000 and 20,000 leaflets.

(b) Calculate the individual cost per leaflet at the various batch quantities.

8 JOB COSTING SYSTEM

45 mins

The management of a large manufacturing company are considering introducing a system of job costing into their plant maintenance and repair department. At present all the expenses incurred by this department, which is regarded as a service function to the production departments, are collected and apportioned to the production departments under the expense heading 'general works expenses'.

REQUIREMENTS:

(a) Describe the benefits to the company which may result from introducing a job costing system into the plant maintenance and repair department.

8 Marks

(b) Outline the information and procedures required in order to establish the total cost of individual repair or maintenance jobs.　**17 Marks**

Total Marks = 25

9　BEAVERS LTD

During its financial year ended 30 June 19X7 Beavers Ltd, an engineering company, has worked on several contracts. Information relating to one of them is given below.

Contract X201

Date commenced	1 July 19X6
Original estimate of completion date	30 Sept 19X7
Contract price	£240,000
Proportion of work certified as satisfactorily completed (and invoiced)up to June 19X7	£180,000
Amount received from contractee	£150,000
Costs up to 30 June 19X7	
Wages	£91,000
Materials sent to site	£36,000
Other contract costs	£18,000
Proportion of head office costs	£6,000
Plant and equipment transferred to the site (at book value on 1 July 19X6)	£9,000

The plant and equipment is expected to have a book value of about £1,000 when the contract is completed.

Stock of materials at site on 30 June 19X7	£3,000
Expected additional costs to complete the contract	
Wages	£10,000
Materials (including stock at 30 June 19X7)	£12,000
Other (including head office costs)	£8,000

If the contract is completed one month earlier than originally scheduled, an extra £10,000 will be paid to the contractors. At the end of June 19X7 there seemed to be a good chance that this would happen.

REQUIREMENTS:

(a) Show the account for the contract in the books of Beavers Ltd up to 30 June 19X7 (including any transfer to the profit and loss account which you think is appropriate) and the personal account of the contractee.

(b) Show how the work in progress would be displayed on the balance sheet.

(c) Briefly justify your calculation of the profit (or loss) to be recognised in the 19X6/X7 accounts.

10　SLAGG AND HEAP LTD

(a) Slagg and Heap Ltd operates two factories, each making a different processed product.

In factory A, the standard processing loss in the single production process is 15%. The scrap from the process, which has a sales value of 20p per kilogram, is delivered immediately to a dealer who has an arrangement with the company to purchase for cash whatever scrap is produced.

In period 9, 26,000 kg of basic raw material was input to the process and 23,200 kilograms of the end product was made. The costs of production were as follows.

Raw material   80p per kg
Labour   £12,090
Overhead   100% of labour costs

There was no opening or closing stock.

REQUIREMENT:

Prepare the necessary accounts to show the result of the process.

(b) In factory B, a product called Golden Grime is made by treating input units through three consecutive and distinct processes. At each processing stage, extra materials are added to the product, and direct labour and overhead costs incurred.

Work in progress at the beginning of period 4 consisted of 12,000 units which had just completed the first process and were about to be input to the second process. The cost of these units up to this point was as follows.

	£
Direct materials	9,300
Direct labour	4,500
Overhead	3,000
	16,800

During period 4, these units were input to process 2, when additional raw materials were added at a cost of £8,400 and labour costs of £3,600 were incurred. Production overhead is applied at the rate of 160% of labour costs; actual overhead incurred during period 4 was £6,200.

During the period, 9,600 units of output were completed and transferred to process 3. Of the remaining units, it was estimated by the works engineer that half were 75% complete and the other half were 50% complete with regard to extra materials and conversion costs.

REQUIREMENT:

Write up the process 2 account for period 4, showing clearly the cost of raw material transferred to process 3 and the value of closing work in progress in period 4. Explain your treatment of production overhead.

11   TWO PROCESSES   *45 mins*

(a) 'Whilst the ascertainment of product costs could be said to be one of the objectives of cost accounting, where joint products are produced and joint costs incurred, the total cost computed for the product may depend upon the method selected for the apportionment of joint costs, thus making it difficult for management to make decisions about the future of products.'

REQUIREMENT:

Discuss the above statement and state two different methods of apportioning joint costs to joint products.   **8 Marks**

(b) A company using process costing manufactures a single product which passes through two processes, the output of process 1 becoming the input to process 2. Normal losses and abnormal losses are defective units having a scrap value and cash is received at the end of the period for all such units.

The following information relates to the four-week period of accounting period number 7.

Raw material issued to process 1 was 3,000 units at a cost of £5 per unit.

There was no opening or closing work in progress but opening and closing stocks of finished goods were £20,000 and £23,000 respectively.

	Process 1	Process 2
Normal loss as a percentage of input	10%	5%
Output in units	2,800	2,600
Scrap value per unit	£2	£5
Additional components	£1,000	£780
Direct wages incurred	£4,000	£6,000
Direct expenses incurred	£10,000	£14,000
Production overhead as a percentage of direct wages	75%	125%

REQUIREMENT:

Present the following accounts.

Process 1
Process 2
Finished goods
Normal loss
Abnormal loss
Abnormal gain
Profit and loss (so far as it relates to any of the accounts listed above)

17 Marks

Total Marks = 25

12   MINT SAUCE LTD

Mint Sauce Ltd manufactures three products, X, Y and Z, in a common process. Operating results of this process in September 19X2 were as follows.

Output		
	Product X	96,000 units
	Product Y	120,000 units
	Product Z	96,000 units

Joint operating costs during the month were £1,560,000. There were no opening stocks, but closing stocks were 6,000 units of X, 24,000 units of Y and 18,000 units of Z.

Costs are apportioned between joint products by the units method. Output was sold at the following prices per unit, to a single customer, Hungry Wolf Ltd.

X : £9   Y : £5   Z : £4

The management of Mint Sauce Ltd have been considering a proposal to carry out further processing operations on products X, Y and Z, instead of selling them to Hungry Wolf Ltd. The estimated unit costs of further processing are as follows.

	X £ per unit	Y £ per unit	Z £ per unit
Direct materials	3.00	0.60	0.90
Direct labour	4.80	2.40	3.60
Variable overhead	6.60	1.80	2.70

Prime costs would be variable, and fixed overheads of £840,000 per month would be incurred as a direct consequence of establishing the further processing operation. In addition, special equipment would have to be rented to process product Z, at a cost (not included in previous figures) of £430,000 per month.

There would be no weight loss in the further processing operation, and output of the end products X, Y and Z would sell for £20.50, £17 and £14 per unit respectively.

REQUIREMENTS:

(a) Calculate the profit made in September 19X2.

(b) Prepare a statement to assist the management of Mint Sauce Ltd in deciding whether to process products X, Y and Z further. You may assume that average monthly sales are equal to the actual sales in September 19X2.

13   STEER AND WHEEL LTD

Steer and Wheel Ltd distributes its goods to a regional dealer using a single lorry. The dealer's premises are 40 kilometres away by road. The lorry has a capacity of 10½ tonnes, and makes the journey twice a day fully loaded on the outward journeys and empty on the return journeys. The following information is available for a four-week budget control period, period 8, during 19X4.

Petrol consumption	8 kilometres per 5 litres petrol
Petrol cost	£0.36 per litre
Oil	£8 per week
Driver's wages and national insurance	£140 per week
Repairs	£72 per week
Garaging	£4 per day (based on a seven-day week)
Cost of lorry when new (excluding tyres)	£18,750
Life of the lorry	80,000 kilometres
Insurance	£650 per annum
Cost of a set of tyres	£1,250
Life of a set of tyres	25,000 kilometres
Estimated sales value of lorry at end of its life	£2,750
Vehicle licence cost	£234 per annum
Other overhead costs	£3,900 per annum

The lorry operates on a five-day week.

REQUIREMENTS:

(a) Prepare a statement to show the total costs of operating the vehicle in period 8, 19X4 analysed into running costs and standing costs.

(b) Calculate the vehicle cost per kilometre, and the cost per tonne/kilometre in the period.

(c) Using the costs you have calculated, arrive at the charge, to cover full costs, for a special delivery of 6 tonnes on an outward and a return journey to a destination 120 kilometres away, if costs are estimated on the following bases.

    (i)   On a kilometres travelled basis
    (ii)   On the basis of tonne/kilometres carried

14   BACKLOG   *45 mins*

You are employed as the administration manager of Weeble Ltd, a medium-sized software consulting and development house. A backlog of software development work has built up due to staff turnover and sickness and the partners have decided it must be cleared. It will require 2,000 software development staff hours to clear the backlog.

Three alternatives have been suggested.

(a) Cancel a development job which is estimated to need a further 2,500 hours work. It would produce a fee income of £47,000 if completed. There is no cancellation penalty clause in the contract. This action would release sufficient staff to clear the backlog within three months.

(b) Sub-contract 2,000 hours of development work to another firm at an estimated fee cost of £35,000.

(c) Employ four extra temporary staff for the next three months.

Set out below is some additional information.

(a) Software development staff are employed at an average salary of £25,000 pa and produce about 2,000 hours work pa each. Employment taxes and employers' pension contributions add a further 25% to salary costs.

(b) When pricing work for clients Weeble Ltd usually add 80% to estimated staff costs to cover overheads and profit.

(c) If the work were to be sub-contracted a senior consultant would need to spend about 80 hours overseeing the contract. Consultants work about 2,000 hours per year at an employment cost of £75,000 pa. Their time is usually charged to clients at £100 per hour.

(d) Temporary staff would be paid for the hours they work at £15 per hour. No pension contributions would be payable by Weeble Ltd.

(e) Employment tax is payable in respect of temporary staff at 15% of salary.

(f) Recruitment costs for the temporary staff (agency fees and interview expenses) are likely to be £750 each.

(g) Four extra personal computers would be needed at a cost of £2,000 each if temporary staff were employed. Their second-hand value after the work has been completed is expected to be £1,500 each. They would have a four-year life if kept. Alternatively computers could be leased for £750 per quarter each.

(h) Weeble Ltd are located in open plan offices on the third and fourth floors of a six-storey office block at a rental cost of £200 per square metre per annum. Each floor comprises 400 square metres. If temporary staff were employed forty square metres of extra space would be needed. This could be obtained by transferring the contents of 20 large filing cabinets to CD ROM at a total cost of £1,300. The cabinets could then be sold for £20 each. An alternative would be to rent a spare office (which has an area of fifty square metres) on the fifth floor of the same building for three months at a rental cost of £1,500 per quarter.

(i) Heating and lighting costs in the office block average £50 per square metre per annum and are not included in the rent.

(j) Weeble Ltd have sufficient spare desks and chairs in store for the temporary staff. This furniture was bought in 19X2 at a total cost of £3,000 and now has a second hand value of £1,500. It is partnership policy to depreciate furniture at 10% of cost per annum.

REQUIREMENTS:

(a) Advise the management which option is the most cost effective. Show your calculations. **10 Marks**

(b) For each of the 'costs' (a) to (j) above, explain why you decided to include it in or exclude it from your calculations for part (a). **12 Marks**

(c) Describe non-cost factors which would be relevant when considering the three options. **3 Marks**

Total Marks = 25

15   DIFFERENT METHODS   *45 mins*

A distribution and marketing organisation sells three products named A, B and C in two areas which are designated as Area 1 and Area 2. The information given below is for 19X0.

	Product A	Product B	Product C
Selling price per unit	£40	£48	£60
Purchase price per unit	£32	£36	£44
Sales, in units			
Area 1	92,000	40,000	28,000
Area 2	30,000	40,000	40,000

	Product A	Product B	Product C
Number of orders			
Area 1	40,000	20,000	10,000
Area 2	6,000	10,000	8,000
Volume in cubic metres per unit	2.0	1.5	1.0

	Variable	*Fixed*	*Basis of apportionment*
Costs	*£'000*	*£'000*	
Selling	188	376	Number of orders
Warehousing/distribution	432	648	Volume sold
Advertising	270	540	Units sold
Administration	64	256	Sales value

REQUIREMENTS:

(a) Prepare a budget for 19X0 showing the profit or loss for each area and in total, using absorption costing. **10 Marks**

(b) Prepare a budget for Area 1 only, using marginal costing and showing relevant information for each product and the total profit or loss for that area. **8 Marks**

(c) Comment on the result shown in your answer to (b) above and suggest action which management ought to take. **7 Marks**

Total Marks = 25

16   MINIMUM PRICING

Toby Ltd is considering replacing the production of jugs by that of cups. The accountant has provided the following figures.

	Jugs	*Cups*
	Pence	Pence
Materials	120	72
Labour	20	6
Variable overheads	10	3
	150	81
Contribution	50	
Price	200	

REQUIREMENT:

Advise the management of Toby Ltd what the minimum price per cup should be in the following circumstances.

(a) Materials are in short supply.
(b) Labour is in short supply.

17   FAST FANDANGO LTD

Fast Fandango Ltd manufactures a single product, a steel poker, which sells for £10. At 75% capacity, which is the normal level of activity for the factory, sales are £600,000.

The cost of these sales are as follows.

Direct cost per unit	£3
Production overhead	£156,000 (including variable costs of £30,000)
Sales costs	£ 80,000
Distribution costs	£ 60,000 (including variable costs of £15,000)
Administration overhead	£ 40,000 (including variable costs of £9,000)

The sales costs are fixed with the exception of sales commission which is 5% of sales value.

REQUIREMENTS:

(a) Calculate the breakeven volume of sales.

(b) Prepare statements to show the revenue, contribution and profit in the following circumstances.

  (i)   At the normal level of activity

  (ii) If the sales price is reduced by 5% and the sales volume thereby increased by $16^2/_3$% above the normal level of activity

  (iii) If the sales price is reduced by 7% and the sales volume thereby increased by 20% above the normal level of activity

(c) Calculate the C/S ratio in each instance in (b) above.

(d) Calculate what the sales volume would need to be under the sales price arrangements in (b) (iii) for the profit to be the same as in (b) (ii).

18   MANUFACTURER'S BREAKEVEN   *54 mins*

A summary of a manufacturing company's budgeted profit statement for its next financial year, when it expects to be operating at 75% of capacity, is given below.

			£	£
Sales	9,000 units at £32			288,000
Less:	Direct materials		54,000	
	Direct wages		72,000	
	Production overhead:	fixed	42,000	
		variable	18,000	
				186,000
	Gross profit			102,000
Less:	Administration, selling and distribution costs:			
	fixed		36,000	
	varying with sales volume		27,000	
				63,000
	Net profit			39,000

REQUIREMENTS:

(a) (i)   Calculate the breakeven point in units and in value.   **4 Marks**

  (ii) Draw a contribution volume (profit volume) graph.   **5 Marks**

  (iii) Calculate the profit that could be expected if the company operated at full capacity.   **2 Marks**

(b) It has been estimated that:

  (i)   if the selling price per unit were reduced to £28, the increased demand would utilise 90% of the company's capacity without any additional advertising expenditure; and

  (ii) to attract sufficient demand to utilise full capacity would require a 15% reduction in the current selling price and a £5,000 special advertising campaign.

  Present a statement showing the effect of the two alternatives compared with the original budget and advise management which of the three possible plans ought to be adopted (the original budget plan or (i) above or (ii) above).   **10 Marks**

(c) An independent market research study shows that by spending £15,000 on a special advertising campaign, the company could operate at full capacity and maintain the selling price at £32 per unit.

  (i)   Advise management whether this proposal should be adopted.
  (ii) State any reservations you might have.   **9 Marks**

                                                          Total Marks = 30

19   OVERSEAS SUPPLIER   *45 mins*

Domestic political trouble in the country of an overseas supplier is causing concern in your company because it is not known when further supplies of raw material X will be received. The current stock held of this particular raw material is 17,000 kilogrammes which cost £136,000. Based on raw material X, your company makes five different products and the expected demand for each of these, for the next three months, is given below together with other relevant information.

Product code	Kilogrammes of raw material X per unit of finished product Kg	Direct labour hours per unit of finished product Hours	Selling price per unit £	Expected demand over three months Units
701	0.7	1.0	26	8,000
702	0.5	0.8	28	7,200
821	1.4	1.5	34	9,000
822	1.3	1.1	38	12,000
937	1.5	1.4	40	10,000

The direct wages rate per hour is £5 and production overhead is based on direct wages cost, the variable overhead absorption rate being 40% and the fixed overhead absorption rate being 60%.

Variable selling costs, including sales commission, are 15% of selling price.

Budgeted fixed selling and administration costs are £300,000 per annum.

Assume that the fixed production overhead incurred will equal the absorbed figure.

REQUIREMENTS:

(a) Show what quantity of the raw material on hand ought to be allocated to which products in order to maximise profits for the forthcoming three months.   **13 Marks**

(b) Present a brief statement showing contribution and profit for the forthcoming three months, if your suggestion in (a) is adopted.   **6 Marks**

(c) Comment briefly on the analysis you used to aid the decision-making process in (a) and give three other examples of business problems where this type of analysis can be useful.   **6 Marks**

Total Marks = 25

20   POPACATAPETL LTD

Popacatapetl Ltd manufactures three products, the Poppa, the Catta and the Pettle which are produced from the same basic type of production process and use similar materials and labour.

The draft budget for the forthcoming year was submitted to the board, and the profit statement was as follows.

	Poppa £	Catta £	Pettle £	Total £
Sales	1,378,545	1,485,000	868,455	3,732,000
Direct materials	269,490	607,500	653,760	1,530,750
Direct labour	207,300	101,250	164,880	473,430
Variable overhead	72,555	101,250	101,695	275,500
Total variable costs	549,345	810,000	920,335	2,279,680
Contribution	829,200	675,000	(51,880)	1,452,320
Fixed overhead				980,000
Profit				472,320

At a meeting of the board it was decided that in view of the pessimistic outlook for the Pettle (sales of which have been gradually falling for several years) and because there was no possibility of raising its selling price, it should become a discontinued product.

Sales demand for the Poppa and Catta, on the other hand, are buoyant, and the company has so far been unable to produce sufficient of either product to meet the full demand potential. It was therefore decided that the labour force released by discontinuing production of the Pettle should be transferred, £40,500 of this transferred labour being switched to producing the Catta and the remainder to producing the Poppa. The increased production of the Poppa and the Catta is not expected to change their cost/selling price relationships.

REQUIREMENTS:

(a) Prepare the revised profit statement which would result as a consequence of the board's decision, and comment briefly on its effect.

(b) If it is believed that potential sales demand for both the Poppa and the Catta is extremely high but that the company is working at full labour capacity, describe other possible courses of action that the Board might wish to consider. You may assume that the additional sales of either product would be at the existing selling price.

21   HYMAN OLD ERSKINE FLINT LTD   *54 mins*

(a) In a few sentences, explain the functions of a cash budget and indicate its importance in budgeting and budgetary control.   **5 Marks**

(b) From the information given below you are required to prepare a cash budget for Hyman Old Erskine Flint Ltd for the months October to December 19X8.

(i)

	July £'000	Aug £'000	Sept £'000	Oct £'000	Nov £'000	Dec £'000
Sales	40	60	100	120	160	200
Direct cost of production and sales						
Materials	30	35	40	40	35	20
Labour	15	18	20	28	18	16
Overheads						
Production	16	19	22	24	18	12
Sales	6	6	12	14	15	18
Administration	8	10	10	12	8	10

(ii)   Suppliers of direct materials allow on average two months' credit.

(iii)   Wages outstanding for direct labour at the end of each month average one week's pay (one quarter of a month).

(iv)   Production overheads include depreciation of £4,000 per month. Of the remaining costs half are paid in the month they are incurred, and half in the following month.

(v)   5% of sales overhead includes a sales commission, payable one month in arrears.

(vi)   Delay in the payment of other sales and administration overhead averages one half of a month.

(vii)   A new machine costing £18,000 will be installed from the beginning of November. 20% of the cost is payable at the commencement of installation work, and the balance is payable on completion (early January 19X9).

(viii) A dividend of £30,000 is payable in October 19X8.

(ix)   A mortgage on a company property will raise £40,000 in November, and repayments of £2,000 per month will begin in December.

(x)   The cash balance on 1 October 19X8 is expected to be £5,000.

(xi)   There has been a problem with debt collection in the past, since most sales are on credit. To encourage early payment, a discount scheme was introduced on 1 July and a cash discount of 2% is offered on all cash sales and for debtors who pay within one week of sale.

(xii) 10% of sales are expected to be cash sales.

(xiii) Of credit sales, 25% are expected to take the discount. You may assume that all debtors who take the discount pay in the month of sale (although more strictly, about one quarter, who buy goods in the final week of the month, are likely to pay in the first week of the month following sale).

(xiv) Of the remainder of credit sales, half will pay in the month of sale and half in the month following sale. There are no bad debts.   **25 Marks**

Total Marks = 30

22   JAK LTD

Jak Ltd is a small company which manufactures a single product, the Anori. The company's directors have just received the actual results for May 19X3 for comparison with the budget for the same period, set out below.

	Budget	Actual results
Production and sales of the Anori (units)	40,000	48,000
	£	£
Sales revenue	50,000	55,200
Direct materials	12,000	16,800
Direct labour	8,000	10,290
Variable o/hds (allocated on basis of direct labour hrs)	5,000	5,560
Fixed overheads	15,000	16,500
Total costs	40,000	49,150
Profit	10,000	6,050

Clearly the directors of the company are concerned about the results, particularly bearing in mind that the following operational changes were authorised after the budget for May 19X3 had been prepared in the belief they would increase the profitability of Jak Ltd.

(a) The unit selling price of the Anori was cut from £1.25 to £1.15 on the 1st May 19X3 in a deliberate attempt to increase sales.

(b) To reduce operating costs it was decided to use a cheaper but more wasteful alternative material - a 15% price reduction was obtained.

(c) The hourly rate for direct labour was increased from £5.00 to £5.25 in order to encourage greater productivity. However, overtime had to be authorised during the month in order to meet demand.

(d) There was a one-off sales promotion campaign costing £2,000.

REQUIREMENT:

Prepare a flexible budget which will be useful for management control purposes.

23   STANDARD COSTS

(a) Briefly explain the term 'standard cost'.

(b) Outline the benefits which a company may obtain from a standard costing system.

(c) Discuss the problems which may arise in the development and operation of a standard costing system.

24   ARCHIMEDES LTD

Archimedes Ltd manufactures Eurekas and you are given the following information regarding the department which manufactures component X for the product.

(a) The departmental budget prepared for standard costing purposes assumes the following.

   (i)   Production: 1,000 units a week

   (ii)   Cost of powder: 1 kg at £1.80 per kg per component X

   (iii)   Cost of resin: 1 litre at £0.35 per litre per component X

   (iv)   Direct labour consists of five workers who are each paid at a rate of £2.50 per hour. In addition a piecework supplement of £10 per hundred units of component X produced is shared amongst the five workers.

   (v)   Indirect labour consists of a full time supervisor who is paid a fixed £120 per week and a cleaner who is paid £1.50 per hour for a 20-hour week.

   (vi)   Fixed overheads amount to £200 per week. This excludes the cost of indirect labour.

   (vii) Variable overheads amount to 20% of the direct wages paid.

(b) The following information is relevant to the week ended 7 April 19X0.

   (i)   1,200 units of component X were produced.

   (ii)   The actual cost of raw materials used in production was as follows.

	£
Powder	2,240
Resin	400

   1,500 kgs of powder were used and 900 litres of resin.

   (iii)   The five workers each worked the budgeted 40 hour shift, but two workers also worked five hours overtime each, which was paid at a premium rate of £3 per hour.

   (iv)   Overhead expenditure (fixed and variable) was as budgeted.

   (v)   Due to illness, the cleaner only worked three shifts of four hours each.

REQUIREMENTS:

(a) Prepare a statement showing the composition of the standard cost of component X.

(b) Prepare a statement of variances for the week ended 7 April 19X0.

25   BACKE AND SMASH LTD

Backe and Smash Ltd manufactures a brand of tennis racket, the Winsome, and a brand of squash racket, the Boastful. The budget for October was as follows.

	Winsome	Boastful
Production (units)	4,000	1,500
Direct materials: wood (£0.30 per metre)	7 metres	5 metres
gut (£1.50 per metre)	6 metres	4 metres
Other materials	£0.20	£0.15
Direct labour (£3 per hour)	30 mins	20 mins

Overheads

		£
Variable:		
power		1,500
maintenance		7,500
		9,000
Fixed:		
supervision		8,000
heating and lighting		1,200
rent		4,800
depreciation		7,000
		21,000

Variable overheads are assumed to vary with standard hours produced.

Actual results for October were as follows.

Production:	Winsome	3,700 units
	Boastful	1,890 units

		£
Direct materials, bought and used:		
wood	37,100 metres	11,000
gut	29,200 metres	44,100
other materials		1,000
Direct labour	2,200 hours	6,850
Power		1,800
Maintenance		6,900
Supervision		7,940
Heating and lighting		1,320
Rent		4,800
Depreciation		7,000

REQUIREMENT:

Calculate the cost variances which should be incorporated into the operating statement for the month of October. Assume that a standard absorption costing system is in operation.

1   CLASSIFICATION AND CODING

(a)   The CIMA *Official Terminology* defines 'classification' as 'The arrangement of items in logical groups, having regard to their nature (subjective classification) or purpose (objective classification)'. A code is defined as 'A system of symbols designed to be applied to a classified set of items, to give a brief accurate reference, facilitating entry, collation and analysis'.

Classifications are therefore groupings, and individual items can be classified according to the groupings to which they belong. Coding is a system for identifying in a shortened symbolised form the grouping that a particular item belongs to.

An example of the distinction is as follows.

Items of inventory might be classified into the broad groupings of raw materials and components and finished goods. Each item of inventory will be given a unique code, but the coding system might be used to identify the classification of inventory to which the item belongs - eg items with a code whose first digit is, say, 1 might be raw materials, whereas a first digit of say, 2 might indicate finished goods.

Coding systems for inventory can be much more elaborate and used to identify the nature of the stock items more exactly, for example, a stock code 135837 might indicate the following.

1	- Raw materials
3	- Wood
5	- Pine planks
8	- Width details
3	- Thickness details
7	- Length details

(b)   The requirements for a practical coding system are as follows.

(i)   It should provide a unique reference code for key items, such as customer account number, supplier account number, stock code number or employee number.

(ii)   It should provide a comprehensive system, whereby every recorded item can be suitably coded.

(iii)   It should be brief, to save clerical time in writing out codes and to save storage space in computer memory and on computer files.

(iv)   The likelihood of errors going undetected should be minimised. For unique reference codes, check digits should be used.

(v)   There should be no duplication of the same code for different items in the same category.

(vi)   Existing codes should be reviewed regularly, and obsolete codes removed.

(vii)   It is preferable in most cases that all codes should be of the same length. There are exceptions, however, where different length codes are used for reasons of logical construction (such as hierarchical codes) or to reflect operational requirements (for example the STD telephone exchange codes, whose differing lengths were partly dictated by the nature of the telecommunications switching system).

(viii)   Code numbers should be issued from a single central point. Different people should not be allowed to add new codes to the existing list independently.

2   REGIMENT OF THE LINE LTD

> *Tutorial note*. Using the high-low method to calculate variable costs, and understanding how contribution is calculated, are important exam topics.

Grenadier factory

The increase in cost between 80% and 90% levels of activity is the same as the increase in cost between 90% and 100% activity. Changes in cost follow a linear pattern in relation to output, that is the variable cost is the same at all levels of activity. We can see that the cost per unit is constant at all activity levels for direct materials and labour and so these are linear variable costs. However the cost per unit does not remain constant for production overhead and so it must be a semi-variable cost.

Production overhead	£
Cost at 100% activity (13,000 units)	67,000
Cost at 90% activity (11,700 units)	63,100
Variable overhead cost of 10% activity (1,300 units)	3,900
	ie £3 per unit

The fixed overhead cost is calculated as follows.

	£
Total overhead cost of 13,000 units	67,000
Variable overheads (× £3)	39,000
Fixed overhead	28,000

The direct material cost is £7 per unit and the direct labour cost is £6 per unit. The sales price is £20 per unit.

Contribution estimate at 75% level of output	£	£
Sales (9,750 units at £20)		195,000
Variable costs		
Direct materials	68,250	
Direct labour	58,500	
Variable production overhead	29,250	
Total variable costs		156,000
Contribution		39,000
Fixed overhead costs		28,000
Profit		11,000

Fusilier factory

The changes in cost at differing levels of output follow a different pattern in the Fusilier factory. The rate of increase in direct material cost declines above the 100% level and the rate of increase in direct labour cost rises above the 100% level. It is probable that some discount on extra materials is obtainable and that the labour force is paid overtime premium on the additional output. It is assumed that variable costs at 115% will be at the new rates.

Production overhead (no change in rate of cost increase above the 100% level of output)	£
Overhead cost at 110% activity (9,900 units)	60,600
Cost at 100% activity (9,000 units)	57,000
Variable overhead cost of 10% activity (900 units)	3,600
	= £4 per unit

The fixed overhead is calculated as follows.

	£
Total overhead cost of 9,000 units	57,000
Variable overheads (× £4)	36,000
Fixed overhead	21,000

The variable costs are calculated as follows.

	£
Direct materials cost at 110% activity (9,900 units)	106,650
Direct materials cost at 100% activity (9,000 units)	99,000
Variable cost of 10% activity (above 100% level) (900 units)	7,650

The variable cost of materials above the 100% capacity level = £8.50 per unit.

	£
Direct labour cost at 110% activity (9,900 units)	81,000
Direct labour cost at 100% activity (9,000 units)	72,000
Variable cost of 10% activity (above 100% level) (900 units)	9,000

The variable labour cost per unit above 100% capacity = £10 per unit

	£	£
Contribution estimate at 115% level of output (10,350 units)		
Sales (10,350 × £30)		310,500
Variable costs		
Direct material (£99,000 + (1,350 units × £8.50))	110,475	
Direct labour (£72,000 + (1,350 units × £10))	85,500	
Variable production overhead (10,350 units × £4)	41,400	
Total variable costs		237,375
Contribution		73,125
Fixed costs (overheads)		21,000
Profit		52,125

3   COST CENTRES AND UNITS

(a) (i)   The CIMA *Official Terminology* provides definitions of cost centres and cost units.

A cost centre is 'A production or service location, function, activity or item of equipment for which costs are accumulated'.

A cost unit is 'A unit of product or service in relation to which costs are ascertained'.

The common feature of the definitions is the process by which costs are ascertained and accumulated so as to provide control information for management. Examples of cost centres might be the various production or service departments in a factory (for example the machining or finishing departments, stores, canteen). Examples of cost units are given in (ii) below.

(ii)   (1)   A cost unit in a hospital might relate to the number of beds occupied or the number of patients treated. Examples might be patient/day (or bed/day) or in a casualty department each patient treated might form a cost unit.

(2)   In a road haulage business, the obvious cost unit is ton/mile, that is the costs involved in transporting one ton of freight over one mile would be accumulated.

(3)   In a hotel, a cost unit would be either bed/day occupied or room/day occupied. A slight refinement would be to treat double room/day occupied and single room/day occupied as separate cost units.

(4)   A public transport authority might want to establish the costs of transporting one passenger one mile. The cost unit would be a passenger /mile.

(b)   REPORT

To:	Managing director	
From:	Cost accountant	
Subject:	Use of computer	Date:01.01.X1

We have the opportunity to use a computer for two of the following three tasks.

Payroll preparation and gross pay analysis
Stores records and stores control
Sales analysis

We need to decide which two of the three tasks should be computerised.

All three tasks are suitable for a computer to deal with. For payroll preparation in particular there are many software packages currently on the market. However, payroll analysis is an area of very limited application. There are few useful spin-offs in terms of analysis and reports which the computer could produce. We would therefore be getting less than full value from the computer's capability. The main reason for using a computer in this area would be to save the time spent in repetitious calculations, and improve accuracy. But this task is already done on keyboard accounting machines and the improvements in timeliness and accuracy might not be very great.

The other tasks are currently done manually. Use of a computer could bring significant benefits to the company.

For stores records and stores control, packages are available which deal with issues, receipts and pricing of materials stocks; valuation of materials, work in progress and finished goods; maintenance of stock levels and calculation of optimum re-order levels. Up-to-date information would be constantly available on prices and stock availability. Eventually, if we were able to expand our computer facilities, a link would be possible between the stores system and new systems for purchase ledger, sales ledger and sales invoicing.

Sales analysis can be carried out by computer to show, amongst other things, the value of sales generated by each salesman. Extensions could cover sales by area, sales by retail outlet and so on. This would assist not only in monitoring the efficiency of salesmen, but also in assessing the value of promotional and advertising campaigns.

My recommendation is to use a computer for the tasks of stock recording and control, and sales analysis.

Signed: Cost accountant

4   SPREADDEM FAIRLEY LTD

Tutorial note. This question emphasises the range of methods that can be used to apportion overheads; you should be able to comment critically on what methods are suitable for specific situations. Note also that different absorption rates are used for the two departments.

(a)   *Building occupancy costs*

	£
Rent	3,000
Rates	800
Lighting and heating	200
Insurance on building	200
Contract costs of cleaning	1,400
Building repairs	400
	6,000

(i)   *Overhead analysis sheet - first stage*

		Total £	Machining £	Assembly £	Finishing £	Stores £
Allocated costs						
Indirect materials		2,800	500	1,700	600	0
Indirect wages		46,600	11,000	21,900	6,700	7,000
Power		2,000	1,500	400	100	0
Maintenance		2,600	1,900	600	100	0
Other expenses		900	300	100	200	300
		54,900	15,200	24,700	7,700	7,300
Apportioned costs	*Note*					
Plant depreciation	(1)	19,800	14,000	3,800	1,500	500
Plant insurance	(1)	1,980	1,400	380	150	50
Pension scheme	(2)	28,000	5,000	15,900	6,100	1,000
Factory admin	(3)	12,500	2,000	7,000	3,000	500
Building occupancy	(4)	6,000	1,800	2,400	1,200	600
		123,180	39,400	54,180	19,650	9,950

Basis of apportionment

(1)   Cost of plant and equipment

(2)   Percentage of total direct and indirect labour costs in the four departments:

	£
Direct wages (24,000 + 89,400 + 36,000)	149,400
Indirect wages	46,600
Total wages	196,000

Pension scheme costs (1/7 of wages cost) = £28,000

	Indirect wages £	Direct wages £	Total wages £	Pension costs (1/7 of wages) £
Machining	11,000	24,000	35,000	5,000
Assembly	21,900	89,400	111,300	15,900
Finishing	6,700	36,000	42,700	6,100
Stores	7,000	-	7,000	1,000
	46,600	149,400	196,000	28,000

(3) Number of employees (£12,500 ÷ 625 = £20 per employee)

(4) Area occupied (£6,000 ÷ 10,000 square metres = 60p per square metre)

(ii) *Overhead analysis sheet - second stage*

	Total £	Machining £	Assembly £	Finishing £	Stores £
Allocated and apportioned overhead	123,180	39,400	54,180	19,650	9,950
Apportionment of stores costs (see note)		2,780	5,820	1,350	(9,950)
	123,180	42,180	60,000	21,000	0

Note. Stores costs are apportioned on the basis of the number of stores requisitions.

$$\text{Stores cost} \quad \frac{£9,950}{(556 + 1,164 + 270)} = £5 \text{ per requisition}$$

(b) *Overhead absorption rates*

	Assembly department	Finishing department
Overhead cost	£60,000	£21,000
Direct labour hours	80,000	35,000
Absorption rate per direct labour hour	£0.75	£0.60

(c) The choice of the basis of apportionment involves an attempt to spread costs on a 'fair' basis, so that each department is burdened with a share of cost which appears to reflect its use of the various shared cost items.

(i) *Plant depreciation.* On the assumption that straight line depreciation is used, and that all items of equipment have the same life and no residual value, apportionment on the basis of historical cost is appropriate.

(ii) *Plant insurance.* On the assumption that the insurance cost relates to the value of the plant and that plant value is in its turn related to plant cost, plant cost would again be the appropriate basis for apportionment.

(iii) *Pension scheme.* Pension scheme costs are almost certainly related to wages and salaries costs, presumably as a percentage of these costs. The only known wages costs are direct and indirect wages in the four departments, and the basis of apportionment was therefore a percentage (or fraction) of these costs.

(iv) *Factory administration.* These costs should be apportioned in relation to the work done by the administration departments (personnel, accounting and so on) for the other departments. Labour hours might be an appropriate basis for apportionment, but given that we are not told the hours of indirect labour in any of the four departments, number of employees is chosen as the most relevant basis available.

(v) *Building occupancy.* Floor area is an apportionment basis commonly used for rent, rates and lighting. It is here assumed that all the other costs may similarly be apportioned.

(vi) *Stores department costs.* The work done by the stores department for each of the three production departments is probably most aptly reflected by the number of requisitions made by each department (on the assumption that requisitions from each department call for roughly equal amounts of stores effort).

(d)   More appropriate ways of allocating or apportioning costs might have been as follows.

    (i)   *Plant depreciation.* Actual depreciation of the plant and machinery in each department (based on expected life, residual value and depreciation method for each item of plant) would have been a better method.

    (ii)   *Plant insurance.* Information from the insurance policy as to the method of valuing plant for insurance purposes would enable a more accurate apportionment to be made.

    (iii)   *Pension scheme.* Actual pension provisions for all employees (in the four departments and in administration) should be used to allocate these costs.

    (iv)   *Factory administration.* If labour hours are preferred as the basis of apportionment, details of indirect labour hours are required.

    (v)   *Building occupancy.* Given that these costs are grouped together in one cost centre, the existing basis of apportionment is probably fair.

    (vi)   *Stores department.* On the assumption stated in (c) (vi) above, the basis of apportionment would be fair. If the assumption is inaccurate, an estimate of the time spent by the stores department in working for each of the three production departments would provide a better basis for apportionment.

As a more general and fundamental comment, it is worth noting that the overhead absorption rate is usually calculated in advance on the basis of budgeted costs and activity levels. Ideally, therefore, information about the budget would be required to calculate the absorption rates in preference to information about actual results.

5   A COMPANY

> *Tutorial note.* The different methods of calculating cost of sales and closing stock under absorption and marginal costing often catch students out in the exam. You should also note that *actual* fixed costs are deducted from contribution in the marginal costing statement.

(a)   Profit statement using absorption costing

	£'000
Sales (114,000 × £36)	4,104.0
Cost of sales (114,000 units × £25.6̇ (W3))	(2,926.0)
Gross profit	1,178.0
Non-manufacturing costs	(875.0)
Net profit (before adjustment)	303.0
Under-absorbed overhead (W4)	(64.6)
Net profit (after adjustment)	238.3

(b)   Profit statement using marginal costing

	£'000	£'000
Sales		4,104
Variable costs (116,000 × 14.5 (W5))	1,682	
Less closing stock (2,000 × 14.5)	(29)	
		(1,653)
Contribution		2,451
Fixed manufacturing costs (£1,340,000 + £20,000)	1,360	
Fixed non-manufacturing costs	(875)	
		(2,235)
Profit		216

(c)   The difference in profit shown by the two costing methods arises because of the inclusion of fixed manufacturing costs under absorption costing. Unit costs under the two methods are as follows.

	Absorption costing £	Marginal costing £
Direct labour	5.500	5.50
Direct materials	7.000	7.00
Manufacturing overhead	2.000	2.00
Department 1	5.053	-
Department 2	6.113	-
	25.666	14.50

The difference of £11.1$\dot{6}$ per unit in the value of stocks accounts for the difference of £22,333.$\dot{3}$ in the profit reported (2,000 units at £11.1$\dot{6}$ per unit).

In general the following points may be made.

(i)   If there are changes in stocks during a period, so that opening stock or closing stock values are different, marginal costing and absorption costing give different results for profit obtained. If there is a net rise in stock over the period, absorption costing will report higher profits; If there is a net fall marginal costing profit will be higher.

(ii) If the opening and closing stock volumes and values are the same, the same profit figure is given by both methods.

Workings

1   Allocation of fixed manufacturing costs

	Department 1 £	Department 2 £	Service department £	General factory £
Initial allocation	380,000	465,000	265,000	230,000
General factory costs (4:5:1)	92,000	115,000	23,000	(230,000)
	472,000	580,000	288,000	
General factory costs (W2)	134,400	153,600	(288,000)	
	606,400	733,600		
Normal production (units)	120,000	120,000		
Absorption rate per unit	5.053	6.113		

2   Allocation of service department costs

The costs of £288,000 (W1) are to be split 60:40 between labour and machines and are then allocated to the two divisions on the basis of machine hours and labour hours respectively.

	Dept 1 £	Dept 2 £	Total £
Labour (8:10)	76,800	96,000	172,800
Machines (1:1)	57,600	57,600	115,200
	134,400	153,600	288,000

3   Total manufacturing costs per unit

	£
Direct materials	7.000
Direct labour	5.500
Manufacturing overhead	2.000
Fixed overhead: department 1 (W1)	5.053
department 2 (W2)	6.113
	25.666

4   Under-absorbed overhead

	£
Department 1: £(20,000 + ((120,000 – 116,000) × 5.053)	40,213.3
Department 2: £((120,000 – 116,000) × 6.113)	24,453.3
	64,666.6

5   Variable costs per unit

		£
Direct materials		7.00
Direct labour		5.50
Manufacturing overhead		2.00
		14.50

6   CAPET

> *Tutorial note.* This question is typical of questions in this area in that raw materials, work in progress and finished goods accounts all contain balancing figures.

(a)   *Note* CLC = cost ledger control account

(i)   RAW MATERIALS

	£'000		£'000
Bal b/f (110-7)	103	Returns - CLC	20
Purchases - CLC	640	Work in progress*	578
		Bal c/f (130 + 15)	145
	743		743

* The transfer to work in progress is deduced as the balancing figure on the account.

(ii)   WORK IN PROGRESS

	£'000		£'000
Bal b/f (25+3)	28	Finished goods (bal)	984
Raw materials	578	Bal c/f (27–5)	22
Direct wages -CLC	240		
Production overhead (^{2}/3 × £240)	160		
	1,006		1,006

(iii)   FINISHED GOODS

	£'000		£'000
Bal b/f (82–9)	73	Cost of sales (bal)	989
Work in progress	984	Bal c/f (72–4)	68
	1,057		1,057

(iv)   PROFIT AND LOSS

	£'000		£'000
Cost of sales	989	Sales (net) - CLC	1,500
Production overheads under-absorbed(162–160)	2		
Gross profit c/d	509		
	1,500		1,500
Admin expenses	200	Gross profit b/d	509
Net profit	309		
	509		509

(b)   In some industries (for example the manufacture of whisky) large amounts of capital are tied up in stock held for a number of years until they reach maturity. A cost accounting system which failed to account for the substantial costs of such an investment in stocks might be seriously misleading.

When the cost and financial profits are reconciled the notional interest should already have been added back or credited in the costing profit and loss account, therefore no adjustment should be necessary. If the notional interest has not been added back then the amount of interest would be added to the cost accounts profit to arrive at the financial accounts profit.

7   BATCH COSTING

> *Tutorial note.* The profit is 25% on selling price ie Cost (75) + Profit (25) = Selling price (100), and thus profit = $^1/_3$ cost).

Expected orders per annum = 2 orders × 50 weeks = 100 orders

∴ Fixed overhead per order = $\dfrac{£1,000}{100}$ = £10

(a)   *Calculation of price per 1,000 leaflets*

Batch size: (leaflets)	2,000	5,000	10,000	20,000
	£	£	£	£
Setting up machine	60.00	60.00	60.00	60.00
Artwork	20.00	20.00	20.00	20.00
Paper	36.00	90.00	180.00	360.00
Other printing materials	3.00	7.50	15.00	30.00
Direct labour cost	4.80	12.00	24.00	48.00
Fixed overhead	10.00	10.00	10.00	10.00
Total cost	133.80	199.50	309.00	528.00
Profit	44.60	66.50	103.00	176.00
Selling price	178.40	266.00	412.00	704.00
Price per 1,000 leaflets	89.20	53.20	41.20	35.20

(b)   Individual cost per leaflet   £0.0069   £0.0399   £0.0309   £0.0264

8   JOB COSTING SYSTEM

(a)   In order to describe the benefits of introducing a job costing system into the plant maintenance and repair department, it is first advisable to consider what is thereby involved.

Job costing means that, as the year develops, all maintenance and repair costs are identified as relating to a number of larger 'jobs' which arise during the year. The expense of these jobs may then be properly attributed to the department(s) responsible for them.

With the above explanation, it may be seen that the following benefits may arise from the introduction of the new system.

(i)   *Realistic apportionment*
Because of the identification of expenses with jobs, and the subsequent attribution of these to the department(s) responsible, costs are then borne by those who incurred them. This is preferable to apportionment with other 'general works expenses' which may be somewhat arbitrary and thus unrealistic.

(ii)   *Increased responsibility*
It is to be hoped that because of the above more realistic apportionment, managers of departments will become more responsible in their attitude to plant maintenance and repair expenses, only incurring such costs when they are needed (or alternatively preempting the need for costly repairs by organising earlier and cheaper, preventative measures).

(iii)   *Expense analysis*
Because of the division of plant maintenance and repair expenses into more manageable 'jobs', it will be possible to determine which of those expenses are 'one-off', and which are to be expected to recur periodically. The greatest use for this facility is described below.

(iv)   *Budgeting*
The above analysis would allow for more realistic budgeting each year, since the make-up of plant maintenance and repair would be more fully understood.

(v)   *Control*
With a more realistic budget, the calculation of variances would then readily highlight actual departures from planned expenditure, and control action could then be promptly taken.

(b)   The answer to this part of the question should contain the following points.

	Information	*Procedures required to retrieve this information*
(i)	The existence of different jobs during the year should be recognised.	A responsible official within the factory should take the decision as to what constitutes a new job (rather than a continuation of an old) for costing purposes.
(ii)	All elements relating to a particular job should be properly identified and collated.	A job card should be raised for each job (probably at the same time as the decision taken above).
	(1) Labour	The work force should enter their hours on the job on the job card.
	(2) Any spare parts, from stores, should be included.	As items are taken from stores, their identity should be noted on the job card.
	(3) Any parts especially bought in for repairs/maintenance should not be over-looked.	All invoices relating to repairs/maintenance should be so identified; details should then be entered on the job card.

The above three objectives would be more easily met if each job had a number ascribed to it; this would be written on the job card itself.

In addition, a 'job log' book should be kept, ensuring no duplication of numbers used and enhancing control over the length of time taken over jobs and so on.

(iii)   The costs relating to (ii)(1), (2), (3) above should be properly calculated...

Once a job has been completed it should be sent to the accounts department for costing.

(1)   Labour should be costed at the standard rate applicable to that grade.

(2)   Parts should be costed at their standard cost.

(3)   The procedures identified at (ii)(3) above might well be carried out at this stage.

(iv)   ...and recorded in the books of account.

(v)   The overheads attributable to the plant repairs and maintenance cost centre should be established.

The same absorption rate for these expenses, probably based on labour hours, should be established and utilised.

(vi)   These overheads should be absorbed into jobs.

This should be done using the above absorption rates.

(vii)   Jobs should then be ascribed to the departments responsible.

9 BEAVERS LTD

> *Tutorial note.* Provided that reasons and assumptions are stated, alternative solutions may be acceptable. In particular, it would be acceptable to apportion the estimated total profit on the basis of the cost of work done instead of its invoice value.

(a)

CONTRACT ACCOUNT X201

	£		£
Wages	91,000	Stock c/d	3,000
Materials	36,000	Plant c/d (£9,000 – £6,400)*	2,600
Other costs	18,000	Costs incurred to date	154,400
Head office costs	6,000		
Plant and equipment	9,000		
	160,000		160,000

* Total expected loss of value of plant = £8,000. Proportion to be allocated to contract to date = 12 months/15 months × £8,000 = £6,400.

CONTRACTEE ACCOUNT

	£		£
Work certified	180,000	Bank	150,000
		Balance c/d	30,000
	180,000		180,000

Working

	£	£	£
Contract price			240,000
Actual costs to date			
Wages	91,000		
Materials	33,000		
Other costs	18,000		
HO costs	6,000		
Plant	6,400		
		154,400	
Expected future costs			
Wages	10,000		
Materials	12,000		
Other costs	8,000		
Plant	1,600		
		31,600	
			186,000
Estimated total profit			54,000

Proportion recognised in the current year:

$$\frac{£180,000}{£240,000} \times £54,000 = £40,500$$

Of this, £180,000 is allocated to turnover and £139,500 is allocated to cost of sales

$$\frac{£180,000}{£240,000} \times £186,000 = £139,500$$

(b) BALANCE SHEET (EXTRACT)

	£
Fixed assets	
Plant	2,600
Current assets	
Stocks: long term contract balances (W1)	14,900
Debtors: amounts recoverable on long-term contracts (W2)	30,000

Workings

		£
1	Costs incurred to date	154,400
	Less allocated to cost of sales	139,500
		14,900

2   Amounts recognised as turnover   180,000
     Less progress payments received   150,000
                                                     30,000

This is effectively the balance on the contractee account.

(c) The contract is nearing completion and so credit has been taken for profit in direct proportion to the work certified as completed. The possible bonus has been ignored on the grounds of prudence as there appears to be an element of uncertainty. It is also assumed that profit is accrued evenly in proportion to the completed work and that no provisions have to be made in respect of penalties or other possible contingencies.

10   SLAGG AND HEAP LTD

> *Tutorial note.* In (a) necessary accounts are the process account, the scrap account, and the abnormal loss or gain account. There is insufficient information to prepare other accounts. Note that scrap value of *abnormal* gain has no impact on the process account.

Workings

(i)   *Expected output and losses*

                                                    Units
      Expected output (85% × 26,000)   22,100
      Normal loss (15% × 26,000)   3,900
      Abnormal gain (23,200 – 22,100)   1,100

(ii) *Costs of input*

                                                      £
      Material (26,000 × 80p)   20,800
      Labour   12,090
      Overhead   12,090
                                                     44,980
      Less scrap value of normal loss (15% of 26,000 × 20p)   780
                                                     44,200

      Costs per unit
      Expected output units   22,100 units
      Cost per unit   £2

(iii) *Total costs*

                                                      £
      Output (23,200 × £2)   46,400
      Abnormal gain (1,100 × £2)   2,200

(iv)   PROCESS ACCOUNT, PERIOD 9

	kg	£		kg	£
Raw material	26,000	20,800	Normal loss (scrap)	3,900	780
Labour		12,090	Finished goods	23,200	46,400
Overhead		12,090			
	26,000	44,980			
Abnormal gain	1,100	2,200			
	27,100	47,180		27,100	47,180

                         ABNORMAL GAIN ACCOUNT

	kg	£		kg	£
Scrap a/c (loss in revenue due to shortfall of scrap)	1,100	220	Process account	1,100	2,200
Profit and loss a/c		1,980			
	1,100	2,200		1,100	2,200

SCRAP ACCOUNT

	kg	£		kg	£
Process account			Cash (actual sales)	2,800	560
(normal loss)	3,900	780	Abnormal gain a/c	1,100	220
	3,900	780		3,900	780

(b) (i) STATEMENT OF EQUIVALENT UNITS

		Equivalent units	
	Total units	Process 1 materials	Added material plus labour and overhead
Output to process 3	9,600	9,600	9,600
Closing work in progress:			
(see note)			
one half (75%)	1,200	1,200	900 (75%)
one half (50%)	1,200	1,200	600 (50%)
	12,000	12,000	11,100

Note. Closing work in progress is complete with regard to input material from process 1, half the units are 75% complete regarding additional material and labour and overhead and half are 50% complete.

(ii) STATEMENT OF COST PER EQUIVALENT UNIT

	Process 1 materials	Added material plus labour and overhead
Cost in period 4	£16,800	£17,760 (note 1)
Equivalent units	12,000	11,100
Cost per equivalent unit = £3	£1.40	£1.60

Note 1	£
Direct material	8,400
Direct labour	3,600
Overhead (160% of labour)	5,760
	17,760

(iii) STATEMENT OF EVALUATION OF COST

		Closing WIP		
	Output to process 3	One half (75%)	One half (50%)	Total
	£	£	£	£
Process 1 material	13,440	1,680	1,680	16,800
Other costs	15,360	1,440	960	17,760
	28,800	3,120	2,640	34,560

The value of closing work in progress is therefore £5,760 (£3,120 + £2,640).

PROCESS 2 ACCOUNT PERIOD 4

	Units	£		Units	£
From process 1	12,000	16,800	Process 3	9,600	28,800
Added materials		8,400			
Direct labour		3,600	Closing WIP c/d	2,400	5,760
Overhead		5,760			
	12,000	34,560		12,000	34,560
WIP b/f	2,400	5,760			

Production overhead	£
Overhead incurred	6,200
Overhead absorbed	5,760
Under-absorbed overhead (taken to profit and loss account)	440

11   TWO PROCESSES

> *Tutorial note.* In (b) the scrap value of normal loss is deducted from other costs in order to calculate cost per unit.

(a)   Where joint products are produced, the total cost of a product will include an arbitrary apportionment of the joint costs which were incurred before the separation point - sometimes called the pre-separation point costs.

These total costs are not useful for management decision making, because they include the joint costs which cannot be altered by any action taken concerning the products after the separation point.

Decision makers should concentrate on any incremental or post-separation point costs, so that they can consider these costs in conjunction with any incremental revenue when making decisions.

Notwithstanding their lack of usefulness for management decision making, joint costs are often apportioned for purposes such as long-run pricing and for stock valuations. Two methods of apportioning joint costs to joint products could be selected from the following.

(i)   Sales value at separation point.

(ii)   Physical measurement at separation point.

(iii)   Notional sales value at separation point (final sales value less post-separation point costs), used when products are not saleable at the separation point.

(b)   (i)   *Expected output and losses*

Process 1

	Units
Expected output (90% × 3,000)	2,700
Normal loss (10% × 3,000)	300
Abnormal gain (2,800 − 2,700)	100

Process 2

	Units
Expected output (95% × 2,800)	2,660
Normal loss (5% × 2,800)	140
Abnormal loss (2,660 − 2,600)	60

(ii)   *Cost per unit*

$$\text{Cost per unit} = \frac{£(15,000+1,000+4,000+10,000+3,000-600)}{(2,800-100)}$$

$$= \frac{£32,400}{2,700}$$

$$= £12 \text{ per unit}$$

$$\text{Cost per unit} = \frac{£(33,600+780+6,000+14,000+7,500-700)}{2,600+60}$$

$$= \frac{£61,180}{2,660}$$

$$= £23 \text{ per unit}$$

(iii)   *Total costs*

See process accounts

(iv)

PROCESS 1

	Units		£		Units		£
Raw material	3,000		15,000	Process 2	2,800	(× £12)	33,600
Additional components			1,000	Normal loss			
Direct wages			4,000	(10% × 3,000)	300	(× £2)	600
Direct expenses			10,000				
Production o/head			3,000				
Abnormal gain	100	(× £12)	1,200				
	3,100		34,200		3,100		34,200

PROCESS 2

	Units	£		Units		£
Process 1	2,800	33,600	Finished goods	2,600	(× £23)	59,800
Additional components		780	Normal loss			
Direct wages		6,000	(5% × 2,800)	140	(× £5)	700
Direct expenses		14,000	Abnormal loss	60	(× £23)	1,380
Production o/head		7,500				
	2,800	61,880		2,800		61,880

FINISHED GOODS

	£		£
Balance b/f	20,000	Cost of sales (balancing figure)	56,800
Process 2	59,800	Balance carried forward	23,000
	79,800		79,800

NORMAL LOSS/SCRAP STOCK

	Units	£		Units		£
Process 1	300	600	Abnormal gain			
Process 2	140	700	- process 3	100	(× £2)	200
Abnormal loss			Cash	400		1,400
- process 2	60	(× £5) 300				
	500	1,600		500		1,600

ABNORMAL LOSS

	Units	£		Units		£
Process 2	60	1,380	Normal loss/			
			scrap stock	60	(× £5)	300
			Profit and loss			1,080
	60	1,380		60		1,380

ABNORMAL GAIN

	Units		£		Units	£
Normal loss/				Process 1	100	1,200
scrap stock	100	(× £2)	200			
Profit and loss			1,000			
	100		1,200		100	1,200

PROFIT AND LOSS ACCOUNT (EXTRACT)

	£		£
Abnormal loss	1,080	Abnormal gain	1,000

12   MINT SAUCE LTD

> *Tutorial note.* In (a) the units method was specified as the method for allocating joint costs. Alternative methods may be specified in the exam. Note in (b) the key calculation was *not* whether further processing was profitable, but whether it was as profitable an option as not carrying out further processing.

(a)

Product	Units produced	% of total	Joint cost apportionment
X	96,000	30.77	480,000
Y	120,000	38.46	600,000
Z	96,000	30.77	480,000
	312,000	100.00	1,560,000

The apportionment of joint costs to products is at the rate of £5 per unit. This is also the value of units of closing stock.

September 19X2	X £'000	Y £'000	Z £'000	Total £'000
Opening stocks	0	0	0	0
Cost of production	480	600	480	1,560
	480	600	480	1,560
Less closing stocks	30	120	90	240
Cost of sales	450	480	390	1,320
Sales	810	480	312	1,602
Profit	360	0	(78)	282

(b)   The revenue from further processing, net of further processing costs, must exceed the sales value of the part-processed products if the new scheme is to be viable.

	X	Y	Z	*Total*
Monthly sales (units)	90,000	96,000	78,000	
Unit price	£20.50	£17.00	£14.00	
Further variable costs per unit	£14.40	£4.80	£7.20	

	X £'000	Y £'000	Z £'000	*Total* £'000
Revenue	1,845.0	1,632.0	1,092.0	4,569.0
Further variable costs	1,296.0	460.8	561.6	2,318.4
	549.0	1,171.2	530.4	2,250.6
Extra fixed costs				(840.0)
Equipment rental				(430.0)
				980.6
Revenue from part-finished products, A, B and C per month (see (a))				1,602.0
Loss of profit from further processing				621.4

Conclusions

There would be a loss of profit from further processing of £621,400 per month and the further processing operation is not viable either for all three products together, or (on the information available) for any product on its own. Further processing of product Y alone, for example, would earn a contribution of £1,171,200 per month, but this would be insufficient to cover both the fixed costs of £840,000 and also the revenue of £480,000 obtainable from the sale of the part-finished product Y.

13   STEER AND WHEEL LTD

> *Tutorial note.* A catch in this type of question is often that kilometres travelled do not equal kilometres travelled fully loaded (as here). Remember when calculating tonne/km the important figure is km travelled *with* a load.

(a)   Kilometres travelled per day $40 \times 2 \times 2 = 160$ km
      Kilometres travelled in the period 160×5 days $\times 4$ weeks $= 3,200$ km
      Kilometres travelled in the period fully loaded
      (½ of 3,200)   1,600 km
      Tonnes carried, per trip   10½ tonnes
      Tonnes/kilometres in the period   16,800 tonne/kilometres

STATEMENTS OF COSTS PERIOD 8 19X4

(i) *Running costs*

	£
Petrol (3,200 kms ÷ 8 km per 5 litres × £0.36 per litre)	720
Oil (£8 × 4 weeks)	32
Repairs (£72 × 4 weeks)	288
Wages (£140 × 4 weeks)	560
Tyres cost ((£1,250 ÷ 25,000 km) × 3,200 km)	160
Depreciation (((£18,750 − 2,750) ÷ 80,000 km) × 3,200 km)	640
Running costs	2,400

* Depreciation is assumed to be a running cost, charged on distance travelled, rather than a fixed charge per period.

(ii) *Standing costs*

	£
Garaging (£4 per day × 7 days × 4 weeks)	112
Insurance (£650 ÷ 13)	50
Licence cost (£234 ÷ 13)	18
Other overheads (£3,900 ÷ 13)	300
Standing costs	480

(iii) *Total costs*

	£
Running costs	2,400
Standing costs	480
Total costs, period 8	2,880

(b) Cost per km travelled $\dfrac{£2,880}{3,200 \text{ km}}$ = £0.90 per km

Cost per tonne/km $\dfrac{£2,880}{16,800 \text{ tonne / km}}$ = £0.171 per tonne/km

(c) To deliver six tonnes to a destination 120 km away, and to return loaded with a further six tonnes, 240 km would be travelled and the tonne/kilometres would be 240 × 6 = 1,440 tonne/kilometres.

The charge would be calculated as follows.

(i) On a kilometre basis of costs, 240 kilometres × £0.90 = £216.00
(ii) On a tonne/kilometre basis of costs, 1,440 tonne/kilometres × £0.171 = £246.24

14 BACKLOG

> *Tutorial note.* Make sure you understand in this question the reasons why some costs are relevant costs, some costs are not relevant.

(a) *Option 1 (cancel job)*

	£
Cost of cancelling job	47,000

Option 2 (sub-contract)

	£
Fee	35,000
Lost revenue from senior consultant's work (80 × £100)	8,000
	43,000

Option 3 (temporary staff)

	£
Temporary staff pay (£15 × 2,000 × 4 × ¼)	30,000
Temporary staff employment tax (15% × £30,000)	4,500
Recruitment costs (£750 × 4)	3,000
Computers, lower of:	
Purchase cost = (4 × £(2,000 − 1,500)) = £2,000	
Lease cost = 4 × £750 = £3,000	2,000
Office space (and heat and light), lower of	
*Transfer to CD ROM = (£(1,300 − (20 × £20) + (40 × £50))) = £2,900	
Spare office = £1,500 + (£50 × 50) = £4,000	2,900
	42,400

*Assume space made free by removal of filing cabinets requires heating and lighting.

Option 3 is the most cost effective.

(b) (i) *Exclude (a)*. The costs associated with the employment of software development staff will be incurred regardless of the option chosen and hence they are not relevant to the decision.

(ii) *Exclude (b)*. Since the employment costs will be paid regardless of whether or not the job is cancelled, the information about the margin is irrelevant. It is the total fee income which is affected by the decision.

(iii) *Include (c)*. If the consultant has to oversee the contract he will be unable to work for other clients and hence the revenue from such work will be lost. The employment costs will be incurred regardless of the decision taken and so are not relevant.

(iv) *Include (d)*. Temporary staff will only be paid if the decision is taken to employ them.

(v) *Include (e)*. Employment tax is only payable if the decision is taken to employ the temporary staff.

(vi) *Include (f)*. Recruitment costs will only be incurred if the temporary staff are employed.

(vii) *Include (g)*. The costs associated with each alternative are relevant since they will only be incurred if temporary staff are employed. The following assumptions are made.

(1) The organisation will sell the computers after the work has been completed so as to recoup some of the cash outlay and hence the information about their life is not relevant.

(2) The organisation will choose the cheapest of the two alternatives.

(viii) *Include (h)*. The costs associated with both alternatives are relevant and it is assumed that the company would choose the cheapest alternative. Either the cost associated with the transfer to CD ROM or the rental cost of the spare office would only be incurred if temporary staff were employed.

(ix) *Include (i)*. If extra space is needed because of taking on the temporary staff then the heating and lighting costs will be incurred.

(x) *Exclude (j)*. The purchase price of the furniture is a sunk cost. The second-hand value has not been included as an opportunity cost since it is assumed that the furniture is not being sold if it is not required. Depreciation is not a cash flow and hence is never relevant in a decision-making situation.

(c) Non-cost factors relevant when considering the three options are as follows.

(i) Cancelling the job may have commercial implications which could affect the long-term profitability of the organisation. Potential customers may be loath to deal with Weeble, fearing that other jobs may be cancelled. Alternatively customers might demand that high cancellation penalty clauses be inserted into future contracts.

(ii) The reliability of any firm subcontracted to do the work should be checked. Weeble will, of course, lose a certain degree of control over the work should it be sub-contracted.

(iii) Weeble would need to ensure that the temporary staff had the necessary skills and expertise to perform the development work.

(iv) The effect on the organisation's software development staff of the option chosen should be considered.

15   DIFFERENT METHODS

> *Tutorial note.* The marginal costing information demonstrates all three products are making a positive contribution in area 1; this is not apparent from the absorption costing statement.

(a)   BUDGET FOR 19X0 - ABSORPTION COSTING

	Area 1				Area 2				Total
	A	*B*	*C*	*Total*	*A*	*B*	*C*	*Total*	*Total*
	£'000	£'000	£'000	£'000	£'000	£'000	£'000	£'000	£'000
Sales revenue	3,680	1,920	1,680	7,280	1,200	1,920	2,400	5,520	12,800
Purchase cost	2,944	1,440	1,232	5,616	960	1,440	1,760	4,160	9,776
Gross profit	736	480	448	1,664	240	480	640	1,360	3,024
Overhead costs (i)									
Selling costs	240	120	60	420	36	60	48	144	564
Wareh/distn costs (ii)	460	150	70	680	150	150	100	400	1,080
Advertising	276	120	84	480	90	120	120	330	810
Administration	92	48	42	182	30	48	60	138	320
Profit/(loss)	(332)	42	192	(98)	(66)	102	312	348	250

Notes

(i)   Absorption costing does not distinguish between fixed and variable costs, therefore the total costs are apportioned using the bases given.

(ii)   Calculation of volume sold, to use as basis of apportionment:

	Area 1			Area 2			Total
	A	B	C	A	B	C	
Sales units ('000)	92	40	28	30	40	40	
× volume in m3 per unit	× 2.0	× 1.5	× 1.0	× 2.0	× 1.5	× 1.0	
Volume sold	184	60	28	60	60	40	432

(b)   A marginal costing statement does not apportion fixed costs to products, but treats them instead as an overall period cost.

BUDGET FOR 19X0 - MARGINAL COSTING

	Area 1			
	A	*B*	*C*	*Total*
	£'000	£'000	£'000	£'000
Sales revenue	3,680.0	1,920.0	1,680.0	7,280.0
Purchase cost	2,944.0	1,440.0	1,232.0	5,616.0
Gross contribution	736.0	480.0	448.0	1,664.0
Variable overhead costs				
Selling costs (iii)	80.0	40.0	20.0	140.0
Wareh/distrn costs (iv)	184.0	60.0	28.0	272.0
Advertising (v)	92.0	40.0	28.0	160.0
Administration (vi)	18.4	9.6	8.4	36.4
Net contribution	361.6	330.4	363.6	1,055.6
Fixed costs				1,153.6
Loss				(98.0)

Notes			Total cost apportioned to area 1 (from a)	Variable cost proportion	Variable cost apportioned
(iii)	Selling costs:	A	240		80.0
		B	120	$\times \dfrac{188}{376 + 188}$	40.0
		C	60		20.0
(iv)	Warehousing costs:	A	460		184.0
		B	150	$\times \dfrac{432}{432 + 648}$	60.0
		C	70		28.0

Notes			Total cost apportioned to area 1 (from a)	Variable cost proportion	Variable cost apportioned
(v)	Advertising:	A	276		92.0
		B	120	$\times \dfrac{270}{270 + 540}$	40.0
		C	84		28.0
(vi)	Administration:	A	92		18.4
		B	48	$\times \dfrac{64}{64 + 256}$	9.6
		C	42		8.4

(c) The result shown in the answer to (b) above indicates that although area 1 makes an overall loss, it does earn a contribution towards the apportioned fixed costs. If it can be assumed that fixed costs would be incurred even if area 1 was discontinued, then management should continue to operate in area 1.

Management should concentrate on improving the contribution earned in area 1, which will involve an investigation of the individual product contributions.

	A	B	C
Gross contribution to sales %	20.0	25.0	26.7
Net contribution to sales %	9.8	17.2	21.6

Product A's profitability in terms of gross contribution is lower than B and C, and the difference in the net contribution percentages is even more marked.

Management actions which could be taken are as follows.

(i) Sell proportionately more of products B and C, as long as sales are not inter-related.

(ii) Raise the price of A, as long as this does not result in a significant drop in sales.

(iii) Seek a cheaper supplier for A, or perhaps negotiate a discount with the current supplier.

(iv) Exercise tighter control over the variable overhead costs associated with product A.

16 MINIMUM PRICING

Tutorial note. The opportunity cost which must be taken into account is the contribution from the alternative foregone.

(a) *Materials in short supply:* at present the production of jugs gives a contribution of 50p per 120p of materials used. Each cup will require 72p of materials and the contribution must be at least $72/120 \times 50p = 30p$.

The minimum price is 81p + 30p = 111p.

(b) *Labour in short supply:* jugs give a contribution of 50p per 20p of labour which is 250% of labour cost. Each cup will require 6p of labour, and the contribution must be at least 250% of 6p = 15p.

The minimum price is 81p + 15p = 96p.

17 FAST FANDANGO LTD

> *Tutorial note.* The vital first stage in this question is to split fixed and variable overheads.

(a) Sales are 60,000 units at the normal level of activity. Variable overheads at 60,000 units of production/sales are as follows.

	£	£ per unit
Production overhead	30,000	0.50
Sales costs (5% of £600,000)	30,000	0.50
Distribution costs	15,000	0.25
Administration overhead	9,000	0.15
	84,000	1.40
Direct costs	180,000	3.00
Total variable costs	264,000	4.40
Sales revenue	600,000	10.00
Contribution	336,000	5.60

At breakeven point, the contribution exactly covers fixed costs.

	£
Fixed costs	
Production overhead	126,000
Sales costs	50,000
Distribution costs	45,000
Administration overhead	31,000
	252,000

The contribution/sales ratio is 5.6/10 = 56%.

Breakeven sales can be calculated in two ways.

$$\frac{\text{Contribution required}}{\text{Contribution per unit}} \quad or \quad \frac{\text{Contribution required}}{\text{C / S ratio}}$$

$$= \frac{£252,000}{£5.60} \quad or \quad \frac{£252,000}{56\%}$$

$$= \quad 45,000 \text{ units} \quad or \quad £450,000$$

(b) (i)

	£
Sales	600,000
Variable costs (as in (a))	264,000
Contribution	336,000
Fixed costs (as in (a))	252,000
Profit	84,000

(ii)

	£	£
Sales (70,000 units × £9.50)		665,000
Variable costs		
Direct costs (70,000 × £3)	210,000	
Production overhead (70,000 × £0.50)	35,000	
Sales costs (5% of £665,000)	33,250	
Distribution costs (70,000 × £0.25)	17,500	
Administration overhead (70,000 × £0.15)	10,500	
		306,250
Contribution		358,750
Fixed costs		252,000
Profit		106,750

(iii)

	£	£
Sales (72,000 units × £9.30)		669,600
Variable costs		
Direct costs (72,000 × £3)	216,000	
Production overhead (72,000 × £0.50)	36,000	
Sales costs (5% of £669,600)	33,480	
Distribution costs (72,000 × £0.25)	18,000	
Administration overhead (72,000 × £0.15)	10,800	
		314,280
Contribution		355,320
Fixed costs		252,000
Profit		103,320

(c) The C/S ratio is:

(i) $\dfrac{£336,000}{£600,000}$ = 56%

(ii) $\dfrac{£358,750}{£665,000}$ = 53.95%

(iii) $\dfrac{£355,320}{£669,600}$ = 53.06%

(d) Under the (b)(iii) scheme, if the required profit is £106,750 the required contribution is £358,750.

	£
Profit	106,750
Plus fixed costs	252,000
Required contribution	358,750

Contribution per unit = £355,320 ÷ 72,000 = £4.935

Required sales units = $\dfrac{£358,750}{£4.935}$ = 72,695 units

18 MANUFACTURER'S BREAKEVEN

(a) (i)

	£'000	£'000
Sales		288
Variable costs: direct materials	54	
direct wages	72	
production overhead	18	
variable administration costs, and so on	27	
		171
Contribution		117

Contribution per unit = $\dfrac{£117,000}{9,000}$ = £13

Breakeven point = $\dfrac{\text{Fixed costs}}{\text{Contribution per unit}}$ = $\dfrac{£42,000 + £36,000}{£13}$

= 6,000 units

6,000 units × £32 = £192,000 sales value

(ii)

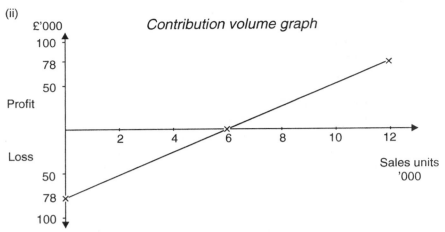

Contribution volume graph

(iii) Assuming that cost behaviour patterns remain the same if activity increases to 100% capacity, a profit of £78,000 can be expected.

	£'000
Contribution (12,000 × £13)	156
Less: fixed production overhead	42
fixed administration costs, and so on	36
Profit	78

(b) *Alternative (i)*

	£'000
Sales (£28 × 10,800 units)	302.4
Variable costs (£171,000 × $\frac{90}{75}$)	205.2
Contribution	97.2
Fixed costs	78.0
Profit	19.2

Alternative (ii)

	£'000	£'000
Sales (£27.20 × 12,000 units)		326.4
Variable costs (£171,000 × $\frac{100}{75}$)		228.0
Contribution		98.4
Fixed costs - budgeted	78.0	
- special advertising	5.0	
		83.0
Profit		15.4

A unit price of £32, as suggested in the original budget plan, should be adopted, as it produces the highest profit of £39,000.

(c) (i)

	£'000	£'000
Sales (£32 × 12,000 units)		384
Variable costs (as (b)(ii))		228
Contribution		156
Fixed costs: budgeted	78	
advertising	15	
		93
Profit		63

The proposed advertising campaign generates a considerable increase in profit and should be adopted.

(ii) Reservations about the recommendation are as follows.

(1) The advertising expenditure has to be incurred before results are known. This increases the risk involved and raises the breakeven point.

(2) How reliable is the market research information?

(3)   Does the company have any contingency plans in case the campaign generates more demand than the company can satisfy?

19   **OVERSEAS SUPPLIER**

> *Tutorial note.* Remember we are interested in *contribution per unit of scarce resource.* Fixed overheads absorbed are not relevant to the decision in (a). It is not necessary in this question to calculate the usage of material if maximum sales are achieved since it is obvious from the data given in the question that this will exceed material available.

(a)   As shown by working 1, product 702 gives the highest contribution per kg of X consumed, followed by products 701 and 822. As X is in short supply, we should aim to maximise profit within this constraint by making the most profitable use of material X. With this in mind, we will manufacture the maximum amounts of 702 and 701 which we can sell, and use the remaining X to manufacture the next most profitable product, 822, as per working 2.

(b)

	702 £	701 £	822 £	Total £
Sales revenue	201,600	208,000	228,000	637,600
Variable costs	(99,360)	(132,000)	(142,800)	(374,160)
Contribution	102,240	76,000	85,200	263,440
Fixed costs	(17,280)	(24,000)	(19,800)	(61,080)
Admin and selling (£300,000 ÷ 4)				(75,000)
Profit				127,360

(c)   The example above is of decision making in a situation where there is a limiting factor. In this it is the shortage of material X. The scarce resource has to be used as efficiently as possible in order to maximise profit. This kind of analysis can also be used in the following types of situation.

(i)   Where labour is in short supply, either because of a shortage of people or skills, so that contribution per labour hour must be maximised.

(ii)   Where machine capacity is a constraint. The most profitable use of machine hours must be adopted.

(iii)   Where sales demand is limited, so that the most profitable products must be sold.

Workings

1   *Cost of product*

	701 £	702 £	821 £	822 £	937 £
Material	5.60	4.00	11.20	10.40	12.00
Labour	5.00	4.00	7.50	5.50	7.00
Variable production overhead					
(40% × wages)	2.00	1.60	3.00	2.20	2.80
Variable selling cost	3.90	4.20	5.10	5.70	6.00
Total variable cost	16.50	13.80	26.80	23.80	27.80
Selling price	26.00	28.00	34.00	38.00	40.00
Contribution per unit	9.50	14.20	7.20	14.20	12.20
Contribution per kg	13.57	28.40	5.14	10.92	8.13
Ranking	2	1	5	3	4

2   *Production schedule*

			Usage kg
1	7,200 units of 702 = 7,200 × 0.5 kg		3,600
2	8,000 units of 701 = 8,000 × 0.7 kg		5,600
3	6,000 units of 822 = 6,000 × 1.3 kg		7,800
			17,000

Suggested solutions

20   POPACATAPETL LTD

(a)   The direct labour force will be switched from producing the Pettle to the Poppa and the Catta.

	£
Production of the Poppa	124,380
Production of the Catta	40,500
	164,880

Sales, direct material costs, variable overhead costs and contribution of these products will all rise in the same proportion as the increase in labour costs.

	Poppa	*Catta*
Increase =	$\dfrac{(207,300 + 124,380)}{207,300}$	$\dfrac{(101,250 + 40,500)}{101,250}$
	= 1.6 times	= 1.4 times

Revised profit statement for the forthcoming year

	Poppa £	*Catta* £	*Total* £
Sales	2,205,672	2,079,000	4,284,672
Direct materials	431,184	850,500	1,281,684
Direct labour	331,680	141,750	473,430
Variable overhead	116,088	141,750	257,838
Total variable costs	878,952	1,134,000	2,012,952
Contribution	1,326,720	945,000	2,271,720
Fixed overhead			980,000
Profit			1,291,720

Note. Compared with the original draft budget, this revised budget shows the following.

(i)   A 14.8% increase in turnover
(ii)   A 56.4% increase in contribution
(iii)   A 173.5% increase in profit
(iv)   A reduction of 11.7% in variable costs

A combination of higher receipts and lower payments must result in a considerable improvement in the cash flow position of the company.

(b)   (i)   If there is potential sales demand for even more units of Poppa or Catta, the company should perhaps consider whether an increase in production capacity is possible.

       (ii)   If an increase in capacity is not possible owing to the limiting factor of direct labour, the company might be able to improve its profit by switching resources from producing Catta, or vice versa.

The contribution per unit of limiting factor (per £1 direct labour cost) is as follows.

	Poppa	*Catta*
Original budgeted contribution	£829,200	£675,000
Original budgeted labour cost	£207,300	£101,250
Contribution per £1 of labour cost	£4	£6.67

Since Catta earns a higher contribution per £1 of labour cost, a switch of production from the Poppa to the Catta would yield a higher profit.

       (iii)   A further possibility would be to produce the Poppa and the Catta at the levels in the revised budget, but to increase the sales price of each product and thereby increase profit.

21   HYMAN OLD ERSKINE FLINT LTD

(a)   A cash budget is used to estimate cash receipts and cash payments during the forthcoming period. The cash flows in this period of time (typically one year) will be analysed into smaller time periods (usually months) for control purposes.

The importance of cash budgeting lies in the fact that a company may be operating profitably, but may still run short of cash. A cash shortage would threaten the company with liquidation. Conversely, a cash surplus can be used more efficiently if management are forewarned of its timing and duration.

It is therefore essential in budgeting that there will either be a sufficiency of cash or a large enough overdraft facility, throughout the budget period. Should actual cash flows differ from the budget in any control period, management is in a position to estimate the consequences of this change on liquidity, and to attempt whatever remedial action might be necessary.

(b)   HYMAN OLD ERSKINE FLINT LTD
      CASH BUDGET

	October £	November £	December £	Total £
Receipts				
Discount sales (W1)	38,220	50,960	63,700	152,880
Non-discount sales (W1)	74,250	94,500	121,500	290,250
Mortgage		40,000		40,000
	112,470	185,460	185,200	483,130
Payments	£	£	£	£
Trade creditors	35,000	40,000	40,000	115,000
Wages (W2)	26,000	20,500	16,500	63,000
Production overhead (W3)	19,000	17,000	11,000	47,000
Sales commission (W4)	600	700	750	2,050
Other sales overhead (W4)	12,350	13,775	15,675	41,800
Administrative overhead (W5)	11,000	10,000	9,000	30,000
New machine		3,600		3,600
Mortgage			2,000	2,000
Dividend	30,000			30,000
	133,950	105,575	94,925	334,450
	£	£	£	£
Receipts less payments	(21,480)	79,885	90,275	148,680
Opening cash balance	5,000	(16,480)	63,405	5,000
Closing cash balance	(16,480)	63,405	153,680	153,680

Workings

1	July £'000	Aug £'000	Sept £'000	Oct £'000	Nov £'000	Dec £'000
Sales	40.00	60.00	100.00	120.00	160.00	200.00
Cash sales (10%)	4.00	6.00	10.00	12.00	16.00	20.00
Credit sales	36.00	54.00	90.00	108.00	144.00	180.00
Credit sales with discount (25%)	9.00	13.50	22.50	27.00	36.00	45.00
Other credit sales	27.00	40.50	67.50	81.00	108.00	135.00
Total sales with discount (cash and credit)	13.00	19.50	32.50	39.00	52.00	65.00
Discount (2%)				0.78	1.04	1.30
Cash receipts				38.22	50.96	63.70
Other credit sales (see above)	27.00	40.50	67.50	81.00	108.00	135.00
Receipts	13.50					
		13.50				
		20.25				
			20.25			
			33.75			
				33.75		
				40.50		
					40.50	
					54.00	
						54.00
						67.50
				74.25	94.50	121.50

Suggested solutions

2

Wages

	Total £'000	Oct £'000	Payable in Nov £'000	Dec £'000
Wages incurred in:				
September	20	5		
October	28	21	7.0	
November	18		13.5	4.5
December	16			12.0
		26	20.5	16.5

3

Production overhead

	Total £'000	Oct £'000	Payable in Nov £'000	Dec £'000
Overhead excluding depreciation:				
September	18	9		
October	20	10	10	
November	14		7	7
December	8			4
		19	17	11

4

Sales overhead	Sept £	Oct £	Nov £	Dec £	Total £
Overhead	12,000	14,000	15,000	18,000	
Commission (5%)	600	700	750	900	
Other costs	11,400	13,300	14,250	17,100	
Which are payable in					
October	5,700	6,650			12,350
November		6,650	7,125		13,775
December			7,125	8,550	15,675

5

Administration overhead

	Total £'000	Oct £'000	Payable in Nov £'000	Dec £'000
Overhead incurred in				
September	10	5		
October	12	6	6	
November	8		4	4
December	10			5
		11	10	9

22 JAK LTD

> *Tutorial note.* The hint dropped in this question is that the report should be useful for management control purposes ie variances should be highlighted.

Comparison of budget and actual results for May 19X3

	Budget	Flexed budget	Actual results	Variance
Production and sales of the Anori (units)	40,000	48,000	48,000	
	£	£	£	
Sales	50,000	60,000	55,200	(4,800)
Direct materials	12,000	14,400	16,800	(2,400)
Direct labour	8,000	9,600	10,290	(690)
Variable overheads	5,000	6,000	5,560	440
Fixed overheads	15,000	15,000	16,500	(1,500)
Total costs	40,000	45,000	49,150	(4,150)
Profit	10,000	15,000	6,050	(8,950)

23   STANDARD COSTS

(a)   *Standard cost*

A standard cost is a predetermined cost calculated in relation to a prescribed set of working conditions, correlating technical specifications and scientific measurements of materials and labour to the prices and wage rates expected to apply during the period to which the standard cost is intended to relate (with an addition of an appropriate share of budgeted overhead if absorption costing is used).

The CIMA *Official Terminology* defines standard cost as 'The planned unit cost of products, components or services produced in a period' whose main uses are 'in performance measurement, control, stock valuation and the establishment of selling prices'.

(b)   *The benefits of standard costing*

   (i)   Carefully planned standards are an aid to more accurate budgeting.

   (ii)   Standard costs provide a yardstick against which actual costs can be measured.

   (iii)   The setting of standards involves determining the best materials and methods which may lead to economies.

   (iv)   A target of efficiency is set for employees to reach and cost-consciousness is stimulated.

   (v)   Variances can be calculated which enable the principle of 'management by exception' to be operated. Only the variances which exceed acceptable tolerance limits need to be investigated by management with a view to control action.

   (vi)   Standard costs and variance analysis can provide a way of motivation to managers to achieve better performance. However, care must be taken to distinguish between controllable and non-controllable costs in variance reporting.

(c)   *Problems of standard costing*

   (i)   Deciding how to incorporate inflation into planned unit costs.

   (ii)   Agreeing a short-term labour efficiency standard (current, attainable or ideal).

   (iii)   Deciding on the quality of materials to be used (a better quality of material will cost more, but perhaps reduce material wastage).

   (iv)   Deciding on the appropriate mix of component materials, where some change in the mix is possible (for example in the manufacture of foods and drink).

   (v)   Estimating materials prices where seasonal price variations or bulk purchase discounts may be significant.

   (vi)   Finding sufficient time to construct accurate standards. Standard-setting can be a time-consuming process.

   (vii)   Incurring the cost of setting up and maintaining a system for establishing standards.

   (viii)   Dealing with possible behavioural problems. Managers responsible for the achievement of standards might resist the use of a standard costing control system for fear of being blamed for any adverse variances.

24   ARCHIMIDES LTD

(a)   STANDARD COST PER UNIT

		£
Material:	powder	1.80
	resin	0.35
Labour:	direct (W1)	0.60
	indirect (W2)	0.15
Variable overheads		0.12
Fixed overheads (W3)		0.20
		3.22

Note. Indirect labour and fixed overheads have been absorbed on a basis of production levels and not on a basis of labour hours.

(b)   STATEMENT OF VARIANCES FOR THE WEEK ENDED 7.4.X0

	£
Budgeted cost of budgeted production (1,000 × £3.22)	3,220
Increased production (200 × £3.22)	644
Budgeted cost of actual production	3,864

	Adverse £	Favourable £	
Raw materials variances (W4)			
Powder price		460	
Resin price	85		
Powder usage	540		
Resin usage		105	
Direct labour variances (W5)			
Efficiency		75	
Rate	5		
Indirect labour variances (W6)			
Volume		30	
Expenditure		12	
Fixed overhead variances (W7)			
Volume		40	
	630	722	92 (F)
Actual expenditure on actual production			3,772

Workings

1   *Direct labour*

$$\text{Budgeted cost per component} = \frac{5 \text{ workers} \times 40 \text{ hours} \times £2.50\,/\,\text{hr}}{1,000 \text{ units}} = £0.50$$

$$\text{Piecework supplement} = \frac{£10}{100} = £0.10 \text{ per component}$$

$\therefore$ Budgeted direct labour cost per component = £0.60

2   *Indirect labour*

$$\text{Budgeted cost per component} = \frac{£(120 + (20 \times 1.50))}{1,000} = £0.15$$

3   *Fixed overheads*

$$\text{Budgeted cost per component} = \frac{£200}{1,000} = £0.20$$

4   *Powder price variance*

	£
1,500 kgs should have cost (× £1.80)	2,700
but did cost	2,240
Variance	460 (F)

Resin price variance

	£
900 litres should have cost (× £0.35)	315
but did cost	400
Variance	85 (A)

Powder usage variance

1,200 units should have used (× 1kg)	1,200 kgs
but did use	1,500 kgs
Variance in kgs	300 kgs (A)
× standard cost per kg	× £1.80
Variance in £	£540 (A)

Resin usage variance

1,200 units should have used (× 1 litre)	1,200 litres
but did use	900 litres
Variance in litres	300 litres (F)
× standard cost per litre	× £0.35
Variance in £	£105 (F)

5   *Direct labour efficiency*

1,200 units should have taken $\left(\times \left(\dfrac{5 \times 40}{1,000} \right) hr \right)$	240 hrs
but did take ((5 × 40) + 10)	210 hrs
Variance in hrs	30 hrs (F)
× standard rate per hour	× £2.50
Variance in £	£75 (F)

Direct labour rate

	£
210 hours should cost (× £2.50)	525
but did cost ((5 × 40 × £2.50) + (2 × 5 × £3)	530
Variance	5 (A)

6   *Indirect labour expenditure*

	£
Budgeted expenditure (1,000 × £0.15)	150
Actual expenditure (£120 + (£1.50 × 12)	138
Variance	12 (F)

Indirect labour volume

(Actual − budgeted volume) × standard rate per unit = 200 × £0.15 = £30 (F)

7   *Fixed overhead volume variance*

(Actual − budgeted volume) × standard rate per unit = 200 × £0.20 = £40 (F)

25   **BACKE AND SMASH LTD**

Materials price variance

	£	£
37,100 metres of wood should cost (× £0.30)	11,130	
but did cost	11,000	
Wood price variance		130 (F)
29,200 metres of gut should cost (× £1.50)	43,800	
but did cost	44,100	
Gut price variance		300 (A)
Wood and gut price variance		170 (A)

Material usage variance

3,700 units of Winsome should use	(× 7m)	25,900 m	(× 6 m)	22,200 m
1,890 units of Boastful should use	(× 5m)	9,450 m	(× 4 m)	7,560 m
		35,350 m		29,760 m
Together they did use		37,100 m		29,200 m
Material usage variance in metres		1,750 m(A)		560 m (F)
× standard cost per metre		× £0.30		× £1.50
Material usage variance				
Wood		£525 (A)		
Gut				£840 (F)

Other materials cost variance

	£
3,700 units of Winsome should cost (× £0.20)	740.00
1,890 units of Boastful should cost (× £0.15)	283.50
	1,023.50
Together they did cost	1,000.00
Other materials cost variance	23.50 (F)

Direct labour rate

	£
2,200 hours of labour should cost (× £3)	6,600
but did cost	6,850
Direct labour rate variance	250 (A)

Direct labour efficiency

3,700 units of Winsome should take (× 30 minutes)	1,850 hrs
1,890 units of Boastful should take (× 20 minutes)	630 hrs
	2,480 hrs
Together they did take	2,200 hrs
Efficiency variance in hrs	280 hrs (F)
× standard rate per hour	× £3
Direct labour efficiency variance	£840 (F)

Variable overhead costs

	Hours	Units
Budgeted hours:Winsome	2,000	4,000
Boastful	500	1,500
	2,500	

	£
Power cost per standard hour (£1,500 ÷ 2,500 hrs)	0.60
Maintenance cost per standard hour (£7,500 ÷ 2,500 hrs)	3.00
	3.60

Variable overhead efficiency variance

= (as labour) 280 hours (F) × £3.60 =   £1,008 (F)

	£	£
Variable overhead cost of 2,200 hours should be (× £3.60)		7,920
but was: power	1,800	
maintenance	6,900	
		8,700
Variable overhead expenditure variance		780 (A)

Fixed overhead

Budgeted fixed costs	£21,000
Budgeted hours (see (f))	2,500 hrs
Absorption rate per hour	£8.40

Fixed overhead expenditure variance

	Budgeted expenditure £	Actual expenditure £	Expenditure variance £
Supervision	8,000	7,940	60 (F)
Heating and lighting	1,200	1,320	120 (A)
Rent	4,800	4,800	-
Depreciation	7,000	7,000	-
Total	21,000	21,060	60 (A)

Fixed overhead volume variance

	£	£
Actual production at standard rates		
Winsome (3,700 × £8.40 × ½ hr)	15,540	
Boastful (1,890 × £8.40 × $\frac{1}{3}$ hr)	5,292	
Budgeted production at standard rates		20,832
Winsome (4,000 × £8.40 × ½ hr)	16,800	
Boastful (1,500 × £8.40 × $\frac{1}{3}$ hr)	4,200	21,000
		168 (A)

Class questions

1   MARGINAL AND ABSORPTION

45 mins

Discuss the relative advantages of accounting systems based upon full absorption and marginal costing principles, and provide a simplified example of the likely format of an income statement for management for each system.

25 Marks

2   THE PARTY SOFA LTD

Collette O'Day, the managing director of The Party Sofa Ltd has asked you, as cost accountant, to prepare certain information about the costs of various production orders (for custom-built furniture).

Work on four orders (job numbers 355 to 358) made up the entire production effort in week no. 38.

You are aware of the following balances at the beginning of week 38.

	£
Raw materials	41,600
Work in progress	82,000
Finished goods (awaiting delivery)	12,000
Under-/over-absorbed overhead account	3,400 (debit balance)

The work in progress account is supported by the following job cost sheets.

Job number	Direct materials £	Direct labour £	Production overhead £	Total cost £
355	11,200	9,500	13,300	34,000
356	16,600	6,000	8,400	31,000
357	5,000	5,000	7,000	17,000
	32,800	20,500	28,700	82,000

During week 38, the following transactions occurred.

	£
Raw material purchases	23,500
Special components for Job No 358	700
Material requisitions from store for	
Job No 355	7,200
356	5,600
357	6,300
358 (excludes special components)	4,100
Transfer of materials from Job no 356 to Job no 358	1,300

Direct labour employees			£
Total time recorded	8,700 hours		18,000
including Job No 355	(1,400 hours)		3,000
356	(2,400 hours)		4,500
357	(1,800 hours)		4,000
358	(2,600 hours)		5,100

	£
Indirect labour employees	4,800
Supervision	2,600
Employer's national insurance contributions	1,800
Depreciation of machinery	2,900
Factory depreciation	1,000
Heating and lighting	500
Power	300
Maintenance	3,600
Indirect materials issued to production from stores	4,700
Other production overhead expenses	2,900

Production overhead is applied at the rate of £2.50 per direct labour hour.

At the end of week 38 Job No 355 was completed and delivered to the customer. The invoiced value of the job was £55,000.

REQUIREMENTS:

(a) Show the raw materials control account for week 38.

(b) Calculate the profit on Job no 355.

(c) Calculate the closing value of the work in progress for each remaining job at the end of week 38.

(d) Calculate the balance in the under-/over-absorption of overhead account at the end of week 38.

(e) Explain briefly how the utilisation and efficiency of the labour force could be measured, for control purposes.

3   BRADMORE BUILDERS LTD

Bradmore Builders Ltd are a firm of building contractors. In the present conditions of slack trade they have only one current contract. Operating data for the contract for the year ended 30 June 19X4 is as follows.

Contract A

	£
Contract price	620,000
Value of work certified	570,000
Cash received from contractee	480,000
Work in progress at 1 July 19X3	447,850
Costs incurred during the year:	
Materials	46,412
Labour	31,283
Overhead excluding depreciation	12,513
Plant - valuation at 1 July 19X3	83,465
Plant - valuation at 30 June 19X4	87,220
Plant - purchased during year 19X3/X4	21,478
Cost of work not yet certified	3,458

The contract is nearing completion and the quantity surveyors estimate that a further £25,000 will be incurred to complete the job, and that any plant remaining on the site will be sold for £70,000 at completion. No further plant purchases are planned for this contract.

The work in progress for the contract as at 1 July 19X3 included an estimated profit of £26,480.

REQUIREMENT:

Draft the appropriate ledger accounts to record the transactions disclosed above in the books of Bradmore Builders Ltd, and show how they would appear in the balance sheet as at 30 June 19X4.

4   PROCESS 3   *45 mins*

The following data are available in respect of Process 3 for the month of April.

	£
Direct materials added in process	776
Direct labour	386
Production overhead	768

Transfer from Process 2: 4,200 units valued at £1,560
Transfer to Process 4:   3,650 units

Stock at 1 April: 600 units valued at £390
    degree of completion:

materials added in process	40%
labour	50%
overhead	60%

Stock at 30 April: 800 units
    degree of completion:

materials added in process	80%
labour	70%
overhead	60%

Units scrapped: 350
    degree of completion:

materials added in process	100%
labour	100%
overhead	100%

Normal loss is 10% of throughput

All units scrapped can be sold for £0.10 per unit.

REQUIREMENTS:

Prepare the following.

(a) A statement showing the cost per unit of production and the value of the output

18 Marks

(b) An account for Process 3   **5 Marks**

(c) An abnormal loss or abnormal gain account   **2 Marks**

Total Marks = 25

5 DISCRETIONARY

(a) A drug company has initiated a research project which is intended to develop a new product. Expenditures to date on this particular research total £500,000 but it is now estimated that a further £200,000 will need to be spent before the product can be marketed. Over the estimated life of the product the profit potential has a net present value of £350,000.

REQUIREMENT:

Advise management whether they should continue or abandon the project. Support your conclusion with a numerate statement and state what kind of cost the £500,000 is.

(b) Opportunity costs and notional costs are not recognised by financial accounting systems but need to be considered in many decisions taken by management.

REQUIREMENT:

Explain briefly the meanings of opportunity costs and notional costs; give two examples of each to illustrate the meanings you have attached to them.

6 LOCAL AUTHORITY   *45 mins*

(a) Identify and discuss briefly five assumptions underlying breakeven analysis.
10 Marks

(b) A local authority, whose area includes a holiday resort situated on the east coast, operates, for 30 weeks each year, a holiday home which is let to visiting parties of children in care from other authorities. The children are accompanied by their own house mothers who supervise them throughout the holiday. From six to fifteen guests are accepted on terms of £100 per person per week. No differential charges exist for adults and children.

Weekly costs incurred by the host authority are as follows.

	£ per guest
Food	25
Electricity for heating and cooking	3
Domestic (laundry, cleaning and so on) expenses	5
Use of minibus	10

Seasonal staff supervise and carry out the necessary duties at the home at a cost of £11,000 for the 30-week period. This provides staffing sufficient for six to ten guests per week but if eleven or more guests are to be accommodated, additional staff at a total cost of £200 per week are engaged for the whole of the 30-week period.

Rent, including rates for the property, is £4,000 per annum and the garden of the home is maintained by the council's recreation department which charges a nominal fee of £1,000 per annum.

REQUIREMENTS:

(i) Tabulate the appropriate figures in such a way as to show the breakeven point(s) and comment on your figures. **8 Marks**

(ii) Draw a chart to illustrate your answer to (b) (i) above. **7 Marks**

Total Marks = 25

7 SPRINGER
45 mins

The management of Springer plc is considering next year's production and purchase budgets.

One of the components produced by the company, which is incorporated into another product before being sold, has a budgeted manufacturing cost as follows.

	£ per unit
Direct material	14
Direct labour (4 hours at £3 per hour)	12
Variable overhead (4 hours at £2 per hour)	8
Fixed overhead (4 hours at £5 per hour)	20
Total cost	54

Trigger plc has offered to supply the above component at a guaranteed price of £50 per unit.

REQUIREMENTS:

(a) Considering cost criteria only, advise management whether the above component should be purchased from Trigger plc. Any calculations should be shown and assumptions made, or aspects which may require further investigation should be clearly stated. **7 Marks**

(b) Explain how your advice would be affected by each of the two *separate* situations shown below.

(i) As a result of recent government legislation if Springer plc continues to manufacture this component the company will incur additional inspection and testing expenses of £56,000 per annum, which are not included in the above budgeted manufacturing costs. **7 Marks**

(ii) Additional labour cannot be recruited and if the above component is not manufactured by Springer plc, the direct labour released will be employed in increasing the production of an existing product which is sold for £90 and which has a budgeted manufacturing cost as follows.

	£ per unit
Direct material	10
Direct labour (8 hours at £3 per hour)	24
Variable overhead (8 hours at £2 per hour)	16
Fixed overhead (8 hours at £5 per hour)	40
Total cost	90

All calculations should be shown.   **7 Marks**

(c)   The production director of Springer plc recently stated the following.

'We must continue to manufacture the component as only one year ago we purchased some special grinding equipment to be used exclusively on manufacture of this component. The equipment cost £100,000, it cannot be resold or used elsewhere and if we cease production of this component we will have to write off the written down book value which is £80,000.'

Draft a brief reply to the production director commenting on his statement.

4 Marks

Total Marks = 25

8   **DOODLE LTD**

Doodle Ltd manufactures and sells a range of products, one of which is the squiggle.

The following data relates to the expected costs of production and sale of the squiggle.

Budgeted production for the year	11,400 units
Standard details for one unit:	
direct materials	30 metres at £6.10 per metre
direct wages	
Department P	40 hours at £2.20 per hour
Department Q	36 hours at £2.50 per hour

Budgeted costs and hours per annum
    Variable production overhead (factory total)

Department P	£525,000 : 700,000 hours
Department Q	£300,000 : 600,000 hours

Fixed overheads to be absorbed by the squiggle

Production	£1,083,000 (absorbed on a direct labour hour basis)
Administration	£125,400 (absorbed on a unit basis)
Marketing	£285,000 (absorbed on a unit basis)

REQUIREMENTS:

Prepare a standard cost sheet for the squiggle, to include the following.

(a)   Standard total direct cost
(b)   Standard variable production cost
(c)   Standard production cost
(d)   Standard full cost of sale

Calculate the standard sales price per unit which allows for a standard profit of 10% on the sales price.

9   **NANOOK OF THE NORTH LTD**

Nanook of the North Ltd manufactures a single product, the SK Mow. The standard cost card for this item is as follows.

	£	£
Direct materials:		
P (8 kg at £0.40 per kg)	3.20	
Q (4 kg at £0.70 per kg)	2.80	
		6.00
Direct labour (3 hours at £2.50)		7.50
Variable production overhead (3 hours at £0.50)		1.50
Fixed production overhead (3 hours at £2.00)		6.00
		21.00

The standard sales price per unit is £25. The budgeted production and sales for period 7 were 3,000 units and the budgeted fixed production overhead (from which the fixed cost per unit was derived) was £18,000. Budgeted administration, selling and distribution overheads of £5,000 are excluded from standard costs.

Actual results for period 7 were as follows.

Sales and production	2,800 units	
Sales revenue	£71,200	
Direct materials purchased:		
P 19,000 kg	Cost £7,500	Materials used 24,100 kg
Q 14,000 kg	Cost £10,250	Materials used 10,100 kg

Direct labour 8,600 hours   Cost £24,100

It is known that 300 hours of this labour was recorded as idle time.

Variable production overhead	£4,100
Fixed production overhead	£18,450
Administration, sales and distribution overhead	£5,200

All stocks are valued at standard cost.

REQUIREMENT:

Prepare an operating statement reconciling the budgeted profit in period 7 with the actual profit.

Glossary
and Index

Abnormal gain The gain resulting when actual loss is less than the normal or expected loss.

Abnormal loss The loss resulting when actual loss is greater than the normal or expected loss.

Absorbed overhead Overhead attached to products or services by means of absorption rates. (CIMA *Official Terminology*)

Absorption costing A method of costing that, in addition to direct costs, assigns all, or a proportion of, production overhead costs to cost units by means of one or a number of *overhead absorption rates*. (CIMA *Official Terminology*)

Activity based costing (ABC) An approach to the costing and monitoring of activities which involves tracing resource consumption and costing final outputs. Resources are assigned to activities and activities to cost objects based on consumption estimates. The latter utilise cost drivers to attach activity costs to outputs. (CIMA *Official Terminology*)

Activity-based management (ABM) System of management which uses activity-based cost information for a variety of purposes including cost reduction, cost modelling and customer profitability analysis.

Activity cost pool A grouping of all cost elements associated with an activity. (CIMA *Official Terminology*)

Activity driver A measure of the frequency and intensity of the demands placed on activities by cost objects. For example, the number of customer orders measures the consumption of order entry activities by each customer. (CIMA *Official Terminology*)

Activity driver analysis The identification and evaluation of the activity drivers used to trace the cost of activities to cost objects. It may also involve selecting activity drivers with potential to contribute to the cost management function, with particular reference to cost reduction. (CIMA *Official Terminology*)

Administrative expenses Cost of management, secretarial, accounting and other services, which cannot be related to the separate production, marketing or research and development functions. (CIMA *Official Terminology*)

Attainable standard A standard which can be attained if a standard unit of work is carried out efficiently, a machine properly operated or a material properly used. Allowances are made for normal losses, waste and machine downtime.

Avoidable costs The specific costs of an activity or sector of a business which would be avoided if that activity or sector did not exist. (CIMA *Official Terminology*)

Basic standard A long-term standard which remains unchanged over the years and is used to show trends.

Batch A group of similar articles which maintains its identity throughout one or more stages of production and is treated as a cost unit. (CIMA *Official Terminology*)

Batch costing A form of specific order costing in which costs are attributed to batches of product. (CIMA *Official Terminology*)

Bill of materials A detailed specification, for each product produced, of the subassemblies, components and materials required, distinguishing between those items which are purchased externally and those which are manufactured in house. (CIMA *Official Terminology*)

Breakeven chart A chart which indicates approximate profit or loss at different levels of sales volume within a limited range. (CIMA *Official Terminology*)

Breakeven point The level of activity at which there is neither profit nor loss. (CIMA *Official Terminology*)

Breakeven (cost-volume-profit (CVP)) analysis The study of the interrelationships between costs, volume and profit at various levels of activity.

Budget A quantitative statement, for a defined period of time, which may include planned revenues, expenses, assets, liabilities and cash flows. A budget provides a focus for the organisation, aids the co-ordination of activities, and facilitates control. Planning is achieved by means of a fixed *master budget*, whereas control is generally exercised through the comparison of actual costs with a *flexible budget*. (CIMA *Official Terminology*)

Budgetary control The establishment of budgets relating to the requirements of a policy, and the continuous comparison of actual with budgeted results, either to secure by individual action the objectives of that policy, or to provide a basis for its revision. (CIMA *Official Terminology*)

Budget committee Ideally comprises representatives from every part of the organisation and oversees the budgeting process by coordinating and allocating responsibility for budget preparation, timetabling, providing information to assist in budget preparation and monitoring the budgeting and planning process by comparing actual and budgeted results.

Budget manual A detailed set of documents that provides information and guidelines about the budgetary process.

Budget period The period for which a budget is prepared and used, which may then be sub-divided into control periods. (CIMA *Official Terminology*)

Budgeted capacity Standard hours planned for the period, taking into account budgeted sales, supplies, workforce availability and efficiency expected. (CIMA *Official Terminology*)

By-product Output of some value produced incidentally in manufacturing something else (main product). *See* joint products. (CIMA *Official Terminology*)

CAD Computer-Aided Design. The use of a computer to assist with the design of a product such that diagrammatic representations of the product may be easily reproduced and amended on display or print. (CIMA *Computing Terminology*)

CAM Computer-Aided Manufacture. The use of computers (and, more specifically, computerised techniques such as computer-aided design, hence CAD/CAM) as an aid to the manufacturing process. (CIMA *Computing Terminology*)

Cash budget A detailed budget of cash inflows and outflows incorporating both revenue and capital items. In Government accounting, budgets for cash expenditure are referred to as *cash limits*. (CIMA *Official Terminology*)

Centre Department, area or function to which costs and/or revenues are charged. (CIMA *Official Terminology*)

Classification The arrangement of items in logical groups having regard to their nature (subjective classification) or purpose (objective classification). (CIMA *Official Terminology*)

Code A system of symbols designed to be applied to a classified set of items to give a brief accurate reference, facilitating entry, collation and analysis. (CIMA *Official Terminology*)

Committed costs Costs arising from prior decisions, which cannot, in the short run, be changed. Committed cost incurrence often stems from strategic decisions concerning capacity, with resulting expenditure on plant and facilities. Initial control of committed costs at the decision point is through investment appraisal techniques. (CIMA *Official Terminology*)

Continuous operation costing *See process costing.*

Contract costing A form of specific order costing in which costs are attributed to individual contracts. (CIMA *Official Terminology*)

Contribution Sales value less variable cost of sales. It may be expressed as total contribution, contribution per unit or as a percentage of sales. (CIMA *Official Terminology*)

Contribution/profit-volume (P/V) graph Graph showing the effect on contribution and on overall profits of changes in sales volume or value. (CIMA *Official Terminology*)

Control account A ledger account which collects the sum of the postings into the individual accounts which it controls. The balance on the control account should equal the sum of the balances on the individual accounts, which are maintained as subsidiary records. (CIMA *Official Terminology*)

Control limits Quantities or values outside which managerial action is triggered. (CIMA *Official Terminology*)

Controllable cost A cost which can be influenced by its budget holder. (CIMA *Official Terminology*)

Cost accounting The establishment of budgets, standard costs and actual costs of operations, processes, activities or products; and the analysis of variances, profitability or the social use of funds. (CIMA *Official Terminology*)

Cost accumulation The collection of cost data in some organised way through an accounting system.

Cost behaviour The variability of input costs with activity undertaken. A number of cost behaviour patterns are possible, ranging from variable costs whose cost level varies directly with the level of activity, to fixed costs, where changes in output have no effect upon the cost level. (CIMA *Official Terminology*)

Cost centre A production or service location, function, activity or item of equipment for which costs may be attributed to cost units. (CIMA *Official Terminology*)

Cost department The department responsible for keeping cost accounting records.

Cost driver Any factor which causes a change in the cost of an activity, eg the quality of parts received by an activity is a determining factor in the work required by that activity and therefore affects the resources required. An activity may have multiple cost drivers associated with it. (CIMA *Official Terminology*)

Cost pool A group of costs that are associated with the same activity or cost driver.

Cost unit A unit of product or service in relation to which costs are ascertained. (CIMA *Official Terminology*)

Cost-volume-profit (CVP) analysis *See breakeven analysis.*

Current standard A standard based on current working conditions (current wastage, current inefficiencies).

Database Frequently a much-abused term. In its strict sense a database is a file of data structured in such a way that it may serve a number of applications without its structure being dictated by any one of those applications, the concept being that programs are written around the database rather than files being structured to meet the needs of specific programs. The term is also rather loosely applied to simple file management software. (CIMA *Computing Terminology*)

Departmental/functional budget A budget of income and/or expenditure applicable to a particular function. A function may refer to a department or a process. (See page 255 of this Study Text for the full CIMA Terminology definition.)

Differential/incremental cost The difference in total cost between alternatives; calculated to assist decision-making. (CIMA *Official Terminology*)

Direct cost Expenditure which can be economically identified with, and specifically measured in respect to, a specific saleable cost unit. (CIMA *Official Terminology*)

Discretionary cost A cost whose amount within a time period is determined by, and is easily altered by, a decision taken by the appropriate budget holder. Marketing,

research and training are generally regarded as discretionary costs. Control of discretionary costs is through the budgeting process. Also known as *managed* or *policy* costs. (CIMA *Official Terminology*)

Dual value *See shadow price.*

Economic order quantity (EOQ) The most economic stock replenishment order size, which minimises the sum of stock ordering costs and stockholding costs. EOQ is used in an 'optimising' stock control system. (CIMA *Official Terminology*)

Engineered cost A cost which varies in proportion to a measure of activity. Direct materials and royalty payments are engineered costs. Control is through flexible budgeting or standard costing. (CIMA *Official Terminology*)

Equivalent units Notional whole units representing uncompleted work. Used to apportion costs between work in progress and completed output. (CIMA *Official Terminology*)

Feedback control The measurement of differences between planned outputs and actual outputs achieved, and the modification of subsequent action and/or plans to achieve future required results. (CIMA *Official Terminology*)

Feedforward control The forecasting of differences between actual and planned outcomes, and the implementation of action, before the event, to avoid such differences. (CIMA *Official Terminology*)

First in, first out (FIFO) The principle that the oldest items or costs are the first to be used. Most commonly applied to the pricing of issues of materials, based on using first the costs of the oldest materials in stock, *irrespective of the sequence in which actual material usage takes place*. Closing stock is therefore generally valued at relatively current costs. (CIMA *Official Terminology*)

Fixed budget A budget which does not include any provision for the event that actual volumes of production may differ from those budgeted.

Fixed cost/fixed overhead/period cost The cost which is incurred for an accounting period, and which, within certain output or turnover limits, tends to be unaffected by fluctuations in the levels of activity (output or turnover). Examples are rent, rates, insurance and executive salaries. (CIMA *Official Terminology*)

Fixed overhead *See fixed cost*

Flexible budget A budget which, by recognising different cost behaviour patterns, is designed to change as volume of activity changes. (CIMA *Official Terminology*)

Flexible manufacturing system An integrated computer-controlled production system which is capable of producing any of a range of parts, and of switching quickly and economically between them. (CIMA *Official Terminology*)

Full capacity Output (expressed in standard hours) that could be achieved if sales order, supplies and workforce were available for all installed workplaces.

Full cost plus pricing Method of determining the sales price by calculating the full cost of the product and adding a percentage mark-up for profit.

Function costing *See service costing.*

Functional budget *See departmental budget.*

Functional classification of costs A group of costs that were all incurred for the same basic purpose.

High-low method A technique for determining the fixed and variable components of a total cost that uses actual observations of total cost at the highest and lowest levels of activity and calculates the change in both activity and cost.

Historical cost The original acquisition cost of an asset, unadjusted for subsequent price level or value changes. (CIMA *Official Terminology*)

Ideal standard A standard which can be attained under the most favourable conditions, with no allowance for normal losses, waste and machine downtime. Also known as potential standard.

Imputed cost Cost recognised in a particular situation that is not regularly recognised by usual accounting procedures.

Incremental cost *See differential cost.*

Indirect cost *See overhead cost.*

Integrated accounts A set of accounting records which provides both financial and cost accounts using a common input of data for all accounting purposes. (CIMA *Official Terminology*)

Interlocking accounts / non-integrated accounts A system in which the cost accounts are distinct from the financial accounts, the two sets of accounts being kept continuously in agreement by the use of control accounts or reconciled by other means. (CIMA *Official Terminology*)

Internal opportunity cost The shadow price of a scarce resource.

Job A customer order or task of relatively short duration. (CIMA *Official Terminology*)

Job cost sheet A detailed record of the amount, and cost, of the labour, material and overhead charged to a specific job. (CIMA *Official Terminology*)

Job costing A form of specific order costing in which costs are attributed to individual jobs. (CIMA *Official Terminology*)

Joint products Two or more products separated in processing, each having a sufficiently high saleable value to merit recognition as a main product. (CIMA *Official Terminology*)

Just-in-time (JIT) A system whose objective is to produce or to procure products or components as they are required by a customer or for use, rather than for stock. A just-in-time system is a 'pull' system, which responds to demand, in contrast to a 'push' system, in which stocks act as buffers between the different elements of the system, such as purchasing, production and sales. (CIMA *Official Terminology*)

Key factor *See limiting factor.*

Limiting factor/ key factor Anything which limits the activity of an entity. An entity seeks to optimise the benefit it obtains from the limiting factor. (CIMA *Official Terminology*)

Line of best fit Represents the best linear relationship between two variables.

Mark-up pricing *See marginal cost plus pricing.*

Marginal cost plus pricing /mark-up pricing Method of determining the sales price by adding a profit margin onto either marginal cost of production or marginal cost of sales.

Marginal cost The part of the cost of one unit of product or service which would be avoided if that unit were not produced, or which would increase if one extra unit were produced. (CIMA *Official Terminology*)

Marginal costing The accounting system in which variable costs are charged to cost units and fixed costs of the period are written-off in full against the aggregate contribution. Its special value is recognising cost behaviour and hence assisting in decision-making. (CIMA *Official Terminology*)

Master budget The budget into which all subsidiary budgets are consolidated, normally comprising budgeted profit and loss account, budgeted balance sheet and budgeted cash flow statement. These documents, and the supporting subsidiary budgets, are used to plan and control activities for the following year. (CIMA *Official Terminology*)

Minimum pricing Price charged that just covers both the incremental costs of production and selling an item and the opportunity costs of the resources consumed in making and selling it.

Mixed cost *See semi-variable cost.*

Non-integrated accounts *See interlocking accounts.*

Normal loss The loss expected during the normal course of operations, for unavoidable reasons.

Notional cost A cost used in product evaluation, decision-making and performance measurement to represent the cost of using resources which have no conventional 'actual cost'. Notional interest, for example, may be charged for the use of internally generated funds. (CIMA *Official Terminology*)

Operating budget A budget of the revenues and expenses expected in a forthcoming accounting period. (CIMA *Official Terminology*)

Operating statement A regular report for management of actual costs, and revenues, as appropriate. Usually compares actual with budget and shows variances. (CIMA *Official Terminology*)

Opportunity cost The value of the benefit sacrificed when one course of action is chosen, in preference to an alternative. The opportunity cost is represented by the forgone potential benefit from the best rejected course of action. (CIMA *Official Terminology*)

Overhead absorption rate A means of attributing overhead to a product or service based, for example, on direct labour hours, direct labour cost or machine hours. (CIMA *Official Terminology*)

Overhead/indirect cost Expenditure on labour, materials or services which cannot be economically identified with a specific saleable cost unit. (CIMA *Official Terminology*)

Period cost *See fixed cost.*

Practical capacity. Full capacity less an allowance for known unavoidable volume losses.

Participative/bottom-up budgeting A budgeting system in which all budget holders are given the opportunity to participate in setting their own budgets. (CIMA *Official Terminology*)

Principal budget factor A factor which will limit the activities of an undertaking and which is often the starting point in budget preparation. (CIMA *Official Terminology*)

Process/continuous operation costing The costing method applicable where goods or services result from a sequence of continuous or repetitive operations or processes. Costs are averaged over the units produced during the period being initially charged to the operation or process. (CIMA *Official Terminology*)

Product cost The cost of finished product built up from its cost elements. (CIMA *Official Terminology*)

Profit centre A part of a business accountable for costs and revenues. (CIMA *Official Terminology*)

Profit-volume (P/V) chart *See contribution chart.*

Rectification costs Costs arising from rectifying sub-standard output.

Relevant costs Costs appropriate to a specific management decision. (CIMA *Official Terminology*)

Relevant range The activity levels within which assumptions about cost behaviour in breakeven analysis remain valid. (CIMA *Official Terminology*)

Rolling continuous budget A budget continuously updated by adding a further accounting period (month or quarter) when the earliest accounting period has expired. Its use is particularly beneficial where future costs and/or activities cannot be forecast accurately. (CIMA *Official Terminology*)

Scarce resource An item that is essential to production activity, but that is available only in a limited quantity.

Scrap Discarded material having some value. (CIMA *Official Terminology*)

Semi-fixed cost *See semi-variable cost*

Semi-variable cost/semi-fixed cost/mixed cost A cost containing both fixed and variable components and which is thus partly affected by a change in the level of activity. (CIMA *Official Terminology*)

Service/function costing Cost accounting for services or functions, e.g. canteens, maintenance personnel. These may be referred to as service centres, departments or functions. (CIMA *Official Terminology*)

Shadow price An increase in value which would be created by having available one additional unit of a limiting resource at the original cost. (CIMA *Official Terminology*)

Spreadsheet The term commonly used to describe many of the modelling packages available for microcomputers, being loosely derived from the likeness to a 'spreadsheet of paper' divided into rows and columns. (CIMA *Computing Terminology*)

Standard cost The planned unit cost of the products, components or services produced in a period. The standard cost may be determined on a number of bases. The main uses of standard costs are in performance measurement, control, stock valuation and in the establishment of selling prices. (CIMA *Official Terminology*)

Standard costing A control technique which compares standard costs and revenues with actual results to obtain variances which are used to stimulate improved performance. (CIMA *Official Terminology*)

Standard hour or minute The amount of work achievable at standard efficiency levels in an hour or minute. (CIMA *Official Terminology*)

Step cost A cost which is fixed in nature but only within certain levels of activity.

Sunk cost A past cost not directly relevant in decision-making. (CIMA *Official Terminology*)

Uncontrollable cost A cost that cannot be affected by management within a given time period.

Under- or over-absorbed overhead The difference between overhead incurred and overhead absorbed, using an estimated rate, in a given period. In a standard costing system, it is the sum of variable production overhead total variance and fixed production overhead total variance. (CIMA *Official Terminology*)

User cost The incremental cost of using machinery.

Variable cost A cost which varies with the level of activity. (CIMA *Official Terminology*)

Variance Difference between planned, budgeted, or standard cost and actual cost incurred; and similarly for revenue. (CIMA *Official Terminology*)

Not to be confused with statistical variance which measures the dispersion of a statistical population.

Variance accounting A method of accounting by means of which planned activities (quantified through budgets and standard costs and revenues) are compared with actual results. Provides information for variance analysis. (CIMA *Official Terminology*)

Variance analysis The analysis of performance by means of variances, whose timely reporting should maximise the opportunity for managerial action. (CIMA *Official Terminology*)

Weighted average process costing method A process costing method that adds the cost of all work done in the current period to the cost of work done in the preceding period on the current period's opening work in process and divides the total by the equivalent units of work done to date.

Zero base budgeting A method of budgeting which requires each cost element to be specifically justified, as though the activities to which the budget relates were being undertaken for the first time. Without approval, the budget allowance is zero. (CIMA *Official Terminology*)

ORDER FORM

For further question practice on Stage 2 *Operational Cost Accounting*, BPP publish a companion Practice & Revision Kit. The February 1998 edition contains a bank of questions, mostly drawn from past examinations, plus a full test paper. Fully worked suggested solutions are provided for all questions, including the test paper. The new edition will be published in January 1999.

You may also wish to make use of our innovative revision product, CIMA Passcards. Published in February 1998, they are designed to act as last-minute revision notes and memory prompters. A new edition will be available in January 1999.

To order your Practice & Revision Kit and Passcards, you can phone us on 0181-740 2211, email us at *publishing@bpp.co.uk*, fax us on 0181-740 1184, or cut out this form and post it to us at the address below.

To: BPP Publishing Ltd, Aldine House, Aldine Place, Tel: 0181-740 2211
London W12 8AW Fax: 0181-740 1184

Forenames (Mr / Ms): _____ Surname: _____

Daytime delivery address: _____

_____

Post code: _____ Date of exam (month/year):_____

Please send me the following books:	*Price* £	*Quantity*	*Total* £
CIMA Stage 2 *Operational Cost Accounting* Kit	8.95	....	....
CIMA Stage 2 *Operational Cost Accounting* Passcards	4.95	....	....

Postage and packaging:

UK: £2.00 for first plus £1.00 for each extra	....	....
Europe (inc ROI): £2.50 for first plus £1.00 for each extra	....	....
Rest of the World: £15.00 for first plus £8.00 for each extra	....	....

We guarantee delivery to all UK addresses inside 3 working days. Orders to all EU addresses should be received within 4 working days. Single Kits/Passcards to overseas addresses are airmailed. All other parcels are sent by courier and should arrive in not more than six days.

I enclose a cheque for £ _____ or charge to Access/Visa/Switch

Card number | | | | | | | | | | | | | | | | | | | |

Start date (Switch only) _____ **Expiry date** _____ **Issue no. (Switch only)**_____

Signature _____

Data correct at time of publication

To order any further titles in the CIMA range, please use the form overleaf.

ORDER FORM

To order your CIMA books, you can phone us on 0181-740 2211, email us at *publishing@bpp.co.uk*, fax us on 0181-740 1184, or cut out this form and post it to us at the address below.

To: BPP Publishing Ltd, Aldine House, Aldine Place   **Tel: 0181-740 2211**
           London W12 8AW   **Fax: 0181-740 1184**

Forenames (Mr / Ms): _____ Surname: _____

Daytime delivery address: _____

_____

Post code: _____ Date of exam (month/year):_____

	Price (£) 7/98 Text	2/98 Kit	2/98 Passcards	Quantity Text	Kit	Passcards	Total £
Stage 1							
1 Financial Accounting Fundamentals	18.95	8.95	4.95				
2 Cost Accounting and Quantitative Methods	18.95	8.95	4.95				
3 Economic Environment	18.95	8.95	4.95				
4 Business Environment and Info Technology	18.95	8.95	4.95				
Stage 2							
5 Financial Accounting	18.95	8.95	4.95				
6 Operational Cost Accounting	18.95	8.95	4.95				
7 Management Science Applications	18.95	8.95	4.95				
8 Business and Company Law	18.95	8.95	4.95				
Stage 3							
9 Financial Reporting	19.95	9.95	5.95				
10 Management Accounting Applications	19.95	9.95	5.95				
11 Organisational Management and Development	19.95	9.95	5.95				
12 Business Taxation (FA 98)	19.95	9.95	5.95				
Stage 4							
13 Strategic Financial Management	19.95	9.95	5.95				
14 Strategic Management Accountancy & Marketing	19.95	9.95	5.95				
15 Information Management	19.95	9.95	5.95				
16 Management Accounting Control Systems	19.95	9.95	5.95				

Postage and packaging:

UK: Texts £3.00 for first plus £2.00 for each extra

    Kits and Passcards £2.00 for first plus £1.00 for each extra

Europe (inc ROI): Texts £5.00 for first plus £4.00 for each extra

    Kits and Passcards £2.50 for first plus £1.00 for each extra

Rest of the World: Texts £20.00 for first plus £10.00 for each extra

    Kits and Passcards £15.00 for first plus £8.00 for each extra

                                                Total [_____]

We guarantee delivery to all UK addresses inside 3 working days. Orders to all EU addresses should be received within 4 working days. Single Kits/Passcards to overseas addresses are airmailed. All other parcels are sent by courier and should arrive in no more than six days.

I enclose a cheque for £ _____ or charge to Access/Visa/Switch

Card number [ ][ ][ ][ ][ ][ ][ ][ ][ ][ ][ ][ ][ ][ ][ ][ ][ ][ ][ ]

Start date (Switch only) _____ **Expiry date** _____ **Issue no. (Switch only)**___

Signature _____

REVIEW FORM & FREE PRIZE DRAW

All original review forms from the entire BPP range, completed with genuine comments, will be entered into one of two draws on 31 January 1999 and 31 July 1999. The names on the first four forms picked out on each occasion will be sent a cheque for £50.

Name: _____ Address: _____

_____

_____

How have you used this Text?
(Tick one box only)

☐ Home study (book only)

☐ On a course: college _____

☐ With 'correspondence' package

☐ Other _____

Why did you decide to purchase this Text?
(Tick one box only)

☐ Have used complementary Kit

☐ Have used BPP Texts in the past

☐ Recommendation by friend/colleague

☐ Recommendation by a lecturer at college

☐ Saw advertising

☐ Other _____

During the past six months do you recall seeing/receiving any of the following?
(Tick as many boxes as are relevant)

☐ Our advertisement in *CIMA Student*

☐ Our advertisement in *Management Accounting*

☐ Our advertisement in *Pass*

☐ Our brochure with a letter through the post

Which (if any) aspects of our advertising do you find useful?
(Tick as many boxes as are relevant)

☐ Prices and publication dates of new editions

☐ Information on Text content

☐ Facility to order books off-the-page

☐ None of the above

Have you used the companion Practice & Revision Kit for this subject? ☐ Yes ☐ No

Your ratings, comments and suggestions would be appreciated on the following areas

	Very useful	Useful	Not useful
Introductory section (How to use this text, study checklist, etc)	☐	☐	☐
Introduction to chapters	☐	☐	☐
Syllabus coverage	☐	☐	☐
Exercises and examples	☐	☐	☐
Exam focus points	☐	☐	☐
Chapter roundups	☐	☐	☐
Test your knowledge quizzes	☐	☐	☐
Illustrative questions	☐	☐	☐
Content of suggested solutions	☐	☐	☐
Glossary and index	☐	☐	☐
Structure and presentation	☐	☐	☐

	Excellent	Good	Adequate	Poor
Overall opinion of this Text	☐	☐	☐	☐

Do you intend to continue using BPP Study Texts/Kits? ☐ Yes ☐ No

Please note any further comments and suggestions/errors on the reverse of this page.

Please return to: Edmund Hewson, BPP Publishing Ltd, FREEPOST, London, W12 8BR

REVIEW FORM & FREE PRIZE DRAW (continued)

Please note any further comments and suggestions/errors below

FREE PRIZE DRAW RULES

1   Closing date for 31 January 1999 draw is 31 December 1998. Closing date for 31 July 1999 draw is 30 June 1999.

2   Restricted to entries with UK and Eire addresses only. BPP employees, their families and business associates are excluded.

3   No purchase necessary. Entry forms are available upon request from BPP Publishing. No more than one entry per title, per person. Draw restricted to persons aged 16 and over.

4   Winners will be notified by post and receive their cheques not later than 6 weeks after the relevant draw date. Lists of winners will be published in BPP's *focus* newsletter following the relevant draw.

5   The decision of the promoter in all matters is final and binding. No correspondence will be entered into.